Writing in Transit

with Readings

by DENISE K. COMER

FOUNTAINHEAD
PRESS

As a textbook publisher, we are faced with enormous environmental issues due the large amount of paper contained in our print products. Since our inception in 2002, we have worked diligently to be as eco-friendly as possible.

Our "green" initiatives include:

Electronic Products
We deliver products in nonpaper form whenever possible. This includes PDF downloadables, flash drives, and CDs.

Electronic Samples
We use a new electronic sampling system, called Xample. Instructor samples are sent via a personalized web page that links to PDF downloads.

FSC Certified Printers
All of our Printers are certified by the Forest Service Council, which promotes environmentally and socially responsible management of the world's forests. This program allows consumer groups, individual consumers and businesses to work together hand in hand to promote responsible use of the world's forests as a renewable and sustainable resource.

Recycled Paper
Almost all of our products are printed on a minimum of 10-30% post-consumer waste-recycled paper.

Support of Green Causes
When we do print, we donate a portion of our revenue to Green causes. Listed below are a few of the organizations that have received donations from Fountainhead Press. We welcome your feedback and suggestions for contributions, as we are always searching for worthy initiatives.

Rainforest 2 Reef
Environmental Working Group

Developmental Editor: Amy Salisbury-Werhane
Cover and text design: Ellie Moore

Copyright © 2017 Fountainhead Press
Stock images provided by Shutterstock.

For information, please call or write:
1-800-586-0330
Fountainhead Press
Southlake, TX 76092

Website: www.fountainheadpress.com
E-mail: customerservice@fountainheadpress.com

ISBN: 978-1-68036-636-5

Printed in the United States of America

Contents

Acknowledgments

Many people have contributed to the shaping and development of *Writing in Transit*. My particular gratitude goes to Scott Timian, whose leadership and vision moved the book forward from the beginning through to publication. Felix Frazier's insights and conceptual ideas were foundational to generating the manuscript. Thank you to both Scott and Felix for believing in me. Amy Salisbury-Werhane, my fantastic developmental editor, provided crucial feedback and encouragement throughout the entire process. My friend and colleague Aftab Jassal offered incredibly astute insights on the manuscript. The inimitable Ellie Moore has granted her creative genius to designing *Writing in Transit*. Shelley Smith has provided her scrupulous eye toward copyediting.

The approach to writing transfer that informs *Writing in Transit* has been shaped through many years of working with the multidisciplinary faculty who comprise the Duke University Thompson Writing Program; exchanges with these talented colleagues have helped make visible cross-disciplinary convergences and divergences, and I am deeply grateful to all past and present Thompson Writing Program faculty. In particular, many productive conversations grounded on writing transfer have emerged through conversations among participants in the Postdoctoral Summer Seminar in Teaching Writing, which I have co-taught for nearly a decade (first with Joseph Harris and more recently with Marcia Rego). Special appreciation goes to my friend Joseph Harris, founding director of the Thompson Writing Program, whose approach to teaching writing has been integral in shaping my writing pedagogy. Kristen Neuschel's mentorship and support over the past several years have helped me come to understand writing itself in much more nuanced ways.

I am extremely thankful for the many writers from around the world who have enrolled in English Composition I: Achieving Expertise and engaged in cross-disciplinary and intercultural conversations about writing. These conversations have greatly enhanced my thinking about writing transfer. My appreciation extends especially to those who have graciously contributed Writer Insights throughout this book.

My close friends and family provide ongoing motivation, inspiration, strength, and space for my writing. They express interest in and enthusiasm for my projects, reassuring, insightful advice, and compassion for my quandaries. My immense gratitude goes to Parag Budhecha; Patty and Mike Comer; David, Paige, Amanda, and Lauren Gotterer; Emily Robbins; Rebecca Ryslik; and Jonathan Wolitz. Particular appreciation goes to Ray and June Wolitz for their guidance. I am also grateful to my mother, Barbara

Gina Garrett, for her ideas and support. My three curious and creative children, Owen, Ethan, and Drew Comer, also deserve special recognition for their patience, interest, and insights. And, to my rock-star husband, David Comer: you have provided honest feedback, helped create time and energy for me to write, and offered courage, inspiration, and laughter.

Preface to Instructors

Archaeoastronomy and Writing Transfer

Each chapter of *Writing in Transit* opens with a different archaeoastronomical site from around the world. Offering a unifying thread for the book—and a metaphor for writing transfer—these chapter openings each include a brief site description and a writing prompt that invite students to consider that particular archaeoastronomical site through the lens of that particular chapter's area of focus. Archaeoastronomy provides an apt inroad for *Writing in Transit* in part because it infuses writing with curiosity and wonder, but also because it holds much in common with writing transfer. As archaeoastronomical sites forge intersections and emphasize difference across disciplines, cultures, time, and space, so too does the kind of active consideration of writing transfer central to *Writing in Transit*. Therefore, with each new chapter of *Writing in Transit*, instructors and students can use the archaeoastronomical sites to sponsor and inform conversations about writing transfer: How do culture, time, discipline, and space yield unique yet intersecting contexts for writing, learning, and knowledge? In what ways do context and individual dispositions shape, reflect, and refract the kinds of questions writers ask and the knowledge writers create? How do writing-related practices and approaches align and depart across, through, and in between the enormous range of contexts writers encounter in academia and beyond?

Writing Transfer

Perhaps more than ever before, twenty-first century college students need to become adept at writing within and across disciplinary boundaries and navigate increasingly complex, overlapping, and varied landscapes of writing. In short, they need to cultivate habits of mind grounded on transfer.

Transfer, according to Linda Darling-Hammond and Kim Austin of the Stanford School of Education, is "the ability to extend what one has learned in one context to new contexts." Writing-related transfer involves students reflecting on what they learn in one context about writing and about themselves as learners and writers, and then applying, extending, rejecting, or otherwise modifying this knowledge for other disciplinary, interdisciplinary, and transdisciplinary contexts.

Writing in Transit foregrounds writing transfer, making explicit the changing, intersecting, and disparate contexts of writing across, within, and beyond our institutions. *Writing in Transit* invites students to actively engage with, reflect on, and position themselves within those varying and overlapping domains so they can become better at transferring their writing-related knowledge, practices, approaches, and skills to whatever contexts they encounter.

Research into writing transfer has a long history, reaching back at least as far as Aristotle's *Rhetoric* in the fourth century BCE (Nowacek). Writing transfer is often based on inquiries into the connected yet divergent values and practices within particular disciplines. David Russell's notion of "activity theory," for instance, suggests that each discipline—and each discipline's (sometimes overlapping) approach to writing—has a highly contextualized and historically grounded set of practices, motives, and approaches:

> [Activity theory develops] metaphors of interlocking, dynamic systems or networks. These systems embrace both human agents and their material tools, including writing and speaking.... An activity system is any ongoing, object-directed, historically-conditioned, dialectically-structured, tool-mediated human interaction: a family, a religious organization, an advocacy group, a political movement, a course of study, a school, a discipline, a research laboratory, a profession, and so on. These activity systems are mutually (re)constructed by participants using certain tools and not others (including discursive tools such as speech sounds and inscriptions). ("Rethinking")

As you can see in Figure 1, Russell maintains that writing thus reflects, shapes, and is shaped by the particular network(s) from which it emerges.

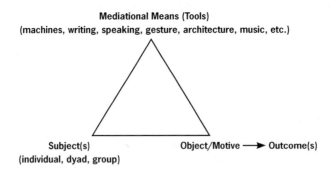

Mediational Means (Tools)
(machines, writing, speaking, gesture, architecture, music, etc.)

Subject(s)   Object/Motive ⟶ Outcome(s)
(individual, dyad, group)

FIGURE 1 An Activity System (Fundamental Unit of Analysis of Social Practices). From Russell, "Rethinking," 510.

Contemporary research into writing transfer often invokes and builds on Russell's notions of activity systems, or what others have since termed "communities of discourse" (Carter) or "language socialization" (Duff).

One of the most important recent ideas about transfer is that it is a highly dynamic process (Bransford, Brown, and Cocking). It can occur deliberately or unconsciously, directly or indirectly, positively or negatively (knowing what *to do* or what *not to do* in particular circumstances). Anne Beaufort's research shows that competing values in discourse communities can sometimes stymie students' abilities to effectively enact writing transfer. Elizabeth Wardle emphasizes the importance of reflection and meta-awareness for transfer. Dana Lynn Driscoll and Jennifer Wells examine "the role of learners' dispositions" in transfer. They emphasize that learners' personalities, dispositions, and identities impact their approach to transfer and that this can shift with time as well. This means that students should reflect meaningfully on their work as learners, thinkers, and writers on a continuing basis. Kathleen Blake Yancey, Liane Robertson, and Kara Taczak's recent work in *Writing across Contexts* emphasizes the importance of designing curriculum in first-year writing courses with an explicit emphasis on enabling students to "foster transfer in writing."

Rebecca Nowacek's research on writing transfer yields particular insights into how students engage with writing transfer. She has resituated binary conceptions of transfer (low-road/unconscious or high-road/deliberate; positive or negative) to unpack a more matrixed approach: "four avenues of connection, four resources that individuals employ as they draw connections among various contexts: knowledge, ways of knowing, identity, and goals." Nowacek foregrounds the agency involved with transfer to emphasize that students are not merely conduits moving from context to context but are instead "agents of integration" who actively reconstruct writing-related knowledge and practices through transfer.

Of significance to point out is that a transfer-based approach to writing is not equivalent to promoting interdisciplinarity. Those involved with transfer acknowledge that activity systems enable scholars to advance knowledge within their disciplines because they can build on the work of others and move forward long-term conversations premised on shared knowledge, conventions, and outcomes. These discourse communities are vitally important, and cultivating attention to transfer does not mean that disciplinary boundaries should necessarily become more porous. Rather, a transfer-based approach encourages students to cultivate the meta-awareness to recognize and participate in and across these discourse communities more effectively.

The diversity and complexity of discourse communities helps us understand why writing, and more broadly academic inquiry, can be so challenging for undergraduates as they move between activity systems. Gerald Graff, for instance, decries that students' perception of their college education can too often seem "a disconnected series of courses." It can be difficult even for faculty to help students make connections across courses because faculty themselves sometimes struggle with or resist developing a more integrated approach to research and writing. Michael Carter suggests that faculty can be so immersed in their particular discipline's activity systems that they may be unlikely to notice the situatedness of writing in their field, much less acquire the perspective to help students understand these contexts: "[B]ecause professors typically learn to write in their disciplines not by any direct instruction but by a process of slow acculturation through various apprenticeship discourses, they are unable to see that writing itself is specific to the discipline." The result, Carter argues, is that faculty may conceive of their discipline's approach toward and values about writing as universal: "Consequently, faculty in the disciplines continue to conceive of writing as generalizable to all disciplines and therefore distinct from disciplinary knowledge, to be learned as a general skill outside the disciplines." This conception of writing as generalizable can then, according to Carter, give way to the idea that learning how to write is primarily only about mastering grammar, punctuation, and spelling rather than about higher order abilities such as posing questions, engaged reading, critical thinking, and effective argumentation.

One way writing faculty and students can move more deliberately and productively among various networks of discourse is by designing courses that integrate transfer-based approaches to learning, writing, and assessment. Informed by these conversations, *Writing in Transit* invites first-year students and faculty to foster just such a transfer-based approach toward writing through pointed areas of focus (see Table 1).

TABLE 1 Pointed areas of focus.

Disciplinary Epistemologies	What kinds of knowledge production and strategies for learning and knowing operate within and across disciplines? What counts as worthwhile, effective questions in particular contexts, and how can we reframe these questions for other contexts?
Discourse Conventions	How can we transfer our awareness of discourse conventions, including matters of genre, voice, tone, and citation, from one writing context to others? How can we transfer our abilities to identify particular discourse conventions as we encounter different contexts?
Individual Epistemology	What kinds of learning work best for us as individuals? How can we learn more about ourselves as learners based on our work in first-year writing? What kinds of approaches to inquiry, peer engagement, collaboration, and research work best for us as individuals and under what circumstances? How might these preferences or affinities change across time as we grow and change?
Writing Process/Practices	Which aspects of the writing process (i.e. research, pre-writing, drafting, feedback, revision, and editing) can be applied and adapted from one context to other writing and learning occasions?
Writing Moves and Skills	How can specific writing moves, such as developing arguments, engaging with the work of others, integrating evidence, crafting introductions and conclusions, structuring arguments, and writing effective sentence-level prose be adapted from one context to other writing and learning occasions?
Content	In what ways might the content-based knowledge we acquire through texts, writing, and research impact concurrent and subsequent learning and writing occasions, be they in the academy or outside?

Writing in Transit invites students to cultivate this transfer-based approach to writing by examining texts and writing practices from across disciplines. The framing material for these texts, though, guides students not toward a prescribed set of conventions, but instead toward thinking about disciplinary epistemologies, asking what we can learn about values and approaches to writing in disciplines. And, even as *Writing in Transit*, draws from the work of scholars in linguistics, such as Charles Bazerman, who identify patterns across texts, it also embraces Carter's notions of "disciplines as ways of knowing."

By providing example texts from across disciplines, and writing concepts situated in a disciplinary based context, *Writing in Transit* can accustom students to think with transfer-based habits of mind, facilitating the agency students have in transfer, and thereby empowering them to find more value and integration in their education, especially through the centrality of writing and writing-related transfer.

Whom *Writing in Transit* is for

This book is primarily aimed toward first-year writing students, but it would also be valuable for writers at other stages of their educational journeys—undergraduates through graduate students, and faculty who are integrating writing (in large or small ways) into their discipline-based courses. It would also offer useful materials for interdisciplinary or multidisciplinary faculty learning communities.

Transfer-Based Features of *Writing in Transit*

Writing in Transit facilitates your exploration of writing transfer with students by providing key pedagogical elements specifically designed to promote a transfer-based approach to writing and learning.

Archaeoastronomical chapter openers

Students' journey exploring the many moving parts of writing finds a corollary journey with each chapter opener, which orients students to the chapter content through a different archaeoastronomical site from around the world. Together, these sites provide a unifying thread across *Writing in Transit*, operating as an alignment in much the same way as the features of writing included in the text. Even beyond this form of alignment, however, archaeoastronomy is a field of inquiry and contains structures that—like writing transfer—transverse disciplines, cultures, and individuals, retaining some common characteristics but also bending slightly (or drastically) in response to these varying contexts.

Opportunities for writing and reflecting

Writing in Transit includes numerous opportunities for writing and reflecting, opportunities that are specifically infused with a transfer-based approach so students can actively engage in the process of writing transfer.

"Write Here"

Appearing with and emerging from each archaeoastronomical site, Write Here writing prompts locate students both geographically within the particular site and position them as writers within the area of focus for that particular chapter. Write Heres invite students to begin thinking and writing about the feature of writing that will be addressed in that chapter.

"Write Now"

Interspersed throughout each chapter and consisting of opportunities for brief writing and reflecting, Write Now writing prompts ask students to engage with elements of writing transfer connected to a particular chapter's area of focus.

"Write Away"

Located after each reading, Write Away ideas invite students to embark on slightly more substantive writing experiences related to the reading and chapter content. These Write Away prompts are designed to ask students to draw upon their transfer-related skills and practices as they write within contexts relevant to the reading. Write Aways include individual opportunities for writing as well as occasions where students can collaborate with peers.

Together, these occasions for writing and reflecting sponsor opportunities for students to transfer writing knowledge within and across disciplinary contexts and writing occasions.

Introductions to each reading

The introductions to each reading address the disciplinary context of that reading through the lens of transfer. Thus, the introductions may address the contours and epistemologies of a particular discipline, but primarily focus on the ways in which writers within these disciplines themselves rely upon writing transfer as they navigate the many contexts for writing in that discipline.

Maps guiding students through each chapter

Since *Writing in Transit* is steeped in movement, it becomes ever more crucial to occasionally pause and take stock, to consider how ideas build on one another and where ideas may lead. Two elements of the text in particular help map this dynamic terrain.

"Pinpointing Chapter [Number]"

Located early in each chapter, these sections show how the elements of writing transfer being addressed in the current chapter build on preceding chapters and how subsequent chapters will, in turn, extend them as well. These Pinpointing sections also provide an overview of the chapter material so students can see the direction in which they are heading as writers.

"Transferring [Chapter Name]"

Appearing at the end of each chapter, these sections re-emphasize how writers transfer the aspect of writing addressed in that chapter to many and diverse writing occasions. These sections also highlight how students can transfer what they have learned in prior chapters to the aspect of writing addressed in that chapter and how they can transfer what they have learned in the current chapter to subsequent chapters. In this way, students can see how writing transfer operates across *Writing in Transit* as a dynamic series of interlocking, sequenced, and recursive concepts and practices.

Multi-disciplinary examples

Each chapter includes multi-disciplinary and multi-contextual examples, perspectives, and readings. These illustrate the range of approaches writers can bring to the element of writing under consideration. In so doing, students can see specific examples of how how writers transfer—borrow, adapt, and reject—aspects of writing from one occasion to others.

Occasions to connect with others

Through "Transfer Hubs," students will have occasion to engage in productive exchanges about writing with others beyond the immediate course setting. The Fountainhead Press Transfer Hub (fountainheadpress.com/transferhub) invites students to visit a wider networked site to contribute their ideas and see what others have written, thereby facilitating even greater degrees of transfer and exchange. Many of the writing and reflecting opportunities are also in and of themselves opportunities for connecting through collaborations with peers.

Insights about writing

National and international writers share their experiences with writing throughout *Writing in Transit*. These Writer Insights provide glimpses into writing from across professions, disciplines, and contexts. The real-world people who contributed provide authentic perspectives on transfer-based aspects of writing.

Amidst all of these transfer points, your students, as writers, will travel, moving through disciplines and writing occasions by exploring and discovering writing in transit.

Why You Should Introduce Students to *Writing in Transit*

Academic writing is hard, even for those of us who are purportedly experts at it. First-year writing students deserve the chance to actively interrogate the ways in which academic inquiry, writing values, expectations, and conventions are shaped by and reflected in the writing that exists within disciplines. They also deserve to contribute to these conversations by learning how to pose meaningful questions and engage with the work of others in ways that are situated within, across, and against disciplinary perspectives.

Perhaps most importantly, students should have the space to think about themselves within, outside of, and alongside these domains. Framing first-year writing around these disciplinary practices and questions will illustrate for students that academic writing itself is dynamic, animated by the shifting, often recursive and overlapping aims, methods, purposes, and ideas scholars bring to their writing.

Your Integral Role with *Writing in Transit*

One of the most important aspects of writing transfer to keep in mind is that faculty have a strong role encouraging, or discouraging, students' aptitude with transfer:

The rich evidence of longitudinal studies also indirectly supports what we have learned from studying the research on transfer, namely, that transfer depends heavily, although not exclusively, on our teaching: when we teach with analogies, encourage metacognition, scaffold student learning, motivate our students effectively, and provide sufficient time for the learning to 'take,' our teaching potentially enables transfer." (Boone, et al.)

Writing in Transit anticipates that you will, and makes room for you to, bring your expertise as a teacher of writing, and your own disciplinary lens, to bear on these texts and ideas as you encounter them with students. *Writing in Transit* relies on your teaching as a key mechanism for supporting and encouraging writing transfer.

You do not, however, need gain expertise in writing for every discipline. Just as writers write better when they write about something they care about, the best writing pedagogy occurs when we teach writing from within our own scholarly perspectives. Students learn best when texts, teachers, circumstances, and they themselves all work together, colliding, intersecting, and overlapping.

Writing in Transit encourages you, therefore, to find your own path through the materials, and to supplement these materials with others that you have created and collected. You and your students can also find a variety of other valuable resources and supplements at the Fountainhead Press website.

About the Author

Denise Comer, Assistant Professor of the Practice of Writing Studies and Director of First-Year Writing at Duke University, has worked with a multidisciplinary first-year writing faculty for more than fifteen years.

Duke University's award-winning and nationally recognized first-year writing program recruits faculty with Ph.D.s across the social sciences, natural sciences, and humanities to teach first-year writing. The program is founded on the premise that cross-disciplinary conversations about first-year writing improve the teaching of writing and help first-year writers learn how to navigate more effectively the variegated landscape of academic writing.

Approaching first-year writing pedagogy as an intellectual endeavor and fostering conversations about writing that actively consider disciplinary perspectives have helped earn Duke University's Thompson Writing Program national recognition with the 2006 CCCC Writing Program Certificate of Excellence and through the 2012 *U.S. News & World Report*, which commended Duke for "making the writing process a priority at all levels of instruction and across the curriculum."

Denise has collaborated on several initiatives for Duke and the Durham community that demonstrate her investment teaching writing to *all* learners: launching a writing course for students who need more time and preparation with college-level writing, many of whom are first-generation or low-income; integrating responsiveness to English Language Learners across all first-year writing courses; developing writing workshops for low-income, high-potential urban middle-school children; and creating a writing-based program for chronically and fatally ill children residing at the Ronald McDonald House of Durham. In 2013, she launched a Massive Open Online Course, English Composition I: Achieving Expertise, funded largely through a grant from the Bill & Melinda Gates Foundation and offered in partnership between Duke University and Coursera. Currently in its third iteration, to date over 200,000 learners from around the world have enrolled in that course. Prior to teaching at Duke, she taught writing at public universities, community colleges, and a military base.

Denise's scholarship explores writing transfer with multidisciplinary inquiries into writing pedagogy, writing program administration, and the intersections between technology and the teaching of writing. Her book, *It's Just a Dissertation: Transforming Your Dissertation from Daunting to Doable to Done*, co-written with Barbara Gina Garrett (Fountainhead Press, 2014), provides guidance to graduate students across disciplines on how to write and complete a dissertation. Her articles, attentive to multidisciplinary perspectives and often grounded on a transfer-based approach, have appeared in such journals as *Writing across the Curriculum*, *Teaching/Writing*, *Pedagogy*, and *WPA: Writing Program Administration*. She has also given presentations about, offered keynote addresses on, and worked as a consultant on multidisciplinary writing pedagogy and writing transfer.

Writing Transfer

Pinpointing Chapter 1

As the introductory chapter of the text, Chapter 1 introduces transfer as a way of approaching writing and as a strategy for learning. To provide you with strategies for *writing transfer*, this chapter addresses the following concepts:

- What is Writing Transfer?
- The Dynamic Nature of Discourse Conventions
- A Transfer-Based Approach to Writing
- Writing Practices that Align, Modify, and Differentiate across Contexts
- Strategies for Becoming Better at Writing Transfer
- Why Writing Transfer Matters

Subsequent chapters each feature and explore a key writing practice that writers align, modify, and differentiate across contexts. These key writing practices align across disciplines and writing occasions, even while also reframing, shaping, and reflecting distinct perspectives and approaches.

Chaco Canyon is one of the most impressive examples of ancient engineering, astronomy, and architecture. Located in what is now a relatively remote area of New Mexico, the structures in Chaco Canyon were built by the Chaco Anasazi people of the Pueblo culture between 850 and 1250 CE.

Representing the accomplishments made possible through interdisciplinary collaboration, Chaco Canyon fuses "architectural designs, astronomical alignments, geometry, landscaping and engineering." Connecting more than 150 communities together, the site stands among "[m]ore than four hundred miles of interlocking ancient roads," suggesting it was a hub of intercultural activity ("Chaco"; Gibson).

Chaco Canyon is especially well known for its Great Houses, which were enormous complexes, multiple stories high, some of which included as many as 750 rooms. Archaeologists believe Great Houses functioned primarily as "important focal point[s] for ritual activity" rather than as residences. While each Great House contained unique characteristics, they also all shared several features in common. One such feature—a precise astronomical alignment between windows and walls—enabled Anasazi people to recognize the summer and winter solstices ("History"; Malville; Ward).

One of Chaco Canyon's most exceptional structures is the Sun Dagger, which consists of three sandstone slabs and spiral petroglyphs that until recently due to a settling of the rock slabs, marked solstices and equinoxes: "[At summer solstice,] a vertical shaft of light passed through the center of the spiral…At winter solstice, two noonday daggers framed the large spiral. During the equinoxes, the smaller spiral was bisected at midday by a lesser dagger" ("Fajada"). With its precise use of shadows to track time, the Sun Dagger remains an exemplar of ancient knowledge, collaboration, and achievement.

Chaco Canyon makes visible the complex intersections between that which may otherwise seem discrete. Great Houses were each distinctive, yet they all shared certain key structural features. Chaco roads each led to a different place, but interlocked to enable movement between and through these locales. People with unique disciplinary knowledge each contributed toward realizing a shared goal of developing Chaco Canyon. The stone slabs around the Sun Dagger existed independently, but then aligned, if only for a moment, to mark time.

The moving, diverging, and intersecting parts that together generated the marvel that became Chaco Canyon illustrate the value of forging connections and collaborating even as difference is preserved. Chaco Canyon thus exemplifies the achievements possible through disciplinary and cultural collaboration, but at the same time reaffirms the value of deep disciplinary and culturally based knowledge production.

Not unlike the alignments transecting Chaco Canyon's Sun Dagger or Great Houses, academic writers engage in many of the same moves, strategies, and practices, even as disparate disciplines and contexts shape each writer's unique approach to any given writing occasion.

The kind of thinking required by this terrain of academic writing is known as **transfer**. Transfer consists of the ability to establish connections, notice confluences, and adapt prior knowledge amid different concepts and contexts, even those that may at times seem widely disconnected.

Writing in Transit will help you become more effective at transfer, especially, though not exclusively, within the context of academic writing. A transfer-based approach to writing will enable you to more effectively transfer knowledge, ideas, and practices about and across writing contexts. Gaining acumen with writing transfer will facilitate your growth as a writer, thinker, and global citizen and empower you to contribute ideas to ongoing conversations, advance knowledge, achieve your goals, and make a meaningful difference in the world around you.

Write Here

Chaco Canyon exemplifies the collaboration and exchange that often occurs across disciplines and cultures. What other structures or sites—historical and/or contemporary—can you think of that exhibit this kind of fusion, transfer, and exchange? For several of the sites or structures you name, identify also the various component cultures, disciplines, or concepts that intersect and align to create that structure/site.

 Transfer Hub: Contribute your ideas and see what others have written at fountainheadpress.com/transferhub.

What is Writing Transfer?

Writing transfer entails customizing your knowledge, practices, and approaches to learning and writing from one writing occasion to other writing occasions. Writing transfer relies on complex, higher-order thinking skills and emerges through practice, awareness, and reflection. With writing transfer, you can adapt what you have learned about writing, and about learning itself, from one context to others.

At the same time, navigating the dynamic and varied landscape of academic writing often can be challenging. The potential for intersections and divergences among writing occasions does not readily lend itself to a compact set of guidelines for becoming a good

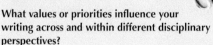

Writer Insights

What values or priorities influence your writing across and within different disciplinary perspectives?

I've written throughout my life, and one pattern that I have noticed is that I write in order to understand my world. When I was younger, "truth" came in the form of political criticism. I remember giving a speech in eighth grade on parallels between America and the fall of Rome...In high school, influenced by my history teacher, I read Chomsky and wrote several essays critical of American hegemony....By my junior year, I joined the debate team and competed in national tournaments. One day...someone introduced me to Richard Feynman, an incredibly brilliant physicist, and [I] was blown away. "This was real truth. Scientific truth!" I applied (and got into) UC Davis Physics. I stopped writing about politics, but I didn't stop writing. For nearly a decade, I wrote peer reviews for scientific papers, published papers in journals, maintained a research blog, and even churned out a doctoral thesis....When I graduated, I continued to write for my job, but now I "wrote" PowerPoint presentations. I was a data scientist for an analytics startup....Recently, I've decided to...write about data analysis on social issues. I still write to understand the world, but my focus is now closer to home and towards bringing about positive changes in my community.

~Jesse Singh, Physicist,
Oakland, California, U.S.

academic writer across the board. Instead, conventions and expectations for writing shift across and within various fields of inquiry, or **disciplines**.

These disciplines and the writers within them create knowledge through shared—albeit shifting—understandings about posing questions, pursuing research, and communicating ideas as effectively as possible. In order to write in a way that resonates with readers in their disciplines, those writing from within a given disciplinary perspective generate texts whose features coalesce to form what scholar James Porter refers to as a **discourse community**, "a local and temporary constraining system, defined by a body of texts (or more generally, practices) that are unified by a common focus. A discourse community is a textual system with stated and unstated conventions [and] a vital history."

Together, the "stated and unstated conventions" within discourse communities generate patterns that help readers and writers in those disciplines advance knowledge (Bazerman). These conventions are known as **discourse conventions**, and they influence the choices people make when writing. When you write a paper for a psychology class, for instance, you will likely invoke writing practices that both resonate with and differ from those you might summon while writing an essay in an English course. Similarly, when you write a biology lab report, you are working within yet another disciplinary context composed of some unique writing features and some crossover elements.

These discourse conventions can even impact seemingly minute aspects of writing. For example, in a study by Ken Hyland, data shows that writers in the disciplines of Philosophy and Marketing refer directly to themselves in their writing (with "I," "we," or the impersonal pronoun) 550 percent more frequently than writers in the discipline of Mechanical Engineering. Amid so many different disciplinary contexts and writing occasions, the criteria for what makes writing effective can seem confusing, if not arbitrary.

Discourse conventions, however, are about much more than just pronouns. Instead, they reflect the values, priorities, and customs for how people in disciplines create and advance knowledge. Discourse communities shape and reflect the values writers embrace, and the expectations and conventions writers bring to writing, reading, and research.

Connecting discourse conventions with the creation of knowledge, Gordon Wells, Professor of Education at University of California, Santa Cruz, writes:

> Each subject discipline constitutes a way of making sense of human experience that has evolved over generations and each is dependent on its own particular practices: its instrumental procedures, its criteria for judging relevance and validity, and its conventions of acceptable forms of argument. In a word each has developed its own modes of discourse.

Modes of discourse emerge from within their respective disciplines, and therefore reflect, shape, and govern the arguments most valued by members of those disciplines. Being able to navigate among these discourse communities requires becoming more sophisticated at writing transfer by adapting prior knowledge, experiences, and strategies to each new writing occasion you encounter.

Write Now

Think of two or three different writing experiences you have had within different disciplinary perspectives. Options might include an English paper, a history essay, a journalistic piece, a math proof, a lab report—any experiences with writing you believe were influenced by a disciplinary perspective. Reflect in writing about the discourse conventions operating within each of these experiences. How would you describe these instances in terms of discourse conventions? Did you notice any shared discourse conventions? Any unique ones? Did anything surprise you in terms of the expectations or conventions for the writing occasions?

The Dynamic Nature of Discourse Conventions

As you consider the nature of discourse conventions, however, it becomes crucial to recognize that they are dynamic rather than static. Discourse is dynamic because disciplines are created and sustained by human beings. This sounds simple enough, but it is worth emphasizing: humans in disciplines create knowledge, rethink approaches, change assumptions, and move ideas forward (or sometimes backward). For that reason, disciplinary writing, by its very nature, grows and changes.

Not only do disciplinary conventions shift, but different people also hold varying individual expectations and values about what constitutes effective writing. These individualistic preferences can be shaped by disciplinary history and context, as well as by particular scholars' unique dispositions, experiences, and approaches to learning, thinking, and writing.

Making discourse communities even more complex, these values, conventions, and expectations about writing shift not only within and between disciplines and people, but often across historical and cultural contexts as well. Twenty years ago, for example, writing in online environments was not as prevalent in academic contexts. Today, nearly every discipline has modes of writing that operate in digital environments. Similarly, what people agreed upon as effective writing in 1820 is not necessarily what we would agree upon now. Scholars in different places around the world can have a diverse and sometimes conflicting range of expectations, approaches, and conventions. Janice Walker, a scholar of writing studies, uses citation as an example to illustrate just how heterogeneous these writing practices can be:

> Strict attribution of sources has not always been necessary, and indeed in many cultures and contexts, it is still not (necessarily) required. Ancient texts often did not follow any formal rules of attribution, since it was assumed that the audience would already be familiar with the body of scholarly work. I have also heard…that in Chinese culture, the words of others are used without attribution as a way of honoring those whose words were considered so important that they needed no attribution.

Walker goes on to outline the many changes in citation practices that have occurred over the past ten years, including shifting rules about italics, citation of online sources, and what does or does not constitute "common knowledge." Walker, herself an expert in writing studies and a highly accomplished writer, exclaims at one point: "I'm *so* confused!"

As Walker's confusion illustrates, disciplinary perspectives, historical context, and writers themselves all occupy important roles in shaping and reflecting discourse conventions. However, other layers of transfer are at play in this landscape as well. Even within particular disciplines, writing expectations and conventions can shift dramatically across and between writing projects.

A writer's particular purpose, for example, significantly impacts what constitutes an effective approach to writing. Depending on whether writers hope to persuade, inform, critique, or define, their discourse conventions shift accordingly. When writers have multiple, overlapping, or even perhaps contradictory purposes, their decisions about how to write effectively become even more complex.

Discourse conventions also change in relationship to whether writing is meant to be private, professional, scholarly, widely accessible, or some combination thereof. Increasingly, writers across disciplines produce and share knowledge not only in scholarly settings, but also in more public contexts, including such forms of writing as blogs, oral presentations, op-eds, captions for museum exhibits or online archives, magazine articles, or reviews of books or films.

Pointing out the ways in which writers transfer writing practices between public and scholarly contexts (distinctions which are themselves frequently blurred), Professor of English Mike Rose suggests that this approach entails "bilingualism." Bilingualism of the sort Rose refers to hinges on a transfer-based approach to writing and learning.

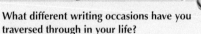
Writer Insights

What different writing occasions have you traversed through in your life?

[I]n high school…I wrote several reports and opinions about classical books. In college [I wrote everything from] book reports to final exams. Today, as a notary, I'm writing constantly: contracts, descriptions of facts and persons, different kinds of affidavits. Also, I have written two monographs, one about trust and [the] other about patrimonial aspects of marriage. Both of them [were] published in legal journals.

~*Gonzalo Toro, Public Notary, Jujuy, Argentina*

Each writing occasion presents unique opportunities and challenges for writers regarding how they might adapt, modify, extend, or otherwise reconsider—in essence, how they will *transfer*—the choices they make about writing from one writing occasion to others. And, because discourse is so dynamic, it would be nearly impossible to articulate precisely what the rules are for writing in particular disciplines or for particular writing occasions, nor can a text such as *Writing in Transit* provide you with neat and tidy formulas for writing in each discipline. What can happen, however, is that writers can invoke a transfer-based approach to writing and learning in order to bring prior knowledge, practices, and experiences to bear on each new writing occasion.

Write Now

Create a timeline documenting your writing history. Begin your timeline with your earliest memories involving writing (even if these entailed "pretend" writing while you were a child, for example), and move through the years to the present day, documenting memorable or meaningful (or mundane) writing experiences. Plot out on your timeline all the many different occasions in which you have written, whether in school, in your personal experiences, and/or in your professional encounters.

A Transfer-Based Approach to Writing

Writing in Transit will help make the complexities of discourse conventions, disciplinary perspectives, and context more manageable for you by preparing you to more effectively transfer your knowledge, practices, goals, individual dispositions, and ideas from one writing context to others. Adopting a transfer-based approach to writing, the concepts in this text will bring to your attention varying disciplinary approaches to writing, illustrating how writers create knowledge and how their dynamic values and priorities inform writing practices and discourse conventions.

This approach embraces a premise whereby disciplines operate as "ways of knowing" (Carter). As such, *Writing in Transit* models the dynamic nature of academic writing. Exploring writing as a network of shifting inquiries, this book invites you to consider the questions asked by scholars of various disciplines, as well as the resulting values about writing that they hold. A transfer-based approach will enable you to anticipate the variable aspects of discourse conventions, empowering you to embrace the twists and turns of academic writing as it generates new knowledge. In so doing, you will be able to explore new writing occasions with curiosity and confidence rather than with confusion and frustration.

But this transfer-based approach not only asks you to reflect on others' writing choices, but equips you with the ability to transfer *your* writing practices across disciplinary contexts. You will learn, for example, strategies for creating knowledge within and between diverse disciplinary perspectives, by turn shaping your inquiries and arguments to these perspectives and also at times deliberately infusing different perspectives into particular discourse communities. Writing with a transfer-based approach will therefore position you to participate actively in ongoing academic conversations, contribute your ideas effectively, and advance knowledge meaningfully in the world around you.

Writing Practices across Contexts

A transfer-based approach to writing explores how writers forge key intersections across writing contexts, even though discipline, writing occasion, and individual disposition will continue to impact how writers approach any given project or situation. As Dawn Youngblood maintains, "No discipline is an island entirely in itself.... [D]isciplines are by no means discrete entities—they necessarily overlap, borrow, and encroach upon one another." Within, across, and beyond disciplines, the writing you encounter may appear quite distinct or idiosyncratic, but it too will "necessarily overlap, borrow, and encroach upon" other writing occasions.

Exploring in more depth the ways in which disciplines borrow from one another, each chapter of *Writing in Transit* considers one of the following aspects of academic writing. Transversing context, these aspects will alternately overlap, intersect, and diverge across disciplines and writing occasions:

- Research and Writing as a Process
- Posing Meaningful Questions
- Reading
- Summary
- Synthesis
- Analysis
- Framing Arguments
- Constructing Arguments
- Designing Arguments
- Choosing and Integrating Evidence
- Citing Evidence

Discovering the ways in which these key aspects of academic writing align across disciplines will enable you to more effectively transfer, modify, and apply your writing-related knowledge from one writing occasion to others.

Keep in mind, though, that despite the ways in which writers might be able to transfer these writing practices across context, *Writing in Transit* cannot offer one perfect, go-to strategy for these writing practices. Instead, this transfer-based approach prepares you to identify which practices (or parts of practices) might work best within particular contexts, and invites you to take into account disciplinary discourse conventions, individual priorities and dispositions, and other relevant aspects of writing occasions to tailor your practices and approaches accordingly.

Strategies for Becoming Better at Writing Transfer

Writing in Transit offers you a transfer-based framework for becoming a better academic writer, preparing you for the complex and multifaceted exigencies of college-level writing across disciplines and writing occasions. Transfer, however, is not composed of a simple formula for success, but functions instead as a habit of mind and a comprehensive approach to writing and learning. As you explore *Writing in Transit*, you learn to deploy certain strategies that improve your writing transfer skills (see Table 1.1).

TABLE 1.1 Strategies to improve writing transfer skills

Consider how people in various disciplines create knowledge.	What kinds of questions do scholars ask in various disciplines? What forms of research do they conduct? What purposes and aims do various writers have within and across disciplines?
Identify shared and unique patterns of writing across disciplines and writing occasions.	As you encounter texts across disciplines and contexts, identify general patterns as well as features that seem unique to a particular discipline or writing occasion. Assess what seems non-transportable as well: are there, for instance, any conventions or expectations within certain disciplines or occasions you believe might be counterproductive in other contexts?
Reflect on your own writing approaches and values.	What are your individual dispositions and inclinations with regard to writing? What approaches seem most meaningful to you when you encounter writing projects? What values do you hold about effective writing? How do your values shift according to context? Which kinds of questions most often spark your curiosity?
Think about yourself as a writer.	Reflect actively on how you as a writer are changing and growing, and identify periodically what is working more or less effectively for you as a learner. Which approaches and practices seem to come more readily to you? As you read others' writing, think about which aspects you would like to emulate, modify, or reject. Keep in mind that your learning and writing approaches will shift across time and context.
Consider this the beginning stage of a lifelong journey enriched through transfer.	Writing is a lifelong enterprise, and you are the individual best positioned to know and track your writing experiences, your writing ambitions, and your writing strengths and limitations. The goal of *Writing in Transit* is to help you cultivate a habit of mind in which you can rely on transfer as you move forward in your education, career, and life.

Carrying these strategies with you as you move within, across, and among all the many writing occasions you will encounter in college and beyond will prepare you to approach each new writing occasion with transfer-based thinking and writing practices.

Why Writing Transfer Matters

A transfer-based approach to writing and learning—the ability to establish connections, notice confluences, and adapt prior knowledge amid seemingly disparate concepts and contexts—has particular value in our increasingly connected twenty-first century. Future studies expert William H. Newell emphasizes just how interconnected the world is becoming:

> Most public intellectuals as well as experts in future studies would agree that the increasingly global society of the first half of the twenty-first century will be characterized by increasing connectivity, diversity, scale, and rapidity of change.... [S]tudents will face challenges in the next several decades unlike those in the past. In general, small events on one part of the planet and in one sphere of human existence can now end up having large and relatively rapid effects on other parts of the planet and in other spheres of human existence.... Coping with this complexity will require a new way of understanding—one that does not rely on having only a single viewpoint.

The increasing "connectivity, diversity, scale, and rapidity of change" to which Newell refers will ask us, perhaps more than ever before, to sharpen and rely on our abilities to engage in transfer-based thinking. In this emerging context, writers will need to become adept at considering multiple perspectives and taking into account the ways in which context shapes and reflects ideas. The rapidity of change and increased connectivity defining contemporary experience asks that writers become accustomed to adapting, borrowing, extending, and challenging their prior knowledge and practices as they encounter new contexts and ideas.

Your educational path—whatever it may be—will likely invite you to negotiate the discourse conventions of courses across a wide range of disciplines, each of which will likely present many diverse writing occasions. According to a study of 179 syllabi from 17 different disciplines, professors assigned 40 different kinds of "papers" in one academic year. The same study found that 83 percent of undergraduates submitted, in one academic year, at least 60 pages of final-draft writing across all of their classes (Graves, et al.).

These figures demonstrate that, throughout your undergraduate experience, you will likely be expected to do a lot of writing across many different contexts, each of

Writer Insights

What different writing occasions have you traversed through in your life?

I am currently a sophomore in college....Back in my elementary school days, most of my writing was done in pencil/pen. Around third grade, I learned to write in cursive, but since middle school began, I have always been writing in print or typing everything out. Throughout elementary and middle school, I mostly only wrote whenever my teachers assigned...In eighth grade, I got a Facebook account, and that was when I started posting or commenting on statuses.... [In] eleventh grade...my brother taught me the importance of a good thesis. [Now] I am searching for internships, which reminds me that I need...good speaking skills. In order to get these speaking skills, I need to learn how to be a better writer. This will help me express my points in a better way when talking to other people, including my friends.

~Dan Hoang, College Student,
Cupertino, California, U.S.

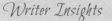

which will likely carry different criteria for success. Faculty assign many different kinds of papers, and their expectations about what effective writing looks like are contingent on the genre of the writing assigned, the purpose of the writing, established discourse practices within their disciplines, and individual dispositions.

Gaining acumen in transfer—an essential and complex habit of mind—will enable you to strengthen your abilities in all sorts of domains (not only writing), so you can be better prepared for the demands and opportunities of the twenty-first century. A transfer-based approach to writing will provide you with the opportunity to more effectively transfer your knowledge, ideas, and practices about and from writing to other contexts, thereby increasing your growth as a writer, thinker, and global citizen.

> **Writer Insights**
>
> **Why is writing important in your life across different contexts and occasions?**
>
> I've been a…writer for many years…at school and university, at work and at home. In my childhood I often…was at the top of the class [for] writing essays, I wrote many letters to my relatives and friends, [and] I had a personal diary. Now I write emails, different kinds of papers for my job (reports, instructions, etc.)…I remember [once] I was asked to write a special thank you letter for an American school principal. To be honest it was not easy at all [but] thanks to collaboration with other people I managed to do it! It was my small success in writing.
>
> ~Marina Leonova, Vice Principal, Russia

Transferring Writing Knowledge, Practices, and Approaches

This text foregrounds the ways in which writing is highly dynamic, moving and shifting across context. Chapter 1 offers an orientation to the text and to writing transfer, emphasizing how transfer will enable you to reflect on your learning abilities, gain increased awareness of what strategies work more or less effectively for you, and strengthen your intellectual acumen. With this approach, *Writing in Transit* empowers you to more effectively contribute your ideas and advance your knowledge through writing across your undergraduate experience and beyond.

Each of the subsequent chapters builds on the foundation established in Chapter 1 by focusing on a key aspect of academic writing that aligns—with its own unique elements—across complementary writing contexts. Moving through the chapters of *Writing in Transit,* you will engage with disparate aspects of writing that include reading, research, and argumentation, all of which cut across distinct yet overlapping disciplinary perspectives and writing contexts. Far from providing one perfect, universal approach, writing transfer instead involves cultivating a habit of mind where you learn to apply, modify, and revisit writing practices from one writing occasion to others, even as you also discover new approaches and strategies.

Consider the content of this book, then, an invitation for you to explore, read, discuss, and write about ideas that matter to you and others, and to discover how writing shifts across and within disciplines, time, and context.

℘ ℘ ℘

Historical Engineering Report: "Johnstown, Pennsylvania, 1889" by Ernest Zebrowski

Transfer Points: Engineering, Science Education

Flooding is among the most devastating of disasters, across regions and time. In 1971, the Hanoi Flood killed 594 people, impacted nearly 600,000 people, and yielded an estimated loss of one billion dollars (Thu). From July 2011 to January 2012, nearly three quarters of Thailand's provinces became flooded, killing more than 800 people, leaving millions homeless or displaced, and costing more than $45 billion dollars (Nindang and Allen). The 1931 Yanzi-Huai Flood in China is widely regarded as the most devastating flood in history: it killed as many as two million people, and impacted an area of land equivalent to the size of England (Courtney).

The Johnstown Flood of 1889 in Pennsylvania was, at the time, the worst disaster in United States history, killing 2,209 people (Wharton-Michael). As you will learn in the Zebrowski selection, the flooding resulted from the failure of the South Fork Dam (Kaktins, Todd, Wojno, and Coleman) and decimated the Johnstown, Pennsylvania, community. Newspaper accounts featured the grisly and heartbreaking devastation. *The Tribune*, for example, described Stone Bridge as "having railroad cars, telephone poles, houses, horses, and human corpses strung along its expanse" (Wharton-Michael). Artists drew images of the aftermath, depicting harrowing scenes of parents carrying coffins to bury their children.

As illustrated by this confluence of art and journalism, a fuller understanding of a complex event such as the Johnstown Flood requires a variety of perspectives. Gaining a fully nuanced understanding would require contributions of yet more disciplines, from history and anthropology to ecology, geography, and psychology.

With the Johnstown Flood, Zebrowski adopts a civil and environmental engineering perspective. This discipline deals with the "built environment": buildings, bridges, roads, railroads, subway systems, airports, water supply systems, and sanitary engineering ("What is"). Scholars and professionals in civil and environmental engineering, also sometimes called structural engineering, work across many industries, from automotive and shipbuilding to construction and space stations.

Scholars in civil and environmental engineering publish research on advances in technologies, practices, and knowledge related to structures and built environments. Often, this knowledge is highly specialized, relying on assumed levels of knowledge and familiarity with the field. Along with discipline-specific terminology and knowledge, writing in this field also adheres to discipline-specific discourse conventions and expectations. Research articles tend to include graphics and data visualization that demonstrate the advances and inquiries.

Zebrowski's rendering of civil and environmental engineering, however, reflects an approach designed for broader publics. While Zebrowski does include discipline-specific terms and knowledge to understand the Johnstown Flood, he does so through an approach grounded more firmly on narrative and explication.

This approach resonates with a set of larger goals affiliated with science education, a wide-ranging discipline that seeks to make science more accessible and understandable. Those in science education are

Ernest Zebrowski has taught disaster science and physics at Penn State, Duquesne University, Louisiana State, and Southern University. He founded the doctoral program in science and math education at Southern University. He holds a Ph.D. from University of Pittsburgh and an M.S. from Carnegie-Mellon University. He has written a number of books designed to narrate scientific perspectives for broader publics, including *Category 5: The Story of Camille; Global Climate Change; The Last Days of St. Pierre: The Volcanic Disaster That Claimed Thirty Thousand Lives; Hydrocarbon Hucksters: Lessons from Louisiana on Oil, Politics, and Environmental Justice;* and *A History of the Circle: Mathematical Reasoning and the Physical Universe.* The selection on Johnstown comes from his book *Perils of a Restless Planet*, which provides scientific perspectives on disasters throughout history. Zebrowski is from Beaver County, Pennsylvania, and now lives on St. George Island, Florida ("Ernest").

invested in science transfer, exploring how people can adapt, reconsider, extend, and/or challenge scientific concepts to a myriad of contexts.

Such research helps those like Zebrowski transfer science to a larger array of contexts. And, in the case of Zebrowski, it helps facilitate efforts to understand the Johnstown Flood from a broader range of perspectives, including art and journalism, as well as civil and environmental engineering.

Write Here

Working with a group of classmates, imagine the varying ways in which scholars from many different disciplines might conduct research about a disaster. You might together decide on a particular type of disaster (flood, volcano, chemical spill, etc.), or a particular instance of a disaster. Then, identify as many different disciplines as you can that might have important perspectives to bear on understanding the disaster. Be as specific as you can about the potential research questions scholars from each of those various disciplines might pose regarding the disaster.

Ernest Zebrowski

Johnstown, Pennsylvania, 1889 from *Perils of a Restless Planet*

In May of 1889, record rains drenched the partially deforested Conemaugh River valley upstream of the small industrial city of Johnstown, population 28,000. Had the Conemaugh been a free-running river, it would have crested high enough to flood a portion of Johnstown's business district, damage the lower stories of a few hundred houses, render several bridges impassable, and interrupt some public services and utilities. Few if any lives would have been lost, for floods in this region usually gave observant people ample time to scamper to higher ground. In fact, Johnstown residents had long learned to expect annoying floods almost every spring, for the Conemaugh and its tributaries had flooded at particularly high levels in 1808, 1847, 1875, 1880, 1885, 1887, and 1888. The flood of 1889 would have been but slightly worse than these earlier floods if the hand of Man hadn't transformed the event into a major disaster. The aggravating factor was a dam that did not do its job.

This was the most devastating dam failure in U.S. history, and it involved a structure that the ancient Romans would have been smart enough *not* to build. The dam was not arched, it did not transmit its load to bedrock, and it was not even built of masonry. The South Fork Dam was originally built to supply water to a section of the Pennsylvania Canal at a location on the South Fork of the Conemaugh River 22 kilometers (14 mi) upstream from Johnstown. This dam was an earthen structure 260 meters (850 ft) in width and 24 meters (80 ft) in height, which impounded a lake some 5 kilometers in length and around 2 kilometers in width. The dam originally failed in 1847, while it was still under construction, and on that occasion the resulting torrent washed out an aqueduct at Johnstown. Completed in 1852, the dam's original function was rendered obsolete within a decade as railroads replaced the canals. By 1889, the structure's fundamental design shortcomings had been aggravated by neglectful maintenance during ten years of private ownership by the South Fork Hunting and Fishing Club, an exclusive group of Pittsburgh millionaires. The spillway had been obstructed by a meshwork designed to keep fish from escaping, pipes originally installed to permit independent regulation of the water level had been removed (a cheaper strategy than repairing and maintaining them), and the breast of the dam had been allowed to sink lower than its shoulders. The failure was predictable, not in terms of the exact date and time, but in view of the statistical certainty that sooner or later the region was bound to be drenched by heavy rains whose runoff would exceed the capacity of the dam's spillway.

When a downpour began on May 30, 1889, it had already rained eleven days that month. Because the saturated earth of the surrounding forests could hold no more water, this rain ran off into the creeks and rivers. Around noon on the thirtieth, many of the more observant inhabitants of Johnstown and upstream villages began to evacuate the low-lying areas; had they not, the death toll would have been much higher. Upstream, the inadequate and obstructed spillway of the South Fork Dam became clogged with flood debris, and the waters of the artificial lake rose until they topped the breast of the dam. A few minutes after 3 PM on May 31, the dam exploded and sent a thundering wave front 15 meters (50 ft) high down the already-swollen river. It took around 36 minutes for the lake to empty, and for those 36 minutes fluid energy poured into the valley below at a rate comparable to the energy flow over Niagara Falls.

Within its first moments, the giant wave ripped up thousands of trees and churned them into a thundering maelstrom of splintered timber. The leading edge of this surge chewed through the forests and villages farther downstream. On the steeper straightaways of the valley, the wave reached speeds of 100 kilometers per hour (60 mi/h), while on sharp curves and shallower drops it slowed to around 15 kilometers per hour (10 mi/h). (According to some observers, it may almost have stopped at times.) Because the bottom of the surge was retarded by friction while the top was not, this great flood wave progressed not as a wall of water but rather as a turbulent, cascading breaker. Victims were pounded downward rather than being swept forward and upward. This was not the kind of flood which would allow anyone to swim to safety.

A few miles downstream stood the Conemaugh Viaduct, a large and substantial stone arch bridge. Here the debris jammed up, temporarily creating a leaky dam 22 meters (71 ft) high, which was about the same height as the dam that had burst. Had the viaduct held at this point, the downstream towns might have experienced only a modest acceleration in the rising

water. Alas, although the viaduct's engineers had planned for floods in their design, they had not anticipated this particular extreme set of conditions. The viaduct held for only a few minutes. As the structure toppled, the flood wave surged forward with renewed vigor and completely wiped away the village of Mineral Point, destroying 30 houses and a furniture factor. It then burst across an oxbow, resculpturing the river's channel, and tore into East Conemaugh, where it carried away whole railroad trains and thirty steam locomotives. Next downstream was Woodvale, where 255 houses were swept completely from their foundations, along with a tannery and a streetcar shed housing eight-nine horses. When the water hit the Gautier Wireworks, boilers and furnaces promptly exploded and contributed a billowing "death cloud" of soot and ash to the churning wave front, along with many miles of tangled barbed wire.

As it thundered into Johnstown, this tumbling mass of debris indiscriminately ground up and swept away most human constructions in its path. Bodies of humans and animals churned in the foam, and even railroad cars were tossed around like footballs. In just a few terrible minutes, thousands of houses and businesses were destroyed, and thousands lost their lives. Ultimately, the official statistics would list 2,209 known dead and 967 missing. If you walk through Johnstown's cemeteries today, you won't fail to notice a particular recurring date on the tombstones: "Died May 31, 1889." One section of Grandview Cemetery has a large granite monument dedicated to the unknown dead, behind which are 777 small white and anonymous marble headstones.

Only one man-made structure survived the direct onslaught of the wave, and paradoxically its survival actually contributed to the horror of the disaster. This structure, a railroad bridge at the lower end of town, had been built as a series of seven low semicircular stone arches that would have looked quite at home in ancient Rome. When the thundering surge threw its debris against this bridge, it once again created a dam, just as it had at the upstream viaduct. Here, however, the individual arches were much shorter in span and heavier; this was a very conservatively built structure (which some engineers would

Figure 3.11. The disaster at Johnstown's Stone Bridge, as depicted in an 1889 photograph.

characterize as inefficient in its use of materials), and it held. Although the Cambria Iron Company and many houses downstream of the Stone Bridge were damaged by the portion of the surge that topped the bridge, relatively few of these structures were totally destroyed.

Unfortunately, although Stone Bridge saved some, it also aggravated the disaster for many others. The sudden blockage of a rapidly moving stream always has its repercussions; on a much smaller scale you may have noticed the "water hammer" effect when the solenoid valve on a washing machine suddenly closes. When the arches of the Stone Bridge were slammed shut by the debris-riding on the wave front, the flood wave was reflected back upriver and into a nearby tributary, Stony Creek, where it swept away even more dwellings in the town of Kernville. In places, this reflected wave may have attained a height of as much as 30 meters (100 ft), roughly double that of the initial wave.

Yet there was more to come. Upstream of the Stone Bridge the river was blanketed with floating trees, the remnants of crushed houses, and many partially intact structures that had been carried off their foundations. As the floodwaters poured over and through the logjam at the bridge, the trapped flotsam piled higher and higher. Some victims apparently did succeed in climbing out of this heap of debris. But then this giant pile of splintered wood caught fire, possibly ignited by an overturned stove in an upper story of one of the many houses that had ridden the floodwaters into the bridge, and possibly fueled further by oil leaking from wrecked railroad tank cars. In spite of the continuing rain, there was enough dry fuel in this massive pileup to sustain a monstrous fire, which continued unchecked for several days (Fig. 3.11). It has been speculated that many of the missing—those whose bodies were never recovered—were consumed in this grisly conflagration at the Stone Bridge. After the floodwaters subsided and the flames finally died out, cleanup workers had to resort to explosives to clear the tangled and charred wreckage at the bridge in order to restore the course of the stream.

Relief poured in from across the country, but Pittsburgh's "Captains of Industry" made relatively token contributions; Andrew Carnegie, a member of the club that owned the dam, contributed just ten thousand dollars on behalf of his steel company, while thirty of the sixty-one club members contributed nothing at all. Ultimately, the courts in Pittsburgh ruled that the disaster had been an act of God, and that the South Fork Hunting and Fishing Club and its members had no legal liability for the damage or loss of life. Particularly galling to the survivors, many of whom had lost everything they owned and loved, was the fact that the dam had served no functional purpose other than to provide recreation for an exclusive private membership. This angry sentiment was captured in a widely quoted contemporary poem by one Isaac Reed:

> Many thousand human lives—
> Butchered husbands, slaughtered wives,
> Mangled daughters, bleeding sons,
> Hosts of martyred little ones,
> (Worse than Herod's awful crime)
> Sent to heaven before their time;
> Lovers burnt and sweethearts drowned,
> Darlings lost but never found!
> All the horrors that hell could wish,
> Such was the price that was paid for—fish!

The dam was never rebuilt, and the club's property was sold off. Today a few of the original club members' houses still stand, privately owned, and one can dine at a restaurant in the former clubhouse, which is now owned by a local historical society. The National Park Service maintains a memorial park and a museum that includes the site of the failed dam, the shoulders of which still remain.

The Johnstown Flood offered a profound lesson: Knowledge by itself is no guarantee of sound engineering. In 1889, all knowledgeable parties were quite aware that the South Fork Dam was unsafe, and that even the ancient technology of the Romans would have created a safer structure (as was subsequently confirmed by the survival of Johnstown's Stone Bridge). But knowledge alone does not guarantee the power to act, or to force others to act. The South Fork Dam was no more than a weekend recreational asset to its owners, and, by being part of a collective, the club members were largely insulated from the concerns that had been voiced over the years by various downstream residents. Members of the club were not necessarily evil people (although some of the officers certainly had misplaced priorities); a better characterization is that most of the members were ignorant of the physical principles, ignorant of the prevailing engineering practices, and/or too distracted with other activities to contemplate the potential human consequences of a failure of their dam. They were mainly uninformed, and, through their insularity, uninformable.

Today, one can no longer build or own a private dam on a public waterway. In the United States, to dam even a small stream on private property requires environmental impact studies, hearings, licenses, engineering reviews, and subsequent inspections. This body of governmental regulation has evolved in response to the historical record of incidents where individuals and private groups had been presumed to be safeguarding the public interest but in fact failed to do so. Those who complain about today's "excessive" government regulation lose all credibility if they ignore the historical disasters that were aggravated by the lack of such regulation. The Johnstown Flood of 1889 stands as a prime example, not to be forgotten.

Joints, Fasteners, and Foundations

The strength of the materials alone does not guarantee the integrity of a structure; in fact, it's quite possible for a building or bridge to collapse even though each of its individual structural members remains intact. To ensure the stability of a structure, its designers must address two additional issues: (1) How are the pieces held together? And (2) What holds the building to the earth?

For small wood-framed structures, the most common fastener is the lowly nail. Nails hold reasonably well, provided they are kept in compression and/or shear by the loads on the building. There is, however, one way a nail will *not* hold: If you pull opposite to the direction in which it was driven, you'll pop the nail right back out. This in fact is why roofs are often lost in high winds; although most of the time a roof bears down on the rest of the structure, a high wind can reverse this direction and pull the roof members *up*. Nails alone are ineffective in preventing this type of failure.

To accommodate possible reversals in the direction of the load, particularly in regions subject to hurricanes, roof rafters and other framing timbers need to be joined by metal tie straps and brackets, and/or by drilling holes through the overlapping members and joining them with threaded bolts and nuts. In addition, triangular bracing can be quite effective in reducing lateral bending and torsional loads on a structure's joints. Such techniques are particularly important when building in coastal areas or on interior floodplains, for when a flood destroys a structure, it is usually the joints and fasteners that fail.

With larger steel and concrete structures, the design of the joints is even more critical. Bridges, elevated roadways, and tall buildings are subject to significant movements from winds and ground tremors. (For example, a long suspension span such as the Golden Gate Bridge can sway laterally as much as 4.5 meters [15 ft] on a gusty day, and the top floors of a skyscraper may move as much as 1 meter [3 ft]). Remember that such structures *need* to move a little, because it is their elasticity that allows them to adapt to changing loading conditions. At the same time, large structures must be allowed to expand and contract with temperature changes; if they don't, the resulting stresses can easily exceed the elastic limit of the steel and concrete. For instance, a 150-meter (500-ft) steel truss in Pennsylvania will expand and contract about 12 centimeters (5 in.) between a cold day in winter and a warm day in summer.

The design of fasteners for large structures is particularly challenging, because we now have two somewhat conflicting design criteria: (1) the requirement that the structural members be held together, and (2) the requirement that the joined members be allowed some degree of relative movement (usually in just one direction). Bridges and large buildings incorporate a variety of clever solutions to this problem: large encased rollers, rocker bearings, offset straps, and pin-and-hanger assemblies, to name a few.[12] In some cases, engineers have cushioned tall buildings on expansion supports that permit the entire building to rock slightly rather than bending. The mechanical details of these joints need not concern us here; my point is that there is no "perfect" method of fastening two large structural members together, because it is quite impossible to simultaneously prevent movement yet allow movement in the same joint. Compromise in design is therefore unavoidable, and in practice this usually amounts to ignoring those combinations of loading conditions that are considered to be highly unlikely to occur during the lifetime of the structure. The Northridge, California, earthquake of January 1994 triggered the collapse of sections of three major elevated freeways, and all of these failures occurred at joints or vertical supports. This does not, however, compel us to conclude that the engineering was deficient in California. Had an earthquake of this same intensity occurred in New England, the damage would have been considerably greater. (And yes, earthquakes do occur in the eastern portion of the United States, just not as often.)

The most important part of any structure is the part few people see: the foundation. A failure here can lead to the collapse of everything above. Although light one-story structures in warm climates are sometimes built on concrete slabs, usually a foundation must be much more than this. In cold climates, the foundation for even a light building must extend below the frost line, to prevent heaving and buckling when the earth expands on freezing. In Arctic regions, foundations must thermally isolate the structure from the ground, to prevent the building's interior heat from melting the permafrost; if the permafrost *does* melt, the structure will be subject to settling (probably unevenly), followed by additional movements when the supporting earth refreezes.

While it's obvious to even the most casual observer that the load-bearing capacity of soil decreases when its moisture content rises, quantitative predictions of this effect are quite difficult to make and are fraught with uncertainties. Foundations that depend on the mechanical properties of soil must therefore be built very conservatively. In coastal construction where the water table is high and the soil is predominantly sand, even relatively light homes need to be built on pilings that extend 3 to 5 meters (10-16 ft) below the ground surface. Such pilings also act as vertical beams that can resist the lateral onslaught of moderate storm surges and will stiffen the structure against high winds.

For the largest and heaviest structures, soil simply cannot be depended on to support a foundation. Most bridges and skyscrapers are therefore held up by pilings that extend through the soil and bear against bedrock, often many meters (even many stories) below the ground surface.[13] This is the best one can do, for no amount of engineering will prevent the bedrock from shifting during an earthquake or a local fault creep. Fortunately, the probability is low that the bedrock will happen to shift directly under a structure; the worst it usually does is vibrate.

If gravity were the only force acting on a structure, it would be quite sufficient to simply build the edifice so it "sits" on its foundation. In fact, around the globe, numerous historical buildings constructed in this manner have survived many centuries. Earthquakes, however, may produce lateral loads capable of knocking even the heaviest building off its foundation, while high winds and floods will transmit both lateral and lifting forces to a structure. Clearly, the engineer needs to be concerned about these possibilities. In most parts of the United States, construction codes require that buildings be rigidly connected to their foundations, in a manner that resists the lifting or base shear forces that have been identified as local disaster hazards.

Unfortunately, there is no easy way to retrofit many older structures that do not meet modern building codes. In some cases, such older non-compliant structures have proven their ability to withstand natural geophysical or meteorological events. In other cases, however, such structures may be time bombs, waiting to be set off by the next windstorm, earthquake, or flood.

Write Away

1. Zebrowski's book, from which this selection is drawn, provides scientific perspectives on natural disasters. Finding one or more specific places in the reading selection, reflect on the impact of this scientific perspective: How has this perspective shaped your understanding of the Johnstown Flood? How do you think your understanding might be different had you instead read an account of the Johnstown Flood that was not informed by science? How has this perspective shaped your understanding of civil and environmental engineering? Using these questions and evidence from Zebrowski, articulate a position on the impact of work such as this for science education, the disciplines involved, and disaster preparedness, response, and/or recovery.

2. As Zebrowski indicates, dams have been in use since at least Roman antiquity. Curate a photographic essay or a visual presentation about dams in which you address one or more of the following questions: What are their functions? What have been their impacts to people and environments? Where have dams been constructed and why? You can take a historical approach, focusing on a particular time period, or a regional approach, focusing on a particular geographic area; or you can decide on a different approach to selection and range. Through your curation, develop a visual argument about dams.

3. Working with a group of classmates, compile a collaborative annotated bibliography with multidisciplinary resources that can inform even deeper knowledge about the Johnstown flood. You can assign particular disciplines to each group member, or work together to gather and annotate sources. You can choose whether to compile historical or contemporary sources from different disciplines that directly address Johnstown and/or that address concepts and ideas that could be applied to the Johnstown Flood but that do not directly address it.

Persuasive Letter: "An Open Letter From Internet Engineers to the U.S. Congress" by Peter Eckersley and Parker Higgins

> Transfer Points: Engineering, Computer Science, Public Policy

Downloading movies, sharing music with friends, copying and pasting images, words, ideas … all are acts that may constitute internet piracy. Broadly defined, internet piracy "refers to the unauthorized copying and distribution (often, though not necessarily, for commercial gain) of copyrighted content" (Yar; 66). This copyrighted content can include movies, photographs, art, graphics, books, articles, music, products, documents ... nearly any sort of human-generated material. According to Google data, during the week of April 16, 2012, Google received requests for 252,490 urls to be removed from Google Search due to copyright infringements. Only four years later, this number has exponentially increased: during the week of April 18, 2016, Google received requests for 22,481,420 urls to be removed due to copyright infringements ("Google").

Learning how to curb internet piracy has become one of the most complex problems of modern life. Internet piracy compromises ownership and integrity, and costs money (Plumer). Some estimate that the film industry loses as much as $6.1 billion from lost movie sales ("Piracy"), the technology sector loses upwards of $10 billion a year (Hess), and the music industry loses $12.5 billion a year ("Music"). Others focus on the loss at a personal level, whereby internet piracy makes it nearly impossible for people to make a living creating creative products such as writing, art, and music (Timberg).

Along with these economic considerations, internet piracy raises a number of other complex questions about freedom of speech, property, democracy, and internet censorship. These questions span many disciplines, including law, public policy, media studies, computer science, engineering, arts and humanities, and philosophy: What is the role of the government in regulating human behavior online and internet content? Who decides what is or is not allowed? How do we protect some people's rights without infringing on others' rights?

One landmark case where these questions emerged was in 2001 with Napster, a peer-to-peer (P2P) music file-sharing network. Another pivotal case, the SOPA-PIPA debates, occurred in 2011 with two proposed pieces of legislation: the Stop Online Piracy Act (SOPA), in the House, and the Pirate IP Act (PIPA), in the Senate. The open letter reprinted here, signed by influential engineers and posted on the Electronic Frontier Foundation (EFF) site, played a critical role in shifting public opinion about the limits and consequences of government efforts to manage internet piracy.

Two aspects of this letter make it especially significant in terms of writing transfer.

First, it shows one of the many ways in which engineers engage with writing transfer. Engineers transfer engineering knowledge across many contexts, from grants, peer-reviewed articles, and textbooks to procedures, reports, analyses, proposals, and reviews. As this letter illustrates, engineers also transfer research through activism and public scholarship, including letters, blogs, and op-eds.

Second, this letter is noteworthy because of its impact after being posted on the EFF website. Established in 1990, EFF aims at "defending civil liberties in the digital world [and championing] user privacy, free expression, and innovation through impact litigation, policy analysis, grassroots activism, and technology development" ("Electronic"). After Eckersley and Higgins posted the letter on the EFF website, public opinion mobilized immensely in opposition to the proposed legislation, prompting congressional leaders to rescind the proposed bills (Benkler).

Such impact has come to be known as the "fifth estate," referring to the influence nontraditional media can have on shaping law and policy. The term builds on feudal conceptions of government as being composed of three estates: the nobility, the clergy, and the commons. In the eighteenth century, Edmund Burke coined the concept of the fourth estate referring to media and journalism. More recently, nontraditional media such as open letters by engineers posted on the EFF website, constitute a fifth estate of influence.

The so-called fifth estate is available to and populated by scholars across disciplines through public scholarship and activism. Scientists fight laws that threaten to restrict access to research data, literary scholars condemn censorship, and sociologists advocate against racism. Scholars compose fifth-estate arguments across genres, from TEDx-like talks, blogs and op-eds, to open letters such as this one. Such

Peter Eckersley is chief computer scientist for the Electronic Frontier Foundation (EFF). He has a Ph.D. in computer science and law from the University of Melbourne. His research examines strategies to legalize P2P file sharing through developing alternative systems of compensation. **Parker Higgins** is an activist who works for Electronic Frontier Foundation. He describes himself as a "free culture and free software enthusiast" (Higgins). He graduated from NYU Gallatin with a concentration in Creativity, Freedom of Speech and Intellectual Property. He lived in Berlin and worked for SoundCloud before moving to San Francisco and joining EFF.

activism and public scholarship demonstrate the value of writing transfer, enabling scholars to transfer their research from academic contexts to broader contexts that can lead to change in the public sphere.

Write Here

Think about an online account you have, and consider the material you post. Have you ever posted something of someone else's—a photo, an image, music, video? Have you ever, inadvertently or intentionally, been an internet pirate? Why or why not?

Peter Eckersley and Parker Higgins

An Open Letter From Internet Engineers to the U.S. Congress

Today, a group of 83 prominent Internet inventors and engineers sent an open letter to members of the United States Congress, stating their opposition to the SOPA and PIPA Internet blacklist bills that are under consideration in the House and Senate respectively.

We, the undersigned, have played various parts in building a network called the Internet. We wrote and debugged the software; we defined the standards and protocols that talk over that network. Many of us invented parts of it. We're just a little proud of the social and economic benefits that our project, the Internet, has brought with it.

Last year, many of us wrote to you and your colleagues to warn about the proposed "COICA" copyright and censorship legislation. Today, we are writing again to reiterate our concerns about the SOPA and PIPA derivatives of last year's bill, that are under consideration in the House and Senate. In many respects, these proposals are worse than the one we were alarmed to read last year.

If enacted, either of these bills will create an environment of tremendous fear and uncertainty for technological innovation, and seriously harm the credibility of the United States in its role as a steward of key Internet infrastructure. Regardless of recent amendments to SOPA, both bills will risk fragmenting the Internet's global domain name system (DNS) and have other capricious technical consequences. In exchange for this, such legislation would engender censorship that will simultaneously be circumvented by deliberate infringers while hampering innocent parties' right and ability to communicate and express themselves online.

All censorship schemes impact speech beyond the category they were intended to restrict, but these bills are particularly egregious in that regard because they cause entire domains to vanish from the Web, not just infringing pages or files. Worse, an incredible range of useful, law-abiding sites can be blacklisted under these proposals. In fact, it seems that this has already begun to happen under the nascent DHS/ICE seizures program.

Censorship of Internet infrastructure will inevitably cause network errors and security problems. This is true in China, Iran and other countries that censor the network today; it will be just as true of American censorship. It is also true regardless of whether censorship is implemented via the DNS, proxies, firewalls, or any other method. Types of network errors and insecurity that we wrestle with today will become more widespread, and will affect sites other than those blacklisted by the American government.

The current bills—SOPA explicitly and PIPA implicitly—also threaten engineers who build Internet systems or offer services that are not readily and automatically compliant with censorship actions by the U.S. government. When we designed the Internet the first time, our priorities were reliability, robustness and minimizing central points of failure or control. We are alarmed that Congress is so close to mandating censorship-compliance as a design requirement for new Internet innovations. This can only damage the security of the network, and give authoritarian governments more power over what their citizens can read and publish.

The US government has regularly claimed that it supports a free and open Internet, both domestically and abroad. We cannot have a free and open Internet unless its naming and routing systems sit above the political concerns and objectives of any one government or industry. To date, the leading role the US has played in this infrastructure has been fairly uncontroversial because America is seen as a trustworthy arbiter and a neutral bastion of free expression. If the US begins to use its central position in the network for censorship that advances its political and economic agenda, the consequences will be far-reaching and destructive.

Senators, Congressmen, we believe the Internet is too important and too valuable to be endangered in this way, and implore you to put these bills aside.

Write Away

1. Internet piracy is a complex problem, one that can benefit from a careful unpacking. Using stasis theory (see Chapter 9), map the stases onto this open letter from engineers. Consider the questions relevant to stasis theory, including: What are the different arguments at stake? Where are the disagreements located? How much harm has been done? What is the nature of the harm?

2. This letter was highly effective in mobilizing public opinion against the proposed SOPA and PIPA legislation. Compose a rhetorical analysis of this open letter. Consider the main components of rhetorical reading, including author, audience, message, purpose, and appeals of *ethos, pathos, logos,* and *kairos.* Your rhetorical analysis can address all of these, or you can choose to focus on one rhetorical component you find to be particularly pronounced or significant.

3. What are the costs of internet piracy? How does internet piracy impact different people? In what contexts does it matter more or less? Conduct interviews with several people whose intellectual property is on the internet to find out their impressions about internet piracy. Decide whom to interview, conduct any necessary preliminary research about their particular property, develop questions and conversation starters, choose a recording or note-taking device, and then, after you have completed the interview, write up the responses. Include prefatory material before the interviews to contextualize them, and a concluding paragraph in which you reflect on the interviews and any significance insights you can glean from them.

Multidiscipline Informatics: "Twitter as a Sentinel in Emergency Situations: Lessons from the Boston Marathon Explosions" by Christopher Cassa, Rumi Chunara, Kenneth Mandl, and John S. Brownstein

Transfer Points: Computer Science, Biomedical Engineering, Health Informatics

While health informatics, computational biology, and biomedical engineering may seem highly specialized, these disciplines actually have direct presence across nearly everyone's lives.

People in these fields, for instance, have developed technologies and information systems that reduce patient waiting times in hospital emergency rooms (ER) by improving health history processing and by developing ways for people to canvas area ER waiting times so they can choose which ER to visit ("3 Ways").

Those in health informatics have also designed many other important health technologies, such as wearable technology. These include fitness trackers to archive data on diet, sleep, and exercise; contact lenses that measure glucose levels in diabetes patients; real-time skin monitors that track exposure to UV rays; and smartwatch apps that speed communication between elderly people, emergency responders, and care providers (Zheng, et al.).

Researchers in these fields, especially those in health informatics, have also been integral in developing, implementing, and improving electronic health record (EHR) systems. These have helped providers improve patient care, patient participation, care coordination, and diagnostics ("Benefits"). Work in this area has also had a vital role in helping health professionals monitor disease outbreaks and manage health threats such as Zika and H1N1.

Health informatics, computational biology, and biomedical engineering are highly interdisciplinary fields that combine knowledge from such disciplines as computer science, information science, engineering, biology, public health, and medicine. Researchers and professionals in these fields rely on innovation and creative problem solving to improve preparation for disasters, to advance the efficacy of health care, and to help people enjoy healthier lives ("What is").

The many helpful areas of research in these fields can be further illustrated through the research areas of the authors who collaborated to create this paper. Christopher Cassa, for instance, one of the co-lead authors, has training in medicine and biotechnology. He has researched such areas as the spatial distribution of diseases (Wieland, et al.), disease surveillance (Hafen, et al.), privacy considerations with healthcare information (Cassa, et al.), and the use of databases for tracking genetic variation data (Tong, et al.). He has a B.S. and Master's in Engineering, and a Ph.D. in Bioinformatics and Integrative Genomics ("Christopher").

Rumi Chunara, the other co-lead author, runs the Chunara Lab at New York University, which uses "computational and statistical methods" in such areas as "data mining, natural language processing, spatiotemporal analyses, and machine learning" to better understand human health (Chunara). Her research has examined how to draw data from internet search queries to detect malaria outbreaks (Ocampo, et al.); how to track social media use to identify youth substance use risk (Salimiian, et al.); how to use mobile phones for health reporting (Freifeld, et al); how to prevent pandemics through a systems approach (Bogich, et al.); and how to use crowdsourced data for disease surveillance (Chunara, et al., "Why"). She has a B.S. in Electrical Engineering, an S.M. in Electrical Engineering and Computer Science, and a Ph.D. in Electrical and Medical Engineering ("Rumi").

The two other authors on the article also demonstrate through their training and research the interdisciplinarity of health informatics and the kinds of research people in this field pursue. Kenneth Mandl's research examines populations and public health, such as detecting outbreaks, tracking disease, and developing crowdsourced knowledge from online patient networks. ("Kenneth"). He has a B.S. in Biology and Psychology, a Master's of Public Health, graduate training in medical informatics, and a Ph.D. in medicine.

Finally, the fourth author of this article, John Brownstein, has a Ph.D. in epidemiology. His research centers on the surveillance, control, and prevention of disease ("John"). For instance, he has conducted studies on how tracking social and news media can provide information about Haitian Cholera outbreaks (Chunara, et al., "Social") and about the use of electronic cigarettes (Ayers, et al.). He has also researched how evaluating online restaurant reservations can help with disease surveillance (Nsoesie, et al.), find-

Christopher Anthony Cassa is an Instructor in Medicine at Brigham and Women's hospital in Boston, Massachusetts and an Instructor of Pediatrics at Harvard Medical School ("Christopher"). **Rumi Chunara** is an assistant professor of computer science and engineering, and in the College of Global Public Health at New York University ("Rumi"). She won the MIT Top 35 Innovator Under 35 Award in 2014 ("Rumi"). **Kenneth D. Mandl** is a Professor of Biomedical Informatics and of Pediatrics at Harvard Medical School ("Kenneth"). **John S. Brownstein** is the Chief Innovation Officer of Boston Children's Hospital and an Associate Professor of Pediatrics at Harvard Medical School and Harvard-MIT Division of Health Sciences and Technology ("John").

ing that an increase in restaurant table availability correlates with upticks in flu. Brownstein's work also includes the creation of HealthMap, an infectious disease intelligence system (Brownstein, et al.).

All of these efforts capture the ongoing innovations in the fields of biomedical engineering and health informatics. Because these fields are tightly woven within quantitative epistemologies, writing in these areas often includes robust data visualizations. And, because much of the inquiry in these fields involves hypothesizing, experimentation, and empirical research, writing often adheres to variations of the IMRAD argument structure. Finally, as evidenced in this article, much research in this field involves intense collaborative. Collaborative research and writing in this context enables different people to lend their expertise to the areas under investigation and provides more people to participate in large-scale projects that often include sizeable datasets.

Alongside all the promise of these fields, though, they also generate risk, particularly in the area of ethics: How do we negotiate individual privacy with public health priorities? Under what public health circumstances might individual privacy be compromised? How can we protect patient confidentiality within global systems infrastructures? Should there be limits to data mining and information gathering? What are the intersections between health technologies and human experiences? These questions, alongside innovations to improve human health, are what will continue to motivate the highly interdisciplinary fields of health informatics and biomedical engineering.

Write Here

How has technology intersected with your health? Examples might be electronic health records, internet searches for symptoms or health conditions, wearable technologies, social media usage and health-related interests, concerns, or activities. Identify as many ways as you can the intersections you have experienced between health and technology. What are your impressions of health-related technologies? What are their potentials, limitations, and/or risks and promises?

Christopher A. Cassa et al.

Twitter as a Sentinel in Emergency Situations: Lessons from the Boston Marathon Explosions

On April 15 at 2:49pm EDT, two bombs improvised from pressure cookers exploded on the sidewalk near the finish line of 117 Boston Marathon. 264 patients were transported to 19 emergency departments throughout Boston.[1]

Public health authorities provided alerts to regional emergency departments approximately nine minutes after the explosions, just as ambulances left the scene[2] via the Massachusetts Emergency Preparedness

Bureau (MA EPB) Health and Homeland Alert Network (HHAN). The Massachusetts Central Medical Emergency Direction (CMED) Center also began communicating to individual hospitals by radio in the minutes prior. We sought to measure the timing of social media reports in relation to those issued through these official emergency response channels.

Social media and other mobile platforms enable individuals to post messages along with specific geographic information. These messages can help track infectious disease outbreaks,[3] aid in natural disaster response[4] and provide insight into conflicts,[5] where data collected through official reporting structures can take weeks to collect and analyze. Twitter streams are routinely used by high frequency trading applications to rapidly assess external factors that may affect market conditions[6] and used in marketing to assess consumer response in real-time to advertisements.[7] Data from informal media are typically available in near real-time and can be combined with geographically encoded news media reports and traditional data sources to improve surveillance.[8] Here, we characterize the early social media response to a geographically-constrained, rapidly evolving critical situation.

Geo-localized social media trend analysis

Our analysis was based on the set of Twitter postings with geolocation data (latitude and longitude) freely available via the Public Twitter API.[9] To increase specificity, we narrowed the radius of the tweets to 35 miles from the Boston Marathon finish line. We observed messages containing the word stems: 'explos*' or 'explod*', just 3 minutes after the explosions (Figure 1). When adding words beginning with 'bomb', a picture quickly emerges of an incident warranting further exploration.

While an increase in messages indicating an emergency from a particular location may not make it possible to fully ascertain the circumstances of an incident without computational or human review, analysis of such data could help public safety officers better understand the location or specifics of explosions or other emergencies. Figure 1 illustrates the timeliness of the social media data, along with initial Twitter postings about the event from pertinent national and local news sources (CNN, the Associated Press, Boston WCVB) and with electronic messages from the MA EPB HHAN. Social media messages directly from individuals on the ground were timely, followed closely by validated public health alerts; messages from news sources followed both of these.

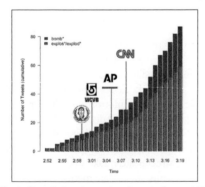

[Fig. 1: Cumulative time series of tweets from within a 35 mile radius of the Boston Marathon finish line selected using the stems "explod*", "explos*" and "bomb*" after the bombings at 2:49. Public health officials alerted regional emergency departments via the HHAN at 2:59. Reports from news stations such as WCVB, the Associated Press, and CNN followed shortly after.]

The baseline level of messages with these included keywords is very low in this area. For the stems 'explos*' and 'explod*', there was only one other message the day prior to the explosions in the same geographic radius.

Geolocation and characterization of the event

Within the first 10 minutes of the bombings, many of the observed messages were from the immediate vicinity of the finish line.

Because of their proximity to the event and content of their postings, these individuals might be witnesses to the bombings or be of close enough proximity to provide helpful information. These finely detailed geographic data can be used to localize and characterize events assisting emergency response in decision-making. In the Supplementary Materials, we include the text of the Twitter messages from individuals (SM Table 1) and (SM Table 2), and Twitter postings from select news sources (SM Table 3). We have redacted expletives and personal identifiers.

Discussion

Each year, the Boston Athletic Association provides a medical tent near the finish line of the Boston Marathon as well as a strong security and media presence. Hence, first responders, law enforcement and reporters were already present near the explosions, and were able to respond to the injuries, activate the emergency response system, and begin the investigation. In other situations, crowdsourced information may uniquely provide extremely timely initial recognition of an event and specific clues as to what events may be unfolding–e.g. "area of 671 Boylston St.", "hundreds hurt…bloody"—that could be used to tailor and refine the response.[2] Here we described how data from Twitter provided localization and characterization of the Boston Marathon explosions.

Caution in the use of social media reports is warranted, however. While social media data can provide timely insight into events as they unfold, they may also produce false positive reports with negative effects, as illustrated by a powerful example from the financial sector. In the recent "flash crash," a spurious Twitter report of a White House attack by the Associated Press was promulgated over 4,000 times.[6] This led automated financial systems to take rapid—but inappropriate—action, which was quickly reversed.[10]

Classification strategies and filtering approaches that have been developed for disease surveillance,[8,11,12,13] geospatial cluster identification,[14] and crime tracking[15] may help refine the sensitivity and specificity as well as classify postings into relevant categories such as personal, informative and other.[16] Additionally, by comparing newly observed data against temporally adjusted keyword frequencies, it is possible to identify aberrant spikes in keyword use. The inclusion of geographical data allows these spikes to be geographically adjusted, as well. Prospective data collection could also harness larger and other streams of crowdsourced data, and use more comprehensive emergency-related keywords and language processing to increase the sensitivity of this data source. The analysis of multiple keywords could further improve these prior probabilities by reducing the impact of single false positive keywords derived from benign events.

In the wake of the explosions, Twitter became a news source for many individuals, which allowed unvetted information to enter the public sphere. For example, in our keyword analysis, we see two tweets that blamed individuals from Korea for the explosions (SM Table 1 and SM Table 2). This misinformation—which may be posted in a practically anonymous fashion—is difficult to correct or expunge once it has been cited by the media or shared extensively on social media platforms.

Given this risk, the sensitivity and specificity of notifications must be optimized using the perceived cost of intervention (e.g. unnecessary investigation) and the opportunity cost of not reacting when appropriate (e.g. delay in care). In events that unfold over a longer period of time, or require more in-depth investigation, it is possible that the dangerous impact of false positives may be reduced, or that the data may be weighted to mitigate unwanted consequences.

There is a real opportunity to make use of Twitter streams and other social media data to expedite public health, safety, or medical response in crises. Approaches to actively survey social media to complement traditional approaches to situation awareness after emergency events should be developed which integrate with existing analysis and alerting infrastructure.

Acknowledgements

We thank Clark Freifeld, John Grieb, James Daniel, Patrick Simon and Steven Climans for their assistance and expertise.

APPENDIX 1
Supplementary Table 1

Keywords beginning with stem word 'explo' within first 20 minutes
There was just an explosion at Copley...seriously. Wtf...
Two explosions just rocked the finish line of the Boston Marathon. Sirens galore. People running in fear. Wonder what happened.
Did something just explode... twice in town? @*****
Just heard two large explosions at the #bostonmarathon
2 explosions just happened here on boylston st. #boston #bostonmarathon
first something exploded and then they made everyone clear the way so an ambulance could go through... #whathappened?
can someone tell me what that explosion was!? #boston #bostonmarathon
Holy **** there was explosions in Copley.
@***** @***** RT: @***** Large explosion on the Boston Marathon route, area of 671 Boylston St. Possibly 60 people injured
That explosion in Boston just shook my house

Multiple explosions @ Boston Marathon
BREAKING NEWS: Two powerful explosions detonated in quick succession right next to the Boston Marathon finsh line this afternoon.
There was just a ****ing explosion on boylston street
Also what exploded
And then this. Why? "@*****: RT @*****: Live video from scene of Boston Marathon explosion http://t.co/mYxdURqnT8
what exploded
BREAKING NEWS: Two powerful explosions detonated in quick succession right next to the Boston Marathon finsh line this afternoon.
I am fine, I was literally by where the explosions happened less than 1 hour ago, my office is right by finish line
@***** I heard a loud BOOM and they are saying there were two explosions, seems many hurt
#BostonMarathon explosion, why why why !!!! http://t.co/eAGDM8F8wH
That explosion was definitely set up ....
were the explosions terrorist attacks?
"@*****: This explosion is scary
Jesus. MT @*****: Aerial shot of the finish line were the explosions happened. (Fox #Boston) http://t.co/8i86l45XlO
Multiple people are injured near the Boston Marathon finish line after two explosions. The #BostonMarathon has been stopped.
What explosion lol
I hope everyone is okay at the marathon from the explosion
Holy ****. Prayers go out to those injured/effected by the explosions at the finish line. Hopefully nothing else happens. 2 explosions at Boston marathon
So scared. Stuck in Boston because my car won't start and probably won't be able to get out bc of the explosions. Hope everyone is okay.
Bomb just exploded at the Boston Marathon #bostonmarathon
Two explosions @ the finish line of the Boston Marathon....horrific scene, hundreds hurt...bloody. On no! This is terrible.
My aunt literally just said she think North Korea is responsible for the Boston Marathon explosion
Two explosions by the finish line of #bostonmarathon
#BREAKING 2 explosions at Boston marathon finish line.
Some of these Boston Marathon explosion pics are gruesome.
**** my moms on the train I'm gunna explode
And then the city started to explode and we couldn't get out...........
@***** two explosions. Some major injuries.
Watching this explosion on the news is reminding me of 9/11
Just heard two huge explosions in Boston. What is going on?

APPENDIX 2
Supplementary Table 2

Keywords beginning with stem word 'bomb' within first 20 minutes
Two bombs just went off on boylston.....
Holy **** did a bomb just go off????
Sounds like a few bombs went off across the street
Two bomb sounds and a building on fire on one of the biggest days in Boston... Coincidence I think ****ing NOT
WTF the boston marathon just got bombed
Marathon got bombed wtf, thats right near my work
Koreans bombed Boston spread the word
I can't believe I just witnessed a bombing #blessedtobesafe
Two men had bombs strapped to themselves and they both went off. Everyone is scrambling.
I hate that my mom works at the airport I always think people are gunna bomb it
@***** it was 2 bombs! You okay?
Omg...omg....I was standing right down from where the bomb went off earlier
A bomb went off at the marathon?
O **** they calling bomb squad and FBI **** got real
Hoards of people being directed away from Copley Square where a #bomb went off at the #BostonMarathon... http://t.co/Aq6v2AqAqs
Two bombs just went off in Boston!? #wtf #BostonMarathon
@***** bombs went off in boston I have so many friends here who are in the area I'm so worried.
Two bombs went off during the marathon? #****edup
@***** I am yes, we only saw two big puffs of smoke and they sounded a lot like bombs

APPENDIX 3
Supplementary Table 3

News and public safety source initial messages regarding the bombings
3:01 @WCVB Explosion reported near Boston Marathon finish line
3:05 @AP BREAKING: Two explosions at the finish line of the Boston Marathon result in injuries BW
3:08 @CNN There has been at least one explosion near the Boston Marathon finish line, according to CNN affiliate WCVB. Details on @CNN TV now.
3:39 @boston_police Boston Police confirming explosion at marathon finish line with injuries. #tweetfromthebeat via @CherylFiandaca
3:47 @bostonmarathon There were two bombs that exploded near the finish line in today's Boston Marathon. We are working with law...http://fb.me/1HdL4nLXX

References

1. Katz D (2013) Injury toll from Marathon bombs reduced to 264. Boston Globe. Boston, MA.

2. Gawande A (2013) Why Boston Hospitals Were Ready. News Desk: The New Yorker.

3. Chunara R, Andrews JR, Brownstein JS (2012) Social and news media enable estimation of epidemiological patterns early in the 2010 Haitian cholera outbreak. Am J Trop Med Hyg 86: 39-45.

4. Lu X, Bengtsson L, Holme P (2012) Predictability of population displacement after the 2010 Haiti earthquake. Proc Natl Acad Sci USA 109: 11576-11581.

5. Heinzelman J, Brown, R., Meier, P. (2011) Mobile Technology, Crowdsourcing and Peace Mapping: New Theory and Applications for Conflict Management. Mobile Technologies for Conflict Management Law, Governance and Technology Series. pp. 39-53.

6. Matthews C (2013) How Does One Fake Tweet Cause a Stock Market Crash? Wall Street & Markets: Time.

7. Labs B (2013) Research at the MIT Media Lab led to Bluefin Labs and Social TV analytics. Mapping the TV Genome.

8. Brownstein JS, Freifeld CC, Reis BY, Mandl KD (2008) Surveillance Sans Frontieres: Internet-based emerging infectious disease intelligence and the HealthMap project. Plos Medicine 5: e151.

9. Twitter (2013) Public Streams. Documentation.

10. Bradshaw T, Massoudi, A., Scannell, K. (2013) Bogus terror tweet sparks shares blip. Equities: Financial Times.

11. Reis BY, Kirby C, Hadden LE, Olson K, McMurry AJ, et al. (2007) AEGIS: a robust and scalable real-time public health surveillance system. J Am Med Inform Assoc 14: 581-588.

12. Reis BY, Kohane IS, Mandl KD (2007) An epidemiological network model for disease outbreak detection. Plos Medicine 4: e210.

13. Mandl KD RB, Cassa C. (2004) Measuring outbreak-detection performance by using controlled feature set simulations. MMWR Morb Mortal Wkly Rep 53: 130-136.

14. Wieland SC, Brownstein JS, Berger B, Mandl KD (2007) Density-equalizing Euclidean minimum spanning trees for the detection of all disease cluster shapes. Proc Natl Acad Sci USA 104: 9404-9409.

15. Levine N (2010) CrimeStat. Ned Levine & Associates.

16. Imran M, Elbassuoni, S., Castillo, C., Diaz, F. and Meier, P. Practical Extraction of Disaster-Relevant Information from Social Media; 2013 May 14th, 2013; Rio de Janeiro, Brazil.

 Write Away

1. Data visualization is central to writing in the discipline of health informatics. First, look back at one of the tables in this article and reflect on why you think the authors chose to visualize the data in the way they did. Then, engage with your own data collection and data visualization. Collect data related to health informatics. You might, for instance, track references to a disease or disaster using hashtags or tags on a social media platform of your choice. Or, you might look up a few statistics related to a health matter of interest to you. Or, you might gather a subset of data related to infectious disease tracking from a database such as ProMED. After you have collected data, design a health informatics graphic (table, chart, map, network image, or other data visualization) about the data you have collected. Write a reflection on what your aims were with the graphic or visualization you selected, as well as any challenges you encountered.

2. Develop a literature review on an aspect of health informatics. Choose a subset of research in health informatics, biomedical engineering, or computational biology, and synthesize the emerging and relevant research related to that area of inquiry. Use your literature review to identify emerging trends, gaps in the field, or areas of further research and inquiry.

3. The ethical complexities of health informatics have wide-ranging impact. Compose an op-ed about ethics and health informatics in which you address a contemporary instance that illustrates the complexities of ethics in the realm of health informatics, and in which you argue a position about these ethical complexities.

Science and Information History: *Prologue from* The Information: A History, a Theory, a Flood *by James Gleick*

Transfer Points: History of Science and Technology, Information Science

725, Zhejiang Province, China: Buddhist monk Yi Xing makes the first model of a mechanical clock ("22 Chinese Inventions").

1543, Frombork, Poland: From his deathbed, Nicholas Copernicus, a Polish astronomer and mathematician, publishes *De Revolutionibus Orbium Coelestium*, his theory of heliocentrism, which asserted that the sun is at the center of the universe and planets revolve around it ("Heliocentrism").

1796, Gloucestershire, England: Edward Jenner grabs a local boy and shoots him with a cowpox concoction to test a theory about vaccines. The boy survives, and vaccines are invented (Marr).

1898, Alabama, USA: George Washington Carver, an ex-slave, publishes a bulletin advising farmers to feed acorns to their animals. The first of 44 such bulletins, Carver's writing would fundamentally change agricultural practices across the United States and economic development in the South ("George").

1962, Maryland, USA: Rachel Carson publishes *Silent Spring*, a book about the harmful impacts of chemicals on the environment, and which would become a foundational text in environmentalism and lead to the elimination of harmful chemical crop dusting such as DDT (Griswold).

Moments that changed the world.

For James Gleick, author of *The Information*, another such a moment occurred in 1948 in New Jersey, in the Bell Labs office building. Here, mathematician Claude Shannon published "A Mathematical Theory of Communication," a paper in which he coined the term "bits." Having thus invented binary code, the quantification of information into 1s and 0s, Shannon would henceforth be considered the "father of information science" (Nunberg).

Momentous as such occasions may be, Gleick emphasizes that any such moment builds on a long history of ideas that have lead to innovation. From the invention of writing in Sumer to African drumming and the telegraph, Gleick suggests that Shannon synthesized and extended centuries' worth of mathematical and technical knowledge to "discover" binary code. In turn, Shannon's innovation paved the way for subsequent "discoveries," including the internet, information technologies, and information-based sciences.

James Gleick (1954–) is a prolific writer who publishes books on the history of science and technology for popular audiences. One of his most well-known books was the national best-seller *Chaos: Making a New Science*, a popular rendering of chaos theory that became a National Book Award and Pulitzer Prize finalist. He has also written best-selling biographies on Isaac Newton and Richard Feynman. *The Information*, published in March 2011, has won several awards, including the 2011 Salon Book Award and the 2012 Royal Society Winton Prize for Science Books. Born in New York City, Gleick graduated Harvard with a Ph.D. in English and Linguistics, founded an alternative newspaper in Minneapolis, and then worked as an editor and science reporter for the *New York Times* for a decade. He taught for one year as a distinguished lecturer at Princeton, and then became a full-time writer. (Gleick)

Through this survey of discoveries based on the synthesizing, communication, and distribution of information, Gleick's book contributes to a broad discipline known as information science. Sometimes termed information theory, informatics, or information systems, this discipline deals with the systems and processes for gathering, storing, communicating, and disseminating information. Applications of information science include library sciences, mathematics, technology studies, engineering, and computer science.

But Gleick's book is not exclusively, or even predominantly, a text within the field of information science. More accurately, it might be labeled a history of information science, and in that sense may be situated more squarely within a discipline known as the history of science and technology.

Historians of science and technology combine historical research and writing with a deep knowledge of scientific and technological inquiry and methods. Writing in the history of science and technology spans the continuum from scholarly writing, to public scholarship, to popular writing. Those conducting research in this field, be they academics, journalists, or photographers, may have training from a large range of disciplines, across English and sociology to engineering, history, and chemistry. They advance knowledge about famous and lesser-known scientists and technologists through a myriad of genres, from Wikipedia entries and TEDx talks to infographics and academic biographies. Historians of science and technology also examine ideas, events, developments, objects, and discoveries, from nuclear physics and DNA to computer graphics and mechanical engineering. Historians of science and technology have, for example, researched Victorians and meteorology (Anderson), the gun in central Africa (Macola), and the recumbent bicycle (Hassaan, Massood, and Khan).

Part of their work illustrates the ways in which scientific and technological advancements are deeply nested in networks of power and privilege. For instance, Vasia Lekka has researched how the *Diagnostic and Statistical Manual of Mental Disorders* has worked to normalize sexuality. And Robert S. Anderson has researched science and power in India.

Learning more about the history of science and technology is critical to helping illustrate the long, complex trajectories that contribute to scientific and technological advancement. These histories help us understand these advancements in more nuanced depth, and also inspire others to pursue aspirations, to resist disillusionment when faced with the frustrations that inevitably accompany innovation. Of equal importance, examining history helps us understand the limitations of innovation, the inequities that often exist around such discoveries, and the many dangers and risks of scientific and technological advancement.

Write Here

Moments that change history are rarely recognized as such in the moment. Think back to a pivotal moment in your life. Describe it in as much detail as possible. Then think about the larger history and context that led to that moment. What experiences helped shape that moment? Finally, think about the arc of impact since that moment. What other significant experiences have emerged for you due to that pivotal moment?

James Gleick
Prologue from *The Information: A History, A Theory, A Flood*

The fundamental problem of communication is that of reproducing at one point either exactly or approximately a message selected at another point. Frequently the messages have meaning.
— Claude Shannon (1948)

After 1948, which was the crucial year, people thought they could see the clear purpose that inspired Claude Shannon's work, but that was hindsight. He saw it differently: *My mind wanders around, and I conceive of different things day and night. Like a science-fiction writer, I'm thinking, "What if it were like this?"*

As it happened, 1948 was when the Bell Telephone Laboratories announced the invention of a tiny electronic semiconductor, "an amazingly simple device" that could do anything a vacuum tube could do and more efficiently. It was a crystalline silver, so small that a hundred would fit in the palm of a hand. In May, scientists formed a committee to come up with a name, and the committee passed out paper ballots to senior engineers in Murray Hill, New Jersey, listing some choices: *semiconductor triode…iotatron…transistor* (a hybrid of *varistor* and *transconductance*). *Transistor* won out. "It may have far-reaching significance in electronics and electrical communication," Bell Labs declared in a press release, and for once the reality surpassed the hype. The transistor sparked the revolution in electronics, setting the technology on its path of miniaturization and ubiquity, and soon won the Nobel Prize for its three chief inventors. For the laboratory it was the jewel in the crown. But it was only the second most significant development of that year. The transistor was only hardware.

An invention even more profound and more fundamental came in a monograph spread across seventy-nine pages of *The Bell System Technical Journal* in July and October. No one bothered with a press release. It carried a title both simple and grand—"A Mathematical Theory of Communication"—and the message was hard to summarize. But it was a fulcrum around which the world began to turn. Like the transistor, this development also involved a neologism: the word *bit*, chosen in this case not by committee but by the lone author, a thirty-two-year-old named Claude Shannon. The bit now joined the inch, the pound, the quart, and the minute as a determinate quantity—a fundamental unit of measure.

But measuring what? "A unit for measuring information," Shannon wrote, as though there were such a thing, measurable and quantifiable, as information.

Shannon supposedly belonged to the Bell Labs mathematical research group, but he mostly kept to himself. When the group left the New York headquarters for shiny new space in the New Jersey suburbs, he stayed behind, haunting a cubbyhole in the old building, a twelve-story sandy brick hulk on West Street, its industrial back to the Hudson River, its front facing the edge of Greenwich Village. He disliked commuting, and he liked the downtown neighborhood, where he could hear jazz clarinetists in late-night clubs. He was flirting shyly with a young woman who worked in Bell Labs' microwave research group in the two-story former Nabisco factory across the street. People considered him a smart young man. Fresh from MIT he had plunged into the laboratory's war

work, first developing an automatic fire-control director for antiaircraft guns, then focusing on the theoretical underpinnings of secret communication—cryptography—and working out a mathematical proof of the security of the so-called X System, the telephone hotline between Winston Churchill and President Roosevelt. So now his managers were willing to leave him alone, even though they did not understand exactly what he was working on.

AT&T at midcentury did not demand instant gratification from its research division. It allowed detours into mathematics or astrophysics with no apparent commercial purpose. Anyway so much of modern science bore directly or indirectly on the company's mission, which was vast, monopolistic, and almost all-encompassing. Still, broad as it was, the telephone company's core subject matter remained just out of focus. By 1948 more than 125 million conversations passed daily through the Bell System's 138 million miles of cable and 31 million telephone sets. The Bureau of the Census reported these facts under the rubric of "Communications in the United States," but they were crude measures of communication. The census also counted several thousand broadcasting stations for radio and a few dozen for television, along with newspapers, books, pamphlets, and the mail. The post office counted its letters and parcels, but what, exactly, did the Bell System carry, counted in what units? Not *conversations*, surely; nor *words*, nor certainly *characters*. Perhaps it was just electricity. The company's engineers were electrical engineers. Everyone understood that electricity served as a surrogate for sound, the sound of the human voice, waves in the air entering the telephone mouthpiece and converted into electrical waveforms. This conversion was the essence of the telephone's advance over the telegraph—the predecessor technology, already seeming so quaint. Telegraphy relied on a different sort of conversion: a code of dots and dashes, not based on sounds at all but on the written alphabet, which was, after all, a code in its turn. Indeed, considering the matter closely, one could see a chain of abstraction and conversion: the dots and dashes representing letters of the alphabet; the letters representing sounds, and in combination forming words; the words representing some ultimate substrate of meaning, perhaps best left to philosophers.

The Bell System had none of those, but the company had hired its first mathematician in 1897: George Campbell, a Minnesotan who had studied in Göttingen and Vienna. He immediately confronted a crippling problem of early telephone transmission. Signals were distorted as they passed across the circuits; the greater the distance, the worse the distortion. Campbell's solution was partly mathematics and partly electrical engineering. His employers learned not to worry much about the distinction. Shannon himself, as a student, had never been quite able to decide whether to become an engineer or a mathematician. For Bell Labs he was both, willy-nilly, practical about circuits and relays but happiest in a realm of symbolic abstraction. Most communications engineers focused their expertise on physical problems, amplification and modulation, phase distortion and signal-to-noise degradation. Shannon liked games and puzzles. Secret codes entranced him, beginning when he was a boy reading Edgar Allan Poe. He gathered threads like a magpie. As a first-year research assistant at MIT, he worked on a hundred-ton proto-computer, Vannevar Bush's Differential Analyzer, which could solve equations with great rotating gears, shafts, and wheels. At twenty-two he wrote a dissertation that applied a nineteenth-century idea, George Boole's algebra of logic, to the design of electrical circuits. (Logic and electricity—a peculiar combination.) Later he worked with the mathematician and logician Hermann Weyl, who taught him what a theory was: "Theories permit consciousness to 'jump over its own shadow,' to leave behind the given, to represent the transcendent, yet, as is self-evident, only in symbols."

In 1943 the English mathematician and code breaker Alan Turin visited Bell Labs on a cryptographic mission and met Shannon sometimes over lunch, where they traded speculation on the future of artificial thinking machines. ("Shannon wants to feed not just *data* to a Brain, but cultural things!" Turing exclaimed. "He wants to play music to it!") Shannon also crossed paths with Norbert Wiener, who had taught him at MIT and by 1948 was proposing a new discipline to be called "cybernetics," the study of communication and control. Meanwhile Shannon began paying special attention to television signals, from a peculiar point of view: wondering whether their content could be somehow compacted or compressed to allows for faster transmission. Logic and circuits crossbred to make a new, hybrid thing; so did codes and genes. In his solitary way, seeking a framework to connect his many threads, Shannon began assembling a theory for information.

The raw material lay all around, glistening and buzzing in the landscape of the early twentieth century, letters and messages, sounds and images, news and instructions, figures and facts, signals and signs: a hodgepodge of related species. They were on the move, by post or wire or electromagnetic wave. But no one word denoted all that stuff. "Off and on," Shannon wrote to Vannevar Bush at MIT in 1939, "I have been working on an analysis of some of the fundamental properties of general systems for the transmission of intelligence." *Intelligence*: that was a flexible term, very old. "Nowe used for an elegant worde," Sir Thomas Elyot wrote in the sixteenth century, "where there is mutuall treaties or appoyntementes, eyther by letters or message." It had taken on other meanings, though. A few engineers, especially in the telephone labs, began speaking of *information*. They used the word in a way suggesting something technical: quantity of information, or measure of information. Shannon adopted this usage.

For the purposes of science, information had to mean something special. Three centuries earlier, the new discipline of physics could not proceed until Isaac Newton appropriated words that were ancient and vague—*force, mass, motion*, and even *time*—and gave them new meanings. Newton made these terms into quantities, suitable for use in mathematical formulas. Until then, *motion* (for example) had been just as soft and inclusive a term as *information*. For Aristotelians, motion covered a far-flung family of phenomena: a peach ripening, a stone falling, a child growing, a body decaying. That was too rich. Most varieties of motion had to be tossed out before Newton's laws could apply and the Scientific Revolution could succeed. In the nineteenth century, *energy* began to undergo a similar transformation: natural philosophers adapted a word meaning vigor or intensity. They mathematicized it, giving energy its fundamental place in the physicists' view of nature.

It was the same with information. A rite of purification became necessary.

And then, when it was made simple, distilled, counted in bits, information was found to be everywhere. Shannon's theory made a bridge between information and uncertainty; between information and entropy; and between information and chaos. It led to compact discs and fax machines, computers and cyberspace, Moore's law and all the world's Silicon Alleys. Information processing was born, along with information storage and information retrieval. People began to name a successor to the Iron Age and the Steam Age. "Man the food-gatherer reappears incongruously as information-gatherer," remarked Marshall McLuhan in 1967.[1] He wrote this an instant too soon, in the first dawn of computation and cyberspace.

We can see now that information is what our world runs on: the blood and the fuel, the vital principle. It pervades the sciences from top to bottom, transforming every branch of knowledge. Information theory began as a bridge from mathematics to electrical engineering and from there to computing. What English speakers call "computer science" Europeans have known as *informatique, informatica,* and *Informatik.* Now even biology has become an information science, a subject of messages, instructions, and code. Genes encapsulate information and enable procedures for reading it in and writing it out. Life spreads by networking. The body itself is an information processor. Memory resides not just in brains but in every cell. No wonder genetics bloomed along with information theory. DNA is the quintessential information molecule, the most advanced message processor at the cellular level—an alphabet and a code, 6 billion bits to form a human being. "What lies at the heart of every living thing is not a fire, not warm breath, not a 'spark of life,'" declares the evolutionary theorist Richard Dawkins. "It is information, words, instructions....If you want to understand life, don't think about vibrant, throbbing gels and oozes, think about information technology." The cells of an organism are nodes in a richly interwoven communications network,

transmitting and receiving, coding and decoding. Evolution itself embodies an ongoing exchange of information between organism and environment.

"The information circle becomes the unit of life," says Werner Loewenstein after thirty years spent studying intercellular communication. He reminds us that *information* means something deeper now: "It connotes a cosmic principle of organization and order, and it provides an exact measure of that." The gene has its cultural analog, too: the meme. In cultural evolution, a meme is a replicator and propagator—an idea, a fashion, a chain letter, or a conspiracy theory. On a bad day, a meme is a virus.

Economics is recognizing itself as an information science, now that money itself is completing a developmental arc from matter to bits, stored in computer memory and magnetic strips, world finance coursing through the global nervous system. Even when money seemed to be material treasure, heavy in pockets and ships' holds and bank vaults, it always was information. Coins and notes, shekels and cowries were all just short-lived technologies for tokenizing information about who owns what.

And atoms? Matter has its own coinage, and the hardest science of all, physics, seemed to have reached maturity. But physics, too, finds itself sideswiped by a new intellectual model. In the years after World War II, the heyday of the physicists, the great news of science appeared to be the splitting of the atom and the control of nuclear energy. Theorists focused their prestige and resources on the search for fundamental particles and the laws governing their interaction, the construction of giant accelerators and the discovery of quarks and gluons. From this exalted enterprise, the business of communications research could not have appeared further removed. At Bell Labs, Claude Shannon was not thinking about physics. Particle physicists did not need bits.

And then, all at once, they did. Increasingly, the physicists and the information theorists are one and the same. The bit is a fundamental particle of a different sort: not just tiny but abstract—a binary digit, a flip-flop, a yes-or-no. It is insubstantial, yet as scientists finally come to understand information, they wonder whether it may be primary: more fundamental than matter itself. They suggest

---

1   And added drily: "In this role, electronic man is no less a nomad than his Paleolithic ancestors."

that the bit is the irreducible kernel and that information forms the very core of existence. Bridging the physics of the twentieth and twenty-first centuries, John Archibald Wheeler, the last surviving collaborator of both Einstein and Bohr, put this manifesto in oracular monosyllables: "It from Bit." Information gives rise to "every it—every particle, every field of force, even the spacetime continuum itself." This is another way of fathoming the paradox of the observer: that the outcome of an experiment is affected, or even determined, when it is observed. Not only is the observer observing, she is asking questions and making statements that must ultimately be expressed in discrete bits. "What we call reality," Wheeler wrote coyly, "arises in the last analysis from the posing of yes-no questions." He added: "All things physical are information-theoretic in origin, and this is a participatory universe." The whole universe is thus seen as a computer—a cosmic information-processing machine.

A key to the enigma is a type of relationship that had no place in classical physics: the phenomenon known as entanglement. When particles or quantum systems are entangled, their properties remain correlated across vast distances and vast times. Light-years apart, they share something that is physical, yet not only physical. Spooky paradoxes arise, unresolvable until one understands how entanglement encodes information, measured in bits or their drolly named quantum counterpart, qubits. When photos and electrons and other particles interact, what are they really doing? Exchanging bits, transmitting quantum states, processing information. The laws of physics are the algorithms. Every burning star, every silent nebula, every particle leaving its ghostly trace in a cloud chamber is an information processor. The universe computes its own destiny.

How much does it computer? How fast? How big is its total information capacity, its memory space? What is the link between energy and information; what is the energy cost of flipping a bit? These are hard questions, but they are not as mystical or metaphorical as they sound. Physicists and quantum information theorists, a new breed, struggle with them together. They do the math and produce tentative answers. ("The bit count of the cosmos, however it is figured, is ten raised to a very large power," according to Wheeler. According to Seth Lloyd: "No more than 10^{120} ops on 10^{90} bits.") They look anew at the mysteries of thermodynamic entropy and at those notorious information swallowers, black holes. "Tomorrow," Wheeler declares, "we will have learned to understand and express *all* of physics in the language of information."

As the role of information grows beyond anyone's reckoning, it grows to be too much. "TMI," people now say. We have information fatigue, anxiety, and glut. We have met the Devil of Information Overload and his impish underlings, the computer virus, the busy signal, the dead link, and the PowerPoint presentation. All this, too, is due in its roundabout way to Shannon. Everything changed so quickly. John Robinson Pierce (the Bell Labs engineer who had come up with the word *transistor*) mused afterward: "It is hard to picture the world before Shannon as it seemed to those who lived in it. It is difficult to recover innocence, ignorance, and lack of understanding."

Yet the past does come back into focus. *In the beginning was the word,* according to John. We are the species that named itself *Homo sapiens,* the one who knows—and then, after reflection, amended that to *Homo sapiens sapiens.* The greatest gift of Prometheus to humanity was not fire after all: "Numbers, too, chiefest of sciences, I invented for them, and the combining of letters, creative mother of the Muses' arts, with which to hold all things in memory." The alphabet was a founding technology of information. The telephone, the fax machine, the calculator, and, ultimately, the computer are only the latest innovators devised for saving, manipulating, and communicating knowledge. Our culture has absorbed a working vocabulary for these useful inventions. We speak of compressing data, aware that this is quite different from compressing a gas. We know about streaming information, parsing it, sorting it, matching it, and filtering it. Our furniture includes iPods and plasma displays, our skills include texting and Googling, we are endowed, we are expert, so we see information in the foreground. But it has always been there. It pervaded our ancestors' world, too, taking forms from solid to ethereal, granite gravestones and the whispers of courtiers. The punched card, the cash register, the nineteenth-century Difference Engine, the wires of telegraphy all played their parts in weaving the spiderweb of information to which we cling. Each new information technology, in its own time, set off blooms in storage and transmission. From the printing press came new species of information organizers: dictionaries, cyclopaedias, almanacs—

compendiums of words, classifiers of facts, trees of knowledge. Hardly any information technology goes obsolete. Each new one throws its predecessors into relief. Thus Thomas Hobbes, in the seventeenth century, resisted his era's new-media hype: "The invention of printing, though ingenious, compared with the invention of letters is no great matter." Up to a point, he was right. Every new medium transforms the nature of human thought. In the long run, history is the story of information becoming aware of itself.

Some information technologies were appreciated in their own time, but others were not. One that was sorely misunderstood was the African talking drum.

Write Away

1. The text reprinted here is the "Prologue" for Gleick's book. Using specific portions of this text as evidence, identify the elements that comprise a "Prologue." Consider the following questions: What goes into prologues? What do prologues accomplish? What purposes might they serve? What, if any, might be the limitations of prologues?

2. Write a scholarly book review about a text in the discipline of the history of science and technology. Include in your review a summary of the main aspects of significance of the text, as well as a broader orientation for your readers about the content. Include as well the limitations and strengths of the text, explicating for readers how the text can be situated within the broader landscape of the history of science and technology as a discipline.

3. Many historians of science and technology write biographies of people who have contributed to scientific and/or technological developments. Interview a person you know who is affiliated with science and/or technology, and write an extended biographical account about that person. To prepare for writing your biographical account, read several biographies about people involved with science and technology, and model your text on these. Remember that the main focus of your biographical text is to illustrate this individual's contributions to science and technology in human terms.

℘ ℘ ℘

Chapter 1 Key Terms

transfer	discourse conventions	modes of discourse
writing transfer	discourse communities	op ed
disciplines	writing occasions	literature review

Write Away

Just as Chaco Canyon's Great Houses contained distinctive features as well as alignments, so too will your writing experiences. Essentially, your journey from one writing occasion to others throughout your college career and beyond will in some ways resemble a visit to a Great House, where you will move from room to room through aligned features. As a writer, you will find yourself transferring various writing practices, approaches, and skills to each new writing "room" you come to occupy, as well as discovering new approaches to writing along the way. This activity invites you to imagine your own writing trajectory as a "Writing Great House" by creating a visual depiction of all the different writing rooms—aligned and yet also discrete—you will likely encounter across your college career and beyond.

Build or sketch out the beginnings of a Writing Great House. You can shape your great house any way you choose. Be as creative as you are inclined to be, selecting colors and design features that resonate with or reflect your experiences with and attitudes about writing.

Gradually add on writing rooms to your Writing Great House. Add "rooms" for all the different writing experiences you have had and that you anticipate having over the next few years of your education and beyond. To identify prior writing experiences, you can return to the Write Now timeline on page 7. To imagine future writing possibilities, consider any core education requirements you will be completing, as well as any potential majors or minors you might choose. Consider as well the writing you will engage in as construed more broadly, such as oral presentations, online writing, professional writing, and personal writing. Label each writing room clearly to indicate what kind of writing experiences it has housed or will house.

Forge connections among rooms. Create connections—passageways, routes of exchange and transfer—among the rooms you have created. Which ones have more overlap than others? Which ones are located farther apart from one another? You, as a writer, will traverse the Great House through these connections and intersections.

Reflect on writing transfer. Reflect in writing about what skills or approaches you think you will need in order to be prepared as you move through all these writing rooms across your college career and beyond, finding alignments but also noticing distinctions. What aspects of writing are you already equipped to draw upon as you move within and between various writing occasions? What features of writing do you anticipate needing to strengthen, or perhaps even discard, as you encounter writing in transit throughout your Writing Great House?

Research and Writing as a Process

Pinpointing Chapter 2

Chapter 2 begins our exploration into the key aspects of academic writing that transverses disciplinary context by addressing an especially central and important writing-related concept: research and writing as a process. Writers throughout all disciplines engage in research and writing processes. These processes may look quite different from one another, but they all share certain core features and phases. To provide you with strategies for *research and writing in transit*, this chapter addresses the following concepts:

- Overview of the Research and Writing Process: Phases and Features
- Research across Disciplines
- Prewriting Strategies across Disciplines
- Drafting across Disciplines
- Revising across Disciplines
- Editing across Disciplines
- Feedback Mechanisms within and across Disciplines
- Transfer and the Final Product

Subsequent chapters of *Writing in Transit* build on this knowledge by introducing you to more specific aspects of writing that occur within and across various disciplines, and that permeate many phases of the research and writing process.

Building J, located at Monte Albán, in Oaxaca, Mexico, has been described as "one of ancient Mesoamerica's most enigmatic structures" (Aveni 26). Shaped like an arrow, Building J holds 40 stone slabs decorated with upside down heads and place names, believed to signify Zapotec conquests of different cities and regions. Building J has long puzzled scholars because of its northeast orientation, which is an anomaly in Zapotec architecture (Marcus). Archaeologists refer to Building J as the observatory since it is aligned with Capella, the sixth-brightest star in the sky (Aveni; Ching, Jarzombek & Prakash; Marcus).

Monte Albán has earned status as a World Heritage Site in part because its buildings and structures were "literally carved out of the mountain." Architectural historians maintain that the "Zapotec elite constructed [Monte Albán as] a new administrative center" around 500 BCE. This date, however, marks only the beginning of an extended, phased process of construction and development across approximately 1500 years. Throughout these centuries, Monte Albán became, by turns, home to several different groups of people, at one point housing as many as 30,000 residents. In 850 CE, for reasons that are still unknown, people began to abandon the area (Ching, Jarzombek & Prakash; "Historic"; Urcid & Joyce).

This lengthy trajectory wherein people built, expanded, and rebuilt Monte Albán foregrounds the cyclical nature of progress and knowledge, the impact of context, and the complexity of process.

Changes in context and knowledge across time, for example, influenced site construction regarding agriculture. To contend with seasonal variations and slope erosion in the land surrounding Monte Albán, farmers "buil[t] terraces [that] retained sufficient soil and moisture to assure adequate and predictable production" (Garcia). To better forecast these seasonal shifts, farmers may have relied on astronomical indicators, perhaps explaining in part Building J's compelling architecture.

Likewise demonstrating the impact of a long-term process and the importance of adapting approaches, be it with farming practices or knowledge itself, one Monte Albán scholar

revised his research claims about Building J after recognizing the centuries-long, phased construction of the site. In 1972, Anthony Aveni argued that Building J was aligned with the five brightest stars and also worked in concert with Building P to track the sixth-brightest star, Capella. Subsequently realizing that different stars gained or lost visibility across the centuries of development, Aveni had to modify his claim to argue instead that Building J only tracked Capella and did so alone rather than with Building P ("Mound J"; "Zapotec").

The extended, iterative, adaptive, and recursive development process of Monte Albán mirrors in important ways people's research and writing processes. Rarely do writers produce discrete writing projects in linear, uninterrupted moments. Instead, and much like Monte Albán, research and writing processes often involve starts and stops, reflections, reconsiderations, adaptations, and additions over long periods of time.

Similarly, the growth process for writers themselves involves long-term effort, reconsideration, and adaptation. People are not generally born "good" writers. Even established writers like Maya Angelou acknowledge that writing is a long-term process: "Some critics have said I'm a natural writer. Well, that's like being a natural open-heart surgeon."

And here's the really tough news: being an effective writer requires this level of effort every time you write and even, retrospectively, after each writing occasion.

Of course, writers grow and improve over time, but writing remains challenging in part because nearly every writing occasion carries different expectations and conventions. Although the writing and research processes writers use have some stable components across contexts, writers generally find it necessary to tailor their processes as they encounter different writing projects. In so doing, writers build a repertoire of writing skills, experiences, and proficiencies that they can then transfer, adapt, and build on for subsequent writing occasions.

Write Here

Monte Albán represents a centuries-long, cyclical developmental process. Brainstorm a few other examples of a structure, concept, or place that has undergone a similarly long and complex developmental process. Choose one of these to explore further by reflecting in writing about the aspects of this structure, concept, or place that have been revised, expanded, or otherwise adapted across time.

 Transfer Hub: Contribute your ideas and see what others have written at fountainheadpress.com/transferhub.

Overview of the Research and Writing Process

Generally speaking, the academic research and **writing process** involves four recursive phases, all of which include research and feedback, and which, together, ultimately yield a final product: prewriting, drafting, revising, and editing.

It is valuable to keep in mind several defining features of these phases of the writing process—the ways by which writers arrive at that final product.

The writing process is dynamic

Writers vary writing processes across time and writing occasion. Writers experiment with different approaches and reflect on what works well and on what might need to be adjusted with their processes. Writing occasion and disciplinary context significantly impact how writers approach process. Collaborative writing projects, for instance, require different approaches to the writing process than do more individual writing projects. With collaborative writing, writers must be open to adapting their writing processes in ways that are most effective for the project and for other team members. This might mean relying on different team members for their unique expertise and contributions, or it might involve pacing the development of a writing project in ways that fit best with everyone's schedules. Similarly, some writing projects involve more extensive focus on prewriting, while others require greater focus on revision. Writing process also varies for writers themselves. Sometimes a writing process that has worked well for a writer before stops being as effective as it once was. This might be because a writer's circumstances have changed. Maybe a favorite place or time to write is no longer available, or maybe a writer's schedule now works for shorter bursts of writing time as opposed to longer pockets of writing time. Writing processes also change because individuals' attitudes and preferences toward writing shift across time. Writers change because people change; what we like and engage with at one point in our lives often shifts across time and circumstance.

The writing process is recursive

Writers rarely proceed in a linear manner from one phase of the research and writing process through to the next. Instead, they circle back or jump ahead, moving betwixt and between the various phases. This continual movement makes the writing process recursive. Writers, for instance, often revise and edit even as they are drafting. And, during revision or editing, writers may return to prewriting to address an aspect of a writing project that needs further development. Similarly, during prewriting, writers might draft portions of a project. Even after writing projects are complete, the writing process often again emerges recursively as writers consider how to transfer ideas from one writing project to others, or consider how to transfer one writing project to other formats, such as moving from an oral format to a written one. Disciplinary context and writing occasion also drive the recursiveness of the writing process. Writing occasions that are longer term, for instance, might facilitate greater recursiveness across all phases of the process, whereas shorter-term deadlines might move that primarily to

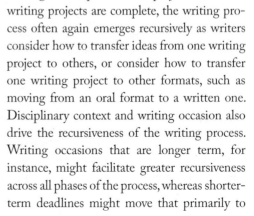

Writer Insights

Describe your research process.

Whenever I am asked to translate an article or a document, the same systematic process starts. First of all, I focus on gathering as much information as possible. I read and analyze data from related books, newspaper articles, and journals, both in English and Spanish.... [W]e, translators have to understand the message properly and... have detailed knowledge of the subject area.

~Lucía Inés Martinez, Translator and EFL Teacher, Tigre, Buenos Aires, Argentina

the drafting and revision stages. Thinking of the writing process as a cyclical endeavor helps emphasize this recursivity (see Figure 2.1).

FIGURE 2.1 Phases of the writing process.

The writing process is social

The idea of a writer sitting alone in a writer's den, toiling away at the craft in painstaking isolation, may seem familiar from some representations of writers in literature and film. And, there may be moments when writers are alone. However, more often than not, the research and writing process is intensely social. Writers rarely engage in the writing process in complete isolation. Many disciplinary contexts for writing involve collaborative teams working on a writing and research project. Members of these teams might conduct research together, analyze data together, compose together, revise together, or brainstorm together. Even in cases of individually authored writing projects, though, writing still remains a social enterprise. In such cases, writers are often engaging with others' texts, either overtly or more subtly through the influence of others' texts. Writers also routinely discuss writing ideas and drafts-in-progress with others. And, across the writing process they get feedback from others about their drafts. After a writing project is completed, readers will likely be reading and engaging with that project, bringing yet another element of

Transfer at Work

Patrick Bahls argues that a writer generating the following mathematical proof goes through prewriting, organizing, outlining, drafting, reviewing, and revising, much like writers in other contexts:

The sum of two even integers is again an even integer.

Recall that we say an integer n is even if there is an integer s such that n = 2s. Suppose that m and n are even. Thus there are integers s and t such that m = 2s and n = 2t. Therefore m + n = 2s + 2t = 2(s + t), using the fact that multiplication distributes over addition. Letting k be the integer s + t, we see that m + n = 2k, so that it is indeed even, as desired. Since m and n were arbitrary even integers, we are done.

Detailing the prewriting stage for this proof, Bahls writes, "If we could see them, earlier drafts of the proof would show us errors, gaps, and indecision as the prover tried to write his way past whatever mathematical obstacles he encountered." However, Bahls also notes that the writing process varies based on the writer and the proof: "For simple proofs, this [prewriting] stage may take only minutes; for difficult ones it may take years." Further emphasizing how context impacts the writing process, Grant Eckstein, Jessica Chariton, and Robb Mark McCollum argue that people writing in a second or third language may find an iterative multi-draft process more beneficial than a sequential multi-draft process.

the social dimension to writing. All of these interactions together make writing an intensely social endeavor.

The writing process is context-dependent

The writing process varies. Contexts that impact the writing process include the writing occasion, disciplinary context, and variations that occur within writers' own circumstances. For instance, writers embarking on a semester-long writing project will approach the writing process differently than those facing shorter deadlines. As another example, writing projects involving humanities-based research and analysis might require more intense concentration with drafting and revising. By contrast, writing in the natural sciences or social sciences might involve writing processes that focus more energy on the prewriting phrase as writers design a study and craft research methods. Writers themselves also adopt different processes at different times. When facing many competing priorities, writers might abridge portions of the writing process, or depend more heavily on revision. Similarly, writers' levels of expertise with a given project, as well as their purposes and goals, also impact how they approach various aspects of the research and writing process. Acknowledging the ways in which context impacts the writing process enables writers to be nimble with how they approach writing projects.

The writing process is individualized

No one, universal writing process exists. What works well for one writer or for one set of writers does not necessarily work for all writers in all contexts. While all writers use the research and writing process, these processes vary drastically. It is important to be experimental and willing to try new approaches, whether writing individually or collaboratively. But it is also important to be aware of one's own preferences and strengths, even as they may change over time and across disciplinary context and writing occasion. To best understand how to craft an effective writing process, writers should reflect often and deeply about their preferences, strengths, and attitudes. If writers recognize, for instance, that they have very little patience for editing, they might decide to give themselves more time for that phase of the process, or to seek feedback more deliberately during that phase. By contrast, if a writer understands that prewriting seems most exciting, then that writer can set a time limit on that process to be sure that the overall project is able to move for-

Writer Insights

Describe your research process.

I find research a great tool to detect and solve teaching and learning difficulties. Research is a systematic inquiry to understand something and make sense of issues of contemporary significance. So, to carry out a valid research project, we must develop some stages for effective research. First of all, this journey starts with a research question that allows us to focus on the matter we want to undertake. Secondly, we must carry out a literature review to support the topic or subject areas we want to develop. Then, we design the appropriate methodology and instruments to measure the study. Finally, it is relevant to analyze the data and come up with relevant conclusions. For developing these significant conclusions and the whole stages of the research project, writing is crucial for the scholar to outline the project. By doing this, the researcher is able to be focused, objective, reflective, and above all to share his/her research work with a specific community.

~ Alexander Izquierdo Castillo,
EFL Teacher and Researcher,
Bogotá, Colombia

ward without delay. In the context of collaborative writing endeavors, where a team works to develop a writing project, individualized processes also must take on new dimensions in response to the entire team's dispositions and attitudes. Across all writing circumstances, it is important to be aware of one's own preferences and strengths with regard to writing and research, even as these preferences may also change over time and across disciplinary context.

Research across Disciplines

Research is perhaps the most critical and ongoing component of academic writing and is deeply nested in disciplinary context.

An ethnomusicologist, for instance, might conduct research by listening to music, talking with people in musical groups, and then listening to the transcripts of those conversations. A literary scholar may instead conduct research by reading literature closely and critically and by locating and reading what other scholars have already written about that literature. A chemist, on the other hand, often conducts much of her research with a team of people, conducting experiments in a lab.

Often, researchers invoke several different kinds of research for a project. In the examples above, for instance, it is likely that all of those scholars, not only the literary scholar, would spend time researching published relevant scholarship so they could build on, push against, or otherwise advance what others have already written.

Research includes many different practices; some of the most common ones include:

- reading, listening to, or viewing the work of others
- analyzing texts, sounds, textures, or images
- conducting fieldwork (i.e., observations, interviews, data collection)
- gathering data and performing quantitative analysis
- conducting experiments and measuring and analyzing the results
- visiting an archive of materials
- collaborating with others who bring different expertise to a writing project

Each of these research strategies asks that the writer follow accepted conventions for what are known as **research methodologies**. Research methodologies are often rooted in disciplinary perspective. While they are highly complex (there are entire graduate-level courses devoted to research methodology!), they can be generally grouped into one of three overlapping categories: qualitative research, quantitative research, and mixed-methods research.

Qualitative research methods

Qualitative research relies primarily on observation, interpretation, and analysis of non-numerical data. Qualitative forms of research operate across the humanities, social sciences, and natural sciences. However, qualitative research occurs with particular frequency by scholars in such fields as literature, psychology, anthropology, and sociology (Saint-Germaine). Non-numerical data for qualitative research might include written or verbal words, images, sounds, body language, and interactions. Examples of disciplinary occasions that involve qualitative research are vast. Musicologists, for instance, analyze songs and music. Ethnographers observe people and places, and conduct interviews. Sociologists conduct focus groups with people and gather qualitative data in those ways. Literary scholars read, interpret, and analyze creative and non-fiction texts such as books, newspapers, websites, and advertisements. Artists and art historians analyze visual texts. Historians explore artifacts as evidence for understanding an event, person, organization, period, or place. These are but a few examples of the many applications of qualitative research methods across disciplines.

Quantitative research methods

Quantitative research involves measurements, observations, and analyses of numerical and quantifiable data. Quantitative research, as with qualitative research, occurs across disciplines. However, quantitative research occurs with particular frequency in such fields as statistics, computer science, engineering, biology, chemistry, and mathematics. Researchers often use quantitative research to test, explore, and generate patterns and hypotheses, and to then make generalizable conclusions. Statisticians, for instance, gather and analyze numerical data about populations, trends, or places. Engineers use quantitative research to help develop and test products and systems. Mathematicians analyze numerical theories and problems. Environmental scientists collect and analyze numerical data related to climate, ocean acidification, coral reef bleaching, and ice flow. And physicists use quantitative research to examine models for motion and relationships between matter.

Mixed-methods research

Mixed-methods research relies on both qualitative and quantitative methods and data. Many research occasions involve mixed-methods research. The disciplines most commonly associated with mixed-methods, though, are such fields as sociology, psychology, health care, education, and business. In a research study in the field of psychology, for instance, researchers might use qualitative research methods by conducting focus groups and observations. Then they might use that qualitative data to design a survey that can be sent to a larger sample size. Finally, they might use quantitative research methods on the survey data in order to understand percentages and trends, as well as statistical significance of the survey responses. This mixed-methods design can be used across many disciplinary contexts from sociology and psychology to business, education, and writing studies. Researchers tend to use mixed-methods research when they realize that mixed methods are required in order to fully answer their research questions.

Another way research can be organized is through what are often overlapping categories between primary, secondary, or tertiary sources.

- **Primary sources**
  These are direct, firsthand sources. Examples of primary sources are interviewees for a survey in political science, art for an art history analysis course, or a novel in an English literature course.
- **Secondary sources**
  Secondary sources include materials that address a primary source. These might include scholarly or popular writing about a topic or subject, such as criticism about a novel.

- **Tertiary sources**

   Tertiary sources include compilations of primary and secondary sources that survey a particular area of research. These might include encyclopedias, almanacs, dictionaries, indexes, or other types of reference materials.

Decisions about which methodology to employ or how to navigate between primary, secondary, and tertiary sources will be shaped largely by the disciplinary context in which you are writing. Different disciplinary contexts use different approaches to research as a means of forwarding knowledge. Disciplinary context and writing occasion can also impact how a particular source might be categorized; for instance, in an analysis of websites, a website would be primary, whereas in another writing occasion that same website might be considered secondary or tertiary. Being effective at research not only means that you can transfer specific research skills from one context to another, but also that you can identify research methodologies and source distinctions within particular disciplines.

Write Now

Read one of the excerpted examples of argument located in Chapter 9: Constructing Arguments, and try to identify what kinds of research went into generating that argument. What methodology or methodologies do you think the author has employed? Where and when do you imagine the research was conducted? Can you tell if the research involved primary, secondary, and/or tertiary sources?

Prewriting Strategies across Disciplines

Prewriting involves everything the writer or team of writers thinks and writes before actually drafting the writing project. It blends deeply with the drafting phase and also overlaps with research. Prewriting may entail thinking about a writing project, posing questions, reading, and conducting research. The purpose of prewriting is to gather evidence, generate ideas, and explore topic ideas in order to move toward the drafting phase. Prewriting also helps to "prime the pump" (Elbow), or get a writer in the mode of writing, and help the writer overcome writing blocks or difficulties getting started. There are many prewriting strategies, some of which lend themselves more fittingly to particular disciplines. Review some of the more common prewriting strategies and their guidelines, which present different approaches to accomplishing this critical phase of the writing process.

Outlining

Outlining entails using a number and/or alphabetic system to briefly summarize, in order, the major and minor aspects of a topic. Outlining enables writers to decide what the main components are of an argument or issue and then to think through each of these main components in more depth. Because outlining typically challenges writers to develop at least two or three sub-elements for each main idea, writers can identify which elements merit more or less consideration. Outlines also offer writers a way of identifying the optimal organization for a text because the outline will help make visible which ideas should go together and which organizational order makes the most sense.

Journaling

Journaling involves a writer using paper or an electronic device to record thoughts about a writing project, often in somewhat brief journal entries over an extended period of time. Journals can (and should) include random observations and ideas, meaning that each entry does not need to be firmly connected to the topic. Sometimes more loosely connected ideas end up inspiring writers to move in new and productive directions. Writers who are more visually oriented might choose to draw images or take photographs in their journals to help further develop a concept. Those who prefer to talk might create audio journals using a recording device. Journaling affords writers the opportunity to think about their projects throughout a period of days or weeks. Some writers may emerge between their projects and other experiences in their daily lives, thereby inspiring new questions or prompting additional consideration. Journaling has the advantage of offering an archive of thought development over time.

Reading

Reading can be one of the most effective prewriting strategies. As writers embark on a project, they can read extensively across related texts, materials, or images. Writers can seek out scholarly texts (academic journals and websites) as well as more popular texts (blogs, newspaper articles, other nonscholarly online sources) and related visual, aural, and tactile materials. Reading provides one of the best antidotes to situations in which writers are unsure about what to write. Through reading, writers can engage with what others have argued about a particular topic. Often, the texts writers read will point to areas for further research or will inspire writers with new ideas and questions.

Note-taking

Many disciplines ask writers to take notes as part of the research prewriting phase. These can include interview/conversation notes in oral history, journalism, or sociology, or field notes in cultural anthropology or biology. Writers in these and other fields also write notes during their reading experiences, identifying ideas that seem significant, erroneous, interesting, and/or curious. Notes can help writers forge connections between ideas and identify gaps in the research. Writers can also be creative with notes, creating mnemonic devices or visual materials to think through complex concepts. To be most effective, notes should be as individualized as possible even as they also adhere to any discipline-specific structures or methods.

Directed talking

Talking through ideas can facilitate idea generation for writers and help them break through any difficulties they might be encountering during the writing process. One talking strategy entails a writer spending two to three minutes talking about his/her writing project with another person or talking into a recording device. In this conversation, the writer can address the project's main ideas, his/her primary purposes or goals with the project, any sticking points or areas of difficulty with the topic, and other main points of the writing project.

This reflection back should not include the listener's opinions about the ideas, but simply a version of what he or she heard the writer say. Talking out loud in one's own words and then hearing those ideas repeated can help the writer both generate new ideas and reconsider their current approaches. If both people are working on the same writing project, or each has a separate writing project, they can take turns and then reverse roles so that both people get a chance to be a talker and a listener.

Walking

Walking, as with many other forms of motion, can provide a valuable kinesthetic prewriting strategy. Be it inside or outdoors, walking can stimulate the brain to generate new ideas and make connections across ideas. Some writers go for walks while they are beginning to think through a writing project, and others make use of walking or motion during other moments of the research and writing process. Writers can ask themselves generative prompts during the walk about such issues as overall argument, main purpose, implications, assumptions, etc.

Some writers will take a recording device with them on the walk to capture any ideas that emerge, others will write notes in a notebook or on an electronic device during the walk, and still others will write notes upon returning from the walk. When integrated into the writing process, walking and other forms of motion can become an integral part of developing ideas and moving forward with a project.

Freewriting

Freewriting is a low-stakes, generative approach to prewriting that invites writers to write about anything for five or ten minutes, not necessarily even their writing project. Writers rarely need to share their freewriting, so they should not focus on grammar, consistency, or even complete sentences. The goal is to maintain momentum and active writing for the entire time. If a writer runs out of something to write during that five minutes, he or she should merely just keep writing "I'm out of ideas" until the next idea comes along. The idea behind freewriting is that the act of writing, even about random thoughts unrelated to a project, will get the brain moving and energized and will either de-clutter the mind in order to make room for the writing project at hand or will eventually prompt idea generation about the topic in some capacity.

Directed quickwriting

Directed quickwriting, also sometimes termed directed freewriting or quickwriting, is a modified version of freewriting in that a writer still aims to write nonstop for five or ten minutes, but instead of writing about anything, the writer focuses on his or her writing project, or on a particular part of that writing project. If the writer gets stuck during that time of writing, he or she should not stop writing but should instead keep writing "I feel stuck" until another idea emerges. Writers often find through quickwriting that they have more ideas about a topic than they may have previously anticipated.

Transfer at Work

Outlines reflect and are shaped by disciplinary context and writing occasion. The following outline for an epidemiology article reflects an argument structure common in scientific writing known as IMRAD (Introduction, Methods, Results and Discussion):

- Introduction
  - Epidemiological studies show a correlation between isoflavone consumption and cancer.
  - Evidence supports the idea that genistein is the most important isoflavone in the diet.
  - Genistein has an anticancer effect in animal models.
- Main Point: Epidemiological studies show that diet, which can vary substantially from one country to another, is one of the major factors in cancer etiology and may account for up to 35% of the differences in cancer rates among different countries.
- Thesis Statement: Genistein, a dietary component, has a novel mechanism of action, whereby it specifically down-regulates MDM2 at both transcriptional and post-translational levels.
- Materials and Methods:
  - Plasmids and reagents
  - Cell lines and cell cultures
  - Reverse transcription-PCR
  - Assays for apoptosis, cell proliferation, cell cycle distribution, and clonogenicity
  - Xenograft models
- Results:
  - Genistein inhibits MDM2 expression in human cancer and primary cell lines, regardless of p53 status. (Figures 1 and 2)
  - MDM2 transcription is repressed by genistein. (Figure 3)
  - Genistein promotes degradation of the MDM2 protein, independent of p53. (Figure 4)
  - Inhibitory effects of genistein on tyrosine kinases are not required for the down-regulation of MDM2. (Figure 5)
  - Genistein has antitumor effects on apoptosis, cell cycle distribution, and cell proliferation, regardless of cellular p53 status. (Figure 6)
  - In vitro antitumor activities of genistein are associated with its capacity to down-regulate MDM2. (Figure 7)
  - In vivo MDM2 inhibition by genistein shows dose-dependent antitumor activity and chemosensitization, independent of p53. (Figure 7)
- Discussion:
  - Reason for interest in genistein.
  - Purpose of study and summary of results.
  - Transcriptional activation of MDM2.
  - NFAT, a specific transcription factor.
  - Post-translational regulation of the MDM2 protein.
  - Lack of effect of tyrosine kinase inhibitors.
  - Importance of MDM2 expression in cancer.
  - The antitumor effect of genistein and its effect on MDM2.
- Conclusion: importance of results in relation to cancer prevention and therapy.

By contrast, the following draft outline about late adopters of technology reflects the disciplinary context of ethnography:

Outline

I. Introduction to gestural interfaces and pertinent vocabulary.
   a. Define gestural interfaces and provide examples.
   b. Explain how they are different from traditional user interfaces.
   c. Describe why they were developed and the problem they solved for users.
   d. Provide basic information about pros and cons and vocabulary of gestural interface design.

II. Even though gestural interface technology has existed for a long time, explain the sudden increase in adoption rates.
   a. Describe the representative demographics for early adoption of gestural interfaces.
   b. Investigate the possible reasons behind those statistics.
   c. Describe the following stages of cultural adoption after early adopters: medical devices, restrooms, kiosks, gaming.
   d. Describe the resistors, the novice tech users, and other late adopters.

III. Possible reasons why certain people are resistors of technology in general and more specifically gestural interfaces.
   a. Explain habits, personality types, opportunities, etc. for novice tech users and resistors of gestural interfaces.
   b. Based on research of existing papers on the subject and my own ethnographic research, explain why I think that personality and opportunities play a large part in the adoption and confidence of using gestural interfaces.

Outlines also shift based on writing format, as in the following outline for a digital story, created as a storyboard so the writer can plan video and audio components:

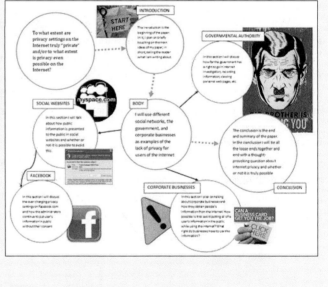

Writers can also adapt outlining practices based on their dispositions, as in the following outline for a research paper on social media and privacy that demonstrates a more visual approach to outlining:

Directed quickwriting allows space for one's ideas to emerge, as well as a structure for generating more ideas. As with freewriting, directed quickwriting is a low-stakes writing strategy, not often shared with others, so writers should not focus on grammar or clarity so much as idea generation.

Looping

Looping is an extended and iterative version of directed quickwriting. In looping, writers complete a directed quickwrite for five or ten minutes, then re-read it and identify one key term that then becomes the starting point for another iteration of directed quickwriting. By re-reading each quickwrite iteration, searching for a new key term that can launch the next quickwrite, writers can engage in a process of discovery to explore the various perspectives and components of a topic, as well as their own interests within a topic.

Typically writers find that three to five iterative loops in one setting works sufficiently to help them move to increasing levels of depth and breadth with a potential topic and to avoid fatigue with too many loops at once. Looping provides writers the chance to explore several aspects of a topic and identify which ones seem most interesting or promising to pursue. After looping, writers can continue to re-read their quickwrites to reflect on which loops seemed most generative, difficult, significant, etc. See Figure 2.2.

Brainstorming

Brainstorming is one of the most widely used forms of prewriting. While many structures exist for brainstorming, the premise is that writers choose a set amount of time (5 minutes, 10 minutes, 30 minutes, etc.) and then generate as many ideas as possible about a topic or concept as quickly as possible, using short phrases or words so as not to get slowed down creating long sentences. Brainstorming can occur on an individual basis or in a group format where everyone works together to brainstorm.

With brainstorming, as with the other forms of prewriting, writers should not regulate or restrict their ideas, but should aim to develop as many ideas as possible in the time permitted. Writers can do this using paper, an electronic device, or a large writable wall, board, or screen. As one of the paramount forms of ideation—or idea generation—brainstorming occurs across numerous fields, not only with writing, but also for any other instance where people want to explore possibilities and identify promising avenues for future exploration. See Figure 2.3.

Concept mapping

Concept mapping is a form of brainstorming that includes more of an explicit capacity for building relationships and connections among ideas. Writers can create concept maps using any of the forms of media described in brainstorming (paper, electronic device, large writable screen, board, or wall) as well as through one of several online concept-map generators. To

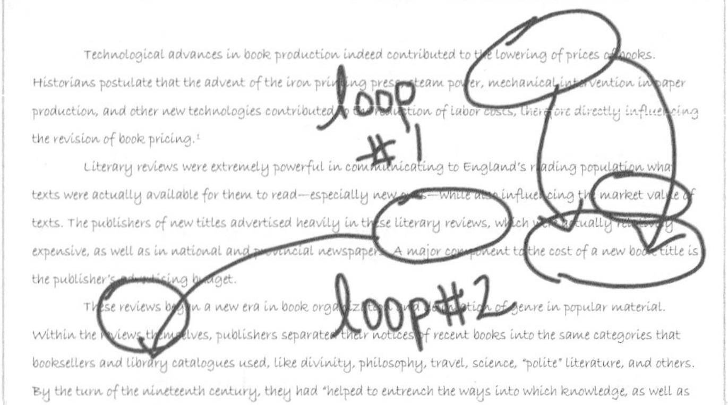

FIGURE 2.2 Example of looping.

FIGURE 2.3 Example of a collaborative brainstorm by a group generating ideas for a writing mashup project.

begin a concept map, writers should write down the main topic or issue in the center using a key phrase or word as the starting point. The writer then begins branching out with subcategories and creating groups of concepts or ideas around the main idea.

In this way, writers create something like a geographic map, whereby similar ideas are more closely related to or connected with one another and the more widely divergent ideas can be positioned farther apart from one another. Writers can use any geometric form for their concept map, perhaps using different forms to designate different levels of ideas, from boxes and circles to squares and triangles. Writers can also use different colors to designate different levels, categories, or groups of concepts. See Figure 2.4.

FIGURE 2.4 Example of a concept map about social media.

Data analysis

Data analysis can emerge as a stage in the research process or as a form of prewriting. When used as a form of prewriting, writers examine their data in order to generate ideas and identify trends, patterns, divergences, and other significant findings. Data can be numerical, aural, verbal, visual, or qualitative in nature, or it can be artifacts and materials.

When writers use data analysis as a form of prewriting, they will often choose a strategy, a theoretical lens, or a methodology to apply to the analysis of their data. During early stages of the writing process, this approach can help writers notice what the data are suggesting about a particular topic or issue. This early form of data analysis can help writers identify subsets or elements of data that they can then pursue in more depth for the remaining work of the data analysis, research, and writing.

Posing questions

Posing and answering questions in an organized way as a form of prewriting provides a generative approach for exploring various dimensions of a topic. Often, this form of prewriting involves a writer using a question heuristic, or guided template, to explore particular questions about an area of inquiry. One useful and frequently used question heuristic is the journalist's 5 Ws and H: Who? What? When? Where? Why? and How? Asking—and then attempting to answer—these questions can help writers determine what aspects of a topic are significant, contentious, or interesting, and what areas might warrant additional research or further exploration in the writing project. Another less structured version of posing questions, involves a writer generating numerous questions about an issue, and perhaps initial responses to these questions, so as to identify what questions may be most important or valuable to the researcher.

Formulating hypotheses

Writing and research across many disciplines emerges from researchers formulating and exploring hypotheses. A hypothesis involves making an educated guess, based on what you know or think about a given issue or topic, about a potential argument, claim, or data result. Writers who formulate hypotheses will spend time writing down what they anticipate will be the outcome of research, followed by a justification of that projected outcome. Although hypotheses do emerge from prior knowledge and experiences, writers must be cautious not to get too attached to a hypothesis. The purpose of research is to either prove or disprove a hypothesis, and writers can learn a significant amount in either case.

Write Now

Think about a writing project you will be completing this term. Choose two of the above prewriting strategies that make sense given the context of the writing occasion (discipline, project, timeline, aims, etc.) and spend five minutes trying out the technique.

Regardless of which prewriting strategy a writer chooses, there are several critical factors that can help make prewriting strategies more effective. Depending on the context, different writing occasions sometimes warrant different prewriting strategies. For instance, if you are writing a personal narrative for a creative writing course about a difficult moment in your life, you may decide to do some freewriting just to get yourself mentally prepared to tackle this subject. If you are writing about an electrical engineering research study for your Introduction to Engineering course, you probably want to generate a hypothesis and pose questions. If you are writing a historical analysis of the civil rights movement for an African and African-American studies course, you might opt for a concept map so you can think through the many aspects of this movement and decide where you want to focus your attention.

Think as creatively as possible so you can have lots of possible ideas to consider. Avoid questioning or limiting your prewriting because you never know if an idea might be worthwhile. The point of prewriting is often to generate as many possibilities and gather as much data as possible within a reasonable amount of time.

Context helps writers determine which prewriting strategies to adopt. **Context** includes such elements as the following:

- **Discipline:** What is the disciplinary context for this writing project?
- **Genre:** What options do you have for the genre of writing with this project? What genre makes the most sense?
- **Aims/Purpose:** To whom are you primarily writing? Why? What do you hope to accomplish with this writing project?
- **Timeline:** When is this writing project due? When should the various phases of the project be completed? When would you like to finish it?
- **Other:** Is this a collaborative or individual writing project?

Write Now

Think about a writing project you will be completing this term. Write for five minutes about your aims and purpose: What do you hope to accomplish with this piece of writing? Who do you hope reads it? Why? Where are you planning on sending/publishing the final version? How will your awareness of purpose and aims help shape your prewriting plans for the writing project?

Transfer Hub: Contribute your ideas and see what others have written at fountainheadpress.com/transferhub.

Drafting across Disciplines

Drafting occurs when writers move from primarily prewriting activities such as researching or brainstorming to composing the sentences and paragraphs of a piece of writing. This phase

Writer Insights

How do you use concept maps?

[When] brainstorming for ideas, I use Mind Maps, which use bubbled maps to generate and record ideas and thoughts. One uses bubbles to jot down ideas and thoughts and connects them to similar ideas branching out of it. This creates a wide networked bubbled map and it makes the flow of ideas very easy and natural without the need to write long sentences that may cause delay in the flow of thoughts. It makes it very easy to select relevant ideas and plots and the rest is easily discarded.

~Sweta Lal,
Creative Writer/Management Research Candidate,
Bentleigh East, Melbourne Area, Australia

overlaps significantly with research, pre-writing, and revision. As with all parts of the writing process, there is no "right" or "wrong" way to draft. Some writers choose to draft an entire piece before revising; other writers will draft a portion of a text, then start revising that section before the whole project is written. Others might start in the middle of a piece of writing and save the beginning or conclusion for the end of the process.

Disciplines and writing occasion also impact drafting. In Archaeology, scholars may spend most of their time researching, and then "write up," or draft, their findings relatively quickly. By contrast, American Literature scholars may spend most of their time drafting to discover insights and develop arguments. Those writing public-policy memos may need to generate documents quickly, abridging the entire writing process, drafting included. Writing collaboratively, in pairs or teams, also impacts drafting. These writers may draft together, or they may distribute drafting, assigning different people to draft different sections, or taking turns with different iterations of a draft. However much drafting time you may need for the writing occasion, there are a few tips for success to keep in mind.

Begin drafting early

Even if a writer does not feel or believe that it is time to begin drafting, it still makes sense to get an early start. For some writers, the drafting process seems to mark an important turning point in the writing and research process—an indication that they have learned everything they can about a topic and are therefore ready to simply and quickly write up an article. Since it is difficult, if not impossible, to actually learn everything one can about any topic, writers often delay the drafting phase because they feel like they need to spend more time doing research, analyzing data, or thinking about the project.

In fact, drafting early can help solidify a writing project and provide direction. Starting to draft sooner rather than later helps a writer get ideas down and nudges a writing project forward. Drafting early can be an important component of writers figuring out what to write, and how to write. Even if writers are still waiting for more research results or need more time for research, they can still likely begin writing certain segments of a writing project. Beginning to draft early in the process will help writers avoid feeling overwhelmed about a writing project or delaying a writing project for long periods of time. It is often much easier to resume work on a draft in progress than to perpetually be on the brink of beginning to draft a writing project.

Establish a writing ritual

Whether you know it or not, you likely have writing rituals you adopt when you write. Some people prefer to write to music, others in silence. Perhaps you have a favorite place to write or a favorite writing implement or equipment. Or maybe you have an activity you engage in prior to writing that offers you a writing transition, such as going for a walk or preparing a cup of tea or coffee.

These habits are not merely quirks but are important rituals writers use in order to be ready to engage with their writing. Sometimes these habits are static for a writer; other times they shift, depending on the kind of writing a writer engages in. They also make writing fun.

Write Now

What are your writing habits or rituals? Do you engage in any activities that help transition you into writing? Where do you prefer to write? When? Write for five minutes on your writing rituals and habits. Share your ideas and see what others have written.

Transfer Hub: Contribute your ideas and see what others have written at fountainheadpress.com/transferhub.

Start anywhere and jump around

A common misconception about the drafting process is that drafting needs to be accomplished in a linear manner, from the beginning of a writing project through to the final sentence. In fact, writers do not need to start drafting at the beginning of a writing project (unless they want to). Writers can instead feel free to dive in anywhere in the project and then move around as they wish. When a writer is more enthusiastic about one particular section of a writing project than others, he or she can begin drafting that section first. Writers might choose to draft a section on background research first, or they can begin drafting a conclusion.

Allowing oneself the flexibility to start anywhere and jump around during the drafting process will sidestep one of the most common difficulties involved with writing: how to begin. Many writers indicate they have difficulty knowing how to start a writing project, but that once they are in the middle of that project the writing becomes more productive and fluid. Perhaps, though, this common difficulty in some cases is not really a matter of how to begin drafting, but literally about how to create an effective introduction to a writing project. If this is the case, then drafting the rest of the project first may solve the problem because the writer can use the drafting process to develop an argument, integrate evidence and research data, and synthesize research, all of which will make writing an introduction easier. By first developing an argument, writers may find it easier to go back and create the introduction because they will then know what it is they are trying to accomplish or argue in the project.

Quiet your "inner critic"

Writing is already difficult, but it is often made more difficult by our own misgivings, insecurities, and ambivalences. Our "inner critic" is the negative voice inside our own heads that challenges our ideas, questions our capabilities, and sometimes prevents us from making progress on our writing. Kathleen Kendall-Tackett, editor-in-chief of Praeclarus Press and former acquisitions and development editor for Hale Publishing, describes the "inner critic":

> For most writers, getting started is the hardest part. You may be bursting with good ideas. But somehow, what comes out on paper is…horrible. Because of that disconnect, it's easy to put writing off. A major reason writers procrastinate is that little voice inside our heads. It's the voice that tells you your writing is awful and will never improve. Talk with other writers and you'll find out what a common experience this is.

Kendall-Tackett, like many others, relies on the advice of author Anne Lamott, who emphasizes in *Bird by Bird*, that all writing begins needing work: "Almost all good writing begins with terrible first efforts. You need to start somewhere. Start by getting something—anything—down on paper."

Transfer at Work

Writing processes vary depending on disciplinary context and writing occasion. Sociologist Hua-Fu Hsu conducted interviews in a Taiwanese prison over four weeks in July 2003, then analyzed data, drafted, revised, and edited the article for approximately two years, until it was published in 2005. Demonstrating a variation of the writing process, Aaron Carpenter—a prisoner taking a class in prison—created an online op-ed, "Does racial injustice still exist? Look at our schools," over several months in the fall of 2014. Carpenter wrote a reflection piece based on a text he read in a class, then re-shaped it into an op-ed through revising and editing, ultimately publishing it on December 1, 2014. Meanwhile, Berit Johnsen, Granheim Per Kristian, and Janne Helgesen traveled to 32 different prisons over four months in 2007, then analyzed data, drafted, revised, and edited the article for approximately four years until it was published in 2011. They found that prisoners in smaller prisons had comparatively higher satisfaction scores across a number of dimensions than prisoners in medium- or large-size prisons:

Table 2. Results for first-line officers by prison size (small, medium and large)

Dimensions	Prison size							
	Small (n=169–96)		Medium (n=139–45)		Large (n=407–26)			
	M	SD	M	SD	M	SD	F-ratio	Probability
Treatment by senior management	3.61*	0.83	3.44*	0.71	2.98	0.76	49.88	.000
Attitudes towards senior management	3.39++	0.85	3.18*	0.76	2.72	0.71	58.20	.000
Perception of prison service	3.24	0.63	3.24	0.62	3.20	0.61	0.32	.728
Relationship with peers	4.07	0.43	4.05	0.36	4.07	0.42	0.15	.859
Relationship with line management	3.81	0.77	3.83	0.54	3.91	0.55	2.14	.119
Treatment by SOs and POs	3.71	0.74	3.66	0.56	3.60	0.57	2.04	.130
Commitment	3.86	0.56	3.87	0.59	3.76	0.61	3.00	.050
Safety/control/security	3.54*	0.65	3.66*	0.56	3.35	0.58	16.88	.000
Recognition and personal efficacy	3.36*	0.64	3.27	0.56	3.22	0.60	3.50	.031
Involvement in prison	3.25**	0.71	2.99*	0.73	2.78	0.68	29.83	.000
Involvement in work	3.74	0.61	3.79*	0.52	3.63	0.59	5.19	.006
Stress	3.32	0.89	3.25	0.81	3.22	0.87	0.80	.449
Relationships with prisoners	3.88*	0.41	3.79	0.40	3.78	0.47	3.39	.034
Social distance	3.34**	0.48	3.21	0.42	3.22	0.47	4.44	.012

*Significant mean difference from large prisons.
**Significant mean difference from both large and medium prisons.

Don't get stuck with details

The drafting phase of a writing project should be considered an extension of the prewriting phase in that writers who are drafting are often still in the process of discovering ideas and exploring possibilities. It is less important to get it "right" during the drafting process than to continue making progress on the draft itself. Writers can avoid focusing on details such as grammar or perfect word choice. Writers can work on these aspects later in the revision and editing phases. Spending valuable time focusing on the exact right phrase or word might end up being a misuse of time if, during revision, a writer decides to jettison an idea or section altogether. Getting bogged down in the details during the drafting phase may hamper a writer's progress, preventing him or her from continuing to generate ideas and develop the fuller writing project.

Instead, when writers find themselves stuck on a detail, they can just insert a bracket with the phrase "return later" (or any other phrase) to stand in for the absent content. Creating this sort of placeholder for details enables writers to easily pass over these small details and instead keep writing the rest of the sentence, paragraph, page, or project. In so doing, writers can draft the overarching organization and structure of a project, without having spent valuable time and energy on small details and then finding themselves left with only part of a project completed.

> ## Writer Insights
>
> **What is your writing process?**
>
> My writing process includes conversations with research providers, data analysis, and development of business implications. I start by creating an outline of key points for the topic at hand. Then I compose a section for each point that details the research findings, explains how they would affect business decisions made by my colleagues, and illustrates the data with graphs. When all topics are complete, I compose a summary that introduces the general topic and touches the main points and their business implications. The next step is editing the draft, removing extraneous details, rewriting sentences to be understandable to both junior and senior colleagues, subtitling each section, and making sure the ideas flow logically and are relevant. The summary is presented at the start of the final version. It is emphasized by enclosing it in a box with a bold border that separates it from the rest of the text. Most of my colleagues will only read the report if they think it affects their own job, so it's important to grab their attention with the summary box at the start or they won't take the time to read beyond the first few paragraphs.
>
> ~Liz N., Advertising Research Director, New York City, U.S.

"Park on the downhill slope"

We all need breaks when writing, sometimes just to stretch or move around, other times to sleep, or most often because other aspects of our life need attending to. Busy college students may not have time to work on one writing project at a time in sustained ways. Expert writing advisor Joan Bolker urges writers to "park on the downhill slope" in order to make it easier to return and pick up the writing project again:

> [Y]ou'll come to a point at which you start to tire and feel like there's not much left in your writing reservoir for the day. This is the time to begin to summarize for yourself where you've been, to write down your puzzlements or unanswered questions, to do what Kenneth Skier, who taught writing at M.I.T. many years

ago, calls "parking on the downhill slope": sketching out in writing what your next step is likely to be, what ideas you want to develop, or follow, or explore when you pick up the writing again the next day. This step will help you get started more easily each day, and it will save you an enormous amount of energy and angst.

As Bolker's suggestion illustrates, writers find it infinitely easier to return to a writing project if they are returning to an easier part of the project. If writers stop writing during a difficult spot, they might run the risk of avoiding or dreading a return to a project. Parking on the downhill slope, at a moment when the writer's ideas are developing easily and rapidly, enables a writer to take a break from writing but be enthusiastic about the prospect of returning to that project. If writers cannot forge through a difficult part before taking a break, they can instead choose to create a downhill slope by writing out notes for themselves about what they will do when they return to the project. Breaks are important. Writers need them to regain energy, take a step back, and think through the writing project. So, take breaks, but do so in conjunction with planning the next writing steps so that it is easier, not harder, to return to the writing project once your break is over.

Revising across Disciplines

Writing is, at its core, about rewriting. **Revision** involves writers rethinking their texts. Revision generally involves global rethinking and restructuring, whereas editing involves smaller, more sentence-level changes and proofreading. Revision involves making changes to the structure, organization, and content of a project. Take a look at some strategies that can make your revising more effective in addition to receiving feedback from other writers, and an extended section on feedback is provided on pp. 62-66. Revision generally requires that a writer have time to rethink a text; this might involve stepping away from a text for a day, or several days, and returning to it with a fresh perspective.

Read aloud

Find a quiet place to read your text aloud. Mark moments in the text where you notice an aspect you would like to adjust. Read to make sure you have accomplished what you hope to have accomplished, or that you have communicated the significance of your ideas. Think about structure, organization, and evidence. Reading aloud can often reveal disconnected thoughts or rough patches of writing. An effective follow up after discovering such areas for revision is developing a reverse outline.

Create a reverse outline

You are likely familiar with what an outline is. This version is called a "reverse outline" because it happens after a piece is written rather than before. A writer notes beside each paragraph a key phrase that captures what that paragraph communicated.

These brief phrases enable the writer to reflect on and, as needed, reconsider several aspects of a writing project. One such aspect that reverse outlines can highlight is organization. Writers can look at the reverse outline and decide if the sequence of paragraphs makes sense. Perhaps an idea is missing, or an idea seems out of place in its current location and would work better in a different location within the project. A second aspect of writing that reverse outlines can help make visible is overall cohesion. Perhaps, for instance, the reverse outline reveals an idea that seems tangential or unconnected to the larger project. Writers can then eliminate it to connect that concept more closely to the main idea. Finally, a third element that reverse outlines can help writers address is paragraph unity. Paragraphs should, ideally, focus on one main idea. If in creating a reverse outline, a writer has difficulty identifying one word or phrase to capture that paragraph, then the writer might have discovered that the paragraph is not unified. The writer can then decide to break the paragraph differently or move some of that paragraph's material to a different location in the project in order to achieve more paragraph unity. In these ways, reverse outlines serve as indispensable tools for writers.

Organization

Does the sequence of paragraphs make sense? Is there anything missing? Does any material seem tangential or unnecessary? If so, that material might be deleted or connected more explicitly. Should the piece be organized differently?

Paragraph unity

Was it possible to develop a word or phrase to capture a paragraph? If not, the paragraphs might need to be divided differently.

Overall cohesion

Do all the parts of the paper work together to advance your main point and overarching purpose?

Be open to change

Perhaps one of the biggest barriers to revision is the writer himself or herself. We get attached to a turn of phrase or concept and may resist considering a new direction for our writing project. Be willing to rethink your piece. Sometimes revision can be frustrating as well because it unravels some of what you have accomplished or makes you realize you are not as far along as you may have hoped. This messiness and recursivity, though, is part of the writing process, and rather than responding with denial or dismay, expect and embrace it.

Perhaps you have other revision strategies. No matter what strategy you adopt, be sure to engage in revision. Revising makes your writing stronger.

Figures 2.5, 2.6, and 2.7 show a writer, Katharine Krieger, moving through the drafting and revision process of an introduction to an article.

Notice in Figure 2.7 how much material Krieger changes during the process of revising. These changes include global-level revisions such as adding more research and expanding ideas. Krieger's revisions also address more local-level aspects of the writing

Draft: Nov 23, 2010

Dating back almost a century, scientists have been interested in the behavior of animals. Information such as their habitat, reaction to environmental changes and interactions with other animals of the same and different species has been little understood until the past decade. The field of biologging has increased and improved exponentially with the improvements in technology. Tracking animals has gone from observing and taking notes on land mammals that could be seen, to satellite and other tracking technologies on marine animals, providing us with, in some cases, real time information of the temperature, salinity, depth and pressure of the water, along with their location, heart rate, and consumption (Roupert-Coudert, Wilson, pp. 438, 2005).

Biologging is defined as the study of animals' behavior, physiology, and ecology of free-ranging animals, especially that which cannot easily be observed (Davis, pp.12, 2008). More specifically, biologging is the study of animals, which are not easily observed, for example nocturnal animals, marine animals or very small animals. Each of these groups cannot be observed using conventional method's as there are restrictions on human's ability to see them for long periods of time.

Google Earth is a virtual globe that brings the user a 3-D interactive view of the earth containing endless information. The newest version, Google Earth 5, now allows users to explore beneath the oceans surface, seeing things such as coral reefs, trenches, and the movements of GPS-tracked marine life (Butler, para. 1, 2009). The importance of this science lies in the advancements that can be made in protecting the animals that are studied. The more that is understood regarding habitat and environments that endangered animals live, and how they react to stimuli such as global warming and pollution will undoubtedly lead to better protection of the animals.

The purpose of this article is to highlight the advancements in biologging marine animals, and show how Google Earth is helping this field to further develop and increase awareness of the issues surrounding these animals.

FIGURE 2.5 Early draft of Katharine Krieger's introduction to "Google Earth's Role in Marine Conservation through Biologging."

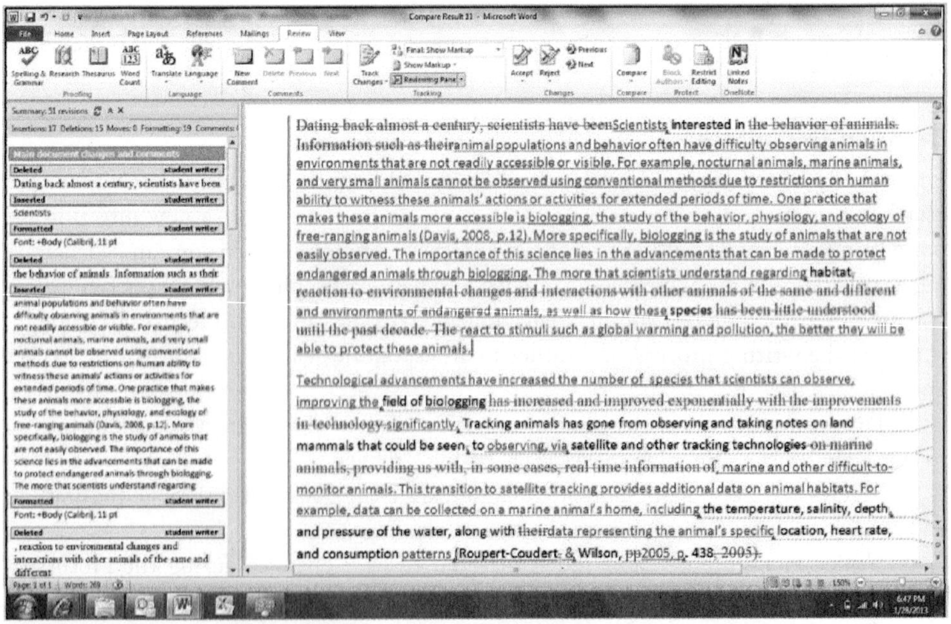

FIGURE 2.6 Krieger's revisions to the introduction to "Google Earth's Role in Marine Conservation through Biologging" (depicted through Microsoft Word's Compare Document Feature).

Published: Oct 28, 2011

    Scientists interested in animal populations and behavior often have difficulty observing animals in environments that are not readily accessible or visible. For example, nocturnal animals, marine animals, and very small animals cannot be observed using conventional methods due to restrictions on human ability to witness these animals' actions or activities for extended periods of time. One practice that makes these animals more accessible is biologging, the study of the behavior, physiology, and ecology of free-ranging animals (Davis, 2008, p.12). More specifically, biologging is the study of animals that are not easily observed. The importance of this science lies in the advancements that can be made to protect endangered animals through biologging. The more that scientists understand regarding habitat and environments of endangered animals, as well as how these species react to stimuli such as global warming and pollution, the better they will be able to protect these animals.

    Technological advancements have increased the number of species that scientists can observe, improving the field of biologging significantly. Tracking animals has gone from observing and taking notes on land mammals that could be seen to observing, via satellite and other tracking technologies, marine and other difficult-to-monitor animals. This transition to satellite tracking provides additional data on animal habitats. For example, data can be collected on a marine animal's home, including the temperature, salinity, depth, and pressure of the water, along with data representing the animal's specific location, heart rate, and consumption patterns (Roupert-Coudert & Wilson, 2005, p. 438). Until recently, however, technology allowing the spatial representation of this breadth of data has not kept up with advances in data collection technology.

FIGURE 2.7 Krieger's final version of the introduction to "Google Earth's Role in Marine Conservation through Biologging."

project such as transitions and clarity. Krieger has also eliminated much material, perhaps deleting portions of text that seemed less specific or less relevant to her argument. And, one can also see in these revisions that Krieger has addressed several proofreading or editing dimensions; in the citations, for instance, Krieger has modified them to adhere more closely to an established citation system.

 Write Now

What did Krieger change through the course of her revision? Can you identify the ways in which she improved her introduction?

Editing across Disciplines

Editing, as opposed to revision, generally involves smaller, local changes to a piece of writing. The editing phase occurs as a piece of writing is nearing the final version. Some depictions of the writing process include a final phase, termed proofreading, but we have decided to include proofreading in the editing phase. Commonly, writers work on the following aspects of writing as they edit:

- clarity
- grammar

- word choice/diction
- proofreading
- titles
- opening sentences
- closing sentences
- topic sentences

Editing usually involves short, small changes in order to polish a piece of writing and make it ready to share in a final version. Try to reserve editing until the latter stages of a piece of writing so you don't spend valuable time getting the words of a sentence just right only to learn later as you revise that you have decided to take out that sentence altogether.

Feedback across Disciplines

Feedback is one of the most crucial parts of the writing process and, like research, is best located throughout every stage of the writing process. Feedback can be verbal or written, it can involve your own feedback to yourself or come from others, and it can be formal or informal. Throughout the process of receiving feedback, keep certain strategies in mind to make feedback more useful.

Integrate feedback throughout the writing process

Writers can request and receive feedback at all points during the writing process, from prewriting through editing. You can share writing-in-progress or ideas you are thinking about writing at earlier stages in the process in order to get feedback from others to help you develop a piece of writing. During the drafting phase, writers can get feedback about portions that are already drafted or about portions of a project that are presenting difficulties. Feedback during the revision phrase is also crucial. Such feedback should be timed when writers have a basically finished draft, but one that is not yet fully polished and finalized. Drafts at this latter stage should be as developed as possible so those providing feedback can have the advantage of reading the entire project. However, drafts should still be in a stage where writers are willing and able to make revisions. While a writer might wish on some level that readers' feedback will simply say that the draft is perfect and complete as is, the reality is that writing is almost never completely polished. Purely positive feedback would not equip writers with the insight to improve a writing project or grow as a writer.

Writer Insights

Why is revision important in your writing?

Writing is the physical manifestation of thoughts, concepts and ideas. Words give form to abstractions bubbling out of the imagination. Laid side by side, these create sentences whose sole task is to impart the reader with a sense of pace and, if all goes to plan, drama. Getting at those right words and placing them in the right order takes time. Writing becomes re-writing, which becomes re-re-writing. All this calls for patience and trust that with a sustained effort, your initial idea will be captured out of abstraction and laid out for all to see.

~Benoit Detalle, Animation Scriptwriter and Animator, Belgrade, Serbia

Feedback at its most effective should occur throughout the writing process so writers can incorporate others' ideas along the way rather than waiting until the last minute before a deadline and then finding themselves unwilling or unable to revise.

Even after a writing project is complete, feedback remains valuable. Writing transfer emphasizes that you will move forward as a writer even after individual pieces of writing are completed. Soliciting and receiving feedback even on a final product will enable you to use that feedback to move forward with other writing projects, extend ideas, and otherwise grow as a writer.

Choose readers purposefully

Different readers will offer different strengths and perspectives. Perhaps there is a disciplinary perspective you would like to include. Perhaps you know someone who is working on a related project. Or, perhaps you've admired an aspect of someone else's writing or thinking, and you would like his or her input. We can't always choose who is giving feedback to us, but if you have any input in the selection process, try to do so purposefully. Also aim for getting feedback from multiple readers. Each reader should have the potential to offer something valuable.

Acknowledge that sharing can be uncomfortable

If you are comfortable sharing your writing with others, good for you! But, if you are like many of us, you may feel nervous sharing your writing. Getting used to sharing your writing, though, will make you a better writer. Receiving feedback helps you grow as a writer overall, and it helps you improve a particular writing project. Writers at all levels in all disciplines, especially professors or researchers, must submit their writing to peers for review before their work is published in academic journals or books. See Figure 4.2 on p. 131 to learn more about this process.

Write Now

Think back to moments in the past when you have provided or received feedback on a piece of writing. The feedback could be from a peer, friend, colleague, or teacher. What makes feedback more or less effective? Do you remember any particular feedback you received? What makes this feedback stand out? What's hard about providing feedback to others?

Transfer Hub: Contribute your ideas and see what others have written at fountainheadpress.com/transferhub.

Offer your readers feedback guidelines

When you ask for feedback, avoid just asking "What do you think?" Also try to avoid asking yes/no questions. Instead, share with them what your main concerns are, what you would especially like feedback on, where you were stuck or uncertain as a writer. For example, you might ask any of the following questions: Which evidence did you find most effective? What other evidence would be helpful for my argument? I struggled on page 4 with the [insert specific] section; what do you think that paragraph is trying to accomplish or communicate? Which elements of my introduction enable you to become interested in the writing project? As much as possible, try to avoid asking readers to copyedit (at least not until later in the process); substantive feedback should really be more about the ideas and substance of the writing, not the more surface aspects.

Be open and flexible, even with challenging feedback

If you think you've written a perfect final version and then you share it with others, you will likely be disappointed. Feedback involves more than just providing a stamp of approval. Be willing to really consider others' ideas, and be open to changing your writing project in accordance with the feedback you receive. Cultivating this receptivity, though, is easier in some instances than in others. It might be easy to be open and flexible to feedback when feedback highlights the strengths of a writing project or when responders suggest a few quick edits, such as fixing typos, changing words, or revising a few sentences. Being open and flexible to feedback can be much more challenging when that feedback is unsolicited, challenging to implement, or emotionally difficult to hear. Writers, for instance, must work harder at being open and flexible with difficult feedback suggestions, such as deleting an entire section, integrating more research, or reframing an argument. In these instances, though, it is even more important for writers to be open and flexible by carefully considering the feedback they receive. Try to listen carefully to what your readers say and consider thoughtfully how you might respond to the feedback in order to strengthen your writing.

Take an active role in making feedback meaningful

Although it may seem that the writer is a passive recipient of feedback, the truth is that writers can and should take active roles in making feedback productive. This is true even when that feedback may seem less than ideal. Some writers, for instance, believe that if they receive feedback that is unhelpful, unclear, too critical, or otherwise unproductive, it is the fault of the reviewers and nothing else can be done. However, writers have many options available to them in order to take active roles in making feedback productive.

Take time reviewing feedback

After you receive feedback, consider waiting a little while before you implement the suggestions. Read and re-read the feedback so you can process the feedback and develop your approach to revising. Sometimes feedback can seem overwhelming at first, but waiting a few days usually enables you to find renewed energy to revise a writing project.

Explain unclear feedback

Do not settle for less than satisfactory feedback. If you can, return to the reader to ask follow-up questions and gain more clarity. If not, find another reader to read that feedback and help you gain more clarity. If you are unclear how to proceed with a project after having received contradictory feedback from two or more different readers, you can also take actions to provide clarity for yourself. Discrepancies in feedback do not usually mean that one responder is right and the other wrong. Rather, feedback discrepancies are often simply a result of individual readers having their own perspectives. Different readers respond differently. You can arbitrate between contradictory feedback by eliciting more conversation between and with the responders. Alternatively, you can aim for a compromise or get another opinion altogether from another responder.

Revise overly harsh feedback

Sometimes writers encounter negative feedback that seems exceedingly harsh. Harsh feedback can be frustrating and discouraging. Some writers respond to harsh feedback by ignoring it. Writers do this for many reasons. Perhaps this harsh feedback is emotionally painful to hear, and avoiding such pain is a natural human reaction. Or, perhaps a writer anticipates that revising in response to this harsh feedback would be too challenging, so ignoring it or the writing project seems more reasonable. Sometimes writers ignore harsh feedback because they believe the person providing the feedback is biased against the writer or writing project. While ignoring harsh feedback is understandable, it is not necessarily the best choice. Harsh feedback can often have value despite the harshness. To access this value, you can revise harsh feedback. For instance, if a responder describes your writing as "awkward and boring," you can revise that to become the following: "Use more precise word choices, vary sentence structure, and add more human-interest elements."

Remember your own authority

If you disagree with feedback, you can reject certain portions of it. Perhaps a responder suggests taking the project in a direction the writer does not prefer, or maybe the responder suggests deleting a segment the writer deems essential. In these cases, writers can always decide to reject portions of the feedback. That said, writers might also recognize that even seemingly unproductive feedback can be valid in some manner: perhaps the suggested new direction would yield a good footnote or an opportunity for future work; or, a suggestion for deletion might signal that the writer needs to connect that material more thoroughly to the main argument. In the end, though, the writer is the author and, as such, has final authority over what to do with a text (at least to a certain extent, depending on context).

Writer Insights

What has been your experience giving feedback?

I fear my feedback will be misconstrued. Some people have lower thresholds for criticism. They feel they're being attacked, but that's not true. I want to help them produce the best writing possible. So I structure my feedback positively to encourage receptivity.

~Yolanda Riley, Writer,
St. Louis, Missouri, U.S.

Provide feedback to yourself

Many writers forget that they too can provide feedback to themselves. Providing feedback to yourself is best accomplished through time away from the text. This is known as re-seeing a text. Set down your project for a day or more in order to create space and distance. Doing so before reappraising one of your drafts will enable you to read with fresh eyes and recognize aspects that can be modified and improved.

Feedback is always valuable

Writing transfer emphasizes that you will move forward as a writer even after individual pieces of writing are completed. Accept and solicit feedback even on a final product so you can use that feedback as a way to move forward with related projects, extend ideas, or grow as a writer.

Provide feedback to others as a way of becoming a stronger writer

Although the benefits of providing feedback are in some ways less immediately visible than the benefits of receiving feedback, they are nonetheless highly present and valuable. Offering to provide feedback to others, whether for writing projects that are similar to ones you are working on, or writing projects that are quite different, will help you with your writing. During the process of providing feedback, you can identify features of writing you would like to model in your own writing (or do differently), or you might come across ideas that resonate with your own thinking or that inspire you to pursue new questions.

Each time you provide feedback to others, reflect on how providing feedback has benefited you and your writing. You can ask yourself what you have learned about a particular topic or about an aspect of writing. Possibilities include anything from style to sentence structure, paragraphing to organization. Every chance you get to provide feedback is another opportunity for you to learn more about yourself as a writer and about your own writing.

Writer Insights

How does providing feedback help you?

I am a biomedical scientist, and my latest writing task is a systematic review paper. Since English is my second language, writing in English has been an exciting challenge. The same way English is the language of the academic world, written communication is the most common form of communication in science. In addition to writing letters, scientific papers and course assignments, I also review the writing of my co-workers which is a great opportunity to improve my writing skills and help people with theirs.

~D., Biomedical Scientist,
Porto Alegre, Brazil

Transfer and The Final Product

In academic writing, a final product is not an end, necessarily, so much as the moment when your writing becomes more public so that others can engage with your ideas and thereby continue the conversation. Of course, some writing is meant only to be read by the person who wrote it, and some writing is written without even the intention of being read at all. But academic writing, for the most part, is generally read by others so scholars can contribute to and advance knowledge based on engaging with others' texts.

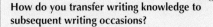

Academic writing takes many shapes and forms across disciplines. Some writing appears in books (or as books), as articles in scholarly journals, or in more popular forms of writing such as op-eds, blogs, memos, policy papers, and reviews. Across all these possible formats, the best academic writing encourages more writing and research, whether by the original authors or by others who are encountering and engaging with that text.

Even though academic writing participates in an ongoing conversation, however, a final product does mark a distinct ending point. Sometimes writers may not feel ready for a writing project to be finished, but a deadline might demand that it be finished. Or, sometimes a writing project has just reached its natural conclusion. It is therefore important to acknowledge that a piece of writing does live on as a final product, a material artifact of your thoughts and research at a given moment in time (even if in cyberspace).

Writer Insights

How do you transfer writing knowledge to subsequent writing occasions?

I am a writer working in Tokyo. Since I first became a copywriter in 1989, I have been changing my writing style and focusing area. I wrote in advertising for about a decade, then I became a writer for a history magazine. After working in the editorial office, I started a web design business by myself in the 2000s. And in recent years, I have co-authored web articles and books with scientists. These works may look similar, but they are diverse in backgrounds, interests, and cultures. So each time I moved to another field, I had to take on a new challenge. Now I am engaged in another one: becoming a writer in English. Through my experience, I think that switching to a new field has only good effects for improving writing skills. I anticipate that it will bring the most revolutionary reform to my writing.

~Rue Ikeya, Writer, Research Administrator, Tokyo, Japan

Even as you take a moment to acknowledge this moment of closure, it is vital you also recognize that you will encounter subsequent writing projects. Because writing transfer hinges in large part on your ability to adapt, modify, reject, or translate what you learn from a previous writing occasion when a new writing occasion occurs, it is important to reflect on your experience with writing at this final juncture. As King Beach advises, transitions are not all created equally, and for a transition to be meaningful, it should include reflection: "A transition is *consequential* when it is consciously reflected on, struggled with, and shifts the individual's sense of self or social position."

To help make your writing transitions between projects as "consequential" as possible, reflect on what you have learned and how you are planning to move forward. You can consider elements about the writing experience you enjoyed, or you disliked, as well as anything you learned about yourself as a writer (strengths and areas for improvement) that you think might be applicable to subsequent writing occasions.

Reflecting on these ideas upon completion of writing projects will help you cultivate a habit of mind grounded in writing transfer, one that enables you to navigate more successfully through the many writing occasions you will encounter both in and outside of school settings.

Transferring the Research and Writing Process

These phases of the research and writing process provide writers with a way to navigate through writing projects that may otherwise seem daunting or overly complex. Prewriting, drafting, revising, and editing, with research and feedback throughout, enable writers to develop worthwhile

Writer Insights

How do you know when you have a final product?

I just received notice that a scientific manuscript for which I am lead author was accepted for publication in a respected peer reviewed journal. The acceptance came after the editor requested a substantial rewrite, which led me to reconsider and reconceptualize the way I presented my study. Applying the peer feedback, engaging in critical thinking and articulating a compelling rebuttal letter were important steps that helped turn a possible rejection into a publication. I am left with a physical feeling of accomplishment and growth.

~Deirdre Dingman,
Postdoctoral Fellow with Public Health Law Research,
Temple University, Philadelphia, Pennsylvania, U.S.

final products that advance knowledge and contribute to ongoing conversations.

As indicated throughout this chapter, it is crucial to keep in mind the ways in which context impacts the research and writing process. With some writing projects, you may find it necessary to focus most of your energies and time on research; with others, revision might take precedence. Still other writing occasions may demand that writers compress these phases into a shorter overall timeframe. Becoming effective at transfer means that you can draw on these general phases of the research and writing process but customize them to meet the particular needs and constraints of any given writing occasion.

Building on what you have learned in this chapter about the research and writing process, the next chapter invites you to consider how writers pose meaningful questions. Questions often actually animate the research and writing process, providing the jumping-off points for research, prewriting, and drafting, and serve as the anchor points for revising, editing, and feedback. As Chapter 3 illustrates, questions also sponsor ongoing inquiry that builds on final, published products.

℮﹆ ℮﹆ ℮﹆

Travel Memoir: *"Trying Really Hard to Like India"* by Seth Stevenson

Transfer Points: Creative Writing, Journalism, English Literature

Across the centuries, travel writing, also termed travel narratives or travel literature, appears in many forms, from memoirs and nature writing to adventure writing and travel guides. Travel writing extends across fiction and nonfiction, and can take the shape of book-length travelogues, feature-length documentaries, unpublished travel diaries, short stories, visual texts, poetry, and magazine articles such as Seth Stevenson's "Trying Really Hard to Like India."

The vast range of texts that constitute travel writing help explain why scholars from across so many disciplines turn to these texts in their research and writing. Scholars across such diverse fields as Environmental Studies, Writing Studies, History, Journalism, American Studies, and Literature use travel writing as primary or secondary materials for their research.

Operating across these many contexts, a central aspect of travel writing involves how travel writers—and those who read travel writing—negotiate power and privilege: In what ways do presuppositions, biases, and predetermined ways of understanding the world impact the impressions travel writers make? Who reads travel writing, and why?

Sometimes termed an "armchair travel," wealthy westerners for centuries traveled to "exotic" locales, writing about their experiences in ways that cast themselves as the protagonists of the narratives. They then delivered their narratives to privileged readers who could read about these exotic lands from the comfort of their living rooms, and, in so doing, often confirm erroneous assumptions and suppositions about cultural superiority. Such elitism, though often less explicit, extends to contemporary travel writing, whereby travel writers describe places for wealthy potential travelers as a means of assisting them in deciding where their next vacations will be.

Catering to the desires of armchair travelers to reaffirm their perceived cultural superiority, many travel writers have historically depicted people and places as inferior, and have often done so without having fully engaged with those people and places. Well-known literary theorists such as Edward Said and Mary Louise Pratt argue that Western travel writers assert dominance through writing by depicting Eastern and South Asian people and places in ways that imply or indicate Western hegemony. The colonial history of India, where Stevenson traveled for the selection included here, is particularly situated within these power dynamics.

Of course, this rendering of travel writing as a genre dominated by power and prestige overlooks the many instances of travel writing composed by and for people from underprivileged or less privileged cultures. It also overlooks travel writers with authentic curiosity and respect for people and places, and readers who turn to travel writing through a genuine interest in learning and understanding. Still, practitioners and researchers of travel writing must grapple with their own privilege, and must be intentional and reflective about their motivations, assumptions, and purposes.

Demonstrating just this sort of metacognition, Stevenson challenges the conventions of travel writing. A predisposition toward positivity is among these

> **Seth Stevenson** has worked as a writer since graduating from Brown University and the Columbia School of Journalism (Potts; "Seth"). He travels around the world and writes about his experiences for such publications as *Slate*, *Newsweek*, and *Rolling Stone*. He has won several awards for his writing. His book *Grounded: A Down to Earth Journey Around the World* (2010) documents his attempt to travel around the world without using any aircraft. Of his profession, Stevenson writes, "I've known I wanted to be a writer since I was a child. From elementary school through high school, I only really lit up when given a chance to write stories or poems" (Potts). This article originally appeared on *Slate.com* in 2004. It was then republished in 2005 as part of an annual anthology of travel writing titled *The Best American Travel Writing*.

conventions. Perhaps as a response to the derisive remarks made by many colonial-era travel writers, or as a way to entice readers to travel to a particular locale, contemporary travel writers often focus on the positive aspects of places, conveying somewhat sanitized versions of their experiences. This is particularly so with places riddled with violence and poverty, since any negative remarks might be construed as participating in a longstanding colonial legacy of perceived superiority.

But Stevenson's approach also gestures to the role of memory. As with any mode of writing that involves experience, travel narratives foreground the challenges surrounding memory and perception: How do people filter experiences through their own ways of knowing and presuppositions? In what ways do bias, motive, and purpose impact what we see, how we understand it, and how we describe it for others?

Such questions are at the heart of creative nonfiction. The term, creative nonfiction, does not suggest a text is untrue, but rather that a writer composes a text with literary craft to enhance meaning and read-ability. Those who write literary journalism, travel writing, and other forms of creative nonfiction rely on literary devices such as tropes, themes, metaphor, diction, imagery, tone, and synecdoche to add dramatic drive and help inscribe and convey meaning. The challenge, though, is to do so in ways that still accurately convey that place and one's experiences. Addressing this challenge, Stevenson also takes issue with the role of literary devices in travel writing, decrying the jargon or trite adages travel writers commonly deploy.

The complexities involved with creative nonfiction, travel narratives, and literary journalism, along with the long history of privilege with regard to travel writing, combine to make travel narratives such as "Trying Really Hard to Like India" worthy of important inquiries into travel writing, power, memory, and representation.

Write Here

Think of a place you have been; this can be in your neighborhood or far away from where you live. First, write a brief description of that place featuring only positive impressions, good experiences, and appealing features. Next, write another brief description of that place in which you instead fea-ture only negative experiences, adverse impressions, and unpleasant features. Then, reflect in writing about what insights you have gleaned about the challenges and choices facing travel writers as they depict people and places. Given the vast range of options for what to include and how to frame experiences, what do you think influences and shapes the choices travel writers make?

Seth Stevenson
Trying Really Hard to Like India

It's OK to hate a place.

Travel writers can be so afraid to make judg-ments. You end up with these gauzy tributes to the "magic" of some far-off spot. But honestly, not every spot is magical for everyone. Sometimes you get somewhere, look around, and think, "Hey, this place is a squalid rat hole. I'd really rather be in the Netherlands." And that's OK.

For example, the last time I went to India I just haaaaaaated it. Delhi was a reddish haze of 105-degree dust. And while, of course, the Taj Mahal was great ... the streets outside it were a miasma of defecating children. I could not wait to go home. (Disclosure: I was there on a previ-ous assignment for *Slate*. And actually, I loved Ladakh, which is in northern India—up in the Himalayas. But I don't really count Ladakh, because it's more like Tibet than like India. Anyway ...)

Now—mostly because my girlfriend wants to come back—I'm back. I'm giving this dreadful place a second chance. And this time I vow I will try really hard to like India.

I'm convinced it's a reachable goal. My plan involves: sticking to South India, far away from Delhi, staying exclusively at beach resorts and luxury hotels, and stocking up on prescription-strength sedatives. But there are other important steps as well, which I will be outlining over the course of this week.

Step 1: Making Peace With Poverty and With Parasitic Worms

After flying into Bangalore and acclimating for a couple of days, we visit a town called Mysore (rhymes with "eyesore"). There's a famous temple here and an opulent palace—big tourist attractions both. But to me, the most interesting thing to see (in *any* place I visit) is the daily life of the people who live and work there.

For instance, from our hotel window in Mysore, we look down on a pile of garbage. Every night, this pile becomes dispersed as it is picked at and chewed on by rats, then crows, then stray dogs, then cows, and then homeless people. Every morning a woman dressed in a brightly colored sari sweeps this masticated garbage-porridge back into a pile. It is the worst job I can imagine. (Previously, the worst job I could imagine was navigator for a rally-car driver, because I get nauseous when I read in cars. But this woman's job is much worse than that. And really, with this added perspective, rally-car navigator doesn't seem so bad anymore.)

When we leave the hotel and walk down the (urine-soaked) street, we get assaulted by autorickshaw drivers, by hawkers, by tour guides … and by tiny children pointing to their own mouths. This last one is rough—at least the first few dozen times. Sometimes these kids are part of a scam. They're forced to beg by adults who run panhandling teams. (We've read stories about teams that cut out kids' tongues, to make them seem more pitiable.) But sometimes these kids are just honestly looking for food. Because they're starving. They might eat out of that big garbage pile tonight. Once the dogs are done.

On the train ride back to Bangalore, monsoon rains slap at the window. I gaze out on wet, destitute slums. Wherever one can build a shanty, someone has. Wherever one could be pissing, someone is. The poverty's on a mind-blowing, overwhelming scale, and you feel so helpless. The money in your pocket right now, handed to any one person out there beyond the window, would be life-changing. But you can't save a billion people and turn the fortunes of this massive country. (You're not Gandhi, you know.) And after all, back in Bangalore we hung out with highly paid IT guys who worked for Infosys. There's a lot of wealth in India, too.

The thing is, if you go to India as a tourist, you'll have to make some sort of peace with all this. Because it's one thing to see poverty on television, or to get direct mail that asks for your charity. It's different when there are tiny, starving children grabbing your wrists and asking for money wherever you go.

For my part, I've resolved to send a check to some worthy Indian charity when I get home. (Suggestions are invited.) It's the best solution I can come up with. Because I'm not going to get through this trip until I've reached an understanding with myself … and until I take some Pepto-Bismol, because my stomach is just killing me. Which brings me to the other thing you'll have to be prepared for.

You *will* get "Delhi belly" soon after touching down in India. And you won't enjoy your trip until it's gone. My illness takes hold on the train ride back to Bangalore, as my intestines suddenly spasm into a clenched fist full of acid. The restroom—should this come into play—is a hole in the floor of the train. (A sign on the door requests that we not use the hole while the train's in a station—for obvious reasons.)

For the next day or two, I find myself playing a game I call "Could I Vomit in This?" The idea is to pick a nearby object and then decide if, in the event of an emergency, it could be puked into. For example, potted plant: Certainly. Water bottle: Sure. Magazine: Iffy, but worth a try.

The good news is that it won't take long before your stomach adjusts to these new microbial nasties, and you're back to feeling fine. Unless, of course, like my friend who was here a few years ago, you've got a parasitic worm and you lose 40 pounds and need medical attention.

Write Away

1. Stevenson refers at several junctures to travel-writing conventions and commonly deployed travel writing phrases or literary devices. Identify several such moments in

Stevenson's text. How do you see Stevenson embracing, extending, amending, or challenging travel-writing conventions and literary devices?

2. Examine the images included with Stevenson's article. Using your skills with close reading of visual texts and visual analysis, write a visual analysis in which you use one or more of those images as evidence to discuss the role of visual images in travel writing. Address such questions as follows: What is in the image? What is the context? What might be outside the frame of the image? How does this image expand upon, modify, or challenge Stevenson's writing?

3. Find several other travelogues about Mumbai (online, in print, book-length, or article length, contemporary or historical). Write a comparative analysis in which you discuss how these travelogues reinforce and/or depart from Stevenson's account and from one another. Examining these texts together, what conclusions might you draw or questions might you pose about travel writing and Mumbai?

Government Document: "Resolution 1738: (2006) Protection of Civilians in Armed Conflict" by the United Nations Security Council

Transfer Points: Public Policy, Political Science, International Relations

Brian Smith, Sportscaster: Shot on August 1, 1995, while exiting the CJOH-TV station building in Ottowa, Canada.

Zezinho Cazuza, Journalist: Shot on March 13, 2000, while leaving a party in Canindé de Sáo Francisco, Brazil.

Dolores Guadalupe García Escamilla, Crime Reporter: Shot while arriving at work on April 16, 2005, in Nuevo Laredo, Mexico.

Paul Kiggundu, Journalist: Beaten to death on September 11, 2010, near Kalisizio, Uganda, while filming a group of motorcycle taxi drivers demolishing a house.

Faisal Arefin Dipan, Newspaper Publisher: Stabbed to death at the offices of a newspaper, Jagriti Prokashoni, in Dhaka, Bangladesh.

These are but several of the hundreds of journalists who have been killed in the line of work. Nearly every year, dozens of journalists are murdered, tortured, and kidnapped for their roles with the media. Some years are especially appalling. Fifty journalists were murdered in 2015, for instance. Eight of these people were killed on January 7, 2015, in the offices of the satirical weekly *Charlie Hebdo* in Paris, France.

Making such dangers more visible, and creating recommendations to protect journalists, the United Nations (UN) Security Council adopted

The UN Security Council was formally established in 1945, as part of an effort to preserve peace and improve upon what were seen to have been the shortcomings of its predecessor, the League of Nations. The UN SC consists of fifteen countries, five of whom are permanent members: China, United States, United Kingdom, Russian Federation, and France. The other ten member countries are elected and nonpermanent, and serve on two-year cycles. There are also more than 60 non-council member states. This organizational structure is significant, because it impacts voting privileges and establishes a hierarchy. Resolution 1738 was published in 2006, developed through a collaboration between France and Greece, with support by Reporters without Borders.

Resolution 1738 on December 23, 2006. Resolutions such as this proceed through a complicated development process involving research, advocacy, debate, drafting, revision, and voting ("What's in Blue"). In the case of Resolution 1738, France and Greece co-authored the resolution, with input from Reporters without Borders (Reporters; "UN Condemns").

UN Security Council Resolutions, which describe problems and make recommendations, address many pressing issues, from terrorism and piracy to democracy and humanitarianism. Resolution 105, for example, from 1954, created an International Court of Justice. And, Resolution 1576, from 2004, recommended continued aid for Haiti, including that which would promote accountability in the Haitian electoral process.

The breadth of issues addressed by UN Security Council Resolutions helps explain the wide range of scholars who research and write about, with, and for the UN and its resolutions. Perhaps most directly among these scholars are those in public policy and international affairs. Public policy relies on analytical tools to implement and evaluate public programs. International affairs, also known as international relations or international studies, carries an explicitly global perspective to questions of policy and interaction. Both fields intersect with economics, ethics, and moral and political philosophy, deal with policies and debates in the public sphere, and rely on quantitative and qualitative social-science research methods.

Academics across public policy and international affairs write in many genres. They might, for example, write position papers, policy briefs, or white papers to describe a problem and make recommendations for action or advocate a position. These documents can help develop a UN resolution, or they might target other policy makers or corporate leaders. Writing in this context requires conciseness, clarity, and accuracy, and an awareness of writing transfer. Policy briefs require synthesizing complex knowledge from different disciplines for readers who themselves carry diverse disciplinary knowledge and expertise.

Writing in public policy and international relations also includes analyses and critiques of UN policies, processes, and resolutions, often in the form of case studies. Examples include an analysis of the implications of Resolution 1325, which called for a mainstream approach to gender during peacekeeping efforts (Pratt), and an argument that Resolution 242, from 1967, has been misinterpreted and is leading to the erosion of Israeli rights (Lapidoth). Researchers in other disciplines, such as history, use UN resolutions as evidence for their work understanding historical events and issues.

For those in media studies and journalism, Resolution 1738 brought visibility to an ongoing, critical problem. A related resolution came in 2013, Resolution 2222, which continued to promote protection of journalists. Sadly, though, as the people named at the outset of this introduction show, violence against journalists continues, illustrating simultaneously the importance of such resolutions, and their limitations.

Write Here

With classmates or individually, learn more about the origins and function of the United Nations Security Council, and about the process of development for UN Security Council Resolutions. Then, write a reflection about the United Nations Security Council and Resolutions in which you address the following questions: What are the overarching aims and functions of the UN Security Council? How do resolutions get developed? What advantages and limitations do you see, if any, with the structure of the UN Security Council and/or with the process for resolutions?

United Nations Security Council
Resolution 1738: Protection of Civilians in Armed Conflict

Deeply concerned at the frequency of acts of violence, including deliberate attacks, in many parts of the world against journalists, media professionals and associated personnel, in armed conflicts, the Security Council today condemned such attacks and called on all parties to put an end to such practices.

Unanimously adopting resolution 1738 (2006), the Council recalled, without prejudice to the war correspondents' right to the status of prisoners of war under the Third Geneva Convention, that journalists, media professionals and associated personnel engaged in dangerous professional missions in areas of armed conflict shall be considered civilians, to be respected and protected as such.

In that connection, the Council recalled its demand that all parties to armed conflict comply with their obligations under international law to protect civilians in armed conflict. It also emphasized the responsibility of States in that regard, as well as their obligation to end impunity and to prosecute those responsible for serious violations. All parties in situations of armed conflict were urged to respect the professional independence and rights of journalists, media professionals and associated personnel as civilians.

Further to the text, the Council reaffirmed its condemnation of all incitements to violence against civilians in situations of armed conflict, as well as the need to bring to justice those who incite such violence. When authorizing missions, the Council also indicated its willingness to consider, where appropriate, steps in response to media broadcast inciting genocide, crimes against humanity and serious violations of international humanitarian law.

The meeting was called to order at 12:42 p.m. and adjourned at 12:45 p.m.

Resolution

The full text of resolution 1738 (2006) reads as follows:

"*The Security Council,*

"*Bearing in mind* its primary responsibility under the Charter of the United Nations for the maintenance of international peace and security, and underlining the importance of taking measures aimed at conflict prevention and resolution,

"*Reaffirming* its resolutions 1265 (1999), 1296 (2000) and 1674 (2006) on the protection of civilians in armed conflict and its resolution 1502 (2003) on protection of United Nations personnel, associated personnel and humanitarian personnel in conflict zones, as well as other relevant resolutions and presidential statements,

"*Reaffirming* its commitment to the Purposes of the Charter of the United Nations as set out in Article 1 (1-4) of the Charter, and to the Principles of the Charter as set out in Article 2 (1-7) of the Charter, including its commitment to the principles of the political independence, sovereign equality and territorial integrity of all States, and respect for the sovereignty of all States,

"*Reaffirming* that parties to an armed conflict bear the primary responsibility to take all feasible steps to ensure the protection of affected civilians,

"*Recalling* the Geneva Conventions of 12 August 1949, in particular the Third Geneva Convention of 12 August 1949 on the treatment of prisoners of war, and the Additional Protocols of 8 June 1977, in particular article 79 of the Additional Protocol I regarding the protection of journalists engaged in dangerous professional missions in areas of armed conflict,

"*Emphasizing* that there are existing prohibitions under international humanitarian law against attacks intentionally directed against civilians, as such, which in situations of armed conflict constitute war crimes, and *recalling* the need for States to end impunity for such criminal acts,

"*Recalling* that the States Parties to the Geneva Conventions have an obligation to search for persons alleged to have committed, or to have ordered to be committed a grave breach of these Conventions, and an obligation to try them before their own courts, regardless of their nationality, or may hand them over for trial to another concerned State provided this State has made out a prima facie case against the said persons,

"*Drawing* the attention of all States to the full range of justice and reconciliation mechanisms, including national, international and "mixed" criminal courts and tribunals and truth and reconciliation commissions, and *noting* that such mechanisms can promote not only individual responsibility for serious crimes, but also peace, truth, reconciliation and the rights of the victims,

"*Recognizing* the importance of a comprehensive, coherent and action-oriented approach, including in early planning, of protection of civilians in situations of armed conflict. *Stressing*, in this regard, the need to adopt a broad strategy of conflict prevention, which addresses the root causes of armed conflict in a comprehensive manner in order to enhance the protection of civilians on a long-term basis, including by promoting sustainable development, poverty eradication, national reconciliation, good governance, democracy, the rule of law and respect for and protection of human rights,

"*Deeply concerned* at the frequency of acts of violence in many parts of the world against journalists, media professionals and associated personnel in armed conflict, in particular deliberate attacks in violation of international humanitarian law,

"*Recognizing* that the consideration of the issue of protection of journalists in armed conflict by the Security Council is based on the urgency and importance of this issue, and recognizing the valuable role that the Secretary-General can play in providing more information on this issue,

"1. *Condemns* intentional attacks against journalists, media professionals and associated personnel, as such, in situations of armed conflict, and calls upon all parties to put an end to such practices;

"2. *Recalls* in this regard that journalists, media professionals and associated personnel engaged in dangerous professional missions in areas of armed conflict shall be considered as civilians and shall be respected and protected as such, provided that they take no action adversely affecting their status as civilians. This is without prejudice to the right of war correspondents accredited to the armed forces to the status of prisoners of war provided for in article 4.A.4 of the Third Geneva Convention;

"3. *Recalls also* that media equipment and installations constitute civilian objects, and in this respect shall not be the object of attack or of reprisals, unless they are military objectives;

"4. *Reaffirms* its condemnation of all incitements to violence against civilians in situations of armed conflict, further reaffirms the need to bring to justice, in accordance with applicable international law, individuals who incite such violence, and indicates its willingness, when authorizing missions, to consider, where appropriate, steps in response to media broadcast inciting genocide, crimes against humanity and serious violations of international humanitarian law;

"5. *Recalls its demand* that all parties to an armed conflict comply fully with the obligations applicable to them under international law related to the protection of civilians in armed conflict, including journalists, media professionals and associated personnel;

"6. *Urges* States and all other parties to an armed conflict to do their utmost to prevent violations of international humanitarian law against civilians, including journalists, media professionals and associated personnel;

"7. *Emphasizes* the responsibility of States to comply with the relevant obligations under international law to end impunity and to prosecute those responsible for serious violations of international humanitarian law;

"8. *Urges* all parties involved in situations of armed conflict to respect the professional independence and rights of journalists, media professionals and associated personnel as civilians;

"9. *Recalls* that the deliberate targeting of civilians and other protected persons, and the commission of systematic, flagrant and widespread violations of international humanitarian and human rights law in situations of armed conflict may constitute a threat to international peace and security, and *reaffirms in this regard its readiness* to consider such situations and, where necessary, to adopt appropriate steps;

"10. *Invites* States which have not yet done so to consider becoming parties to the Additional Protocols I and II of 1977 to the Geneva Conventions at the earliest possible date;

"11. *Affirms* that it will address the issue of protection of journalists in armed conflict strictly under the agenda item "protection of civilians in armed conflict";

"12. *Requests* the Secretary-General to include as a sub-item in his next reports on the protection of civilians in armed conflict the issue of the safety and security of journalists, media professionals and associated personnel."

Write Away

1. UN Security resolutions consist of two parts: 1. reasoning statements, also known as the perambulatory statements, which lay out the background and justification, and 2. operative clauses, which lay out the resolution's recommendations (Nadin 12). Conduct a close reading of the reasoning statements and operative clauses of Resolution 1738: What forms of reasoning or persuasion shape the reasoning statements? What aims are the operative clauses accomplishing? How are the reasoning statements aligned with the operative clauses?

2. Write a policy brief in which you describe a problem and advocate for a security council resolution. You can focus your brief around an issue of your choice, but it should be an issue you care about and which you can show has global significance. Specify the components of the resolution you would hope to be included.

3. Choose a disciplinary perspective, such as environmental studies, health sciences, cultural anthropology, media studies, or women's studies, and write an analysis of UN resolutions related to that discipline. How does the UN intersect with that discipline? What has the UN accomplished with relation to that discipline? What challenges remain with regard to the UN, the relevant resolution(s), and that discipline?

Technical Document: Excerpt from "Emergency Management Plan: Classifications of Emergencies" by Southern Illinois University Edwardsville

Transfer Points: Public Policy, Criminal Justice, Public Health, Emergency Management, Technical Writing

"Preparedness 101: Zombie Apocalypse." This was a May 16, 2011, blog post by a staff member of the Centers for Disease Control (Khan). The CDC website server soon crashed from all the traffic. Inspired by the surge of public interest, the CDC subsequently published a manual titled *Preparedness 101: Zombie Apocalypse*. Alongside zombie images, photographs from the Toronto Zombie Walk, and links to *Walking Dead* discussions, one can also find step-by-step guidelines for surviving zombies: "Once you've made your emergency kit, you should sit down with your family and come up with an emergency plan. This includes where you would go and who you would call if zombies started appearing outside your door step" ("Preparedness"). Other government agencies followed suit. War planners at U.S. Strategic Command created a 2011 contingency plan titled "Counter-Zombie Dominance," FEMA held a 2012 webinar about zombie preparedness, and the Kansas Department of Emergency Preparedness launched October zombie awareness month with activities and events designed to fortify zombie resilience.

Emergency planning asks people to imagine—even anticipate—the most horrifying circumstances. It asks people to suspend fear in order to plan for and dwell upon what is, for many, unimaginable. Couching emergency planning in zombies provides an imaginative way of engaging with the murkiness of facing risk and anxiety.

Zombie preparedness also highlights the ways in which writing transfer plays an especially key role in emergency planning. Grafting preparedness onto a zombie landscape relies, at an essential level, on writing transfer. To do so requires that a writer draw on multidisciplinary knowledge and multidisciplinary approaches to writing. "Zombie Preparedness 101," in fact, fuses

> Southern Illinois University Edwardsville (SIUE) (SIUE) is a liberal-arts university with approximately 14,000 undergraduate and graduate students. It is located near St. Louis, Missouri. SIUE offers undergraduate degrees across arts, sciences, education, business, and health. SIUE is also home to the Schools of Dental and Pharmacy. The "Classification of Emergencies" text included here is part of a longer document produced by the SIUE Emergency Management and Safety (EMS) office.

thinking and practices from cultural anthropology, public policy, and psychology to technical writing, criminal justice, and public policy.

As a highly transferable and transfer-based field of knowledge, practice, and writing, emergency planning transects an enormous range of contexts, operating across local and national government organizations, businesses, educational institutions, performance·venues, neighborhoods, and families. Across these contexts, those who produce plans and accompanying texts for emergency planning must collaborate extensively with others, including those in public policy, security, health care as well as experts across fields that have knowledge that might come to bear on planning for various disasters, such as chemistry, history, geology, cultural anthropology, and sociology.

The "Classification of Emergencies" text included here is part of a longer document produced by the SIUE Emergency Management and Safety (EMS) office. Nearly every educational institution has an office such as this, and the people involved with this office address all aspects of emergency management: "hazard mitigation, emergency preparedness, emergency response, and recovery activities." At SIUE, these hazards include earthquakes, severe weather, and flu, as well as Homeland Security and hazardous material incidents. Such offices are also responsible for safety recommendations for employees and students, and making sure institutions operate in environmentally and locally conscious ways ("Emergency").

Although each of these instances signals a unique context, they all intersect through transfer. All of these instances require expert knowledge about the discipline of emergency planning, transferred to particular contexts through nuanced understandings. Emergency planning, for instance, can involve the collaboration of many disciplinary perspectives, from technology and culture, to training and infrastructure. Such work also requires ongoing assessment, analysis, and evaluation in order to identify shortcomings, respond to new developments, and strengthen operating procedures and plans. Emergency planning also involves transfer across modes of communication and genres, moving information across multiple modalities, from written, verbal, and visual and including virtual and face-to-face contexts.

The transfer evident across emergency planning reflects, more broadly, the transfer-based dimensions of a field that those in emergency planning draw upon: technical writing and communication. Technical communication involves communication that is about technical or specialized topics, that uses technology to communicate, and/or that provides instructions about how to do something (STC). Examples include training manuals, technical illustrations, medical instructions, and software instructions (STC, "Defining")

Technical communication privileges clarity of message and design and involves an extensive process of development, feedback, and revision. Technical communicators must design materials for people who speak many different languages, have widely divergent levels of education and literacy, and who may have learning differences or disabilities that impact the ways in which they process information.

Technical communication within emergency management often gains public attention. On August 3, 2016, for example, Emirates Flight 521 crash-landed at Dubai International Airport. Videos soon went viral of passengers stopping to grab their luggage before evacuating. Debates ensued about how airlines approach emergency planning: How much carry-on luggage should be allowed? Should overhead bins be automatically locked during emergencies, takeoff, and landing? Should the pre-flight safety instructions include more emphasis on leaving luggage in the event of an emergency landing? In what ways, more generally, should pre-flight instructions be improved? (Flottau)

Such questions, and ongoing incidents that raise more such questions, form the basis of emergency planning and make it one of the most complex and transfer-based of disciplines. It is also one of the disciplines most grounded in our everday lives, even if it does sometimes venture into imaginative realms filled with zombies.

Write Here

Think about a moment when you encountered an emergency planning and management text. This might be an evacuation map in a hotel room, a weather alert, a safety drill, a pre-flight emergency presentation on an airplane, or another instance. Describe in as much detail how you responded to and engaged with that text: Did you pay careful attention? Why or why not? What feelings, if any, did it evoke for you? How do you imagine other people might respond to or engage with that document? What are various human behaviors with regard to emergency planning and what do you think accounts for these behaviors?

Southern Illinois University Edwardsville
Classifications of Emergencies

The Director of University Police and Director of Emergency Management and Safety are the designated Campus Emergency Directors during any major emergency or disaster. The following classifications of emergencies are provided as guidelines to assist the campus emergency staff in determining the appropriate level of response:

Levels of Emergency Response

    Level 1—*Minor Emergency:* A minor department or building incident that can be resolved by the responding service unit with existing University resources. (Example: Facilities Management is called to respond to a broken water pipe.)

    Level II—*Major Emergency:* Any event that affects an entire building or buildings and that will disrupt the overall operations of the University. (Example: A Building Fire or Chemical Spill during which outside emergency services will probably be required.) Level II emergencies may also include imminent events that may develop into a Major Emergency or Disaster. (Example: An extended power outage or severe storm.) The lead duty officer, the Director of University Police, or the Director of Emergency Management and Safety will seek approval from the Chancellor or Vice Chancellor for Administration to activate the Emergency Operations Center.

    Level III—*Disaster:* A catastrophic event or occurrence that has taken place and has seriously impaired or halted the operations of the University and possibly the surrounding communities. (Example: A Tornado or Earthquake) In some cases, mass personnel casualties and severe property damage may be sustained. A coordinated effort of all campus-wide resources is insufficient to effectively control the situation. Outside emergency services will be essential. In all disaster cases, an Emergency Operations Center will be activated by the Director of Emergency Management and Safety, and the appropriate support and operational plans will be executed. The lead duty officer, the Director of University Police, or the Director of Emergency Management and Safety will seek approval from the Chancellor or Vice Chancellor for Administration to activate the Emergency Operations Center.

TYPES OF EMERGENCIES

The types of emergencies covered in this manual are:

A. Airborne Releases	N. Infectious Disease Outbreak
B. Airplane Crash	O. Life Threatening Emergencies
C. Bomb Threat	P. Medical and First Aid
D. Chemical Spill	Q. Natural Gas Leak
E. Civil Disturbance/ Demonstration	R. Pipeline/Transportation Accident
F. Death on Campus	S. Psychological Crisis
G. Earthquake	T. Radiation Emergency
H. Elevator Malfunction	U. Rape or Sexual Assault
I. Evacuation	V. Terrorism and Other National Security Emergency
J. Explosion	W. Tornado/Severe Weather
K. Fire	X. Unsafe Water Supply
L. Hostile Intruder	Y. Violent or Criminal Behavior
M. Inclement Weather	

Write Away

1. One of the key components of emergency planning is hazard assessment. Use the different levels of emergency identified in the text here as a starting point for developing your own hazard assessment. Working with a team of classmates, conduct a hazard assessment for the area in which you reside. This endeavor involves identifying and defining the various types of hazards facing the region, as well as evaluating the likelihood of each of these hazards occurring and the range of risk and damage they might yield. Synthesize your hazard assessment into a graph or chart depicting your research in visually accessible ways.

2. Design a public preparedness text for a potential emergency. Identify a potential emergency you would like to address, and conduct research to learn about its causes and impacts, contextualized within a particular place. Then, produce your text. Decide what format will be most effective. It can be written, verbal, visual, or tactile. You might, for instance, create an infographic for preparedness for a particular context, or a video, or an in-person demonstration. After you have designed and developed the text, write a reflection that articulates what your primary aims are for the text, what challenges you faced, how you intend to disseminate it, and what else would be needed in terms of accompanying that text in order to most effectively prepare people for the potential disaster under consideration.

3. As illustrated by the efforts taken to develop and design *Preparedness 101: Zombie Apocalypse,* those involved with preparedness and emergency planning must acknowledge and respond creatively to human emotions and behaviors. Conduct research on your campus about people's perceptions of, knowledge about, and attitudes toward preparedness and emergency planning. Your research design will address research methods (will you use survey instruments, focus groups, interviews, observation?) as well as study populations (whom will you research and why) and final product options (a presentation, a report, a researched article, etc.). Develop specific research questions, and, in consultation with your instructor, conduct research by doing secondary research, data collection and analysis, drafting, revision, and editing.

ℂ ℂ ℂ

Chapter 2 Key Terms

writing process	qualitative research	revising
recursive	mixed-methods research	editing
research methodologies	prewriting	feedback
quantitative research	drafting	

Write Away

Context deeply impacts the research and writing process. This chapter's activity asks you to conduct and produce an interview of another writer in which you find out about his or her research and writing process. Follow these steps (notice that these steps themselves involve phases of the research and writing process).

Find a writer to interview (pre-write and research). Think about a person you might interview in order to learn more about his or her research and writing process from the perspective of his or her particular discipline or context. This writer can be a faculty member, administrator, or graduate student at your institution whom you would like to get to know, or it can be a peer acquaintance. You might interview a family member, friend, or other acquaintance, someone younger or older than you, and you can conduct the interview virtually, by phone, or in person.

Develop interview questions (pre-write, research, and feedback). To develop your interview questions, work in small teams with your classmates. Think about what questions you will ask (and how many) that will enable the interviewee to share specific details about his or her research and writing process. Since your interviewee is likely to write across several different contexts, you might invite him or her to think in particular about one or two recent writing occasions as he or she describes his or her process. Keep in mind as well that your interviewee might not know as much about the phases and features of the research and writing process as you do!

Select an interview format (pre-write, research, and feedback). Decide, in consultation with your interviewee, what format you would like to use for creating your interview: a brief written article, a PowerPoint or Prezi, an audio account (such as a podcast), a video, or some other format or combination. Deciding in advance will enable you to procure any necessary technology. Use a format with which you have some experience, so you are not taking on too many new challenges at once.

Conduct the interview (research). Conduct the interview, using your interview questions as a guide, but allow yourself the flexibility to also let the conversation move forward organically. During the interview, take particular care to understand the context (genre, discipline, aims, audience, etc.) surrounding the particular research and writing process your interviewee is describing. Be sure to have a way of archiving the interview so you will not lose the material.

Create and develop your final product (draft, revise, edit, and feedback). Create and develop the final version of your interview, using the format you have decided upon. Verify with your interviewee whether you should use his/her name or use a pseudonym. Share a somewhat polished draft of the interview with your interviewee, and invite that individual to make any adjustments or changes she or he believes would better capture what she or he had to say.

Share your interview (feedback). Share the interview final product with your classmates.

Transfer Hub: Contribute your ideas and see what others have written at fountainheadpress.com/transferhub.

Reflect (transfer). After you have examined the interviews created by your classmates, write for ten minutes to reflect on what you have learned from this experience about the interview process and/or what you have learned from the interviews about how you might transfer portions of the research and writing process across contexts and disciplines.

Posing Meaningful Questions

Pinpointing Chapter 3

Chapter 3 deepens and extends the ideas from Chapter 2 by addressing how writers develop and pose questions as part of their research and writing process. The parameters of questioning and the process for developing them may vary extensively, but writers throughout all disciplines pose questions, sometimes explicitly and sometimes implicitly. To provide you with strategies for *posing questions in transit*, this chapter addresses the following concepts:

- Disciplinarity and Questions
- Writers Posing Questions: Examples from across Disciplines
- Characteristics of Effective Questions
- Strategies for Posing Meaningful Questions

Chapter 4 advances these strategies by exploring how academic writers read others' texts and, in so doing, have occasion to see how writers actually pursue the questions they pose through their research and writing.

The Egyptian pyramids at Giza, constructed between 2600 and 2450 BCE, have fascinated humans for centuries. The largest pyramid on the site, the pyramid of Khufu, is composed of 26 million limestone blocks, some of which weigh as much as 70 tons each. Mystified by the pyramids' enormity and precision, some people have surmised that aliens must have built the pyramids, or that residents of the mythical land of Atlantis had a hand in the construction. Most scholars, however, agree that the pyramids were built as part of a royal undertaking ("Giza"; "Introduction"; Magli).

Herodotus, in one of the earliest known writings about the pyramids, claims that King Khufu enslaved the laborers who built the pyramids and, to help pay for the enormous construction costs, forced his daughter to work in a brothel. Modern Egyptologists, however, have suggested that Herodotus's narrative of Khufu's oppression and cruelty was erroneous, and that those involved with the pyramids' construction did so on a voluntary basis in order to be affiliated with an endeavor they believed to be glorious and worthwhile (Clark).

Whether Khufu motivated those who built the pyramids through cruelty or inspiration, most scholars agree that the Great Pyramid of Khufu served as his royal tomb. Mathematical physicists have noted that the pyramid, oriented precisely to true north, aligns with the sun and has symbolic significance, representing Khufu's power over the horizon. The area, called Akhet Khufu, can be translated as Khufu's horizon or the horizon that belongs to Khufu ("Giza"; Magli).

As scholars learn more about who built the pyramids and why, remaining mysteries endure, prompting scholars to continue posing and pursuing new questions about the pyramids. Recently, a team of engineers and computer scientists, curious to learn what was in the depths of the pyramids, used a robot (named Djedi) to explore hidden areas and discovered long-unseen hieroglyphics (Richardson, et al.). Physicists, wondering how Egyptians moved the heavy limestone, recently determined that Egyptians could have transported building materials with far fewer people than previously believed by adding water to sand and thereby enabling greater sliding friction (Fall, et al.). And archaeologists, seeking to learn more about how ancient Egyptians used the pyramids, have recently identified buildings that likely served as grain silos or bakeries, and they have discovered cattle bones at the site, which indicate that ancient cult worship and offerings likely took place at the pyramids (Jarus).

As illustrated by this research, scholars from many different disciplines continue to pose and pursue questions regarding the pyramids. Classics Professor Donald Redford, for instance, asks questions about how the pyramids were built. Professor of Theology and Religious Studies, Jeremy Naydler, poses questions about the intersections between religion and Egyptology. Professor of Oriental Studies, Kate Spence, pursues questions about how the Egyptians were able to so accurately align the pyramids to true north (McCauley).

But the pyramids are not unique in sponsoring this preponderance of questions. Scholars across all fields spend much of their time posing questions about all sorts of ideas, entities, people, periods, and texts. Answers, when discovered, serve more often than not as jumping-off points for new questions: "[I]n research," remarks Nobel Laureate Salvador Edward Luria, 1969 Winner for Physiology or Medicine, "there are no final answers, only insights that allow one to formulate new questions."

Asking meaningful questions, pursuing avenues of curiosity, and discovering new areas of **inquiry** are among the most important and rewarding aspects of academic writing. Unfortunately, many students become accustomed instead to teachers posing questions, such as with assignment prompts or essay exams. These students may then perceive that questions are not part of their own work. These students may regrettably assume that their main responsibility is not only to drum up answers, but to find the right answers and defend them as vigorously as possible.

Writing in Transit works against that model by showing how writers across disciplines—at all levels of experience—pose questions in order to advance knowledge.

Write Here

What research questions might a biologist ask about the pyramids? An anthropologist? An economist? Brainstorm as many questions, from as many different disciplinary perspectives as you can, about the Giza Pyramids.

 Transfer Hub: Contribute your ideas and see what others have written at fountainheadpress.com/transferhub.

Disciplinarity and Questions

Disciplines are in many ways defined by **questions**. According to the website physics.org, for instance, "Physicists ask really big questions like: How did the universe begin? How will the universe change in the future? How does the Sun keep on shining? What are the basic building blocks of matter?" Similarly, the website for the English Department at Illinois State University describes its discipline in the form of questions: "In English Studies multiple and interdisciplinary perspectives are used to examine and produce texts for audiences communicating in English: how do cultures shape language and how does language shape culture; how do intersections of cultures affect communication

Writer Insights

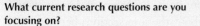

What current research questions are you focusing on?

The questions that occupy my thoughts are those about ways to empower students to learn a new language in an unprivileged context. Also, those about how to teach English to students in an EFL context and how to help them change their lives in the process! As a teacher trainer, I ask myself about how to help teachers become better professionals who can generate change in our nation. I wonder about how to make a better country every day and I know it is through education and better opportunities!

~Carolina R. Buitrago, Lecturer and Researcher,
English Language Teaching Master's Program,
Universidad de La Sabana, Bogotá, Colombia

across borders; what forms can we create to connect and enter into dialogue with each other?"

Many questions, of course, traverse disciplinary boundaries. John Brockman, founder of edge.org, poses these kinds of more universally applicable questions each year, inviting prestigious thinkers from different fields to share their thoughts on such queries as, "What should we be worried about?"; "What have you changed your mind about? Why?"; and "What are you optimistic about?"

While widely applicable questions sponsor engaging cross-disciplinary conversations, they offer only a partial glimpse of the role of questions in academic writing. Most academic questions emerge from within and are shaped by disciplinary context.

Brockman's 1998 query, in which he asked, "What Questions Are You Asking Yourself?" illustrates how disciplinary perspective shapes academic questions. Notice in the following "answers" how each scholar poses a question that emerges from within his or her disciplinary frame.

Christopher Stringer
research paleoanthropologist at the Natural History Museum, London; Author, *Lone Survivors*; Co-Author of *In Search of the Neanderthals*; Co-Author of *African Exodus*

"What was the key factor in the success of Homo sapiens compared with other human species such as the Neanderthals?"

Charles Simonyi
chief architect, Microsoft Corporation; software engineer; computer scientist; entrepreneur; philanthropist

"Does reality have real numbers?"

Elaine Pagels
Harrington Spear Paine Professor of Religion at Princeton University; Author, *Revelations*; Author, *The Gnostic Gospels*; Author, *The Origin of Satan*

"Why are religions still vital?"

Of course, sometimes scholars step outside of their disciplinary boundaries, as in the following question submitted by technology correspondent Katie Hafner, who opts to ask about history.

Katie Hafner

technology correspondent, *New York Times;* **Author,** *Where Wizards Stay Up Late*

"Why does history matter?"

But Hafner's case and others like it aside, most scholars' questions emerge from within a disciplinary context.

Using Pompeii art as an example, the following excerpts from different disciplines pose the kinds of questions scholars can ask about a single topic. As you read, look for both implicit and explicit questions.

Consider, too, the ways in which each excerpt illustrates how academic writers advance knowledge through questions, as well as how they articulate the significance of their lines of inquiry.

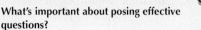

Writer Insights

What's important about posing effective questions?

Science is a field where writing is a very powerful tool. A well-written question is the key for a complete research in fact, everything orbits around the right question, so a mistake using a wrong verb or noun, can mean a disaster.... [W]riting is not only a combination of words, but also a collection of interpretations. A question can be grammatically correct, even elegant, and fail when other researchers read it. That makes language a complex process.

~ Alma Dzib Goodin, Neuroscientist,
Chicago, Illinois, U.S.

Write Now

I wonder…? What if…? How does…? Why did…? What are you curious about? What questions matter to you? Why? Brainstorm several general questions—about anything or several things—that you find interesting and/or important. Then, for each of these questions, identify a smaller subset of questions that might emerge from various disciplinary perspectives as a way of gaining practice refining and tailoring questions inflected by perspective.

Writers Posing Questions: Examples from across Disciplines

Example 1: Disciplinary Questions, Chemistry, and Pompeii Art

Excerpt from "Evaluation of Corrective Measures Implemented for the Preventive Conservation of Fresco Paintings in Ariadne's House (Pompeii, Italy)" by P. Merello, F. Garcia-Diego, and M. Zarzo

The long-term preservation of wall paintings in open-air sites or semi-confined environments is a challenge due to the difficulty in providing optimum ambient conditions. In such cases, the deterioration process of paintings is determined by many factors such as petrographical and chemical characteristics of the materials, presence of mineral salts and organic

> Merello, Garcia-Diego, and Zarzo are asking questions here about how chemicals in the atmosphere impact the deterioration process of Pompeii art.

substances on the surfaces, air pollution, sunlight, heating, water content of the surface, etc.... The house of Ariadne or dei capitelli colorati (of the colored capitals) is one of the most interesting places in ancient Pompeii (Italy).... Although most interior walls were originally ornamented with frescoes, the paintings have suffered severe damages since the excavation of Ariadne's house in 1832-1835. At present, original frescoes are only conserved in three rooms that were sheltered with transparent polycarbonate sheets in the

> In 2008 researchers in chemistry asked, how can we assess the "conservation state" of murals in Ariadne's house?

1970s...Mural paintings of Ariadne's house have undergone deterioration processes in the last decades, and a research project was launched in 2008 to assess their conservation state by means of microclimate monitor-

> Here they are asking, what is the effect of roof change on microclimate conditions around the paintings?

ing, thermography, study of materials, solar radiation, characterization of salt efflorescence, etc.... The present work performs a comparative statistical analysis of data recorded in 2008 and 2010 (summer periods) aimed at evaluating the effect of roof change

> We learn that these chemists care about this question in order to advance long-term preservation through chemical "corrective measures."

on the microclimate conditions surrounding the valuable fresco paintings. Results provide guidelines for additional corrective measures.

From *Chemistry Central Journal*, 2013.

Example 2: Disciplinary Questions, Art History, and Pompeii Art

Excerpt from "Before Pornography: Sexual Representation in Ancient
Roman Visual Culture" by J. Clarke

The study of ancient visual representations of sexual activity reveals the modernity of the

> Clarke is here asking, what is the history of erotica collection in museums?

term 'pornography.' Not only is pornography a modern word, its genesis lies in modern collecting practices that so isolated ancient erotic objects from their contexts as to render them meaningless.

> Clarke asks, what are the origins of the term pornography and how have people decided to categorize certain art as pornographic?

Beginning with the Renaissance, wealthy collectors assembled collections of Greek and Roman sculptures, vase paintings, mosaics, ceramics, small bronzes and gems with sexual representations, calling them 'erotica.' The discovery of Herculaneum (1738) and Pompeii (1748) brought about an explosive proliferation of such objects…. We have the German scholar, Karl Otfried Müller, to thank for the term 'pornography,' borrowed from the Greek word *pornographos*. We know that *pornographos* was literally a 'whore-writer,' that is, an author who wrote about the famous accomplished prostitutes of the time, called *pornai*…. What prompted Müller to coin the word 'pornography' was embarrassment. With increasing rapidity the excavations of the cities buried by Vesuvius turned up paintings, mosaics, bronze objects and terracottas that

> Clarke here is interested in the following questions: what are the social and cultural influences on museum collecting practices? How do social and cultural influences shape collecting practices?

shocked the excavators…. In 1819, during the period

> Clarke asks, what were ancient Roman attitudes toward sexual images?

of the Bourbon restoration, Ferdinand, King of the Two Sicilies, ordered his curator of antiquities, Michele Arditi, to sequester all objects that could be considered obscene by the standards of his time. In 1823 the name of this collection was changed to the Cabinet of Secret Objects and sealed with a brick wall for good measure…. [A]t about the same time the British Museum formed the so-called Museum Secretum, and the museums in Florence, Madrid and Dresden followed suit. All of these rooms were filled with ancient Greek and Roman objects considered to be obscene. Rather than seeing this as a common-sense curatorial decision, I would like to question the social and cultural forces that or-

From *Pornographic Art and the Aesthetics of Pornography*, 2013.

phaned these objects, separating them not only from their architectural and archaeological contexts, but also keeping them from public view...My main concern in both of my books on ancient sexual representation was to understand ancient Roman attitudes towards sexual images with Roman eyes...I wanted to put aside modern notions of pornography and the obscene. One of my strategies was to find out where the sexually explicit objects in the Pornographic Collection in Naples came from and put them back into their original settings. In this way, I could reconstruct the ancient experience, the situations where men, women, and children originally looked at what we today consider pornographic.

> Clarke explains that his questions are significant because they enable us to "reconstruct the ancient experience."

Example 3: Disciplinary Questions, Literature, and Pompeii Art

Excerpt from "Imperial Decadence: The Making of the Myths in Edward Bulwer-Lytton's The Last Days of Pompeii" by W. St Clair and A. Bautz

Ever since the discovery in 1749 of the remains of Pompeii, ... the excavations have yielded rich materials for understanding the daily life of the Roman Empire. They also featured as themes in contemporary European design, art, and music, including opera. In the nineteenth century, previously diverse elements were unified into a romantic mythic narrative, fixed in material form, disseminated, consolidated, imported to Pompeii, naturalised, and then re-exported. This process is evident in the publication history of Edward Bulwer-Lytton's novel, *The Last Days of Pompeii* (1834). Taking in the spin-offs and feedbacks of theatre, songs, opera, pantomime, the circus, high and popular art, and book illustrations, we use quantified information about readerships and viewerships from archival and other primary sources to show how, within the economic and technological governing structures of the Victorian age, cultural consumers cooperated with producers to invent myths and clichés still vigorous today.

> St Clair and Bautz ask, how have excavations been depicted and represented in art and artistic productions?

> St Clair and Bautz are asking questions about publication history of a novel.

From *Victorian Literature and Culture*, 2012.

The *Last Days of Pompeii* begins with a scene of wealthy Pompeians sauntering through the streets of Pompeii where they encounter Nydia, a blind slave girl selling flowers. This casual meeting between her and the rich Greek Glaucus introduces the storyline. Nydia, who soon loves Glaucus across the insuperable social divide, is purchased by him and presented as a gift to the beautiful and virtuous Greek heiress, Ione, who is the ward of Arbaces, an Egyptian priest of the religion of Isis.... Suddenly the volcano erupts and buildings shake and fall to the ground as the city is torn open by earthquakes.... In the darkness and confusion of the last day only the blind Nydia can find her way through the rubble-strewn streets, and she leads Glaucus and Ione to the port. On the voyage to Athens, however, Nydia throws herself into the sea, suicide being allowed by ancient ethics.... Her death makes way for the socially matched, newly converted, Christian couple to live together happily ever after.

> St Clair and Bautz ask, what are the traditions within which authors position themselves and from which they draw?

When Bulwer wrote and published *The Last Days of Pompeii*, he was inserting himself into a tradition … He was able to draw on and adapt a wealth of cultural production relating to Pompeii and its destruction as offered to different types of cultural consumers in a variety of media across Europe. And in some cases it can be shown from the biographical record that he had direct knowledge of his predecessors, both ancient and recent. Among recent predecessors were paintings, volcanic spectacles, literature and travel writing, and opera, yet none of these, either individually or together, came close to being as influential as his novel was to become.

> Here, St Clair and Bautz ask direct questions about the text and its publication history, and indirect questions about the reception and influence of "adaptations and spin-offs."

The main focus of this essay is on the materialities of the production and diffusion of the ideas in the *Last Days*, asking questions such as how did the text come to be written in the form that it was, who had access to the book, when, in what numbers, in which versions, and with what consequences? The essay also explores the materiality of the adaptations and spin-offs—theatre, songs, opera, pantomime, the circus, high and popular art, and book illustrations—that both influenced the text of the novel by being anticipated, and then helped to shape readerly and viewerly responses to and interpretations.

> St Clair and Bautz show that the significance of their questions is that art can shape our responses to and interpretations of historical events.

Example 4: Disciplinary Questions, Archaeology, and Pompeii Art

Excerpt from "Painted Birds at Pompeii" by B. A. Sparkes

Birds come in all shapes and sizes, and the evidence for their study is similarly diverse. When studying birds for archaeological purposes, the remains of the actual bones are obviously of the utmost significance. However, it is also important to consider written evidence from previous periods to see what earlier writers observed or inferred about the appearance, habits and habitats of birds. Allied to this is the visual evidence in the form of objects such as stone carvings, bronze figurines, coin dies, gem engravings, mosaics and paintings on different materials such as wood, canvas, silk, and terracotta. When we turn our attention to the visual images of the Mediterranean cultures of the Greeks and Romans in classical antiquity (1000 BC to AD 500), we see that the Greeks showed a serious interest in birds in their literature and art. They appear as the 'familiars' of the gods and goddesses, such as Zeus's eagle, Athena's owl and Aphrodite's doves, and they are also part of their myths and legends, such as Leda and the swan, and Prokne and Philomela as nightingale and swallow. Their coins carry birds as symbols of various cities; their tombstones show birds as pets of children and adults or as symbols of another life; and vase-paintings include birds as elements in patterns and as characters in narratives of myth and everyday life. When we move down to the Roman period, the evidence is equally full. We have Roman writers such as Varro, Columella and Pliny the Elder, who give basic information on the varieties of birds and their habitat, and the artists of the day had a much greater interest than the Greeks in representing nature for its own sake in their art. Trees, plants, animals and birds form the subject matter of many of their works of art, particularly their wall-paintings. In the cities, towns and country villas of Roman Italy in the first centuries BC and AD, house and villa owners were enthusiastic in having the walls in the different rooms of their houses covered with complex wall-paintings: dining rooms, bedrooms, halls, courtyards and others. The wall-paintings acted as one way of demonstrating their status and position in society. The best preserved examples of this decoration are to be found in Pompeii and the other Campanian towns that were buried by the volcanic eruption of Vesuvius in AD 79.

> Sparkes asks, what evidence can we use to learn more about ancient birds?

> Sparkes wonders, what roles did birds play in ancient civilizations?

> Sparkes asks, what kinds of wall-paintings existed and in what ways were they markers of social status?

From *International Journal of Osteoarchaeology*, 1997.

Write Now

Using a research-based text of your choosing, identify the main questions informing that text. What explicit questions are included in the text? What are the underlying, or implicit, questions sponsoring the research?

Although none of these examples fully represents the discipline from which it emerges (disciplines are far too varied and dynamic), we can nonetheless glean a considerable amount about how scholars pose questions and construct knowledge within disciplinary contexts. From these examples, we learn that chemists (these chemists, anyway) ask questions about chemical elements and test which ones are most effective for their purposes; art historians ask questions about museum collecting practices and about the role of social and cultural forces in shaping perceptions about art; literary scholars ask about how events are represented in art and literature, and about the publication history of literature; finally, archaeologists ask questions about ancient civilizations and how we can learn more about them through the artifacts we find. All of the scholars locate their questions within a larger frame of questioning, and all articulate the significance of their questions. They also all have larger and smaller questions. Perhaps most evident from these excerpts is just how very *many* questions are being asked.

Characteristics of Effective Questions

Although you may have heard before that no question is a bad question, the truth is (sorry to have to tell you…), in academic writing, some questions are in fact more effective than others. Jane Agee writes, "Good questions do not necessarily produce good research, but poorly conceived or constructed questions will likely create problems that affect all subsequent stages of a study." Becoming a better academic writer requires learning how to develop strong, meaningful questions.

Originate from a disciplinary context

Meaningful academic questions often emerge from within a **disciplinary context** and take into account prior disciplinary knowledge so scholars can continue advancing knowledge.

This can take many forms. It might be that a scholar borrows questions from one discipline and applies it to his or her own. One can imagine, for instance, that St Clair and Bautz raise questions that might be applicable as well to performance or theatre studies. Situating questions within a disciplinary frame may also entail a scholar using prior questions to generate new questions, such as when Merello, Garcia-Diego, and Zarzo build on a 2008 research study. Linking questions within disciplinary frames can also sometimes involve a scholar duplicating or revisiting prior questions. The questions Clarke asks, for example, are steeped in cultural context, and so might need to be revisited across time and culture as attitudes toward pornography shift.

Transfer at Work

Questions sponsor nearly all academic writing, but the particular questions scholars ask depend on such matters as disciplinary conventions, available resources, and research methods. In "Bone Preservation in Human Remains from the Terme Del Sarno at Pompeii using Light Microscopy and Scanning Electron Microscopy" archaeologists research the following questions: "What diagenetic processes affected Pompeian bones? How might these diagenetic processes be suitable for future biomolecular research?"

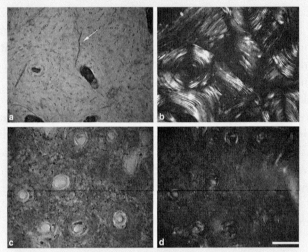

Figure 1 Cross section of untreated archaeological bone

Meanwhile, Professor of Classics Charlotte Potts researches Pompeii with a quite different question: "How does our understanding of the significance of the painted façade on the Via dell'Abbondanza change when its physical, social, and civic contexts are taken into account?"

Figure 2 Façade at IX.7.1, Pompeii. From V. Spinazzola,
Pompei alla luce degli Scavi Nuovi di Via dell'Abbondanza (anni 1910–1923) (Rome, 1953), ii, Tav. XIII.
Courtesy of the Istituto Poligrafico e Zecca dello Stato, Rome.

The way in which a question is posed should likewise be connected to a disciplinary context—scholars phrase their questions to fit into, or sometimes to deliberately resist, a disciplinary model.

It should also be noted that over time, certain questions will seem to *trend* within a discipline, where scholars will become occupied with a particular set of questions. For instance, before artifacts began to erode, chemists such as Merello, Garcia-Diego, and Zarzo likely would have been asking different questions. They might be motivated to undertake these questions due to advancements in knowledge about preservation practices or, alternately, from a growing urgency to preserve artifacts in the light of rapidly changing environmental conditions. As time moves forward, chemists may still be asking these same questions, but they will also discover new kinds of questions to ask.

Maintain significance

Good questions can be simple or complicated, but they should always have **significance**. They do not need to be of significance to everyone—but they should at least be significant to some subset of people. A good example of this is in the bird excerpt above; not everyone may care as much about birds as Sparkes, but birds are linked in his article to larger questions about how we can reconstruct the ancient experience. One can imagine that more people may be interested in ancient life and culture more broadly conceived, and can therefore appreciate the birds as one piece of that larger effort.

Sometimes the significance of a question is fairly self-evident, as with questions about how chemicals can improve long-term preservation methods. There may be times when academic writers need to convince others that a question is important. Perhaps, for instance, Clarke may have needed to make a case at some point as to why learning more about ancient views on sexuality is of significance.

Perhaps of most importance is that the questions you ask should matter to you. Figure out what you care about and why you think others should care as well. Doing so will enable you to feel motivated to pursue a question and invested in learning and writing more about it.

Keep a pointed scope

Even as meaningful questions have larger significance, they are also manageable, addressing one part of a larger question. St Clair and Bautz, for instance, look at Bulwer-Lytton's novel *The Last Days of Pompeii*, which is one part of Bulwer-Lytton's larger set of writings, and which is one part of a larger set of literature about Pompeii and Pompeii excavations. St Clair and Bautz have opted to treat a smaller part of this larger set of inquiries in order to achieve depth in pursuit of their research question about the publication history and reception of Bulwer-Lytton's novel.

Even book-length texts focus on one part of a larger set of questions. Clarke, for example, alludes to his books on Roman attitudes toward sexuality; one can see that this project is part of a larger set of questions about cultural attitudes toward sexuality across other moments of time and place.

Returning briefly for inspiration to the Pyramids at Giza, one helpful way of thinking about how writers tailor and narrow questions to make them more effective is through the very notion of a pyramid, whereby the most general questions are located at the bottom, and increasingly specific questions emerge toward the top. In this way, one might think about Clarke's research questions as involving a general question about cultural attitudes toward sexuality in general at the bottom of the pyramid. Then, a more specific question about Roman attitudes toward sexuality would be found at the middle of the pyramid, followed by even more specific questions about erotica collections in museums or about visual erotica from Pompeii at the top of the pyramid (see Figure 3.1).

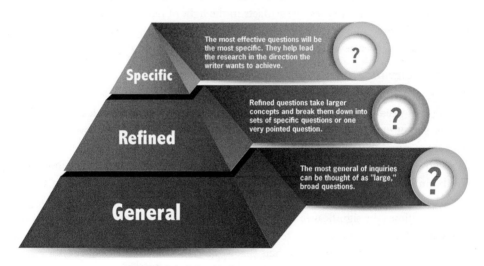

The most effective questions will be the most specific. They help lead the research in the direction the writer wants to achieve.

Specific

Refined questions take larger concepts and break them down into sets of specific questions or one very pointed question.

Refined

The most general of inquiries can be thought of as "large," broad questions.

General

FIGURE 3.1 Pyramid of narrowing questions.

Spur further research

A question should be sufficiently complex that it could sponsor at least some degree of multiplicity and complexity, perhaps even disagreement, in the ways in which people might approach that question. That is, meaningful questions have multiple branches of inquiry leading to and from them. For example, the questions Sparkes asks about the role of birds in ancient civilizations might be examined through other means than wall-paintings; inquiries into literary artifacts or animal husbandry practices may lead to different ideas about the role of birds. Similarly, scholars could pick up on where St Clair and Bautz stop by examining the publication and reception history of other novels about Pompeii excavations.

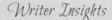

Writer Insights

How do you design and develop your research questions?

I work on experimental condensed matter physics, and developing research questions in writing in my field not only depends on our personal understanding of general topics such as plasmonics, quantum dots, nano-photonics, thin magnetic films, etc., but also relies on the specific experimental process, especially on our experimental data. The final answer of a research question is a resonant explanation of the underlying physics which is well-supported by our experimental data.

~Yikuan Wang, Associate Professor, Physics, Yancheng, Jiangsu Province, China

Write Now

Add to this list of criteria for effective questions by reading several texts of your choosing, perhaps from different disciplines, and identifying the components of questions that make them more or less effective. Why are certain questions more engaging? What, if anything, makes certain questions less effective?

Transfer Hub: Contribute your ideas and see what others have written at fountainheadpress.com/transferhub.

Strategies for Posing Meaningful Questions

Learning how to pose effective questions is of critical importance to academic writing across disciplines. While different writing occasions and disciplinary contexts impact how academic writers shape and frame their questions, the underlying disposition toward inquiry transfers across contexts. Because context influences the particulars of questions in nuanced ways, writers can often face challenges when developing effective questions across and within writing occasions. Posing questions involves both sustained reflection and research to figure out what to ask, as well as careful attention and consideration toward figuring out how to ask. Even though writers infuse their questions with unique perspectives, different conventions and expectations can shape how they develop questions across a range of writing contexts. The following strategies can help you learn how to navigate these complexities as you discover and pose your own meaningful questions across varying disciplinary contexts and writing occasions.

Examine other writing

Use a subject-specific database (for example, PubMed, International Index to the Performing Arts, or Political Science Complete—ask a librarian for help!) to find several examples of recent academic writing from the discipline in which you are writing. Skim through these examples to identify the kinds of questions scholars are asking in that discipline, and how they are posing those questions. Do they tend to ask questions directly or indirectly? What kinds of questions are being asked in that discipline over the most recent five-year period? How do these scholars articulate the significance of their questions? Because disciplines can be so amorphous and dynamic, there will always be variation and overlap, but if you read enough examples with questions in mind, you will likely be able to identify some trends or approaches that you can adopt and/or modify for your own questions.

Consider publication medium and platform

Examining the kinds of questions asked by scholars in a particular discipline will get you only so far because even within disciplines, the publication medium affects the ways in which questions are asked. Are you writing a piece intended for scholarly readers only, or is it geared toward a broader public? Will you be writing for an online

95

or print publication? Who do you imagine is likely to read your writing? How much do they already know or not know about your line of inquiry? The kinds of questions a neuroscientist asks in a peer-reviewed research journal such as the *Journal of the American Medical Association* will look different from the kinds of questions he or she might ask when writing for WebMD or Medicine Net. More popular kinds of publication mediums tend to ask more widely applicable questions and make the significance of those questions more self-evident. Digital platforms also often hold different expectations from print platforms.

Use a question heuristic

A question **heuristic** is a general template or guide for generating questions. Heuristics often include a specific set of questions designed to explore the many facets of a general area of inquiry or topic. These can offer good beginning points to help you explore an idea and identify which questions are more relevant or valuable to you. With heuristics, though, it is important to adapt them to better fit your particular writing occasion.

Question heuristic #1: Journalists' "big six" questions

These questions enable writers to explore various dimensions of a topic. Table 3.1 employs a disciplinary dimension to the journalistic "big six" questions by exploring Pompeii artwork through the perspective of economics.

TABLE 3.1 Journalists' "big six" questions.

Who	Who collects Pompeii art now? Who were art collectors in Pompeii? Who decides the value of Pompeii art?
What	What was the economic impact of the production and distribution of art in ancient civilizations such as Pompeii?
Where	Where are the most valuable collections of Pompeii art located?
When	When have the peak periods of value for Pompeii art occurred? When did the large-scale production and distribution of art in ancient Pompeii begin to impact its economy?
Why	Why has the value of Pompeii art fluctuated?
How	How was art produced and distributed in Pompeii?

Question heuristic #2: Interpretive questions

Librarian Holly Samuels has developed a framework for brainstorming and designing what she has labeled "interpretive questions." Table 3.2 includes a series of interpretive questions from the perspective of someone in environmental studies exploring Pompeii art.

TABLE 3.2 Interpretive questions.

Hypothetical	"How would things be different today if something in the past had been different?" Example: How might slight shifts in intensity, duration, or direction of the volcanic eruption have impacted Pompeii, its structures, and its art? How might the preservation of Pompeii's art have been different if climatic conditions had been different in the centuries following the eruption?
Prediction	"How will something look or be in the future, based on the way it is now?" Example: What will happen to Pompeii's sculptures and wall paintings as the climate continues to change? If carbon dioxide levels rise, how will that impact the long-term preservation of art in Pompeii?
Solution	"What solutions can be offered to a problem that exists today?" Example: How could environmental conditions be improved in Pompeii so as to better preserve the city? What can be done to ensure that climate change does not negatively impact Pompeii?
Comparison or Analogy	"Find the similarities and differences between your main subject and a similar subject, or with another subject in the same time period or place." Example: In what ways was the impact of Mt. Vesuvius on Pompeii's structures and art similar to or different from its impact on Herculaneum? What are the differences between the preservation of art in Pompeii and the preservation of art in other areas of the world under different environmental conditions?
Judgment	"Based on the information you find, what can you say is your informed opinion about the subject?" Example: How has the environment impacted Pompeii's structures and art? How have changing climatic conditions shifted preservation methods for Pompeii's art and structures?

Question heuristic #3: Fundamental disciplinary questions

Table 3.3 from Michael Quinn Patton's book, *Qualitative Research and Evaluation Methods*, is organized by discipline to show the kinds of questions scholars in particular disciplines tend to ask. Since Patton is dealing with qualitative research, he has focused primarily on disciplines that make heavy use of qualitative research methods.

TABLE 3.3 Patton's fundamental disciplinary questions.

Anthropology	What is the nature of culture? How does culture emerge? How is it transmitted? What are the functions of culture?
Psychology	Why do individuals behave as they do? How do human beings behave, think, feel, and know? What is normal and abnormal in human development and behavior?
Sociology	What holds groups and societies together? How do various forms of social organization emerge and what are their functions? What are the structures and processes of human social organizations?
Political science	What is the nature of power? How is power organized, created, distributed, and used?
Economics	How do societies and groups generate and distribute scarce resources? How are goods and services produced and distributed? What is the nature of wealth?
Geography	What is the nature of and variations in the Earth's surface and atmosphere? How do various forms of life emerge in and relate to variations in the Earth? What is the relationship between the physical characteristics of an area and the activities that take place in that area?
Biology	What is the nature of life? What are variations in the forms of life? How have life forms emerged and how do they change?

You might use Patton's fundamental disciplinary questions to generate possible questions for your area of inquiry (Table 3.3). For instance, if you were writing a research essay for a psychology course and were interested in Pompeii art, you could model your questions on the questions Patton provides for that discipline: Why did ancient Romans collect art? How might Pompeii art reveal how ancient Romans behaved?

Question heuristic #4: Quantitative questions

Researchers Burke Johnson and Larry Christensen have developed a guideline for developing questions in disciplines that make considerable use of quantitative research methods. The following quantitative questions in Table 3.4 continue to draw out the illustration by providing examples of someone writing about Pompeii art in a statistics course.

TABLE 3.4 Quantitative questions.

Descriptive	"Descriptive research questions seek answers to 'How much?,' 'How often?,' or 'What changes over time or over different situations?'"…They also seek to identify the degree of relationship between two variables.
	Example: How much have particular pieces of Pompeii art eroded over the past 1,500 years? What is the relationship between the number of visitors to Pompeii and levels of deterioration?
Predictive	"Predictive questions are questions that seek to determine whether one or more variables can be used to predict some future outcome."
	Example: Does income level predict the likelihood of members of ancient Roman civilizations producing or collecting art?
Causal	"Causal questions…compare different variations of some phenomenon to identify the cause of something."
	Example: Does variation in the amount and duration of sunlight produce a change in the long-term preservation of Pompeii art?

Transferring Questions

One of the most important aspects to note with developing effective questions is that writers across disciplines pose and pursue questions that matter to them. Not every question will matter equally to you or to your readers, and your motivations for asking certain questions might sometimes be varied. But do try to ask questions about which you harbor at least some degree of curiosity. Following your intellectual interests will enable you to create more meaningful academic writing. This chapter has also illustrated that it is entirely possible to apply your own particular areas of interest to multiple disciplinary inquiries. It's even possible, for instance, to bring an interest in Pompeii art into a statistics course. Using questions as a framework for academic writing enables writers to capture their own interests and use a disciplinary lens to discover, explore, and learn about ideas from a wide variety of perspectives. In the subsequent chapter, you will see, through reading, how writers develop scholarship based on the meaningful questions they pose.

℮ ℮ ℮

Historical Presentation: "Roman Addiction: The Changing Perception of Problem Gaming in the Roman World" by Suzanne B. Faris

Transfer Points: History, Sociology, Public Policy

While the phrase "ancient history" may sometimes dismiss the relevance of something, historians such as Suzanne Faris instead emphasize the enduring significance of ancient history.

Faris's history of problem gaming in the Roman World, for instance, has bearing on contemporary understanding of addiction and gaming. Through her research into how Romans approached addiction and problem gaming, Faris enables us to ask more questions about current practices: What are the intersections and disparities between historical and contemporary approaches? What have we inherited in terms of Roman attitude and law? What practices warrant reconsideration?

In this way, Faris's work illustrates one of the main ways in which historians pose questions. They ask questions about how the past intersects with and contributes to the present. Working within these sorts of inquiries enables greater understanding about current practices.

Many of historians' questions focus on historical events—not for their impact on the present, but more so for history's sake itself. These questions include the following: "What were the causes of past events?" "What has changed or remained the same across history?" "How did past decisions or actions affect future choices?" "How did people in the past view their world?" (OAH).

Historical research also encompasses a vast range of contexts. Historians can specialize in a specific time period, geographic region, or other area of expertise. Faris, for instance, focuses on Roman antiquity, while other historians focus on the Civil Rights Era, medieval history, or World War II. Historians also fuse history with other disciplines, pursuing scholarship in such areas as the history of science, the history of music, the history of food, or the history of economics. Journals in the discipline of history illustrate the broad range of specialty areas. Journal titles in history, just to provide a small set of examples, include the *Journal of Victorian Culture,* the *Journal of Modern History,* the *Journal of the History of Sexuality,* and *Environmental History.*

Historians use many different kinds of primary sources as evidence in their research. They might turn to letters, newspaper clippings, oral accounts, photographs, drawings, maps, songs, diaries, or other material artifacts such as pottery, coins, or battlegrounds. In an article titled "Capturing the Moment, Picturing History: Photographs of the Liberation of Paris," historian Catherine E. Clark examines photographs of the August 1944 liberation of Paris. However, because these photographs were also widely exhibited and circulated, Clark also uses the pamphlets, books, and museum archives that shared those photographs as evidence for how photographs not only document history, but also shape perceptions of history.

Some history is harder to discern. People who existed in the lower social strata or who were otherwise oppressed often have fewer public records. Historians, therefore, often pose questions about the challenges of history: How can we access the histories of underprivileged people and incorporate perspectives of underprivileged people within historical accounts? Examining official public records, for example, will not reveal information about individuals who are not in the public record, such as undocumented migrants. And, researching the history of an era by relying solely on public records will yield only a partial account of that era. In many cases, historians must instead access other forms of historical evidence, such as diaries, photographs, and material artifacts. Amy Stanley, for instance, researched the history of Japanese maidservants from 1600-1900 by using letters, marriage records, and diaries.

Suzanne B. Faris is an independent researcher and speaker with specialties in ancient history, especially textual, epigraphic, and legal sources. She has taught history, Ancient Greek, Elementary Latin, and Western Civilization at several institutions, including Tulane University, Southern Illinois University, University of Cincinnati, and Ohio University. She has a B.A., M.A., and J.D. from Tulane University, and a Ph.D. from Bryn Mawr College. Ongoing research projects include ancient tips on effective communication and public relations, Roman concepts of addiction, and Roman law and policy regarding gambling.

Some of the most important questions historians ask center around these matters of perspective and power: Whose histories are being told? Whose histories remain invisible? Historian Matthew Restall, for instance, argues that in order to understand Mayan history, we must resist the dominant narratives about the Maya and instead learn more about Afro-Yucatecans who have heretofore been "rendered invisible by historical processes and lack of scholarly attention" (393).

As they pursue these important questions about the past, historians write in many formats and modalities. Faris's argument, for instance, takes the form of a PowerPoint, delivered as a lecture in Las Vegas, Nevada. In addition to PowerPoint presentations and public lectures, historians also compose op-eds to offer correctives to popular misconceptions of history. Historians also often write reviews of recent books in the discipline of history, and research essays on historical periods, events, or persons. Significantly, historians write across public contexts and more scholarly contexts. Popular books on history may be found in bookstores, and many people even consider themselves to be amateur history buffs. But, history also reaches into the more conventional echelons of scholarship, with peer-reviewed articles and books. Historians may present their research as oral histories (verbal recounts of an experience), as researched articles, or in the form of biographies.

Finally, historians also conduct research into historical methods, examining how historians access and interpret various sources. Such work is sometimes termed historiography for its focus on the process of historical research.

Amid all of this variety and applicability, though, there is one aspect of history that remains important to acknowledge: its dynamic nature. For, although history by default has already occurred, our knowledge of what has occurred, and our practices based on what we know to have occurred, are always shifting. Therefore, a phrase like "ancient history" in many ways belies the continual movement of historical knowledge. The ways in which we understand history are continually shifting based on new discoveries about the past. As such, works such as Faris's may be in the realm of ancient history, but, precisely because of their historical footprints, will also always be among the most contemporary sorts of research.

Write Here

Faris created her PowerPoint for a presentation at the University of Nevada Las Vegas. Why might people in Las Vegas be interested in the history of problem gaming? What is at stake in understanding historical perspectives such as this?

Suzanne B. Faris

Roman Addiction: The Changing Perception of Problem Gaming in the Roman World

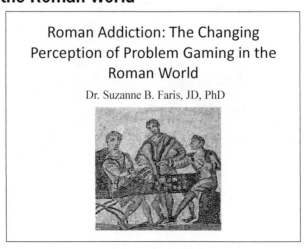

Roman Addiction: The Changing Perception of Problem Gaming in the Roman World

Dr. Suzanne B. Faris, JD, PhD

The Ancient Roman World

The Lure of the Dicing Table

- Roman Youth:
  - deemed to be esp. susceptible
  - concern for protecting family assets, reputation (of elites)
  - fear of "syndrome of vice" (dicing, drinking, illicit sex)
- Senatorial Elites:
  - Excessive, habitual or inappropriate gambling seen as road to ruin
- The Poor:
  - initially viewed as part of the problem, *not* victims
    - lumped in w/criminal element (& presumed guilty)
  - awareness, concern for poor increased in Christian period

Roman Gamblers

- Caligula (Suetonius Gaius 41.3)
- Claudius (Suetonius *Claudius* 33)
- Commodus (HA *Commodus* 3)
- Licinius Lenticula (Cicero *Philippics* 2.23.56)
- Roman "Gamblers Anonymous":
  - "Young Wastrels": (Horace Hor. *Odes* 3.24.58 ; cf. Seneca *De Vita Beata* 7)
  - "Betting the Coffers": (Juvenal *Satires* 1.88-93)
  - "The Idle Poor": (Ammianus Marcellinus 6.25)

Understanding of Pathological Gambling: Then & Now

Early Christian Tract*:
- Deceptive speech
- Wild impatience
- Fraternal discord
- Mindless raving/quarrelsome displays
- Continuous gambling ("day and night")
- Risks large amounts/entire family fortune
- Does not cease after losses/desire to increase wealth
- Shameful crime/false witness

DSM IV Definition**:
- Lying to others
- preoccupied w/gambling
- Restless, irritable when not gambling
- Jeopardizing important relationships
- Risks increasing amounts of money
- "chasing losses" leads to further gambling
- resorts to forgery, fraud, etc.

Points of Comparison: the Ancient Romans on Alcoholism

- Seneca on habitual alcohol consumption (1st C CE)
  - Distinction: *ebrius* vs. *ebriosus**
  - description of long-term effects of habitual drinking**
    - Loss of neuromuscular coordination (tripping,stumbling, etc.) :
    - Pallor
    - Trembling hands
    - Weight loss (thinness)
      - attributed to inability to digest
    - Abdominal bloating
    - Sluggishness/stupefaction
  - Pliny the Elder on effects of habitual drinking (1st C CE)
    - Sores/inflammation in eyes
    - Pallor
    - Trembling hands
    - Insomnia
    - Excitability/aggression
    - Shortened lifespan

- NIAAA Brochure***:
  - Hepatic encephalopathy
    - loss of neuromuscular coordination
      - Shaking or flapping of hands
    - Anxiety
    - Mood/personality changes
    - Coma
  - Conjunctival Injection (eyelids)
  - Gastritis
    - abdominal bloat)
  - Pancreatitis
    - digestive dysfunction
    - sweating,
    - pain
  - Weakened immune system
  - Cancer Risks

Roman Criminal Statutes on Gaming

- General prohibition on gambling, 3rd C BCE
  - *Lex Talaria* (or *lex Alearia*)
    - known only from references in literary sources
    - Little is known of content of prohibition, sanctions
      - evidence suggests a fine on gamblers of 4x amount wagered
      - gambling under general jurisdiction of aediles (city officials)
      - In practice, state enforcement at best sporadic & selective
    - Law of early 1st C BCE created exception to prohibition:
      - for betting on "contests of strength" (running, javelin-throwing, etc.)
      - potentially opened the door to sports-betting (on chariot races, gladiatorial games, etc.)
        - » Likely, however, that sports betting of that type had always gone in Rome on without any state interference
        - » Considered strictly private matter between friends

Adolescent Gambling in Ancient Rome

- Adolescent males thought especially susceptible to lure of gambling by Romans:
  - challenge of defining "youth gambling" in Rome
    - *adulescens* & *iuvenis* used very loosely by Romans
    - Adolescent males: under age and *in potestate*
      - Actual age range: appr. 13-18
      - typically had discretionary funds (*peculium*) from *pater familias*
  - Evidence from literary sources suggests adolescent males engaged mainly in dice games, *not* sports betting
    - *NB*: literary & legal sources take little note of "sports betting"
    - some varieties of dice games involved high levels of skill
    - Very little evidence in sources with respect to gambling by women or girls

Roman Vices: Gambling, Drinking and Prostitution as a Trap for the Unwary

Legal Response to Youth Gambling

- General criminal law prohibition (3rd C BCE)
- Civil Liability/Rights of Action (*Just. Dig.* 11.5):
  - in favor of youth's *pater familias* for his losses
  - against youth's *pater familias* for his winnings
  - against party deemed responsible for "corrupting" a youth by inducing him to gamble:
    - for "insult" (*iniuria*), a type of tort (delict)
    - in favor of his *pater familias*

Justinian's Anti-Gambling Edicts

- Stated Policy Objective: to protect people from their own folly, playing dice "day and night," then losing substantial sums, leading ultimately to "blasphemy" as they executed promissory notes
- Content of Law: playing dice in public or private for real stakes or not, declared illegal, but not subject to penalty; losses on permitted types of "sports betting" limited to one gold piece (equivalent of $)
- Effect: to prevent chief evils (loss of wealth & "blasphemy") associated with gambling by limiting the potential financial losses.
  - Recovery of gambling losses made actionable for gamblers and their heirs;
  - earlier practice (however sporadic) of imposing fourfold fine on gamblers officially abandoned.
- Sanctions for owners/operators of establishments w/gambling
- Special penalties for clergy dicing or watching dice games

Sources

- American Psychiatric Association(2000) Diagnostic and statistical manual of mental disorders 312.31 (4th ed., text rev.).
- "Beyond Hangovers: Understanding Alcohol's Impact on your Health." http://pubs.niaaa.nih.gov/publications/Hangovers/beyondHangovers.
- Berger, Adolf. Encyclopedic Dictionary of Roman Law. Transactions and Proceedings of the American Philological Association, 1953.
- Carcopino, Jerome. Daily Life in Ancient Rome: the People and the City at the Height of the Empire. Trans.E.O. Lorimer. Yale, 1968.
- Disney, John. A View of the Ancient Laws against Immorality and Profaneness. Crownfield and John Crownfield, 1729.
- Harnack, Adolf, Ed. Der pseudocyprianische Tractat de Aleatoribus. Gorgias Press, 2010.
- Horsfall, Nicholas. The Culture of the Roman Plebs. Routledge, 2003).
- Leibowitz, J.O.,"Studies in the History of Alcoholism II: Acute Alcoholism in Ancient Greek and Roman Medicine " Br.3. .Addict,1967, Vol. 62, pp. 83-86.
- McGinn, Thomas. Prostitution, Sexuality and the Law in Ancient Rome. Oxford, 1998.
- Robinson, O.F. The Criminal Law of Ancient Rome. Johns Hopkins, 1995.
- Rolleston, J.D., "Alcoholism in Classical Antiquity," British Journal of Inebriety 24.2 (1927).
- Carl Schoenhardt, Uber die Bestrafung des Glucksspiels im alteren romisches Recht. Ecke, 1885.
- Schwartz, David. Roll the Bones: The History of Gambling. Gotham, 2006.
- Toner, Jerry P., Popular Culture in Ancient Rome. Polity Press, 1995.

Write Away

1. Create an artifact related to Faris's historical argument. Using the history Faris has provided, design and develop an artifact, such as dice, a legal edict, or a poster, that enables your class, collaboratively, to recreate items that might have been in an archive about Roman gambling.

2. Using an event, person, or concept of your choosing, create a PowerPoint like Faris's in which you present the history of that event, person, or concept. Write a reflection in which you articulate your intended audience for this PowerPoint and your aims for the history.

3. Oral histories offer individual perspectives and provide a sense of human experiences. Oral histories have helped expand our knowledge of what it was like to experience Civil Rights, women's reproductive rights, and the Vietnam War. In consultation with your instructor, identify an aspect of history that interests you and conduct an oral history.

Disaster Medicine Research: "Ethical Issues in the Provision of Emergency Medical Care in Multiple Casualty Incidents and Disasters" by Pinchas Halpern and Gregory L. Larkin

Transfer Points: Ethics, Health Sciences, Public Policy

"Is getting an abortion immoral?" ... "Is euthanasia immoral?" ... "Is affirmative action right or wrong?" ... "What are human rights, and how do we determine them?" ... "Do animals have rights as well?" (Mastin)

These are but some of the many questions posed by people writing and researching in the discipline of ethics. Ethics, broadly construed, involves the study of how people and cultures develop, understand, change, adhere to—or reject—ethical codes of behavior. The field of ethics includes many approaches and subfields, including ancient Greek ethics, normative ethics, which examines how ethical rules or norms evolve, comparative or descriptive ethics, which studies people's actions and beliefs, and applied ethics, which applies ethics theories to real-world contexts (Mastin).

While ethics is perhaps most closely associated with the discipline of moral philosophy, it is also highly transferable. One broad area of ethics transfer involves the ethics of research methodologies. Ethics plays an especially significant role across disciplines in research involving human subjects, where researchers grapple with such matters as the use of deception, the protection of personal data, and the dissemination of research results. Information technologists Michael Zimmer and Nicholas Proferes, for instance, write about the ethics of using Twitter for data collection. Scholars in psychology and pediatrics have examined the ethics of conducting sexuality research with children (Robinson and Davies). And anthropologists have explored the ethics surrounding ethnographic research methods (Weber).

The ethics of research methodologies across disciplines, though, is only one dimension of the transferability of ethics. Those in psychology, for instance, explore ethics in such contexts as military psychology (Kennedy and Moore) and clinical practice (Pillay). Scholars also examine ethics in religions, such as Geoffrey Ashton's comparative critical analysis of the ethics of Confucianism and the Bhagavad Gita. And, those working in public policy, political science, and international relations also examine ethics, such as in the context of humanitarian aid (Bouvier).

The field of ethics is so transferable, in fact, that many disciplines publish journals specifically dedicated to disciplinary-specific ethics. These include, for example, the *Journal of Business Ethics;* the *Journal of Religious Ethics; Legal Ethics; Journal of Information, Communication and Ethics in Society*; and the *Journal of Ethics, Economics, Finance, and Society.*

In the article included here, authors Halpern and Larkin are writing within an area of research known as bioethics. Bioethicists pose and pursue complicated questions about a variety of health-related issues. For instance, with regard to parenting and procreation, bioethics yields such questions as: "What is good parenting in the age of genomics?" and "What is the role of society in setting and implementing standards for the children's environments, food, and rearing?" With regard to aging, those in bioethics

Pinchas Halpern is the director of emergency medicine at the Tel-Aviv Sourasky Medical Center in Israel. His areas of expertise include Anesthesiology, Critical Care and Emergency Medicine, and Hyperbaric and Diving Medicine. He was born in Romania, and raised in Israel, receiving his M.D. from Tel-Aviv University, and then training in a Navy diving unit in Haifa for five years (Leichman). **Gregory Larkin** is a Professor and chair of emergency medicine at the University of Auckland in New Zealand. His expertise includes "prevention, public health, EMS, disaster preparedness, injury/trauma prevention, substance abuse, mental health, bioethics, professionalism, mHealth/health IT, medico-legal issues, and medical education" ("Gregory Larkin"). He received a B.S. in Chemical Engineering from the University of Notre Dame, an M.S. in Chemical Engineering & Molecular Biology at Penn State University, and his M.D. from Penn State University.

explore such questions as: "What does our society owe to those living with chronic conditions?" and "How do we help people age with respect, dignity, and inclusivity?" (*Hastings Center*)

While bioethical questions have informed healthcare research and practice for centuries, the sustained study of bioethics is somewhat more recent, having crystallized around a 1968 panel discussion among theologians and anthropologists regarding the first human heart transplant (Hanson).

Bioethicists write across many genres. They compose scholarly work such as reviews and research articles. They also write in more public contexts, writing op-eds and developing websites to advocate and educate healthcare providers, policy makers, patients, and families. Bioethicists also work in verbal modalities, engaging in public lectures, talks, dialogues, and conferences with scholars, practitioners, leaders, and administrators involved with health care. When the April 15, 2013, Boston Marathon massacre occurred, for example, doctors at the Beth Israel Deaconess Medical Center called Halpern for advice since he had previously consulted with them on disaster preparedness (Leichman).

The specific area of bioethics addressed by Halpern and Larkin centers on disaster medicine. This field, as with ethics, is largely grounded on transfer-related thinking. Gregory R. Ciottone, the editor of the book *Disaster Medicine,* in which Halpern and Larkin's article originally appears, explains how transfer is uniquely situated at the core of disaster medicine:

"[T]he care of casualties from a disaster requires the healthcare provider to integrate into the larger, predominately non-medical multidisciplinary response. ... [t]o operate safely and efficiently as part of a coordinated disaster response" (3).

Scholars and professionals involved with disaster medicine conduct research and write about a wide array of matters. In the *Disaster Medicine and Public Health Preparedness Journal*, for instance, research includes the following range: voluntary medical support after nuclear disasters (Morita et al.); guidelines for healthcare workers responding to Ebola (Wiwanitkit); the effects of community participation for earthquake preparedness in Tehran, Iran (Jamshidi et al.); and disaster preparedness in rural families of children with special healthcare needs (Hamann et al.).

As these diverse examples of bioethics research demonstrate, the field, as with the larger field of ethics, carries remarkably broad transferability. And this range of reach makes ethics among the most impactful areas of scholarly inquiry.

Write Here

Describe a moment when you or someone you know faced a complicated choice regarding ethics. What were the ethical complexities involved? How did you or the person you know navigate these quandaries? Drawing on this experience, why are ethics so complex and dynamic?

Pinchas Halpern and Gregory L. Larkin

Ethical Issues in the Provision of Emergency Medical Care in Multiple Casualty Incidents and Disasters

Disasters and multiple casualty incidents (MCIs) affect every corner of the globe. Although natural disasters and wars have plagued humanity for thousands of years, manmade MCIs comprise a relatively new and growing threat with which medicine must content—even in peacetime. Citizens of all nations have increasingly encountered MCIs that, without warning, can instantly overwhelm the capacity of both prehospital and hospital-based systems, imposing significant clinical, organizational, and even ethical challenges. Disasters and MCIs introduce unique moral, triage, resource allocation, and public health issues. The disaster paradigm demands rapid reorganization of medical systems and, in tandem, a recalibration of familiar ethical and moral codes that govern providers during times of stability. Many of the most crucial moral dilemmas can be anticipated, however, and policies can be developed in advance that clearly delineate the duties and priorities for medical support personnel during MCIs and disasters. Prospective ethical deliberation, advance austerity planning, and prophylaxis policy can streamline moral medical decision-making and ensure optimal service delivery downstream to both individual patients and the public at large.

The chronology of preparedness for MCIs and disasters involves three stages: (1) pre-event, (2) event, and (3) postevent. Each stage may be addressed by different medical caregivers, and each poses somewhat different management, clinical, and ethical dilemmas. Major dilemmas within the context of these three timed stages include adequate preparation for eventualities, scene triage and transport, duty to treat, scope of practice off site, stewardship of resources, and ethical long-term goals of fairness in matters of rehabilitation. This chapter will focus mainly on overarching ethical challenges and event-based dilemmas that face emergency medical services (EMS) and emergency medicine (EM) providers in the throes of MCIs and disasters.

HISTORICAL PERSPECTIVE

Over the years, sets of ethical rules have been developed to guide medical personnel in their work, but they usually do not address MCIs and disasters, thereby creating potential uncertainty. Many of the accepted practices have little scientific basis and therefore compel physicians to use common sense. However, common sense may sometimes contradict generally accepted ethical guidelines or leave physicians no choice but to apply some intuitively created adaptation of the ordinary ethical rules to a situation that was not considered when the rules were originally formulated.

In the following are some examples of sets of ethical rules composed throughout history, according to which medical personnel are expected to practice. The Hippocratic oath[1] has been taken by newly appointed physicians in the West for centuries. Inspired by the Pythagoreans, this classic treatise dictates that the physician must be ready and willing to assist a patient with any medical problem under any circumstances, without any economic or other stipulation: "The regimen I adopt shall be for the benefit of the patient according to my ability and judgment and not for their hurt or for any wrong....Whatsoever house I enter, there will I go for the benefit of the sick refraining from all wrongdoing or corruption."

The Geneva Conventions[2] are also concerned with the obligation of integrity and respect of the physician toward the practice of medicine. They regard the patient's health as being the first priority for the physician, who is mandated to use the power of medicine for the general good and maintain good relationships with his or her colleagues, while forbidding any kind of discrimination among patients.

Basic Principles

Borrowing from Beachamp and Childress's concepts of ethical principlism, Priel and Dolev[3] define four principles on which routine medical ethics are based:

1. *Beneficence:* This important Judeo-Christian concept enjoins medical staff members to do their best to optimize outcomes and prolong the life of the patient/victim.
2. *Nonmaleficence:* This is the classic notion of *primum non nocere,* or "the first thing (is) to do no harm." This is the ordering principle of most emergency medical ethics.
3. *Respect for autonomy:* The medical staff must engage in full discourse with patients and honor their own informed decisions regarding their own medical care.
4. *Justice:* The resources and means of medical personnel must be equitably distributed among all victims.

These four principles are not absolute, and shifting circumstances may dictate their reordering or prioritization. They may even contradict each other. For example, a surgeon's desire to do good for a patient through an operative procedure may also cause the patient some short-term discomfort or even harm from complications. Therefore, providing both beneficent and nonmaleficent care can create a conflict of principles, whereupon the clinician must choose one principle over another.

Medical Organizations

Many medical organizations have developed ethical codes, but few have specifically addressed the issue of MCIs and disasters. The World Medical Association (WMA) code of ethics has a specific section on disaster care.[4] The code of ethics of the American College of Emergency Physicians (ACEP) specifically addresses situations in which "the resources of a health care facility are overwhelmed by epidemic illness, mass casualty, or the victims of a natural or manmade disaster" and states that it is the duty of the emergency physician to "focus health care resources on those patients most likely to benefit and who have a reasonable probability of survival."[5] The American Academy of Emergency Medicine's code of ethics does not address disaster/MCI situations.[6] The ethics code of the American College of Physicians does not contain specific mention of the care of victims of disasters or MCIs,[7] whereas that of the American Medical Association (AMA) states in its ethics code as follows: "...physicians and other health professionals should be knowledgeable of ethical and legal issues and disaster response. These include: (a) their professional responsibility to treat victims (including those with potentially contagious conditions); (b) their rights and responsibilities to protect themselves from harm; (c) issues surrounding their responsibilities and rights as volunteers, and (d) associated liability issues.[8] Since studies have demonstrated the poor state of preparedness of medical professionals for disasters and MCIs, such as in the event of bioterrorism,[9] the AMA code also states that "...a social obligation for physician response can be defined, then certainly a derivative obligation can be placed on the profession—an obligation to ensure that its members are prepared...to effectively respond. This obligation of the profession must be not only clearly defined but expeditiously met."

The European Society of Emergency Medicine (EuSEM) has no explicit code of ethics. The World Association for Disaster and Emergency Medicine's Health Disaster Management (WADEM) states[10]:

> Triage...means that scarce resources will be used to provide the maximum benefit to the population at large, even if it means that single victims who might have been

saved under other circumstances are sacrificed for the greater good. However, when the triage concept is expanded into other management areas, the concept becomes more difficult to accept. For example, should limited water resources be distributed in a manner so as to provide the minimum amounts needed to sustain life to only a part of the population, and accept the high probability that the rest will die of thirst? Or should 1 litre (less than the critical threshold) be distributed to everybody, well aware that then everybody will succumb, but at a later stage in the disaster? Since ethics, as such, are not natural laws, but human 'inventions', how is what decided deemed to be ethically correct?

The ethical principles of the Israeli Medical Association (IMA) state: "In an emergency, the physician may act according to his best judgment, thus effectively absolving the physician of requirements such as informed consent, privacy, the patient's right to choose a caregiver and provision of information."[11] U.S. common law does not impose any duty to render aid or assistance to a person in need, even if one could do so with no risk to oneself. However, experts point out that health providers could be required to provide care in the event of an emergency through licensure requirements.[12] In addition, even though individual physicians do not have a duty to provide care, hospitals and other institutions sometimes do, particularly for emergent situations. The current legal establishment, including the requirements of the Americans with Disabilities Act, seeks to expose physicians while still encouraging them to act. The system provides weak incentives to be a hero. So far, only the Model State Emergency Health Powers Act (MSEHPA) has systematically addressed the duty to care issue.[13] Even though the MSEHPA is not law, it does serve to offer guidance to state legislators and may influence what types of laws and schemes will be enacted. For example, MSEHPA would allow states to *require* healthcare providers to provide care in the event of emergencies. The duty does vary with risk, since a scheme that would overburden healthcare providers would be unacceptable.[12] Israeli common law (1988) states that "it is the duty of a person to assist another person...

in immediate severe danger to his life…when he can do so without endangering himself or other."

The International Red Cross and Red Crescent Movement's code of conduct in disaster relief states: "Aid is given regardless of the race, creed or nationality of the recipients and without adverse distinction of any kind….Aid priorities are calculated on the basis of need alone….We hold ourselves accountable to both those we seek to assist and those from whom we accept resources."[14] The ethics code of Magen David Adom (MDA), the Israeli national EMS organization, includes the following text regarding disaster and MCI: "…to treat victims by priorities set according to medical criteria, without any other considerations such as age, sex, religion, nationality, social or economic status…caregivers will, as a rule, attempt to save the largest number of victims possible, even at the possible detriment of the chances of saving an individual victim…to treat victims while guarding the victims' and the caregivers' safety as well as possible. Determining the correct balance between risk to victim and risk to caregiver is the responsibility of the caregiver and the event commander's." (Personal communication, Pinchas Halpern, MD.) The ethical code of the Israeli Army Medical Corps assumes that the operational protocols governing the administration of medical care in the field cover potential ethical dilemmas and does not deal with the issue specifically.

MCI AND ETHICAL ISSUES ARISING FROM IT

All the ethical codes presented here demonstrate a continuity of principles involving patient-caregiver relationships as well as physician-system relationships. Thus, according to these more classic codes, the physician must be professionally and logistically prepared to manage disasters and do what is best for the patient, including doing everything in his or her power to save the patient's life. The physician should not discriminate among patients but treat them with a uniform, balanced, and just approach. The physician ought to share his or her decision-making with patients and provide them with truthful information about treatment and prognosis, except when sharing information is expected to cause any delay in or otherwise negatively affect patient care. How an MCI changes the order of these

principles and relative contribution of each level of obligation is discussed next.

MCI is defined as a state in which there is an imbalance between the numbers or types of injured who need medical care and the medical ability of the emergency systems to deliver *optimal* care to each individual. Disasters may be defined as MCIs that involve significant disruption of the infrastructure (human, logistic, or medical) of the region/nation coping with the event (e.g., natural disaster, war). The effects of disasters, such as famine and epidemics, may be prolonged and result in an extended need for medical care, with a more complex interaction between purely medical and logistic support (e.g., water and food supplies, shelter). In an MCI or a disaster, some of the ethical principles previously mentioned may not be realistically applicable and therefore raise some interesting ethical issues:

- *Beneficence:* If the physician were to act according to this principle of maximizing the good, he or she would be expected to spend an inordinate amount of time on only one or a few patients and would essentially fail to fulfill his or her ethical obligations toward the rest of the patients who require care. Should the caregiver then focus treatment on one person, or partially take care of a maximum number of patients, or perhaps only take care of patients for whom it is cost-effective to intervene, thereby only partly fulfilling the beneficence principle?

- *Distinction without discrimination (nondiscrimination):* It is generally agreed on that patients must not be discriminated against with regard to receiving medical care and the allocation of resources. This issue takes on greater significance during an MCI since it is, by definition, a situation in which there are not enough resources relative to patient requirements. Discrimination among patients must occur, but on what basis should this be done and in a way that does not introduce any form of unfair or improper discrimination? Should medical treatment be administered according to the criterion of severity of injury or according to the patient's age/social status/benefit to society, ethnic group, etc.? Decision rules that optimize outcomes for all concerned in disasters have not been validated. If the decision was made to deliver medical assistance

111

according to the criterion of injury severity, would it be appropriate to favor patients who are injured severely and whose lives can most likely be saved if they receive immediate care, or would it be better to favor potentially fatally injured patients whose odds of survival are low but who may have a remote chance at survival? This question of treatment priorities is one of the most difficult ethical issues during an MCI.

- *Nonmaleficence:* Due to the nature of an MCI, caregivers may be forced into making critical decisions regarding treatment and evacuation of individual casualties based on superficial evaluation and without the guidance of diagnostic techniques that are normally available in modern medical practice. In addition, caregivers may be under special duress due to personal risk or discomfort. As a result, errors may occur in the diagnosis (e.g., undertriage or overtriage), which may harm certain patients. Should providers in MCIs be liable for these harms, and does the liability of a volunteer differ from that of a nonvolunteer?

- *Patient autonomy and right to information:* During an MCI, this principle may need to be subjugated due to the overarching need for expediency in administering care because medical personnel may not have enough time to share decisions regarding treatment with the patient. Professional and policy considerations regarding the type of injury or available hospital facilities will dictate where the patient will be evacuated, even against a patient's wishes or best interest from other perspectives (e.g., closeness to home). When a person refuses to receive medical care, the medical personnel will have no time to decide whether the person is rational, thus raising the question whether coercion or force should ever be used to administer medical care during an MCI. Also how and to what extent should the patient's requests to choose a hospital or to be evacuated with relatives be considered? Should more time be devoted to every patient to explain to him or her the medical care that will be given? Should the explanations be foregone to care for more patients faster and more efficiently?

- *Staff safety:* There are situations in which the cause of danger has not yet been neutralized (e.g., rescue of wounded persons from a collapsing building; terrorist activity in which there might be an additional explosive charge; care of a chemically, radiologically, or biologically contaminated patient). How should medical personnel behave in such cases? Should they administer care while risking their personal safety, or should they wait until the cause of danger is eliminated? How much personal risk is acceptable? Should medical personnel be compelled to receive vaccination for potential bioterrorism weapons (e.g., smallpox) before or even after an event has occurred? Should nonvaccinated personnel be forced to treat contagious patients even though these physicians had previously refused (or were unable) to receive the vaccine? Which medical personnel should receive limited prophylactic antibiotics in case of an attack with anthrax? Should physicians be forced to respond to a call to manage a chemical incident even though their hospital may not be completely prepared for the event and personal protection equipment may be suboptimal or lacking?

- *Use of nonstandard or investigational procedures and drugs:* Advancement of medical knowledge is based on experimentation. For example, many new MCI triage methodologies have been proposed by public and private sources. How should they be tested? Should physicians accept grants or other inducements to study an unproven technology in a personal experience with an MCI? Experimenting in a disaster/MCI situation produces specific ethical issues not usually addressed during Institutional Review Board processes, and there are few contemporary guidelines.

The unique reality during an MCI creates difficult ethical issues arising from the fact that life is often threatened at an alarming rate; in the heat of a novel disaster, old platitudes and even widely accepted medical ethical codes may no longer apply in their original form.

CURRENT PRACTICE
Real-Time Ethics During MCIs and Disasters
TRIAGE

Some authors agree with the ethics of utility and would counsel medical personnel to reduce morbidity and mortality as much as possible during an MCI.[15] The concept of utility attempts to maximize the general good and may seem to be at variance with the traditionally accepted principle of doing the utmost for the individual patient, even when ignoring some patients may raise the level of the cumulative benefit. During an MCI, providers must be prudent stewards of the limited resources entrusted to them. It would, therefore, be wrong for a clinician to devote his or her energies to only one patient since, by doing so, the odds of survival for other casualties may be unfairly limited. In an MCI, equitable sharing of resources based on need may eclipse the first-come, first-served practice of routine operations in peacetime.

Assuming that a utilitarian sharing of resources is an appropriate paradigm shift for an MCI, there is still a need to set treatment priorities. Fortunately, there is broad agreement on which victims a clinician should approach first. Those with a lethal injury or in a perimorbid status will be managed expectantly, whereas those with serious but nonlethal injuries are often given high priority. The literature offers a number of suggestions to determine the order of treatment, but studies have documented the high rate of overtriage and undertriage in MCI situations.[16, 17] Before we accept this evolution in attitude, it behooves us to consider other potential ways of setting treatment priorities in an MCI:

1. *Randomly choosing the order of patients to treat:* This position is based on the concept that every person has an equal right to receive medical treatment and, as such, it affords every casualty an equal chance to be chosen via random selection. The problem is that it does not allow every person an equal right to survive: caregivers may invest their time in treating individuals whose lives are not at risk while the other untreated patients may die. This approach is not consistent with the principle of reducing the mortality in as many cases as possible or with the principle of fair and just distribution, which correlates the extent to which a person needs treatment with the extent to which he or she is actually treated.

2. *Choosing according to "first-come, first served":* This model may appear fair and, like the previous method, may connote a certain randomness. It may, however, portend greater casualties over time, and it is also inconsistent with the principles of equitable distribution of resources based on need. Also, rules set according to the sequence when casualties arrive on site—thereby determining who will be "first"—seem unacceptably arbitrary.

3. *No treatment to anybody:* Team members are not capable of making a decision of whom to treat first; therefore, they prefer not to administer any treatment until sufficient personnel reach the scene so that all patients can be treated equally. This theoretical solution contradicts the principles of beneficence and nonmaleficence. Withholding time-sensitive benefits and causing harm are both antithetical to the clinician's ethical duty.

4. *Using nonmedical standards (e.g., gender, age, profession, social status, contribution to society, ethnic origin):* In times of national crises or war, saving a president or a general may have collateral benefits for the good of the nation-state, and it seems natural to first help a wounded child or an esteemed public personality. However, given that all people have equal rights to live regardless of status, age, gender, origin, creed, or disability, physicians must not discriminate against patients who have legitimate needs for care. Ideological issues must not eclipse the humanistic priorities embodied in ethical rules.[18, 19]

5. *Urgency of need:* The priority of treatment is determined according to the severity of the injury and the likelihood of benefit from care. The World Medical Federation has suggested the following scale of priorities:
   - *First priority:* victims whose lives are at risk and can be saved by an urgent medical treatment
   - *Second priority:* victims whose lives are not at immediate risk but who need immediate medical treatment
   - *Third priority:* victims whose treatment may be delayed for an extended period
   - *Fourth priority:* victims who suffer from emotional reaction to the event
   - *Fifth priority:* victims who are too severely injured to be rescued

Such a scale of priorities may be considered immoral at first glance, like "abandoning a victim in the field."[15] However, herein is the major difference between an MCI and a routine event. The exigency of an MCI dictates the rule of reduction of morbidity and mortality as well as significant suffering in as many cases as possible. Adhering to this rule means preferring several severely injured victims who might be rescued over a near-fatally injured person who has only a slim chance of survival. Healthcare does not have to be equally distributed; it has to be *equitably* distributed, with each victim receiving care according to medical need. This system determines treatment priorities at the scene, but it is also valid in determining the priority of evacuation to hospitals.

Based on these two principles—reduction of mortality and permanent morbidity in as many cases as possible and giving priority of treatment according the severity of injury—a working scheme has been in place for years in all EMS/ EM protocols for MCI triage. Triage is from the French word *trier*, "to sort," and sorting patients according to need is critical to "determining the order of priorities to medical treatment, based upon prognostic observations and evaluation."[15, 17] Triage is performed at the scene in parallel (observing the entire scene simultaneously) and in tandem at the medical facility (triaging patients as they arrive). In practice, scene triage implies that before medical treatment begins, medical personnel will scan the scene and sort the victims into various categories according to the severity of their injury. Medical personnel begin treatment and evacuation only after the evaluation of all the wounded and consideration of extant resources have been completed. This brief planning stage is not "wasted" since it allows the medical personnel to evaluate the situation and determine who needs them most. The evacuation of victims from an MCI scene will take place according to the principle of the severity of injury. First to be evacuated will be unstable victims— those who suffer from a severe breathing disorder, an uncompensated situation of trauma, or a deteriorating state of consciousness. Following will be the stable but urgent victims, and lastly will come nonurgent cases. Often, the priority of evacuation is not identical to the priority of treatment (e.g., a patient with a pneumothorax

needs extremely urgent treatment; however, once treated on-scene, he or she is no longer defined as requiring urgent evacuation).[20] Both treatment and triage during an MCI must be orchestrated by well-trained and experienced disaster medical personnel. Minimizing the number of under-triage and overtriage situations will maximize goods and minimize harms. Triage must take into account patients who arrive at hospitals, patients already there, patients expected to arrive, and the resources available to them all on a dynamic, minute-by-minute basis.

PATIENT AUTONOMY

A recent medical newsletter opined: "In a massive epidemic, such *niceties* as patient autonomy, detailed record keeping, personalized care…" will be sacrificed.[21] Indeed, the principle of respect for patient autonomy may be overruled in certain disaster situations if it contradicts the main objective of providing the most good to the greatest number of victims.[22] This is not to say, of course, that respecting patient autonomy is not terribly important; rather, all attempts should be made to listen to the patient's specific medical wishes when possible, even though there will be little time. Specific wishes may be respected when they do not contradict the benefit of the majority of casualties and/or the operational requirements and protocols in force during the event. An exception to this rule may be the attempt to evacuate small children together with a parent or relative.

PERSONAL SECURITY OF MEDICAL PERSONNEL DURING AN MCI

Medical personnel work in cooperation with additional emergency authorities, such as the police and security forces. Scene safety includes not only the site of the event, but also the care sites. Thus, hospitals may be damaged and rendered unsafe by natural disasters. Hospitals have come under attack in battle zones, and water and food contamination endangers medical personnel as well as the populace. Terrorists have targeted hospitals, and chemical and biological agents pose grave risks to medical personnel both on-site and in care facilities. Balancing personnel safety and casualty needs is usually an ad-hoc decision to be made on-site by the medical commander in consultation with security and other rescue force commanders. Principles, however, must be set a priori. The principle of utility (i.e., maintaining the safety and thus functionality of medical forces who are usually not trained rescuers or fighters) must be balanced with the duty of the medical personnel to offer time-sensitive care as soon as practical. Noteworthily, the Israeli National EMS, MDA, forbids its thousands of underage volunteers to enter the scene of a disaster, but many have still participated in MCI care by functioning on the periphery of the site in areas declared safe by scene commanders. In this way, medical service is given to the victims while minimizing risk to the medical personnel. Having said that, 12 EMS personnel were injured and two killed in the line of duty in MCIs in Israel between September 2000 and September 2003.

BIOTERRORISM AND EPIDEMICS

Despite the 2002 anthrax attacks in the United States and the SARS mini-epidemic of 2003, no modern nation has had to deal with large-scale epidemics with modern means. Even though there is lack of experience and evidence-based information, it is important to at least mention the ethical issues likely to arise from such a situation, which presumably would have a potentially huge impact on a society and its medical system. An abbreviated listing includes:

1. The intrinsic dialectics between the good of society and that of the individual, as evidenced by the questions of whether to limit an individual's movement or his or her autonomy to decide whether to receive a vaccine or care versus society's need to isolate the contagious sick and to treat a contagious individual, perhaps by force
2. The application of experimental treatments during the epidemic, in lieu of existing therapy (pure research) or when other viable therapies are lacking
3. The responsibility of society toward those suffering side-effects of coercive (or even voluntary) therapies, medical personnel family members who contract a disease, affected caregivers, etc.
4. Forcing physicians to receive prophylactic antibiotics or vaccines

5. The right of physicians to refuse to care for contagious patients if these physicians refused (or were unable to or were not offered) vaccines/prophylactic treatment
6. Forcing physicians to remain in the hospital for extended periods to minimize disease transmission
7. Allocating scarce resources to the public versus medical/rescue personnel or politicians/defense forces, etc.
8. Forcing patients to seek care at community clinics by denying access to hospitals
9. Disseminating classified research information to the civilian sector
10. Withholding or modifying information to preserve public order and compliance
11. Manufacturing scarce medications in infringement or patent rights
12. Forcing private companies to produce needed medications
13. Forcing hospitals to take in contagious patients even though it will likely affect their income by turning away other patients
14. Permitting the government to take over stocks of vital supplies from private companies
15. Administering needed therapy to nonmentally competent, institutionalized patients; prison inmates; etc.

Natural Disasters

The deaths of patients in hospitals submerged by floodwater in New Orleans, LA, by Hurricane Katrina in 2005 have highlighted the issue of physician responsibility to his or her patients in times of extreme natural disasters. The physician faces at least three dilemmas under such circumstances: (1) balancing personal, family, and colleague safety with the duty to ensure patient safety and ongoing medical care, (2) providing adequate or at least life-saving care under conditions of severe infrastructure disruption, and (3) the responsibility to mitigate the consequences of disasters by adequate prior preparation for such emergencies. The most acute problem seems to be the immediate or even slightly delayed malfunction of life-sustaining equipment, such as ventilator shut-off due to lack of electrical power or oxygen, or dialysis machine dysfunction due to lack of electricity and dialysate. The lack of air-conditioning, degradation or destruction of stores of medicines, death, incapacitation or desertion of staff, destruction of all or parts of the medical facility, etc., may create an environment that renders the provision of adequate medical care impossible or tenuous.

What is, then, the duty of the physician under such circumstances? It seems futile to provide advice such as "patients first" or "save yourself and/or your loved ones first." It is the physician's duty to do his utmost, under the specific circumstances, to save the patient's life or prevent irreversible injury or organ damage. It seems reasonable to demand that any decision to withhold life- and limb-saving care should be taken only after due deliberation, discussion with peers and superiors, and, whenever feasible, documentation. Admittedly, sometimes the relevant time frame is extremely short (e.g., avalanche, tsunami), in which case it would seem that it is the physician's duty to save as many patients as is compatible with saving his own life. Finally, it is the duty of physicians (and managers, of course) to prepare the medical facility for disasters by appropriate planning, equipping, and staff training, in order to minimize or obviate some or all of these problems. Such mitigation activity is taken, by definition, prior to the event, and is therefore done under less or no time constraints. This makes the physician's duty in this respect much more binding, and any failure to fulfill it much less pardonable.

PITFALLS

The number and complexity of potential dilemmas are too numerous to address in their entirety in this chapter. Moreover, it is both impossible and unnecessary to have a policy for every situation that arises. Technical confusion, professional paralysis, and emotional numbing can seriously impair provider response, and even the classic codes of ethics fall short of a formulaic "one-size-fits-all" approach to moral challenges during mass casualty events.

Specific obstacles may be encountered before an event, during the event, and after the event. Professional ennui and lack of preparedness may be encountered at the individual and system levels. Ethical pitfalls during the event include all of those previously discussed regarding triage, resource allocation, safety, and fairness, as well as duty to care issues when the only contract is of the unwritten, Lockean, social contract variety. In the wake of an event, there are opportunities for fame and fortune and the chance to change practice.

However, there are overarching virtues and vices that can help or hinder a properly ethical MCI response, respectively. Virtues inform a wide variety of behaviors well beyond the reach of most ethics codes, principles, and policies. Around 330 BCE, Aristotle made virtues the basis for all ethics and discussed in his famous *Nicomachean Ethics* that the exercise of virtue was properly the middle ground or "golden mean" between deficiency and excess. Courage, for example, is vital for a healthcare provider to respond bravely to dangerous disasters and MCI situations. Ill-tempered or overexuberant foolhardiness to rush into a contaminated area without proper personal protection equipment when the equipment is available is not considered courage; it is merely foolishness. At the other extreme of this spectrum is the frightened provider who is afraid to act, immobilized by fear. Courage is a willingness to respond in the throes of danger, and it demands that we bravely treat both the perpetrators and the victims of MCIs and have the inner fortitude to take a stand for moral principles when it is difficult or unpopular to do so. Saying "no" to esteemed members of society, family, and friends for the greater good; allowing expectant patients to die under austere conditions; enforcing quarantine and reporting provisions with friends and colleagues; willingly responding to the call for help without fear of malpractice threats, infectious disease exposure, or economic risk are all examples of courage in action.

Justice is vital to promote fairness and the proper allocation of scarce resources according to need. Justice also enjoins providers to adhere to the mandate of the World Medical Association's Declaration of Geneva to treat patients regardless of "age, disease or disability, creed, ethnic origin, gender, nationality, political affiliation, race, sexual orientation or social standing."[4]

Similarly, prudence, or sound judgment, is the practical wisdom required to weigh competing interests and apply technical and moral facts to particular scenarios. Determining who to triage, refer, transport, and decontaminate all require prudential wisdom.

Stewardship is similar to prudence because it requires common sense using scarce resources. This has application to everyday health resource distribution, but it is especially important under the resource and time limitations of a disaster to use personnel and equipment optimally.

Vigilance was perhaps the virtue most evidently lacking on Sept. 11, 2001. Around-the-clock guardianship does not relax on nights, weekends, and holidays. Surveillance activities and MCI preparedness plans mandate an ever-ready, argus-eyed vanguard of medical personnel who are prepared and able to respond before they are ever activated in the field. "Closing the stables after the horses are free" is a meaningless gesture—too little, too late.

Although the foregoing discussion may readily suggest that prudence, courage, justice, stewardship, and vigilance are central for responding to and being prepared for disasters and MCIs, their opposites—impulsivity, cowardice, prejudice, profligacy, and procrastination—are dangerous pitfalls to avoid. As Thomas Aquinas pointed out many centuries ago, for every virtue there is an antagonistic vice that hinders its expression. One way to avoid these vices is to prospectively draft policies and procedures that define role expectations that virtuous persons would manifest.

SOLUTIONS

Virtue, or character, is an important antidote to the many pitfalls and vices. The following principles for administering medical assistance amplify the core virtues of justice, prudence, courage, stewardship, and vigilance and take into account the tripartite obligations of medical professionals to patients, the profession, and the society in an MCI.

1. It is the ethical as well as the professional duty of society and the medical establishment to provide the infrastructure and timely local means to healthcare to minimize the disparity between demands and capabilities, thereby minimizing the number of casualties receiving suboptimal care, even in an MCI. At the same time, providers have parallel obligations to prudently manage and distribute scarce medical resources to avoid waste and to maximize the benefits for all victims.

2. It is essential to be prepared for a designated role in an MCI by continued study, drills, vigilance, and training, even in the face of financial and organizational constraints.

3. The principles of utility and justice mandate that care be distributed equitably and in a manner that maximizes survival and minimizes suffering for the greatest number of victims. Therefore, triage must be carried out fairly and without bias toward individual patients regardless of gender, age, race, creed, ethnicity, or role in the conflict. Medical and operational consideration should be the only factors determining the priority of care. The identity of the victim should play no role in decision-making, except in very extreme situations and those to be determined by policy set forth before the event.

4. Caregivers have a duty to treat MCI victims even in the face of personal danger. Balancing the needs of patients with the right of the caregiver to personal safety should be discussed and spelled out by the authorities before the event. Keep patients, other providers, and oneself safe to the extent that it is compatible with timely and efficient care of the majority of victims. Administer maximal amounts of medical care compatible with the operational limitations. At the very least, strive to minimize suffering.

5. Respect for patient autonomy, dignity, and right to privacy and to information are important even in an MCI. However, these rights may be subordinate to the exigencies of the situation when expeditious care for all patients is the first consideration.

6. Guard the identity, privacy, and confidentiality of victims of an MCI.

7. Work cooperatively with others who care for and about MCI victims and safeguard the public health.

8. Honor your profession by serving in an MCI without self-concern or demands for compensation or remuneration for service. Avoid opportunism and the lures of fame and fortune.

CONCLUSIONS

MCIs and disasters introduce numerous ethical challenges in triage, resource allocation, and patient care at the microlevel (patient care), mesolevel (professional principles), and macrolevel (societal). Prospective consideration of these challenges, disaster drills, and development of ethical MCI policies and protocols can help medical personnel function in a manner compatible with most of the basic ethical principles that guide medicine. To guarantee widespread commitment, ethical MCI policies and procedures must be drafted in advance with the input of both medical leadership and the people delivering actual care in the field. The realities of MCI are difficult to comprehend for anybody who has not "been there"; thus, learning from the experience of those who have been personally involved in MCI and disaster care can benefit medical professionals in all parts of the world who are only now preparing for their first MCI.

REFERENCES

1. Zuger A, Miles SH. Physicians, AIDS, and occupational risk. Historic traditions and ethical obligations. *JAMA*. October 1987;258(14): 1924-8.
2. United Nations High Commissioner for Refugees. Geneva Convention relative to the Treatment of Prisoners of War. Available at: http://www.unhchr.ch/html/menu3/b/91.htm.
3. Priel J, Dolev E. [Ethical considerations in mass casualty situation.] *Harefuah*. July 2001;140(7): 574-7, 680.
4. World Medical Association. Medical ethics in the event of disasters. *Bull Med Ethics*. October 1994;102: 9-11.
5. Larkin, GL, Moskop, J, Derse A, Iserson K. Ethics manual of the American College of Emergency Physicians. Available at: http://www.acponline.org/ethics/ethicman.htm.
6. American Academy of Emergency Medicine. Code of ethics. Available at: http://www.aaem.org/codeofethics/index.shtml.
7. Ethics manual. Fourth edition. American College of Physicians. *Ann Intern Med*. 1998:128(7): 576-94.
8. American Medical Association. Code of medical ethics. H-130.946 AMA Leadership in the Medical Response to Terrorism and Other Disasters. Available at: http://www.ama-assn.org/apps/pf_new/pf_online?f_n=resultLink&doc=policyfiles/HnE/H-130.946.HTM&s_t=disaster&catg=AMA/HnE&catg=AMA/BnGnC&catg=AMA/DIR&&nth=1&&st_p=0&nth=3&, last accessed July 2, 2005.
9. Alexander GC, Wynla MK. Ready and Willing? Physicians' sense of preparedness for bioterrorism. *Health Affairs*. 2003;22: 189-97.
10. World Association for Disaster and Emergency Medicine. Health Disaster Management: Guidelines for Evaluation and Research in the Utstein Style. Available at: http://wadem.medicine.wise.edu/Ch9.htm.
11. Israeli Medical Association. Available at: http://www.ima.org.il/EN/.
12. Garland B. Bioethics and bioterrorism. *J Philosophy Sci Law*. March 2002;Volume 2. Available at: http://www.psljournal.com/archives/newsedit/bioethics_bioterrorism.cfm.
13. The Center for Law and the Public's Health at Georgetown and Johns Hopkins universities. The Model State Emergency Health Powers Act. Available at: http://www.publichealthlaw.net/MSEHPA/MSEHPA2.pdf.
14. International Federation of Red Cross and Red Crescent Societies. Humanitarian ethics in disaster and war. Available at: http://www.ifrc.org/publicat/wdr2003/chapter1.asp.
15. Trotter G. Of terrorism and healthcare: jolting the old habits. *Camb Q Healthc Ethics*. Fall 2002;11(4): 411-14.
16. Kilner T. Triage decisions of prehospital emergency health care providers, using a multiple casualty scenario paper exercise. *Emerg Med J*. July 2002;19(4): 348-53.
17. Hirshberg A, Holcomb JB, Mattox KL. Hospital trauma care in multiple-casualty incidents: a critical view. *Ann Emerg Med*. June 2001;37(6): 647-52.
18. Resnik DB, DeVille KA. Bioterrorism and patient rights: 'compulsory licensure' and the case of Cipro. *Am J Bioeth*. Summer 2002;2(3): 29-39.
19. Raymond NA. Medical neutrality: another casualty of the intifada. *J Ambul Care Manage*. October 2002;25(4): 71-3.
20. Parmet WE. After September 11: rethinking public health federalism. *J Law Med Ethics*. Summer 2002;30(2): 201-11.
21. *Ramifications* [Newsletter of the Richmond Academy of Medicine]. December 2001;13(17): 19. Available at: http://www.msv.org/public/articles/Ramifications_December_01.pdf.
22. Wynla MK, Gostin L. Medicine. The bioterrorist threat and access to health care. *Science*. May 2002;296(5573): 1613.

Write Away

1. Using one of the questions raised in Halpern and Larkin's article, write an op-ed about this ethical dimension of disaster medicine. Ground your op-ed with a recent event or news item relevant to disaster medicine.

2. Halpern and Larkin cite several different codes of ethics related to medicine, each from a different organization. Write a comparative analysis of these codes of ethics. As you develop your analysis, consider the following sorts of questions: What are the similarities and differences among these various codes? What is the significance of any distinctions between the codes? What patterns do you notice across codes? Why do different organizations develop different codes? What would be problematic with one, universal code of ethics related to disaster medicine?

3. Using archival research, write a research-based essay about disaster medicine, drawing on one or more previous disasters, to further explore the longer trajectory of disaster medicine from which Halpern and Larkin's text emerges. You can, for instance, locate old newspaper accounts or photographs, poetry, music, or personal narratives. Or, if you have access to other material artifacts you can include those as well in your research. Contextualize disaster medicine and the disaster(s) you are researching both culturally and historically. In what ways does culture or historical context impact disaster medicine?

Blog Entry: *"It was a special day."* by Salam Pax

> Transfer Points: Journalism, English, History, Digital Studies

"My name is Salam Pax and I am addicted to blogs" (Pax, "I Became").

This is how the Baghdad blogger, Salam Pax, describes his relationship to blogs:

"Some people watch daytime soaps, I follow blogs. I follow the hyperlinks on the blogs I read. I travel through the web guided by bloggers. I get wrapped up in the plots narrated by them. I was reading so many blogs I had to assign weekdays for each bunch, plus the ones I was reading daily" (Pax, "I Became").

His addiction, in part, inspired the 2003 creation of his own blog, "Where is Raed?," which would soon propel Salam Pax to become the "most famous blogger in the world." Salam Pax began his blog in Iraq as a way to communicate with his friend, Raed Jarrar, who was in Jordan working on a master's degree. Apparently, Raed would not respond to emails regularly, so Salam Pax created a blog to provide Raed updates about his life without the expectation of immediate response. As the Iraq invasion soon unfolded, though, "Where is Raed?" would instead become one of the most well-known blogs around the world, providing thousands of readers a first hand, Iraqi citizen's perspective of the Iraq invasion and aftermath.

Creating this blog was no easy feat. Salam Pax took great risk overcoming state-imposed internet censorship and access restrictions, tunneling clandestinely into the internet. Readers were keen to understand daily life in a war zone: "There were days when the Red Crescent was begging for volunteers to help in

> **Salam Pax** (1973-) is a pseudonym for a man named Salam Abdulmunem. He grew up in Iraq, spent time studying in Austria, and then returned to study architecture at the University of Baghdad. He started *Where is Raed?* when he was 29, living at home with his parents in Iraq. After the success of his blog, he began working as a writer for *The Guardian,* and then studied journalism at City University London. After some time living in Beirut, he returned to Baghdad, where he resides now and works as a Communications Officer for UNICEF in Iraq ("Salam Pax").

taking the bodies of dead people off the city street and bury them properly. The hospital grounds have been turned to burial grounds" (Salam Pax, "A Post").

These sorts of unique, on-the-ground, citizen insights found on blogs such as "Where is Raed?" ushered in and solidified a large, growing field of reporting now known as citizen journalism. Also called network journalism, participatory journalism, or Web 2.0 journalism, citizen journalism consists of media coverage by people who are not professional journalists (Matheson). Citizen journalism has challenged and influenced traditional forms of media, disrupting mainstream media, and privileging more civic forms of journalism (Matheson).

Citizen journalism exists alongside similar initiatives in other disciplines. For instance, citizen scientists conduct scientific research, and citizen historians curate historical artifacts and create historical narratives. Across disciplines, such efforts dismantle barriers between those who are perceived to be experts and nonexperts, and enable many different forms of experience and knowledge to work together in advancing understanding and awareness.

Much citizen journalism, as with Salam Pax's, emerges through digital technologies such as microblogs or blogs, relying on social media networks to disseminate information to thousands of people. They can appear in the form of photographs, videos, prose, or blended formats. Written microblog posts can consist of a few characters, written blog posts can contain 200 words, and long-form blog posts can be 1,000 words or more.

Blogs can be personal in nature, documenting one individual's experiences, they can be organized around a central topic or theme, such as food, travel, or politics, or they can operate as news feeds or filters, by compiling news items from and about other sources (Rettberg). Blogs often transect these broad categories, and they can be authored by individuals or groups, experts, professionals, or amateurs. Many scholars create blogs as a way of engaging in public scholarship, sharing their research with broader publics.

Blogs also vary widely in reach. Salam Pax's blog, for instance, began with 26 hits a day, and then ascended to 20,000 hits a day after a widely read blogger linked to "Where is Raed?" (Dane).

Scholars in literature, digital culture, cultural studies, and American studies, might examine blogs such as Salam Pax's by posing questions about genre and culture: How are blogs authentic and inauthentic? How might we understand networks of interaction through blogging? What stylistic features of writing inform blogging? How does blogging influence other forms of writing? In what ways do blogs reflect and shape culture?

Many other scholars across disciplines engage in research about and with blogs. For example, those in science communication or environmental studies research how science is disseminated and understood through blogs. Cultural anthropologists conduct virtual ethnographies, participating in and analyzing digital texts to understand a culture, community, or group of people. Scholars in computer science, engineering, and information science use data analytics to improve platforms and understand usage. Scholars in health sciences examine blogging's impact on health support, education, and communication. And, scholars in business analyze blogs for research about product development, marketing, and advertising.

As these many examples suggest, blogs are among the most transferable genres of writing. They are applicable to and of interest to nearly all disciplines. Such broad range also helps explain how people like Salam Pax can actually become addicted to blogs. In point of fact, psychologists have even studied addictive behaviors in online contexts. But, actual addiction aside, blogs such as "Where is Raed?," enabled by digital platforms, have provided an unprecedented range of and access to perspectives and experiences around the world. In so doing, citizen journalism such as Salam Pax's has vastly expanded our understanding of events and our awareness of how these events impact people who might otherwise be less visible through traditional media coverage.

Write Here

What blogs, if any, do you read? Describe why you read them and what your reading practices are with them? If you do not read any blogs, describe what you have heard about blogs.

Salam Pax
"It was a special day."

THURSDAY, JANUARY 22, 2004

It was a special day.

Here I am, drinking vodka alone at 3 in the morning, in the house of my family. One year ago I was staying in Amman, waiting for my visa to go to Saudi Arabia to marry my first love and ex-fiancé, I was finishing my studies for Masters Degree, and I was working as an architect in a small engineering office.

I will not exaggerate and pretend this is my first jump between my parallel universes, because I had previous heroic hyper jumps in the past.

But this year witnessed two jumps.

Jump raed jump jump jump

The first was on the 19th of Feb. of last year, when I decided to leave my work, my house, and to leave heba and come to Iraq.

Why?

She didn't answer my calls, so I pushed the disappear button.

This is when everyone starts to wonder "where is raed"

I came to Baghdad, I was completely destroyed, without energy, sleeping all the day and night waiting for war to happen, to conceder it the as the "reason" for my miserable life. The war started and explosions helped me forget the rest of my feelings towards heba.

War stopped, and statues were pulled in a dramatic way.

My national feelings pushed me to start something that can make the world see how bad this war was, so I started working on a massive scale survey on war casualties, for months, going on trips to the nine cites of the south weekly, and establishing a huge network of volunteers, monitor them, designing the survey forms and administrating the data input procedure.

More than 4000 injured, more than 2000 killed, just from civilians, all with full documentation and details about the time and place of incidents, and their addresses. My American partner was supposed to publish the results, but she didn't.

After we finished the survey, I started establishing another network of volunteers .. Emaar

.. in the nine cities of the south and Baghdad. 100 volunteers were the result of one month selection period that I met around 1500 persons in, around 30 of the 100 were girls, working all together in teams to identify small problems in the neighborhoods and implementing micro projects depending on the local people's contribution, to give them more trust in themselves and to market the political idea of giving Iraqis the chance to rebuild their countries by themselves.

Meanwhile I had a romantic story that was getting more serious day by day, and making me a worse person day by day too.

After the UN explosion, fund raising started being impossible, and our only funding agency stopped to fund us for political reasons.

My private life was falling apart in parallel to Emaar, slowly and painfully.

Even working with salam, for the BBC, and writing stuff on this blog wasn't making me comfortable. For many reasons.

Today was a special day

I stood in front of everyone in the NGOs meeting, and told them "I'm sorry to announce the death of Emaar in 9 of the 10 governorates that we used to work in" We still have work in the marshes of Nasrya.

I'm tired, and I cant knock more doors

The team of Nasrya are arranging themselves without needing me for support.

Good for them

Emotional wise.

I erased her phone number from my phonebook, preventing other stupid attempts of going back.

Why?

Because she cannot say good morning. I want her to say good morning when we wake up.

But she can't.

Salam:

I'll stop blogging here. Without swimming in the mud of details: you are not the best partner in the world, and I'm not the best blogger too.

I emailed the Jordanian University to tell them I'm not going to resume my masters degree studies. Its way too complicated for me now. I'll take my diploma certificate and stop.

And I emailed a friend in London telling her about my great achievements of today.

I burned out myself. Wzzzzssssss……

Today was a special day, but this Russian vodka made it better.

Jump jump jump
:")

Write Away

1. Melissa Wall defines citizen journalism as "news content (text, video, audio, interactives, etc.) produced by nonprofessionals. Such content may capture a single moment (e.g., witnessing an event), be intermittent (e.g., a Twitterfeed), or be regularly produced such as by hyper-local news operators" (798). Using Salam Pax's text as evidence, write an essay in which you discuss the limitations, advantages, and features of citizen journalism. Consider such questions as: What does this blog accomplish that traditional media might not be able to? Why do you think citizen journalism has become so popular? What, if any, are the limitations of citizen journalism?

2. Several theoretical frames exist for examining blogs. One might look at genre, narcissism, authenticity, and/or performance. Choose a theoretical frame and a blog, and write a synthesis essay in which you apply that theoretical frame to an analysis of the blog. In what ways does the blog you have selected illustrate, challenge, or otherwise prompt insights about the theoretical frame? How does your analysis generate insights about the blog or about blogs more generally?

3. "Where is Raed?" can be considered part of a subset of texts known as war correspondence, and which includes not only blogs, but also soldiers' diaries and letters, current and historical. Write a literature review about war correspondence. You can choose a particular war, a time period, particular people, or a particular region. Identify relevant primary and secondary materials. What is the field of research on war correspondence? Where are the gaps in research or opportunities for future research?

❧ ❧ ❧

Chapter 3 Key Terms

questions

inquiry

significance

disciplinary context

heuristic

modalities

Write Away

Form a team with three to five classmates to engage in pyramid building with questions. In so doing, you will gain experience with the process of developing and narrowing questions and with the ways in which questions are influenced by disciplines.

Establish a pyramid base. Person A writes down a general question that matters to him or her, along with the kind of research one would need to conduct in order to pursue that question. This question will serve as the pyramid's base.

Add a second layer to your pyramid. Person B takes Person A's question and refines it in order to create another level of the pyramid, narrowing the question and inflecting it with a related disciplinary perspective and also indicating what kind of research would now need to be done in order to successfully pursue that question.

Continue building your pyramid. Person C takes Person B's question, and so on, repeating the process until all members of the group have had the opportunity to refine and reshape a question.

Round two. Repeat the process again, using a different Person A and beginning with a different question to build a second pyramid. Or, as an optional challenge, instead see how high you can get your first pyramid to go, by adding on increasingly specific questions with each new turn.

Transfer Hub: Contribute your ideas and see what others have written at fountainheadpress.com/transferhub.

Reflect. As a group, reflect on how the questions shifted across context and what you learned about the process of posing meaningful questions (what was challenging, surprising, inspiring, etc.?).

Reading

Pinpointing Chapter 4

Chapter 4 expands on Chapter 3 by providing you the opportunity to explore how to use the questions you develop for your writing to motivate your choices about which texts to read and how to read them. To provide you with strategies for *reading in transit*, this chapter addresses the following concepts:

- Choosing What to Read: Primary, Secondary, and Tertiary Reading Materials
- Deciding How to Locate Reading Materials
- Deciding How to Read: Shallow and In-Depth Reading Strategies
- Invoking Discipline-Specific Reading Skills

After exploring reading, the next chapter addresses summary, one of several specific ways in which writers respond to, extend, challenge, and otherwise make use of the reading they engage with throughout the research and writing process.

Chichén Itzá, located in the Yucatan Peninsula, was once a thriving city. The Mayans settled there in the sixth century CE. The Pyramid of Kukulcan, also known as El Castillo, is one of the seven wonders of the world, in part because of the precise astronomical features of its design. On the first day of spring and the first day of fall (the Vernal Equinoxes), the setting sun casts a shadow across the stairs in the image of a long snake that appears to be "slithering" down the stairs. This snake is said to represent the god for whom the temple is named: "The feathered snake, Kukulcan, was the most important god for the people who lived here" (Lopata).

Other buildings at Chichén Itzá also illustrate Mayan expertise with astronomy: El Caracol, "the observatory," has "narrow shaftlike windows [that] frame important astronomical events. One...window marks an appearance of Venus at a particular point on the horizon...once every eight years" ("About Alignments").

Another well-known structure at Chichén Itzá is the Great Ball Court, where Mayans played tlachtli, or in Mayan, pok-ta-pok. This game involved a ball that players kept in the air "by hitting it with the hips, thighs or upper arms and bouncing it off the side walls. Use of the hands or feet was forbidden." Scholars hypothesize that the ball had symbolic astronomical significance: "preventing the ball from hitting the ground may have represented maintaining the orbit of the Sun or Venus."

Tlachtli was violent. The ball was so heavy that it killed some players upon impact. Myth holds that "the winning Captain would present his own head to the losing Captain, who then decapitate[d] him" as an act of great honor to facilitate his entry to heaven ("Great Ball Court"). Depictions of the game found on three detailed stone carvings on site, however, suggest that it was actually the losing team's captain who faced beheading. Whoever actually was decapitated at the end of a game, their bones apparently may have been crushed to create a white powder that was then used as a dusting to cover a flint game ball known as "White Flint" ("General"; "Great Ball Court"; "Mayan Ball Game").

Scholars have been able to acquire this knowledge about Chichén Itzá by *reading* all sorts of *texts:* anything from wall carvings, hieroglyphics, and Maya Codices to bones, ancient chronicles, travel narratives, prior scholarship, and architecture itself. Reading broadly, in this way, is a cornerstone of academic writing, and scholars across disciplines read numerous kinds of texts in the course of their research. They build on, extend, examine, modify, revisit, rebut, and otherwise respond to what others have written or produced. They read evidence and data to draw conclusions and make arguments.

Still, as ubiquitous as reading is, it nevertheless can present deep challenges. Nicholas Carr, himself an author of several books, confesses that sustained reading, for him, can be difficult: "[M]y concentration often starts to drift after two or three pages. I get fidgety, lose the thread, begin looking for something else to do. I feel as if I'm always dragging my wayward brain back to the text."

Reading closely, as Carr suggests, requires energy and sustained concentration. But another issue that makes reading especially challenging is that nearly everything about how we read and what we read can shift depending on our disciplinary perspective, the writing occasion, and our aims and purposes. Reading well demands that academic writers be reflective and deliberate in taking context into account on a continuing basis.

Fostering this kind of deliberateness requires an approach to reading that centers on making choices… choices about what to read, how much to read, how closely to read, when to read, and who to read.

Write Here

Archaeologists read all sorts of texts for their research—stones, bones, buildings, images, garments, etc. Imagine you are an archaeologist thousands of years from now and have just discovered your campus, perfectly preserved, though without human presence. What different kinds of texts—broadly defined to include words, material artifacts, and abstract concepts—would you read to understand the campus? What might you learn from reading each of these different texts? Might any of these texts yield conflicting or contradictory insights about your campus?

Choosing What to Read: Primary, Secondary, and Tertiary Reading Materials

What do academic writers read? Everything! If you think academic reading only involves specialized texts with elevated language, minimal pictures or images, and scores of footnotes, think again. While these kinds of texts certainly do accomplish important work and play a significant role in academic writing, academic writers read a broad and varied array of texts.

They *read* visual images, websites, data sets, social media, newspapers, magazines, novels, speeches, poetry, comics, artwork, policy briefs, musical soundtracks,

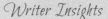

Writer Insights

What kinds of texts do you read?

I read cartoons for a living. People often say: "You get to just look at cartoons all day—that's not work!" But it is—and lots of it. I research nearly 5,000 editorial cartoons: one artist's body of work for the last 20 years of South African democracy. Visual analysis is serious stuff. Not all political cartoons are funny, and my goal is to better understand them. I'm looking for links, patterns, trends—none of which I know for sure I'll find. They're there, but will I see them? It can be daunting, exciting, sobering, terrifying—some days all four.

~Gregory Paitaki, Ph.D. Candidate, Film & Media Studies, Cape Town, South Africa

performances, and even human and animal actions and interactions. Scholars "read" numbers, solids, liquids, gasses, and earth matter.

Choosing what to read and where to look depends on the context of the writing project. There are four questions you can use to help you determine more specifically your writing context so you can make reading choices that best fit your aims.

1. What is the disciplinary context for your writing project?

If you are working within a particular discipline, it's likely a good idea to read texts that emerge from that discipline. The psychology student writing the paper we imagined earlier, for instance, would likely read scholarly articles about violence and video games that are written from a psychological perspective, and he would engage in research methods that are consonant with psychology research. Academic writers also will apply frameworks from one discipline to another, or engage with multiple disciplinary perspectives, but in these cases they also ground their research in some way within their disciplines.

2. What are your research questions?

Your research questions will help you make choices about what to read. For instance, our psychology student will likely be searching library databases and internet search engines for materials that have to do with video games and with violent behavior among adolescents. He will need to decide how to define the word "violent" (only extreme, or also milder forms?) and may decide to narrow the research question to an age range of 13- to 15-year-olds or only adolescents with a particular socioeconomic background. Developing a specific and relevant research question (see Chapter 3: Posing Meaningful Questions) will enable you to identify a more manageable range of potential reading materials.

3. What is your research methodology?

Chapter 2: Research and Writing as a Process discusses different kinds of research methodologies (quantitative, qualitative, or mixed). If you were writing the psychology paper, would you plan to conduct interviews, distribute surveys, engage in observation, or conduct a review of existing research? If you decided to conduct interviews, you'd expect to analyze the interviews and also read other examples of interviews in psychology so you can build on and draw from that research. As you decide upon your research methods, you will be better able to choose the kinds of readings with which you may want to engage.

4. What kind of writing project are you creating?

The amount and type of reading you do depend on the length, style, and tone of your writing project. Writing projects that are more scholarly in nature require more scholarly reading. The writer in psychology would likely draw on a variety of sources, reading about how popular culture portrays violence in video games alongside reading interview transcripts and actual scenes from video games, as well as more scholarly articles and books about violence and video games.

Once you have asked and reflected on these questions, you will be in a better position to actually choose your reading materials. The three main categories of reading from which academic writers choose, each outlined in more detail, are as follows: primary materials, secondary materials, and tertiary materials.

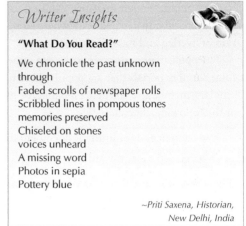

Writer Insights

"What Do You Read?"

We chronicle the past unknown through
Faded scrolls of newspaper rolls
Scribbled lines in pompous tones
memories preserved
Chiseled on stones
voices unheard
A missing word
Photos in sepia
Pottery blue

~Priti Saxena, Historian,
New Delhi, India

Primary Materials

Primary materials are direct, original, firsthand sources, texts, or data. They include data sets, statistics, letters, novels, speeches, photographs, artifacts, etc. The writer working on violence in video games might read any number of primary materials, like:

- transcripts from interviews with adolescents
- results from a survey sent to people in mental health care, adolescents, parents, people affiliated with the K-12 public school system, or members of the judicial system
- images and scenes from actual video games, such as *Call of Duty* or *Grand Theft Auto*
- data from a heart-rate monitor or blood-pressure cuff measuring the rates of people before, during, and after playing the games
- statistics on violence and video games
- posts in an online gaming forum such as gtaforums.com

Secondary Materials

Secondary materials are those written about a particular question or idea. The University of California at Berkeley Library describes secondary materials in this way: "Secondary sources describe, interpret, analyze, evaluate, explain, comment on, or develop theories related to a topic. They are often written after-the-fact, with hindsight." Secondary materials can further be differentiated along the continuum of popular to scholarly as shown in Figure 4.1.

Popular Secondary Sources   Public Scholarship Secondary Sources   Scholarly Secondary Sources

FIGURE 4.1 Continuum of secondary materials.

Keep in mind, though, that texts will rarely be located at either end of the spectrum; they instead are usually perched somewhere along the continuum, and there is usually some measure of overlap and multiplicity.

Popular secondary sources can appear online or in print; nearly all disciplines have some set of materials that are popular in nature. Popular secondary sources can be written by scholars, members of the general public, or professional writers. They often have one or more of the following characteristics:

- absence of (or limited) documentation, bibliographic citations, and footnotes
- geared more toward the general public in tone, style, and content

The writer who is working on the video games and violence research essay in her psychology course might use any or all of the following as popular secondary sources:

- a "60-Minutes" broadcast titled "Can a Video Game Lead to Murder? Did *Grand Theft Auto* Cause One Teenager to Kill?"
- an article from *Newsweek*, "This Is Your Brain on Alien Killer Pimps of Nazi Doom," by journalist Karen Springen
- a blog post on computerworld.com by freelance writer Darlene Storm, "Not Again: Stop Blaming Violent Video Games for Mass Shootings"
- a book by writers Dave Grossman and Gloria DeGaetano titled *Stop Teaching Our Kids to Kill: A Call to Action against TV, Movie & Video Game Violence*

Public scholarship is becoming increasingly prevalent as scholarship becomes more accessible through online platforms. Public scholarship is geared toward a general readership, but is written, created, or produced by a scholar and contains some attentiveness to documentation, bibliography, and citation. It is not what we might label fully *scholarly*, though, because public scholarship usually does not go through as rigorous or as official a peer review process.

Our student writing on video games and violence for her psychology class may use the following kinds of public scholarship sources:

- a podcast titled "Violent Video Games—What Does the Research Say?" by Michael (Ph.D. Psychology) on the website "The Psych Files"
- an article by Professor of Psychology at San Diego State University, Jean M. Twenge, published in *Psychology Today*, titled "Yes, Violent Video Games Do Cause Aggression"
- a video titled *Game Over: Gender, Race and Violence in Video Games*, by Nina Huntemann, associate professor of media studies at Suffolk University
- a brief summary of previous research on this topic, titled "Violence in the Media—Psychologists Study TV and Video Game Violence for Potential Harmful Effects," posted on the American Psychological Association website (apa.org)

Scholarly secondary sources appear online or in print and are, like public scholarship, written by academics. Scholarly secondary sources, however, are distinguished by the following characteristics:

- published by university presses or scholarly organizations
- documented extensively with citations and footnotes
- geared in tone, style, and content toward a postsecondary reader
- vetted through the formal peer review process. This process (depicted in Figure 4.2) involves review and approval of a manuscript by peer experts. These peers decide whether a manuscript deserves to be published by whether it meets publication and disciplinary standards for research and academic integrity.

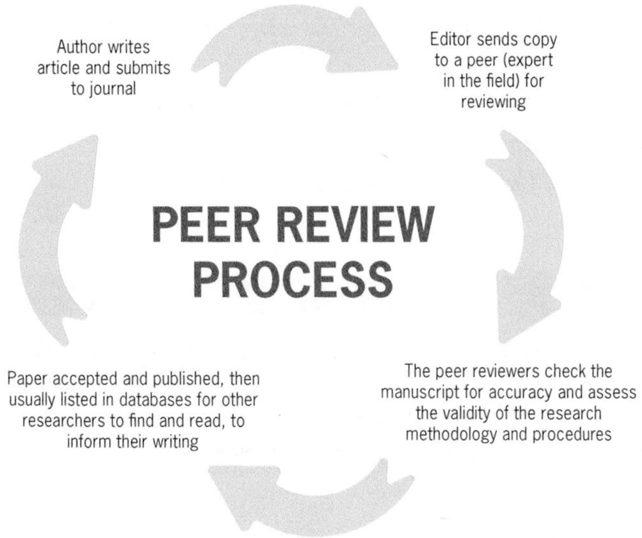

Author writes article and submits to journal

Editor sends copy to a peer (expert in the field) for reviewing

PEER REVIEW PROCESS

Paper accepted and published, then usually listed in databases for other researchers to find and read, to inform their writing

The peer reviewers check the manuscript for accuracy and assess the validity of the research methodology and procedures

FIGURE 4.2 Peer review process.

Our student writer researching violence in video games might read the following scholarly sources:

- an article by scholars Brad J. Bushman and L. Rowell Huesmann published in the peer-reviewed journal *European Psychologist*: "Twenty-Five Years of Research on Violence in Digital Games and Aggression Revisited: A Reply to Elson and Ferguson (2013)"
- an article by scholar Tobias Greitemeyer published in the *Journal of Experimental Social Psychology:* "Intense Acts of Violence During Video Game Play Make Daily Life Aggression Appear Innocuous: A New Mechanism Why Violent Video Games Increase Aggression"

- a book by scholars Craig A. Anderson, Douglas A. Gentile, and Katherine E. Buckley, published by Oxford University Press: *Violent Video Game Effects on Children and Adolescents: Theory, Research, and Public Policy*

Tertiary materials

Tertiary materials include reference works about a certain area of research. They can include such items as encyclopedias, dictionaries, or indexes. The writer working on violence in video games might read any of the following kinds of tertiary materials:

- the *Encyclopedia of Video Games: The Culture, Technology, and Art of Gaming*, edited by Mark J. P. Wolf. This encyclopedia has more than 300 entries on terms, games, and people related to the video game industry
- the *Encyclopedia of 20th-Century Technology*, edited by Colin A. Hempstead and William E. Worthington
- the *Wikipedia: WikiProject Video games/Reference library*
- the *Guinness World Records Gamer's Edition*
- *A Dictionary of Video Game Theory* by Jesper Juul

Write Now

Think about a research question you will be exploring this term. For that question, brainstorm several ideas for primary, secondary, and tertiary materials you might choose to read. For the secondary materials, be sure to include a range of texts that exist throughout the continuum of popular writing, public scholarship, and scholarly writing.

Deciding How to Locate Reading Materials

Given that academic writers draw upon so many different kinds of reading materials for their research and writing, they face numerous options for locating those materials. While it may seem that mastering a few strategies would suffice, writers should build a flexible repertoire of options for locating materials. From this, they can tailor their approaches with each new writing occasion. Perhaps some disciplines will use certain strategies to a greater or lesser extent, but over time, writers will likely have the opportunity to incorporate a wide range of materials.

A transfer-based approach to writing emphasizes that writers learn how to identify what kinds of reading materials will best enable them to pursue their research for any given writing project, and, from there, make optimal decisions about how best to locate, explore, and discover those reading materials. You will encounter a diverse range of writing occasions in undergraduate work and beyond, many of which will require you to seek primary materials, popular or scholarly secondary materials, public scholarship, and tertiary materials. To do this, you will likely make use of many of the following search strategies.

Transfer at Work

Psychologist James Hartley surveyed 156 scholars across the arts, social sciences, and sciences about how they use book reviews for their teaching and research. Almost all reported reading one to five book reviews each month, but more writers in the arts and social sciences labeled book reviews useful or very useful:

TABLE 5. Ratings of the value of book reviews for teaching and research.

Question: How useful are book reviews for your teaching/for your research?

		Teaching	Research
Arts	Useful or very useful	60%	85%
Social sciences	Useful or very useful	51%	72%
Sciences	Useful or very useful	25%	50%

Hartley's research shows that scholars across disciplines use the same kinds of reading materials, but that disciplinary context impacts why they do so and how integral particular reading materials are for their work.

Data collection

Data collection serves as a large, umbrella concept referring to a variety of strategies, approaches, and study designs for collecting data that researchers across disciplines enact. Scholars across many disciplines acquire their primary reading materials through experiments, field research, interviews, or other forms of data collection. The datasets, research results, field notes, and other data they collect then become the primary reading material these researchers use to explore their research questions and develop their arguments. The particular type of data collection, field research, or experimentation, along with the methods a researcher uses, will depend on the writing occasion and the particular research questions being pursued.

Often, disciplinary context influences how writers collect data. Writers in disciplines such as anthropology, environmental studies, and archaeology, for instance, might visit field sites in order to collect their primary reading materials. Meanwhile, an evolutionary anthropologist might travel to South America to collect data on primate behavior through observation, and an environmental scientist might travel to Alaska to measure ice flow. Data collection also includes the results researchers gather from interviews, surveys, and focus groups. A sociologist or marketing analyst might collect interview or survey data for primary reading material. The psychology student exploring video games might set up a controlled experiment to measure users' blood pressure during violent moments of a particular video game, or she might conduct field research by attending a video game convention, such as PAX, the Penny Arcade Expo, to interview game manufacturers and users. Of course, all of these forms of data collection and primary reading materials are transferrable, and a scholar in any field might draw on any sort of data collection, so long as it fits his or her aims and works to yield effective data for primary reading purposes.

Libraries and archives

Libraries and archives are among the most frequently utilized repositories for locating reading materials across disciplines. Libraries contain not only books, but also many other sorts of reading materials, including magazines, journals, maps, images, and artifacts. Since libraries are frequently organized by subject area, writers can use the library catalog or the library shelves to find a text that works for their research, and then browse around that text to locate other related texts. Many libraries also house archives, which are specialized collections of materials and artifacts. Many scholars locate reading materials by visiting important archives (online or in person), such as the Archives of African American Music and Culture at Indiana University, Bloomington. Our writer in psychology, for instance, might decide to include some archival research by visiting the Computer and Video Gaming Archive at the University of Michigan, where they house an impressive collection of video games from the 1970s to the present (Carter).

Because of their enormous range and quantity of holdings, libraries and archives can seem daunting to researchers, and it can sometimes be challenging to find relevant items among so many different materials. As such, libraries and archives should be approached as spaces for discovery and exploration, where researchers can read among and around items as a way of moving toward developing and understanding their research inquiries. Library catalogs and research databases (see section below) help researchers explore and discover the reading materials that will best assist them with their research. Another helpful resource is academic librarians, who are highly skilled with information science and welcome the opportunity to help students find reading materials. Many librarians have even created **library guides**, which are online resource documents created to supplement undergraduate courses by outlining research methods in specialized disciplines or topics. Figure 4.3 is an example of a library guide created by librarian John Holmes for a psychology course at the University

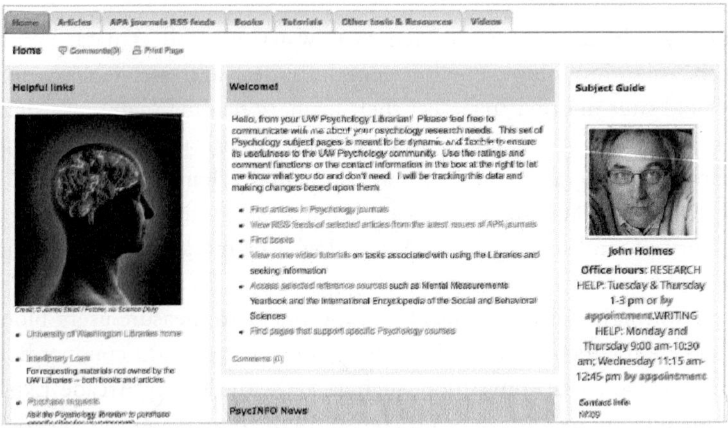

FIGURE 4.3 University of Washington library guide.

of Washington. From this library guide, our violence and video games writer could explore articles, books, and specialized journals in psychology.

Internet search engines

Although internet searching alone is not sufficient for research in most academic contexts, it can be a useful starting point for some research endeavors. Since many people are accustomed to using internet search engines for everyday queries, they can approach research as an opportunity to transfer their personal experiences into academic contexts. Typing in a random key term to Google or Bing might yield many unrelated results, and so finding relevant materials requires careful consideration of what key terms to deploy. Key terms should be as precise as possible in order to maximize the likelihood that the results will be related to your research.

Researchers should also keep in mind that internet search engines are governed by complex algorithms that determine what results will emerge from a particular search. These algorithms include measurements of popularity and commercial influence, alongside relevance and other factors. In addition, internet search engines do not return every single result possible for a search, and so internet searches leave much undiscovered. Finally, results from most internet searches must also be carefully evaluated for authenticity and reliability, since internet search engines do not necessarily measure for these factors, either. For these reasons, if you choose to begin your research with an internet search, you will at some point need to move on from internet searching to research databases.

Research databases

Research databases are more specific and far reaching than general internet search engines in that they identify more scholarly research and yield more focused results. Research databases can be general in nature or highly specialized according to discipline or topic. General research databases include, for example, Google Scholar, JSTOR, ProQuest, or AcademicOne. These research databases often have additional tools that can help researchers, such as citation assistance (which also warrant double-checking since they can contain errors), or advanced search components that can assist with research. For instance, when you conduct a research database search and get a list of results, you might encounter "cited by" or "related articles" links, which show you other relevant texts that have cited or are related to the original text result. Another advanced tool involves tailoring your search to include only particular types of materials, such as only popular (i.e., magazines and newspapers) or only peer reviewed, or a mix. Research databases also enable you to specify a certain date range

Writer Insights

Why is knowing how to conduct research important in your field?

Compared to other literary genres, perhaps Historical Fiction is the most tedious to write. In my work, I spend most of my time doing research. I want to make sure that my story sticks to accurate historical facts up to the smallest detail—like what kind of soap did eleventh century Europeans use; and did they use the same soap to wash their clothes? If you know how to do proper research, you'll find the answers you seek—I did.

~Anna Teodoro-Suanco, Novelist,
Manila, Philippines

for results should you want to focus on more contemporary research or should you have a historical date range with which you are working.

Discipline-specific research databases

These databases will provide a range of sources pertinent to a particular discipline. You can identify discipline-specific research databases through one of the library guides mentioned above or by asking a librarian. When you search in a discipline-specific research database, you can narrow results to return only popular sources (such as magazines and newspapers), only peer-reviewed journals, or a combination of both. You can also specify a certain date range for results. In contrast to more general research databases, these databases will likely offer a larger set of relevant materials and offer more flexibility with tailoring your search. For example, databases relevant to video games and violence in psychology might include any the following: Psycinfo, Web of Science, PubMed, or PsycCRITIQUES. From here, the writer would use one of these discipline-specific research databases to search for articles and materials on violence and video games.

#followthebreadcrumbs

One of the savviest ways to identify and explore reading materials is to follow the bread crumbs from other scholars. Look to see what others working in your area of research have been reading and use these materials as a starting point for your own research. You might think of this process of interconnection as resembling hashtags in Twitter or tags on a blog. For instance, each time you find a relevant text, look through that text's bibliographies to see what reading materials are included. You can then accumulate and explore those reading materials for your work. Examining others' bibliographic sections will also give you a sense of who the major academic figures are in a given scholarly conversation. For instance, in the field of violence and video games one of the more well-known scholars is Douglas A. Gentile, a developmental psychologist at Iowa State University, Ames, and editor of the book *Media Violence and Children*. Researchers can surmise Gentile's popularity because a preponderance of texts on video games mention and make use of his work. It is likely that our student writer would probably want to refer in some capacity to Gentile's work since he is a major figure in this area of research.

Another strategy for locating and exploring reading materials is to use others' bibliographic research as tertiary material. For instance, a search for a literature review on a particular topic or issue may yield several promising results that can offer you starting points for your own materials search. In our example case, a literature review on violence and video games, titled "Literature Review on the Impact of Playing Violent Video Games on Aggression," was prepared for the Australian government by the Attorney General's Office. It describes the current research on video games and violence. Keep in mind, though, that what is current now may soon be outdated, so you should always be aware of the dates of materials on literature reviews so you can supplement, if needed, with additional current research.

Another helpful bibliographic and tertiary source that enables you to follow others' bread crumbs is an **annotated bibliography,** which is a list of relevant sources on a particular topic with brief summaries or descriptions. Researchers often prepare annotated bibliographies as a way of compiling research on a given topic or issue so other scholars can benefit from their bibliographic research.

Deciding How to Read: Shallow and In-Depth Reading Strategies

Given how very much there is available to read, academic writers must not only choose what to read, but they must make continual choices about which materials to devote considerable energy to and which materials they can devote less energy to. While you may have thought that all academic reading requires intense concentration and effort, academic writers often make use of other reading strategies. Sometimes they need to get up to speed quickly on a topic, or sometimes they are looking for one particular portion of a text that is more closely relevant to their research.

The bottom line is this: you cannot possibly read everything about a topic, and academic writers make continual choices about where to devote their reading energy. The key is learning to make good decisions about what warrants different levels of reading effort.

This set of choices creates a continuum of reading practices that can be usefully differentiated by the terms shallow and in-depth as shown in Figure 4.4.

Shallow Reading   **In-Depth Reading**

FIGURE 4.4 Continuum of reading practices.

It's important to note that the most effective academic writers combine these reading strategies rather than practicing only one kind of strategy.

Shallow reading

The name might seem derogatory, but **shallow reading** really does play a large, important role in academic writing. Alice Horning offers the following explanation for the importance of learning how to read faster while at the same time demonstrating how fast reading does not equate to sloppy or poor reading: "People need to read faster, just because the amount of material is growing exponentially. People need to read better, too, because it's no good to read fast if readers can't recall and use the information. That is, readers must be able to go beyond main ideas to analysis, synthesis and evaluation." While the in-depth reading strategies outlined will offer additional ways of getting "beyond main ideas," readers also need to hone their skills with shallower reading practices.

Anne Mangen, a professor at the Reading Centre at the University of Stavanger, Norway, describes "shallower" forms of reading as being characterized by "scanning and browsing." Ziming Liu, professor of library science at San Jose State University, further describes shallower forms of reading as that which includes "browsing and scanning, keyword spotting, [and] one-time reading."

Writer Insights

How do you ready shallowly?

I read IT blogs at mssqltips.com and sqlbog.com, twitter feeds #SQLHelp, and *ComputerWorld* magazine. I read the first 2 paragraphs first and the last 2 paragraphs next. Then I skim the middle.

~*Ameena Lalani, Database Administrator, Chicago, Illinois, U.S.*

This kind of shallower reading occurs in our daily lives as we browse the sports, news, or entertainment sections of a website, or as we scroll through social networking sites. But academic writers also make use of shallower forms of reading quite often. We skim through texts or data sets quickly for various reasons:

- to determine if the texts or data are relevant for our research
- to identify the main points, arguments, or key terms
- to look for the portions that are most important for our research
- to get a quick sense of the landscape of research on which we can build

Reading a text quickly and efficiently, or shallowly, often involves:

- reading the abstract
- reading the signposts of the text (i.e., title, section headings)
- looking for signals of phrases indicating significance, such as: I argue that…or the main point is
- reading the introduction and conclusion

Write Now

Reflect for ten minutes on what kinds of texts you have recently read in shallower ways and what kinds of texts you have recently read in more in-depth ways. What drove your decision on how to read these texts? Which kinds of reading practices worked more effectively for you to accomplish your particular purposes?

In-depth reading

At the other end of the reading spectrum, and also a strategy of great importance, is what Liu calls "**in-depth reading** [or] concentrated reading" (700). This form, Liu maintains, is characterized by "sustained attention...[a]nnotating and highlighting" (700). We engage with in-depth reading, also known as active reading, in our leisure reading as well, particularly if we come across a post or image that interests us or motivates us to understand it more fully. Academic writers make use of in-depth forms of reading quite often, particularly

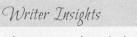

Writer Insights

What are some of your in-depth reading practices?

When writing for research, I read and take notes, organize my notes thematically, and write reflections.

~Y., English as a Foreign Language Teacher,
Kyiv, Ukraine

when we want to really grapple with ideas or think carefully about the ideas in the readings. We read texts or data sets using in-depth strategies in order to:

- interpret and analyze
- remember more carefully what we are reading
- find quotes or data to integrate into our own arguments
- pose questions

To read materials in more in-depth ways, first start with the shallow reading practices outlined above, then read the material multiple times. These multiple encounters with a text will enable you to process ideas more completely, taking the time to think about the ideas and let them percolate. Reading in-depth often includes annotating readings and writing about what you read.

Annotating a text, also known as marginal note-taking, involves taking notes while reading. As you read, engage with the text as though you were having a conversation with the author(s). Think about your annotations in terms of both noting main points and recording your thought process while reading. Figure 4.5 is a page of text illustrating annotations. The page is a selection of text from an article called "Arts of the Contact Zone," by Mary Louise Pratt. The specifics of the annotations might not make complete sense to you, but the point is not for you to be able to understand another's annotations so much as to get a general sense of how a scholar engages with a text during in-depth reading. Note that annotations do not entail merely highlighting sentences but active thought through your reading of the text. The annotations address points such as:

- questions you have about the text
- words/terms with which you are unfamiliar
- connections you are noticing between this text and other texts
- points of tension within the text/moments of contradiction
- key terms/ideas from the text
- aspects/ideas that elicit some kind of emotion or affect from you (i.e., surprise, frustration, happiness, agreement, disagreement)

FIGURE 4.5 Annotating during in-depth reading.

Again, Figure 4.5 is not intended to be entirely transparent—it's one writer's personal notes from a highly individual form of in-depth reading. Instead, the image is intended to illustrate what one reader's deep engagement with a text looks like. As a student, you can also engage deeply in this manner in handwritten contexts or by making a separate record of reading notes in a document of your own. If you do use your own document, though, make sure to make specific notes of page numbers or locations of significant passages so you can recall later when reviewing your notes where the passages in question can be found.

Write Now

Choose a text you are currently reading and practice annotating the text. After annotating, reflect for ten minutes about the experience. What did you find challenging about annotating? What worked really well? What do you think you might do differently if you were annotating a different sort of text, for a different course, for example?

Whereas annotating a text and taking notes like those in Figure 4.5 amount to brief moments of writing for in-depth reading, more sustained writing over a period of five or ten minutes (or longer) can further enable you to process what you read. Spending longer periods of time writing about what you read, though still in an informal manner, such as through a directed quickwrite, enables you to discover, analyze, and explore ideas.

Exactly what you choose to write about when you read depends on why you are reading a particular text. Some of the following general questions are possibilities for ways that you can write about what you read.

- What do you take to be the author's purposes?
- What themes do you notice across the data set or field notes?
- What worked well?
- What seemed confusing?
- What seems significant and why?
- What questions do you have and why?
- Which portions shed new light on your research questions?

Two specific strategies for in-depth reading are important to feature here because they are generally applicable to and important for academic writers across disciplines.

Featured in-depth reading strategy: Read like a writer

Composition scholar Mike Bunn argues that students who are interested in developing as academic writers should not only read for content, but should also read texts as writers. Bunn describes the process in this way:

> [I]dentify…the choices the author made so that you can better understand how such choices might arise in your own writing. The idea is to carefully examine the things you read, looking at the writerly techniques in the text in order to decide if you might want to adopt similar (or the same) techniques in your writing…. You are reading to learn about writing.

Bunn's point is that the texts we read must always serve two purposes: to help us learn about and explore a line of inquiry and to provide a model of writing we can then follow, adapt, or

---

Transfer at Work

Disciplinary context shapes how writers approach text annotation. In *Critically Reading the Theory and Methods of Archaeology*, Guy Gibbon advises archaeologists to annotate and critically read texts by considering the following kinds of questions:

"What kind of archaeology is it?"

"How are the observations summarized?"

"Is there a population estimate from a sample?"

"Which research program is my reading an example of?"

"Are concepts given archaeological interpretations?"

By contrast, according to an English professor interviewed for Lisa Bosley's "'I Don't Teach Reading': Critical Reading Instruction in Composition Courses," the approach to text annotation in the context of English Literature includes the following types of questions:

How does the author persuade the reader?

What stylistic, grammatical, or technical devices does the author use?

How does the author appeal to the reader?

How does the author get the reader's attention?

How does the author unfold the argument?

How does the author organize the argument so the reader can access it?

How does the author keep the reader in mind when trying to explain something?

Does the author use poignant examples, comparisons, contrasts, or analogies? (291)

reject in our own work as writers. Reading like a writer focuses on the latter of these purposes, asking that you conduct in-depth reading strategies on the writing choices themselves as made by the author(s). In-depth reading as a writer might include making notes in the text and in a writer's journal of your own about such aspects of the text like:

- overall structure and organization
- types of secondary and primary sources
- integration of evidence
- use of quotes or data
- approaches to introductions and conclusions
- articulation of the argument or position
- integration of visual elements (graphs, charts, tables, images, media, etc.)
- use of signposts. Signposts are phrases that indicate to readers where a writing project is moving. Signposts include such phrases as *For instance…In this essay I will argue …To summarize…Historically…More recently…*
- other aspects specific to a discipline and/or writing occasion

One helpful strategy for in-depth reading of a text's overall structure and organization would be to do a reverse outline of the text (for guidelines on reverse outlining, see Chapter 2, p. 58). Use the texts you are reading as an opportunity to gain more familiarity with writing in particular disciplines and/or in particular writing contexts. For example, if you are learning how to write in the discipline of history, make note of the key features of historical scholarship as you read it for your research. Likely, you will discover a range of (perhaps even conflicting) approaches that you can consider as you develop your own writing acumen.

Again, consider keeping a writer's journal (print or electronic) for you to track ideas about writing that emerge as you read like a writer. Note down the text, the page or section, and what you noticed about the writing. You may not know at a given moment how you might put one of these ideas to use in your own writing, but you will have them collected together. Keeping a writer's journal will also help you acquire the habit of mind of thinking of yourself as a writer.

Featured in-depth reading strategy: Reading rhetorically

Rhetoric can be understood to be the art of persuasion. Reading rhetorically asks that readers approach a text by thinking about how and why the text is attempting to persuade or influence readers. Compositionists Christina Haas and Linda Flower define rhetorical reading as "an active attempt at constructing a rhetorical context for the text as a way of making sense of it" (167-8). Reading rhetorically empowers readers not only to develop a deeper understanding of a text, but also to generate meaning within the text. Reading rhetorically invites readers to consider the rhetorical situation from which the text has emerged. (Chapter 7: Analysis and Chapter 8: Framing Arguments both expand on the concept of rhetorical reading.)

To explore rhetorical reading, let's look at how to utilize the following three aspects of reading rhetorically: exigence-audience-constraints, rhetorical triangle, and the argumentative appeals.

Exigence-audience-constraints

The framework concept of exigence-audience-constraints provides a structured way of examining the rhetorical components that give shape to texts. This structured way of reading rhetorically emerges from the work of Lloyd Bitzer, a rhetorician and professor emeritus at University of Wisconsin-Madison. Bitzer argues that exigence-audience-constraints together form three crucial elements of the "rhetorical situation":

- **Exigence:** the problem that gives rise to an argument
- **Audience:** who can or will be in a position to hear the argument and/or be influenced by the argument
- **Constraints:** the limitations, form, and context within which the argument will be developed and delivered. This includes such matters as discipline, publication context, form limitations, time constraints.

All of these elements shape an argument. The exigence impacts how a writer defines his or her area of inquiry; the audience and constraints work together to shape what a writer chooses to include in his or her argument, and how he or she makes the argument.

Rhetorical triangle

Another way of reading rhetorically is through what is known as the **rhetorical triangle** (Fig. 4.6).

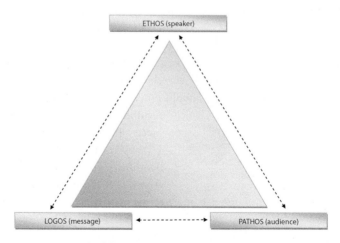

FIGURE 4.6 Rhetorical triangle.

Considering the rhetorical triangle enables readers to understand more about how and why an argument emerged through considering the elements of the triangle. Reading rhetorically means asking questions about these elements in order to construct and create meaning in a text as well as to understand the text more thoroughly.

- **Author:** Who is the author? Why does she care about this topic? What may be influencing her perspective or approach?
- **Audience:** Who is being or can be influenced by a particular text? How is the text shaped in ways that are directed toward these readers? Who do you think is the intended audience and why?
- **Purpose/Message:** What do you understand to be the aim of the text? What is it attempting to accomplish? What are the messages of the text? How is the text organized? What evidence does the writer use to convey the message(s)? How does the writer situate the message(s) within ongoing research and current debates? What might the message(s) reveal about the writing occasion or rhetorical context?

Reading through the lens of Aristotle's argumentative appeals

Aristotle developed a scheme for the ways that rhetoricians can persuade their audiences.

Ethos: persuasion by appealing to readers on the basis of the author's character and authority

Pathos: persuasion by appealing to readers' emotions

Logos: persuasion by appealing to readers' sense of reason and logic

Depending on the context of a particular writing occasion, the frequency of one appeal over the others might be more apparent. Reading rhetorically in this vein, though, asks that readers consider these appeals even if it is only to recognize that one is privileged over the others.

Another term also operates with central importance to Aristotle's approach to rhetoric: *kairos*. **Kairos** can be roughly translated as time. In this context, the concept of time indicates that an argument should emerge at the appropriate time, when that argument will have the highest likelihood of success in persuading its audience.

According to Phillip Sipiora and James Baumlin, *kairos* can be thought of in two ways: (1) Adhering to matters of propriety in terms of writing in such a way as to observe the expectations of any given context and (2) Demonstrating timeliness in that the text is shown to emerge at a "uniquely timely" moment. *Kairos* might thus be understood as the way that a writer situates his or her argument within an awareness of time (timeliness

Transfer at Work

Scholars across disciplines engage with rhetorical analysis. Psychologists Warren Thorngate and Mahin Tavakoli, for example, use rhetorical analysis with their research in public policy, technology, and psychology. In "Simulation, Rhetoric, and Policy Making," they argue that those who develop simulations use rhetorical strategies to accomplish their aims of using the simulations to influence the beliefs and practices of policy makers and to change their attitudes.

for the argument itself and a sense of being contemporary by recognizing the historical moment in which he or she is writing).

Translating these four concepts into a way of reading rhetorically would direct readers to ask the following about a given text (see Table 4.1).

TABLE 4.1 Argumentative appeals questions.

Ethos	How does the writer establish her credibility and/or expertise? What gives her the right to construct and deliver this argument? Why would readers be inclined to consider being persuaded by her?
Pathos	What emotions does the writer invoke for readers? Does the writer appeal to readers' sense of justice, sympathy, love? How does the writer encourage readers to become emotionally invested in the argument?
Logos	What elements of reason and logic are included in the text and how do they work to persuade readers? How does the writer address opposing or modified views?
Kairos	How does the writer attend to content, format, style, and structure in ways that adhere to, modify, or reject conventions and expectations of the discipline, publication context, etc.? How does the writer establish the timeliness of the argument?

These approaches to rhetorical reading can work together as a range of concepts for you to use with in-depth reading. As you can see, they require time and patience and re-reading.

Example of Rhetorical Reading

Review this annotated article about video games to demonstrate rhetorical reading. In this annotation, several approaches to rhetorical reading are fused as a means of illustrating a blended approach. The article, written by undergraduate student Obaid Rashed Aleghfeli at Kaist University in South Korea, was originally published in the *Undergraduate Research Journal for the Human Sciences*. Note that not every rhetorical aspect is annotated here, just a few to provide an example. It is also possible to argue that a rhetorical feature can have multiple components at once. For instance, a particular aspect of the text could be appealing to *logos* and *kairos* simultaneously, or message and purpose could overlap.

Writer Insights

How do you integrate *ethos* in your writing?

How I write cover letters by midnight:

- Off Tweets and research in the target company, especially "About Us" page and qualification requirements

- Drafting time: remember to sound polite but not affected, confident but not pompous, neither above nor below who I am

- Review and ask myself: does it sound good to my ear?

- If not, make changes; if yes, chances are my readers may like it, too

~Jing Hu, Freelance Translator, Urumqi, Xinjiang, China

Rhetorical Reading of "Video Games" by O. Aleghfeli

At the root of the notion of video games is the word "video," which originally meant a kind of electronic device that can show images (Stiles, 2010). In fact the first video games were sometimes called TV games. Having appeared as an experiment for human interaction, video games have changed dramatically and now have become an example of art and a form of business industry (Gladwell, 2000).

> Aleghfeli establishes *ethos* by invoking others' published scholarship and, later in this paragraph, well-known writers such as Malcolm Gladwell. This shows he has conducted research and has expertise.

All you need to have to play a video game is an input device, a joystick (or any other kind of game controller, such as a keyboard, a mouse etc.), and a particular video game. Speakers and headphones are not obligatory; they just make the effects more impressive.

> Since Aleghfeli begins with a general overview and physical description of video games, he assumes his audience includes those who are very unfamiliar with video games. It also suggests that his purpose is to provide an overview of video games, to inform.

Original video games could be found in a number of formats; everything depended on the electronic device it had to fit. The first widely sold game was called "Computer Space" and was created by T. Dabney and N. Bushnell. In fact, it played only on the black and white TV. This type of video game was developed and transformed into "Brown Box," which appeared in the 1960s and could be used with a standard TV. The enormous success came after the appearance of the "Space Invaders" in 1980s. The game inspired thousands of movie and storytellers and became a well-known brand. In fact, it opened a golden era of video games that is still continuing.

> He establishes *kairos* here by showing that video games are prevalent and have been since the 1980s.

Because video games are a form of art, we can divide them into different genres due to different aspects (the level of interactivity which the game presents, ways of playing this game, types of devices, the style of playing the game, etc.). Educational video games are considered to be the most useful ones. In fact, in 2009 President Barack Obama supported a program called "Educate to Innovate," which included the development of technology in the sphere of education. According to this program, video games helped students to gain knowledge in an interactive way.

> *Ethos* is again established through expertise on these details and with this informed historical account. *Kairos* emerges through the reference to Obama, suggesting an inquiry worthy of contemporary politics.

From *Undergraduate Research Journal for the Human Sciences*, 2012.

The second type is casual games that are usually played on telephones and a PC. These types of games may seem to be useless, but some psychologists still consider them to develop skills of time management and reaction time. One more type is serious games (Winegarner, 2005), created to develop some kind of learning experience and not usually intended for simple entertainment. They are dedicated to development of specific professional skills and knowledge. One of the most prominent examples of this type is a game called "Microsoft Flight Simulator," which was developed for the military (Roberts, 2001)....

> Throughout the article, Aleghfeli demonstrates *kairos* (as in propriety) by including a blend of scholarly citations, his own ideas, and, later in the text, popular literature such as *Forbes Magazine*. This meets readers' expectations about a topic like video games, which spans the popular to scholarly continuum.

There is no doubt that games can educate people by providing them not only pure knowledge but also skills that are hard to gain. Knowledge received from playing will not be static; this knowledge will develop "cognitive maps," which create strategies to manage time, to count resources, and to find solutions to hard problems (Layford, 2008). On the other hand, it is necessary to remember that the virtual world still differs greatly from the real one. For example, learning how to drive a car in a video game does not mean you can really drive.

Professor B. Griffiths, from the University of Nottingham, noted that playing video games helps disabled people, in particular disabled children, to gain social and educational skills (Aarseth, 2004). In fact, some medical departments in the U.S. recover individuals' motor skills and develop coordination by giving them opportunity to play video games. What is more, research shows that playing such kinds of games makes people think more creatively and faster. Children are also thought to gain some amount of self-confidence, motivation, and inspiration not to search for easy solutions while dealing with hard problems (Blodget, 2006).

> These two paragraphs demonstrate *logos* as he cites specific examples of video games that cultivate knowledge and skills and describes how video games accomplish this.

> This paragraph illustrates *logos* with specific examples, *ethos*, by citing scholars and establishing expertise, and *pathos*, by appealing to readers' emotions about the education of children and people with disabilities.

> By addressing violent video games, he shows that his *purpose* is not only to show the educational purposes of video games, but also to address the potential negative impact of video games. His *ethos* emerges therefore as trustworthy and judicious.

Although there are positive outcomes of playing video games, it is also a double-edged sword. There are many educative outcomes, but what are the outcomes of violent games (Greg, 1994)? If players are killing other creatures, they may unconsciously change their psychological condition and become more aggressive and uncontrollable. Psychologists think that there is enough blood, violence, and death in movies and television for children today. They have no need to play murderers.

Too much of something can never be useful. While playing any type of video games, it is necessary to have a healthy environment (Miller, 2005). Many people claim video games to be the main reason of destruction for the family relationships, as this kind of amusement takes too much time away from family activities that keep people close together (Crawford, 1992). Moreover, there are claims that video games are the main cause of children's mental imbalance; kids are easily addicted to playing games that keep their attention for long hours. This makes children isolated from the world of doing their homework and family duties. This is why parents need to control and limit the time their children spend on playing this type of game. Certainly, game addiction may not be compared to drinking alcohol and taking drugs, but it still destroys health (Dolan, 2009). Children and adults who are addicted to games not only fail to do their work or school duties, they also forget about sports, eating, and even sleeping.

Spending too much time eye-to-eye with a computer will also cause a "social withdrawal" effect, where a person is left out of the social circle and without friends. Moreover, it effects the development of natural talents and the amount of time spent on hobbies (Wills, 2002).

Many people working in the video game industry today have become concerned about the question: "What is the future of the video games?" Making predictions about the future is never an easy task in the fast-moving video game business. Michael Noer, from *Forbes Magazine*, said that the graphics of video games will continue to develop, especially concerning colors and details. The demographics and motion-sensitive controllers are also expected to change greatly. Huge video game corporations will divide into smaller ones, and

> The focus of this paragraph and the next is largely on children and families, which suggests that his audience might include those who are parents of children who play video games.

> *Logos* appears here as he cites experts on claims about the damaging impact of video games.

> These sections invoke *pathos* as he appeals to readers' sympathy for those in the throes of addictive behavior and fear of the destructiveness of that behavior and the "social withdrawal" effect.

> Because he spends considerable time outlining the potential negative impact as well as the positive impact, Aleghfeli's audience likely includes those who are skeptical about video games as well as those who are enthusiasts. He might be offering a dual message, suggesting a middle-ground approach to video games that recognizes their potential and their drawbacks.

> This paragraph speaks to the business and industry side, suggesting that people in those sectors are also among his audience. This paragraph also invokes *kairos* by showing that video games have a future presence.

the competitiveness of producing high-quality video games will rise greatly. Games will include more possibilities to actually "feel" what you are playing; for example, they will include sensitive instruments, pedals, new types of wheels, and other innovations (Noer, 2007)....

Kairos emerges here since video games are likely to play a role of some sort in our lives. This shows it is worth our while to consider the effects and use of video games.

This concluding paragraph reveals his message: that video games have positive and negative effects and must be controlled by the user or parent. His audience is people who play video games and parents of children who do.

All in all, no matter how bad or good you think the role of video games play in present-day life, they are definitely an active part of it. If one listens to the people who specialize in this industry, games will remain popular. Counting all the advantages and disadvantages of playing these games leads to a conclusion that a video game can have both positive and negative effects. Video games are a double-edged sword; everything depends upon how you manage to use them (Lieu, 1997). One thing remains clear: individuals have to control the time they spend playing a game and be sure that the game is worth it. Parents should not only take care of how much their children play, adults should also watch what children are playing in order to avoid further social and health problems described in this essay. Have fun playing, but make sure not to cross the boundary between "being entertained" and "becoming addicted."

He ends with a clear message of playing with moderation. His purpose, thus, seems to be to help his audience (gamers and parents of children who game) play safely and have fun, while recognizing the educative potential and avoiding the risks of addiction.

[References omitted here; available at http://www.kon.org/urc/v11/aleghfeli.html]

Write Now

Choose a text you are currently reading and practice one of the above strategies: either reading like a writer or reading rhetorically (or practice a combination of each). After you have completed this in-depth reading strategy, reflect in writing for ten minutes: What did you learn about the text and/or about yourself as a writer and reader by having adopted this in-depth reading strategy?

Invoking Discipline-Specific Reading Skills

Alongside the aforementioned strategies for reading, academic writers also need to make decisions about which discipline-specific reading skills they might invoke in different contexts. Researchers have identified and developed a range of discipline-specific reading skills, to which readers should be attuned. Charles Bazerman, for example, conducted research about physicists' reading practices and identified that they "generally do not read articles sequentially." Instead, Bazerman found they often "looked at the introduction and conclusions," "scann[ed] figures," and often "skipped over...detailed mathematics." Understanding how you might approach texts based on these discipline-specific elements should help you become a more effective and efficient reader.

Structure

Scholars in some disciplines tend to adopt particular kinds of structures for much of the writing in those fields. For instance, one common structure for academic articles across several disciplines is known as IMRAD. IMRAD involves dividing an article into the following sections: "introduction, methods, results, and discussion." While writing in many contexts follows the IMRAD structure, writers in the medical sciences and the natural sciences make particular use of this structure. The IMRAD format is so popular, in fact, that according to researchers it grew in use over the twentieth century until becoming, in the 1980s, "the only pattern adopted by original papers" (Sollaci and Pereira).

Another structure frequently used by writers across many disciplines involves creating a section for a literature review or discussion of prior research that precedes the new argument. In some disciplines this section is explicitly marked as such, while in other disciplines it is embedded in the text. Understanding structurally how to recognize a literature review section will enable you to differentiate more efficiently between a writer's review of prior scholarship and that writer's new argument or contribution to the field. Learning about structures such as IMRAD and literature reviews will help you read more accurately and effectively within and across disciplines. As you encounter reading materials across disciplines, make it a standard practice to reflect on the structures you see emerging across the texts.

Discipline-specific reader questions

Discipline-specific reader questions might be thought of as a range of reading questions that people within disciplines tend to ask as they read. For example, in science-oriented disciplines that rely heavily on up-to-date research, readers may be accustomed to routinely posing questions about the dates for secondary materials used in a text or about the dates when the text's writers conducted experiments. In a discipline such as history, readers might tend to ask questions about what kinds of evidence a writer has used to draw conclusions. Readers in sociology or statistics might be accustomed to asking questions about research methodology. Finally, readers in disciplines such as literature or English may tend to ask questions that probe and elicit a text's analytic frame or that examine a text's contradictions, tensions, or inconsistencies.

Discipline-specific reading questions are not necessarily intended to yield tidy, quick answers, but they are instead constructed as a way for readers to interrogate texts and evaluate what they are reading. Actively questioning the texts you read will, in turn, enable you to engage with what others have written as you develop your own writing projects. Learning to think about the questions your readers may ask will also help you shape your own writing. Through this process, you will become more attentive and responsive to the ways in which readers will likely approach your text through discipline-specific questions.

Visual literacy

Many disciplines require understanding visual texts and graphics as you read. Visual components of texts can include images, charts, graphs, and tables, as well as other forms of media, such as videos, animation, and interactive multimedia elements. While some texts consist entirely of prose, writing in many academic disciplines includes visual components as a crucial element of texts. In some cases, these visual components provide a supplement to the prose, and in other cases the visual components have equal importance to the prose or even take precedence over written text in terms of conveying information and articulating the argument.

Reading visually asks that you consider how the visual elements intersect with other elements of the text, what their purpose is, and how they contribute to the overall argument. Visual literacy also invites you to think about the choices writers have made in assembling, curating, and developing visual elements in their texts. Choosing to visualize data as a bar graph instead of a pie chart can impact the story that data conveys. Similarly, choosing one image over another can alter the nature of the argument or the reader's impression of an issue. Chapter 7: Analysis and Chapter 10: Designing Arguments both expand on visual literacy from the perspectives of visual analysis and visual argument.

Mathematical literacy

Many disciplines also require a certain level of facility with mathematical calculations and numerical data. This is true not only in math or statistics, which might be expected, but also across the social sciences in such fields as economics and sociology, as well as in the natural sciences, business, environmental studies, and engineering fields. People reading in psychology will likely need to be able to differentiate between mean, median, and mode. Those reading in sociology might need to understand the concept of N in reference to survey respondents. Even some writing in the humanities includes statistics and numerical data.

Mathematical literacy enables readers to understand data with greater accuracy and nuance, including what the data suggest and the arguments that people are making about their data. One way of gaining knowledge in mathematical and statistical data would be to take a course in statistics or math. Another alternative would be to refer to any one of several online resources that define basic mathematical operators and statistical measures. As you read, develop a running list of mathematical and statistical elements you encounter so you can begin constructing your own personal reference list to enhance your mathematical literacy.

Technical vocabulary

Academic writers will often encounter terms within a discipline that are more or less particular to that discipline. Examples of technical vocabulary would be the concept of "proof" in mathematics or "anomie" in sociology. Other examples of technical vocabulary include "primary source documents" in history or "climate change" in environmental studies. Technical vocabulary also exists in humanities disciplines, such as the concept of "ethnographic inquiry" in cultural anthropology. Technical vocabulary, sometimes referred to as discipline-specific terminology, should be differentiated from the notion of jargon, which has negative connotations. Whereas jargon tends to refer to catch phrases or overused terms deployed with little discrimination, technical vocabulary actually includes terms, concepts, and phrases that are of critical importance to knowledge in a particular discipline.

As you newly encounter reading in various disciplines, you can expect to spend some time learning any such technical vocabulary. Readers build their familiarity with this vocabulary by reading texts across time in particular disciplines and by learning to recognize word patterns, phrases, or terms that appear with frequency across these texts. In this way, readers can build a lexicon of technical vocabulary for the disciplines in which they are reading. This technical vocabulary, however, can change across time as researchers build knowledge and add new terms, eliminate outdated terms, or change the definitions of existing terms. Therefore, it is important to pay attention to technical vocabulary every time you read, not only as you are beginning to build your lexicons for technical vocabularies within and across disciplines.

Transferring Reading

Reading well in academic contexts requires a deliberate approach. Chapter 3 discussed how varied and numerous academic questions can be. In the same way, with every new and different question, writers face decisions about how to best pursue that question through reading. Recognizing and learning to navigate through the many different decisions of what to read and how to read will enable you to become a more effective and efficient academic reader. Each writing occasion—each time you pose and pursue a question—necessitates that you consider carefully what kinds of text you will read and how you will read them.

And, although this chapter began with an admission that reading can be challenging, it can also be quite exhilarating: Reading enables you not only to learn from others, but also to begin to formulate your own thoughts as you move toward contributing your ideas through your writing. Helping you move in this direction, Chapter 5—which addresses summary—will introduce you to a key component of engaging with others through writing, as well as becoming a participant in the very conversations about which you are now reading.

☙ ☙ ☙

Disaster Archaeology: *"Ethnoarchaeology and the Aftermath: The Process of Memorialization" by Richard A. Gould and Randi Scott*

Transfer Points: Archaeology, Cultural Anthropology

"It's almost impossible … to make plans anymore" ("Digging"). So says Richard Gould regarding the increasing demand for his expertise in disaster archaeology. Over the years, Gould has worked with a range of disasters, from shipwrecks and airline wreckages, to fires and terror attacks. With the preponderance of disasters, Gould's work has become simultaneously unpredictable and certain: unpredictable in that disasters are largely unanticipated, but also certain in that disasters do, nevertheless, continue to occur.

Disaster archaeology is an emerging subfield within archaeology, which is itself a discipline nested within anthropology. Archaeology involves the excavation, examination, and analysis of artifacts as a means of better understanding human experiences.

Archeaology has many subfields. Prehistoric archaeology, for instance, examines Egyptian pyramids and structures such as Stonehenge. Classical archeology addresses Greek and Roman sites. And other subfields include biblical archaeology, underwater archaeology, urban archaeology, and bioarchaeology.

Disaster archaeology, as its name implies, examines artifacts specifically from disasters in order to improve understanding of human experiences. Pompeii is one of the most famous sites of disaster archaeology. More contemporary sites include New York City after the 2001 World Trade Center attacks and the regions impacted by the Great East Japan Earthquake of 2011.

While archaeologists work primarily with inanimate objects, their motivating drive is human-centered inquiry. The Society for American Archaeology, for instance, defines archaeology as "the study of the ancient and recent human past through material remains" ("What is").

In keeping with this human-centered motivation, one overarching aim for disaster archaeology is to help people better understand, prevent, and prepare for future disasters. One example involves Japan, which experienced two devastating earthquakes in a relatively short time span: the Great Hanshin Awaji Earthquake of 1995, in which 5,502 people died, and the 2011 Great East Japan Earthquake, which killed more than 15,500 people (USGS).

Helping explain these two earthquakes, disaster archaeologists identified through excavations a layer of 2,000-year-old tsunami deposits in rice fields from an ancient area of the region known as Taga-jo. Disaster archaeologists were thus able to analyze the deposits and explain the historical vulnerability of the region to earthquakes and tsunamis (Okamura, et al.).

Another human-centered dimension of disaster archaeology entails preserving material artifacts as a record of human experience. During the aftermath of disasters, disaster archaeologists help preserve and rescue vital cultural and museum artifacts that are damaged or at risk for loss. In this way, disaster archaeologists help preserve cultural heritage.

Richard Allan Gould is Professor Emeritus of Anthropology at Brown University. He received his B.A. from Harvard University and his Ph.D. in Anthropology from University of California Berkeley. Before joining the faculty at Brown, he was an Associate Professor of Anthropology at the University of Hawaii at Manoa, Honolulu. His areas of expertise include examining how humans adapt to stressful or risky situations, as well as underwater fieldwork in shipwrecks and other losses at sea. His research has been conducted in Bermuda, Finland, New York, Rhode Island, Louisiana, and the Dry Tortugas (Gould, "Richard"). **Randi Scott** is Deputy Director of the Forensic Archaeology Recovery (FAR) unit, a Rhode Island-based organization Gould founded. She has also worked as the organization's public relations officer and administrative coordinator. She has a B.A. in Anthropology from the University of Rhode Island ("Profiles"). She was recognized by Cambridge Who's Who in 2012 for "demonstrating dedication, leadership and excellence in forensic archaeology ("Randi").

Disaster archaeologists also provide an important role for people directly impacted by earthquakes, be they survivors, families, and/or people who have lost loved ones. Gould writes in his book *Disaster Archaeology* that, through victim identification, disaster archaeology is "an instrument of recovery for the families and others affected by a disaster." Such work is affiliated with forensic anthropologists and forensic police officers; disaster archaeologists, however, approach this work primarily as a means of providing solace to those impacted by a disaster rather than doing so as part of a criminal investigation ("Digging").

Disaster archaeologists publish research in public genres such as reports, interviews, websites, and lectures, and in peer-reviewed journals and books. Such work addresses a broad range of contexts, including, for example, social resilience and adaptation to volcanic disasters in Papua New Guinea (Torrence); the archaeology of El Nino events (Van Buren); the impact of the Bam, Iran, earthquake on families (DezhamKhoy and Leila); and the cultural processes that shape maritime disasters such as the Salvage and Muckelroy (Gibbs).

While disaster archaeology relies on carefully crafted methods and practices, much of the research and writing in this field is highly transferable to and from other disciplines.

One transferable element of disaster archaeology reasearch is knowledge of context. As they study artifacts and sites, archaeologists must develop expertise in the particular contexts surrounding those items. Doing so enables them to develop more reasonable analyses of the sites and artifacts, and more reasonable hypotheses about how humans might have interacted with those material artifacts.

Another transferable research practice involves in-depth reading and analysis. Archaeologists pay close attention to detail and conduct in-depth analysis of objects. This emphasis on close examination of artifacts is so profound that some have described archaeology as the "discipline of things" (Olsen).

Beyond even the practice of close reading, the role of materiality provides a highly transferable dimension of research and writing between disaster archaeology and many other disciplines. Material-culture studies involve a consideration of the interactions between people and things. From art history and fashion studies to history, technology, and museum studies, material culture studies enable us to better interpret, design, and compare the very many objects that surround, reflect, and impact us on a daily basis (Center). And, in the face of what may seem utter devastation from disasters such as earthquakes, floods, mass murder, and volcanoes, material studies in the context of disaster archaeology offer the opportunity for some degree of preservation, recovery, and understanding of the human experience before, during, or after disaster.

Write Here

Memorials abound: in the form of buildings or exhibits, or more impromptu memorials on roadsides or at other locations. What memorials have you seen or heard of? Describe several memorials you have encountered, focusing in particular on the objects and scenes of the memorial. Describe the sites and the objects in as much detail as possible, considering design and layout. What might the significance be of some of these objects and sites?

Richard A. Gould and Randi Scott

Ethnoarchaeology and the Aftermath: The Process of Memorialization

In the weeks that followed the World Trade Center attacks, homemade messages headed "Have you seen…?" or "Missing…," often accompanied by a picture and description of someone who was missing and not yet identified, were a common sight in New York City. They proliferated at bus stops, in public areas such as Grand Central Station, and at public gatherings. In

First responders comb through smoldering remains of the Twin Towers soon after the terrorist attack on Sept. 11, 2001.

some locations, such as Union Square and St. Paul's Chapel, people placed candles and floral offerings in front of these signs and added messages of their own. The weeks that followed the attacks of 9/11 were perhaps the most painful in the history of the city.

This behavior was matched on a smaller scale by similar signs on fences surrounding the Station nightclub fire scene in West Warwick, R.I., shortly after the disaster there on February 20, 2003. In some cases these notices included descriptions of victims' clothing and personal effects. The presence of these signs at both disaster scenes attested to the immediacy of the need in the minds of the families for prompt and accurate victim identification, and in each case the national Disaster Mortuary Operations Team assisted the local authorities—primarily the Medical Examiner's Office—with the identifications. As these identifications progressed, the "missing" notices were gradually replaced by memorial messages and displays containing such items as flowers, teddy bears and other stuffed animals, and religious symbols. At the Station these persisted until the crime scene there was closed and the fences were taken down in March 2003. In New York most of the homemade memorial messages lasted until the weather obliterated them or they were removed.

Most people are already familiar with this kind of behavior at roadside memorials commemorating victims of road trauma,[1] at air-crash scenes, and sometimes at murder and kidnap scenes.[2] The bombing at the Alfred P. Murrah Building in Oklahoma City on April 19, 1995,

was followed by similar public displays,[3] as was the death of Princess Diana[4] and the shootings at Columbine High School in Colorado. The deaths of twelve college students when wood poles for a campus bonfire collapsed at Texas A&M University in 1999 were memorialized in a like manner. The behavior and character of the A&M memorials was studied and described by folklorist Sylvia Grider.[5] In 2005 ephemeral memorials began to appear at locations affected by the disastrous tsunami in the Indian Ocean.[6]

Spontaneous memorialization of this kind is now reported as a common feature of the emotional landscape in the United States, the United Kingdom, and Australia. Impromptu memorials characteristically occur in cases of violent death in location separate from those where the physical remains of the victims are deposited (in a cemetery or some other permanent setting) and apart from more culturally or religiously sanctioned ceremonies. They are often (but not always) found near the scene of the tragedy. Kenneth Thompson, whose mother died in the bombing of the Murrah Building, commented on how important it was for him and others who had lost relatives in the Oklahoma City bombing to be allowed to visit the scene as often as possible and to memorialize the event there.[7] In cases such as the crashes of TWA Flight 800, Swissair Flight 111, and Alaskan Airlines Flight 261, the mourners could not visit the site itself, which was offshore and under water, but they could view the area from the nearest point of land and place displays of flowers, photographs, and other items. Although such memorialization is usually a private expression of grief, it takes place in public view and often draws in people who are unrelated to the victims or their friends and families. The physical objects in these memorial displays tend to be eclectic, with unusual combinations of religious symbols and mundane items such as teddy bears.

This kind of spontaneous memorialization following a mass-fatality incident sometimes precedes more durable memorials such as monuments, signs, or plaques. Geographer Kenneth Foote has explored the conditions that have fostered or discouraged the formation of durable memorials in relation to various events in American history, noting that the result depends

Friends and family members of both victims and first responders march through New York City honoring those who were killed on Sept. 11.

primarily on the collective cultural meaning attached to the disaster event.[8] It is still too early to tell what, if any, durable memorials will emerge from the World Trade Center tragedy or the Station nightclub fire. There is nothing inevitable about the process that occurs during and after spontaneous memorialization. It can follow a course that leads to neglect and abandonment, with the result that the site is obscured by the restoration of the area for other purposes or completely obliterated, just as readily as it can lead to the construction of a monument or other memorial landmark. As events unfolded following the Station nightclub fire, an opportunity arose to apply archaeological skills of a special kind—called *ethnoarchaeology*—to explore, record, and perhaps begin to understand this complex process.

ETHNOARCHAEOLOGY

Ethnoarchaeology is generally, if not universally, regarded as an archaeologically controlled way of observing present-day human behavior in order to explain the patterning of cultural remains in the past.[9] Ethnographic research is performed with the goal of constructing hypotheses and developing theories that can be compared with and tested against the archaeological record. Most debates and discussions among ethnoarchaeologists are intended to lead to better approximations of a knowable human past.

Many ethnoarchaeologists have sought resemblances between present-day and ancient material remains in order to establish *analogues* to account for past behavior that could have produced such similar results. Such analogues range from superficial similarities of appearance to more carefully constructed arguments based on structural parallels arising from comparable modes of adaptation by similar kinds of societies (such as mobile hunter-gatherers) to similar environments (such as deserts). An alternative ethnoarchaeological approach explores *contrasts* between the material by-products of present-day behavior and the physical remains of the past, generally in the context of similar environmental or social contexts. In other words, the goals of ethnoarchaeology tend to divide sharply over how much one seeks to explain similarities or differences in past and present human behavior.

These goals apply to ancient mortuary assemblages just as they do to more frequently studied aspects of culture such as technology, economic behavior, architecture, and trade and exchange. For example, Grider's account of the Texas A&M bonfire tragedy drew generalized parallels to ancient Maya funeral offerings from a grave at Tikal, Guatemala, with the subhead: "Today's Grief May Help Explain Ancient Funeral Offerings."[10]

One of the basic issues concerning practices of disposal and memorialization of the dead was addressed by anthropologist A.L. Kroeber in his monumental survey of the ethnology of the California Indians.[11] Basing his conclusions on historic and ethnographic accounts over the length of the entire state, Kroeber proposed that mortuary practices—specifically, whether particular groups habitually buried or cremated their dead—were fashions that varied independently of other aspects of culture, in a manner resembling the way hemlines on women's dresses rose and fell through time.[12]

A restudy of this issue in the 1960s, using historical and ethnographic accounts that had not been available earlier, determined that the controlling variable in such activities was a universally shared belief among Native Californians that a person's remains must be deposited at or as close as possible to where he or she was born. Groups that normally buried their dead, for example, might cremate in situations such as hunting or war parties if a member died while the task group was far from its home village. The overriding imperative was to transport the remains back to the place of birth, usually the village. It was easier to carry the ashes than the body, especially over mountainous terrain. The mode of disposal of the dead in aboriginal California was linked to other elements of the cultural system, in the context of situations that might require adjustments to general practices of burial or cremation.[13] However variable or arbitrary the mode of disposal of the dead may have seemed to Kroeber, this traditional behavior was not an autonomous statement of fashion but was connected to and dependent on other beliefs and behavior within the cultural systems of Native Californians.

A similar issue arises in cases of spontaneous memorialization following a disaster: one might conclude that the idiosyncratic and ephemeral character of the displays is a form of "fashion," as originally proposed by Kroeber. Ethnoarchaeology can be used to examine this proposition and to determine to what, if any, extent the complex and idiosyncratic expressive behavior at postdisaster memorials represents something more than mere fashion. The ethnographic case of burial versus cremation among Native Californians suggests that disposal and memorialization of the dead should be viewed as an open, rather than a closed, cultural system. Events in the wider community during the aftermath need to be observed and correlated with events occurring within the memorial site and among the people directly affected by the disaster.

Although ethnoarchaeology continues along with the rest of archaeology to address our understanding of the human past, it should not stop there. It was not obvious what role ethnoarchaeology could play in disaster archaeology, even after the events surrounding the World Trade Center attacks. At the start of the recovery efforts at the Station it was still unclear. The counsel of Irving Owens, Rhode Island state fire marshal, during our initial walkover of the fire scene on February 26, 2003, proved to be prophetic. He advised me that mass-fatality disasters have aftermaths that last for years and that in taking on the task of recovering human remains and personal effects, FAR would also need to consider how to respond to the aftermath. His own principal concern was with changes to the existing state fire code and with legal cases that would follow from the

Visitors to the Sept. 11 remembrance site look on one of the many displays memorializing victims of the attacks.

disaster, and these became major issues of public interest in Rhode Island. The Comprehensive Fire Safety Act of 2003 contained radical changes from the earlier rule and was signed into law on July 7, 2003, following some of the most emotionally intense public hearings imaginable.[14] The Station fire also produced the largest single rush of litigation in the state's history, with three criminal indictments and forty-six civil suits,[15] all of which are currently under review as preparations go forward for the trials.

The role of the ethnoarchaeologist in relation to disaster archaeology became clearer a few months after the crime scene at the Station was closed on March 9, 2003. Ethnoarchaeology embodies the same empirical assumptions as the rest of archaeology. Archaeological skills produce detailed and controlled recording of physical associations at regular intervals along with interviews and observations of behavior linked to those associations. As we now know, ethnoarchaeological skills are ideally suited to recording ephemeral elements of material culture associated with the aftermaths of such events.

With memorials, we are dealing with the physical associations of expressive behavior. Understanding elements of symbolic and emotional expression in ethnoarchaeology requires a participant-observation approach familiar to anthropologists and ethnographers generally. This "insider's" view of the group being studied must be coupled, whenever possible, with the scientific ("outsider's") approach provided by archaeology. Because of FAR's earlier direct involvement with the recovery efforts at the

Station, we were already insiders to a degree rarely encountered in this kind of study. After all, this disaster occurred to members of our own community, some of whom were known to FAR volunteers personally. We found ourselves struggling with the same emotional and practical issues as our friends and neighbors. Just as happened to New Yorkers more than a year earlier, the citizens of our tiny state were faced with one of the most painful aftermaths to a disaster in its history.

Who were the people who were present at the club that night and who later died in the fire or survived? Many were devoted fans of the Great White band, which had its heyday during the 1980s. This fact is reflected indirectly in their age and residential profiles. The mean age of the 100 victims who died is 32.92 years (standard deviation = 6.35), and that of the 181 survivors whose ages were given is almost the same, 32.69 years (standard deviation = 6.75). Among the dead, the youngest victim was 18 and the oldest was 46. Among the survivors, the youngest was 19 and the oldest was 53. With a few exceptions, this was an older crowd than one usually sees at rock concerts. The partygoers came from communities all over southeastern New England, including Massachusetts and Connecticut, although 57 of the 100 who died were from Rhode Island. Of the 192 survivors identified by the *Providence Journal*,[16] 131, or 68 percent, were from Rhode Island. The relatively high proportion of out-of-state residents who died (43 percent) or survived (32 percent) suggests a strong regional following for the band. As one often sees at rock concerts, there were fans who wore special costumes and carried special paraphernalia, and many of them had extensive tattooing and body piercing. Many of the messages at the memorial site displays contain specific references to Great White and other bands. All the members of the band survived except for Ty Longley, the lead guitarist.

From a personal point of view this experience of recording the memorial site was both easy and difficult. The easy part was the recognition that ethnoarchaeological experience gained in earlier work among Tolowa and other Native American groups in northwestern California, Aborigines in the Western Desert of Australia, and farmers in Finnish Lapland was relevant to

the Station aftermath. The difficult part was the direct encounter with the emotional distress of survivors as well as relatives and friends of the victims. What comfort could they find in these fragile displays? Could simply listening to them voice their grief and anger help in some way? When and how does closure come, if at all, for people affected by a disaster like this? As of 2006, more than two years after the event, the memorial displays continue in place and are being tended. People still come. They hold vigils, play guitars, hug, and cry. Many come in good weather, but some come in bad weather, too, and simply sit in their cars looking at the memorial site. When will it end?

A SPONTANEOUS MEMORIAL

After the fences came down at the Station fire scene, the public swarmed over the site looking for souvenirs. For several evenings on the television news, one could watch investigators hired by lawyers to prosecute civil suits against various parties associated with the disaster as they walked through the debris field looking for anything they could identify or seize as evidence.[17] The lawyers arranged to have much of the debris, including the drummer's alcove and other bits of structure, hauled off to a warehouse for use in the trials to follow. Finally, earth-moving machinery was used to clear the site completely, obliterating virtually all traces of the nightclub. By May 2003 the site of the club was a vacant lot. Except for a section of concrete retaining wall alongside Kulas Road, the asphalt parking lot, and the sign standing next to Cowesett Avenue (the main highway), few visible traces remained. The site appeared quiet and abandoned.

During this period Triton Realty, the landowners, offered to donate the property to the city of West Warwick for a memorial park to the fire victims. The landowning company should not be confused with the club owners, Michael and Jeffrey Derderian, who face indictments for criminal negligence along with the former tour manager of Great White. The offer from Triton Realty was welcomed by most parties, but at least one of the plaintiffs' lawyers blocked the donation because she saw the property as a possible asset to be seized in the litigation to follow. It became increasingly clear that any plans for a permanent memorial at the site would remain on hold until these suits were settled.[18]

While everything looked quiet down at the site, an emotional issue was building. Sometime during the last week in June, a neighbor living nearby on Kulas Road heard a pounding noise coming from the nightclub site and went over to investigate. She found a woman there driving 100 homemade wooden crosses upright into the ground in an oval-shaped pattern about 110 feet long by 73 feet wide that approximated where the nightclub had stood. The woman hammering the crosses into the ground had not lost anyone close in the fire but said she had been a frequent patron at the club. The crosses were relatively small and plain. They were made from tongue-and-groove planks originally taken from the nightclub floor and piled up in the weeds near the site after the cleanup. Within a day or two someone had painted the crosses lavender, and immediately afterward paper or plastic butterfly stickers were attached to most of them along with strings of plastic Mardi Gras beads.

Family and friends created a makeshift memorial at the site of the Station night club.

By July 1, when we first visited the memorial site, 48 of the 100 crosses had names inscribed on them, and 17 individual family displays had already appeared. We immediately began inventorying, photographing, and recording the memorial displays. At the time we had no idea how long the activity at the site would continue or how it would evolve. We realized, however, that a detailed record of the memorial site and associated activities was needed. When reporters and state officials asked why, the facile answer was that a detailed historical record was necessary so people in Rhode Island would not forget what happened after the disaster. This is true, of course, but the complete answer to this question is more complex. We visited the memorial site a total of 64 times, or almost one visit per week, from July 1, 2003, until January 24, 2005.

In the days that followed the appearance of the 100 wooden crosses, visitors came in ever-increasing numbers. The busiest day we observed was 80 to 100 visitors per hour, but 20 to 30 per hour was more usual, including families who brought flowers (real and artificial—some with plastic dew), balloons, teddy bears, candles, food (especially boxes of pizza and soft drinks in cans and plastic bottles), American flags, inflat-

able vinyl guitars, cigarette packs, coins, ceramic angels, rings, plastic angles on wands, and personal messages and photographs. Balloons appeared on birthdays and anniversaries at individual displays. The symbol that emerged most prominently, however, was the butterfly. Butterflies appeared in various shapes, sizes, and styles and multiplied as the number of individual family displays increased. Within a week or two, four free-standing displays were present within the area enclosed by the oval. We assigned feature numbers to these displays and others that appeared later, and we recorded and photographed them in detail at regular intervals to note changes. The contrast between general and individualized displays was apparent from the beginning and has continued, although individualized memorials have increasingly filled in the displays along and inside the oval.

By July 20 a solar-powered light, similar to those used in home driveways, appeared at the foot of each cross in the oval. They were placed there by a single individual, who spent close to $500 for them. By July 26 there were 102 crosses at the memorial, 76 of which now had names inscribed on them. We conducted interviews with visitors who wanted to talk, but there was no systematic effort to follow a formal interview schedule. Whenever possible, however, we encouraged people to discuss the changes they were making to the memorial displays and to explain why they thought these changes were important. Sometimes this led to a free-flowing stream of memories and associations connected to the deceased relative or friend and to the elements of the memorial display. The interviews were productive but were so emotional that we found that we had to spell each other and take periodic breaks from this activity in the weeks that followed. Not all visitors were relatives or friends of victims. There were also people from other areas who had heard about what was happening here and wanted to see it for themselves.

On August 20 there was a well-attended unofficial memorial concert at the site to mark the six-month anniversary of the fire. By this time our interviews indicated a vague but growing awareness by the families and other visitors that their actions were a response to the failure to create a permanent memorial at the site, a failure brought on by the legal injunction against Triton Realty's offer to donate the land for such a memorial. We should emphasize, however, that the memorials that appeared shortly after late June 2003 were not part of any organized protest by the victims' families or anyone else. They arose spontaneously.

DISPUTES ARISE

Forty-six days after the fire a special legislative Fire Safety Commission was appointed to hear testimony and review the existing state fire code.[19] The commission met regularly during the spring and early summer at the state capitol and later produced sweeping revisions to the code. During these hearings fire survivors and relatives of victims spoke of their experiences and vented their feelings. Raw expressions of grief were mixed with a growing but unfocused sense of anger. Expressions of anger had been present earlier among some of the people at the fire scene while the recoveries conducted by FAR were in progress, but at the hearings these took the shape of an emergent but as-yet-unstructured dispute between individuals whose anger was overtaking their sense of grief and those who simply wished to grieve. After a particularly emotional hearing the state fire marshal told me that he doubted that any changes to the fire code, no matter how sweeping, would quell the sense of anger among some of the victims' families. Like his earlier comment, this one proved to be prophetic.

By mid-September a crisis had developed at the memorial site. Two crosses and other items at the memorial display for Ty Longley, guitar-

ist for Great White who was killed in the fire, were removed from the site and were reported to the West Warwick police as stolen property. By this time a consensus had emerged among most of the families and visitors, revealed by the messages they posted as well as through interviews, that the memorial site was sacred ground.[20] The woman who removed the items later confessed, arguing that it was wrong for a member of the band that started the fire to be memorialized along with the other victims. The police did not prosecute her, pointing out that articles left at the memorial were in the public domain and could not be regarded as private property—that is, the removal was not a case of theft.[21] The incident led to the replacement of Ty Longley's original wooden crosses with a robust, welded metal cross set solidly into a cement base in the ground.[22] The diffused anger seen earlier at the hearings was now becoming more firmly focused on the physical items displayed at the memorial site, and more was to follow.

Coincidentally, this incident occurred while more permanent crosses, mainly of wood, were already starting to replace some of the original ones. By September 7 there were 13 of these in place, 3 of them within the area enclosed by the oval. By September 18 there were 7 of these more durable crosses (6 wood, 1 metal) within the oval, and four large memorial displays appeared along the oval as well. A hurricane watch was posted for southeastern New England at this time, prompting another emotional dispute—this time between individuals and families who wanted to remove their displays temporarily to a more protected location and those who opposed the idea of anyone even touching their displays, let alone moving them. A group had formed called the West Warwick Fire Memorial Association to promote the construction of a permanent memorial at the site, and they organized the removal of 13 displays for those who wanted it done. Forty-six other families, however, left their displays in place and tied plastic bags over them to protect them. As it happened, the storm weakened and did little damage. Two days later, on September 20, all the memorial displays were fully restored to their original, prestorm condition.

As inconsequential as these issues might seem to an outsider, the whole sequence of events sur-

Visitors to the Ty Longley display look through crosses placed in his memory.

memorials. As the first anniversary of the disaster approached, however, this uncertainty evaporated and the competing emotions of grief and anger began to diverge more clearly. The memorial site was turning into a kind of emotional centrifuge for the affected community.

Throughout the late fall and winter the displays were tended and even expanded. It was a hard winter with heavy snows, but visitors continued to come—so many, in fact, that the perimeter along the oval of crosses became solidly packed into an icy, elevated pathway. From the start of activity at the memorial site, we watched mourners and visitors as they moved around the displays in a shuffle that resembled the way people were seen walking around the area near the World Trade Center in New York in the weeks following 9/11. The body language around the WTC site was unusual. Many people there walked in a dreamlike fashion around Ground Zero, seemingly bound for some mysterious destination as if they were part of a strange pilgrimage from which others were excluded. Similar kinds of movement occurred at the Station memorial site as mourners and visitors circulated alongside the oval. There was one mourner at the WTC who walked along the perimeter of Ground Zero enclosed in a hooded cape, and an almost identical hooded figure appeared at the memorial site in West Warwick. At both places couples and families would sometimes stop and cling fiercely to each other, sobbing uncontrollably. Our initial expectation that worsening winter conditions at the site would discourage visitors and maintenance of the memorial displays was not borne out.

Shortly before the first anniversary of the fire, the first of a new assemblage of signs appeared at the location of the original sign for the nightclub next to Cowesett Avenue. These signs, placed there by the father of fire victim Tammy Mattera-Housa, were large and well made. They stood in a location that was visible to hundreds of motorists who passed the site each day and announced that Mr. Mattera's daughter's death was no accident. Anger and a need to attach blame were now messages for all to see. The signs were temporarily removed for the memorial service at the site on the night of February 20,

rounding the "nonstorm" was punctuated with emotional outbursts in the same way as the Ty Longley display had been. This episode showed the importance of close, empirical monitoring of behavior associated with the memorial displays. In the space of only four days, the memorial site was altered substantially and then changed back to its original configuration, amid much vocal disagreement. We wondered if tensions might be getting out of control. On the evening of September 20, nine months after the event, an impromptu gathering took place at the site. There was no program of any kind, but as it grew dark large numbers of people came to mourn. Each cross was lighted with its little solar lamp and a group of candles. Families hugged and cried as it grew darker. At this time all emotions were focused on the shared sense of loss.

As we look back over those days, it seems clear that we were witnessing an emotional tug of war between grief and anger, as expressed in the physical changes to the memorial displays at the site. There was no linear progression from one set of emotions to the other, nor were the physical changes to the site linear. Like our famously unstable New England weather, the displays shifted back and forth in ways that reflected shifting emotions within the grieving community and changing circumstances that impinged on the

2004,[23] but were replaced immediately afterward. These signs have been maintained with a few additions in this same location, while the displays at and inside the oval continue to proclaim the grief felt by the families of the victims (including Mr. Mattera, whose display cross stands along the oval). In other words, a year after the fire, emotions felt by a few families had crystallized to the point where the displays expressing anger were clearly separate from those showing grief. The latent layering of emotions following the disaster was now overtly displayed.

Sporadic demonstrations of anger have appeared at the site since then, most notably on May 7, 2004, when a small group appeared with the media in tow. The demonstrators could not understand why "the fire marshal" was not facing criminal indictments along with the Derderian brothers and the former band manager. It was not clear, however, from the responses of the demonstrators exactly which fire marshal they were accusing. Was it the state fire marshal, the West Warwick fire marshal, or another of the forty-six fire marshals in Rhode Island? Asked this question by a reporter, they seemed surprised to learn that there was more than one. Three days later this question was resolved when three additional posters appeared at the "anger display" with messages demanding "a 'cry' for justice" and "accountability," directed specifically at the West Warwick fire marshal. These sad incidents brought the divergence between the displays at the original oval of crosses—now the "grief display"—and the "anger display" out by the road (103 feet from the oval) into sharp relief, where they continue as of 2006.

THE FIRST ANNIVERSARY OF THE FIRE

In the days leading up to February 20, 2004, the pace of activities at the memorial site increased dramatically. Memorial displays already in place were freshened up and added to, with fresh flowers present in abundance. An entire genre of larger and more durable displays appeared, including a large Christmas tree that had been set up earlier in the season by the Station Fire Memorial Association, a table-like display anchoring a white arched trellis with 100 small crosses and artificial roses attached to it (provided by the

Fraternal Order of Eagles), and a temporary tent with a painted plywood heart-shaped panel containing 100 electric lights. These displays all appeared in the area inside the oval along with some of the earlier displays there.

Two of the earliest displays (which we called Features 2 and 3) within the oval were now completely obliterated by displays that were put up during this period. Both original displays had been well tended during the first few months of the memorial site but were now effectively abandoned. The Feature 2 display contained a large sign that was blown down repeatedly and finally had to be moved away. The Feature 3 display consisted originally of numbers right feet high displaying the figure 100, and a heart outlined in candles set in small holders resting flat on the ground. The heart was additionally outlined by 25 upright wands topped with plastic angels, and there were also bouquets of plastic flowers and cloth angels, glass candle holders, an American flag, and printed messages anchored with stones. By the anniversary this display was overlaid by several wooden crosses, and the only visible trace of the original feature consisted of bits of melted candle wax adhering to the soil in a few places where the "100" and heart had been. These two memorial displays presented an example of physical superposition of features, as one set of displays faded and others replaced them. The layering of emotions of grief and anger at the site could be compared with the stratigraphic layering of memorials within the oval.

On the date of the fire anniversary there were two major ceremonies: an officially sponsored remembrance ceremony held indoors at Rhodes-on-the-Pawtuxet in Cranston, R.I., and an unofficial outdoor ceremony at the memorial site in West Warwick sponsored by the Station Fire Memorial Association. About 900 to 1,000 people attended each ceremony, including officials such as the governor and the state attorney general of Rhode Island, the governor of Massachusetts, and local officials and representatives of law-enforcement and emergency-services agencies. The official ceremony was notable for its conspicuous use of the butterfly theme, indicating a degree of organized acceptance of this image to represent the tragedy. Survivors, family members, and friends filed past photographs of the victims, and a bell was tolled 100 times, once for each victim. Throughout the day there were public announcements and special programs on radio and television along with a special newspaper insert devoted to photographs of the victims and articles about the fire's aftermath.[24]

The ceremony at the memorial site was preceded by an open period for families and people who had been involved to visit memorials, place flowers, visit among themselves, and observe the new displays prepared for the event. As on the night of the fire, it was bitterly cold. The program, which started around 11:00 p.m.—approximately when the fire began—consisted of brief statements by representatives of the West Warwick Police Department, the Rhode Island Victims' Advocacy and Support Center, and the Station Fire Memorial Association, along with recorded music. Perhaps the most memorable moment came with the arrival of some of the survivors who were most seriously burned. For some of these people, this was their first public appearance since the fire, and it was hard to bear. A more positive personal moment came when members of FAR encountered emergency-services workers we had met at the fire scene in the course of our duties there. It was not always possible to get the names of the individuals working at the scene during the recovery efforts there, but now we had a heartfelt reunion. On February 20, 2004, the memorial site served as the venue for personal connections of many kinds within the community.

ANOTHER YEAR, AND STILL GOING

As the second anniversary of the fire approached, the memorial site continued in the same general configuration that was established earlier. The oval bounded by crosses and individual memorials enclosing several large displays still expressed grief in various ways, while 103 feet across the parking lot near Cowesett Avenue stood the display of signs and posters publicly proclaiming the anger felt by some families that criminal charges were not extended beyond the original three individuals named in the indictment. During the fall of 2004 serious efforts were made to landscape and clean up the site. On September 20 we observed a major display of living shrubs and trees being installed inside the oval in what

the family doing the planting called a butterfly garden. They were putting in live plants because the place "seemed too sad all the time," and they felt it needed a change. The plants, they said, would attract butterflies in the spring. A more elaborate butterfly garden was also constructed at Roger Williams Park in Cranston in honor of the fire victims during this same period, so the idea of the butterfly as a symbol of the fire victims has expanded and become more routinized within the community since it first appeared. On October 31, 2004, we counted a total of 122 butterfly images, mainly plastic, distributed throughout the memorial displays, making it the dominant symbol present at the site (plastic and ceramic angels came in a distant second with a total of 59 that day).

Memorial displays continue to be highly individualized, with unique associations of personal and seasonal items. Many of these displays express the interests of the victims during their lives. Some, like the elaborate shrine we designated Feature 13, emphasize religious themes. In this case there is an eight-foot-high wooden cross standing on a glass-fronted wooden cabinet, flanked by plastic buckets containing plastic roses and two American flags, all resting on a two-tiered platform of compacted stones. A plastic urn with plastic flowers rests on the top of the cabinet in front of the cross, and a crucifix hangs from the cross. Inside the cabinet there are family photographs taken on religious occasions along with images of Christ and the Virgin Mary as well as another small crucifix. Religious articles and messages and images of a religious character occur in many other displays, too, but Feature 13 appears to be almost entirely religious in its content. Feature 13 was blown down during a powerful winter storm in 2004 but was put back up and repaired soon afterward.

There are also memorial displays that contain sports-related items such as baseball caps, T-shirts, and coffee mugs with team logos; stuffed bears with baseball team insignia; a football team keychain; and a baseball batter's helmet. Some memorials reflect musical interests. Inflatable vinyl guitars were among the earliest display items to appear at the site, and they continue along with guitar picks and a drumstick, T-shirts with logos of popular bands, inscriptions of musical notes,

"The Last Column" memorial consists of a piece of steel that is signed by the Sept. 11 victim's families.

a ticket stub from a rock concert, and an autographed photograph of someone who appears to be a performer in a band. One display reveals an interest in mythical figures, with a figure of Frodo from *The Lord of the Rings*, two large elf statues, and a plastic elf; another display contains what appear to be occult symbols in plastic.

As we followed the evolution of specific displays, we were able to conduct on site interviews with family members attending to these displays. Most of these discussions focused on changes that each family or individual was making to the memorial displays. The conversations quickly entered such intense domains of emotion and family history, however, that they cannot be published. Nowhere else did the connections between FAR's earlier work at the site and the emotional needs of the victims' relatives and friends become as obvious. Specific questions about a valued object such as a ring or a necklace would be discussed. We would tell them about our wonderful volunteers, and they in turn expressed appreciation for the efforts that took place on their behalf. These conversations closed the circle by providing friends and family members with an understanding of how these objects were recovered and repatriated to them, and for us it was just as important to realize the extent to which these results had affected theme. We did not, however, discuss anything to do with FAR's "cleanup" at the site or the common tissues encountered there.

Listening to these outpourings of personal emotion was like standing under a waterfall. Somehow the physical properties of the memorial and its associations released questions that had tormented some of these people since the event. Did a son or daughter suffer in the fire? (Probably not, since there was evidence that smoke inhalation— really a rush of superheated toxic gases that kills instantly, often at the first breath—was responsible for killing man, if not all, of the victims before the fire reached them.) Why did my friends die that night and I didn't? (Answer: His friends invited him to the club for his birthday to hear the band, but his wife coaxed him out to dinner instead at the Cowesett Inn, across the street, where he saw the fire break out and watched as survivors escaped and burn victims were brought out.) Am I the only one who feels this pain? (Clearly not, and at the memorial site several individuals pointed out how the other visitors who come there to mourn have become "like family" to them.) How is it that my sister's age when she died in the fire exactly matches the number of miles from her home to the nightclub? And that the location of my house, of her house, and of the nightclub form a perfectly straight line on the map? (Many family members and friends of victims discerned otherwise obscure patterns in the way this tragedy occurred and affected them. Written messages attached to the memorial displays revealed similar views.) Who did this to us? (Almost everyone had an opinion about who was to blame for the fire and for the loss of life, although only a few were prepared to make specific accusations and fewer still were prepared to act on those accusations.)

My question is, can specific information like this ever be used in research of this kind, even anonymously for purposes of analysis? The answer: Probably not—at least not in print or in any public forum. The situation here is akin to what happened to the wreckage of TWA Flight 800. After salvaging many pieces from depths of around 80 feet in one of the most difficult underwater recovery operations ever attempted, the NTSB reconstructed the fuselage of the Boeing 747 on a frame inside a hangar. The reconstruction provided a three-dimensional view of the damage to the aircraft structure and helped the investigators identify a probable cause for the crash. Today the reconstructed fuselage of TWA 800 sits inside a cavernous, hangar-like building at the NTSB Academy in Virginia, where it serves as a training aid for accident investigators.[25] It also serves as a memorial for the families of the 230 people killed in the crash. Families have access to the building and sometimes visit. Because of the families' wishes, no photographs of the reconstructed fuselage are allowed. One message of TWA 800 is that we must learn from these events and experiences in such a way as not to retraumatize the people most affected by them, namely, the families and friends of the victims.

LESSONS FROM THE STATION FIRE MEMORIAL SITE

Our work at the memorial site points out the degree to which the memorialization process is connected to the aftermath of the disaster as experienced throughout the wider community. Specific displays and events at the site were linked chronologically at every step with public issues, including postdisaster investigations, criminal indictments, civil litigation, on-site squabbles, storms, and changes to the state fire code. The physical associations as they evolved over almost two years at the memorial site were prompted by these issues in the minds of the individuals and families affected by the tragedy, as expressed in numerous interviews and the memorial displays themselves. Kroeber's earlier claims notwithstanding, changes to the memorial displays were not mere statements of fashion that could be expected to vary independently of systemic changes in the society following the disaster.

At the level of symbology and meaning, it is harder to see these connections. We do not know what prompted the precise patterning of the memorial crosses when they were first place at the site or many of the elaborations that followed. Who chose the butterfly to symbolize what happened here? And how did this symbol gain such rapid and widespread acceptance among the mourners? One could speculate that butterflies evoked images of both fragility (of life) and flight (of the soul), which were certainly present in the minds of some of the people affected by the disaster. The butterfly could also be viewed as a neutral image—that is, not specific to any particular religious affiliation—while having generalized spiritual connotations. Even when asked, visitors to the memorial site

could not seem to agree on the meaning of this image. None of the ideas expressed about the butterfly representation can explain this choice of imagery and symbolism over other possible candidates. Despite the lack of shared meaning, the butterfly spontaneously became the agreed-on image during the early days of the memorial site to represent the Station fire tragedy and has now become routinized (approaching the sense originally advocated by Max Weber in his discussion of the "routinization of charisma")[26] to the point where it has emerged as an archaeological fact. Do people coping with intensely felt loss following a mass-fatality disaster generally tend to seize on a symbol to encapsulate and project their individual emotions? What factors can account for the choice of a specific symbol in such situations? Beyond documenting what happened in this particular case, we cannot offer general explanations that convincingly answer such questions.

The material associations at the memorial site displays provide clear indications, however, of the competing emotions of grief and anger following a mass-fatality tragedy. The emotions were eventually expressed in the form of physically separate displays containing very different messages. They also accurately indicated the relative degrees of support by the affected families for these emotional points of view. The layering of emotions referred to earlier is one way to describe this patterning. An overwhelming majority of the families still preferred to maintain their memorials as pure expressions of grief while a few families went ahead with their own displays expressing their anger at the authorities. These latter families, however, also maintain grief displays in the oval. As we began to conduct our interviews, these emotions were expressed to us verbally but not visually. It was not until shortly before the first anniversary of the fire, when two major ceremonies occurred, that the anger displays first appeared.

Another variation in this layering of emotions appeared in the timing of the anger displays following the outbursts of anger by individual families surrounding the Ty Longley display and the conflicts that arose before the storm. Once criminal indictments were handed down, the diffuse anger of these earlier episodes became focused on the authorities, resulting in two separate displays. The question remains, what were the proximate causes of this separation? After the criminal indictments were announced, there was a noticeable increase in the way people at the memorial site expressed their views about who should have been indicted. This was a major topic of discussion all over Rhode Island then. The approaching anniversary events provided an immediate opportunity to express these views visually at a location where they would be noticed.

Mixed emotions of grief and anger always seem to be present in the aftermath of mass-fatality disasters, especially among the families and individuals directly affected by the tragedy.[27] Ephemeral memorials appear to be a good litmus test of how and to what degree these emotions are operating within the community of victims. This kind of visualization is possible, however, only if one keeps a close empirical watch on the events surrounding the memorial site as well on what is happening in the wider community. An ethnoarchaeological perspective is well suited to this kind of observation. There were several instances at the Station fire memorial site when changes were rapid and nondirectional. It would have been easy, for example, to miss the reversal that took place with some of the displays before and after the storm or how certain major displays faded and were obliterated by later ones before the first anniversary of the fire.

Ethnoarchaeology, like archaeology, works best when it adheres to minimalist, empirical assumptions about human behavior in relation to material culture. In the context of disaster archaeology, ethnoarchaeology aided in understanding and in actively engaging the aftermath of a mass-fatality disasters in the months—and now, years—following the Station fire. The role of ethnoarchaeology following a disaster appeared unexpectedly, rather like the disaster itself. Perhaps the most important general lesson of our experiences following the Station disaster is to expect the unexpected: be ready to draw on the widest possible range of skills, ranging from site recording to interviews, to monitor events as they change in specific and often unpredictable ways.

Write Away

1. Spend time looking closely at one of the images in Gould and Scott's article and conduct a visual analysis. To guide your visual analysis, consider such questions as the following: What objects do you notice in the image? What people do you notice, and what are their expressions? What is in the background and foreground? What do you notice about the frame of the image? What is included? What do you think is excluded or exists right outside of the frame? What emotions does this image evoke for you? What can you learn about the historical and cultural contexts surrounding the image? How do those contexts inform, shape, or challenge your understanding of the image? What might the photograph reveal about the complexities and central issues of ethnoarchaeology as articulated by Gould and Scott?

2. Design a photographic essay about memorials. Decide the range and scope for your photographic essay, as well as how you will choose to integrate text throughout. In developing your photographic essay, consider what argument you would like to make about memorials. After you have completed your photographic essay, write a reflection about the process of developing your essay: What were your aims and purposes? How did you go about making selections and crafting text? What did you take into consideration with layout? What challenges did you encounter? What surprised you? What will you be able to take with you from this experience for subsequent learning and writing occasions, be they about memorials or with photographic essays, or not?

3. Choose a site near you and conduct an ethnoarchaeological research study and analysis. Your site can be related to memorials or it can emerge from a different context. As much as possible, adopt the same blended research strategies that Gould and Scott do, combining methods from archaeology and cultural anthropology. Engage in close observation of

material artifacts you're planning, decide how you will approach the selection process and which aspect of the site you will write about. Write up the results into an article that resembles the interdisciplinary genre adopted by Gould and Scott. Afterward, write a reflection about your experience with this blended research strategy and what you have learned about ethnoarchaeological methods.

Epidemiological Study: "Zika Virus Infections in Three Travellers" by AT Maria, et al.

Transfer Points: Public Health, Health Professions, Public Policy

Public health and epidemiology are of critical importance. Those working in these fields monitor the distributions and spread of disease across the world and within particular geographic regions or demographic populations. Epidemiologists help us recognize when and where outbreaks are taking place, and how we might best manage and treat them.

Those in healthcare professions and public policy use the knowledge produced by epidemiologists to enhance treatment plans, engage in crisis prevention, and create policies and procedures to improve the health care and welfare of people around the world. Because of their global focus, epidemiologists often consider disease as a worldwide human issue, one that must supersede national borders and individual nation-state politics.

The people who contribute to the field of epidemiology work in many professions, such as healthcare providers, policy makers, engineers, and statisticians. Increasingly, the work of human geography, sociology, and cultural anthropology intersects with epidemiology, as researchers must track the movement of people and viruses, and the impacts that cultural practices and human experiences have on the spread and treatment of disease and illness.

This article appears in a journal called *Eurosurveillance*. This journal publishes peer-reviewed research in an open-access format, enabling the research to be available to all readers. They have also, beginning in 2016, made their work part of the Creative Commons database, which means that anyone can reuse, distribute, or adapt any of the research. Typically, when an author submits research to a journal, the journal owns the rights to that research. This journal, however, is foregoing the rights, and possible income, in a move that signals that this sort of epidemiological data and research is created in the service of public good.

Each issue of the journal features several different kinds of writing, including opinion pieces, reviews, research articles, and what is termed "rapid communication." This article appears in the rapid communication section, a section designed to enable those on the front lines treating patients a way to communicate potential outbreaks to others in the healthcare field. A key facet of epidemiology is the time-sensitive nature of the work. Sometimes disease outbreaks take shape over a matter of days. Therefore, those working in epidemiology rely on frequent canvassing and amassing of information, and respond rapidly to emerging developments. Because of the time-sensitive nature of this material, one can see why it would be counterproductive for those who want to pass information along to have to wait through a lengthy peer-review and revision process, or to have to secure permissions.

This article is formatted as a case study, where the authors report on three cases that seem related to one another and significant. The headings and graphic elements are standing components for rapid communication articles in this journal. This

These authors are physicians and faculty working at several different hospitals and universities in France, including the Department of Infectious Diseases and Tropical Medicine at Montpellier University Hospital and the Institut de Recherche Biomédicale des Armées in Marseille, France.

prescribed structure facilitates the timely dissemination of the information, enabling the researchers to present their information clearly, without requiring too many decisions about how and where to order that information.

Such a format also increases the article's accessibility and navigability for readers; these readers, who are likely busy healthcare providers and policy makers, become familiar with this structure and form, and can therefore read through the material quickly getting the information they need as efficiently as possible.

The article's tone and style, exuding clarity and conciseness, also reflect the time-sensitive nature of the content. Unlike writers in many other contexts, these authors are not necessarily considering strategies for drawing readers in, nor are they evaluating how best to establish rapport with readers. Instead, their focus is clearly on message, emphasizing the main points as clearly and efficiently as possible and working under the assumption that readers who have a stake in this material will read it. Their expertise as authors, their *ethos*, emerges through their affiliations with established universities, institutes, and hospitals.

The authors present the information, include the medical figures, and then provide background and conclusions. Presumably, some readers might be more or less interested in particular sections, and these sorts of headings provide easily navigable signposting so readers can approach the text with their own priorities.

Those who go in to medical practice might be inclined to think that writing skills are less valuable. However, this article demonstrates how writing is central to the practice of medicine, and how communicating clearly and quickly, and collaborating with other providers, can help strengthen the worldwide sharing of knowledge about how to identify, manage, and treat illness and disease.

Write Here

Transferring epidemiological research to public contexts, the Centers for Disease Control regularly issue warnings about health. Some of these warnings involve travel alerts about health risks in particular destinations, other warnings involve updates about domestic health issues, such as Zika, hot weather, or salmonella. How have you been impacted by epidemiology in your life? How do you imagine epidemiology might impact you in your future?

AT Maria, M Maquart, A Makinson, O Flusin, M Segondy,
I Leparc-Goffart, V Le Moing, V Foulongne

Zika Virus Infections in Three Travellers Returning From South America and the Caribbean Respectively, to Montpellier, France, December 2015 to January 2016

We report three unrelated cases of Zika virus infection in patients returning from Martinique, Brazil and Colombia respectively, to Montpellier, France. They developed symptoms compatible with a mosquito-borne disease, and serological and molecular investigations indicated a recent Zika virus infection. Considering the recent warning for the likely teratogenicity of Zika virus and the presence of competent mosquito vectors in southern France, these cases highlight the need for awareness of physicians and laboratories in Europe.

Since early 2015 there has been a rapid spread of Zika virus infections in South America with a subsequent threat for importation of that emerging disease in other regions of the world. Here we describe three cases in travellers returning to France from affected areas.

Description of cases

Case 1

On 24 December 2015, a woman in her sixties presented at the Department of Infectious and Tropical Diseases at the University Hospital of Montpellier, France. Three days earlier she had developed sudden fever associated with myalgia, maculopapular rash located on face, trunk and limbs, and conjunctivitis. Symptoms onset occurred two days after having returned from a three-week vacation on Martinique Island (French West Indies). Blood cell count, liver enzymes and renal function were normal. Fever and rash resolved on day 3, but fatigue and mus-

cular symptoms lasted for seven days. Zika virus (ZIKV) real-time polymerase chain reaction (RT-PCR) was negative in blood on day 5 after symptom onset; urine samples were not collected for testing. ZIKV IgM antibodies were detected on 24 December (day 5 after symptom onset) with an increasing level in subsequent samples, whereas the rise of ZIKV IgG antibodies was noticed three weeks later.

Case 2

On 13 January 2016, a man in his twenties was examined in the same department. He had experienced gradual onset of fever, myalgia, diarrhoea,

TABLE

Temporal and virological data related to three imported cases of Zika virus infection, Montpellier, France, December 2015 to January 2016

Cases		Case 1	Case 2	Case 3
Temporal information				
Returning country		Martinique	Brazil	Colombia
Duration of stay		3 weeks	1 weeks	4 weeks
Date of return		18 Dec 2015	4 Jan 2016	10 Jan 2016
Symptoms onset		20 Dec 2015	5 Jan 2016	11 Jan 2016
Viral investigation				
First sample date		24 Dec 2015 (D5)	13 Jan 2016 (D9)	13 Jan 2016 (D3)
Dengue virus	RT-PCR[a] plasma	Negative	Negative	Negative
	RT-PCR urine	NS	Negative	Negative
	IgM[b] (OD[c] 1/200)	Negative (0.096)	Positive (0.241)	Positive (0.106)
	IgG[d] (OD 1/500)	Negative (0.061)	Positive (1.139)	Positive (0.209)
Chikungunya virus	RT-PCR[a] plasma	Negative	Negative	Negative
	RT-PCR urine	NS	Negative	Negative
	IgM[b] (OD 1/200)	Negative (0.077)	Negative (0.089)	Negative (0.064)
	IgG[d] (OD 1/500)	Negative (0.048)	Negative (0.047)	Negative (0.052)
Zika virus	RT-PCR[a] plasma	Negative	Negative	Positive (Ct=37.0)
	RT-PCR urine	NS	Negative	Positive (Ct=33.2)
	IgM[b] (OD 1/200)	Positive (0.264)	Positive (0.501)	Negative (0.104)
	IgG[d] (OD 1/500)	Negative (0.047)	Positive (0.301)	Negative (0.061)
Second sample date		4 Jan 2016 (D14)	18 Jan 2016 (D14)	18 Jan 2016 (D8)
Dengue virus	IgM (OD 1/200)	Negative (0.095)	Negative (0.191)	Positive (0.364)
	IgG (OD 1/500)	Negative (0.049)	Positive (0.899)	Positive (0.823)
Zika virus	RT-PCR plasma	ND	Negative	Negative
	RT-PCR urine	NS	Negative	Positive (Ct=33.9)
	RT-PCR saliva	NS	Negative	Positive (Ct=30.3)
	IgM (OD 1/200)	Positive (0.895)	Positive (0.446)	Positive (0.433)
	IgG (OD 1/500)	Negative (0.065)	Positive (0.406)	Positive (0.368)
	Zika virus neutralising antibodies[e]	1/320 (<1/40)	1/640 (1/160)	1/40 (<1/40)
Third sample date		14 Jan 2016 (D21)	NS	NS
Zika virus	IgM (OD 1/200)	Positive (0.313)	NS	NS
	IgG (OD 1/500)	Positive (0.155)	NS	NS
	Zika virus neutralising antibodies[e]	1/640 (<1/40)	NS	NS

Ct: Cycles threshold; D: days from symptom onset; ND: not determined; NS: not sampled; OD: optical density; RT-PCR: real-time polymerase chain reaction.

[a] RT-PCRs were performed with the RealStar dengue RT-PCR kit 2.0, the RealStar chikungunya RT-PCR kit 1.0 and the RealStar Zika virus RT-PCR kit 1.0 (Altona Diagnostic, Germany).

[b] Flaviriruses IgM and chikungunya virus IgM detections were performed with in house IgM antibody-capture ELISA (MAC-ELISA) assays.

[c] At 1/200 or 1/500 working dilutions.

[d] Flaviriruses IgG and chikungunya virus IgG detections were performed with in house indirect ELISA assays.

[e] Zika virus neutralising antibodies (result of West Nile virus neutralisation antibodies assay performed as control) with the titre of serum neutralising 90%.

arthralgia and cutaneous rash on trunk and limbs, starting on 5 January, one day after his return from a one-week stay in Rio de Janeiro, Brazil. Upon examination in hospital, fever and cutaneous rash had disappeared, but arthralgia persisted, in association with asthenia, non-productive cough and conjunctivitis. On the day of admission (13 January), laboratory tests showed normal blood cell count and normal renal function, while transaminases were slightly increased. RT-PCR for ZIKV was negative in blood and urine samples. ZIKV IgG and IgM antibodies were detected in serum concomitantly with DENV antibodies; however, the specificity of these anti-ZIKV antibodies was confirmed by a neutralisation assay. Three of the patient's relatives living in Brazil were concurrently diagnosed with symptomatic ZIKV infection.

Case 3

A man in his fifties progressively developed myalgia in lower limbs, pruriginous rash and fever, two days after returning from a three-week vacation in Columbia. He was examined in the same hospital department on the third day (13 January), and showed intense fatigue, extensive maculopapular eruption on the face, trunk and both upper and lower limbs, ulcerative pharyngitis, and conjunctivitis. Results of the neurological examination were normal. Blood cell count showed mild leucopenia (3,800 cells/μL; norm: >4,000 cells/μL), with normal liver enzymes and renal function. RT-PCR for ZIKV was positive in blood, urine and saliva samples. ZIKV seroconversion was detected in the second sample (day 8 after symptom onset) with observation of cross-reactivity with flaviviruses including dengue. Interestingly, two relatives who travelled with him were subsequently tested, and the results were negative for ZIKV.

Symptoms disappeared completely within one week in all patients. Temporal and viral investigation data are summarised in the Table.

Background

Zika virus is a mosquito-borne flavivirus related to dengue virus (DENV), yellow fever virus (YFV) and West Nile virus (WNV). A large outbreak of ZIKV infections involving the ZIKV Asian lineage is ongoing in Brazil since April 2015 [1] with up to 18 countries affected as at 23 December 2015 [2]. By the first week of December 2015, nine additional South American countries and Cape Verde islands had reported locally acquired cases [3]. Furthermore, a link between ZIKV infection and neurological disorders or congenital malformations has been suspected in Brazil, and an epidemiological alert from the Pan American Health Organization (PAHO) has been issued [4]. ZIKV which is transmitted by Aedes aegypti has been isolated from several Aedes mosquito species [5] and transmission by Ae. albopictus has been documented in Gabon [6], leading to the threat of a worldwide spread. In the last week of December, the French Ministry of Health issued a warning about the detection of autochthonous cases of ZIKV infections in French Departments of America, French Guyana and Martinique Island, confirming the spread of ZIKV in the Caribbean [7]. Given that South American and Caribbean countries are highly touristic regions and that European overseas districts in that area have close connections with their related European mainland countries, there is a risk for imported cases to occur in Europe.

Discussion and conclusions

No autochthonous case of ZIKV infection and a limited number of cases related to the South American outbreak have been reported so far in Europe. The first one was observed in Italy, at the beginning of the Brazilian outbreak, in a traveller returning from Brazil [8] and, more recently, in November 2015, in a traveller returning to the Netherlands from Surinam [3]. Interestingly, similarly to Case 1 returning from Martinique, these imported cases were concomitantly detected close to the first reported locally-acquired cases. Since most ZIKV infections are asymptomatic or mild, this suggests that, at the time of the first autochthonous cases, the overall burden of ZIKV infection has been underestimated.

Since its first introduction in 2004, the mosquito vector *Ae. albopictus* has been well established in southern France. Autochthonous transmissions of chikungunya virus (CHIKV) or DENV previously occurred in Europe [9,10], such as in Montpellier, with an outbreak of 12 locally acquired CHIKV infections in October 2014 [11] or in Nimes, a nearby town, with an outbreak of six autochthonous DENV infection cases in 2015 [12]. Thus, prerequisites for ZIKV autochthonous transmission are likely met in southern France. However, despite the fact that *Ae. albopictus* is an in vitro competent vector for the ZIKV African lineage [13] and was identified as an efficient vector for this lineage in Gabon [6], its vectorial capacity for the ZIKV Asian lineage remains to be clarified. Furthermore, in the cases reported here, the risk of local transmission can be ruled out, considering the vector inactivity during winter time.

However, this description of imported cases, including one case from a French Overseas Department, should reinforce the preparedness plan for arboviral outbreaks which is implemented each year since 2006, during the *Ae. albopictus* activity period (May to November), in all *Ae. albopictus*-colonised areas in France [11]. This means that the network of laboratories that currently propose CHIKV and DENV diagnosis should add ZIKV diagnosis to their panel, with regular reports to regional surveillance boards, and that practitioners' awareness of clinically-suspected cases must be raised; moreover, they should be required to report to regional health authorities. However, as illustrated here, the laboratory diagnosis of ZIKV infection might be challenging due to the transient viraemia, the antibody rise that might be delayed, and the IgG flavivirus cross-reactivity that may interfere in serological testing. This will be a concern for the surveillance of pregnant women [14] as well as for blood safety policy [15].

Conflict of interest
None declared.

Authors' contributions
Managed the patients: ATM, AM, VLM; performed laboratory investigations: MM, OF, ILG, VF; wrote the manuscript: ATM, MS, VLM, VF.

References

1. Campos GS, Bandeira AC, Sardi SI. Zika virus outbreak, Bahia, Brazil. Emerg Infect Dis. 2015;21(10):1885-6. DOI: 10.3201/eid2110.150847 PMID: 26401719

2. Ministério Da Saûde (Brazil). Monitoramento dos casos de dengue, febre de chikungunya et febre pelo virus zika até a seman Epidémiologica 48, 2015. [Monitoring cases of dengue, chikungunya, zika virus infections as of epidemiological week 48]. Brasília: Ministério Da Saûde. [Accessed 23 December 2015]. Portuguese. Available from: http://portalsaude.saude.gov.br/images/pdf/2015/dezembro/23/2015-049---Dengue-SE-48---para-publica----o-21.12.15.pdf

3. European Center for Disease Prevention and Control (ECDC). Communicable disease threats report, week 51, 13-19 December 2015. Stockholm: ECDC. 2015. Available from: http://ecdc.europa.eu/en/publications/Publications/Communicable-disease-threats-report-19-dec-2015.pdf

4. Pan American Health Organization (PAHO). Epidemiological Alert. Neurological syndrome, congenital malformations, and. Zika virus infection. Implications for public health in the Americas Organization. Washington: PAHO. [Accessed 1 Dec 2015]. Available from: http://www.paho.org/hq/index.php?option=com_content&view=category&layout=blog&id=1218&Itemid=2291&lang=fr

5. Diallo D, Sall AA, Diagne CT, Faye O, Faye O, Ba Y, et al. Zika virus emergence in mosquitoes in south-eastern Senegal, 2011. PLoS One. 2014;9(10):e109442. DOI: 10.1371/journal.pone.0109442 PMID: 25310102

6. Grard G, Caron M, Mombo IM, Nkoghe D, Mboui Ondo S, Jiolle D, et al. Zika virus in Gabon (Central Africa)--2007: a new threat from Aedes albopictus? PLoS Negl Trop Dis. 2014;8(2):e2681. DOI: 10.1371/journal.pntd.0002681 PMID: 24516683

7. European Center for Disease Prevention and Control (ECDC). Communicable disease threats report, week 52, 20-26 December 2015. Stockholm: ECDC. Available from: http://ecdc.europa.eu/en/publications/Publications/Communicable-disease-threats-report-26-dec-2015.pdf.

8. Zammarchi L, Tappe D, Fortuna C, Remoli ME, Günther S, Venturi G, et al. Zika virus infection in a traveller returning to Europe from Brazil, March 2015. Euro Surveill. 2015;20(23):21153. DOI: 10.2807/1560-7917.ES2015.20.23.21153 PMID: 26084316

9. Grandadam M, Caro V, Plumet S, Thiberge JM, Souarès Y, Failloux AB, et al. Chikungunya virus, southeastern France. Emerg Infect Dis. 2011;17(5):910-3. DOI: 10.3201/eid1705.101873 PMID: 21529410

10. Marchand E, Prat C, Jeannin C, Lafont E, Bergmann T, Flusin O, et al. Autochthonous case of dengue in France, October 2013. Euro Surveill. 2013;18(50):20661. DOI: 10.2807/1560-7917.ES2013.18.50.20661 PMID: 24342514

11. Delisle E, Rousseau C, Broche B, Leparc-Goffart I, L'Ambert G, Cochet A, et al. Chikungunya outbreak in Montpellier, France, September to October 2014. Euro Surveill. 2015;20(17):21108. DOI: 10.2807/1560-7917.ES2015.20.17.21108 PMID: 25955774

12. Institut National de Veille Sanitaire (INVS). Surveillance sanitaire en Languedoc-Roussillon. Point épidémiologique au 4 Novembre 2015. [Medical surveillance in Languedoc-Roussillon. Epidemiological point 4 Nov 2015]. Paris: INVS. [Accessed 11 November 2015]. French. Available from: http://www.invs.sante.fr/fr/Publications-et-outils/Points-epidemiologiques/Tous-les-numeros/Languedoc-Roussillon/2015/Surveillance-sanitaire-en-Languedoc-Roussillon.-Point-epidemiologique-au-4-novembre-2015

13. Wong PS, Li MZ, Chong CS, Ng LC, Tan CH. Aedes (Stegomyia) albopictus (Skuse): a potential vec-tor of Zika virus in Singapore.PLoS Negl Trop Dis. 2013;7(8):e2348. DOI: 10.1371/journal.pntd.0002348 PMID: 23936579

14. Petersen EE, Staples JE, Meaney-Delman D, Fischer M, Ellington SR, Callaghan WM, et al. Interim guidelines for pregnant women during a Zika virus outbreak- United States, 2016. MMWR Morb Mortal Wkly Rep. 2016;65(2):30-3. DOI: 10.15585/mmwr.mm6502e1 PMID: 26796813

15. Marano G, Pupella S, Vaglio S, Liumbruno GM, Grazzini G. Zika virus and the never-ending story of emerging pathogens and transfusion medicine.Blood Transfus. 2015;5:1-6.PMID: 26674815

http://eurosurveillance.org/ViewArticle.aspx?ArticleId=21374

Write Away

1. Create a personal narrative, written from the perspective of one of the patients in these cases. Expand the narrative account to convey not only the medical experience, but the person's entire experience both during and after travel. Your personal narrative can take the form of a prose narrative, a series of blog posts, or another format of your choosing, in consultation with your instructor.

2. Identify discipline-specific terminology in the article, including terms found in the table, and, together with a team of peers, create a collaborative slide deck to explain each of these terms for lay readers.

3. Write your own rapid-communication case study, using a real virus but imagined cases. Where did the persons travel and why? When did the individuals present with the illness? Compose your case study in the format of this article, as though you were submitting it for publication in *Eurosurveillance* or a similar journal.

Video Game Screenshot, Poster:
"Grand Theft Auto V Automobile" by Brenna Hillier;
World of Warcraft Poster

Transfer Points: Visual Studies, Design, Computer Science, Marketing

"For ages, the fallen titan Sargeras plotted to scour all life from Azeroth. To this end, Sargeras possessed the human sorcerer Medivh and compelled him to contact Gul'dan, an orc warlock on the world of Draenor. There, Sargeras' demonic servants among the Burning Legion worked to corrupt the once-peaceful orcs and forge them into a bloodthirsty army known as the Horde" ("Warcraft").

So begins the story of *Warcraft: Orcs and Humans*, a video game initially released in 1994 and that went on to become a gaming sensation. Re-branded and released in 2004 as *World of Warcraft (WoW)*, this video game now holds status as one of the longest running and most popular multiplayer video games of all time (Braithwaite).

Grand Theft Auto (GTA), the game from which the other image depicted here emerges, was first released in 1997, and, like *WoW*, also stands as a groundbreaking video game, renowned for its privileging of violence and crime. Its images and content were deemed so extreme at first, that "British, German and French officials condemned it [and] Brazil banned it outright" (McLaughlin and Thomas).

The popularity of these video games makes them much more than leisure-time play. Video games such as *WoW* and *GTA* are big business, and they integrate the latest technologies and computer graphics. The images included here represent what is often referred to as concept art or graphic design. Concept artists have expertise in art, visual studies, and/or digital technologies, and they put their talents and skills to use by designing video games.

Video game design emerges through an iterative process of development, much like the writing process. For instance, where writers might begin a project by brainstorming or mind mapping, concept artists might embark on a design project by using thumbnail sketches, either in word or visual form (Kay and Tudor). Concept artists often work in teams, exploring several different possibilities before narrowing in on a design plan. And, they provide and receive feedback on drafts in progress, much like writers.

Video game design operates through several distinct principles. Veteran designers Rob Kay and Andy Tudor emphasize that designers abide by such concepts as the "Golden Ratio," whereby nature, architecture, and biology appear in equal thirds on the screen at all times. Kay and Tudor also note that concept artists often adhere to the principles of animation stemming from the 1930s, which include a sequence framework of anticipation-action-reaction.

Those who work in the field of video game design or concept art might have degrees in visual studies or computer science. Computer science is a broadly applicable field across many sectors and industries, from health care and economics to video game development and design. Game development, from the computer science perspective, focuses on the scientific and technological aspects of video game development. Computer scientists write codes for games, and imagine the pathways and human behaviors within intricately constructed and responsive gaming worlds. The multiplayer capacities of games such as *WoW* and *GTA* hinge on a computer logic that facilitates human-human interaction within the confines of a digital world.

The other discipline most closely linked to video game design is visual studies, also termed visual arts. This field focuses on the production, dissemination, analysis, and reception of all forms of visual content. Visual studies is closely linked with an area of research known as visual culture. Visual culture argues that contemporary culture is more heavily steeped in the visual as opposed to the written.

Those in visual studies apply various theories to the ways they read visual texts. Such theoretical apparatus might include gender theory, postmodern theory, or critical race theory. In an article about gender and video games, for instance, sociologist Xeniya Kondrat argues that some video games use "wrong, disrespectful and sometimes even violent representations of both genders." Asking users in surveys how video games represent the female gender, Kondrat concludes that many video games do create female characters who are "sexually provocative" and that few include female protagonists. Kondrat also finds, though, that the trends are shifting, albeit slowly, to include more female protagonists and more positive female role models.

As work such as Kondrat's suggest, scholars across disciplines conduct research through and with

Grand Theft Auto (GTA) is a video game created by Rockstar Games, which is a subsidiary of Take2Games. Rockstar Games began in 1988. *GTA* was first released in 1997, developed by computer game designer David Jones. He had initially named it *Race-n-Chase*, but the two brothers who first bought the rights to develop *GTA*, Sam and Dan Houser, renamed it *GTA* (McLaughlin and Thomas). *World of Warcraft* is an online video game, first released in 2004. It is developed by Blizzard Entertainment, and designed by Tom Chilton, Rob Pardo, and Jeffrey Kaplan.

video games. *WoW*, for instance, has been the subject of numerous articles and books, from purchasing behavior (Guo and Barnes), mythology (Geraci), and philosophy (Cuddy and Nordlinger), to therapy (Jordan). Similarly, *GTA* has also been the subject of inquiry across disciplines, including geographers (Salter), psychologists (Teng, et al), and legal scholars (Martin and Adams).

The peer-reviewed scholarship and research about video games is but one form of writing circulating around this industry. Users also often write reviews of their gaming experiences. The *GTA* screenshot, for example, was included in a blog by gamer Brenda Hillier, who is a Deputy Editor at *vg247.com*, a company that reviews video games and highlights news about the industry. Writers are also involved directly with video games, helping to script characters' lines and writing the narratives that drive the game worlds. Such work demonstrates the intersections between visual and written texts in the complicated but highly popular worlds of video game play.

Write Here

Working with a small group of classmates, develop a mind map documenting your collective knowledge about the video game industry. You might think about the following questions as starting points for your mind map, but be sure to also allow your group to add all sorts of dimensions and areas to the mind map: What do you know about video games? What fields of scholarship have a stake in research about video games? What conversations about video games circulate in popular news? How are video games developed? What are the most popular video games right now?

Brenna Hillier
Grand Theft Auto V Automobile

World of Warcraft **Poster**

Write Away

1. Using techniques of visual analysis (see Chapter 10), conduct and write a visual analysis of one of these images. Consider such questions as the following: What do you notice most about the image? What is in the background and foreground? What do you notice about the frame of the image? What is included? What do you think is excluded or exists right outside of the frame? What emotions does this image evoke for you? What argument might this image make? What might the image suggest about the video game industry or about this particular video game?

2. Write a review of a video game experience. First, look at samples of video game reviews to determine the components of that genre and to develop some terms of art used in such reviews. Then, choose a video game, play it, or a portion of it, and then write a review of your experience. Be sure to address as many components of the video game as you can, in order to provide a robust review.

3. Create a portfolio of visual images related to video games. You can choose to use a particular theme, or a particular subset of video games. Develop an introduction to your repository in which you articulate the aims of the portfolio you have assembled, draw on relevant research about video games, and introduce readers to the contexts in which these images emerge. Annotate each image to include full citations as well as other information as determined by you. Portfolios can create strong arguments, so think carefully about what argument you are making with this portfolio, and select, organize, and annotate the images accordingly.

Chapter 4 Key Terms

primary materials	in-depth reading	*kairos*
secondary materials	research databases	literature review
tertiary materials	rhetorical triangle	annotated bibliography
popular secondary sources	*ethos*	rhetoric
scholarly secondary sources	*pathos*	visual literacy
public scholarship	*logos*	mind map
shallow reading		

Write Away

This activity invites you to explore and reflect on discipline-specific reading strategies so you can become more adept at approaching reading from a transfer-based perspective.

Pose a question. Pose a general research question. You can use one of those you developed in Chapter 3, or you can pose an entirely new one. Your question should be broad enough that you will be able to apply it to several different disciplines.

Find (at least) three different disciplinary perspectives. Using several different discipline-specific databases at your institution, find three different articles related to that topic, each from a different disciplinary perspective. For instance, you might find one article from an English literature perspective, one from sociology, and one from chemistry. Focus specifically on scholarly articles from whichever particular disciplines you are choosing.

Read and annotate. Read in-depth and annotate each of those articles, looking specifically for moments where you as a reader find yourself using discipline-specific reading skills. For example, do you notice any particular structures? Where are you finding technical vocabulary? Do any of the articles require you to use visual, mathematical, or data-based literacy skills?

Reflect. After annotating the articles, reflect in writing for ten minutes about what you have learned about discipline-based reading strategies and about how you will transfer your approaches to reading across contexts.

Summary

Now that you have encountered throughout Chapters 2, 3, and 4 several foundational aspects of academic writing that transverse disciplines—research and writing as a process, posing questions, and reading—our exploration now focuses on a more specific writing practice: summary. Chapter 5 offers you a glimpse into how academic writers across disciplines and contexts make use of the many varied forms of summary. To provide you with strategies for *summary in transit*, this chapter addresses the following concepts:

- Correcting Common Myths about Summary
- Prerequisites for Writing Summary
- Varied Components of Summary across Context
- Varied Criteria for Effective Summaries across Context
- Different Occasions for Summary

Chapter 6 focuses on synthesis, a writing strategy that uses summary as its foundation by making connections between and across different ideas and texts, thus supporting both analysis and arguments, which will then be the areas of focus for the remaining chapters.

Days 1 & 2—Kathmandu, Nepal
Arrive in Kathmandu and transfer to our hotel, where we'll gather for an orientation. Spend the following day discovering medieval Kathmandu. Venture into Pashupatinath and visit Nepal's largest Buddhist stupa, the Boudhanath Stupa, both part of the UNESCO's World Heritage site. Shangri-La Hotel (*National Geographic Expeditions*).

That these expeditioners chose to feature their visit to the Boudhanath Stupa in even the briefest of journal entries demonstrates its impressiveness and the now-iconic presence it occupies in Kathmandu, Nepal. Those on Mount Everest expeditions often stop at the Boudhanath Stupa to spin prayer wheels and, according to custom, travel the perimeter in clockwise circumnavigation.

The Boudhanath Stupa is one of a number of stupas that exist across Asia, some of which date from as early as 250 BCE and which were often erected as burial monuments in honor of Buddha. Those who study and write about stupas have conveyed many intricacies about these structures. Many feature remarkable astronomical accuracy, oriented so that the moonrise and sunset can mark time and built so that the center pole, which is often the highest point, tracks the sun's zenith…each day. Looking down from the top of a stupa, one can discern an axis point, from which emerge four directions pointing east, north, south, and west ("History"; Kak; Rao; Shelby).

Nearly all the aspects of the stupa have symbolic significance, from the pyramid with 13 steps, "representing the ladder to enlightenment" to the "two circular plinths supporting the hemisphere of the stupa, symbolizing water." The route for clockwise circumnavigation along the bottom of a stupa also holds symbolic importance: "If one thinks of the stupa as a circle or wheel, the unmoving center symbolizes Enlightenment" ("Boudhanath"; Shelby).

The origins of the Boudhanath Stupa have given rise to several legends from varying cultural traditions that have been passed down across generations and that, together, reflect the multiculturalism of Kathmandu, a city known to sponsor the "greatest intermingling" of Hindus and Buddhists in what is otherwise officially a Hindu country. One legend describes a woman outwitting a king: "[A] woman...asked the king for land to build a shrine to [B]uddha. He agreed to let her have enough land that a buffalo's skin could cover. The woman cut a buffalo's hide into strips and made a large circumference" ("Guide"), thereby winning more land than the king had anticipated.

Another legend holds that a female poultry farmer, Shamvara, and her four sons built the Boudhanath Stupa. However, according to legend, villagers began to complain about the construction, but Shamvara refused to stop and died on the spot, thus attaining Buddhist salvation. Yet another legend, emerging from Hinduism, maintains that "the great stupa was built by King Manadeva I in the fifth century CE to absolve himself from the sin of patricide" ("Cultural").

Conveying origin myths such as these, relaying architectural features of stupas, and journaling about travel experiences all rely on one of the most valuable, pervasive, and varied features of academic writing: summary. Summary enables people to share knowledge, data, observations, experiences, and ideas.

While summaries such as a three-sentence travelogue might suggest that summary is quite easy, the reality is that summary—even the most concise versions—requires a number of complex writing decisions about what to include and how to incorporate it most effectively for a particular aim or purpose. Far from being simplistic, summary is one of the most powerful, challenging, and central skills you will encounter in academic writing across disciplines and contexts. In fact, it would be difficult to overstate just how vital summary is to academic writing, and just how varied are its forms.

The act of summarizing involves condensing another's text (or your own) into a smaller amount of text. The notion of what constitutes a text in this case, as in Chapter 4: Reading, must be broadly construed because writers routinely summarize all sorts of texts, be they written, verbal, visual, material, auditory, or some combination thereof.

With multiple, sometimes overlapping purposes, summaries can work to share key information, encourage others to examine a text for themselves, discuss the uses and limits of a text, or provide a platform of knowledge from which writers and their readers can build. Sometimes summaries stand alone, and other times they are embedded as part of larger writing projects.

Write Here

Locate two or three other travel accounts of Kathmandu, read them, and then compare them to the brief one excerpted from the *National Geographic* expedition on the first page of this chapter. What sites and experiences in Kathmandu do these other travelers document? What do you think influences the decisions different travelers make for how to summarize their experiences and how to select which experiences to include or omit as they develop their travelogues?

Correcting Common Myths about Summary

Summary carries with it a somewhat unforgiving reputation in part due to some common, negative myths about what summary is and what it is not. Such negative myths about summary can divert writers from considering the complexities of summary and, therefore, can end up contributing to ineffective summary. These myths also negatively impact writers' transfer of summary across writing contexts by preventing writers from examining how the conventions and expectations of summary are shaped by those contexts. So, as a point of departure for developing an in-depth, nuanced, and transfer-based approach to summary, let's begin by debunking some of these common myths about summary.

Myth #1: Summary is objective

Because summary is often contrasted with other modes of working with texts, such as evaluation or criticism, many people erroneously believe that summary is an objective type of writing that operates in contrast to more subjective modes of writing. This myth of objective summary maintains that writers can somehow cleanly pull out the most central components of any text and readily summarize it, without infusing any disciplinary, individual, or context-specific perspectives or purposes. In fact, summary is rarely objective. Since all humans understand texts and experiences based on their perspectives, summary looks different depending on who is writing the summary and why he or she is writing it.

Every occasion for summary presents unique goals and purposes, and every person who summarizes will also bring his or her own individual preferences and aims. Different individuals notice different details, for varying reasons, and different writers have varying priorities for what to include in a summary. Summaries also emerge from and respond to varying contexts, and these contexts play a large role in shaping what summaries look like. Writing occasion and disciplinary context influence which aspects a writer will choose to summarize of any given text, as well as how many details to include in the summary. These choices will change what the resulting summary includes and excludes, what it features and obscures, and what it either suggests or makes explicit. Summaries nearly always reflect these highly subjective, individual, and diverse nuances.

Myth #2: Summary is easy to write

Perhaps the myth that suggests summary is easy to write originates from summary being among the first modes of writing instruction offered for working with texts. Students in early education, even as early as preschool, are often asked to summarize a text. These early associations with summary leave an imprint on popular conceptions about summary and suggest that summary is so easy that even a kindergartener or first grader can summarize. However, summary, particularly in academic writing at the undergraduate level and beyond, actually involves a number of complex choices the writer must make: How much detail should I include? How much background information should I offer? How do I integrate a summary into a longer writing project? What kind of tone do I need to convey?

Writers decide how to navigate these choices with summary by taking into consideration the publication context, the disciplinary perspective, and any particular aims and purposes the writer may have. But even beyond the challenges posed by these

Transfer at Work

Writers adjust their approaches to summary in response to disciplinary context and writing occasion. For instance, Nicholas A. Jones and Jungmiwha J. Bullock summarize results from Census 2000 and Census 2010 by focusing on the geographical distribution of people who self-identified as being multiracial. Jones and Bullock summarize the Census data by emphasizing that "about one out of six multiple-race individuals lived in 1 of 10 states" (10):

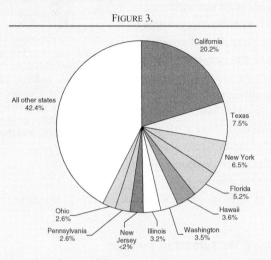

FIGURE 3.

Summarizing Census 2000 data from a different perspective, Jason C. Booza focuses on the geographical distribution of Polish Americans, summarizing that "major concentrations of [Polish Americans] are still found within the historic immigrant destinations such as Chicago, New York, and Detroit" (64):

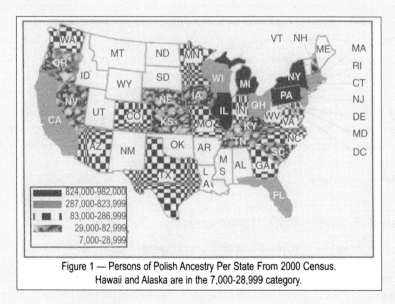

Figure 1 — Persons of Polish Ancestry Per State From 2000 Census.
Hawaii and Alaska are in the 7,000-28,999 category.

sorts of choices, summary is challenging because it asks you to fully understand the text you are summarizing. To summarize effectively, you must be able to recognize and comprehend the main argument or plot (which in itself can often be challenging), as well as many of the supporting elements and evidence. Effective summary also requires an understanding of structure, complexity, nuance, influence, and context, as well as an ability to capture the text's more amorphous qualities such as tone and voice. In addition, writers must not only position this summary to align with their own purposes and goals, but also shape it according to disciplinary context and writing occasion—all within what is often a quite brief amount of text. Summary viewed from this perspective requires considerable sophistication.

Writer Insights

How and when do you use summary in your writing?

As a consultant for workforce development, my writing starts with knowing my audience. For example, when I develop a curriculum, I include more instructions in simpler language if the teachers are likely to be inexperienced. If people who can easily interpret statistics are the targeted audience, I provide less explanation of the numbers than I do for a general readership. Sometimes a bulleted list is desirable as denser text would be a barrier or ignored. Most often I provide an introduction and a summary so potential readers can quickly assess whether the material is relevant to their needs.

~Laura Wyckoff, Workforce Development Consultant, Portland, Oregon, U.S.

Myth #3: Summary isn't used in college

This third myth suggests summary does not deserve considered attention and practice at the postsecondary level. Summary, in fact, appears in countless ways throughout academic writing at the postsecondary level and beyond. Writers routinely summarize texts during the prewriting phases of writing in order to generate ideas about their own projects. Writers also summarize texts within their writing projects as a way of advancing or bolstering their own arguments, typically by situating their project within the context of prior scholarship or existing theoretical perspectives. Most arguments can be connected to larger academic conversations about a topic or issue. Summarizing enables writers to tap into that contextual material. Summary also appears in postsecondary contexts in the form of tertiary research materials such as annotated bibliographies or literature reviews. Far from being unnecessary or infrequent, summary actually operates as a foundational practice that is not only in and of itself complex and rigorous, but that also enables writers to advance their arguments and contribute knowledge to ongoing scholarly conversations.

Prerequisites for Writing Summary

Approaching summary requires two critical prerequisites:

1. **Careful reading.** Writing effective summaries hinges on your critical reading skills, so you are encouraged to review Chapter 4: Reading, especially the section on reading rhetorically. It is exceptionally difficult to summarize a text effectively if you haven't

read it thoroughly, taking into account matters of context, purpose, and other aspects of the text.

2. **Understanding the occasion for the summary.** This involves gaining a nuanced understanding of the occasion giving rise to the summary. Why are you writing the summary? What do you hope to accomplish? The following section includes several key questions writers should ask and answer before creating summaries.

Key questions for determining the occasion for summary

Because the occasion for a summary will determine nearly every aspect of that summary, it is crucial for writers to understand several key aspects and considerations related to the occasion. Doing so will enable writers to craft the most effective summaries for whatever the occasion demands.

TABLE 5.1 Key questions for determining the occasion for summary.

Purpose	Is your purpose primarily to inform readers, ostensibly in lieu of their reading, viewing, or listening to the text themselves? Or, is your purpose primarily to persuade readers to read or purchase the text? Is your summary connected to a larger argument or aim in a piece of writing?
Audience	How knowledgeable are they about the subject matter and/or text you are summarizing? What do you hope your readers learn from the summary? Why might they be reading the summary?
Length requirements	How long should the summary be? Will the summary be more effective in a highly brief format, even perhaps as short as 140 characters (as in a tweet), or will the summary work better in a full-length, highly detailed form?
General to specific	How detailed should the summary be? Is it sufficient to provide a broad, sweeping overview, or should the summary include material about evidence, methods, quotes, and/or more specifics?
Background material	How much background material should be included in a summary? Which aspects of the cultural, historical, social, geographical, or biographical influences that have shaped a text warrant inclusion in the summary of that text?
Disciplinary context	What is the disciplinary context that is giving rise to the summary, and how will that impact the shape of the summary? What is the disciplinary context surrounding the text being summarized, and how has that impacted the content of that text?
Tone	What tone will work most effectively for the summary? Should the tone be positive, negative, encouraging, discouraging, ironic, or should it convey some other tone altogether?

Write Now

Choose a long text you have read, or written, and summarize it into a 140-character tweet.

Transfer Hub: Contribute your ideas and see what others have written at fountainheadpress.com/transferhub.

Varied Components of Summary across Context

Your answers to the previous questions help shape the summary you produce. Depending on how you answer these questions, you might include any or all of the following in your summary:

- main argument/features of the text
- key terms of the text
- evidence and/or main examples from the text
- significance of the text
- key quotes from the text
- purpose of the text
- methods used in the text (see "Research across Disciplines" in Chapter 2: Research and Writing as a Process)
- political, social, and cultural context or background
- assumptions guiding the text
- probable audience of the text
- tone of the text
- related texts

Criteria for Effective Summaries across Contexts

Given the drastic variation in purpose, discipline, format, and style among summaries, it would be challenging to develop an exhaustive list of criteria that make summaries more or less effective. Still, there are some general criteria that might be applied across disciplines. Each occasion for summary may have its own nuances, conventions, and purposes, but writers can nevertheless craft effective summaries by attending to criteria that span different contexts and disciplines. Effective summaries, regardless of discipline or format, will generally benefit from the consideration and integration of the following criteria.

Captures ideas accurately

Be as accurate as possible in your summary. Accuracy in summary means you have identified the main points or arguments of a text and you have done so as completely as possible. Omitting crucial elements of a text or suggesting that a minor point is instead a major point can lead to inaccurate summary. You can work toward accuracy by reading thoroughly and carefully. One way to test your accuracy is to imagine that the author of the text being summarized will be reading your summary. Ask yourself if the author(s) would agree that the summary captures the text honestly and thoroughly.

Readers are relying on your accuracy in order for them to adequately appraise your argument as well as to inform their own research. You might be familiar with the negativity and mistrust engendered by inaccurate summaries in the political arena. In that context, those affiliated with one political agenda might take a snippet of text from someone with different political priorities and then publicize that snippet, out of context, using it as a way to mischaracterize how that individual approaches an important issue. Such a tactic amounts to both an underrepresentation and a mischaracterization and ultimately damages integrity and can stymy the process of knowledge development.

Reduces appropriately

One of the overarching aims of summary, regardless of context, is to consolidate, condense, and reduce another text. The degree to which one reduces a text can shift according to the context for the summary. It is possible to reduce enormously large texts to a few sentences, or even a few words. Likewise, one can choose to create a rather in-depth summary of an expansive text. As a general guideline, though, in most cases, if your summary is the same length or longer than the text you are summarizing, then you have likely not achieved summary. Some exceptions to this might be when writers are summarizing poetry, music, verbal texts, films, or visual texts and are translating these forms of communication into written prose summary. These forms of summary might require that the length of the summary occupy more space than the original text being summarized.

Including too many details will make a summary ineffective. By increasing its length, the writer risks distracting from its focus. Readers across disciplines expect a clear, concise approximation of the original work; otherwise, they could easily spend their time reading the original source. Reducing appropriately in the context of summary requires that you sift through a text to identify the most critical and salient components. However, if the purpose for summarizing is to provide a bibliographic resource for other researchers, you might want to devote more length and include more details, thereby increasing its potential usefulness to a wider variety of readers. Even in these cases, though, summaries should still accomplish the main priority of condensing the original text.

Responds to context

Every summary emerges from within a particular context and should respond effectively to that context. For instance, in some disciplinary contexts, readers expect that summaries will make extensive use of direct quotations. In other disciplinary contexts, direct quotations would be perceived as an anomaly since paraphrasing is that discipline-specific norm. Other contexts that shape an occasion for summary include the purpose for that summary. A writer creating a summary as part of an annotated bibliography on a particular issue may focus on the unique contribution of that particular text to the larger conversation. By contrast, a writer developing a summary of several texts to illustrate a common perspective or approach to an issue may instead choose to summarize by grouping texts together to demonstrate aligned arguments.

Responding to context appropriately with summary helps your readers by meeting their general expectations for what a summary might include, as well as why it might exist or be necessary in that particular context. To do this effectively, it is important to identify the purpose and occasion for the summary, and then tailor your writerly choices to these elements. This includes ensuring that such matters as length, level of detail, and tone are appropriate for the context.

Expresses ideas clearly

Clarity is an important feature of writing across all occasions, but especially so with summary. When you write a summary, you are taking on the weighty responsibility of conveying in your own words ideas from another text. Whether that text is complex and convoluted or simple and elementary, your aim with summary should be to make the summary as clear as possible. Choose words precisely to capture the main ideas. Use signifiers such as "Jones's main point is…" or "Walters includes evidence from…" as ways of helping your readers understand the summary clearly.

Your aim is to make your summary clear enough so readers who have not or will not actually read, view, or listen to the original text can still understand that text. Clarity with summary is critically important, especially if you are using that summary as part of your argument, as evidence that you will be analyzing, as framing material, or as background material that will help you launch your own argument. Clarity of ideas in the summary will provide your readers with the knowledge and background they need to engage productively with the original argument you put forth in the paragraphs or pages to follow.

Addresses the text's main points

Summaries should be sure to address a text's main points or main arguments. Including these main points or arguments helps readers get an overarching sense of the larger vision of a text. Even if a writer intends to focus in more depth on subsidiary points for much of the summary, he or she should still address the main points of that text. Through this, readers will be in a better position to understand how those smaller components fit with the larger argument. Addressing a text's main points includes conveying as clearly as possible the theme or thesis of the text. Include as well any key terms or concepts from the text that participate in developing the main point.

Addressing main points or arguments does not mean you need to spend the entire summary doing so. Rather, it means that before moving to focus on the elements of the summary that work best for your particular purpose, you spend a bit of space in the summary addressing the main points. Part of writing within an ongoing scholarly conversation involves you providing readers with materials they can then use in ways that best fit their aims and purposes. Your readers are, therefore, relying on your summary to capture the main points and significance of the text being summarized, even if your particular purpose for the summary involves other priorities.

Conveys voice and tone (if relevant)

The context for summary impacts significantly whether a writer should make an effort in a summary to convey voice and tone. Voice and tone are features of texts that emerge through language and can play a role in shaping an argument or communicating a point. Tone may be considered to be the emotional dimension or inflection of a text, whether a text conveys irony, disdain, elation, or another emotion. Voice, a concept that is connected to tone, refers to a text's unique argument and approach. However, voice is not only the particular author's voice of a text, but also the other voices within that text that have influenced its development. When writers in a summary situate a text under consideration within the larger landscape of relevant scholarship and literature, they are attending to the text's voice. Doing so enables readers to see how the particular text being summarized relates to and fits within larger relevant debates and conversations about that issue.

Conveying tone and voice can involve situating a text within a larger conversation, or it can include other ways of attending deeply to language within the text. You can convey voice and tone by quoting portions of the text or by using the author's own terms as you summarize. Also consider directly addressing tone or voice in your summary, identifying the emotional register shaping a text, or indicating the ways in which an author's voice emerges.

Manifests purpose

Writers create summaries for particular, and sometimes multiple, purposes. Perhaps a writer is summarizing his or her own argument in the form of an abstract. This purpose might encourage the writer to craft a summary that helps readers see quickly and clearly the significance and main findings of a text. Perhaps a writer is summarizing a text in order to make an argument about why the author of that text has adopted a misguided or shortsighted approach to an area of study. In this case, the writer's summary of the text might include elements that will prepare readers for that argument, perhaps noting the absence of current scholarly research or focusing in detail about the author's methodological choices.

Manifesting purpose while writing a summary enables you to make clearer why you are summarizing that text. If you are summarizing in order to show that your argument is aligned with others' ideas, then summarize several texts together in a comprehensive or sweeping manner to show this network of scholarly solidarity. By contrast, if you are using summary in order to differentiate your argument from another text, then summarize in such a way that highlights those distinctions. Keeping your purpose in mind as you summarize will enable you to make that purpose more explicit for your readers. They will then understand why you were summarizing a text, what you hope they will do with that summary, and how you anticipate that the summary will enable them to more readily engage with and respond to your writing project.

Different Occasions for Summary

Summary occurs in many different occasions and for many different purposes across disciplines. Here are examples and discussions of the following common occasions for summary, many of which you will likely be called upon to make use of in your academic writing at various junctures:

- Summary in Reviews
- Summary as Abstracts
- Summary and Bibliographic Annotation
- Executive Summary
- Summary in Introductions
- Summary in Conclusions
- Summary as Narrative: Events and Lives

Together, these examples illustrate the degree to which summary transverses disciplinary boundaries even as it also reflects and is shaped by disciplinary context. In this way, writers must rely on transfer-based writing and reading strategies as they engage with summary across writing contexts.

Summary in reviews

In a **review**, a writer summarizes (and usually evaluates) a movie, performance, exhibit, or book. Sometimes the summary portion of the review is called a **synopsis**. You likely have some familiarity with summary through various reviews you may have encountered. You may have read, heard, or watched a review of a song, book, album, movie, or performance in order to learn more about that text or to decide if you wanted to attend the event or purchase the item.

Write Now

Have you ever read a review? If so, write for a few minutes about what reviews you have read and why you did so. What were you hoping to learn from a review? How much detail did you hope was or wasn't included? What do you think are the purposes of reviews? If you haven't ever read a review, have you ever asked friends to tell you about a movie they saw or book they read? Write for a few minutes about why you did so, what you hoped to learn, and what you learned from that conversation.

Reviews vary considerably in terms of the amount of detail, opinion, and background or contextual information. Depending on the disciplinary and publication context, some of the summaries that appear in reviews are deliberately lacking in detail because the reviewer knows that his or her readers do not want to know every detail about the text or item under consideration. Take for example an online movie review: a reviewer might provide a warning like a "spoiler alert" to those who haven't seen the movie yet.

Study these four examples of summary in reviews, drawn from different disciplines and demonstrating a range of approach from popular through more scholarly modes of writing. As you read through the following examples, make note of elements that seem to move from summary into evaluation in terms of revealing the author's attitude toward or assessment of the text. Notice also how the authors' disciplinary perspectives influence their approach toward what they summarize and how they summarize.

Example 1: Popular Book Review, Nonfiction

The following example of summary in a review is an excerpt from a book review of Jon Krakauer's *Into Thin Air*, a journalistic account of the May 10, 1996, Everest disaster. On this day, a blizzard killed eight climbers, making it at the time the single deadliest day in the history of expeditions on Everest. The review is written by Alastair Scott, himself a prolific writer, traveler, and photographer. That Scott is the writer of this review demonstrates that a certain degree of expertise about the subject matter is often required in order to make summary as effective as possible.

Excerpt from "Fatal Attraction" by A. Scott
(Review of *Into Thin Air* by J. Krakauer)

"With enough determination, any bloody idiot can get up this hill," observed Rob Hall, the leader of a commercial expedition, on his eighth tour of Mount Everest. "The trick is to get back down alive."

> At the beginning of the review, Scott attempts to provide a clear and concise overview of the content.

The particular descent ahead of those on the "hill" on May 10, 1996, resulted in the greatest loss of life in the history of mountaineering on Everest....

Jon Krakauer was one of the survivors, and in "Into Thin Air" he relives the storm and its aftermath...As he sees it,...the root of the problem lies in the famous explanation George Mallory gave when asked why he wanted to climb the mountain, an explanation that still holds true, albeit with a slight amendment. People climb Mount Everest because it—and the money—is there....

> Here, Scott offers a brief rendition of Krakauer's main argument in the book.

"Into Thin Air" is a step-by-step account of how a diverse group of people try to conquer a mountain whose majesty is utterly dwarfed by the hardship required to ascend it. "The expedition...became an almost Calvinistic undertaking," Mr. Krakauer remarks, adding that he "quickly came to understand that climbing Everest was primarily about enduring pain." Most people who publish mountaineering books are more skillful as adventurers than they are as writers; Mr. Krakauer is an exception....

> Summaries often, as this one does, include quotes from the text. At the end of this excerpt, Scott begins to move from summary to analysis.

From *The New York Times*, 18 May, 1997.

Example 2, Part A: Popular Review, Documentary Television Series (Longer Version)

This next example is an excerpt from a review written by Susan Stewart about a documentary television series called *Everest: Beyond the Limit*, which aired on the *Discovery Channel* November 14, 2006 to December 30, 2009. This review demonstrates how to translate something that is visual into a written summary. This review, like Scott's, also appeared in *The New York Times*. Stewart is a Professor of Humanities at Princeton University.

Excerpt from "Why Climb a Mountain? It's There, and It's Hard to Do" by S. Stewart
(Review of *Everest: Beyond the Limits*)

> Notice the details Stewart chooses to include as she orients readers to the documentary. Why do you think she chose these details as opposed to others she might have included?

"Everest" follows a crew of climbers who paid approximately $40,000 apiece to attempt the summit in the spring of 2006. The expedition is managed by Russell Brice, a silver-haired New Zealander whose rugged good looks are only partly diminished by his chapped lips, and whose machismo is not weakened by his propensity for choking up, as when he mourns the death of a favorite Sherpa guide.

Terry O'Connor, the expedition's physician, excels at describing the effects of altitude sickness, which can strike anyone at any time in the high Himalayas.

"You get used to suffering, frankly," he says. The suffering starts at advanced base camp, where insomnia and nausea accompany the men as their bodies acclimate to the thin atmosphere. Their blood thickens, which helps them not to pass out but increases the risk that they will have strokes....

> Stewart quotes from the documentary even though it is not a written text. She also includes here a sense of one of the main areas of focus: personalities.

The documentary, filmed by Sherpa guides wearing helmet-mounted cameras, invests in personalities early on....

From *The New York Times*, Nov. 14, 2006.

Example 2, Part B: Popular Review, Documentary Television Series (Shorter version)

Even a review can be summarized as in this case, where Stewart's longer review is also linked on the website for *The New York Times* to a briefer overview.

Review Summary: "Why Climb a Mountain? It's There,
and It's Hard to Do" by S. Stewart
(Review of *Everest: Beyond the Limits*)

A group of climbers from all over the world and one veteran guide climb to the world's tallest peak in an attempt to reach the summit. Partially filmed with cameras mounted to Sherpas' helmets, and two camerapersons who also summited with high-altitude cameras, it offers an unflinching look at this incredible expedition through a zeroing in on the experiences of the climbers.

From *nytimes.com*, Nov. 14, 2006.

Write Now

Imagine the editor of *The New York Times* has asked you to write a "review summary" for another's review. Choose a review of either a book, performance, movie, or album and, using the above "review summary" as an example, write a review of the summary in 50-75 words.

 Transfer Hub: Contribute your ideas and see what others have written at fountainheadpress.com/transferhub.

Example 3: Public Scholarship, Academic Review of a Popular Book, Library Science

In this example of a slightly more academic book review than those that appear in *The New York Times*, Margaret Heilbrun, senior editor for *Library Journal,* reviews a coffee-table book composed of photographs of Mount Everest. *Library Journal* emerges from the discipline of library science or information technologies.

Excerpt from M. Heilbrun's Review of *Conquest of Everest:*
Original Photographs from the Legendary First Ascent

Lewis-Jones (Arctic) clarifies in his prolog that this book was originally intended to mark the 50th anniversary of the 1953 Everest ascent, but there were delays. The foreword by Edmund Hillary, a 2007 tribute to his friend George Lowe, is one of the last pieces Hillary wrote. Lowe was the expedition's "cine cameraman." This coffee-table book is not just a treasury of Lowe's photographs; it introduces readers fully to this "forgotten man of Everest." The bulk of the text is Lowe's

> Heilbrun focuses here on the key details of the text and conveys the main significance.

From *Library Journal* (138.7), 2013.

memoir of his life as it relates to that expedition, with "portfolios" of his photographs, many not previously published, between the chapters. Lowe, who was the last surviving member of the expedition (he died last month), writes of his first encounters with fellow New Zealander Hillary as they climbed together in the years before being chosen for the expedition: 13 men (plus "an army of Sherpa") tasked with putting the two of them on the summit. A final chapter contains "Reflections" by others, including sons of Tenzing and of Hillary. Jan Morris, who as correspondent for the *Times* was attached to the expedition, provides the epilogue.

VERDICT: Essential for all Everest collections as one of the expedition's last primary sources and a deserved testament to Lowe's contributions. He proves himself, as Jan Morris puts it, "a man of sweet charm and courtesy."

> Readers of the journal likely work for libraries and make decisions about new books to purchase. Notice in this review, therefore, that Heilbrun concludes with a "verdict" that recommends libraries purchase the text.

Example 4: Scholarly Review, Environmental Studies

The fourth example of summary in a review involves a more academic book review. Here Sebastian Interlandi, from the Department of Environmental Science, Engineering & Policy at Drexel University, writes a review of a book on environmental research. Readers of the journal in which the review appears may use the summary in the review to decide whether to read the book themselves, but they are also likely interested in using reviews to stay current in recent research in their field.

Excerpt from S. Interlandi's Review of *Top of the World Environmental Research*

> Notice in this paragraph that Interlandi shifts from summary to analysis. Where do you see that shift occurring?

This book compiles a broad range of articles that concern high elevation research on the Himalayan Plateau. The contributors have been working in conjunction with a facility called the Pyramid Laboratory, established in the Khumbu Valley by Italy's Consiglio Nazionale delle Ricerche (CNR). Most of the information presented is general in nature, and ranges from simple descriptions of Himalayan geology and biota to assessments of regional water quality.

The first two chapters detail how the Pyramid Laboratory and this book came into existence. A brief history of European exploration in the region and an overview of Himalayan geology follows. Himalayan terrestrial ecology and aquatic ecology are discussed in a vari-

From *Quarterly Review of Biology* (75.2), 2000.

ety of chapters, including a reasonably complete paleolimnological analysis of Himalayan lake sediments including geochemistry, fossil pigments and diatom frustules. The final chapter is an overview of the development of a GIS database of the region. Unfortunately, many chapters are too general in scope. Some are merely reviews of the topic they cover (for example, chapters on high altitude organic micropollutants, exercise at high altitude, and GIS systems) and present only a few paragraphs of information on the Himalayan system in particular. While reading this book, one gets the feeling that only a few thorough studies in the Himalayas are described and placed amid some rather fluffy review material.

The editors carefully reviewed the articles for style and language. Although most authors of the book do not share English as their native language, the chapters are well structured and easily readable with few stylistic errors. Although no conceptually novel research is presented in this volume, the comprehensive coverage of an underappreciated region makes this book interesting for those concerned with alpine research or science in developing regions. In a sense, the aura of mystery surrounding the Himalayan region is unveiled here, and for those simply curious about the area, this book would be worthwhile.

> Interlandi includes here a description of what he takes to be the primary usefulness and contributions made by the volume.

Summary as abstracts

Academic writers often create **abstracts** of either their own or others' texts. The Writing Center at the University of North Carolina defines an abstract as, "a self-contained, short, and powerful statement that describes a larger work." Many academic journals require abstracts for their published articles so busy readers can skim the abstracts in order to decide whether to read an entire article or not. Abstracts can also be called by other terms, such as **précis** or synopsis.

The amount of material academic writers include in an abstract varies considerably and depends on disciplinary and publication context. Sometimes an abstract is quite brief, perhaps a sentence or two. At other times, an abstract includes a much more detailed account of one's argument, evidence, methods, and conclusions.

Abstracts are most commonly found in articles emerging from disciplines in the sciences and social sciences, though the practice is also becoming more common in the humanities. In these contexts, journals often ask authors to write abstracts of their articles for the publication because they anticipate that busy readers will want to read an abstract in order to determine whether to read an article more thoroughly, as well as facilitate a quick skim of a journal in order to stay current in their field.

What follows is an example of an abstract that appears at the beginning of an article in a journal geared toward biology and medicine called *High Altitude Medicine & Biology*. This article involves a case study examining high-altitude amputation on Mount Everest. As you read the abstract, you might consider how the authors might have adjusted the abstract under different length requirements. For instance, what details might they have excluded if their abstract needed to be no more than 50 or 100 words?

Abstract from "Mount Everest and Makalu Cold Injury Amputation: 40 Years On" by S. Morrison, J. Gorjanc, and I. Mekjavic

Freezing cold injuries (frostbite) of the extremities are a common injury among alpinists participating in high altitude expeditions, particularly during inclement weather conditions. Anecdotally, a digit that has suffered frostbite may be at greater risk to future cold injuries. In this case study, we profile a 62-year-old elite alpinist who suffered multiple digit amputations on both his hands and foot after historic summit attempts on Makalu (8481 m) and Mt. Everest (8848 m) in 1974–1979. We describe the clinical treatment he received at that time, and follow up his case 40 years after the first incidence of frostbite utilizing a noninvasive evaluation of hand and foot function to a cold stress test, including rates of re-warming to both injured and non-injured digits. Finger rates of recovery to the cold stress test were not different (0.8 vs. 1.0°C·min−1) except one (injured, left middle finger, distal phalanx; 0.4°C·min−1). Toe recovery rates after cold-water immersion were identical between previously injured and non-injured toes (0.2°C·min−1). Thermocouple data indicate that this alpinist's previous frostbite injuries may not have significantly altered his digit rates of re-warming during passive recovery compared to his non-injured digits.

> The authors describe their case study.

> Here, they offer a description of the data they provide.

> The authors include the conclusions they arrive at in their article.

From *High Altitude Medicine & Biology* (15.1), 2014.

Transfer at Work

Abstracts vary in length, purpose, and content across disciplinary context and writing occasion. Professor of Medicine Robert E. Leach advises the following regarding abstracts in the sciences: "An Abstract with no conclusions that only serves as a teaser to the reader is worthless and annoying. Include the elements that will tell the reader what you did and what you found" (229). Accordingly, abstracts in science-related journals such as the one Leach edited, the *American Journal of Sports Medicine*, are typically 250-300 words and thoroughly summarize each section of the article, from Introduction and Methods to Results, Analysis, Discussion, and Conclusions. By contrast, abstracts in the *Journal of General Education*, such as the following one from Seth S. Pollack's "Knowledge at the Intersection of Career and Community," are typically 50 words and focus only on the main argument:

> Traditional approaches to civic engagement have been marginalized and have had little impact on the core curriculum. *Critical civic literacy* is an alternative curricular approach to civic engagement that explicitly moves departments, disciplines, and degree programs to examine issues of social responsibility and social justice from the context of their particular field of study. (223)

Thus, an abstract that functions somewhat like a "teaser" might be ideal for one context but labeled "worthless and annoying" in another context.

Summary as annotation

Summary in academic writing also appears in another format closely related to abstracts, known as bibliographic annotations. Unlike the prior instance, where authors write an abstract about their own work, the summaries that appear in relationship to bibliographic annotation are generally written by authors who are writing about other people's research.

A bibliographic annotation is a short summary of a text, somewhat similar to an abstract, but generally occurs as part of a longer list of texts, found perhaps in a list of references or in a library catalog or research database.

Example 1: Bibliographic Annotation, Annotated Bibliography

Annotated bibliographies sometimes appear in the back of books, where authors will provide summaries (annotations) of references or provide them as suggestions for further reading. Some academic writers compose annotated bibliographies as part of their research process in order to learn about relevant research in more depth. Others compose annotated bibliographies as the end product itself.

One main purpose of annotated bibliographies is to provide other researchers with a

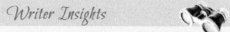

Writer Insights

When do you write annotations?

I always write annotations to help the organization of my work, main points and topics, the data and details I will include in the paper, and to guide me in all the process of research and writing. Furthermore, I write annotations to memorize important concepts for an exam or other assignment.

~Vinicius S. Carvalho, ESL/EFL Student, Osasco, São Paulo, Brazil

Writer Insights

How do annotations help you with your research?

When it comes to writing my thesis, ... I start by creating a list of references for all the sources I depend on. I [then] make an annotated bibliography, and [next] an outline for every chapter.

~Lubna Adel, Ph.D. Candidate & ESI Teacher, Cairo, Egypt

clear picture of the texts relating to a given area of inquiry. Annotated bibliographies can help researchers decide what texts they will read for their own research.

Following are two annotated bibliographic entries from one online annotated bibliography. The author, Bill Buxton, is a technology expert with a passion for mountaineering; he approaches Mount Everest scholarship from the perspectives of history and cultural anthropology. One of the entries reproduced here is longer and one is shorter, demonstrating that bibliographic annotations come in many forms.

Excerpt from "Books on History and Exploration, with a Focus on Central Asia … [and] The History of Climbing and Mountaineering" by B. Buxton

Norgay, Tenzing & Ullman, James (1955). *Tiger of the Snow*. New York: G.P. Putnam's and Sons.

This is an autobiography of Tenzing Norgay Sherpa. See also his second autobiography, *After Everest*. As part of the 1953 expedition led by John Hunt, along with Hillary, Tenzing was the first to summit Everest. While Tenzing could neither read nor write, he was clearly an exceptional man, not only for his climbing, but for his character and intelligence in general. While his story has been put down on paper by Ullman, his voice and thoughts come through convincingly.

> Here Buxton offers a concise description of who Tenzing is and his connection to Everest.

This is clearly a motivated man. He climbed and traveled in Chitral, Kashmir, Garhwal, and Tibet. His finding himself on the top of Everest was also no accident. He had been to Everest 6 times before. He went to the North Side in 1935 with Shipton, 1936 with Ruttledge, 1938 with Tilman; and 1947 with Denman. He then went to the South Side in the spring of 1952 with Swiss team led by Wyss-Dunant, and back again in the autumn on their second attempt led by Chevalley (Dittert et al., 1954).

> Notice the terms such as "convincingly" and "motivated" that convey not only a distanced perspective but also Buxton's assessment of the text.

As Ortner points out, almost all of our history of Himalayan mountaineering comes from westerners, since they were the ones with the skills and means to write the books. From the earlier period, there are only four first person accounts "from the other side," this one by Tenzing, his second autobiography *After Everest*, *Mémoires d'un Sherpa* by Ang Tharkay, and finally the remarkable *Servant of Sahibs*, written in 1923 by Ghulam Rassul

> Here, and in the paragraph above, Buxton situates Norgay's work among other related texts, and demonstrates how Norgay's work offers a unique contribution to the array of texts.

From *billbuxton.com*, 2014.

Galwan, who had worked for Younghusband, among others. Due to their scarcity, insights, and perspective, these books make fascinating reading.

What is interesting about this book is that it spends very little time describing the actual climbing in 1953. Tenzing simply says that others have written extensively about it, so there is no need to cover the details of the expedition, other than to shed light on things that have been neglected. What he does do, which Hunt (perhaps understandably) does not, is discuss not only the issues of conflict between the Sherpa and "Sahibs," but also the repercussions (since many of these caused much controversy under the spotlight that fell on the expedition after its success.) He also talks a lot about the impact of the whole thing on his life, which was significant, given the attention given to the expedition.

> Here Buxton describes what Tenzing focuses on and thereby enables a scholar who may be interested in the impact of the disaster on survivors' lives to see that this book would be relevant for his or her research.

Finally, one cannot read this book without being touched by the love that he had for the mountains, and the bond that he shared with those of similar spirit (not the least of whom was Lambert, of the 1952 Swiss team, with whom—despite a language barrier—he clearly had an outstanding bond.) In this there are strong echoes of Rébuffat's fellowship of the rope. For me, this spirit extended beyond the printed page, bonding author to reader.

See also Tenzing's son Jamling's book, *Touching My Father's Soul*, Tashi Tenzing's *Tenzing Norgay and the Sherpas of Everest*, Malartic's early biography, *Tenzing of Everest*, and the most recent biography, Douglas' *Tenzing: Hero of Everest*.

Excerpt from "Books on History and Exploration, with a Focus on Central Asia … [and] The History of Climbing and Mountaineering" by B. Buxton

Noyce, Wilfrid & Richard Taylor (1954). *Everest is Climbed.* Harmondsworth: Puffin (Puffin Picture Book,

No. 100).

This is a brief (30 page) soft-cover picture book for children. The text is by Noyce, and the images are all drawings by Taylor.

> In this second, very brief example, Buxton has chosen to summarize concisely, omitting background material or assessments of the text.

———

From *billbuxton.com*, 2014.

Example 2: Bibliographic Annotation, Library Catalog

The following example is a bibliographic annotation that appears in a library catalog. These kinds of annotations also sometimes appear on the back covers of books. As with many other occasions for summary, they often include an assessment of the text, or comments on its potential usefulness, because scholars generally use these summaries to decide whether to locate and read the item on the library shelves or through an electronic distribution.

This annotation summarizes a book called *Everest and Conquest in the Himalaya*, co-written by travel writer Richard Sale and Professor in the School of Nursing at the University of Utah, George Rodway. The summary was provided to the library by a company called Syndetic Solutions, Inc., which creates "unique descriptive data components" for online catalogs ("Syndetic Solutions"). As you read, pay attention to terms and phrases in the summary that create a particular tone or convey a certain attitude—elements perhaps intended to shape readers' perceptions of the text.

Excerpt from "Title Summary"
Everest and Conquest in the Himalaya: Science and Courage on the World's Highest Mountain
by R. Sale and G. Rodway

A century ago the summits of the world's highest peaks, Everest included, were beyond reach. Pioneering attempts to overcome the dangers of climbing at extremely high altitudes ended in failure, sometimes with disastrous consequences. Yet today high-altitude ascents are frequent, almost commonplace. Everest can be conquered by relatively inexperienced mountaineers, and their exploits barely merit media attention—unless they go fatally wrong. In this fascinating study of the dramatic history of Everest climbs, Richard Sale and George Rodway describe in vivid detail the struggle to conquer the mountain and the advances in scientific knowledge that made the conquest possible. Their account gives a compelling insight into the science of mountaineering as well as the physical and psychological challenges faced by individuals who choose to test themselves in some of the harshest conditions on earth.

From *library.duke.edu*, 2014.

Write Now

Write a bibliographic annotation for a text you have recently read. Write it as though you were doing so for the back cover of the book and/or for a library catalog.

Executive summary

Executive summaries appear at the front of policy briefs or memos and are intended to serve the exact purpose the name suggests: to provide a brief summary of the most critical aspects of a longer text so busy executives or managers can skim the material quickly. The Writing Center at Texas A&M University defines an executive summary as:

> [A] brief overview of a document's purpose, results, and conclusions condensed for the quick reading of an executive or manager. It is placed at the beginning of a longer report or proposal and summarizes specific aspects of its content. The reader of the summary is usually not interested in the technical details.

Writing that emerges from the disciplinary perspectives of public policy and business are likely to make extensive use of executive summaries.

The following example comes from the United States Department of State, Bureau of Democracy, Human Rights, and Labor. It is a 32-page single-spaced document offering details on Nepal's human rights climate for 2013. The executive summary portion, reproduced here, comprises the first one and one-half pages of this much longer report.

Excerpt from: United States Department of State, Bureau of Democracy, Human Rights, and Labor

EXECUTIVE SUMMARY

For the first few sentences, the executive summary provides a general overview of Nepal's government and political system. Midway through the paragraph, the summary begins to address human rights in elections.

Nepal is a federal democratic republic. The political system is based on the Interim Constitution of Nepal 2063 (2007), with a prime minister as the chief executive and a Constituent Assembly, which is responsible for drafting a new constitution. On November 19, Nepal held national elections to replace the Constituent Assembly, which was suspended in May 2012 after it did not draft a new constitution by the deadline established by the Supreme Court. Domestic and international observers characterized the Constituent Assembly election results as credible and well conducted, and the Asian Network for Free Elections (ANFREL) characterized them as essentially free and fair. There were reports of political violence, intimidation, and some voting irregularities, although many fewer than in the previous Constituent Assembly elections in 2008. Authorities maintained effective control of the security forces. As in previous years, there were reports that security forces committed human rights abuses.

From *state.gov*, 2014.

The most significant human rights problems were exacerbated by the country's continuing delay in promulgating a permanent constitution (reflecting the absence of an elected legislature for most of the year); the continued absence of transitional justice mechanisms, such as a truth and reconciliation commission to account for past human rights abuses; and the related failure to implement court ordered arrests of military personnel, Maoists, and other individuals accused or convicted of human rights violations stemming from the country's 10-year insurgency.

> Notice the different types of "human rights problems" addressed in this paragraph and the next and how the summary emphasizes some as more prevalent or significant than others.

Other human rights problems included poor prison and detention center conditions. Corruption existed at all levels of government and police, and the courts remained vulnerable to political pressure, bribery, and intimidation. There were problems with self-censorship by members of the press. The government sometimes restricted freedom of assembly. The government limited freedoms for refugees, particularly for the Tibetan community. Discrimination against women was a problem, and citizenship laws that discriminate by gender contributed to statelessness. Domestic violence against women remained a serious problem, and dowry-related deaths occurred. Violence against children was widespread, although rarely prosecuted, and sex trafficking of adults and minors remained a serious problem. Discrimination against persons with disabilities, some ethnic groups, and persons with HIV/AIDS continued. Violence associated with caste-based discrimination occurred. There were some restrictions on worker rights, and forced, bonded, and child labor remained significant problems.

A decreasing number of armed groups, largely in the Tarai region, attacked civilians, government officials, members of particular ethnic groups, and each other. Members of the Maoist-affiliated All Nepal National Independent Students Union-Revolutionary (ANNISU-R) were responsible for extortion, intimidation, and school bus burnings. Armed groups were responsible for abductions to obtain ransom, mainly in the Tarai region.

Impunity for conflict-era human rights violations continued to be a serious problem in the absence of a truth and reconciliation commission and a disappearances commission.

Summary in introductions

One of the most frequently found occasions for summary is in introductions. While introductions contain a number of elements, they also often include a summary of what will follow in the text. Sometimes this is in the form of a brief overview of the paper, where a writer shares in a brief sentence or two what the paper will address. In the following introductory passage, authors Robin Canniford, Professor of Business and Economics at the University of Melbourne, and Avi Shankar, Professor of Consumer Research at the University of Bath, provide an overview of the rest of their article, titled "Purifying Practices: How Consumers Assemble Romantic Experiences of Nature," which appeared in the *Journal of Consumer Research*:

> Through data gathered during an 8-year ethnography of surfing culture, we answer [our primary research question] and make three contributions to consumer research.

Other times, summaries appear in introductions to anthologies, or collections of essays, where the person writing the introduction (usually the editor) provides summaries for each of the articles or chapters in the collection.

The following such excerpt comes from the introduction to an anthology about sports and tourism edited by Mike Weed, Professor of Applied Policy Sciences at Canterbury Christ Church University. The anthology includes a variety of reprinted texts, and in the introduction, Weed provides a summary overview of each article. This summary is for Karin Weber's "Outdoor Adventure Tourism: A Review of Research Approaches," which is the fourth chapter of the anthology. Notice the in-depth nature of the summary Weed has written, sharing with readers Weber's main argument in extended detail.

Excerpt from "Introduction"
Sport & Tourism: A Reader, M. Weed, ed.

The fourth chapter…focuses on outdoor adventure tourism…[W]ritten in 2001, Karin Weber's paper, *Outdoor Adventure Tourism: A Review of Research Approaches* argues for a greater focus on adventure experiences in the study of outdoor adventure tourism. Weber suggests that adventure tourism has traditionally been seen as an extension of adventure recreation and, consequently, the tourism element has been overlooked…. In analyses of adventure tourism, Weber suggests that risk has been too narrowly conceived as physical risk, whereas psychological and social risk can be equally important in the adventure experience. In fact, Weber believes that adventure tourism can be conceptualized as being as much about the quest for insight and knowledge as the desire for elements of physical risk. Furthermore, Weber advocates a greater focus on interpretive qualitative methodologies in understanding adventure experiences.

From *Sport & Tourism: A Reader,* 2007.

Summary in conclusions

As with introductions, conclusions contain many different elements, summary among them. Writers routinely use conclusions to summarize the important elements of their arguments because they recognize that a conclusion marks the final opportunity in a text to convey and emphasize their arguments to readers. One challenge writers face with summaries in conclusions is that, in summarizing a text, writers should aim to avoid repeating what they have articulated earlier. The conclusion, instead, should be seen as an occasion to echo the main points or significances of the text through summary.

In the following excerpt, Linda Allin concludes her text by summarizing her argument about women and Mount Everest. Allin chooses to summarize her main findings, as well as their significance for having contributed knowledge to the field. Notice that Allin also uses the conclusion to summarize another text that aligns with hers, and in so doing shows how her own text participates as part of a larger network of scholarship moving forward with a shared vision and perspective.

Excerpt from "Climbing Mount Everest: Women, Career and Family in Outdoor Education" by L. Allin

Summary and conclusions

> Allin reviews her findings as well as the way in which her article has built on prior knowledge.

This study shows the connections and disconnections for women outdoor educators in combining career and family relationships. Joint involvement in the outdoors was illustrated as important in maintaining some partnerships, but the findings show clearly the dilemmas and contradictions for women outdoor educators, especially after motherhood. While the issue of combining career and family is not new, the study highlights the ways in which women's ability to negotiate career and family relationships in outdoor education is made more difficult by the centrality of the body to outdoor education careers. Women outdoor educators were actively negotiating career and family relationships in a variety of ways, but tensions were compounded for women as they negotiated their career identities within outdoor organisations where the material and social realities of women's bodies were not openly acknowledged. Giddens (1991) suggests that the construction of a coher-

> Allin summarizes another study of particular relevance to her own findings.

ent self-identity involves an orientation towards the future as well as the past. In this study, the fragility of women's career identities in the outdoors is evident where mothers struggled to identify a coherent sense of their occupational future. As a consequence of changing legislation in the UK, as from April 2003, all workers who meet qualifying criteria in length of service are now entitled to request flexible working hours, something outdoor organisations will need to implement. The findings from this study suggest that outdoor organisations also need to support women, including providing time for maintaining technical competence, if they are to retain women in and through outdoor education careers.

From *Australian Journal of Outdoor Education* (8.2), 2004.

Summary in biography

Biographical work involves many academic research and writing skills, including summary. Writers across many disciplines engage in biographical work, not only in history, as one might expect, but also in any discipline or in any writing occasion where one needs to provide a narrative of a central figure, person, or group of people whose work or contributions have impacted an idea or concept. As such, biography, in longer or shorter forms, pervades every discipline. Because summary in the context of biography offers a narrative of someone's life, it includes a highly ethical dimension. Choosing what to include and what to exclude, which perspectives to privilege and which to minimize, will drastically shape readers' impressions of this individual or of these groups of people. Writers engaged in biographical summary should take care to make these choices with an awareness of the implications summary has on constructing a narrative about another human being.

The following example is a summary of the life of Richard William George Hingston, who served as the "medical officer and naturalist" (Pyz) for a 1924 expedition to Everest by George Mallory and Andrew Irvine. Written by Justyna Pyz, a research associate at Trinity College, Dublin, this example has a historical disciplinary perspective. Notice in the example how concisely Pyz summarizes the biography of Hingston, including only the most relevant details related to the current purpose. Another biographer, working for another purpose, might have chosen to focus on different aspects of Hingston's life.

Excerpt from "The Mallory Mount Everest Expedition of 1924: An Irish Perspective"
by J. Pyz

The global career of Major Hingston

R.W.G. Hingston was born in London in 1887 but spent most of his early life in the family home at Horsehead, Passage West, Co. Cork. He was educated at University College Cork, from which he graduated with first-class honours in 1910. He subsequently passed into the Indian medical service.

Notice how nearly every detail in this summary has to do with Hingston's global experiences. The summary, therefore, is shaped according to purpose. We do not learn, for example, about his personal life at all.

From *History Ireland* (19.5), 2011.

In 1913 he joined the Indo-Russian Pamir triangulation expedition as a surgeon and naturalist. With the outbreak of the Great War in 1914, Hingston was recalled for military service and saw action in East Africa, France, Mesopotamia, and the North-West Frontier. He was appointed medical officer and naturalist to the expedition to Mount Everest in 1924. From 1925 to 1927 Hingston acted as a surgeon-naturalist to the marine survey of India on HMS *Investigator* and then, aged 40, retired from the Indian medical service on pension and joined the Oxford University expedition to Greenland. The following year he took part in the Oxford expedition to British Guiana. In 1930 he embarked on a mission conducted by the Society for the Preservation of the Empire Fauna that took him through Rhodesia, Nyasaland, Kenya, Uganda and Tanganyika, investigating methods of preserving the indigenous wildlife. Major Hingston was recalled to military duty in India in 1939 and, after World War II, he retired to his home in County Cork, where he died in 1966.

Summary of events

Writers across disciplines invoke summary as a way of archiving and describing events, be they past, current, or future. Writers in journalism or history might engage in this work with comparative frequency, but writers in all fields, from sociology and engineering to literature and religious studies, summarize events important to their field. Writers engaged with summary of events must distill an enormous amount of potential material into a condensed rendition that serves the writer's larger purpose or his or her particular context. In so doing, summary of events shares the ethical responsibilities that inform summary in biographical writing. The way an event is summarized—including the narrative it depicts, the details that are included or excluded, and the contextual materials that are provided or not—will work together to shape people's impressions and understandings of the event. Slanting a summary through a particular lens or with a particular purpose in mind will necessarily change the story people perceive of that event. In this way, summary provides a critical and complex role in conveying historical, contemporary, and future events.

Example 1: Historical Event Summary

The following example, written by Peter Hansen, Professor of Humanities & Arts at Worcester Polytechnic Institute, offers a summary of a historical event in which a film, *Conquest of Everest*, depicts Tenzing Norgay, Edmund Hillary, and John Hunt receiving awards and public recognition for their successful 1953 Everest summit. Thus, Hansen is simultaneously summarizing both a scene from the film and the historical event it depicts.

> Excerpt from "Confetti of Empire: The Conquest of Everest in Nepal, India, Britain, and New Zealand" by P. Hansen
>
> Kathmandu welcomed the climbers with an official parade and state reception at the Royal Palace. Newsreel footage of their arrival shows thick crowds blocking the procession as the climbers acknowledged the cheers. At the Royal Palace, Tenzing, Hillary, and Hunt received the first of their honors. As King Tribhuvan gave Tenzing the Nepal Tara, the Star of Nepal, the highest decoration not reserved for royalty, he told him in Nepali, "you have added to the prestige of Nepal." The Prime Minister, M.P. Koirala, then awarded Hillary and Hunt the Gorkha Dakshina Bahu, Order of the Gurkha Right Hand, First Class, a lesser award, telling them in English, "You have added to the prestige of Nepal and Great Britain."
>
> ———
> From *Comparative Studies in Society and History* (42.2), 2000.

Example 2: Current Event Summary

What follows is a summary of the April 18, 2014, Mount Everest avalanche that killed sixteen people. The summary appears in a longer blog posting written by Jon Krakauer, author of *Into Thin Air*.

> Excerpt from "Death and Anger on Everest" by J. Krakauer
>
> On April 18th, shortly before 7 A.M. local time, an overhanging wedge of ice the size of a Beverly Hills mansion broke loose from the same ice bulge that had frightened Brice into leaving Everest in 2012. As it crashed onto the slope below, the ice shattered into truck-size chunks and hurtled toward some fifty climbers laboring slowly upward through the Khumbu Icefall, a jumbled maze of unstable ice towers that looms above the 17,600-foot base camp. The climbers in the line of fire were at approximately nineteen thousand feet when the avalanche struck. Of the twenty-five men hit by the falling ice, sixteen were killed, all of them Nepalis working for guided climbing teams. Three of the bodies were buried beneath the frozen debris and may never be found.
>
> ———
> From *thenewyorkeronline.com*, 2014.

Write Now

The choices writers make when summarizing events and people's lives have ethical and moral implications. Based on these summaries, what impressions do you have of the kind of person Hingston was, or the kind of work he did, or the circumstances surrounding the avalanche? Identify aspects of the summaries of Hingston's life and the Mount Everest avalanche that might shape readers' perceptions. What other kinds of details might have been included that could have impacted or changed your impressions of Hingston and his work? Choose either an event or a person from your life, one that is likely relatively unknown to others, and write a brief (100-150 words) summary of that event or person's experience. Imagine you are writing for general readers such as those who visit Wikipedia.

 Transfer Hub: Contribute your summary and see what others have written at fountainheadpress.com/transferhub.

Transferring Summary

In many cases, the aspects of an effective summary for one writing occasion are not readily applicable to other writing occasions. Transferring your abilities with summary across discipline and context, therefore, requires thinking carefully about the writing occasion and your particular aims and purposes for any given summary. In this sense, summary resonates with what we learned about effective reading strategies in Chapter 4: what you read and how you read it also hinge on context.

Regardless of the particular version or form for summary, though, this skill is one of the key ways in which writers make use of what they read. Learning more about summary also paves the way for the material in Chapter 6, which builds on knowledge about summary by examining synthesis, a feature of academic writing that relies in great measure on using summary in the service of combining different ideas or concepts to create something new.

ᘒ ᘒ ᘒ

Physics Research and Reporting: "Physicists Discover Long-Sought 'Pentaquark' Particle" by the National Science Foundation, and abstract from "Observation of J/ψp Resonances Consistent with Pentaquark States in $\Lambda^{o}_{b}{\rightarrow}$J/$\psi$K$^-$p Decays" by R. Aaij, et al.

Transfer Points: Physics, Science Communication, Journalism

Relative density … Wien's displacement law … Gamma ray … Cyclotron … Pentaquark

These are but several of the many specialized terms that constitute knowledge in physics and that can create significant barriers for communication. If a physicist, for instance, wants to explain a discovery that emerged with a cyclotron, non-physicists may have difficulty appreciating that discovery without also understanding more about cyclotrons. What is a cyclotron? What is it most often used for? What are the affordances and limitations? Who developed it, when did they do so, and why? What prior discoveries have occurred with the cyclotron?

Although addressing these questions might be informative, it would also waylay the physicist from the original aim: communicating a discovery. Instead, the physicist would be spending ample energy explaining the cyclotron.

The challenge, then, for physicists, as for scholars in other disciplines, is one of writing transfer: How can they effectively communicate advances in their field to people unfamiliar with discipline-specific terminology and disciplinary expertise? This question is what shapes the development of a press release for a peer-reviewed academic article, such as the texts reprinted here.

For physics, the challenge of writing transfer is particularly salient, given that the field relies on specialized terms and concepts. Most broadly, physics involves research into everything around us, from matter and energy to the universe. Physicists tackle big questions: What is the universe made of? How did it start? ("About CERN"). While largely theoretical, physics can be applied in numerous ways. Physics has been central, for example, in advancing sustainable forms of energy production, in treating cancer through radiotherapy, and in developing computer games ("What is").

Advances in physics tend to occur in labs, through extensive collaboration and ongoing financial support. The pentaquark discovery, for instance, discussed in the peer-reviewed article abstract and the accompanying press release reprinted here, occurred at the Large Hadron Collider beauty (LHCb) experiment in Geneva. Primarily associated with CERN, the European Organization for Nuclear Research, the LHCb experiment involves exploring "what happened after the Big Bang that allowed matter to survive and build the Universe we inhabit today" ("Welcome").

Physics endeavors like the LHCb experiment are grounded on deep collaboration. The academic version of the pentaquark article, for example, for which Aaij is the lead author, names dozens of contributing authors. Some of these individuals may have specifically participated in the writing, others might have contributed ideas or knowledge. And, although the LHCb experiment resides in Geneva, the National Science Foundation (NSF) has also helped sponsor it, demonstrating how scientific collaborations often extend across geographic and national barriers.

Roel Aaij, the lead author on this paper, is an Applied Fellow at CERN, in Geneva, Switzerland. His areas of specialty include particle physics, scientific computing, and statistics. Prior to working at CERN, Aaij worked as a Ph.D. student at Nikhef, the National Institute for Subatomic Physics in Amsterdam (Aaij). The National Science Foundation, the organization that holds the credit for the press release, is a federal agency that provides funding to researchers at American colleges and universities in many fields, including math, computer science, chemistry, physics, biology, and social science (NSF). The organization is currently headquartered in Arlington, Virginia.

The NSF's stake in the project explains why it published a press release about the pentaquark on its website. Press releases operate as a staple genre in the field of science and in science communication, communicating discoveries and new research initiatives. Because of their visibility, press releases have enormous influence in shaping public opinion about science and increasing the potential for additional collaborations, funding, and support.

These impacts are among those that scholars in the field of science communication investigate. Broadly defined, science communication explores communication between communities of scientists, interest groups, policymakers and various publics. Scholars in this field, though, also examine communication about science between and among scientists, as well as between non-scientists (Trench and Bucchi 1).

Science-communication scholars research and write about the forms and impacts of science communication. The June 2016 issue of the journal *Science Communication*, for instance, includes an article about how scientists communicate in newspaper op-eds (Parks and Takahashi), an article about how the children's magazine *Highlights* represents scientists in terms of gender and race (Previs), and an article about policy maker perceptions of science credibility (Berdahl, et al.).

Scholars have also conducted research about press releases themselves. They have investigated, for instance, how press releases frame news and integrate emotional appeals (Lee and Basnyat), and how linguistic choices point to the future without making overly risky predictions (McLaren-Hankin).

Press releases, though, are but one genre through which scientists communicate. Others include blogs, op-eds, museum displays, nature exhibits, books, articles, and columns. Science communication also includes public lectures, workshops, and interviews. Physicists write within many of these genres, as well as in academic genres, such as reviews, academic articles, lab reports, grant proposals, and assessment reports.

Across all these genres, science communication facilitates the transfer of complex, discipline-specific knowledge to broader publics. In so doing, science communication enables others to extend and apply science knowledge and paves the way for future generations of scientists to continue advancing knowledge about technical concepts like pentaquarks, cyclotrons, and gamma rays.

Write Here

Why do scientists need to communicate with the broader public? What's at stake? Who cares the most about such advances and why? What might have been some of the particular reasons the scientists in this context may have communicated their research in a press release?

National Science Foundation
Physicists Discover Long-Sought "Pentaquark" Particle

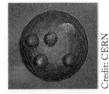

Credit: CERN

Now that NSF-funded researchers have discovered the long-sought pentaquark, their next step is to study how quarks are bound together within this remarkable particle. They could be bound together tightly, as seen in this image.

July 14, 2015
CERN's Large Hadron Collider (LHC) announced Tuesday that researchers discovered a remarkable class of particles, known as pentaquarks, that could reshape scientists' understanding about the properties of matter.

Physicists have been searching for pentaquarks for almost 50 years, but the research group that made the discovery, a Syracuse University team funded by the National Science

Foundation (NSF), wasn't specifically looking for them. According to Syracuse physicist Sheldon Stone, graduate student Nathan Jurik was studying the decay of a different particle when the pentaquark was detected.

"We asked a graduate student to examine what we thought was an uninteresting and minor source of background events, just in case it happened to be a nasty source of experimental noise," Stone told *Symmetry Magazine*. "He did it begrudgingly but came back with a big smile on his face because there was a huge and unexpected signal. We told him to forget about what he was working on and focus on this instead."

Atoms, and the protons and neutrons that make up their nuclei, are familiar terms in science. But quarks are even smaller particles--the building blocks of protons, neutrons and other subatomic particles known as baryons.

Baryons, including protons and neutrons, are composed of three quarks. A pentaquark is something different--a "composite state" that groups four quarks and one antiquark, the associated antimatter particle for a quark. Studying composite states can give scientists additional insight into the properties of ordinary baryons.

"Benefitting from the large dataset provided by the LHC, and the excellent precision of our detector, we have examined all possibilities for these signals and conclude that they can only be explained by pentaquark states," said CERN Large Hadron Collider b-quark (LHCb) physicist Tomasz Skwarnicki of Syracuse University, whose research group was a leader in the analysis. "More precisely the states must be formed of two up quarks, one down quark, one charm quark and one anti-charm quark."

The discovery was made by the LHCb experiment group, one of several ongoing particle physics experiments at the laboratory. LHCb studies antimatter and its relationship to matter. The group has submitted a paper reporting its findings to the journal *Physical Review Letters*.

U.S. participation in the experiment is funded entirely by NSF, which supports the research through nine awards to scientists from Syracuse University, the University of Maryland College Park, the Massachusetts Institute of Technology and the University of Cincinnati working at the LHC.

"The pentaquark is not just any new particle," said LHCb spokesperson Guy Wilkinson. "It represents a way to aggregate quarks, namely the fundamental constituents of ordinary protons and neutrons, in a pattern that has never been observed before in over 50 years of experimental searches. Studying its properties may allow us to understand better how ordinary matter, the protons and neutrons from which we're all made, is constituted."

Years' worth of other experiments searching for pentaquarks have proved inconclusive, leading some scientists to question their existence. LHCb's research looked for the particles from many perspectives, with all results pointing to the same conclusion. The group found the pentaquarks by examining the decay of a particular kind of baryon, known as Lambda b.

"While existence of pentaquarks was speculated on since the beginning of the quark model in 1964, it has taken 51 years to find a solid experimental evidence for their existence," Skwarnicki said. "A series of dubious experimental claims of their discoveries over a decade ago, which were not confirmed by subsequent measurements, made many physicists doubt their existence. The observation by the LHCb collaboration reverses this trend and will lead to a better understanding of quark formations created by nuclear forces, with possible implications in astrophysics."

The group's next step will be to study how, exactly, quarks are bound together in pentaquarks--loosely or tightly. The answer to that question will play a key role in determining what pentaquarks can teach about the composition of ordinary matter.

-NSF-

Aaij, R. et al.
Abstract from "Observation of $J/\psi p$ Resonances Consistent with Pentaquark States in $\Lambda_b^0 {\to} J/\psi K^- p$ Decays"

Observations of exotic structures in the $J=\psi p$ channel, which we refer to as charmonium-pentaquark states, in $\Lambda_b^0 \to J=\psi K^- p$ decays are presented. The data sample corresponds to an integrated luminosity of 3 fb^{-1} acquired with the LHCb detector from 7 and 8 TeV pp collisions. An amplitude analysis of the three-body final state reproduces the two-body mass and angular distributions. To obtain a satisfactory fit of the structures seen in the $J=\psi p$ mass spectrum, it is necessary to include two Breit-Wigner amplitudes that each describe a resonant state. The significance of each of these resonances is more than 9 standard deviations. One has a mass of 4380 ± 8 ± 29 MeV and a width of 205 ± 18 ± 86 MeV, while the second is narrower, with a mass of 4449.8 ± 1.7 ± 2.5 MeV and a width of 39 ± 5 ± 19 MeV. The preferred J^P assignments are of opposite parity, with one state having spin 3/2 and the other 5/2.

Write Away

1. Write a comparative analysis between the abstract of the peer-reviewed article and the press release about that research. What features do you notice that are similar to one another? Which features seem disparate? What accounts for these similarities and differences? What transpires within writing transfer between the peer-reviewed abstract and the article?

2. Select and read a peer-reviewed scientific article of your choosing about a topic of interest to you. Then, write a press release for that article. Make choices about what information to include in the press release and how to frame the material. Compose a headline for your press release as well.

3. Grant proposals, like press releases, rely on writing transfer. In grant proposals, scientists must communicate the significance and viability of their projects to people who may not share their disciplinary expertise. Write a grant proposal for a physics-related project you would like to conduct. Brainstorm possible physics projects and draw upon established physics research methods. Think about what you might need grant support for: travel, equipment, collaborators, etc. Include relevant background literature. When you are ready to write the grant, choose a potential funding organization, and follow as closely as possible the guidelines specified by that organization.

Photojournalism: "Cuban Refugee Elián González" by Alan Diaz

Transfer Points: Journalism, Documentary Studies, Visual Studies

"Winning the Pulitzer Prize for photography is sort of a double-edged sword. On one hand, you've achieved an amazing honor. On the other, you probably witnessed something that you'll never forget" ("Photography").

This must surely have been the case for photographer Alan Diaz, whose photograph of Elián González won the 2001 Pulitzer Prize for Breaking News. Describing the experience, Diaz recalls, "I have four kids of my own … I've heard my children cry because of tantrums … because they are sad … because they are hungry …The cry I heard that day I had never heard in my life. A cry like that will haunt anyone forever" (qtd. in "Photography").

Elián was a five-year-old boy discovered clinging to an innertube three miles off the Florida coast on Thanksgiving Day, November 25, 1999 ("A Chronology"). His mother had drowned during their attempt to escape communist Cuba. Miami relatives of the family took Elián in, but his father in Cuba initiated legal proceedings for Elián's return. A fierce custody battle ensued, culminating on Easter weekend 2000, when Diaz photographed U.S. federal agents who had come to the Miami home where Elián had been living in a pre-dawn raid to take him into custody and return him to his father in Cuba (Padgett).

Elián, now in his twenties, is pursuing engineering in Cuba (Padgett) and has since lived a relatively private life. But Elián's story, and Diaz's photograph, proved pivotal for mobilizing public debate about immigration law, U.S.-Cuban relations, and Cuban-American experiences.

Photographs such as Diaz's frame events in human terms, capturing the personal complexity—and trauma—interwoven through political and social issues. The potential impact of photojournalism, quite apart from whether it wins a Pulitzer or not, is its ability to make stories heard and influence public opinion.

Photojournalism is part of the larger field of journalism and carries an extensive disciplinary history. In 1924 a dean at the University of Missouri-Columbia's Journalism School, Frank Luther Mott, defined photojournalism as "the visual reporting of news for publication in newspapers and magazines" (qtd. in Cartwright 339). Today, this "visual reporting of news" stands apart from more personal forms of news, such as social media newsfeeds. The difference hinges on "who is doing the seeing, how and why they see, and how and why they publish" (Newton 236).

Photojournalists have training across many disciplines, from anthropology, history, and English, to documentary studies, public policy, and international affairs. Such broad disciplinarity enables photojournalists to research a vast range of events and experiences to prepare for photograph assignments and equips them to transfer many practices related to other disciplines. They develop sharp capacities with observation and interpretation of human behavior, for instance, and they hone talents with spatial recognition. At every stage in their process, photojournalists edit and revise, from deciding what to photograph to choosing how to frame images.

While visual media comprise much of their work, photojournalists also engage in writing. They create captions for their photographs and compose accompanying prose segments. They also write reflections about the circumstances surrounding their photographs, and share details about their process for others interested in photojournalism.

Ethics stands as one of the most important aspects of photojournalism. As such, photojournalists must be acutely aware of their own motivations, responsibilities, and biases, as well as potential risks and benefits. What photographers choose to capture, when and where they choose to be present, and how they manipulate and edit images has direct impact on public perceptions, on themselves, and on the people, places, and events they photograph.

Sometimes photojournalists face difficult decisions about whether to help other human beings in a given moment or photograph what is transpiring. Publishing images can make people vulnerable to punishment, repercussions, or even death. Photojournalists put themselves at great risk as well during volatile occasions, through retribution from publishing contentious images, or from intellectual and copyright complexities.

Because of the virtually boundless contexts for photojournalism, scholars across a range of disciplines integrate photojournalism into their research and writing. Scholars in history examine images as primary source material and those in fine arts, documentary studies, and literature conduct visual analysis on images. Scholars in public policy, political science,

Alan Diaz (1947–2013) was an American photographer who won the 2001 Breaking News Pulitzer Prize for this photograph of Elián González. Diaz was born and raised in New York and moved to Cuba with his family in 1964, where he studied photography. In 1978, he moved to Miami, where he taught English and became a photographer. He joined the Associated Press as a freelance photographer in 1994 and became a staff photographer in 2000. ("Alan Diaz"; "Alan Diaz Videos / Interviews") and international affairs use photojournalism to research policies, politics, and political relations, and academics in such fields as gender and sexuality studies and Latino/a studies use photojournalism to research depictions of people. In the case of the Elián González photograph, scholars in law, Latino/a studies, sociology, psychology, and rhetoric have invoked this image within their research.

Across all of these contexts, those engaged with photojournalism ask pressing questions: What stories do images tell, and why? What stories remain untold? What are the ethical responsibilities of and challenges for photojournalists? What role do photographs play in shaping public perception? These are the underlying questions that sparked the immense public response to Diaz's photograph of a young boy caught in a complex personal, political, legal, and social battle.

Write Here

If you were a photojournalist and could go on assignment anywhere, at any time past or present, where would you go, and what or whom would you photograph? Write a response in which you describe your imagined plans, and explain why you think these places, people, or events deserve photographic attention. What would you hope to be able to capture with the photographs you would take, and what impact would you hope they might have? What risks would you need to take into consideration for others and yourself?

Write Away

1. Write a visual analysis of the Elián González photograph. Use the techniques of visual analysis from Chapter 7. Situate your analysis within the historical context of the image by including research about the events and issues surrounding the González story.

2. Embark on a photojournalist assignment in an area near you. Work through the entire research and writing process, from site selection, ethical considerations, close observation, and field notes, to thick description, writing a scene, and crafting a narrative. After drafting, feedback, and revision, reflect on your experience: What was challenging? What surprised you? What did you learn about yourself as a writer and researcher? What

aspects of photojournalism might you apply, repurpose, or otherwise adapt for subsequent writing occasions?

3. Select and examine a subset of news photographs. These can be a set of photographs taken at a particular region or place, of a particular event, or by a particular photographer. You could even draw a subset from photographs that have won the Pulitzer Prize. Using the images in this subset as evidence, write an argument-based essay that provides insights into the values, challenges, and risks involved with this subset of photojournalism. Consider such questions as: What is the potential value of photojournalism in this context? What challenges exist related to photojournalism in this context? What ethical considerations are particularly pronounced in this context? How might this subset of images generate new insights about photojournalism?

Blog Entry: "Why I Was One of the Few to Survive I Won't Ever Know" by John Thompson

Transfer Points: Creative Writing, English Literature, Media Studies, History

On December 26, 2004, a 9.1 magnitude earthquake struck in the Indian Ocean, generating a tsunami of epic proportions. Generating massive waves, now known as the Indian Ocean Tsunami or the Asian Tsunami, this 2004 event leveled entire towns. Approximately 228,000 people died (Rodgers and Fletcher).

Tsunamis are "giant waves caused by earthquakes or volcanic eruptions under the sea" (NCOA). The word tsunami comes from the Japanese word "tsu," for harbor, and "name," for wave (ITIC, "What"). Tsunamis have occurred regularly across history, from as early as the 2000 BCE tsunami in Syria (EIGHTD). More recently, the deadliest and most destructive tsunamis have included the 2004 Asian Tsunami, which was the third largest earthquake ever recorded on a seismograph, as well as the 2011 Tohoku tsunami, which killed 20,000 people ("Deadliest").

Personal accounts of the 2004 Asian Tsunami, composed by survivors as well as rescuers who participated in recovery, began emerging in the days and weeks following December 26, 2004. Their stories provided nuanced details about the disaster. According to witnesses, the approaching tsunami sounded like "three freight trains or the roar of a jet" ("Deadliest"). They reported that animals sensed imminent danger and rushed away, which resulted in very few animal fatalities. Someone saw a 20-day-old baby girl floating, alive, on a mattress in Malaysia (Morrison). Others described watching the ocean receding and seeing curious people going out onto the exposed ocean floor, only moments later to be swept away as the force of incoming water descended (Meadows).

John Thompson, whose personal account of the tsunami is included here, had been visiting Thailand for his brother's wedding. Thompson was, at the time, 28. He had been staying in Khao Lak, a coastal town on Phuket Island. His vacation had begun normally, with him renting a motorbike, taking photographs of

John Thompson is from Santa Rosa, California (Campbell). He is an attorney with the northern California law office, Sonoma County Law. He graduated from the Santa Clara University School of Law in 2001. Before starting his own firm, Thompson worked at the District Attorney's office in Stanislaus County, as well as several other District Attorneys, a major law firm, and private law offices. His experiences of the tsunami have been captured in several places (About) including his own website: http://www.sonomacountylaw. com/tsunami/index.htm. He also contributed his story to a collection of survivor narratives compiled by Rick Von Feldt, himself a tsunami survivor. That website, www.phukettsunami.blogspot.com, aims to "educate many about the strength of the survivors" (Von Feldt). Von Feldt is a consultant on workplace development and has served as a coach and advisor for the Stanford University Graduate School of Business Communications. Von Feldt is also a longstanding writer and blogger. He lives in the Bay Area of California (Von Feldt).

tourist sites, and lounging in his hotel. But all of this changed on December 26. Remarkably, Thompson survived in an area that is now regarded as one of the hardest hit: nearly 4,000 people died in Khao Lak, many of whom were tourists vacationing at the coastal town (Ryall).

Thompson's survival narrative appears on a website, phukettsunami.blogspot.com, developed by Rick Von Feldt, himself a 2004 Asian Tsunami survivor. Von Feldt had compiled this site to archive a wide range of personal accounts of the 2004 Tsunami.

Von Feldt's efforts to compile personal accounts, and Thompson's narrative itself, are indicative of people's ongoing investment in using personal accounts to better understand and experience events. Personal accounts and eyewitness testimony provide a human-centered perspective.

Personal narratives also serve an important function in research across disciplines. Those in history and journalism, for instance, make frequent use of personal narratives in their scholarship, but many others do as well. Irish Studies scholars, for instance, have investigated narrative accounts by Irish women in the diaspora (Bronwen). Sports medicine scholars have researched personal narratives to better understand injury rehabilitation (Joy et al). Philosophers have researched personal narratives to examine personal identity (Schroer and Schroer). Psychologists have researched personal narratives to understand how people process stressful experiences (Klein and Boals). And, scholars in Russian Studies have researched personal narratives of the 2004 Beslan hostage-taking to understand how translation from Russian to English impacts the narrative (Harding).

As many of these examples illustrate, personal narratives often emerge around traumatic experiences. In this way, Thompson's account falls under a more specific genre of personal narrative known as survival narratives. These, as their name suggests, are personal accounts of experiences in which people survive a trauma. Examples include survival narratives associated with asylum confinement (Hanganu-Bresch and Berkenkotter), fiction such as *Life of Pi* (Dodeman), single motherhood (Katz), and cancer (Kim, Hyun, and Kang).

Some scholars have researched the impact of survivor narratives. Scholars affiliated with the medical humanities argue that survival narratives provide positive psychological benefits to the authors (Pennebaker). And, communications scholars have examined common themes, such as optimism, growth, grief, and loss, to better understand the various dimensions of survivor narratives (Kosenko and LeBoy).

Like Thompson's, many survivor narratives are widely accessible. These public forums enable the many people interested in understanding human perspectives on such disasters to have access to them. In so doing, survivor narratives often become part of the fabric of cultural memory. They document and illustrate in rich detail the finer textures of large, unfathomable events.

Write Here

Have you ever read someone's personal account of a shocking or traumatic experience? If so, why? If not, why not? What purposes do such personal accounts of trauma serve? What are their limitations? What do you like and dislike about reading them? What do you think people hope to gain from these accounts? What do you think people composing such texts stand to gain or lose? What might be motivating them to compose such narratives?

John Thompson
Why I Was One of the Few to Survive I Won't Ever Know

Thailand: 8,245 Dead

Why I was one of the few to survive I won't ever know. My fortune was partially due to luck and partially due to a few calculated gambles. This website tells the story of how I survived one of the world's most destructive natural disasters in modern history.

Having narrowly cheated death, I am left with a sense of extreme optimism for my future.

Perhaps because I came so close to losing everything, that now every day of life seems like a new beginning. Being laid off from my job upon my return home was not a crisis. Combined with surviving the tsunami I saw it as an opportunity to reassess where my life has been going and how I could rebuild my career in a meaningful way.

This website is dedicated to the memory of the thousands who were less fortunate than I on the fateful day of 26 December 2004. Special thanks go to those I was with during and after the disaster—Petra, Bob, and Timothy.

Here is a timeline of what happened to me those days in Khao Lak, Thailand.

Saturday, 25 December 2004 16:53:25

Arrived at Khao Lak. Explored area north of bungalow at Khaolak Orchid Beach Resort.

Enjoyed Christmas dinner at Ristorante Da Gorgio and then later had desert at a beach front bar.

Sunday, 26 December 2004 08:00

While laying on mattress, contemplating whether or not to sleep in longer, felt vibrating sensation for about two minutes. Did not think it was an earthquake and thought nothing of it after vibrating stopped.

9:00 Enjoyed breakfast at Mai's Quiet Zone on open patio overlooking the beach. Watched two boys from English family I had met when checking in the previous day playing frisbee in the waves.

9:45 Stopped by motorbike rental shop and paid 200 Baht for one more rental day.

10:00 Purchased souvenir shirt and some food at market across the street from motorbike rental shop.

10:10 Began motorbike journey with eventual goal of checking out the Poseidon Bungalows which had been recommended to me. Also intended on visiting the Ton Pling Waterfall on the way.

10:17 Unsuccessful attempt at finding "View Point" as listed on the map. Continued driving down the road.

10:21 Parked motorbike at Sea Gull Andaman Resort and walked down to inspect beach and what appeared to be an extremely low tide.

10:26:16 Noticed wooden longtail boat struggling in the water and eventually turn over. Also saw many people standing on the shore looking at something, which I then assumed was the struggling boat (but in retrospect I think they were looking at the approaching wave or the bay empty of water). Took camera out of bag to take picture of boat.

10:26:23 Seven seconds later: After taking picture of boat, the bay had already completely filled with water and I took picture of what I thought was just an extra large wave.

10:27:14 Fifty two seconds later: When I realized the wave was not stopping at the shore I and others at the beach began running as fast as possible. Since I already had the camera out, I took a picture over my shoulder as I ran, hoping to capture the rushing wave.

Running from the Waves—Photo by John Thompson

10:28:04 Fifty seconds later: It was obvious that the wave was not stopping and that I was not going to be able to outrun the wave so I ran up the front entrance to the nearest big building, dodging falling roof tiles, and hoping that the building would not be washed away or collapse. Took photo of now flooded street as I ran into the hotel.

10:31:41 Climbed up on wooden balcony railing and prayed I was high enough above the water.

The water eventually came up to the top of the railing and then started receding. Started taking photos as the water drained out.

View of the Courtyard—Photo by John Thompson

Woman on mattress in the water

2004 11:01:04 Sought refuge in alcove at highest point in the building. Was bracing for additional waves which never came.

John Thompson, On the Roof—Waiting for the water to recede—Photo by John Thompson

12:04:16 Almost 2 hours after seeing the struggling boat, the water finally drained out far enough so that it seemed safe to walk out.

Walking Through The Rubble—Photo by John Thompson

12:20:34 Hitched ride on a passing pickup truck back into main beach of Khao Lak. Photographed some of the devastation as seen from the road.

Sunday, 26 December 2004
14:11:14 Photographed what was believed to be a second wave but which turned out to be a false alarm. Spent the rest of the day and night in safety on top of high hill.

Monday, 27 December 2004
09:27:39 After being scared back to the hill by several false alarms, Tim and I finally made our way through the wreckage to retreive some of his belongings from his third floor hotel room before beginning hike out of the area.

11:26:50 During another false alarm we were driven to military staging area where we were finally taken by private car to a bus station to catch VIP bus to Bangkok.

Friday 31 December 2004
06:59:32 Solomon and I inspected donated goods at military side of Bangkok airport while waiting for transport plane back to Krabi.

Saturday 1 January 2005
09:39:23 Distributed donations to owners of damaged longtail boats in Krabi area.

Saturday 1 January 2005
12:18:37 First return vist to Khao Lak area to determine extent of damage. Toured area and local hospitals with Jenny, a relief worker for American medical aid organization.

Sunday 2 January 2005
12:18:25 Toured ruined resort island of Phuket. Photographed destruction at Patong beach.

Daily Collection of recently found bodies—Photo by John Thompson

Uncovered bodies waiting to be identified—Photo by John Thompson

Monday 10 January 2005
14:55:03 Second return trip to Khao Lak. Distributed thousands of dollars of relief aid to refugee camp near Takua Pa.

Tuesday 11 January 2005
09:08:11 Final bit of aid work. Distributed donated money to Monitee Temple in Krabi.

Saturday 22 January 2005
07:12 Returned home to California after continuing trip to southern Thailand, Malaysia, and Singapore.

December 26, 2005
MY STORY—ONE YEAR LATER
After coming within 15 seconds of an almost certain death one year ago today, one of the most common questions I am asked is "How did that experience change your perspective on life?" To answer that question, I look back on how I have lived during this past year.

As all people realize who come so close to losing everything, the only thing that really matters is life. While it is nice to have physical things without life none of those things matter. In recognition of this simple premise, I try to make the most of life, by continuing to travel, mixing work with play when possible, and developing new hobbies.

After returning from Thailand, I spent some additional time traveling, spending a month in Peru exploring the Amazon and climbing peaks high in the Andes. In May I came into possession of a new sailboat and have sailed almost every weekend since then. Beginning in July I started working again as an attorney. Although I currently work for a law firm, I continue to explore other career opportunities.

As for the future, I am sure the lessons from the tsunami will stay with me forever. Not one day has gone by where I have not somehow been reminded of the traumatic and overwhelming events of one year ago. I have not been able to answer the question as to why I survived when over 223,000 people did not, including the fact that 80% of Thailand's tsunami casualties occurred in Khao Lak.

Write Away

1. Using specific evidence from Thompson's narrative, write a rhetorical analysis that identifies the rhetorical elements of his narrative and how they function to contribute to

his overall account. In your rhetorical analysis, address what the purposes might be of Thompson's narrative, likely and potential readers, and the *ethos* the text constructs of Thompson. Address both the written and visual content in Thompson's narrative.

2. The aftermath and recovery period after the Asian Tsunami has intersected with research from many different disciplines. Create an annotated bibliography in which you document resources from across disciplines that have engaged with recovery efforts and analysis of the Asian Tsunami.

3. Develop a collection of personal/survival narratives to document an event. Then, using that compilation as evidence, write an essay in which you articulate the various purposes, forms, conventions, and affordances of personal/survival narratives. You might, for instance, identify common themes, connections, or disconnects across the narratives. Draw on relevant research to contextualize the event and the narratives. Address in your essay the following questions: What do personal/survival narratives accomplish? What, if any, are the limitations of personal/survival narratives?

Chapter 5 Key Terms

summary	abstract	executive summary
review	*précis*	tone
synopsis	annotated bibliography	voice

Write Away

Choose a landmark or site in or near your locale and write several different versions of summary about that site. Doing so will help you explore how you might transfer summary across context.

Select a landmark or site. Choose a site or landmark in your area or at your institution you can use for this Write Away. It can be one that is very well known or one that deserves recognition but is not yet as well known. It could also be a site that may be primarily familiar only to people at your institution or in your locale. The site, though, should be one about which you can find some information fairly easily, such as background, history, significance, or other aspects of the site.

Select three to four versions of summary and potential readers. Choose three to four of the different versions of summary described in Chapter 5 to use for summarizing this landmark. For instance, you might choose to write a brief abstract about the historical significance of the site, such as would appear on a plaque located onsite. You might also choose to write a more extended summary of the site, such as would appear on a Wikipedia page. A third option might be an executive summary aimed at a Preservation Board or Architectural Committee considering making changes to the site. A fourth option might be a summary of the site that would appear as part of an introduction to a research essay about that landmark.

Share your summaries. Share your different summary versions with classmates and ask for their feedback about which elements of your summaries seem to work most effectively.

Reflect. Reflect in writing for ten minutes about which aspects of summary transected the different occasions for summary, and which elements of summary seemed more uniquely adapted to one particular occasion over others.

Synthesis

Pinpointing Chapter 6

Where Chapter 5 addressed how writers across disciplines engage in varied forms of summary, Chapter 6 demonstrates how writers build on summary with synthesis to advance conversations and carve out more space for their own perspectives. Across disciplines, writers use synthesis to generate new understandings, create new ideas, and revisit former assumptions. To provide you with strategies for *synthesis in transit*, this chapter addresses the following concepts:

- What is Synthesis?
- Purposes of Synthesis
- Questions that Shape Synthesis
- Criteria for Effective Synthesis
- Modes of Synthesis across Disciplines

After exploring synthesis here, Chapter 7 offers the opportunity to engage with the work of others through analysis and create something new by thinking in a different direction. Synthesis, as Chapter 6 establishes, is counterpart to analysis, which invites academic writers to break apart ideas into smaller component parts for extended consideration.

Stonehenge, located near Salisbury in central southern UK, is estimated to have been built in 3100 BCE. Theories about its purpose have ranged from a site of human sacrifice to an astronomical calculating tool. The site was constructed in stages; one of its most enigmatic aspects involves "the issue of how people achieved the almost unimaginable feat of hauling the sarsens [bluestones], weighing 25 tons or more, over 30 km from the Marlborough Downs in the north" (Ruggles). Alexander Thom provided one of the earliest investigations into the geometry of Stonehenge, observing that it was oriented in such a way as to be both a lunar and solar observatory. Gerald Hawkins argued in a bestselling book, *Stonehenge Decoded*, "that the megaliths made up a sophisticated observatory in which the stones served to record solstices and equinoxes and even to predict lunar eclipses" ("About"; Roberts). Clive Ruggles, although acknowledging "axial alignment upon midsummer sunrise and midwinter sunset," challenged Hawkins's ideas about Stonehenge being an astronomical observatory, suggesting instead that the monument "may have symbolized cyclical time through alignments on the sun or moon, or that astronomical considerations formed part of the sacred principles." Recent research has found that as many as 240 people were buried at Stonehenge and that the site also had ceremonial significance for herders and farmers. An avenue at Stonehenge, aligned with the solstice, links Stonehenge with the River Aven, and researchers believe that pigs were brought along this avenue to be slaughtered in December and January, possibly as a way of marking the winter solstice (Jarus).

One recent area of research has involved using acoustics to learn more about the purpose and use of Stonehenge.

> Researchers...tested thousands of stones on Carn Menyn in the Preseli Hills, and found a large number of the rocks ring when they are struck. Usually, stones produce a disappointing clunk when hit, with microscopic cracks making it difficult for vibrations to travel within the rock. But certain bluestones have the right microscopic structure—and sound like a metallic gong. They also found a few of the rocks remaining at Stonehenge rang as well. (Cox)

Research on what musicologist Bruno Fazendo calls "archaeoacoustics" shows that learning more about archaeological sites such as Stonehenge often involves asking questions from across disciplines. Researchers working with Fazendo have created real-life and computer-simulated models of Stonehenge to learn more about what it sounded like to stand within the structure when it existed in its entirety.

One finding is that the circular position of the stones provided "the perception…of a reverberant space,…supportive of speech activity since a speaker can be heard reasonably well from anywhere in the space." This archaeoacoustic research enhances previous research about the astronomical alignment of the site to facilitate new understanding about the site's design and function. The kind of multidisciplinary fusion engineered through archaeoacoustics, combining archaeology, musicology, and computer science, among other disciplines, illustrates the concept of synthesis, a kind of scholarly **mash-up** that transects writing across disciplines. Well-known musical mash-ups include *The Grey Album*, a fusion of Jay-Z and the Beatles by Danger Mouse, and "Radioactive Swimming Pools," a mash-up of Imagine Dragons and Kendrick Lamar. Mash-ups also abound in fiction with such works as *Pride and Prejudice and Zombies*, by Seth Grahame-Smith, and *William Shakespeare's Star Wars: Verily, A New Hope*, by Ian Doescher. Various academic disciplines likewise engage in mash-ups, such as in computer science, where a mash-up is defined as "a web application that uses content from more than one source to create a single new service…[such as combining] addresses and photographs…to create a map mash-up." In each of these cases, mash-ups do not merely combine elements; they do so by "mashing them together to create something new" (Fichter).

The kind of innovation engineered through mash-ups is part of what makes synthesis so vital in academic writing. Synthesis enables scholars to generate new ideas and create new approaches. Akin to an actual musical synthesizer, which combines "fundamental properties of sound…in a way that forms a new whole" (Harder), synthesis in academic writing involves putting together two or more ideas, concepts, or elements in order to create something new.

Write Here

Pretend you are part of a world-renowned interdisciplinary team of scholars researching Stonehenge. Form a small group with several of your peers, and appoint each person as a representative for a particular discipline (i.e., an anthropologist, a physicist, a literary scholar, etc). Ask each team member to find three or four examples of how members of their discipline have advanced knowledge about Stonehenge. After sharing with one another what you've learned, write for five minutes about disciplinary intersections and divergences around Stonehenge. What new areas of inquiry on Stonehenge might emerge from interdisciplinary collaboration?

❧ ❧ ❧

What is Synthesis?

Synthesis is defined by the *Oxford English Dictionary* as "The putting together of parts or elements so as to make up a complex whole." Synthesis involves combining and integrating. It emerges across disciplines as academic writers put together two or more ideas, concepts, or materials to create new ideas, products, or entities. At its essence, synthesis is based on forging, naming, and exploring relationships between ideas and elements.

You are likely already familiar with synthesis through school; the art of compiling materials and ideas for a course is a form of synthesis. Your professor has synthesized concepts, theories, topics, materials, and assignments in order to create space for the class members to learn and create new knowledge.

Similarly, most academic research and writing relies heavily on synthesis as academic writers gather materials, summarize ideas, read and analyze data, and then synthesize these elements in the formation of new knowledge.

Purposes of Synthesis

Academic writers use synthesis across disciplines in myriad ways, sometimes as a stand-alone writing project, and other times as part of a larger project. The purposes of synthesis are deeply tied to the writing occasion in which synthesis emerges. Synthesis can involve one or more of the following purposes:

- to make connections between ideas
- to apply one or more ideas to one or more other contexts
- to show disagreement among ideas
- to combine ideas or concepts
- to demonstrate a gap in knowledge
- to create a fuller understanding of a concept
- to produce something new

Many disciplines have particular purposes for synthesis. For instance, according to the website *Biology Online*, synthesis is used in the natural sciences in order to accomplish the creation of new, complex entities:

Biochemistry: "The production of an organic compound in a living thing, especially as aided by enzymes"

Chemistry: "The act or process of forming a complex substance by combining or integrating two or more chemical entities, especially through a chemical reaction"

Psychiatry: "The integration of different elements of the personality" ("Synthesis")

Synthesis is also a key aspect of STEM disciplines. According to Gregory McColm, Associate Professor in the Department of Mathematics at the University of South Florida, synthesis in these disciplines serves the dual purposes of "construct[ing]…

entirely new things from old parts" and in helping us come to greater "cognizance and knowledge." In the following passage McColm describes synthesis in mechanical engineering and math:

> There are two faces of synthesis. First, creative acts usually consist of combining notions that one usually doesn't imagine having much to do with each other. For example, a carburetor is merely a very large [perfume] atomizer. ... Second, many things cannot be understood in isolation ... Consider the problem: find all solutions to:
>
> $$3x + y = 2$$
> $$-2y - z = 2$$
> $$x = 1$$
>
> This can be solved by substitution: $x = 1$, so $y = 2 - 3 = -1$, so $z = 2 - 2 = 0$ ... But what about:
>
> $$x - y + 2z = 2$$
> $$3x + 2y + z = 1$$
> $$x + y + z = 0$$

Transfer at Work

Writers across all disciplines engage with synthesis as an area for research and as a component of their writing. Martin Gruebele and Devarajan Thirumalai argue that a synthesis between chemical physics and biology can yield important insights, particularly when applying experimental tools, algorithms, and fundamental theoretical models developed by chemical physics to biological problems. One example they note is that biologists are using chemical physics to conduct experiments with recent research in HIV viral capsid simulation.

The viral capsid of the AIDS-causing virus (HIV-1) unveiled at the atomic level by a synthesis of experimental techniques and computations between chemical physics and biology.

Substitutions don't work so well here: we need to use a method that deals with the entire system at once: Cramer's rule, or the Gauss-Jordan method. (McColm)

As McColm's calculations demonstrate, in the fields of mechanical engineering and math, synthesis enables people to apply known solutions or rules from one context to others as a way of solving new and complex problems. McColm demonstrates above that Cramer's rule or the Gauss-Jordan method can be applied to a new context in order to find a solution. Such an application is an act of synthesis, bringing strategies used in one context to another in order to build knowledge.

In the field of health care, synthesis can involve examining findings from a set of studies in order to make advances in disease prevention and treatment: "Synthesis [in health-care related reviews] should...explore whether observed intervention effects are consistent across studies, and investigate possible reasons for any inconsistencies" (Center for Reviews and Dissemination).

Synthesis in the humanities and social sciences often involves application, which entails applying one theory or concept to another context. In English literature, this might involve a theoretical reading of a text from a feminist perspective. In the social sciences, it might involve applying a theory to a new primary source, context, or culture.

Often, synthesis appears in the form of a literature review, where an academic writer makes connections among and between relevant research reports. Sometimes literature reviews function as stand-alone writing projects, designed to inform others about the field of research on a given area of inquiry. Other times, the purpose of literature reviews is to enable the writer to carve out a space for his or her own research, showing gaps, disagreements, and overlaps in knowledge. In these ways, literature reviews resonate with the ways in which academic writers use summary in referring to others' research (as discussed in Chapter 5). Synthesis, however, involves a focus on making connections between these various summaries.

Just as synthesis itself involves a combining of elements, academic writers have multiple and often intersecting purposes for using synthesis. This section will help you identify these purposes for yourself as you embark on synthesis.

Questions that Shape Synthesis

As you engage with your own academic writing mash-ups in the form of synthesis, you will need to navigate through a variety of choices for how to shape your synthesis. Writers develop synthesis by considering aspects such as disciplinary context and purpose. Synthesis, as we learned earlier in this chapter, is intended to generate something new. Having a sense of what that something new might be, or what you hope it might be, will help shape your approach to synthesis. So too will an awareness of how the component parts might generate this new knowledge. To help you strengthen and tailor your approach to synthesis, you might ask yourself questions that fall within certain categories.

TABLE 6.1 Questions that shape synthesis.

Disciplinary context	What is the disciplinary context for the synthesis? What do other forms of synthesis in that disciplinary context accomplish? How do writers tend to construct and integrate synthesis in writing throughout that disciplinary context?
Purpose	What is your purpose for the synthesis? What do you hope readers can learn or do based on your synthesis? How do you anticipate the synthesis advancing your larger purpose and aims?
Relationship between components	What is the relationship between the component parts? What points of agreement, overlap, or connection exist among the component ideas or elements? Where do component ideas or elements disagree, differ, or diverge?
New understandings	What new understandings, concepts, or knowledge are you hoping to discover from your synthesis? How does your synthesis create something new? What can your synthesis uncover or illustrate that could not likely have emerged without that synthesis?

Write Now

Practice using a synthesis matrix with a current writing project. Identify two or more main ideas (subtopics) for the writing project, and track what four different texts argue about those main ideas. An alternative approach to experimenting with the synthesis matrix would be to formulate a question or two about your writing project (i.e., how are women represented in hip-hop?) and ask four different people. Record across the matrix what they say, and then look for connections and divergences among and between their answers.

Criteria for Effective Synthesis

Given the drastic variation in purpose, discipline, format, and style in synthesis, it would be challenging to develop an exhaustive list of criteria that make synthesis more or less effective. The effectiveness of synthesis depends almost entirely on what a writer's purpose is, and how well that writer accomplishes that purpose within the disciplinary context and writing occasion. As you will see later in this chapter from the many examples of synthesis, there is no one method or template for how to create the perfect synthesis. Instead, synthesis should be seen as an opportunity to explore in writing the generative nature of noticing connections, developing patterns, juxtaposing ideas, and joining seemingly disparate concepts together. The resulting syntheses should advance knowledge in a purposeful way. Although the precise manner in which that can be accomplished will vary, the following are some general criteria for effective synthesis that might be applied across disciplines and writing occasions.

Demonstrates relationships between ideas

The main difference between summary in an annotated bibliography and the kind of work synthesis does in a literature review or other mode of synthesis is that relationships are named and forged. It might be helpful to consider these relationships through the lens of a dinner conversation. Imagining the component parts of the literature review speaking to one another is one way to think about naming the relationships between them. If you personified the component parts and they sat around a table, who would argue with one another? Who would become fast friends? Which guests might talk all night due to a spark of a new idea?

To help identify relationships among and between ideas and elements, you might want to organize your thoughts in such a way that facilitates your understanding of these relationships. One such strategy to help you prepare a synthesis is to use a visual organizer such as the "synthesis matrix" developed by the Writing and Speaking Tutorial Service at North Carolina State University (see Figure 6.1). This type of matrix can help you examine how various texts are each approaching the same main idea. For example, if you were researching women in hip-hop, you might have Main Idea A focus on female rappers, then trace what various sources (1–4) say about female rappers. Main Idea B might be the representation of women in hip-hop songs, and you might likewise trace what each source (1–4) argues about that. Using a matrix such as this will enable you to make explicit the connections between component elements and ideas that are occurring in the synthesis you create.

Topic: _____

Main Idea A	Source #1	Source #2	Source #3	Source #4
Main Idea B				

FIGURE 6.1 Synthesis matrix.

Reflects disciplinary context and writing occasion

Although disciplinary expectations and writing contexts overlap, many academic writers deliberately opt to modify or challenge these expectations and contexts. Nonetheless, synthesis should still take them into account. Writers often approach synthesis in discipline-specific ways. This might involve synthesizing research that emerges from the discipline in which you are writing (and thereby leaving out research from other disciplines), or it might involve shaping the synthesis in a way that takes disciplinary expectations into account (i.e., more or less detail, quotes or no quotes). In the sciences and social sciences, for instance, a literature review tends to move rapidly, with a writer synthesizing numerous relevant ideas from a large quantity of sources. In the humanities, synthesis often involves a more detailed approach, with quotes and specific details from the various ideas to demonstrate the connections and applications with greater specificity.

Becoming aware of these discipline-specific approaches will enable you to craft a synthesis that is appropriately shaped for that discipline and writing occasion. As you begin a writing project that uses synthesis, you should review examples of synthesis in the discipline in which you are writing so you can model your approach to synthesis on these examples; if you break with or modify disciplinary convention, do so in an informed and deliberate way.

Represents each component text, idea, or concept accurately

Effective synthesis hinges on accurately understanding and representing the component parts. Be sure you have a full grasp of the main thesis or points of each component text, as well as any subsidiary points in each text. Take into consideration other elements of the component texts as well, such as disciplinary context, biographical context, tone, voice, and sociocultural context. The assumptions and purposes driving each component part will also play a role in accurate representation.

Representing the original texts accurately and comprehensively is crucial not only as a matter of ethics and academic honesty, but also so that the relationships you forge and identify between and among the component elements are valid. If you have mischaracterized or misunderstood any of the component parts, then your synthesis will be erroneous. Representing each component part accurately will enable you to navigate the connections and divergences among them. With these in mind, you can move forward more productively and confidently with the synthesis.

Emerges in an organized, integrated manner

Because synthesis can involve many different parts or an in-depth examination of complicated components, readers may get confused or lose track of important ideas while reading a synthesis. This is exacerbated by the likelihood that some readers of a synthesis have likely not encountered the ideas or elements being synthesized. For that reason, it is especially important to organize and integrate a synthesis in a way that makes sense and that helps readers process the connections you are making. Effective organization and integration of your synthesis will avoid the risk of readers spending unnecessary time juggling concepts and figuring out where relationships are emerging; instead, they can devote their energy and attention to processing the information you provide and the ideas you generate.

Effective organization and integration refers to how you are illustrating the relationships between component parts as well as how well the synthesis itself is integrated with the larger writing project. Sometimes syntheses are stand-alone writing projects. When this

---

Writer Insights

How does synthesis inform your scholarship?

"The original idea for [my book, *A Synthesis of Qualitative Studies of Writing Center Theory*] came when [I] prepared questions for [my] doctoral comprehensive exam in writing centers. One of the questions was, 'Is there a writing center theory, and if so, what is it?' [I] found that there was no one common writing center theory, but rather a set of practices and a pattern of taking theories from other disciplines and applying them to writing centers... [I] realized that in order to find out what a unified theory of writing center tutoring would look like, it would be necessary to look at actual studies of tutoring and see what theories emerged."

~Rebecca Day Babcock, English Professor, Odessa, Texas, U.S.

is the case, organize it in such a way that readers can keep up with the conclusions you are drawing. You might want to first thoroughly discuss one text, then another, and so on. Or you might choose to organize by grouping texts together through common ideas or questions. When synthesis operates as part of a larger writing project, the writer should integrate it into his or her project as thoroughly as possible. Effective integration involves making explicit to readers how you are using the synthesis to advance the larger argument or purpose of the writing project rather than simply inserting it into a larger writing project as though it could stand alone.

Remains focused

When synthesizing, academic writers face a risk of including too much material. With any given topic or line of inquiry, there is often an abundance of relevant literature and component parts, and writers can sometimes enjoy the process of noticing connections and divergences across the many ideas they are exploring. While such enthusiasm is laudable, writers must nevertheless remain focused primarily on those component parts that are most directly relevant to the synthesis and writing project at hand. Otherwise, these writers and their writing projects may get diluted and convoluted, and the synthesis will become merely a vast, complex network of connections without an overarching direction or sense of purpose.

Having a clear sense of your aims and purposes for synthesis will help you focus your synthesis and guide your readers productively through it. If your purpose is to show disagreement, then you'll want to focus primarily on synthesizing opposing and/or divergent points of view. By contrast, if your purpose is to show overlap, then you'll want to focus mainly on synthesizing ideas that are tightly related to one another. In efforts to remain focused during synthesis, academic writers must also sometimes make difficult decisions about what to include or exclude. Aim to bring together only the most representative component parts, or the most well-known, or even perhaps the least well-known. Remember that syntheses rarely need to be exhaustive and comprehensive (nor, arguably, could they ever be). Instead, syntheses should include sufficient amounts of component parts and sufficient explication of the relationships in order to effectively accomplish the writer's primary aims and purposes.

Advances knowledge

While academic writers often bring a wide variety of purposes to synthesis, at its core, synthesis involves the generation of something new. Both the writer and his or her readers should gain new knowledge from the synthesis. Rather than making readers engage in guesswork, however, academic writers should name that new knowledge or conclusion directly in the synthesis. At the same time, readers will sometimes generate their own new knowledge based on the synthesis—perhaps knowledge that the writer may not have foreseen.

Perhaps the something new is a fuller or fresher understanding of a concept. Or, perhaps a synthesis uncovers a new, pressing question or an important gap in knowledge. In these cases, the writer should use the process of synthesis as a way of exploring and discovering a potentially generative advancement of knowledge. Other times, writers might approach synthesis by already having an advanced idea about what the something new will be. In these cases, the writer can develop the synthesis by exploring the implications and smaller details of that new knowledge. However, these writers should still be open to new ideas that they may not have anticipated.

Modes of Synthesis across Disciplines

Numerous modes of synthesis exist across and within academic disciplines. It would be nearly impossible even to name, much less describe, all the modes of analysis that operate across disciplines.

In an article offering guidance on how to conduct literature reviews in healthcare settings, the Center for Reviews and Dissemination names two primary approaches for how writers approach data synthesis: quantitative and narrative. "Synthesis involves bringing the results of individual studies together and summarising their findings. This may be done quantitatively or, if formal pooling of results is inappropriate, through a narrative approach." Within these broad categories, though, their guidelines name "descriptive synthesis," "synthesis of findings of included studies," and "quantitative synthesis of comparative studies" (CRD).

Within this large range of types of synthesis, however, there are some modes of synthesis that do emerge more commonly across disciplines. This list offers some of the most common modes of synthesis you may encounter in your undergraduate academic writing career:

- Synthesis as Literature Review
- Synthesis of Application
- Synthesis as Interdisciplinarity
- Synthesis as Curation of Collections
- Synthesis of Resources
- Synthesis as Comparison
- Synthesis as Definition
- Synthesis in Bibliographic Essays

In keeping with the overarching line of inquiry in this chapter and with the spirit of synthesis as a form of mash-up, each of the included modes of synthesis contains examples that show academic writing synthesis related to hip-hop music. While each of the sections illustrates a particular mode of synthesis, the modes also intersect and overlap with one another. As you read through the examples, consider conducting a supersynthesis: a synthesis of modes of synthesis. What are the intersections and differences among and between various modes of synthesis? Where do you notice overlap? What elements seem distinctive to a particular mode of synthesis?

Transfer at Work

Literature reviews appear in different forms and by different titles across contexts. Student Affairs faculty members Wilma J. Henry, Nicole M. West, and Andrea Jackson designate their literature review with the title: "Hip Hop's Influence on the Identity Development of Black Female College Students: A Literature Review." Educational scholar Emery Petchauer also brands his article as a literature review in his title, "Framing and Reviewing Hip-Hop Educational Research." Sociologist Philip Kavanaugh, however, integrates elements of a literature review within his article by using key phrases such as the following: "A number of studies have shown that commercial nightlife venues are among the most salient contexts for this kind of gender construction and performance..." and "There is a sizable and growing literature indicating that nightlife spaces such as bars and clubs are intensely sexualized social spaces..." (21). Illustrating yet another format, S. Ojofeitimi, S. Bronner, and H. Woo begin their literature review for research on hip-hop related injuries with their very first sentence: "Originated in Bronx, New York by African American and Latino youth, (Pabon, 1999; Wiggles, 2009) hip hop dance has become an international art form" (347). They continue the literature review throughout the first two paragraphs of their article to develop a taxonomy of hip-hop subcategories, which they then use for their research into hip-hop-related injuries:

Fig. 1. Subsets of hip hop dance.

Literature reviews can also appear as separate sections within articles. These might be labeled by a generic heading (i.e., "literature review," "background," "prior scholarship," "related research") or a more content-specific heading, such as the section labeled "The Place of Hip Hop in Current Research" in Sharon Lauricella and Matthew Alexander's article analyzing spirituality in comments made on Lil Wayne's blog from prison, www.weezythankxyou.com.

Table 2. Most Frequently Occurring Categories in Comments to the Weezythanxyou Blog

Category	% in Comments from Fans
Encouragement	35
Admiration	35
Love	32
Anticipation (of Wayne's release and/or new music)	24
God/prayer	17
Communication (references to the blog or receipt of letters/ mail, "shout-outs")	16
Music/Young Money/Cash Money Label	14
Inspiration	11
Location (fan's city/country)	11
"Free Weezy" slogan	11
Positive comment about a specific blog post	8
Missing (Wayne and/or his music)	7
Gratitude	6

Synthesis as literature review

Because academic writers build on, adapt, counter, and otherwise modify the research of others in order to advance research, they must synthesize prior research through a **literature review** in order to move forward with their own projects. A literature review is also sometimes referred to as a **background synthesis** (Jamieson). Literature reviews can be stand-alone writing projects or can be part of larger writing projects.

Literature reviews, therefore, are not merely series of summaries. They offer a new way of understanding an area of inquiry by putting others' ideas in conversation together.

Given the many directions in which a conversation can take place, one challenge with a literature review is deciding how to organize it. The Writing Center at the University of North Carolina, Chapel Hill names four methods of organizing a synthesis in the form of a literature review: chronological by publication, chronological by trend, thematic, and methodological. Since multiple forms of organization might be applicable to any given writing occasion, academic writers must choose deliberately how to organize their literature reviews.

Literature reviews can serve multiple purposes, which can often be overlapping as well. Included here are three examples, each of which demonstrates a different purpose:

- Example 1: Literature Review, Extending Others' Research, Nursing
- Example 2: Literature Review, Demonstrating a Gap in Prior Research, Business
- Example 3: Literature Review, Debates in the Field, Sociology

Example 1: Literature Review, Extending Others' Research, Nursing

The authors of the excerpt have chosen to organize their literature review by theme in order to demonstrate how they will build on existing knowledge. The excerpt illustrates a portion of the literature review from an article about using hip-hop to prevent the spread of human papillomavirus (HPV). The corresponding references are also included in order to illustrate further how the writers are synthesizing the work of others through citation. (For more explanation about citing the work of others, see Chapter 12; for more discussion of integrating evidence, see Chapter 11.)

> ### Writer Insights
>
> **Describe your process of summary, synthesis, and analysis.**
>
> In our field, we design our experiment scientifically, collect data carefully, process and analyze the data correctly, and write a paper effectively. While writing, we review relevant literatures and write the methods and introduction first. Then, we write the result section after analyzing data in some reliable statistical software (like R). Now, we write the discussion, synthesizing/interpreting our results and comparing with the previous studies, if any. We also include citations/references at the end of our paper recognizing others' work, while following the academic honesty. Lastly, we write an abstract/summary, which includes an overall synopsis of our study.
>
> ~Subodh Adhikari, Agroecology—Ph.D. student, Montana State University, Bozeman, Montana, U.S.

Excerpt from the Literature Review for "Hip-Hop, Health, and Human Papilloma Virus (HPV): Using Wireless Technology to Increase HPV Vaccination Uptake" by T. L. Thomas, D. P. Stephens, and B. Blanchard

Thomas, Stephens, and Blanchard synthesize research about using technology in education and taking into account "unique cultural methods." See the next page for their references, numbers 24-28.

Researchers across disciplines emphatically agree that interventions seeking to achieve changes in the attitudes toward and beliefs about racial/ethnic-minority sexuality that fail to recognize the unique cultural messages that influence these processes are likely to fail.[24] For example, young women have grown up with technologies allowing faster and more direct information consumption, particularly as it relates to health outcomes, making Internet, cell phone, BlackBerry, iPhone, and iPod devices important tools for education.[25-28] Furthermore, the ways in which these wireless technology tools and culture-specific messages influence behavioral outcomes can differ across racial/ethnic groups, making it important to integrate frameworks that reflect values and expressions relevant to these young women.[29-30] Recognizing this, we have chosen to integrate two cultural tools that that been identified as playing central roles in young adult African American women's daily lives: wireless technology tools, namely cell phones; and hip-hop culture frameworks.

Next, Thomas, Stephens, and Blanchard show that hip-hop in particular is a cultural message that might have an important bearing on education. Again, they synthesize multiple sources (see References).

Research on sexual health decision making and outcomes among African American adolescents and females highlights the relevance and importance of integrating hip-hop specifically into sexual health promotion contexts. A growing body of psychological and public health research has examined the influence of hip-hop culture on African American women's sexual health outcomes clearly indicating their sexual health decision making processes and beliefs are influenced by this culture. Viewing hip-hop images with high levels of sexual content was also found to increase women's negative attitude toward condom use and increase their desire to conceive.[39-40] Stephens and Few [30,33] found that African American adolescents not only recognized stereotypical sexual scripts in mainstream hip-hop videos but saw them as accurate portrayals of real-life sexual behavioral guidelines for their peers.

From *The Journal for Nurse Practitioners* (6.6), 2010.

Here Thomas, Stephens, and Blanchard show how their synthesis of prior research led them to develop this feasibility project about hip-hop as a "vehicle to send positive health promotion messages."

These research findings substantiate hip-hop's important role in health education in combination with wireless technologies as a successful vehicle for health promotion.... This feasibility project chose hip-hop music and images as the vehicle to send positive health promotion messages.

Notice through this references section, which shows the scholarship that Thomas, Stephens, and Blanchard used in their synthesis, that the authors have taken a large number of sources and put them into conversation with one another in order to develop their feasibility project.

References

[24]Kirby D. Effective approaches to reducing adolescent unprotected sex, pregnancy, and childbearing. J Sex Res. 2002; 39(1): 51-57.

[25]Donnerstein E, Smith S. Sex in the media: theory, influences, and solutions. *Handbook of children and the media.* Thousand Oaks, CA: Sage; 2001: p. 289-307.

[26]Skinner H, Biscope S, Poland B, Goldberg E. How adolescents use technology for health information: implications for health professionals from focus group studies. *J Med Internet Res.* 2003; 5(4).

[27]Stokes C. Representin' in cyberspace: sexual scripts, self-definition, and hip-hop culture in Black American adolescent girls' home pages. *Cult Health Sex.* 2007; 9(2): 169-184.

[28]Strouse J, Buerkel-Rothfuss N. Media exposure and the sexual attitudes and behaviors of college students. *J Sex Educ Ther.* 1987; 13(2): 43-51.

[29]Few A, Stephens D, Rouse-Arnett M. Sister-to-sister talk: transcending boundaries and challenges in qualitative research with Black women. *Fam Relat.* 2003; 52(3): 205-215.

[30]Stephens D, Few A. The effects of images of African American women in hip-hop on early adolescents' attitudes toward physical attractiveness and interpersonal relationships. *Sex Roles.* 2007; 56(3): 251-264.

[33]Stephens D, Few A. Hip-hop honey or video ho: African American preadolescents' understanding of female sexual scripts in hip-hop culture. *Sexuality & Culture.* 2007; 11(4): 48-69.

[39]Wingood G, DiClemente R, Harrington K, Davies S, Hook III, E, Oh M. Exposure to X-rated movies and adolescents' sexual and contraceptive related attitudes and behaviors. *Pediatrics.* 2001; 107(5): 1116.

[40]Wingood G, DiClemente R, Bernhardt J, et al. A prospective study of exposure to rap music videos and African American female adolescents' health. *Am J Public Health.* 2003; 93(3): 437.

Example 2: Literature Review, Demonstrating a Gap in Prior Research, Business

The second example of a literature review shows a writer demonstrating that many scholars have addressed a particular question and have done so from a variety of different angles, but that nobody has yet considered one important angle or approach. In the passage, Damien Arthur, a lecturer in business at the University of Adelaide, grounds his synthesis around a concept known as glocalization, a marketing term referring to the process by which people adapt global products or services in ways that make them more marketable to local cultures or people. Specifically, Arthur pursues the question, how does glocalization of hip-hop culture impact consumer behavior with hip-hop in Australia?

Excerpt from the Literature Review for "Authenticity and Consumption
in the Australian Hip-Hop Culture" by D. Arthur

Over the past two decades the Australian hip-hop culture has been fighting a stigma, perpetuated by the media, that its members are imitating U.S. culture. Only in the past four years has that stigma begun to dissipate, as the culture has glocalized. Previous research has found evidence of this glocalization in Australian hip-hop culture (Masters, 2001; Maxwell, 2003). For example, many Australian MC's now rap in Australian accents and about Australian issues. However, to date, no research has investigated these effects of such glocalization on the consumption practices of what the press describes as the fastest growing youth culture in the nation (Donovan, 2004). Furthermore, no research has investigated the role of authenticity on youth subcultures despite its effect on increasing brand loyalty (Kates, 2004). In order to fill this gap this study examines the effect that the local interpretations of foreign brands and the glocalization of the Australian hip-hop culture have on the consumption practices of members, explores the reasons for such effects with a particular focus on authentic self-expression and draws some marketing implications.

> Arthur uses synthesis to outline what previous research has accomplished: evidence of glocalization.

> Arthur shows that in examining this synthesis, he finds that there has been no research on "consumption practices" or on the "role of authenticity." And it is these areas of research that his study will now go on to address.

From *Qualitative Market Research* (9.2), 2006.

Example 3: Literature Review, Debates in the Field, Sociology

The third example of a literature review focuses on debates within the field. Nearly all fields of inquiry have debates and disagreements, and a literature review can map this terrain. Here, author Peter Katel, a sociologist, writes a literature review that asks, what are the main areas of disagreement and debate in hip-hop studies?

Excerpt from the Literature Review for
"Debating Hip-Hop: Does Gangsta Rap Harm Black Americans?" by P. Katel

Debates over hip-hop have taken place mostly within the black community. Some of hip-hop's fiercest critics, including black intellectuals and entertainers, argue that hip-hop presents a caricature of black America that damages how young black people view themselves and how they're viewed by others.

> Katel first identifies one position in the debate and provides an example.

From *Issues for Debate in Sociology: Selections from CQ Researcher*, 2010.

Author and jazz critic Crouch has decried for years what he calls the ravages of hip-hop. In a 2003 column in the New York Daily News—one of dozens he has devoted to them—he lamented that ordinary African Americans were bearing the consequences of a genre in which "thugs and freelance prostitutes have been celebrated for a number of years." The result: "Thousands upon thousands…have been murdered or beaten up or terrorized. After all, the celebration of thugs and thuggish behavior should not be expected to bring about any other results." [18]…

Younger cultural critics, even those who partly agree with Crouch, reject such sweeping condemnations. Instead, they insist on distinguishing between mass-marketed hip-hop and what they see as a purer, original form, less tainted by the demands of the marketplace.

> Now Katel shows how a younger generation of critics disagrees with the prior position, though not entirely, just in terms of "sweeping condemnations."

"I like conscious hip-hop and the stuff that you just dance to," says Lisa Fager, a former promotional specialist at commercial radio stations and record labels, "but I don't like stuff that demeans me as a black woman, or a woman, period—or degrades my community. People don't want to be called bitches, niggas, and hos."…

Rapper Banner doesn't dispute Fager on what gets played. "The labels don't want to deal with anything that creative," he says. "They don't want to develop an artist; they want the quickest thing people will buy. And as soon as one feminist gets mad, they back up."

But Banner reacts explosively to African Americans who attack hip-hop as degrading. Hip-hop mogul Simmons's proposal to ban offensive words is "stupid," Banner says. "There was a time in history when we didn't have a choice about being called a nigger. Now that we're making money off it, it's a problem."

> Here, Katel integrates a third perspective, from someone who argues not over the condemnations, but who has the right (or not) to issue the condemnations.

Synthesis of application

One of the most common modes of synthesis involves applying one concept to another context or entity in order to yield a new understanding of that entity. Scholars apply theories, approaches, and concepts to new contexts in order to reaffirm, challenge, or otherwise expand or modify them. Sometimes this is called reading through a **critical lens** or reading from a critical perspective. Synthesis of application might be termed **thesis-driven synthesis** (Jamieson) or **argumentative synthesis** (Carter) because it synthesizes in order to forward an argument. For instance, scholars in English might apply feminist theories to the reading of hip-hop lyrics, thereby creating a synthesis between hip-hop and feminist theory. Synthesis through application enables scholars to generate new questions: what happens if the ideas of x are applied to situation y or z? Importantly, synthesis through application often not only involves gleaning new insights about the idea or object to which a concept has been applied, but also invites readers to reconsider the concept being applied as well.

In this excerpt, James Stewart creates a synthesis by applying the ideas of Zora Neale Hurston, W. E. B. Du Bois, and Alain Locke to twentieth-century black popular music. This excerpt comes from Stewart's introduction. The remainder of the article goes on to apply in more detail the ideas of Hurston, Du Bois, and Locke.

Excerpt from "Message in the Music: Political Commentary in Black Popular Music from Rhythm and Blues to Early Hip-Hop" by J. B. Stewart

There are a variety of classical and more contemporary commentaries about the role of music in African American culture that provide useful insights for the development of a framework for understanding the political role of R & B. Early twentieth century perspectives advanced by Zora Neale Hurston, W. E. B. Du Bois, and Alain Locke remain relevant for interpreting contemporary African American musical forms. Hurston insisted that African American folklore was the core component of authentic African American culture.[3] Extending this idea, the most authentic political commentary in music lyrics should originate in the organic everyday experiences of people of African descent. In *The Souls of Black Folk* Du Bois maintained that the "sorrow songs" provided one of the most useful documentations of the long history of oppression and struggle against that oppression.[4] Thus, this form of music became a bearer of historical memory, similar to the role of griots in many West African societies. In addition to the sorrow conveyed in these songs, Du Bois argued that there was also a "faith in the ultimate justice of things" and that "minor cadences of despair change often to triumph and calm confidence."[5] Similar shifts in moods and assessments can be observed in R & B

> Stewart discusses Hurston and shows that he will extend (or apply) Hurston's ideas to political commentary in music lyrics.

> Stewart suggests that R & B lyrics demonstrate the "shifts in moods and assessments" that Du Bois identified in "sorrow songs."

From *The Journal of African American History* (90.3), 2005.

lyrics. Philosopher Alain Locke went even further than Du Bois by proposing that changes in predominant African American musical genres were closely correlated with major transformations in the sociopolitical and economic milieu for African Americans.[6] Locke's views suggest that in the absence of external efforts to shape the content of African American music, changes in lyrical content should be correlated with changes in the social, political, and economic circumstances for African Americans. Moreover, Locke emphasized that African American music was deeply ingrained in the American cultural fabric to the point that it "furnish[es] the sub-soil of our national music."[7] Locke's perspective suggests the need to explore political commentary in black music in terms of not only its impact on African Americans, but also on Americans of European and Asian descent.

> Lastly, Stewart applies Locke's ideas to show that the political commentary impacted all Americans, not only African-Americans.

Synthesis as interdisciplinarity

An extension of synthesis of application that deserves particular mention is synthesis as **interdisciplinarity**. This mode involves researchers actively drawing on and bridging the research methodologies and practices of multiple disciplines. Interdisciplinarity has been a feature of academic research across disciplines for years. In 1943, Henry Ozanne wrote about the phenomenon in his article, "'Synthesis' in Social Science":

> Sociological pilfering on the part of psychology is not a new form of scientific delinquency … Dr. Kardiner [has] achieved … a significant integration of two separate fields of social science, anthropology and psychology; or more specifically, culture and psychoanalysis. … Six years ago [Kardiner] announced the attempt to "join the resources of psychology and those of sociology"…In his latest study Kardiner reapplies what he terms his operational tool, basic personality structure, to the analysis of three [cultures]. They are the Comanche,…the Alorese…and Plainville…. Kardiner insists repeatedly that his work is primarily a contribution in methodology. Two aspects of Ozanne's description bear noting: the concepts of "pilfering" and "methodology." Regarding the latter, Ozanne emphasizes that Kardiner's contribution is primarily methodological, which underscores the fact that interdisciplinary research yields contributions of content as well as methodology.

Second, Ozanne initially describes interdisciplinarity as a form of "pilfering," underscoring the tensions that can emerge as scholars blend methodologies. While tensions continue today, most fields now embrace interdisciplinarity. Disciplines such as American Studies, Women's Studies, and African and African-American Studies are inherently interdisciplinary. Many institutions hire faculty who can work across disciplines and have established interdisciplinary studies departments or centers. Some areas of inquiry especially warrant interdisciplinarity. For instance, a committee from the National Institutes of Health created a book in which the second chapter argues for "The Potential of Interdisciplinary Research to Solve Problems in the Brain, Behavioral, and Clinical Sciences." Similarly, Stuart C. Carr and Malcolm MacLachlan argue for interdisciplinarity in the field of development economics: "The Millenium Development Goals (MDGs) focus on a range of human freedoms, and these reflect the inherent inter-disciplinarity of human poverty reduction." In the following excerpt, linguist H. Samy Alim describes his interdisciplinary approach to hip-hop studies. He outlines the many disciplines he has used for his book, *Roc the Mic Right*. Notice that, as we saw in Ozanne, Alim addresses the methodological contributions of this research.

In addition to offering an example of synthesis as interdisciplinarity, Alim's excerpt also shows another form of synthesis: code-switching (DeBose). In code-switching, writers toggle between different types of speech patterns. In Alim's case, he code-switches between more academic-sounding language and language that is more the style of hip-hop language itself. As you read, identify the moments when you see Alim engaging in code-switching.

Excerpt from *Roc the Mic Right* by H. Samy Alim

As an interdiscplinary area of inquiry [hip-hop studies] includes studies of language and language use from various methodological and theoretical perspectives. While studies are grounded in the streets, contributions come from cultural studies, communications studies, ethnic studies, literacy studies, philosophy, sociology, anthropology, sociolinguistics, poetics, literary analysis, and discourse analysis, among other approaches to the study of language. We begin with language as power, that is, the view that language *is* the revolution, a powerful discourse in and of itself. We know that the most powerful people in society tend to control speech and its circulation through mass media. We know, cuz the Wu-Tang Clans Rza told us, that "words kill as fast as bullets." Words are far more than parts of speech; they're weapons of mass culture to be deployed in the cultural combat that we, invariably, as humans, find ourselves in. Unfortunately, with teachers of young Hip-Hop Heads still sayin that the language of their students is the very thing tat they "*combat the most*," we learn this lesson very early on. In this sense of cultural warfare—the micro and macro forms of social control through culture—Hip-Hop Linguists are "combat linguists." Yeah, we know it's a war goin on, but

> Alim identifies numerous disciplines that work together to inform hip-hop studies.

> Alim shows how an inquiry into language involves multiple disciplinary perspectives in order to fully appreciate its linguistic and cultural elements.

From *Roc the Mic Right*, 2006.

don't get it twisted. We are never the aggressors. The task of the Hip-Hop Linguist is to both analyze and mediate the struggle …

The hiphopography paradigm integrates the varied approaches of ethnography, biography, and social, cultural, and oral history to arrive at an *emic* view of Hip-Hop Culture. It is hiphopography that obligates [hip-hop studies] to directly engage with the cultural agents of the Hip-Hop Culture-World, revealing rappers as critical interpreters of their own culture. We view "rappers" as "cultural critics" and "cultural theorists" whose thoughts and ideas help us to make sense of one of the most important cultural movement of the late twentieth and early twenty-first centuries.

> Alim adopts the term "hiphopography" to name the multidisciplinary approach that combines culture, history, sociology, and language. He uses the term "emic" to suggest that this interdisciplinary approach evolves from a consideration of all the elements internal to hiphopography.

Synthesis as curation of collections

Collections in the context of academic writing can refer to any number of synthesized materials. Collections can emerge in the form of anthologies that compile a variety of readings together around a common theme or issue, or they can be blogs that amass a variety of different posts (from different people or one person). Collections in the context of academic writing also include art installations and museum or archive exhibits, where a person or a team of people has compiled, curated, and synthesized a variety of component parts to create a new perspective, frame of reference, or exploration. This section offers three examples of how academic writers across disciplines synthesize in the service of curating collections.

Example 1: Synthesis as Curating Collections, Blogs and Websites, African and African-American Studies

Bloggers often synthesize what others have produced as material for their own blog; Jill Rettberg terms these "filter blogs." Similarly, people often curate websites or synthesize material about themselves on social networking sites such as Facebook, Twitter, and Instagram. The example, from the blog *NewBlackMan (In Exile)* by Mark Anthony Neal, shows a synthesis of events, ideas, and news. The blog demonstrates synthesis not only with content, but also with form, combining print, images, and videos.

Excerpt from *NewBlackMan* by M. Anthony Neal

April 15, 2014:

HuffPost Live

In this first example, Neal draws material from the *Huffington Post* about Nas.

Legendary hip-hop artist Nas joins HuffPost Live with Marc Lamont Hill to celebrate the 20th anniversary of his debut album, Illmatic. He reflects on his illustrious career, the state of hip-hop and what Illmatic XX means to him.

———

From *NewBlackMan*, 2014.

Excerpt from *NewBlackMan* by M. Anthony Neal

April 10, 2014: Hop, Grit, and Academic Success: Bettina Love at TEDxUGA

TEDx Talks

This impassioned talk explains how students who identify with hip-hop culture have been ignored or deemed deficient in schools because of mainstream misconceptions associated with hip-hop culture. Through hip-hop, these students embody the characteristics of grit, social and emotional intelligence, and the act improvisation—all of which are proven to be predictors for academic success. So where is the breakdown between formalized education and the potential for success for these students? Dr. Bettina Love argues that ignoring students' culture in the classroom is all but an oversight; it's discrimination and injustice that plays out in our culture in very dangerous ways.

This second example illustrates Neal drawing his blog followers' attention to a recent TEDx Talk about hip-hop culture.

———

From *NewBlackMan*, 2014.

Example 2: Synthesis as Curating Collections, Anthologies, Communication Studies, and African and African-American Studies

Anthologies exist across all disciplines as a way of providing depth and breadth of knowledge, from the *Norton Anthology of Literature by Women* or *Environment: An Interdisciplinary Anthology* to *An Anthology of Theories and Models of Design* and *A Reader in Medical Anthropology: Theoretical Trajectories, Emergent Realities*. Anthologies also exist as explorations of single authors or concepts, as in *The Henry Louis Gates, Jr. Reader* or *Communicating Colonialism: Readings on Postcolonial Theory(s) and Communication*.

Anthologies rely on the work of synthesis. In all these instances, academic writers conduct curatorial work as editors, making decisions about what to include in an **anthology** and how to organize it. The synthesizing skills used in producing anthologies are summed up in this definition of synthesis by Anton Popovič and Francis Macri: "synthesis is … a configuration of texts according to the principles of combination, selection, and linking."

The example is from the promotional flyer for the second edition of an anthology titled *New Book! That's the Joint! The Hip-Hop Studies Reader*. In this edition, the editors Murray Forman and Mark Anthony Neal make a concerted effort at synthesizing old with new to "conjoin essays from hip-hop's earlier phases with more recent scholarly interventions, facilitating a productive historical dialogue."

Excerpt from promotional flyer for *New Book! That's the Joint! The Hip-Hop Studies Reader*, M. Anthony Neal and M. Forman, eds.

I. Hip-Hop Ya Don't Stop: Hip-Hop History and Historiography

1. The Politics of Graffiti | *Craig Castleman*

2. Zulus on a Time Bomb: Hip-Hop Meets the Rockers Downtown | *Jeff Chang*

3. B-Beats Bombarding Bronx: Mobile DJ Starts Something with Older R&B Disks and Jive Talking NY DJs Rapping Away in Black Discos | *Robert Ford, Jr.*

4. Hip-Hop's Founding Fathers Speak the Truth | *Nelson George*

5. Physical Graffiti: The History of Hip-Hop Dance | *Jorge "Fabel" Pabon*

6. Hip-Hop Turns 30: Watcha Celebratin' For? | *Greg Tate*

> Here is the selection of readings Murray and Neal chose for Part I (referred to in Murray's excerpt above). As you can imagine, there were likely a variety of possible choices, but their work of synthesis involved selecting which ones to include so that the historical dialogue would be as productive as possible.

This newly expanded and revised second edition of *That's the Joint!* brings together the most important and up-to-date hip-hop scholarship in one comprehensive volume. Presented thematically, the selections address the history of hip-hop, identity politics of the "hip-hop nation," debates of "street authenticity," social movements and activism, aesthetics, technologies of production, hip-hop as a cultural industry, and much more. Further, this new edition also includes greater coverage of gender, racial diversity in hip-hop, hip-hop's global influences, and examines hip-hop's role in contemporary politics.

> The final sentence indicates the difficulty of synthesizing large amounts of material. They chose to increase coverage of these areas in the second edition in order, presumably, to address lesser coverage in the first edition.

From *NewBlackMan*, 2014.

Example 3: Synthesis as Curating Collections, Exhibits and Archives, Musicology

The work of synthesis in this domain (be it online, face to face, or blended) requires choosing what to include, how to organize it, and how to present it. Together, exhibits or archives provide viewers or visitors with a perspective on the topic. The excerpt is from a page of the Hiphop Archive website, which is part of an archival collection at Harvard University.

Excerpt from "The Geoff Ward Collection"

The Hiphop Archive is proud to present our extensive "Geoff Ward Collection." Comprised of a large donation of hiphop-related periodicals and VHS cassette tapes, the collection provides a valuable historical account of hiphop culture from a popular perspective. Additionally, they give any student or researcher a glimpse of the issues and concerns surrounding the hiphop community throughout various periods of its development.

> Here, the curators of the archive describe the collection and its components. The collection is a synthesis of artifacts related to hip-hop.

The collection features an extensive range of magazine titles, ranging from mainstream publications like Vibe and Source to lesser-known magazines such as *4080, F.E.D.S.,* and *The Rap Pages. The Source* magazine is the most comprehensive title in the collection with copies ranging from 1993 to 2003. A decade packed with fascinating and immensely important landmarks in the history of Hiphop, articles about the contentious "East Coast/ West Coast" discussion (interviews with Ice Cube and Suge Knight), the first appearance and subsequent rise of contemporary artists (Nas, Mos Def, and Eminem), the contributions of hiphop's fallen stars (Notorious B.I.G., Tupac, and Big Pun), and many more can be found.

From *hiphoparchive,com*, 2014.

Write Now

Curating an exhibit relies on the ability of the curator to demonstrate what insights, ideas, or impressions might be newly generated from bringing various objects together. This work of curation becomes clear through the item descriptions in the exhibit; through these descriptions, curators can make visible the intersections and disparities between the items, as well as show how their being brought together yields new perspectives. Locate four or more images, artifacts, and/or items about a topic of interest to you, and create a mini exhibit. You can do this with an online site, such as Pinterest, or through a different nonvirtual format. Write captions and an overarching introduction to your exhibit that exemplify the synthesis informing the exhibit.

Synthesis of sources as evidence

Academic writers synthesize a variety of resources in order to generate an argument. The discipline of history offers a cogent example of this, with historians synthesizing a breadth of research sources and evidence to generate a fuller understanding of a person, era, or event. Historians make use of personal remembrances, artifacts, and other types of evidence. They synthesize them to generate conclusions and narratives.

In *A Pocket Guide to Writing in History*, Mary Lynn Rampolla emphasizes that historical questions "require [the exploration of] many different kinds of sources":

> [Historians] will read books and articles written by modern historians. [They] may examine maps, photographs, paintings, and pottery.... [H]istory often takes its practitioners into all manner of related disciplines: literary criticism, art history, and archaeology; political science, economics, and sociology."

Rampolla goes on to list the following as examples of the vast range of primary sources historians examine:

> {…} letters; diaries; newspaper and magazine articles; speeches; autobiographies; treatises; census data;…marriage, birth and death registers[;] art films, recordings, items of clothing, household objects, tools, and archaeological remains. For recent history, oral sources, such as interviews with Vietnam veterans or Holocaust survivors and other such eyewitness accounts, can also be primary sources.

In addition to these primary sources, historians also work with secondary sources (i.e., other scholarship) and even tertiary sources such as encyclopedias and textbooks. The work of synthesis in history involves bringing this array of primary, secondary, and tertiary resources together, "mashing" them up to generate a narrative and understanding of a particular historical period, person, or event.

The excerpt shows historian Derrick Alridge synthesizing several different kinds of primary and secondary sources to answer questions about the connections between the civil rights movement and hip-hop. Although this example is from history, academic writers use synthesis of resources across disciplines.

Writer Insights

How do you use synthesis in your writing?

I am a traveler, photographer, and writer. For me, writing travelogues is like drawing from wells of nostalgia buckets full of sights, sounds, smells and vapors of places that I have visited. Travel writing helps both my audience and me. It helps quench the measureless thirst of curious minds. But it also offers me an extraordinary chance to let the tide of old travel experiences ebb so that new ones may flow freely and spontaneously within me. My writing process is fairly straightforward: I research extensively about a place or people before each trip. While on the road, I observe my surroundings keenly and take copious notes. Finally, I synthesize and organize my observations to create an original and personal memoir of my travel.

~Kartik, Travel Writer

Excerpt from "From Civil Rights to Hip-Hop: Toward a Nexus of Ideas" by D. P. Alridge

The most radical ideas often grow out of a concrete intellectual engagement with the problems of aggrieved populations confronting systems of oppression.

The preceding quotation from historian Robin D. G. Kelley captures the manner through which socially and politically conscious (SPC) hip-hop emerged from the social, economic, and political experiences of black youth from the mid- to late 1970s. Hip-hop pioneers such as Kool Herc, Afrika Bambaataa, and Grandmaster Flash and the Furious Five, among others articulated the post-civil rights generation's ideas and response to poverty, drugs, police brutality, and other racial and class inequities of postindustrial U.S. society. In many ways, early hip-hoppers were not only the progenitors of a new form of black social critique, they also represented the voice of a new generation that would carry on and expand upon the ideas and ideology of the civil rights generation.

> In both paragraphs, Alridge notes that hip-hop has emerged from a variety of resources, indicating that it synthesizes sources.

Since the early years of hip-hop, SPC hip-hoppers have continued to espouse many of the ideas and ideology of the Civil Rights Movement (CRM) and Black Freedom Struggle (BFS), but in a language that resonates with many black youth of the post-industrial and post-civil rights integrationist era. For instance, on Michael Franti's 2001 compact disc (CD) *Stay Human,* Franti uses rap and reggae-style lyrics to critique U.S. capitalism, imperialism, racism, and globalization and to offer analyses of discrimination, prejudice, and oppression similar to those of activists and theorists of the CRM and BFS. In his song "Oh My God," Franti lays out what he believes are the hypocrisies of U.S. democracy by pointing out its discriminatory practices against the poor and people of color, its use of the death penalty, its indiscriminate bombing of other countries, and its counterintelligence activities that subvert the rights of U.S. citizens. He states:

> Notice how Alridge links together Franti's lyrics with an interview and historical scholarship. Alridge synthesizes these sources in order to illustrate the political and ideological connections between hip-hop and the CRM.

> Oh my, Oh my God,
> out here mama they got us livin' suicide,
> singin' oh my, oh my God
> out here mama they got us livin' suicide....
> Stealin' DNA from the unborn

From *The Journal of African American History* (90.3), 2005.

and then you comin' after us
'cause we sampled a James Brown horn?
Scientists whose God is progress,
a four headed sheep is their latest project,
the CIA runnin' like that Jones from Indiana,
but they still won't talk about that Jones in Guyana...

In an interview with "underground" Atlanta rapper John Lewis, Jr., son of civil rights leader and icon John Lewis, Sr., Lewis, Jr. provides a firsthand account of the organic ideological connections between hip-hop and the CRM. In discussing the influence of his father and the CRM on his ideas and work, Lewis, Jr., recalled that:

> With me, I grew up around it [civil rights]. Like all I knew really was what was out here. Both of these worlds [civil rights and hip-hop] was [sic] together within me. You know it's hard as hell growing up in the house and, you know, you got pictures of your pops getting hit with billy clubs and getting dogs sicked on him, that shit goes into your head.

Lewis asserts that the stories he heard about the movement from his father are etched into his mind and have profoundly influenced his lyrics as a SPC rapper.

Synthesis as comparison

Writers across disciplines routinely invoke **comparison**, a well-known version of synthesis, in their writing. Comparison is a key strategy for people to use as they are seeking to understand concepts. Some disciplines are even grounded in comparison, such as Comparative Religions or Comparative Literature. Certain research methodologies also rely heavily on comparison, such as in anthropology where some ethnographers use fieldwork to compare cultures or peoples. One can also consider the use of precedent in legal contexts as another example of comparison, whereby people examine prior cases and their resolutions to inform decisions about current litigation. Venn diagrams are another common, visual form of comparison used across many disciplines.

The genre of comparison and contrast may be well known to you since it tends to be assigned across many subjects throughout all levels of education. Perhaps because of its popularity, some people can sometimes approach a comparison-contrast essay without focusing on the outcomes of the synthesis. For comparison to be most effective, it needs to accomplish more than just comparing, or just contrasting, and it should instead hinge on the creation of new insights.

This excerpt shows a writer successfully using comparison as a form of synthesis, comparing digital music piracy in the United States with that in Japan in order to understand a problem and recommend a policy adjustment. Using comparison to yield policy recommendations, though, is but one possible outcome from this form of synthesis. Others could include using comparison with synthesis in order to yield explanations, definitions, or even critiques.

247

Excerpt from "Cultures of Music Piracy: An Ethnographic Comparison of the U.S. and Japan" by I. Condry

I begin with an ethnographic consideration of the music sharing in the U.S. to unpack the overly simplistic image that people are sharing music 'just to get something free.' A peer-to-peer perspective on popularity reveals that the boundaries between piracy, promotion, and sharing are far from clear. ... Then we turn to Japan, the second largest music market in the world, to consider what a cross-national comparison reveals about the intersections of culture, technology, legal setting, and business practices....

> At the end of this paragraph, Condry conveys his purpose for synthesizing/comparing U.S. and Japanese digital music piracy. He aims to compare—to synthesize—in order to glean new understandings about the intersections between "culture, technology, legal setting, and business."

Japan shows that the 'culture of piracy' transcends national boundaries, and does not depend on online peer-to-peer networks. In the U.S., the debate over music piracy largely revolves around peer-to-peer (p2p) file-sharing software, beginning with Napster, and later Kazaa, Bit Torrent, Freenet, and so on. But as of the beginning of 2004, Japanese record companies have largely avoided an online file-sharing epidemic. Sales have nevertheless plummeted more sharply than in the U.S. Yet Japan uses the law differently. By spring 2004, hundreds faced lawsuits in Europe (Lander, 2004), but Japan's legal action against file sharers is limited to three arrests. Instead some business leaders are taking a hard look at the intersection of fan attitudes and promotion strategies. Japan is also instructive because some Japanese popular culture industries, namely *manga* (comic books) and *anime* (Japanese animated movies), may have benefited substantially from copyright infringement that was not prosecuted.

> Here, Condry shows that comparison demonstrates a widespread culture of piracy, rather than being representative of one national culture.

> Condry outlines several similarities and differences to find that Japanese businesses see digital piracy as yielding income (through promotion and other culture industries), even as it reduces sales. Note how Condry argues Japan is "instructive," again illustrating that synthesis as comparison yields new insights and generates recommendations for new "possible directions" in the United States.

Then I return to the U.S. to analyze some possible directions for moving beyond the current impasses between record companies and recalcitrant pirates....

From *International Journal of Cultural Studies* (7.3), 2004.

Synthesis as definition

Academic writers often invoke synthesis in order to define an idea or concept, showing how movements or ideas are often a synthesis of other related concepts. One might term this type of synthesis as **explanatory synthesis**. This mode of synthesis involves demonstrating the antecedents of a particular concept or movement in order to illustrate how the various parts combined to create the new movement or concept. The purpose of this mode of synthesis is to gain a fuller understanding of the context surrounding ideas.

In the excerpt, Yvonne Bynoe explains how hip-hop itself emerged from a synthesis of various parts that combine to create hip-hop.

Excerpt from "Introduction" *Encyclopedia of Rap and Hip-Hop Culture* by Y. Bynoe

Hip-hop is not only music. It represents at least four different, interrelated art forms: MC-ing, or rap—the oral element; B-boying, break dancing, as it is commonly known—the dance element; DJing—the musical element; and graffiti, or aerosol art—the visual element. The acknowledged birthday of hip-hop is November 11, 1973, the date that Afrika Bambaataa, one of the most important hip-hop figures, established the Zulu Nation. This former Black Spades gang member formed a communal organization that intended to eradicate street violence by using the arts as a means to squelch rivalries. Under the Zulu Nation, street gangs transformed into crews, whose members vanquished foes in battles using superior turntable skills, dance, or lyrical talents instead of weapons....

From *testaae.greenwood.com*, 2006.

Synthesis in bibliographic essays

Bibliographic essays, often used in library studies, are another example of a synthesis of different materials. For example, in "The Kaleidescope of Writing on Hip-Hop Culture," Gail Hilson Woldu "distinguish[es] three categories of writing about hip-hop—works by academics, works by journalists and cultural critics, and works by hip-hop's devotees." Similarly, in "'One Day It'll All Make Sense': Hip-Hop and Rap Resources for Music Librarians," Andrew Leach "provides descriptions of a wide array of resources relating to hip-hop culture and rap music," including works that define hip-hop, bibliographies of hip-hop, histories of hip-hop, scholarly literature, and biographies of hip-hop artists.

In the example, we see an academic writer in the discipline of librarian studies synthesizing the wide range of kinds of writing about hip-hop. Andrew Leach is a librarian and archivist at the Center for Black Music Research at Columbia College Chicago.

Excerpt from "'One Day It'll All Make Sense':
Hip-Hop and Rap Resources for Music Librarians" by A. Leach

This bibliographical essay provides descriptions of a wide array of resources relating to hip-hop culture and rap music, and its final section is devoted to the collecting of hip-hop and rap materials by libraries. While the essay is primarily intended to serve as a guide for music librarians who provide reference service and library instruction, and to those with collection development responsibilities, it may also prove useful to educators, students, and those beginning to conduct research on hip-hop or rap.

> Here, Leach presents his purpose for the bibliographical essay and also discusses his choices for organization.

Several…noteworthy essays and encyclopedia entries provide overviews of rap music. One such essay is "The Rap Attack: An Introduction," written by leading hip-hop scholar William Eric Perkins in the anthology for which he served as editor, *Droppin' Science: Critical Essays on Rap Music and Hip-Hop Culture*. Perkins's essay provides an excellent examination of rap music's early history and many of the musical origins of the rap tradition. Tricia Rose's essay "Rap Music," in *The Hip-Hop Reader*, provides another superb scholarly account of rap music's early years while taking into account its connections to culture, identity, gender, and technology. Rose's essay is based on an excerpt from her seminal book *Black Noise: Rap Music and Black Culture in Contemporary America*…David Toop's entry "Rap," in *The New Grove Dictionary of Music and Musicians* and in *Grove Music Online*, provides a useful overview of rap music, covering the genre's history from its beginnings to the present day and providing a short bibliography. Rob Bowman's succinct and well written entry "Rap" in *The Harvard Dictionary of Music* briefly discusses rap music's precursors in African and African American cultures, the use of turntables and samplers, copyright issues, political messages, censorship, and rap's broadening appeal among mainstream music listeners. Finally, the concise entry "Rap" in Bynoe's *Encyclopedia of Rap and Hip-Hop Culture* addresses rap's place within hip-hop culture, its musical antecedents, prior uses of the term "rap" within African American culture, and the music's origins and early history.

> Notice here that as Leach summarizes each article, he focuses on the ways in which each article approaches the same general topic (an overview of hip-hop) from a slightly different vantage point. The result is that the synthesis of all of them generates a deeper understanding of hip-hop.

From *Notes* (65.1), 2008.

Transferring Synthesis

The modes of synthesis addressed in this chapter represent only some of the many kinds of synthesis you will likely be asked to write across your undergraduate career. The very notion of synthesis, in fact, underpins transfer itself: synthesis invites you to apply, adapt, compare, overlay, reject, etc. what you learn about writing and learning when you move from one occasion to other occasions. Synthesis is grounded in advancing knowledge.

This chapter on synthesis has built upon the preceding chapters by providing strategies you can use as you pursue research questions, read others' texts, and deepen what you have learned from summarizing those texts throughout their reading encounters. Chapter 7, in turn, will expand this work by addressing a corollary strategy—analysis—that writers across disciplines also use. While synthesis invites readers to combine ideas to create something new, analysis invites readers to break apart the component parts of concepts also to create something new, be it an insight, recommendation, definition, understanding, critique, or other sort of argument.

And, as you may be starting to discover, the sequence of concepts across Chapters 5, 6, and 7, which move from summary to synthesis to analysis, also equips you with increasing autonomy to contribute your own ideas and advance knowledge as you pursue research questions and engage with texts.

℃ ℃ ℃

Computer Engineering Study: "How Physics is Used in Video Games" by David M. Bourg

Transfer Points: Physics, Computer Engineering

Whether it's soccer balls, rocket-propelled racecars, spaceships, or warheads, video games rely extensively on the laws of physics.

Developers of *XO*, for instance, a video game in which players command a Starfleet to save humanity, calculated actual space velocity to make the experience more realistic. Rather than players simply starting, slowing, and stopping their spaceships, the game instead requires a reverse thrust to slow down or stop a spaceship. This reverse thrust is more consonant with Newtonian physics, whereby objects in space move with increasing speed unless and until force is introduced in the opposite direction (Jamison).

Certainly, some armchair Starfleet commanders might not know (or necessarily care) whether their spaceships are or are not following Newtonian physics. However, other players do prefer that physics follow natural laws to maximize game experience satisfaction.

Sometimes video-game developers deliberately challenge the laws of physics. In *Rocket League*, for instance, a game in which rocket-powered cars race in a field, developers created entirely unrealistic scales for velocity and gravity (Psynoix_Dave). And, in *Call of Duty: Infinite Warfare*, developers created sound-enabled space suits to counteract the absence of sound in space and a grappling hook to make up for how slowly people actually move in a zero-gravity environment (Makuch).

As demonstrated by these diverse examples, physics is a wide-ranging science discipline that addresses how and why objects move and how objects interact with one another through time and space.

The physics involved with video games emerges from a branch of the discipline known as applied physics (as opposed to pure physics). Within this discipline, physics, math, and engineering are applied to a vast array of industries, from video games and space exploration to automobile windshields, eyeglasses, and lighting. Those who work with applied physics help create lasers, which facilitate operations across medicine and defense, and they work with condensed matter, which includes such applications as X-rays and electromagnetic circuitry ("Condensed").

People involved with physics—pure and applied—write across many genres and occasions. They create scholarly books and articles, such as Roger Penrose's *Fashion, Faith and Fantasy in the New Physics of the Universe*, and textbooks, such as J. Lilley's *Nuclear Physics: Principles and Applications*. Physicists also write for more general audiences interested in physics concepts such as time and space. Bestselling popular books on physics include Stephen Hawking's *A Brief History of Time* or Neil deGrasse Tyson's *Welcome to the Universe*.

David Bourg has written two books about intersections between physics, computer engineering, and video games: *Physics for Game Developers* (2001; 2013) and *AI for Game Developers* (2004). His areas of expertise include ship design, construction, and analysis ("David"). He has a Ph.D. in Engineering and Applied Science from the University of New Orleans (Mino). He has taught physics as an adjunct professor at the University of New Orleans School of Naval Architecture and Marine Engineering. His areas of specialty include computational fluid dynamics and he has an independent consulting business, Mino, that provides naval architecture and marine professional services (Mino).

Bourg's article emerges as part of applied physics as well as the broader field of science education. Physicists interested in how to improve the teaching and learning of physics, and garner more interest in physics, write articles about innovative approaches to physics pedagogy. Researchers, for instance, have found that exploring physics in video games improves undergraduate engagement (Rose, et al.) and that asking students to develop their own video games through physics principles improves student interest in physics (Like).

Alongside their peer-reviewed and public scholarship in physics and physics education, physicists also engage in advocacy-related writing and public policy, writing op-eds to influence public opinion, white papers to contribute to decision making, news releases to showcase discoveries and developments, and reports to summarize their research for public and private funding organizations and oversight agencies.

While writing in the field of physics varies according to occasion, it often includes visual elements, such as tables, boxes, figures, and images. These visual elements often play a central role in the text by communicating key results, data, and information. Physicist James McLean, from State University of New York at Geneseo, notes that sometimes these visual elements might even provide an alternative option for readers to understand the content: "the overriding fact about Figures and Tables is that they must 'float' [and in that sense must be] self-contained objects" (n.p.).

Other defining features of writing in physics include discipline-specific terminology and mathematical equations. Key concepts in physics include such ideas as dark matter, the big bang, and quantum theory. Writers in this discipline often refer to one or more of these sorts of specialized terms and will vary on whether they define these terms or not, depending on whether the text is peer reviewed or more public. Writing in physics also often relies on mathematical equations. Physicists have developed mathematical equations, for instance, to understand such concepts as velocity, acceleration, momentum, power, and heat flow (Elert).

While these specialized equations and discipline-specific terminology may create the sense that physics is a discipline that is esoteric and removed from everyday life, the reality is that physics impacts our lives in many important ways. The 2010 Nobel Prize in Physics, for instance, went to Andre Geim and Konstantin Novoselov for their work with the material graphene. Graphene is simultaneously the lightest and strongest of any material currently known, and it can conduct heat and electricity better than anything else. Applications for graphene in health care and bioengineering include fast and efficient monitoring of glucose levels, cholesterol, and anticancer treatments (Graphena). And, graphene can also improve opto-electronics such as touch screens and LCD displays for smartphones, tablets, and televisions (Graphena). This sort of groundbreaking work in physics demonstrates how many applications are possible within this discipline, from video games and health care, to computers and space exploration.

Write Here

What are the educational possibilities and limitations of video games? Have you learned anything from video games? If so, identify what you have learned. If not, what do you think people could learn from video games and/or what do you think might be counterproductive in terms of learning from video games? Of the ideas, concepts, or skills that video games can teach, how would you rate their value: are they positive or negative? Be as specific as possible as you write about the possible intersections between education and video games.

David M. Bourg
How Physics is Used in Video Games

Immersiveness

I was 16 years old driving my white Escort up a winding road along the Mississippi River on my way to work in the local mall. It was hot and drizzling—typical Southern Louisiana weather—but my window was rolled down since I had no air conditioner. The road wasn't too busy, and I was speeding with "I'll stop the world and melt with you" blaring on my stereo.

I couldn't carry a tune but was singing my lungs out as raindrops dotted the left side of my face. I was day-dreaming about getting off from work and hitting Bourbon Street. It was Saturday and the French Quarter was sure to be hopping.

As I started into a sharp bend in the road, I suddenly lost control. With the back end of my car swerving out sideways I was headed towards a canal. My heart was pounding. There was nothing I could do to stop.

CRASH!

Time slowed to a crawl as I watched the horizon through my windshield spectacularly rotate and then invert. I didn't even feel the impact. It seemed like forever, but mere seconds later I found myself on the roof of my car buried under my seats and piles of debris—spare change, books, floor mats and trash. I was turned around, upside-down in the canal.

At near panic speed, I scurried out of the window and ran 50 yards in any direction certain that my car was about to explode. Surprisingly, a police officer was already on the scene; he was on his way to the mall too when he saw the whole thing. First thing he asks me: "can you crawl back in there and turn that music off please. . .".

I am sure this is a rather unusual beginning to a technical article, but I am telling you this story to illustrate a point. My story is complete with visual and emotional imagery as well as a realistic description of the crash itself. Now, what if I ended the story with something like "...and my car bounced 15 metres into the air, landed upright and kept going?" It would spoil the story wouldn't it? Video games are no different. To paraphrase Steven Collins, CEO of Havok: It's all about immersiveness.

Game developers tell their stories using stunning graphics, mood-setting music, rich sound effects and realistic behaviour. The idea is to immerse you in visual, emotional and physical realism—to bring you into the game without jolting you back to reality with a ridiculous special effect or quirky stunt.

So how do game developers create such physical realism? They borrow knowledge and techniques from other fields, in this case physics. More specifically, the techniques used to realistically simulate car crashes belong to the subject of classical dynamics.

Here's how it's done. While your virtual car is racing down the highway, the game's so-called physics engine constantly tracks the acceleration, velocity and position of the car. At the same time, the physics engine is also constantly checking the car to see if it has run into anything else in the game world, for example another car, a road sign or even a telegraph pole. When a collision is detected, the physics engine kicks into overdrive.

Each bounce, flip and roll is precisely calculated by the physics engine to yield a smooth, realistic crash event. When done properly, the results are impressive—the horizon jostles, rotates, even inverts as your car goes tumbling through the air just like it would in the real world. I should know.

These calculations are based on the application of fundamental impulse and momentum principles along with a healthy dose of mathematics. At the instant of impact an impulse force is calculated and applied to the car, and whatever it ran into, at the points of impact. This impulse force is a function of the relative velocity between the car and whatever it ran into—the higher the relative velocity the higher the impulse. Once this impulse is calculated, the car's acceleration, velocity, position and orientation are recalculated thousands of times to step the crash event through time.

The game's physics engine is tied to its graphics engine so that you can see the results in all their glory. The beautifully rendered 3D scenes combined with realistic physical behaviour yield a truly immersive experience second only to the real thing, but a whole lot safer and a heck of a lot more fun.

So, when your lead-footed, speed-hungry students are breaking all known virtual traffic laws in their favourite driving game, they might be getting a good lesson in the laws of physics. With that in mind, the remainder of this article explores some of the technical aspects of how physics is used in modern video games.

'Real' physics examples

So-called 'real' physics is used in video games to achieve a wide variety of realistic effects. Some applications of real physics are almost obvious, while other applications may surprise you.

Flight simulations

Flight simulations are probably one of the first game genres that come to mind when you think of how real physics can be used in games. These games use real-world physics to simulate the lift and drag on the aircraft's components and control surfaces in an effort to mimic the real plane's capabilities and handling characteristics. Some flight simulation games strive for ultra realism where the details of the flight model are meticulously tuned so as to be as realistic as possible. Other games aren't so concerned about realistically modelling any particular aircraft and instead aim to yield a simple, enjoyable virtual flight experience. Such a game could be one where the plane is a paper airplane that you fly around the interior of a house.

Billiards

A game like billiards is another good example of a game where real physics is crucial to the playability and believability of the game. Billiards simulations use real physics to model the striking of the cue ball and its impact with other balls on the table. The physics does not stop there. Realistic friction between impacting balls and rolling resistance are critical in order to properly account for spin. Without properly handling spin and rolling, shots that use 'side' (or 'english' as it is known in north America) would not be achievable.

Projectiles

Projectiles such as sports balls, grenades, cannonballs, bullets, rocks or anything else that can be shot, launched or thrown in a video game use realistic ballistics or projectile motion. Projectile motion isn't limited to these more traditional ballistic scenarios.

In this adventure game, the fires shown in the fireplace and under the large kettle are simulated using buoyant particles that rise and change colour. The bubbling material shooting up from the kettle consists of a collection of particles that are launched upward at some velocity and fall back down under the influence of gravity. The Beholder beast in the upper right of the figure is casting a fireball spell that is essentially another collection of particles launched towards the player and falling under the influence of gravity.

Artificial intelligence

Perhaps an even more unexpected use of physics in games is in the area of artificial intelligence (AI). A good example of how physics can be applied for game AI is in potential-based

movement. Potential functions, like the well known Lennard-Jones intermolecular potential function, are used to model repulsive and attractive forces between game agents. The potential function produces both attractive and repulsive forces depending on the proximity of the two molecules being acted upon. It is this ability to represent both attractive and repulsive forces that makes this function useful for game AI.

These forces can be used to cause one agent to chase or evade another, resulting in seemingly intelligent behaviour by application of a few simple calculations. Potential functions are also used to allow game agents to avoid obstacles in their path. Here the obstacle would repel the approaching game agent such that the agent would essentially steer around the object. Potential functions can even be applied to collections of moving agents to achieve a swarming effect.

Other examples

These are just a few examples of how physics is applied in video games. Other examples include simulating the motion of barrels or boxes being pushed along the floor in a first-person action game; simulating the physics of skateboard stunts such as vertical jumps and Ollies (raising all four wheels of the board off the ground); and simulating the flight dynamics of sports balls such as baseballs in order to achieve curve balls. Clearly the use of real physics in games is quite diverse. I should point out that while the aim of incorporating real physics is very often to achieve realistic behaviour, it isn't always the first priority.

Ultimately games must be fun and sometimes realistic behaviour just isn't as fun. Take Tony Hawk's Pro Skater game series as an example. In this skateboard game players can perform the usual skateboarding stunts with realistic-looking results. However, it's far more fun to be able to Ollie over a bus than a roadside kerb. Likewise, it's much more exciting to make a 18 m vertical jump as opposed to a more realistic 3 m jump. The developers realized this and so they built-in a 'moon gravity' option that allows players to perform their tricks in a gravity field that is about one-sixth that of the Earth's. Clearly, this isn't realistic since the game is set on Earth, but it is a whole lot of fun!

Newton's laws

While the examples discussed so far all aim to achieve different effects, they all share one thing in common, which is that they all rely on Newton's laws of motion. All of the effects mentioned earlier can be broken down into interacting masses, applied forces and torques, and resulting accelerations. This is how game developers are able to apply the equations of motion based on Newton's laws to model the motion of particles and rigid bodies representing various game elements.

Let's take a closer look at the equations of motion:

$$F = m\alpha$$

$$M = I\alpha$$

The first equation shown here is the familiar F = $m\alpha$ equation for linear motion. For particles, this equation is all that is required. However, for rigid bodies that can rotate as well as translate you must also consider the angular equation of motion.

Clearly, dealing with particles is far easier than dealing with rigid bodies—you only have mass and translation to deal with. Particles are great for modelling things such as bullets or grenades. They're also quite useful for modelling more complicated things such as fire, smoke and cloth among others. For other objects such as tables, chairs, boxes, airplanes, cars or hovercraft, rotation is very important for realism so rigid bodies are a better choice.

Rarely is the angular equation of motion as shown earlier ever applied in that form for rigid-body motion in games. The reason for this is that the inertia tensor, **I**, is expressed in global, Earth-fixed coordinates in that equation. Thus, the inertia tensor would have to be recomputed as the object moved. This computation is too costly for real-time video games, so a different form of the angular equation of motion is used instead:

$$M = I \, d\omega \ dt \ + (\omega \times (I\omega)).$$

In this case, the inertia tensor is expressed in body-fixed coordinates and need only be calculated once for the object (unless it changes mass or shape at some point). The ω term in this equation is the angular velocity of the object in terms of body-fixed coordinates. The $d\omega/dt$ term is the time rate of change in angular velocity, that is, its angular acceleration.

With these equations of motion in hand, game developers must tally the mass properties—mass, centre of mass, mass moment of inertia—of the simulated game elements and then compute all of the forces and torques acting on them in order to solve the equations of motion. Ultimately, developers need to know the new positions of the moving objects so the next frame can be drawn.

Solving the equations of motion

Solving the equations of motion relies on fundamental kinematic relationships between acceleration, velocity and displacement.

These relations provide the means to work backward from instantaneous accelerations to velocities to changes in position. This approach is in fact how developers simulate object motion in games—they work backward from acceleration to changes in position and rotation for each object. Accelerations are obtained by solving the equations of motion.

Notice that these steps discretize the time step from an infinitesimally small dt to something more finite, though still small. This is an important point. The equations of motion are not solved analytically, instead they are solved numerically and the procedure described here relies on numerical integration techniques.

If you were to implement the procedure for numerical integration exactly as developed in the previous discussion you would end up with what is known as Euler's method for numerical integration. This would be a rather casual development of Euler's method, albeit relatively easy to grasp. A more rigorous development of Euler's method would consider Taylor's theorem. Taylor's theorem provides a way to predict the value of some function at some point, knowing only the value of the function at another point and something about the derivatives of the function at that point.

Equation of motion = $F = m\alpha$

Rewrite it as: $dv = (F / m)dt$

Use discrete time step: $\Delta v = (F / m)\Delta t$

Estimate new velocity: $v_t +_{\Delta t} = v_t + (F / m)\Delta t$

Estimate new position: $8_t +_{\Delta t} = 8_t + v_t +_{\Delta t}\Delta t.$

Basic steps to solve the linear equation of motion.

Without going into too many details, the Taylor series expansion of a function is an infinite series consisting of terms involving successively higher order derivatives of the function whose value you're trying to find. Euler's method involves taking the partial sum of the series only to the terms including the first derivative of the function. This corresponds to the process I described earlier.

Euler's method is conceptually very important but it is not the most accurate or stable numerical integration method. In practice, using Euler's method usually requires taking very small step sizes (Δt). This results in more computations, which is not good for real-time video games.

There are other methods that give more stable and more accurate results. There are far too many to consider all their details here; however, they all have in common the aim of improving accuracy, stability and efficiency by allowing larger step sizes. You can refer to any good textbook on numerical methods for examples of a variety of methods and the strategies they employ.

Ultimately, game developers must choose a numerical integration scheme that gives them stable and efficient performance for their particular application. Stability is crucial since it would be very difficult to recover gracefully from a divergent solution in the midst of gameplay, not to mention the subsequent loss of realism that would surely ruin the immersive experience for the gamer. Efficiency is crucial because real-time games operate at relatively high frame rates required for smooth animation.

Summary

In practice, solving the equations of motion for game objects is a great deal more involved that what I've summarized in this article. For each object being simulated, developers must first select or calculate appropriate mass properties. Further, depending on the object being simulated, for example an airplane or a race car, a great deal of time is spent developing appropriate models for all of the forces and torques that will act on those objects during the simulation. These are crucial considerations since the forces and torques essentially define how the object will behave.

If collisions are to be modelled, then developers must also prepare accurate geometric models and collision detection algorithms to enable them to detect when objects collide and extract appropriate data on the collision. Dealing with collisions adds a great deal of complexity to simulating objects in games above and beyond that already inherent in solving the equations of motion as described earlier.

Finally, once all of these models and algorithms are developed, game developers spend a good bit of time tuning their simulation to make sure it performs satisfactorily. This step is not looked upon lightly as it involves a great deal of trial and error to yield stable, efficient, believable and, most importantly, fun results.

Further reading

Bourg D M 2002 *Physics for Game Developers* (Sebastopol, CA: O'Reilly) www.ora.com

Bourg D M 2002 *Five Steps to Adding Physics Based Realism to Your Games* (Sebastopol, CA: O'Reilly) www.ora.com

Bourg D M 2003 *Physics for Game Developers Course Notes* (Game Institute) www.gameinstitute.com

Bourg D M and Seemann G 2004 *AI for Game Developers* (Sebastopol, CA: O'Reilly) www.ora.com

Bourg, David M. "How Physics is Used in Video Games." *Physics Education.* 39(5): 2004. *ProQuest.* 13 Nov. 2013.

Write Away

1. Using one of the physics concepts in Bourg's article, develop and conduct an experiment that enables you to further explore that concept. After you have done the experiment,

write a lab report documenting the experiment. In your lab report, include the following sections: an introduction that outlines the background of the experiment, objectives, and a hypothesis; materials and methods used in the experiment; results of the experiment; a discussion section in which you interpret the results; and a conclusion in which you identify the significance of what you have learned and next steps of possible research that could extend this experiment. Be sure to include a title for your lab report and to include tables, figures, and/or images as appropriate. These can be embedded within the report or appended at the end.

2. Write a research proposal for an extensive study that integrates science and video games. Imagine you are writing to a large funding organization that is interested in research related to video games and science. In your research proposal, include an introduction, a methods section, a proposed timeline, and relevant research. Include a budget as well, in which you document proposed costs such as labor, equipment, and travel. And, be sure to indicate the significance of your proposed research.

3. What sorts of disciplinary knowledge can video games teach? To what extent can video games teach? Choosing a particular video game or subset of video games, and one or more discipline(s), compose an argument in which you address how and what people can learn from video games and what, if any, limitations and/or advantages might exist in the context of video games and learning.

Gaming Literacy: "Telling and Doing: Why Doesn't Lara Croft Obey Professor Von Croy?" by James Paul Gee

Transfer Points: Education, Composition

"Thou didst beat me and knowledge entered my head" (Lieberman 3). So wrote an Egyptian child in 3000 BC on a clay tablet to describe his learning process.

James Paul Gee specializes in digital literacies and learning, discourse analysis, and educational linguistics. He has a Ph.D. in Linguistics from Stanford University and is the Mary Lou Fulton Presidential Professor of Literacy Studies in the Department of English at Arizona State University. Prior to this appointment, he was a professor of reading at University of Wisconsin, Madison, in the Educational Psychology department, and Chair of Education at Clark University. He has written many textbooks on discourse analysis (*How to Do Discourse Analysis* and *An Introduction to Discourse Analysis: Theory and Method*), and he has composed a number of books related to gaming and literacy. These include *Language and Learning in the Digital Age* (with Elisabeth Hayes, 2011), *Women and Gaming* (2010), and the book from which this selection emerges, *What Video Games Have to Teach Us about Learning and Literacy* (2007) ("James").

Ideas about how people best learn have a long and varied history. People in sixteenth-century England believed that education should involve extensive hours, so children attended school six days a week, from 6:00 a.m. to 5:00 p.m. (Lambert). Albert Einstein preferred learning outside of conventional school settings: "Education is what remains after one has forgotten what one learned in school" (Meltzer xiii). Ernest Hemingway emphasized listening as a learning strategy: "I like to listen. I have learned a great deal from listening. Most people never listen" (Grant 51). Maria Montessori suggests that independence is key: "The greatest sign of a success for a teacher … is to be able to say, 'The children are now working as if I did not exist'" (283). And Richard Branson maintains that learning requires independent thinking, active engagement, and failure: "You don't learn to walk by following rules. You learn by doing, and by falling over."

As illustrated by these varied approaches and contexts, education is among the most transferable of disciplines. Education scholars conduct research all over the world and in many contexts, from elementary through secondary and into higher education, adult education, and professional development. Education researchers investigate and shape education policy, teacher training, and higher ed administration.

Within school contexts, researchers in education study teaching and learning across nearly all fields, from languages, science, and statistics to art, music, writing, and history. In the context of math, for instance, researchers have examined how confident teachers are with math instruction (Chen, et al.), how to make mathematics teaching culturally relevant for indigenous populations (Abrams, Taylor, and Guo), and how family engagement at home increases math learning (Muccio, Kuwahara-Fujita, and Otsuji). Education researchers have also explored math anxiety (Kirkland), math education in online and face-to-face contexts (Imas, Kaminskaya, and Sherstneva), and how technological tools such as motion sensors impact math learning (Urban-Woldron).

Many disciplines contain subfields focused explicitly on education, such as science education, music education, language education, and literacy education. The history of education is also a robust area of research, exploring how people have taught and learned across cultures and time.

One emerging, interdisciplinary area of inquiry in education involves educational technologies. People with expertise in education, computer science, and engineering collaborate to design, implement, and assess educational tools and platforms that facilitate learning and teaching. Areas of research in this subfield include work with, for example, podcasts, flipped classrooms, and gaming. The *International Journal of Game-Based Learning*, for instance, publishes research on how gaming intersects with teaching, from algebra and chemistry to sociology and ethics. Scholars in this journal have explored 3-D collaborative games (Mavridis, Tsiatsos, and Terzidou), mobile learning (Foster, et al.), and alternate-reality games for learning history (Lynch, Mallon, and Connolly).

The study of teaching and learning, however, extends far beyond school settings. Many professions include continuing education. People in such fields as accounting, real estate, economics, and health care must complete continuing education credits in order to gain or maintain licensure. Education research also factors into outreach efforts across many sectors, from public health, pet care, and home maintenance, to safety and science. Research into effective learning also informs leisure pursuits, helping people learn such activities as skydiving, chess, swimming, and woodworking. According to James Paul Gee, even video-game developers use education research to help them develop effective instruction within their systems so people can learn to play—and keep playing—video games such as *Tomb Raider*.

Research methods in education are highly varied. Researchers use qualitative and quantitative methodologies, relying on everything from ethnography, close reading, and interviews to statistics and data mining.

Those who write in the field of education compose books, presentations, reports, and articles for peer-reviewed journals, government organizations, and broader publics. Scholars and professionals in education also write grants to secure funding for new projects and initiatives.

Texts on education address theories about pedagogy, empirical research and assessment on current practices and innovations, and reviews of ongoing projects and scholarship. Book-length publications on education include a wide array of research and arguments. Examples of these include Fareed Zakaria's *In Defense of a Liberal Education*, Horacio Sanchez's *Education Revolution: How to Apply Brain Science to Improve Instruction and School Climate*, and Christopher Emdin's *For White Folks Who Teach in the Hood … and the Rest of Y'all Too: Reality Pedagogy and Urban Education*.

As these titles suggest, education is not only highly transferable, but is also among the most public of disciplines. Most major news outlets include sections devoted specifically to education news, and education is regularly a topic of debate in local, regional, and national elections. The discipline of education takes an active role in shaping and responding to policies and trends at the local, national, and international levels.

Increasingly, research in education involves international collaborations around educational inequities. According to UNESCO (the United Nations Educational, Scientific and Cultural Organization), in 2016, 17 percent of the world's adult population was not literate, and 122 million young people were illiterate. Women and girls make up a disproportionate number of these people ("Statistics"). UNESCO has set a goal for universal primary education by 2030. But this goal requires a vast amount of research and resources, including developing strategies to grow and maintain the number of qualified teachers, improving access through infrastructure and supplies, and understanding culture as a component of educational values and practices.

Such goals present formidable challenges. But, through robust research and advocacy, those working in the field of education can lead the way to increase awareness of and interventions with ongoing educational inequities, not only around the world, but also locally, in our own communities and neighborhoods.

Write Here

How do you best learn? Think about learning occasions when you have had the most success with learning, be they in or out of school. Describe in as much detail as possible how you learned, what the components were of that learning experience, and why you think those learning occasions were successful for you.

James Paul Gee
Telling and Doing: Why Doesn't Lara Croft Obey Professor Von Croy?

OVERT INFORMATION AND IMMERSION IN PRACTICE

In terms of human learning, information is a vexed thing. On one hand, humans are poor at learning from lots of overt information given to them outside the sorts of contexts in which this information can be used. This problem can be mitigated if the learners have had lots of experience of such contexts and can simulate the contexts in their minds as they listen to or read the information. Humans tend to have a very hard time processing information for which they cannot supply such simulations. They also tend readily to forget information they have received outside of contexts of actual use, especially if they cannot imagine such contexts.

On the other hand, humans don't learn well when they are just left entirely to their own devices to operate within complex contexts about which they know very little. Children who have no mathematical tools but who are nonetheless left to discover Galileo's laws of the pendulum on their own by mucking around with bobs, string, and pendulums are likely only to be frustrated. In fact, since Galileo used his deep knowledge of geometry to discover these principles, the children are actually being asked to engage in a harder task than the one Galileo (a genius if there

ever was one) faced, since they lack both his prior knowledge and sophisticated tools.

The dilemma then is this: For efficacious learning, humans need overt information, but they have a hard time handling it. They also need immersion in actual contexts of practice, but they can find such contexts confusing without overt information and guidance. This is just the dilemma between overt telling versus immersion in practice that has characterized educational debates for years. Educators tend to polarize the debate by stressing one thing (telling or immersion) over the other and not discussing effective ways to integrate the two. They tend to associate support for overt telling in education with conservative politics and support for immersion in practice with liberal politics. The basic problem remains unsolved. The makers of video games—good capitalists that they are—have no such luxury. If they don't solve this problem, no one is going to learn to play their games.

In this chapter—through a discussion of two video games—I take up some of the ways in which video games deal with overt information and guidance on one hand and immersion in practice on the other. Their solution to our dilemma is to deny there are two hands here and to see overt information and immersion in practice as two fingers on the same hand.

LEARNING TO BE LARA CROFT

Lara Croft, the heroine of the *Tomb Raider* series of games (and movies), is one of the most famous video-game characters. Lara is the pampered aristocratic daughter of Lord Henshingly Croft, and she has wanted for nothing in her (virtual) life. When Lara was a young girl, a lecture by the noted archaeologist Professor Werner Von Croy triggered in her a lifelong desire for travel to remote places in search of adventure. Some time after hearing that lecture, when Lara was 16 and away at boarding school, she came across a copy of *National Geographic* magazine that featured an article by Von Croy. From the article, Lara learned that he was preparing for a new archaeological tour across Asia.

Lara showed the article to her parents and demanded to accompany Von Croy on his expedition. Lord Henshingly then wrote Von Croy offering him financial assistance if he would let Lara join him. Von Croy replied that he remembered Lara's incessant but insightful questions at his earlier lecture. Her company as an assistant was welcomed, as was the offer of financial support. Thus, Von Croy became Lara's mentor. *Tomb Raider* games depict Lara as an adult using the skills she learned as a young girl from Von Croy and pursuing danger, knowledge, and adventure across the world.

Lara—one of the few female lead characters in video games—is one of the most physically agile characters in the world of games (and she was one of the first such very agile characters). The player can manipulate Lara to engage in more physical maneuvers than many other heroes in adventure and shooter games. She can walk, run, do both standing and running jumps, jump back, crouch, duck, roll, climb, cling to ledges and maneuver along them, and even jump and swing on vines and branches. She (the player) uses all these skills to defeat enemies and to explore the treacherous landscapes of ancient tombs and temples, deserts, jungles, and foreign cities.

So far what I have described—the story of Von Croy and Lara—is only back story, a story that gamers are told (in the booklet that comes with a game or in bits and pieces they have learned while playing the games) but haven't experienced for themselves. However, *Tomb Raider: The Last Revelation*, a game relatively late in the series, returns to this back story as part of the game. The first episode in *Tomb Raider: The Last Revelation* shows Lara as a 16-year-old being trained by Professor Von Croy after they have just broken into an ancient and sacred royal tomb in Cambodia. The player now actually gets to live and play Lara's apprenticeship when she was a girl.

This first episode is a real part of the game. (An episode is like a chapter in a book.) The player must search for treasures and avoid many pitfalls and dangers, just as in any other episode, though things are easier here than they are in the later episodes. At the same time, however, this episode is also meant as a training module where the player is explicitly coached on how to play the game. This coaching is done in a fascinating way. As Von Croy trains Lara to be an adventurer, he is also simultaneously training the player to operate the computer controls and play the game. While similar things appear in other games, they are handled here in a particularly nice way.

After an opening video showing Von Croy bursting into the ancient Cambodian tomb (a very large building with many levels and twisting paths) and a display of the words "Cambodia 1984," we hear Von Croy say, "And so we breech the sanctum of the ancients, the first footfalls in this tomb for centuries." We then immediately see the young Lara next to him, looking around in awe, and hear her say, "This place gives me the creeps, [pause] after you." This sort of not-so-respectful patter is typical of Lara, a rather spoiled and self-satisfied young girl.

Von Croy proceeds to tell Lara to be careful, that not all is as it seems. Concealed traps and pitfalls are everywhere. She is to stay close to him and follow his instructions. Since good men have died for the information contained in this tomb—and bad ones have "bartered the information for their own ends"—Von Croy insists that "[f]or this we must respect it, we will not deviate from its route and you will not deviate from my instruction." Altogether, Von Croy comes across as an intimidating and dominating professor.

But, of course, Lara is not cowered by him. The game encourages the player not to be too deferential to Von Croy, either. Even though Von Croy has told Lara to stay close and not deviate from the straight route ahead, the only way that the player can find hidden treasures (like golden skulls) is to wander away from him and explore things a bit. In fact, as Von Croy is commanding Lara to stay close, a willful player is probably looking behind a group of pillars to see if they hide anything interesting. If players are not willful in this way, by the end of the episode they will have missed lots of good stuff and probably will want to play it over again.

Players are placed, by the very design of the game, in the same psychological space as Lara—learning from Von Croy but not subordinating themselves entirely to his old-fashioned professorial need for dominance. The game's design encourages the player to take on a certain sort of attitude and relationship with Von Croy—and, more generally, a certain sort of personality—that represents, in fact, just the sort of person that Lara is.

When I played the game, I was a bit intimidated by Von Croy. Based probably on a lifetime of (trying to look as if I am) following the orders of authority figures like deans, I found myself wanting to follow his orders to the T. But I also wanted the treasures and found myself guiltily sneaking down paths off Von Croy's route and thereby becoming more like Lara and less like myself.

The game has a neat way to ensure that even inept player will discover that they can find good things if they are willing to disobey the professor. For example, when I was playing the game, at one point Von Croy ordered Lara to jump across a cavern; in doing so, she fell in the water below, due to my ineptness in controlling her (via the computer's keys). She can climb back up again and try the jump again (indeed, she needs to do this to follow Von Croy and eventually complete the episode). But, low and behold, as Lara swam toward land, she discovered a golden skull in the · water. A player cannot help but think: What if I purposely disobey orders and jump and climb other than where I am told? What other good things will I find? Soon one is just a bit more like the willful and spoiled Lara herself (and practicing yet more jumps and climbs). In such video games, players get practice in trying out new identities that challenge some of their assumptions about themselves and the world. A good science class should do the same.

STRANGE LANGUAGE: VON CROY TEACHES LARA HOW TO PLAY A VIDEO GAME

After Von Croy has told Lara to follow closely and has pushed a hidden stone in a wall to lower a floor-full of sharp spikes ahead, they come to a small obstacle. Von Croy says, "The first obstacle, a small hop to test your—how do you say—pluck. Press and hold walk, now push forward."

Now this is, if you think about it, a strange thing to say. However, it does not seem the least bit strange when one is actually playing the episode. Von Croy is talking to the virtual character Lara, a character who walks and jumps in the virtual world but has no computer whose keys she can press, push, or hold. However, the player who is playing as the character Lara does have a computer and must learn to manipulate its keys to make Lara come alive. (I played *Tomb Raider: The Last Revelation* on a computer, but *Tomb Raider* games are also available, and probably more often played on, game platforms, which, of course, have controls of their own—controls on a handheld controller—that the player needs to learn.) Thus, Von Croy's remark perfectly melds and integrates talk to Lara and talk to the player. This melding is part of what marries the player's real-world identity as a player and his or her virtual identity as Lara. This type of talk is very common in video games.

But things are even yet more interesting here. When Von Croy says, "Press and hold walk," he means for the player to press and hold the Shift key on the computer, which is the key that makes Lara walk rather than run. (When she walks she automatically stops at ledges; when she runs, she runs past them and falls. It is easier to have her walk up to dangerous ledges than to run up to them.) When Von Croy continues with "now push forward," he means for the player, who is now holding down the Shift key, to press the Arrow key pointing up on the computer, which is the key that moves Lara forward. When the player does this combination of keystrokes, Lara walks up to the obstacle and automatically stops at its edge. She is now ready to jump.

At this point Von Croy says, "Come, come, child, do not fear, this is merely an appetizer for the perils ahead. Push forward and jump together." This tells the player to press the Up Arrow key (the move forward key) and the Alt key (the key that makes Lara jump) together. When the player does so, Lara easily jumps over the obstacle.

Here Von Croy is using the functional names for the keys, named for the actions they carry out in the virtual world, actions like "walk," "forward," and "jump," rather than the computer names for the keys, things like "Shift key," "Up Arrow key," and "Alt key." So, then, how does the player know what keys to press? A player can know this in three ways:

1. The player can do as I did and look in the booklet that comes with the game. This means that when the player is listening to Von Croy, he or she is simultaneously looking up the computer key equivalents of his commands (another way in which the virtual and real worlds are married).

2. The player can make intelligent guesses from having played other *Tomb Raider* games or games like them.

3. The player can do as my child does in similar circumstances and press all the plausible keys until he or she gets the right result and thereby finds the right key.

Throughout the first episode, Von Croy continues to talk this way, telling the player (Lara) about even more complicated actions that he or she (and Lara) can do, saying things like: "This gap is wider and the edge is treacherous. First walk to the edge. Then press forward and jump together. When you are in midair, press and hold action. You will grab the outcrop." By the end of the episode, the player has both finished the first episode of the game and learned how to operate the basic controls. The player also has learned some basic strategies of how to explore the virtual world and avoid certain dangers.

LARA AND LEARNING

Why is this "strange" language not actually strange when one is playing the game? In a good many video games, players hear such language,

language that "confuses" the virtual world (e.g., "walk") and the real world of the player at the computer (e.g., "press the walk key"). Such language, in fact, represents a very basic and crucial learning principle, one regularly ignored in schools. Learners cannot do much with lots of overt information that a teacher has explicitly told them outside the context of immersion in actual practice. At the same time, learners cannot learn without some overt information; they cannot discover everything for themselves.

The solution is to give information in context and to couch it in ways that make sense in the context of embodied action. Consider a simple real-world example. Telling someone "When your car is skidding, turn the wheel in the direction of the skid" works less well than saying, "When your car is skidding, look in the direction of the skid." (Of course, when the driver looks in that direction, he or she will turn the wheel in that direction.) The latter formulation couches the information in a way that allows it to be integrated with embodied action both in the learner's mental simulation and in actual action on the spot.

In good classroom science instruction, an instructor does not lecture for an extended period and then tell the learners to go off and apply what they have learned in a group science activity. The learners won't remember most of what they have heard. And, in any case, none of it will have made much sense in a situated and embodied way that is actually usable. Yet good science instructors don't just turn learners loose to engage in activities with no help at all.

Rather, as group members are discovering things through their own activity, the good science instructor comes up, assesses the progress they are making and the fruitfulness of the paths down which they are proceeding in their inquiry, and then gives overt information that is, at that point, usable.

However, there is more at stake in Von Croy's "mixed" language—language that mixes talk to Lara about the virtual world and to the player about the game's controls. Such language is one among many devices in a good video game that encourages the player to relate, juxtapose, and meld his or her real-world identity (actually, multiple real-world identities) and the virtual identity of the character he or she is playing in the virtual world of the game. Such a process also encourages the player to adopt what I called in chapter 3 a projective identity.

I argued earlier that projective identities are the heart and soul of active and critical learning. Children who take responsibility for the sort of classroom virtual scientist they are and will become throughout the school year and relate this proactively to their real-world identities (some of which may have started as virtual identities in other play or school domains) are engaged in real learning, learning as a refashioning of self. Of course, no child can do this if no such virtual identity and world—a world of imagined scientists and science enacted in words, deeds, and texts—is present in the classroom.

But let me return to our game. As is typical of training modules in good video games, this first training episode of *Tomb Raider: The Last Revelation* does not tell the player everything he or she needs to know and do in order to play the rest of the game. All the episode does is give the player enough information and skill to play and learn from the subsequent episodes. Since each episode gets more difficult, the player is, in fact, always both playing and learning. Indeed, the distinction between playing (doing the actual activity) and learning is blurred in a video game, as is the distinction between master and beginner, since players always willingly face new challenges as a game progresses and as new games do new things, make new demands, and get better and better at challenging players in creative ways.

When the second episode of *Tomb Raider: The Last Revelation* begins, Von Croy challenges Lara to put your newly acquired skills to the test in a race against him through unfamiliar territory to grab a sacred stone in another part of the temple. Unfortunately, after he says, "We will race for the Iris, on the count of three: one, two," he takes off without saying "three," giving himself a good head start.

If you've found and collected all eight golden skulls in the first episode, Von Croy races down the Path of the Heretical, a more difficult test. If you haven't found all the skulls, then he races down the Path of the Virtuous, an easier test. This is typical of good video games and represents several of the learning principles discussed

earlier: A good video game adapts to the level of the player, rewards different players differently (but rewards them all), and often stays at the edge of the player's regime of competence.

It is also interesting and an important fact that the game rewards the player for finding the golden skulls. Finding them requires the player to disregard Von Croy's commands to stay close and follow his every command. As we said earlier, the player is encouraged by the very design of the game to be more Lara-like—playful and willful—leaving behind fears and hesitations about authority and the risks of exploration.

LEARNING IN A SUBDOMAIN OF THE FULL DOMAIN

The third episode of the game starts with Lara, now an adult, off adventuring in Egypt. Von Croy, older as well, returns from time to time in the story. By now the player has learned and lived through Lara's back story—even learned where and how she got her famous backpack (indeed, the player playing Lara as a teenager has picked it up). So, are the first two episodes "training" ("learning") or a "real" part of the game? They are, of course, both. In a good video game, the player learns to play the game by playing in a "subdomain" of the real game. This is an important learning principle and, again, one regularly ignored in school.

Many video games have an explicitly labeled training module. For example, many shooter games have such modules where instructors— sometimes sergeants shouting at you, sometimes more gentle instructors, even peaceful-looking female holograms as in the training module for the first *Half-Life* game—talk to the player just as Von Croy talked to Lara. These modules are not episodes in the game, but the player moves through the same sorts of landscapes, performs the same sorts of actions, and engages with the same sorts of artifacts as in the "real" game (except the only way you can get killed in the training module is by blowing yourself up while trying to learn how to use dynamite and similar items, something I have done on more than one occasion).

Once the game proper starts, the first episode (sometimes several early episodes) is almost always something of a training module, even though it may not be labeled explicitly as such. In this episode, things are less hectic and demanding than they will get later on. (This is not to say that things aren't hectic and demanding enough to provide a feel for the game world and what is to come.)

In the first episode, the player is rarely under any sort of time pressure and generally pays only a small price for mistakes. Usually no demanding enemies—often none at all—attack the player. Furthermore, this episode usually offers a concentrated sample of the most basic and important actions, artifacts, and interactions that the player will need to deal with throughout the game.

Nonetheless, these early episodes are very much part of the game and its story. *Tomb Raider: The Last Revelation* combines the training module and the early episodes as places where demands are lowered enough so that lots of fundamental learning can be done "on site" in the "real" world (i.e., in this case, the "real virtual world") of the game (and not, say, in books or through lots of overt instruction out of context).

By saying that in a good video game, players learn to play the game by playing in a "subdomain" of the real game, I mean that training modules and early episodes, where fundamental learning gets done, are built as simplified versions of the same world in which the player will live, play, and learn throughout the game. Learning is not started in a separate place (e.g., a classroom or textbook) outside the domain in which the learning is going to operate. At the same time, the learner is not thrown into the "real" thing—the full game—and left to swim or drown.

Because good video games have training modules, early episodes as further training in the fundamentals, and more advanced learning throughout the game as one is ready, all done in the game's virtual world, something interesting happens to the learner. Let me tell you a little story to make the point: Once when I was giving a talk about video games and learning, there were two excellent game players (and computer experts) in their mid-20s in the audience—dragged to the talk by the academic whose research they assisted. After my talk, this academic asked them publicly what they thought about what I had said. Were the sorts of learning principles I had talked about really operating in these games? The two play-ers both said that, yes, they were aware that such principles were at work when they were playing video games, but that they had never thought of what they were doing as "learning."

This is what is magical about learning in good video games—and in good classrooms, too—learners are not always overtly aware of the fact that they are "learning," how much they are learning, or how difficult it is. Learners are embedded in a domain (a semiotic domain like a branch of science or a good video game) where, even when they are learning (and since the domain gets progressively harder, they are always learning), they are still in the domain, still a member of the team (affinity group), still actu-ally playing the game, even if only as a "newbie."

TRANSFER AND BEYOND IN VIDEO GAMES

Of course, there are times in a video game where players recognize that they are learning. These are the times—and, as the game progresses, such times become more common—where learners see that their now-routinized mastery, developed earlier in the game and in playing similar games, breaks down. They face a new challenge for which their now-routinized skills don't work. In cases like this, a form of learning happens that is just the sort we want to encourage in school but often have little success doing: transfer of prior knowledge mixed with innovation. Let me make this point with an extended example from my own game playing.

By the end of the first-person shooter game *Return to Castle Wolfenstein*, I had learned a strat-egy for killing Nazi "Super Soldiers" (robotlike, mechanically and biologically enhanced beings who can take and give a great deal of damage) of which I was quite proud. In fact, I had gotten quite good at this strategy.

Here is what I did: I positioned myself quite far from a Super Soldier, behind good cover, and then sniped at him using a long-distance rifle with a good scope, ducking below cover each time the Super Soldier fired back. After many shots, the Super Soldier died, and I had suffered little or no damage. Suffering little or no damage is important—it does little good to win a battle but have so few health points left that you will easily die in the next battle, even with a weak opponent, before you can find a health kit to heal yourself. In a closer battle with a Super Soldier, even if I won, I tended to take lots of damage, which left me too weak for the fights to come. However, I do know other players who learned good strategies for defeating the Super Soldiers up close without taking too much damage.

At the end of *Return to Castle Wolfenstein*, the player (playing U.S. Office of Secret Actions' Agent Major B.J. Blazkowitz—a very famous video-game character, because he originally appeared in one of the early first-person shooter games, *Wolfenstein 3D*, a game some consider the "mother" of all first-person shooter games) must face Heinrich I, an ancient deadly knight the Nazis have raised from his grave through dark mysterious rituals. Heinrich is one heck of a Super Soldier. He can cause zombies to rise from the ground to attack you. Furthermore, he can cause a myriad of spirits to fly through the air, find you wherever you are trying to hide, and attack you. If you get close to Heinrich, he can cause rocks from surrounding pillars and arches to fall on you; he can pull you in closer to him by smashing his sword on the ground; and he can easily kill you with one blow of his massive sword.

Trying to hide behind cover and snipe Heinrich does not work—trust me, I tried it many times. The flying spirits find you every time and kill you. So, I discovered that my routinized strategy was no good. At this point, the game forced me—at its very end, to boot—to try other things and learn something new, or not finish it.

Of course, in such a situation, players can call on experiences they have had in other games, adapting them to the current circumstances, or they can try something entirely new. The first strategy, calling on previous experience, is an example of what learning theorists call "transfer." An example of transfer at work would be a case where a student applies something he or she has learned about reasoning in biology to a new problem faced in a social studies class. Transfer does not always work and can be dangerous. (Maybe social studies is better off not being done in the style of biological thinking; then again, maybe not.) Transfer requires active learning and, if it is not to be dangerous, critical learning.

At one time, cognitive psychologists considered transfer to be a fairly easy phenomenon.

Then they went through a stage of thinking that people were, in fact, quite bad at transfer and it was, for all practical purposes, impossible to trigger transfer in school learning. Now they believe transfer is crucial to learning but not at all easy to trigger in learners, especially in school. Getting transfer to happen typically requires making the learners overtly aware of how two different problems or domains share certain properties at a deeper level. That is, it requires thinking at a design level, thinking about how two problems or domains are structured or "designed" in similar ways, ways that may be obscured by the more superficial features of the problems or domains.

Facing Heinrich, and having failed many times, I decided to call on what I had learned in playing other video games. I tried a strategy I had learned from *American McGee's Alice* when trying to kill "bosses" (particularly powerful enemies). I moved wildly around, zigzagging around and away from Heinrich, stopping only quickly to shoot him a couple of times with my most powerful weapons, moving again to avoid his fire and the zombies and spirits he sent after me, all the while frantically searching for health kits laying among the fallen rocks and rubble that would repair the damage I was taking.

This strategy had worked to kill bosses like the Duchess, the Centipede, and the Queen of Hearts in *Alice*. It almost worked here. I survived longer than I had in all my other attempts. But, alas, Heinrich got me in the end. I went down with more pride and dignity (remember, in my projective identity, I care about such things), but I went down nonetheless.

Since some of the *Alice* strategy seemed to work, I needed to think about which parts to keep and which to change. Here is where transfer marries innovation. In this type of situation, the player has to think of something new (new to the player, at least; others may have already hit on it) in the context of keeping what is useful from past experience. This is a key moment for active and potentially critical learning. It is the place where previous experience is, at one and the same time, recruited and transformed, giving rise to newer experiences that can be used and transformed in the future.

Here is what I did. First I used another instance of transfer and did something I have done in a good many shooter games: I ran out of a tunnel I was in, quickly pounded Heinrich with four rockets from my rocket gun, and then ran quickly back into my tunnel. Often in shooter games some of your enemies will follow you into the tunnel or other such narrow space, and they become easier targets, since they are not all spread out and you see them coming at you in a direct line. Some of Heinrich's key helpers (three Dread Knights and the Nazi who had brought him back to life) ran after me, and I easily killed them.

Heinrich was momentarily without helpers, though that would soon change. Now I knew I had to run out and face him—he was not about to follow me back to the tunnel and would have killed me there, in any case, by sending his spirits at me from afar (his version of my sniping strategy). The *Alice* strategy wasn't going to work without some serious modification. What to do? There is, of course, only one way to proceed: Think and try something. If you die, you go back to the drawing board.

I figured that I had to do my wild moving-around strategy from *Alice*, but closer in to Heinrich. If I stayed close, the flying spirits flew over my head for the most part (since they are really a device to stop people from trying to kill Heinrich from a distance). Yet if I stayed too close, he would draw me into him by hitting the ground with his sword and then, as I flew toward him, he would slay me with one blow. What seemed to be called for was a more constrained version of the *Alice* strategy, stressing moving toward and quickly away from Heinrich in straight lines more than the wider and more circular motion I had used in *Alice*. (Other players have had success with circular strafing when fighting Heinrich, but I was at the time no good at tightly controlled circular movements.)

I ran out of my tunnel and tried my new part-transfer, part-innovation strategy. After four direct battles with Heinrich, interrupted by wild runs to find health kits to repair my damage, I had him seriously weakened. Things appeared to be working and I had gotten farther than ever before. But by then I had just less than half my health, even after I had used the last health kit to be found.

Then something happened that can be added to transfer and innovation as a learning strategy:

a lucky discovery. As I used the last health kit, I realized I was out of ammunition for my Venom gun and switched to my Telsa gun, which fires electric rays. I had found the last health kit behind some boxes, and, as I stood behind them, I noticed that the rather slow-moving Heinrich was moving toward the boxes to finish me off. Thus, I quickly ran around the boxes and around behind Heinrich, who was now staring over the boxes at where I had been standing. His back momentarily turned to me, I ran right up to him and blasted him from behind with the Telsa.

It was risky, but he had already taken enough damage that this finished him off. He died in a rage and I immediately saw a cut scene (a short video). The Super Soldier project and the Heinrich project had been Himmler's babies. In the cut scene I saw Himmler looking through binoculars. He had obviously been watching my battle with Heinrich from atop a far away hill.

Himmler says with dismay, "This American, he has ruined everything." His aide then says, "Herr Himmler, the plane is waiting to take you back to Berlin." Himmler is reluctant to go; he obviously does not want to have to explain his failure to Hitler. The aide pushes him: "Sir, the Fuehrer is expecting your arrival." Himmler walks very slowly back to the car. It was quite satisfying to have finished off Heinrich and to have pissed off Himmler at one and the same time.

Though this example may seem trivial—with its talk of Super Soldiers and risen dead—it represents several components of one very important type of active learning.

1.   The learner realizes that a more-or-less routinized, taken-for-granted strategy does not work and quits using it.
2.   The learner transfers skills and strategies from previous experience by seeing underlying similarities between that experience and the current problem (*American McGee's Alice* and *Return to Castle Wolfenstein* are, at the surface level, quite different games, though both are shooter games—*Alice* is a third-person shooter and *Wolfenstein* is a first-person shooter).
3.   The learner learns that, while school sometimes sets up problems so that earlier solutions transfer directly to later ones,

this rarely happens in other situations. The learner adapts and transforms the earlier experience to be transferred to the new problem through creativity and innovation.

4. The learner also uses (and is prepared to use) what he or she discovers—often "by accident"—on the spot, on the ground on practice, while implementing the new transformed strategy (as I did when I circled behind Heinrich looking for me over the boxes). This requires reflection not after or before action but in the midst of action. The learner remains flexible, adapting performance in action.

Write Away

1. What is active learning? When is it most effective? Why does it matter? What else might matter as well to make learning effective? Using Gee's article, address the uses and limits of active learning. Define active learning and provide evidence from Gee's article that illustrates what active learning entails. Then, address the possible applications and uses of active learning beyond *Tomb Raider*, as well as any limitations of active learning. Might Gee have overlooked any aspects of learning, in *Tomb Raider* or elsewhere, that are also important? What, if any, learning occasions are there when active learning might be counterproductive? Or, what, if any, features of a learning occasion might sometimes get in the way of active learning?

2. Develop a teaching plan that relies on active-learning strategies. First, work individually or with a small group of peers, and in consultation with your instructor, to decide on a topic, idea, or skill for the lesson plan and an intended context (i.e., length of lesson/ number of learning moments, age of students, etc.). Second, develop a lesson plan that relies on active learning. Third, write a reflective statement in which you address your choices and intended learning outcomes.

3. Conduct and write a case study that addresses in detail one of the many ongoing challenges in the field of education. To develop your case study, learn more about various education challenges, drawing on research and policy in such areas as equity, access, assessment, teacher training, or another challenge of your choosing. This challenge could be one that is widely applicable, or unique to a particular disciplinary or geographic context. Once you have narrowed your focus, compose a case study about that challenge. This can be on a location, group, or issue. Develop your case study with as much detail as possible, and frame your case study with relevant research about the larger challenge that it addresses. Steps toward developing your case study will include a proposal and an annotated bibliography.

Pop Music: *"Paper Planes"* by M.I.A.

Transfer Points: Music, Cultural Studies, Immigration Studies

Rock journalism, concert and album reviews, biographies and exposés about famous musicians and bands … music sponsors a considerable range of writing. While scholars in the fields of musicology and ethnomusicology hold particular investment in exploring music as a text, many others across academia also research and write about music, from those in English and American Literature, African and African-American Studies, and

Latino/a Studies, to those in History, Cultural Anthropology, Marketing, and Health Professions. While it may seem in some ways paradoxical that so much writing can emerge around a sonic form of communication, writing and research around music in fact adds immense layers of depth and knowledge about music, musicians, and the role of music in the world around us.

One of the most central concepts to keep in mind with regard to research and writing about music is context, the political, social, historical, biographical, and cultural context surrounding a particular piece of music. Musical compositions emerge out of a particular time and place and have currency with that context. This does not mean that songs cannot be relevant outside of that context, but that those who seek to understand songs and their impact will explore that context as a way of deepening understanding. M.I.A., for instance, wrote "Paper Planes" after several years of difficulties stemming from her status as immigrant in the United States. These challenges included a denied work-visa application and a brief stint on the Department of Homeland Security's danger list.

Describing the ways in which immigrants are often met with derision, and why this inspired her to write "Paper Planes," M.I.A. said the following in an interview:

> I was thinking about living [in Bed-Stuy], waking up every morning—it's such an African neighborhood. I was going to get patties at my local and just thinking that really the worst thing that anyone can say [to someone these days] is some shit like: 'What I wanna do is come and get your money.' People don't really feel like immigrants or refugees contribute to culture in any way. That they're just leeches that suck from whatever. So in the song I say 'All I wanna do is [sound of gun shooting and reloading, cash register opening] and take your money.' I did it in sound effects. It's up to you how you want to interpret. America is so obsessed with money, I'm sure they'll get it." (qtd. in Wagner)

M.I.A.'s commentary, then, demonstrates how a particular context and set of personal experiences influenced her to create the song and the argument within the song.

While context can deepen our understanding of a musical text, songs also carry unique, discrete components that add meaning. M.I.A.'s commentary also gestures to her use of particular sonic strategies to accomplish her aims within the song. As part of a larger system of musical components, such aspects as sound effects, melody, harmony, timbre, rhythm, arrangement, and even silence are critical for exploring songs. People studying music examine the structure of songs, the pauses and silences within songs, the choice of instruments, and the arrangement. Together, these musical elements enable those who research and write about music to engage in deep analysis and close reading of songs as texts.

"Paper Planes," though, also raises another important aspect of music scholarship because it is a mash-up of The Clash's "Straight to Hell" and Wreckx-n-Effect's "Rumpshaker." Considering prior musicians, musical genres, and songs that have combined to generate a new song, whether explicitly through a mash-up, or more subtly through implicit influence, also helps unpack the complexities within a song. Musicians frequently draw on a vast field of musical history and knowledge to revise, challenge, revisit, honor, and extend, even as they also create new sounds and ideas.

Alongside this rich tapestry of influence, context, and experience that work together to impact exploration of music, the medium in which a song emerges also holds critical value. The ways in which an artist performs a song, music video versions, written lyrics, audio versions, instrumental versions, live or recorded renditions, acoustic ... all of these various formats and modalities contribute to and impact a song.

> **M.I.A.**, Mathangi "Maya" Arulpragasam, is a British singer and songwriter of Tamil descent who became well known in 2004 when she launched two popular singles: "Sunshowers" and "Galang" ("M.I.A."). She is known for being political: "Her political statements have led to her being described as a terrorist. Her pop videos are analyzed for propaganda ...[one of her videos] was immediately removed from YouTube for its violence" (Sawyer). The song "Paper Planes" initially appeared on M.I.A.'s album "Kala" in 2007, and won several awards ("M.I.A."; "Paper Planes").

These many intersecting vectors work together to make music one of the most frequently used texts across numerous fields of academic research and writing.

Write Here

Identify an issue of importance to you (a question, debate, or matter of local, national, or global significance). Then, imagine you are in the process of developing a mash-up of two or more songs as a way of articulating your position on or concerns about that issue. Which songs would you use for your mash-up? Why? From which musical genres would they be drawn? Why? How would you hope they work together to convey your position or concerns?

M.I.A.
Paper Planes

[x2]
I fly like paper, get high like planes
If you catch me at the border I got visas in my name
If you come around here, I make 'em all day
I get one down in a second if you wait

[x2]
Sometimes I think sitting on trains
Every stop I get to I'm clocking that game
Everyone's a winner, we're making our fame
Bona fide hustler making my name

[x4]
All I wanna do is (BANG BANG BANG BANG!)
And (KKKAAAA CHING!)
And take your money

[x2]
Pirate skulls and bones
Sticks and stones and weed and bombs
Running when we hit 'em
Lethal poison for the system

[x2]
No one on the corner has swagger like us
Hit me on my burner prepaid wireless
We pack and deliver like UPS trucks
Already going hell just pumping that gas

[x4]
All I wanna do is (BANG BANG BANG BANG!)
And (KKKAAAA CHING!)
And take your money

M.I.A.
Third world democracy
Yeah, I got more records than the K.G.B.
So, uh, no funny business

Some some some I some I murder
Some I some I let go
Some some some I some I murder
Some I some I let go

[x4]
All I wanna do is (BANG BANG BANG BANG!)
And (KKKAAAA CHING!)
And take your money

Write Away

1. An interviewer once noted the following about M.I.A.: "[In] an age where 'immigrant' is an insult rather than a description, she uses the word proudly to describe herself: a refugee who started from nothing and became internationally successful by the time she was 28" (Sawyer). What argument does this song makes about immigrants? For evidence, point to specific aspects of the lyrics, video, and music. You might also draw for evidence on the songs M.I.A. mashed up for "Paper Planes," the Clash's "Straight to Hell" and Wreckx-n-Effect's "Rumpshaker."

2. A music review involves description, analysis, and evaluation of a song, performance, or album. Write a review of "Paper Planes." Imagine you are writing for readers who may be unfamiliar with M.I.A's song, but who are interested in music, such as those who might read *Rolling Stone* or visit Billboard.com. Make choices about whether to include any of the following, and, if so, in what ways: the origin of the song, similar songs by M.I.A. or others, prior writing or interviews about "Paper Planes," analysis of musical elements, your perspective on and evaluation of the song. For sample music reviews, speak with a librarian or search on IIMP Full Text (International Index to Music Periodicals), a database frequently used by scholars of music. (Hint: on the IIMP, narrow your search to return only "reviews.")

3. Write a research essay on immigrants, immigration, and music, in which you position "Paper Planes" within that larger conversation. What are some of the historical connections between immigration and music? What other musicians or songs address immigration and immigrant status? You can choose to focus on a particular immigrant group or region of the world, or you can research immigration more broadly. As you develop your research essay, work in stages and with ongoing feedback and exchange, beginning with prewriting and brainstorming, then moving on to a research proposal, an annotated bibliography, a literature review, and then a cycle of drafting, revision, and editing.

Chapter 6 Key Terms

mash-up	critical lens	anthology
synthesis	thesis-driven synthesis	comparison
literature review	argumentative synthesis	explanatory synthesis
background synthesis	interdisciplinarity	bibliographic essay

Write Away

Create your own mash-up (synthesis) as a way of gaining a more nuanced understanding of how synthesis combines elements, ideas, or concepts in order to create something new.

Find a partner. Work in teams of two for this project as a way of enhancing the creative process through collaboration.

Choose a medium for your mash-up. Together with your partner, you can decide to do a mash-up in any medium you wish, provided you have relatively easy access to any needed materials or have the technological acumen necessary for the project. Media options for your mash-up can include songs, videos, poetry, creative nonfiction, nonfiction, art, images, maps, clothing, objects, or any medium or combination of media you want.

Create the mash-up. Generate the mash-up in whichever form you have chosen. As you generate the mash-up, think deliberately about what you are hoping to accomplish from the mash-up. *Why* are you combining these particular ideas, elements, or concepts? What larger purpose might this synthesis serve?

Generate a brief (100- to 150-word) summary and analysis of your mash-up. Using the summarizing skills you have learned from Chapter 5, and practicing in advance the analysis skills you will gain in Chapter 7, write a brief (100- to 150-word) summary and analysis for your mash-up. This brief text should accomplish the following aims: summarize the elements, ideas, concepts, etc. you chose to mash up, explain why you did so, and reveal, from your perspective, the "something new" generated by this mash-up (synthesis). What new insights, critiques, illustrations, questions, etc. emerge from this mash-up? Your brief written text should be modeled after the kinds of texts that can sometimes accompany art exhibits: brief, readable texts that provide a bit of background, general information, and often some small analysis or suggestions for interpretation. Because effective synthesis hinges on the "something new," be explicit about the "something new" generated by this mash-up.

Share your mash-up with the other teams. Share or present your mash-up and your brief written text with the other teams, and learn about their mash-ups as well.

Reflect on transfer and synthesis. After having seen the other teams' mash-ups, and by invoking a comparative approach—itself a form of synthesis—reflect in writing for ten minutes about what you have learned regarding transfer and synthesis: What skills with synthesis seem more or less important across different media? How did other teams go through the process of synthesis, and how do their processes compare with the process you and your partner followed? What do you now know about synthesis from having completed your own mash-up project *and* from having seen other teams' mash-ups? What elements of synthesis do you anticipate transferring across occasions throughout your academic career?

Analysis

Pinpointing Chapter 7

Moving from the synthesis addressed in Chapter 6, Chapter 7 focuses on analysis, where writers combine and also unbundle component parts to generate deeper understandings. Writers conduct and develop their research with *and* through analysis, using it to pursue the questions they pose, as well as to engage with the texts they read. To provide you with strategies for *analysis in transit*, this chapter addresses the following concepts:

- What Is Analysis?
- The Purposes of Analysis
- Types of Data Academic Writers Analyze
- Questions that Shape Analysis
- Criteria for Effective Analysis
- Modes of Analysis

Subsequent chapters, which focus on argument, extend knowledge about analysis by showing how writers move from analysis to constructing and shaping their arguments as effectively as possible.

Petroglyphs, engravings carved into rock, can be found across the world, from New Mexico to Australia. Strategies for analyzing and calculating the age of petroglyphs have become a hotly contested issue. Depending on the strategy used, some scholars have suggested that petroglyphs in Pilbara, Australia, are among the oldest in the world, created as many as 60,000 years ago. Other scholars date most petroglyphs to, at most, 30,000 years ago (Pillans and Fifield; Watchman).

As with debates over the dating of petroglyphs, scholars also argue about how to interpret or analyze petroglyphs. Many scholars associate astronomical significance to some petroglyphs, hypothesizing that they depict solar entities or were designed taking astronomical alignment into consideration. Ray P. Norris and Duane W. Hamacher describe some of these possible interpretations: "A 'bicycle-wheel' or 'sunburst' petro-glyph...may represent the sun, or perhaps even a supernova...crescent shapes are also common, and may represent the moon." Norris and Hamacher, however, are careful to point out that such interpretations are speculative. Marinus Anthony van der Sluijs and Anthony L. Peratt surveyed petroglyphs in 139 countries around the world, noting that "all the sites allowed for the rock artist to look to the South Pole of the sky." They believe that abstract representations such as the sunburst may actually be illustrations of intense auroral storms: "Auroras are centered on the poles. In this case, our observations suggest that an auroral storm of unprecedented proportions may have occurred over the South Pole. The light associated with such storms is unbearably bright and is called synchro-tron radiation light."

Providing a different analytical perspective, other petroglyph research suggests that some "sites may have been places where medicine men, community, or spiritual leaders went to meditate to receive visions or guidance to lead or heal their people." Other research suggests instead that petroglyphs provide a visual "type of storytelling or

recording of history and events [or a form of] artistic expression" ("About Petroglyphs"; Carr and Nevin).

Still other researchers focus on the spirituality of petroglyphs and argue that we should not spend time analyzing or interpreting petroglyphs as a way of maintaining respect and honor for petroglyphs. The National Park Service, for instance, resists interpretation: "We usually do not try and interpret the images or assign specific meanings. Some meanings were not meant to be known or understood today. Some meanings were not meant to be known or understood by the uninitiated" ("Petroglyph").

As demonstrated by this wide range of interpretations and research about what petroglyphs may have symbolized or accomplished, scholars conduct analyses across an enormous variety of different data and texts, from geological analysis of rock to cultural or historical analysis of ancient images. This discussion of ancient petroglyphs illustrates that it is not only the objects or texts of analysis that vary broadly, but also the strategies for analysis (as in the dating methodologies) and the results of analysis (as in the many, often competing conjectures about the purposes and origins of petroglyphs).

The array of data academic writers analyze, the methods they use to analyze, and the outcomes of their analysis vary broadly as one can imagine. Paleontologists can choose to analyze fossils virtually, in person with chemical compounds, or by using other models. Scholars have been analyzing Shakespeare's plays for centuries and continue to come up with widely varying interpretations from their analyses. Two different economists might conduct gender analysis on CEO salaries, using different models and emerge with two markedly different assessments.

Analysis forms the basis of some of the most engaging debates and disagreements across all sorts of issues. Often, how we analyze, what we analyze, and the conclusions we reach from analysis provide the material writers use to make arguments, suggest policy, and convince decision makers. In this sense, analysis is not only widely variable, but also widely significant. In fact, analysis is one of the most significant elements of the research and writing process.

Write Here

Researchers disagree about how or whether to analyze the depictions on petroglyphs. What is your opinion? Why and under what circumstances might analysis of petroglyphs be inadvisable? When might petroglyph analysis be advantageous, and how can it be conducted in a responsible manner? What can be gained from analyzing petroglyphs? Are there other kinds of texts or artifacts (contemporary or historical) you think might sometimes be better left unanalyzed? Why or why not?

What is Analysis?

Analysis occurs around you every day in ways that directly impact your life. Professionals at area water treatment plants analyze water samples to make sure drinking water is safe. Transportation specialists analyze traffic patterns to make adjustments in traffic light rotations. Police officers analyze crimes. You yourself likely engage in analysis on a daily basis with such everyday occurrences as deciding why you prefer one song over another, or as you try to better understand a friend's behavior.

In the broadest sense, **analysis** involves examining data closely, breaking down larger concepts, texts, images, events, and artifacts into smaller pieces. Through analysis, we then scrutinize these smaller components in order to notice patterns, anomalies, significant findings, and observations. We also use analysis to draw conclusions and thereby arrive at a greater understanding of the data.

Analysis typically involves asking such questions like:

- What are the component parts of the data?
- What patterns do you notice?
- What tensions or contradictions can you identify?
- Are there any underlying assumptions in the data?
- What seems significant about the data?
- What is the context surrounding the data?

These general questions, however, blur the nuances and specifics of analysis within the disciplines. Definitions about analysis are highly contingent on disciplinary perspective and the specific writing occasion.

Chemists, for example, employ chemical analysis, defined by the Department of Chemistry at the University of Arizona as "the science of making chemical measurements and characterizations."

Philosophy provides an even more complex example of the contingent nature of analysis. The *Stanford Encyclopedia of Philosophy*, for example, provides eight different definitions of the term "analysis" and quotes more than fifty different people across history, from Plato to Clifford Geertz, each offering his or her own unique descriptions of the term. Michael Beaney explains the range of definitions for analysis in philosophy through variations in analytical method:

> Analysis has always been at the heart of philosophical method, but it has been understood and practised in many different ways. Perhaps, in its broadest sense, it might be defined as a process of isolating or working back to what is more fundamental by means of which something, initially taken as given, can be explained or reconstructed.... This allows great variation in specific method, however. The aim may be to get back to basics, but

there may be all sorts of ways of doing this, each of which might be called 'analysis.'

Part of what accounts for varying definitions of analysis, then, is that academic writers employ a range of analytic methods, each of which impacts both the implementation and the results of analysis. The term analysis, in fact, might be best conceived as an umbrella concept referring to a numerous array of strategies and approaches writers can adopt to examine ideas, texts, and objects in more depth. The particular fundamentals uncovered through analysis will vary depending on what those fundamentals are and what methods writers use to discover them.

Many of these methods for analysis within disciplines require some measure of discipline-specific expertise. For instance, physicists use dimensional analysis, which the Department of Physics at the University of Guelph defines as "a useful method for determining the units of a variable in an equation [and/or for] checking the correctness of an equation which you have derived after some algebraic manipulation."

Alongside these discipline-specific methodologies, however, academic writers across disciplines also employ more transferable types of **analytic methods**. Chemists, philosophers, and physicists, for example, also employ content analysis, depending on the writing occasion and their research questions.

Learning how to conduct and write analysis effectively requires recognizing the degree to which disciplinary perspective and writing occasion shape the analysis academic writers conduct. Effective analysis requires the flexibility to redefine what analysis involves as you move from one writing occasion to others across and among disciplines.

The Purposes of Analysis

Analysis can sometimes become the brunt of derision and resistance, as in the Urban Dictionary's definition of overanalyze: "to over think things to the point of it being annoying or ruining your relationships with people." Because it can be difficult to identify the precise point at which analysis devolves into overanalysis, keeping the purposes of analysis in mind is key.

Analysis serves many vital roles in academic writing across disciplines and helps academic writers achieve a complex range of goals. Without analysis academic writers

Writer Insights

How and why do you analyze data?

Part of my job is to analyze data about our campus writing center. I look at the number of visits in a semester, the ten most common student challenges, the most common courses tutored, the busiest times of day, and so on. I usually start by asking myself a research question, like "How often do students have MLA and APA citation questions?" Then, I use the search tool on my spreadsheet to check the tutor's reports for mentions of these terms. There are about 1,800 reports to sort through! I report my findings to the dean and the president's office.

~Brenna Dugan, College Administrator/
Writing Center Manager/English Professor,
Ohio, United States

would not be able to sufficiently understand data, make arguments, or advance knowledge.

Analysis in academic writing can serve one or more of the following purposes:

- to understand data more deeply
- to explore relationships between two or more entities
- to explain data to oneself and/or others
- to draw conclusions from data
- to make decisions based on data
- to identify patterns or anomalies across and among data

Along with these general purposes, however, there are also discipline-specific purposes for analysis. These discipline-specific purposes are often connected to the very essence of foundational lines of inquiry within disciplines.

The Department of Chemistry at the University of Arizona, for example, explains that the purpose of chemical analysis is to answer four "fundamental questions about a substance or a sample of material. What is the identity of this substance? How can I separate the various components? How much of each component do I have? Is substance X present in the sample?" Chemists, then, use analysis in order to move the work of their discipline forward and to better understand the interactions between various substances.

Cultural anthropologists, by turn, also have discipline-based purposes for conducting analysis. Researchers in this field may conduct cross-cultural analysis, also known as holocultural analysis, which can be defined as "statistical cross-cultural comparisons…used to discover traits shared between cultures and generate ideas about cultural universals" (Kinzer and Gillies). Through cross-cultural analysis, cultural anthropologists can move forward the main areas of inquiry within their discipline.

The great range of these discipline-specific examples demonstrates the value of approaching analysis through a transfer-based framework. Adopting this approach enables you to see how analysis in any disciplinary context can be tailored to serve the overarching purposes of inquiry in that discipline.

Often, academic writers have multiple purposes, some explicit and some implicit. But, as with most matters in academic writing, one should have some sense of aim or purpose when writing because it infuses academic writing with value and significance. Since academic writers can sometimes get mired within the component parts required by analysis, it is important to keep in mind the larger purposes for analysis, purposes that enable academic writers to achieve important disciplinary goals.

Types of Data Academic Writers Analyze

Academic writers analyze an enormously wide range of data. Nearly anything and anyone can be analyzed. This list provides a glimpse into the many different types of data that academic writers analyze.

- **Visual:** photographs, images, art, graphics, observations
- **Aural:** music, spoken language, animal sounds, environmental sounds
- **Tactile:** physiological actions and reactions, forces, vibrations
- **Textual:** language in fiction, nonfiction, poetry, songs, criticism, websites, field notes, archives
- **Quantitative:** numbers, equations, statistics
- **Other:** liquids, solids, events, human or animal behaviors

These types of data often overlap. A film, for instance, has visual, aural, and textual components to it. Depending on your perspective, you might even argue that a film involves tactile data (viewers' responses) and quantitative data as well (costs, revenue, distribution, viewer attendance, length of availability).

To further illustrate the many different types of data that academic writers analyze, and how they work together to advance knowledge, examine this article from the magazine *Science News*. The section excerpted discusses the MERS and H7N9 viruses. It appeared as part of a larger article titled "Science News Top 25." The "Top 25" identified the top-ranked 25 articles from *Science News* across the year 2013. The excerpt here was #5 on this list.

The annotations point to the many types of data academic writers across disciplines might analyze in relation to this topic.

Excerpt from "A Double Dose of Virus Scares"
by T. Hesman Saey

Outbreaks of two deadly viruses captured the world's attention in 2013, but neither turned into the global pandemic expected to strike one of these years.

Scholars in public health analyze data sets about pandemics.

One of the viruses, known as MERS, causes Middle East respiratory syndrome. The other, H7N9, is a new bird flu virus from China. Each virus has infected fewer than 200 people, but both kill a sizable number of the people who contract them. Although the viruses have not spread far from where they started, the scientific effort to decipher and combat them has had global reach.

Engineers and computer scientists analyze data to determine which news stories from a given year are the most "popular."

Statisticians examine data about disease risk and death.

Journalists analyze other news stories to understand how to research and write as effectively as possible.

Scholars in English or Literature analyze data about "outbreak narratives" and "patient zero."

The MERS virus was first isolated from a patient in Saudi Arabia by an Egyptian physician who sent the sample to the Netherlands to be tested. The researchers in the lab of Ron Fouchier (who made headlines in 2012 for work on the bird flu virus H5N1) deciphered the MERS virus's genetic makeup. It turned out that MERS is a coronavirus related to SARS, a virus identified in 2003 as the cause of severe acute respiratory syndrome (*SN 3/23/13, p. 5*).

Geographers analyze data to produce maps representing the spread of disease.

Chemists and biologists analyze data sets about test samples and genetics.

Since it first appeared in people in 2012, MERS has sickened 163 people, killing 71. Most of the victims live in Saudi Arabia, Qatar or the United Arab Emirates, or had recently traveled to the Arabian peninsula.

Scholars in visual studies analyze data sets consisting of medical images.

A transmission electron micrograph shows the Coronavirus responsible for Middle East respiratory syndrome in action.

From *Science News* (184), 2013.

H7N9, a new strain of avian influenza, began circulating in China in February. The outbreak peaked by early April, nearly halting after Chinese officials closed live poultry markets.

Economists analyze data about the economic impact of closing live poultry markets.

Still, sporadic cases appeared in the summer and fall, raising concerns that the virus could make a resurgence in the coming flu season (*SN Online: 10/15/13*). By early December, of the 139 people with confirmed H7N9 infections, 45 had died.

It came as a surprise that this type of bird virus was seriously sickening and killing people. Experts have been worried for a long time that the H5N1 bird flu would sweep the globe as the 1918 Spanish flu did.

Historians analyze data about the prior pandemics.

If H5N1 gained the ability to spread from person to person through the air while retaining its potency, it could potentially kill millions. But until this year, no serious human infections with H7N9 had ever been recorded.

As more and more cases of MERS and H7N9 infection appeared, scientists and health workers scrambled to investigate basic questions about the viruses: Where did they come from? How did they get into humans? How do they infect cells?

Sociologists analyze data about surveillance and public health policy.

And perhaps most important, do they spread easily from person to person, becoming a candidate for a pandemic? Only partial answers have emerged, and some are not comforting.

Researchers found molecular handles on human cells that the MERS virus grasps during infection (*SN Online: 3/13/13*). One study re-

Cultural anthropologists analyze data about human interactions and behaviors that can contribute to the spread of disease.

Molecular biologists or biochemists analyze data about cells.

vealed that H7N9 can grow well in human lung cells (*SN Online: 7/3/13*).

Studies of ferrets revealed that H7N9 can spread through the air from one of the animals to another, raising the possibility that it might also pass from person to person that way (*SN Online: 5/23/13*). But so far, the virus

Ethicists analyze data about medical research on animals.

hasn't been easily transmitted between people. A few people may have spread the virus to their relatives, but most people probably caught it from chickens, ducks, pigeons or other birds at live poultry markets (*SN Online: 4/12/13, 4/15/13*).

71
MERS deaths
since September
2012

45
H7N9 deaths
in 2013

Statisticians analyze data about the number of infections and deaths to generate mathematical models for the spread of and impact of disease.

But the MERS virus does spread from person to person, particularly among people who are elderly or have other health problems. Hospital dialysis wards proved important for at least one big outbreak (*SN Online: 6/19/13*).

Veterinarians and evolutionary anthropologists analyze data about bat and camel behavior.

Researchers have been using DNA data and old-fashioned health sleuthing to track down the source of the MERS virus. It probably originated in bats and may have spread to camels and other animals before infecting humans (*SN: 9/21/13, p. 18; SN Online: 8/8/13, 10/9/13*). Whatever its origin, MERS probably made the leap from animals to people multiple times

Scholars in public policy analyze data about pandemics in order to create policies for global pandemic cooperation.

Psychologists analyze data about anxiety and concern among people.

(*SN: 10/19/13, p. 16*). New cases of the virus continue to emerge, and there is ongoing concern that it could become a worldwide problem.

Again, it is important to emphasize that academic writers from different disciplines often analyze the same types of data with different, but sometimes overlapping, approaches. For instance, while the economists in the example above might analyze agricultural market exchanges, they might also analyze the same data as psychologists do about anxiety; economists, though, might examine that same data to learn the economic impact of public anxiety. While no one individual academic writer has mastered analysis across all the different types of data, academic writers must nevertheless be equipped to analyze multiple different data types.

Writer Insights

What analytical tools do you use?

With websites, there are four main technologies that can be used to collect data about website traffic, or "clickstream data": web logs, web beacons, JavaScript tags, and packet sniffing.

~Kyle James,
Internet Marketing and Web Development Consultant,
Boston, Massachusetts, United States

Transfer at Work

Academic writers across disciplines draw on data from the American Time Use Survey (ATUS), but with different methods and for different purposes. Economists Nany Folbre and Jayoung Yoon, for instance, use the Tobit statistical method with ATUS data to emphasize the importance of terminology between "child care activity" and "child in your care" in understanding how child care is distributed among men and women:

Table 7 Variations in child care activities and supervisory responsibility for children by day of week (married and cohabiting persons in a household with the youngest child under 6 but no child over 12), hours per day, 2003 ATUS

	Weekday			Weekend		
	Male ($n = 1158$)	Female ($n = 1344$)	Male/female	Male ($n = 1276$)	Female ($n = 1460$)	Male/female
Primary child care activity	1.04 (0.05)	2.69** (0.08)	.39	1.13 (0.06)	1.81 (0.06)	.63
Child "in-your-care"	3.41** (0.12)	6.63** (0.14)	.51	7.75 (0.18)	9.79 (0.14)	.79

Note: standards errors in brackets

** Differences in means of each definition of child care for subgroups of men and women between weekday and weekend statistically significant at $p < 0.01\%$

Meanwhile, biologists and health psychologists use ATUS data with SUDAAN 9.0 statistical analysis to examine differences in the intensity and duration of adolescents' sports and exercise:

Table 2. Differences in the intensity and duration of adolescents' sports and exercise bouts across physical and social environments

	Intensity				Duration			
	% Vigorous (boys)†		% Vigorous (girls)†		Minutes (boys)‡		Minutes (girls)‡	
	M	SE	M	SE	M	SE	M	SE
Physical environment								
Outdoors	40.0	1.0^a,b,c,d	54.0	2.0^a,b,c,d	120.91	2.34^a,b,c	89.46	2.59^a,b,c
Home	47.0	1.0^a,e,f,g	49.0	2.0^a,e,f,g	78.72	1.78^a,d,e,f	60.69	1.94^a,d,e,f
Someone else's house	55.0	2.0^b,e,h,i	14.0	3.0^b,e,h,i	98.27	2.52^b,d,g,h	89.55	4.08^d,g,h
School	64.0	1.0^c,f,h,j	35.0	2.0^c,f,h	119.30	1.85^c,g,i	119.39	2.05^b,e,g
Other/unspecified	37.0	1.0^d,g,i,j	37.0	1.0^d,g,i	105.87	1.87^c,f,h,i	80.29	2.20^c,f,h,i
Social environment								
Alone	46.0	1.0^a,b,c	48.0	2.0^a,b,c	76.78	1.55^a,b,c	58.04	2.03^a,b,c
Family	33.0	2.0^a,d,e	44.0	2.0^a,d,e	95.58	2.96^a,d,e	73.55	2.37^a,d,e
Friends/acq./other	54.0	1.0^b,d,f	35.0	1.0^b,d	117.96	1.25^b,d,f	109.14	1.87^b,d,f
Multiple categories	38.0	2.0^c,e,f	34.0	2.0^c,e	124.69	2.78^c,e,f	85.56	2.54^c,e,f

Note. M = mean; *SE* = standard error; from 2003–06 American Time Use Survey; Other/unspecified physical environments = place of worship, work, gym/health club, and other; acq. = acquaintances; Multiple categories = more than one type of companion (e.g., friends and family together); superscripts (e.g., ^a,b,c) indicate differences between values are statistically significant at *p* < .05, as tested by the planned contrasts. Total bouts for boys = 816; bouts for girls = 405.
†Predicted marginal proportions describing the percent of bouts reaching vigorous intensity (> 6.0 metabolic equivalents) from multinomial logistic regressions, which are adjusted for age, race/ethnicity, season, day of the week, and time of day.
‡Predicted marginal means describing the mean duration (minutes) of bouts reaching from linear regressions, which are adjusted for age, race/ethnicity, season, day of the week, and time of day.

Write Now

Select a news article on a topic of interest to you. Using the excerpt as a model, annotate the article you have selected by noting the different types of data that could be analyzed in relation to that topic.

Transfer Hub: Contribute your summary and see what others have written at fountainheadpress.com/transferhub.

Questions that Shape Analysis

Learning how to conduct and write analysis requires both posing and answering key questions about the writing occasion in question. With each new writing occasion, your transfer-based approach to writing invites you to take into account such matters as purpose, disciplinary context, tools, and data as you develop a plan for analysis. There are likely discipline-specific or content-specific analytic questions that will help frame your analysis appropriately for any given writing occasion. In a literary essay, for instance, it would be customary to use in-depth textual analysis, and so you could develop your analysis plan accordingly. Therefore, if you are seeking to explore the use of metaphor in Herman Melville's *Moby Dick*, you would likely conduct textual analysis of passages in the novel and perhaps of other academic articles about the novel. With a scientific article, it would be uncommon (though not unheard of) to use in-depth textual analysis. Instead, your research questions might lead you to use statistical analysis to analyze quantitative data generated from research experiments.

Your data set and disciplinary purpose will help you determine the type of analysis you might adopt. Sometimes analysis is conducted exclusively through thinking, but many modes of analysis rely on tools, technologies, or specific theoretical approaches. In statistics or ecology, for example, academic writers might use a software program called "R" for analyzing graphics and statistics ("What is R?"). If you are conducting a rhetorical analysis of an advertisement for an English course, your tools will likely involve using the terminology from the Aristotelian appeals and the rhetorical triangle. Taking into consideration these important matters of context will enable you to conduct and write your analyses more effectively across disciplinary occasions.

TABLE 7.1 Questions that shape analysis.

Purpose(s)	Are you hoping to understand a text, concept, or artifact in more depth? Or, are you trying to predict an outcome of some sort? Are you testing a hypothesis? What multiple purposes might you have for conducting analysis?
Disciplinary perspective and publication context	What is your disciplinary perspective for this writing project? What forms of and methods for analysis do other writers in that discipline engage with? What are the overarching inquiries driving that discipline and how can analysis help writers build knowledge toward those questions?

Research questions	What are your research questions? How can you tailor your approach to analysis to help you pursue those questions most effectively? What analytic methods will enable you to fully explore your research questions?
Data	What data do you currently have? What data will you need to collect? What are the best methods for analyzing the data that you have or will collect?
Tools and technologies	What tools, equipment, and technologies might you need for this anlaysis? Will you be relying primarily on in-depth reading practices or observer impressions, or might you use a software such as NVivo or Provalis? What tools, equipment, and technologies do you have access to and knowledge about? Which tools, technologies and methods will best facilitate your analytic goals?

Criteria for Effective Analysis

Criteria for effective analysis are contingent on the writing occasion, disciplinary context, and individual purposes. Writers can achieve effective analysis by understanding their purposes, collecting relevant data, and then tailoring their approaches within an acceptable framework. Recognizing that different contexts warrant different analytic approaches may require you to learn new methods and strategies with each new occasion for analysis. However, over time, you will likely come to see crossovers, differentiations, and parallels among the many different sorts of analytic work you will be conducting. As a beginning point, you might think of these broad criteria as being important components of effective analysis across disciplinary context, writing occasion, and writer aims.

Grounded on the available data

Whatever analysis you do, it should remain connected to and engaged with the data you have collected and compiled. This means that if you have collected survey responses or field notes, your analysis should be done with these data sets. Whenever possible, avoid making conjectures such as what might have been the results of your analysis if you only had additional data to consider. While some disciplines or writing occasions warrant slightly more conjecture or inference than others, analysis should nonetheless be as closely connected to the data at hand as possible. Disciplines also define data differently, with data including anything from numbers and artifacts to poems and images. Regardless of what the data includes, the analysis should be designed in such a way that it can be readily applied to that data.

The reason writers must link their analytic work to the data at hand is to ensure that they can draw evidence-based conclusions in their arguments. To assert any conclusions about these texts, issues, or concepts with confidence, writers must be able to demonstrate they have arrived at their arguments by examining the evidence-based results of data analysis.

Transfer at Work

Psychology researchers Elisa Gambetti and Fiorella Giusberti conducted a study of 214 people to evaluate the relationship between anger and anxiety traits and financial behavior such as risk attitude and investment decisions. They found that a personality trait of anger predicts risky financial decisions and a personality trait of anxiety predicts conservative financial decisions (1066):

Appendix A

A.1. Instructions for personality traits tests

   A number of statements which people have used to describe themselves are given below. Read each statement and then choose the appropriate number to the right of the statement to indicate how you generally feel. There are no right or wrong answers. Do not spend too much time on any one statement but give the answer which seems to describe how you generally feel.
   [answer on scale from 1 = "almost never" to 4 = "almost always"].

A.2. Trait anxiety (STAI-Y2; Pedrabissi & Santinello, 1989)

   1. I feel pleasant.
   2. I tire quickly.
   3. I feel like crying.
   4. I wish I could be as happy as others seem to be.
   5. I am losing out on things because I can't make up my mind soon enough.
   6. I feel rested.
   7. I am "calm, cool and collected."
   8. I feel that difficulties are piling up so that I cannot overcome them.
   9. I worry too much over something that really doesn't matter.
   10. I am happy.
   11. I am inclined to take things hard.
   12. I lack self-confidence.
   13. I feel secure.
   14. I try to avoid facing a crisis or difficulty.
   15. I feel blue.
   16. I am content.
   17. Some unimportant thought runs through my mind and bothers me.
   18. I take disappointments so keenly that I can't put them out of my mind.
   19. I am a steady person.
   20. I get in a state of tension or turmoil as I think over my recent concerns and interests.

A.3. Trait anger (STAXI-2; Comunian, 2004)

   1. I am a hotheaded person.
   2. I am quick tempered.
   3. I am an impulsive person.
   4. I get angry when I have to wait because of other's mistakes.
   5. I feel annoyed when I am not given recognition for a job well done.
   6. I fly off the handle.
   7. When I get mad, I say nasty things.
   8. I get angry when I'm told I'm wrong in front of others.
   9. When I am frustrated, I feel like hitting someone.
   10. I feel infuriated when I do a good job and get a poor evaluation.

Conducted thoroughly and repeatedly

Effective analysis takes time and often involves a degree of repetition and recursivity. Writers can conduct analysis at varying points in the research and writing process, from the very beginning of the process as a way of prewriting, to midway through the process, as data are emerging, and/or at the end of the research process after all the data have been collected. Analysis also requires a measure of patience as the methods and results might shift in response to new data that emerge during the research and writing process.

   Imagine a writing occasion in which a researcher is analyzing data from an ethnographic study in cultural anthropology about the intersections between culture and medical care. Perhaps a researcher in medical anthropology is collecting data through fieldwork at a clinic and conducts analysis along the way based on her field notes. With each new conversation she has, she will receive additional data to analyze. The process of qualitative coding, for example, might involve her reading notes to determine possible categories and then reconsidering, adapting, adding to, or deleting those categories as she moves forward with the analysis and acquires additional data. Perhaps after she has herself coded the data, she will decide to use qualitative coding software and thereby discover features of the data she might not have uncovered without that additional layer of analysis. All of these elements of analysis, repeated and reconsidered, will enable her to conduct thorough analysis that can lead her to develop nuanced, well-articulated arguments.

Explicated fully

Although the person conducting the analysis might think much of the analysis will be readily apparent to others, readers will likely need a thorough explication in order to understand an analysis; this refers in part to a full explication of your methodological approach to data. A methods section is found in many writing projects and describes in detail how the researcher(s) collected or sampled data, the analytic framework or methods used, and any limitations posed by those methods.

Explicating analysis fully also means including copious and clear discussion and detail about the results of the analysis. Many writers will even present analysis results in multiple formats, such as a table and an explication of the table. Those in the humanities conducting qualitative analysis will explicate fully by including a quote or excerpt and then drawing out for readers how the analysis yields particular insights or implications from that evidence. If analytic results seem altogether entirely self-evident, then the researcher may do well to return to the data and conduct more analysis. Ideally, most occasions for analysis should illustrate ideas that would not be immediately obvious to those who have spent less time (or no time) examining the data. Explicating data fully is your opportunity to demonstrate your expertise and knowledge based on having conducted the research.

Oriented toward discovery

Researchers should approach analysis in the interest of discovery. Since research is driven by questions, analysis should be approached as a process of inquiry and learning. If you approach a set of data with a predetermined, inflexible agenda for your analysis, it is likely you will miss important results from the analysis. It is also likely you may only find confirmation of your agenda. Humans are curiously capable of finding exactly what they want in data, whether inadvertently or explicitly.

Embracing an approach to analysis grounded on discovery means that if you find contradictions in the data, you should address them directly rather than discounting or ignoring them. If you notice a trend in the data, but one subset of the data does not fit with the trend, you can use that atypical data to generate a qualification in the conclusion or to raise the possibility of additional research. Discovery might also lead you to decide to use a different approach toward analysis altogether. Effective analysis should be open-minded and flexible, responsive to the data you investigate and the insights you uncover.

Aligned with disciplinary methods

Analysis should generally be linked to methods in the discipline in which you are writing. In English literature, scholars might analyze texts through rhetorical analysis or critical discourse analysis. In mathematics, academic writers might use real or complex analysis. In sociology, academic writers often use dynamic network analysis or frame analysis. These discipline-based methods are not exclusive to these disciplines, but they have come to be widely adopted within those disciplines because the methods fit well with the kinds of data being collected and the research questions often being explored.

In order to align your analytic method to that of your discipline, read others' scholarship and determine the methods that writers in those disciplines tend to use. You will likely find that researchers use a variety of analytic methods, so you can compile this list and then choose from among the options the one(s) that fits best with your data, research questions, and available resources. If you decide to depart from accepted analytic methodologies or tools in a field, do so explicitly by expressing why you are applying a somewhat atypical or anomalous analytical method.

Focused on argument and purpose

Once you have conducted analysis, you will likely have a large array of findings and results. When you write the analysis as part of your argument, you will need to focus your analysis so that it includes only the aspects most relevant to or significant for your overall argument and your main purpose. Neglecting to narrow your analysis appropriately can result in an argument that veers off track into complicated details, thereby losing your readers' attention.

When you choose which aspects of analysis to include in any given writing project, select the elements that carry the most significance or importance; you can always save the other elements for another, subsequent writing project. Then, as you move through the analysis in your argument, remind readers frequently what the overarching implications are of this analysis for your argument. Be careful not to assume readers will easily understand how data and analysis will work together to advance a perspective, position, or argument.

Modes of Analysis

Numerous modes of analysis exist across and within academic disciplines. It would be nearly impossible to name, much less describe, all the modes of analysis that operate across disciplines. In the list provided, you will find overviews of the most common forms of analysis you are likely to encounter in your undergraduate academic writing career:

- rhetorical analysis
- critical discourse analysis
- content analysis
- visual analysis
- scientific data analysis
- statistical analysis
- Big Data analysis

And, in keeping with the overarching line of inquiry in this chapter, each of the example readings is related to the *Science News* article excerpt that was first discussed.

Rhetorical analysis

Rhetorical analysis examines how text (written, verbal, or visual) influences readers. Nelson Graff, a writing faculty member at San Francisco State University, describes rhetorical analysis as follows:

> [R]hetorical analysis [means] examining not only what authors communicate but also for what purposes they communicate those messages, what effects they attempt to evoke in readers, and how they accomplish those purposes and effects. Rhetorical analysis often involves the study of rhetorical appeals (*ethos*, *pathos*, and *logos*), the purposes and aims of symbolic communication, and the structure of arguments.

Graff's definition illustrates that rhetorical analysis centers on the elements of the rhetorical situation, or the rhetorical triangle, as described in Chapter 4: Reading. While the key terms affiliated with rhetorical analysis include *ethos*, *pathos*, and *logos*, Graff makes it clear that rhetorical analysis is also grounded on matters of purpose and how communication impacts readers.

When writers engage in rhetorical analysis, they focus on one or more of the following elements (described in brief here; for more expansive descriptions, see Featured In-Depth Reading Strategy: Reading Rhetorically in Chapter 4, p. 142):

- **Author:** Who created/wrote the text? How might a person's background or circumstances inform the text?
- **Audience:** Who do you think are the primary readers/viewers of the text? Why?
- **Message:** What is the author seeking to communicate through the text? What is being argued or shared in the text? In what ways might metaphors, similes, and other figures of speech play a role in communicating that message?
- **Purpose:** What do you think are the primary aims or purposes of the text?
- ***Ethos:*** What kind of character does the writer construct?
- ***Pathos:*** How does the writer appeal to readers' emotions?
- ***Logos:*** How does the writer appeal to readers' sense of logic and reason?
- ***Kairos:*** How does the writer establish the timeliness of the text and address propriety through conventions and features of the text?

Academic writers conduct a rhetorical analysis on texts, speeches, artifacts, events, film, advertisements, and images. Rhetorical analysis can be applied to written, oral, or visual texts, in print or digital environments.

To demonstrate how rhetorical analysis can be applied across a wide range of texts and to illustrate the significance of rhetorical analysis, two examples are provided.

Example 1: Rhetorical Analysis, Rhetoric

The first example comes from an article published in the *Rhetoric Review,* titled "The New Smallpox: An Epidemic of Words?" written by Barbara Heifferon, a rhetorician at Clemson University. Heifferon uses rhetorical analysis to examine historical and contemporary medical rhetoric about smallpox vaccinations. She examines a variety of texts, including letters to the editor, seventeenth-century medical nonfiction, and contemporary advertisements.

The excerpt illustrates Heifferon's rhetorical analysis of visual discourse. The paragraphs come from a subsection of her article titled "The Role of Visual Communication in Smallpox Vaccinations."

Excerpt from "The New Smallpox: An Epidemic of Words?" by B. A. Heifferon

On the December 11, 2002 airing of *60 Minutes* on CBS, the smallpox report included graphic pictures showing side effects of the complications resulting from smallpox vaccination. The pictures, in full color, represented the most extreme results and

> Heifferon describes the ways in which the *60 Minutes* report persuades viewers by way of *pathos,* evoking emotion—fear in this case.

could easily scare even the most medically sophisticated citizens away from vaccinations. There was little mention of the fact that the vaccine itself does not result in smallpox (thus the graphic pictures were not of smallpox), but in a less harmful form of virus called vaccinia, … commonly referred to as cowpox. Yes, it too is ugly. But the results are less threatening and very much less common than infection with the actual smallpox virus in an epidemic. The rash occurs in very few people and is not life threatening. It would have given a more complete picture and

> She emphasizes that the rhetoricians who designed the "graphic pictures" made choices designed to influence their audience to be fearful of the vaccinations.

been a better use of visual communication to show graphic pictures of smallpox itself, that is, what happens if one doesn't get vaccinated and contracts the disease.

Because smallpox has been eradicated in the world, what we have not seen or experienced recently has little valence for us. If active cases were part of our recent memory, as they are in Africa and other [locations around the world], we would have a more realistic context into which to place today's discussions. In other [locations] like Africa in which people remember smallpox cases in their not-so-distant past, there are graphic pictures in their memories of the suffering and disfigurement from this disease. In addition, constant reminders, often viewed daily, in the form of scarred bodies, still signal and visually communicate

---

From *Rhetoric Review* (25.1), 2006.

> Heifferon discusses who the audience is and why they might be particularly susceptible to fear about vaccinations, namely because Americans do not have "recent memory" of the impact of smallpox itself.

the reality of smallpox, unlike the visuals we experience only through our media in this culture....

Thus our Western experience decontextualizes the disease itself. The corrective would be to visually communicate the experiences of smallpox in countries where the epidemic ended more recently, interview members of this population, or at least show graphic pictures of cases of smallpox on U.S. programs rather than graphic pic-

> At the end of this section, Heifferon reiterates her main point of this rhetorical analysis: the discourse creates fear about the vaccine instead of the disease.

tures of complications from vaccinia. However, because our recent American experience does not include the visual and physical memories of active smallpox cases, the risk factors of the vaccination itself take center stage. Through such discourse more fear is created about the vaccine than about the disease itself.

As Heifferon's analysis demonstrates, audience plays a critical role. She makes the argument that the *60 Minutes's* rhetoric is only as effective as it is because most Americans who are watching *60 Minutes* lack a cultural memory of the devastating effects of smallpox to offset fears about vaccine-related side effects. In turn, understanding more about the role of audience in shaping meaning within a message enables readers or viewers to be more self-aware and reflective about the ways in which they might be influenced by subsequent messages.

Example 2: Rhetorical Analysis, Composition and English

Where Heifferon focuses on audience, this second example illustrates how advertising uses the Aristotelian appeals and *kairos* to influence consumers. In this article, Jessica Lundgren, an undergraduate at Pennsylvania State University, University Park, at the time of her publication, conducts a rhetorical analysis on the "Fresh Fit" online Subway restaurant advertising campaign. Through her examination of eight online advertisements that are part of this campaign, Lundgren pursues the question: how does Subway's "use of rhetoric...cause consumers to misunderstand the nutritional value of Subway's menu items?" She makes the argument that Subway's approach misleads customers into thinking the restaurant chain's items are healthier than they are.

Excerpt from "'Eating Fresh' in America: Subway Restaurant's Nutritional Rhetoric"
by J. Lundgren

No fast food restaurant has focused on the "healthiness" of its products to the extent that Subway Restaurant has over the past near decade. In 2000, the restaurant's famous "Jared" campaign first shared the story of Jared Fogle, who lost 245 pounds in one year by following a diet that consisted primarily of Subway sandwiches ("The Subway Diet").... While Subway's sales continue to grow rapidly (and with Jared still appearing in many of its commercials), America's obesity rates also are increasing at a shocking pace.... To understand how restaurants like Subway influence the American diet, it is critical

> Lundgren establishes just how persuasive the campaign has been, showing that their rhetorical methods worked quite successfully. This discussion establishes *kairos* by showing how timely this inquiry is given the "obesity crisis."

to examine their advertising strategies in order to ascertain specifically how their advertisements work to persuade potential customers....

> Lundgren demonstrates that rhetorical analysis serves a valuable purpose by helping forge a link between advertising and nutrition. She coins the phrase "nutritional rhetoric" to describe this mode of communication.

For the purposes of my study, I define rhetoric as the persuasive methods applied by Subway Restaurant to entice television viewers to purchase its products. I specifically concentrate on ads that make a deliberate appeal to the nutritional and health concerns of the average television viewer; I designate this rhetorical focus as "nutritional rhetoric."...

Rhetoric of Comparison

MacArthur and Cuneo take note of the current trend of "comparative ads," which are used in attempts to demonstrate why one company's product is superior to a related company's product.... The Fresh Fit campaign in particular uses comparison to present the argument that Subway's food is healthier than other restaurants' fast food options....

> Rhetorical analysis involves looking at figures of speech, such as the comparisons in advertisements. In this case, Subway uses comparative language to suggest it provides healthier food than its competitors. Lundgren demonstrates that this is part of the *logos* of the advertisements—part of the way in which the message is effective at promoting Subway over others.

In an advertisement featuring Subway's Jared and the champion figure skater Kimmie Meissner, the announcer states that "the delicious Subway Foot-Long Club" has "less than half the fat of a Big Mac."

These comparisons establish the logos of the advertisements. They present the television viewer with negative images or facts related

From *Young Scholars in Writing* (6), 2008.

to rival companies, and then contrast this information with the "better-for-you" nature of a specific type of Subway meal. This approach may influence a consumer to feel that he or she has received strong evidence that Subway Restaurant sells healthier food than other fast food restaurants. Equipped with this understanding, a person may feel that he or she is prepared to make informed and health-conscious decisions concerning future fast food meals....

Implied Undesirability of Weight Gain

The premise of several of the Fresh Fit commercials is that greasy fast food items will result in weight gain, and that this increased amount of body fat is undesirable primarily because of its physical appearance. The rhetorical nature of the perception of body fat in American culture is explored by Sonya Christine Brown, who asserts, "Body shape and size are aspects of physical ethos that Americans focus on" (10). She states: "Fat is ...perceived as the visible, physical evidence that a body is likely to be unhealthy, unwell, unfit" (39), and adds that "to be fat is to be scorned." The relationship between fat and ethos clearly is a rhetorical basis of Subway's advertisements. In one ad, a man pulls up to a drive-through window and asks, "Can I get the love handles, double chin, and some blubber?" The female in his car requests the same, but substitutes for the blubber "thunder thighs and a badonkadonk butt." Another, similar advertisement is located in an office setting, where one character announces his intention to go to "Burger Town." He takes the orders of his coworkers, which include "the can-my-butt-look-any-bigger meal," "the extra-tight-pants combo," the "feel-so-bloated-I-just-want-to-sleep-for-three-days meal," and "a-bucket-of-please-keep-your-shirt-on."

> Lundgren builds on Brown's assertion about body shape contributing to the construction of *ethos*. Lundgren shows that Subway capitalizes on how other fast food restaurants contribute to this negative *ethos* of unhealthiness.

> By providing details about the focus on fat, Lundgren demonstrates how "the relationship between fat and *ethos* clearly is a rhetorical basis" for the advertising campaign.

In addition to its appeals to ethos, this aspect of Subway's advertisements employs pathos to get the consumer's attention by insinuating that (1) if people consume certain types of fast food, they likely will become overweight or obese and that (2) the consumer himself should fear becoming overweight or obese and (3) as a way to protect himself from this fate, he should choose instead to eat the healthier fast food options that are offered at Subway. This approach attempts to plant in the

> Lundgren demonstrates that the ads appeal to *pathos* by invoking fear of obesity and suspicion of other restaurants.

consumer's mind suspicion regarding other fast food establishments, and then asks the consumer to consider that Subway actually can prevent him or her from acquiring "blubber."

Lundgren's rhetorical analysis shows the complex ways in which language can work to persuade consumers. While some may wonder if the creators of the advertising campaign were deliberate in invoking this "nutritional rhetoric," Lundgren's points about the significance of rhetorical analysis make questions about intentionality of less consequence. For Lundgren, the possible impact of the campaign on viewers, the potential for them to be misguided, and the continued prevalence of obesity in America make the rhetorical analysis meaningful. As Lundgren shows the many ways in which rhetorical appeals function in advertising, she also demonstrates the significance of rhetorical analysis as a means of understanding how language and images persuade consumers, often in subtle but powerful ways.

Write Now

Locate a website or advertisement about a topic of interest to you, perhaps involving medical rhetoric, or about some other area of inquiry. Practice conducting a rhetorical analysis on the website by focusing on the elements of rhetorical analysis described above in this section: author, audience, message, purpose, *ethos, pathos, logos,* and *kairos.*

Critical discourse analysis

Academic writers can define **critical discourse analysis** (CDA), also termed discourse analysis, quite differently. In *The Discourse Reader*, editors Adam Jaworski and Nikolaus Copeland offer eleven differently nuanced definitions of the term. Despite these different perspectives, however, many can agree that discourse analysis concerns itself, at heart, with the ways in which language reflects and shapes larger social, historical, and ideological forces. Put another way, CDA "explicitly draws our attention to issues of power and privilege" (Huckin, Andrus, and Clary-Lemon). Note also how the *Foundations of Qualitative Research* website from Harvard University defines CDA:

> Discourse analysis is based on the understanding that there is much more going on when people communicate than simply the transfer of information. It is not an effort to capture literal meanings; rather it is the investigation of what language does or what individuals or cultures accomplish through language. This area of study raises questions such as how meaning is constructed, and how power functions in society.

This definition emphasizes the ways in which critical discourse analysis intersects with notions of power and perspective. By raising questions about how language and communication participate in constructing meaning and influencing perspectives, critical discourse analysis demonstrates the power language can have over knowledge, perception, and thinking.

Scholars deploy discourse analysis across a wide range of texts, including written and spoken. In *The Handbook on Discourse Analysis*, editors Deborah Schiffrin, Deborah Tannen, and Heidi E. Hamilton, all linguists, examine discourse analysis on political discourse, the media, and racism, as well as litigation discourse, medical discourse, educational discourse, and institutional discourse. Scholars can employ qualitative or quantitative approaches to discourse analysis.

The example demonstrates discourse analysis both on the media and on medical discourse. The excerpt is from Priscilla Wald's book *Contagious: Cultures, Carriers, and the Outbreak Narrative*. In *Contagious,* Wald analyzes historical and contemporary discourse from media texts and medical journals to argue that they turn diseases and narratives about the outbreak of diseases into narratives with significant social implications, often involving stigmatization and hierarchical power divisions among certain social classes or ethnic groups.

In the chapter from which this segment emerges, Wald analyzes the way early twentieth-century media and medical journals wrote about Mary Mallon, an immigrant who worked as a cook in New York at the turn of the twentieth century and who was identified as the first person to carry typhoid without having symptoms of the disease herself. Wald argues that the outbreak narrative surrounding Mallon, also known as "Typhoid Mary" led to "society's blaming and stigmatizing immigrants because of their association with communicable disease (especially venereal disease)."

The excerpted reading demonstrates Wald's critical discourse analysis as she discusses the language in Dr. George Soper's early twentieth-century accounts of his investigation into Mallon and the typhoid outbreak.

Excerpt from *Contagious: Cultures, Carriers, and the Outbreak Narrative* by P. Wald

Mary Mallon's recalcitrance, her reluctance to believe she was spreading typhoid and her unwillingness to meet with public-health officials became more central and elaborately recounted each time Soper told the story. With each version, Soper fleshed out the details of her life, shifting his emphasis from the detection of the carrier to a more comprehensive portrait of the woman. In his 1919 version, from an article titled "Typhoid Mary," Soper described the help that he had had in arranging a surprise interview with the reluctant cook from "a friend whom

> Here, Wald frames the analysis as reflecting a larger trend in Soper's narrative that added details about Typhoid Mary's life.

From *Contagious: Cultures, Carriers, and the Outbreak Narrative*, 2007.

she often visited at night in the top of a Third Avenue tenement." Twenty years later, he would elaborate on their relationship, noting that at the end of her workday, Mallon retired "to a rooming house on Third Avenue below Thirty-third Street, where she was spending the evenings with a disreputable-looking man...[whose] headquarters during the day was in a saloon on the corner. I got to be well acquainted with him," Soper admits. "He took me to see the room. I should not care to see another like it. It was a place of dirt and disorder. It was not improved by the presence of a large dog of which Mary was said to be very fond." The dirt and disorder mark social margins and the hint of categorical breakdown, which Soper casts in sexual terms. Typhoid is not a sexually transmitted disease, but with his attention to the evident sexual activity of this unmarried Irish woman whose affection for her lover's dog adds to Soper's disgust, he summoned the conventions of a venereal-disease narrative. Mallon inhabited the spaces and indulged in the behavior of a fallen woman, and Soper's depiction implicitly coded her disease as a result of her illicit behavior.

> Wald analyzes Soper's text by pointing out how details like the dog, dirt, and disorder resonate with venereal disease narratives and position Mallon as a "fallen woman" who had somehow brought typhoid on herself.

Content analysis

Academic writers conduct **content analysis** across disciplines as a way of categorizing and organizing data in a wide variety of texts. Academic writers who conduct content analysis create categories, sometimes conceived of as conceptual "bins," for their data, and then "code" the data by placing parts of the data into these predetermined categories. Content analysis helps researchers understand the quantity of certain kinds of data and relationships across that data. Nearly any written or verbal content can be used for content analysis, from books and interviews to commercials and magazines.

Authors Stefan Timmermans and Steven Haas, both professors of sociology (UCLA and Penn State, respectively), use content analysis to analyze issues of a journal called *Sociology of Health and Illness* to point out a research gap in their discipline and to "argue for a sociology of health, illness, and disease." The excerpted reading discusses results from "a content analysis of the 10 most recent years of original articles published in *Sociology of Health and Illness* (1997–2006)." The authors likely created a coding schema for their research, identifying categories and key terms, and then identified which articles fit into particular categories.

Excerpt from "Towards a Sociology of Disease" by S. Timmermans and S. Haas

> Timmermans and Haas use content analysis to identify how many original articles address a disease category.

The [underrepresentation in the literature of engagement by medical sociologists with diseases] can easily be found in the contributions to *Sociology of Health and Illness*. Between 1997 and 2006, 21 percent of original articles (82 out of 387 articles) published in SHI involved a specific disease category, meaning that the overwhelming majority did not deal with diseases. The most written-about diseases were HIV (16 articles) and various cancers (14 articles), stroke (6 articles), heart disease (5 articles), and depression (4 articles), followed by anorexia, asthma, and chronic back pain (3 articles). These figures do not necessarily mean that the authors paid attention to disease as a biological phenomenon because they included every possible topic related to disease such as, for example, the media representation or historical development of a disease classification. If we further limit the articles to those dealing with disease as a health issue for patients and/or clinicians, the pool shrinks to 16 per cent (60 out of 387).

> Here, Timmermans and Haas have looked through each article to identify which diseases are mentioned the most. Such diseases as cancers, stroke, heart disease, etc. likely represent the disease categories they created in their content analysis.

From *Sociology of Health & Illness* (30.5), 2008.

Visual analysis

While visual analysis overlaps with several other modes of analysis (rhetorical analysis and data analysis in particular), it also merits a focused consideration because of its prevalence across disciplines. This section is also connected to the section on reading visual images in Chapter 4: Reading, and visual arguments in Chapter 10: Designing Arguments.

Visual analysis involves an in-depth consideration of the component parts of an image, be it a photograph, advertisement, painting, digital image, cartoon, graphic, or even a moving image such as a film, video game, documentary, performance, or video. Note that film studies and performance studies are entire disciplines with well-established modes of analysis. This section is intended to offer you a starting point you can extend, modify, and build upon with further exploration into visually oriented disciplines such as these.

Visual analysis treats visual images as a form of text, in the sense that images can contribute to (or form the foundation of) arguments in many of the same ways as written text. Visual images, though, also have unique features that warrant additional analytic tools.

For instance, when conducting a visual analysis, a writer might draw on the same rhetorical strategies described above. However, because of the unique features of visual images, visual analysis also asks that a viewer consider other questions in particular.

TABLE 7.2 Questions to consider for visual analysis.

What message is the visual image conveying?

What is the purpose of the visual image?

How does the visual image evoke emotions (*pathos*)?

How does the visual image appeal to viewers' sense of reason and logic (*logos*)?

How does the creator of the image (author) establish her credibility or construct her character?

How does the visual image establish *kairos*?

Who do you think is the primary viewer for this image? Why?

Who created the image? Why? How might his background impact viewers' interpretation of the image?

What is in the foreground? How does it help the image achieve its aim?

What is in the background? Why do you think the image's creator included it?

What might be beyond the frame of the visual image? Why do you think the creator of the image chose to make the boundaries/frame in this way?

What is the relationship between the visual image and text (if there is text)?

What is the purpose of the visual image whether in its original context and/or in a repurposed context?

Where are the visual images located in a text/document? How does that positioning impact their efficacy?

Where is the focal point of the image?

If there are humans in the image, where are they looking, and why?

What details do you notice about the objects in the image?

What details do you notice about the subjects in the image?

Conducting a thorough visual analysis with the kinds of questions in Table 7.2 requires significant time. As with written texts, those conducting an in-depth analysis should be prepared to spend considerable time thinking about the image, returning to it on many occasions and allowing the analysis of it to percolate with time and deliberateness.

This visual analysis example comes from an article in which Anita Helle discusses photographer Dorothea Lange's photographs depicting rural health care during the Great Depression. Helle is working in a branch of inquiry called narrative medicine, which bridges medicine and the humanities. In this article, Helle pursues the question: how did Lange's photographs work to shape and impact perceptions about New Deal healthcare initiatives?

Excerpt from "When the Photograph Speaks:
Photo-Analysis in Narrative Medicine" by A. Helle

Stricken with childhood polio, [photographer Dorothea] Lange was left with talipes equines ("drop foot"), a distorted leg, and an acknowledged desire, from an early age, for a "cloak of invisibility."[46] ...[Linda] Gordon's biography [of Lange] helps us see ...that Lange's body of photographic work, like her life, is "haunted by feet."[47] ...The photographs depict feet splayed in dirt, feet dancing and playing, mothers' and children's feet, calloused feet against rough boards (with "healing" bracelet) seen at eye level (see figure 2), bare feet on donkey riders, feet seen from a distance and close up, feet from Lange's trips to Alabama and Mississippi as well as her later travels in Asia.

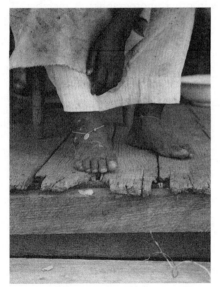

Helle shows through Figure 2 how the feet are the focus of the image. In this case, we have a greater sense of the significance of the focal point based on Lange's biographical history.

Figure 2.   Dorothea Lange. Fifty-seven year old sharecropper woman. Hinds County, Mississippi, 1937. Thin dimes around the ankles to prevent headaches. Library of Congress, Prints and Photographs Division, LC-DIG-fsa-8b32018.

...Consider another of Lange's photographs which bears directly on health care and rural poverty, ... (see figure 3). This remarkable, neglected photograph appears in John Stoeckle and George Abbot White's collection, *Plain Pictures of Plain Doctoring: Vernacular Expression in New Deal Medicine and Photographs....* The stakes of these photographs were

From *Literature and Medicine* (29.2), 2011.

high, sociologically, medically, ethically, artistically. While the administrators of rural "agrarian concerns" wished to build an archive of new health care initiatives as a "good thing," it becomes apparent to anyone who comes to this material for the first time that the relationships between doctors (mostly from volunteer physicians' associations), nurses, and patients have more complex connotations.

The details, frames, and perspectives of the Klamath Falls photograph exceed the FSA-dictated neutral narrative documentary-style caption. We see a typical makeshift trailer, repurposed as the examining room (there are pictures of barns and storefronts in other photographs). A member of the co-op local physicians' association in a formal suit is examining a young girl, while in the background another figure identifiable in the sequence as the "camp nurse," also formally dressed, adjusts the clothing of a young boy sitting on a woman's lap (his mother perhaps) who has just been examined or is waiting his turn. In taking the picture from an angle that keeps the doctor's bulky figure high and in the foreground, Lange's eye has zeroed in on the power differential between doctor and patient. The girl, at three or four, a pale figure, is seated on an examining table—we see from a discrete angle, but can tell she is undressed. The examination table appears also to have been repurposed from a locker or sideboard. It is a delicate situation: the line of vision as the child looks up at the doctor, seeking eye contact as he looks down at her, is structured a priori by the visual template narrative of Madonna and child, a template often at play in Lange's work. In the months that I have studied this photograph, learning more about it, adding narratives and adjusting my vision, the photograph has continued to make me squirm.

> Helle elicits the *kairos* of the photographs, showing that the photographs were part of a larger purpose of seeking to advance perceptions about New Deal healthcare initiatives by influencing viewer perceptions. Given that in 2011, when Helle published this article and debates about Obamacare were occurring, this focus on how public perceptions about health care are shaped has additional *kairotic* appeal.

> Helle describes the photograph in significant detail, from the background to the clothing that the people are wearing.

> Helle addresses the angle of the photograph and how that conveys a power differential.

> Helle addresses the direction of the gaze of the child in the photograph as well, adding to the argument that the physician has complete control over her. This final sentence illustrates the *pathos* that Helle experienced as she considered the image. One can see that she has spent significant time studying the photograph, noticing new aspects over time.

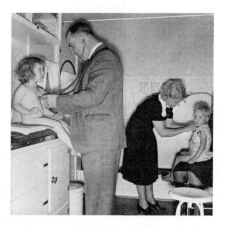

Figure 3. Dorothea Lange. Doctor Examining Child. Kalmath County, Oregon, 1937. Library of Congress Prints and Photographs Division, LC-USF34-021833.

The girl's look evokes the need for approval in a situation that demonstrates her social distance from the doctor, yet also opens up the moment to unfathomable possibilities of shame, embarrassment, confusion. The photograph for me has become more than a singular image, it has become a narrative screen, stirring my own memories of a first visit to the doctor in a different era, a small girl in another smallish, uninteresting room under the scrutinizing gaze of a strange, large man without anyone else anywhere near my size or state of undress or social standing. Perhaps a subliminal rage is stirred, too, because in the subset of photographs of which this one is a part are other photographs which depict makeshift waiting rooms crowded with people; it is all too easy to imagine that in the moments prior to the scene of examination, the small girl may have been among that crowd, having waited a long time for the suited gentleman to appear....

> Helle here refers to that which is outside the frame of the photograph, a waiting room crowded with people.

Write Now

Locate an image of your choice and practice conducting visual analysis by selecting several of the visual analysis questions in Table 7.2 and use them to guide your reading of the image.

Scientific data analysis

Academic writers in scientific fields such as biology, chemistry, and physics analyze data using a wide range of approaches, tools, and methodologies. These writers may at times make use of content and discourse analysis, but their work typically involves more specialized forms of analysis, many of which require technology, lab equipment, and mathematical and statistical knowledge.

In *A Practical Guide to Scientific Data Analysis*, David J. Livingston defines scientific data analysis as "mathematical and statistical procedures which scientists may use in order to extract information from their experimental data." **Scientific data analysis** often results in tables, graphs, and charts that offer a visual depiction of patterns, findings, and other relevant findings.

Each branch of science has multiple analytical methods, many of which overlap. In this example, we look more closely at data analysis in biology. According to Haixu Tang and Sun Kim, scientific data analysis in biology can be divided into two general approaches, hypothesis-driven or data-driven:

> In [the conventional] hypothesis-driven approach, experiments are intentionally designed to collect data only relevant to the to-be-tested hypothesis. [By contrast, the] technology-driven or data-driven approach [emphasizes] a high throughput technique platform, a blind collection of a large amount of data, and a plan of free data sharing to the community.

Tang and Kim develop the term bioinformatics as an important development in data-driven analysis in biology.

This example of analysis emerges from an article about how MERS spreads within various tissues. The team, led by Emmy de Wit, a lecturer and researcher in Earth and Life Sciences at VU University Amsterdam, analyzed tissue samples from rhesus macaques, small primates native to southern and southeast Asia. They argue that animal models "are instrumental for the development of prophylactic and therapeutic countermeasures."

According to their methods section, they used a combination of discipline-specific tests and analytical methods, including histopathology, transmission electron microscopy, microarray data and functional analysis, and serum cytokine and chemokine analysis.

Two segments are included, one excerpt from the "Results" section and one excerpt from the "Discussion" section. Scientific articles often follow a structure known by the acronym IMRAD, which stands for Introduction, Methods, Results, and Discussion.

Excerpt from "Middle East Respiratory Syndrome Coronavirus (MERS-CoV) Causes Transient Lower Respiratory Tract Infection in Rhesus Macaques" by E. de Wit, et al.

Results

We have previously reported the presence of viral RNA and infectious virus throughout the lungs of inoculated macaques, with viral load decreasing between 3 and 6 dpi [days post inoculation]...In addition to the different lung lobes, we have previously

> De Wit, et al. note that they have previously conducted analysis on tissue samples. This suggests that they are operating from a hypothesis-driven approach to analysis in which they are further testing a hypothesis about tissue samples and the presence of viral RNA and infections virus.

analyzed several other tissues, including tissues of the upper respiratory tract, lung lesions, and kidney...Although there was some variation between the different macaques with regard to the presence of viral RNA, we could consistently detect the virus by qRT-PCR in the nasal mucosa, trachea, and mediastinal lymph nodes on 3 dpi (Fig. 3). Furthermore, we could detect viral RNA in conjunctiva, tonsils, oronasopharynx, and in the left and

> De Wit, et al. present the results of their analysis, noting where they detected the virus across the various tissue samples.

right bronchus. Viral loads were lower in these tissues by 6 dpi and viral RNA could no longer be detected in the nasal mucosa or conjunctiva at that time (Fig. 3). Viral RNA could not be detected in kidney or bladder tissue samples.

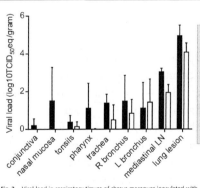

> In Figure 3, de Wit, et al. present the results of their analysis visually, in a graph, which offers a corollary presentation of results to the textual description above.

Fig. 3. Viral load in respiratory tissues of rhesus macaques inoculated with MERS-CoV. Rhesus macaques were euthanized on day 3 (black bars) and day 6 (white bars) postinfection and tissue samples were collected. RNA was extracted and viral load was determined as $TCID_{50}$ equivalents by qRT-PCR. $TCID_{50}$ equivalents were extrapolated from standard curves generated by adding dilutions of RNA extracted from a HCoV-EMC/2012 stock with known virus titer in parallel to each run. Geometric mean viral loads were calculated; error bars represent SD. R, right; L, left; LN, lymph node.

Figure 3

From *Proceedings of the National Academy of Sciences* (110.41), 2013.

Discussion

In this rhesus macaque model, virus shedding as indicated by qRT-PCR occurred predominantly via the nose and, to a limited extent, the throat. In nasal swabs and BAL, viral loads were highest day 1 postinfection and decreased over time. However, at 6 dpi [days postinfection], two of three animals were still shedding virus from the respiratory tract. Although MERS-CoV was detected in the upper respiratory tract and the lymphoid tissue draining the lungs, replication of MERS-CoV was most prominent in the lower respiratory tract. MERS-CoV replicated predominantly in type I and II pneumocytes in the alveoli. These two cell types form the main component of the architecture of the alveolar space around the terminal bronchioles. This predominant replication of MERS-CoV in alveoli may explain the limited amount of virus shedding observed in our rhesus macaque model. In addition, the fact that human-to-human transmission so far seems limited to a few family clusters in Saudi Arabia (6), the United Kingdom (7), and Tunisia and nosocomial transmission in Jordan, Saudi Arabia (6), and France (9) might be explained by the propensity of the novel coronavirus to replicate deep down in the lower respiratory tract.

> Where the first excerpt presented the results of their analysis on the tissue samples, this section illustrates a second level of analysis performed on those results. They likely used statistical and mathematical analysis to generate these conclusions about which bodily tissues showed the greatest amount of viral replication.

Statistical analysis

Statistical analysis can be applied to nearly any data set. This mode of analysis involves not only choosing which statistical measures to generate from a data set, but also analyzing the results of those statistical tests. In his "Introduction to Statistical Analysis," David Rossiter, from the Department of Earth Systems Analysis in the International Institute for Geo-information Science & Earth Observation (ITC), differentiates between two different kinds of statistical analysis, both of which he deems significant forms of the study: "descriptive statistics: numerical summaries of samples (what was observed)," and "inferential statistics: from samples to populations (what could have been or will be observed)."

The example of statistical analysis is from an article on the European Centre for Disease Prevention and Control website titled "Epidemiological Update: Middle East Respiratory Syndrome Coronavirus (MERS-CoV)."

Excerpt from "Epidemiological Update: Middle East Respiratory Syndrome Coronavirus (MERS-CoV)" by the European Centre for Disease Prevention and Control

In June 2012, a case of fatal respiratory disease in a previously healthy 60-year-old man was reported from Saudi Arabia ...The cause was subsequently identified as a new coronavirus that has been named Middle East respiratory syndrome coronavirus (MERS-CoV).

> Notice the focus on quantitative data nearly from the beginning of the article, signaling that statistical analysis will play a large role in the researchers' findings.

By 22 November 2013, 160 cases of MERS have been reported. All cases have either occurred in the Middle East or have direct links to a primary case infected in the Middle East....

As of 22 November 2013, the case-fatality ratio is 43% and is increasing with age. The male to female ratio is 2:1. Among the 155 cases with known age, the median age was 52 (IQR 39-64) and 142 (91.6%) were older than 19 years. We classified cases as primary or secondary based on the information provided publicly by WHO and KSA MOH [Kingdom of Saudi Arabia Ministry of Health]. Primary cases were

> Here is an example of descriptive statistical analysis, sharing the demographic traits of MERS cases. Notice that the information in this paragraph is then depicted visually in the included graph.

classified using the following criteria: no reported exposure to other known cases, occurring in an area with no cases close in time and/or reported as primary case in a cluster. Secondary cases were classified based on the epidemiological link to other confirmed cases. Thirty-seven cases could not be classified based on the information available and they were left out from the analysis.

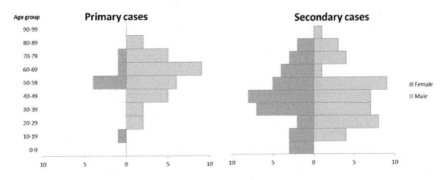

Figure 3. Distribution of confirmed cases of MERS-CoV by primary (N=39) and secondary cases (N=83) by gender and age group, March 2012 - 22 November 2013

*Among secondary cases, 3 cases were not included in the analysis due to unknown age.

From *European Centre for Disease Prevention and Control,* 2013.

Thirty-nine cases were classified as primary cases and of these, 79.5% (31/39) were male with a median age of 59 years (Table 1). The male to female ratio of 3.9 among primary cases is significantly differing from an even gender distribution (p=<10-3), reflecting potentially a gender related difference in exposures. Among the 83 secondary cases with documented age and sex, the median age is 45 years and the sex distribution does not sig- nificantly differ from an even distribution (p=0.44), with 38 (45.8%) cases being females. The more even male to female ratio of 1.2 among secondary cases can be explained by the enhanced surveillance systems in tracing close contacts of the confirmed cases.

> This section layers an additional element of statistical analysis by examining gender alongside primary and secondary cases.

Table 1. Epidemiological characteristics of confirmed cases of MERS-CoV comparing primary (N=39) and second-ary cases (N=83), March 2012 - 21 November 2013.

Epidemiological characteristics	Primary cases	Secondary cases	P value
	n=39 (%)	n=85 (%)	
Gender			0.004 a
Male	31 (79.5)	45 (54.2)	
Female	7 (17.9)	38 (45.8)	
Unknown	-	2	
Outcome			0.003 a
Dead	23 (59.0)	25 (29.4)	
Alive	16 (41.0)	60 (70.6)	
Comorbidities b			<0.001 a
Yes	27 (90.0)	39 (50.6)	
No	3 (10.0)	38 (49.4)	
Unknown	9	8	
Nosocomial transmission			<0.001 a
Yes	2 (5.7)	38 (50.7)	
No	33 (94.3)	37 (49.3)	
Unknown	4	10	

a. Two-tailed Fisher's exact test (unknown cases were excluded from the statistical analysis).
b. Comorbidities including, among others, diabetes, hypertension, chronic cardiac and chronic renal disease.

Big Data analysis

Big Data is a term gaining increasing prevalence across a wide variety of disciplines and economic sectors. It has particular applications in business and technology-driven fields, such as information technology and computer science. Rekha Mishra and Neeraj Kaushik define **Big Data** as follows:

> Big Data refers to relatively large amounts of structured and unstructured data that require machine-based systems and technologies in order to be fully analysed.... [W]hat turn[s] data into Big Data is the amount of information, and the speed at which it can be created, collected and analysed.

In the Big Data analysis example, a research team of computer scientists and software engineers introduce a method for analyzing Big Data in relation to influenza. They address the ongoing question, how can we improve early detection, prevention, and treatment of influenza? This paper, published in the "Letters" section of the journal *Nature,* has led to an ongoing debate in health care, public policy, and epidemiology about the use and value of what has now become known as Google Flu Trends.

The excerpt indicates the significance of their work and their methods of analysis, showing where they get their Big Data from and how they analyze it.

Excerpt from "Detecting Influenza Epidemics using Search Engine Query Data"
by J. Ginsberg, et al.

The authors first establish the significance and prevalence of the problem they are addressing, showing why it lends itself to Big Data analysis.

Seasonal influenza epidemics are a major public health concern, causing tens of millions of respiratory illnesses and 250,000 to 500,000 deaths worldwide each year. In addition to seasonal influenza, a new strain of influenza virus against which no previous immunity exists and that demonstrates human-to-human transmission could result in a pandemic with millions of fatalities. Early detection of disease activity, when followed by a rapid response, can reduce the impact of both seasonal and pandemic influenza. One way to improve early detection is to monitor health-seeking behaviour in the form of queries to online search engines, which are submitted by millions of users around the world each day. Here we present a method of analysing large numbers of Google search queries to track

They introduce the Big Data they will use (Google search queries) and show that their contribution has been to develop a method to analyze it in order to "track influenza-like illness in a population."

From *Nature* (457.7232), 2009.

influenza-like illness in a population. Because the relative frequency of certain queries is highly correlated with the percentage of physician visits in which a patient presents with influenza-like symptoms, we can accurately estimate the current level of weekly influenza activity in each region of the United States, with a reporting lag of about one day. This approach may make it possible to use search queries to detect influenza epidemics in areas with a large population of web search users.

Traditional surveillance systems, including those used by the U.S. Centers for Disease Control and Prevention (CDC) and the European Influenza Surveillance Scheme (EISS), rely on both virological and clinical data, including influenza-like illness (ILI) physician visits. The CDC publishes national and regional data from these surveillance systems on a weekly basis, typically with a 1-2-week reporting lag.

> The authors show that although Big Data has been crucial in CDC work prior to this, the analysis has had a "1-2-week reporting lag," making their method, Big Data analysis, more timely and up to date.

In an attempt to provide faster detection, innovative surveillance systems have been created to monitor indirect signals of influenza activity, such as call volume to telephone triage advice lines and over-the-counter drug sales. About 90 million American adults are believed to search online

> They will be using online activity from 90 million American adults.

for information about specific diseases or medical problems each year, making web search queries a uniquely valuable source of information about health trends. Previous attempts at using online activity for influenza surveillance have counted search queries submitted to a Swedish medical website (A. Hulth, G. Rydevik and A. Linde, manuscript in preparation), visitors to certain pages on a U.S. health website, and user clicks on a search keyword advertisement in Canada. A set of Yahoo search queries containing the words 'flu' or 'influenza' were found to correlate with virological and mortality surveillance data over multiple years.

Our proposed system builds on this earlier work by using an automated method of discovering influenza-related search queries. By processing hundreds of billions of individual searches from 5 years of Google web search logs, our system generates more comprehensive models for use in influenza surveillance, with regional and state-level estimates of ILI activity in the United States.... By aggregating historical logs of online web search queries submitted between 2003 and 2008, we computed a time series of weekly counts for 50 million of the most common search queries in the United States. Separate

> Here, Ginsberg, et al. describe their Big Data analysis, which involves aggregating queries by state and developing a list of "common search queries" related to influenza.

aggregate weekly counts were kept for every query in each state. No information about the identity of any user was retained. Each time a series was normalized by dividing the count for each query in a particular week by the total number of online search queries submitted in that location during the week, resulting in a query fraction.

Write Now

Based on a profession of interest to you, write down a number of possible sources of Big Data and their potential usefulness. What kinds of Big Data might be available to or of interest to people in this profession? Why do you think people in this profession might need (or not need) Big Data?

Transferring Analysis

Because analysis can include so many different modes, it is also important to note that academic writers do not necessarily need to become experts in all the modes, nor even in any particular mode of analysis. Instead, writers should aim to be able to recognize that disciplinary perspective and writing occasion shape the choices they make about analysis.

Building on Chapter 3: Posing Meaningful Questions, effective analysis hinges on learning how to pose the most precise and targeted questions in order to determine how best to analyze a given data type for a particular writing occasion. Analysis relies on the approaches outlined in the preceding chapters in that it forms a vital part of the research and writing process, is grounded in modes of in-depth reading, and often overlaps with summary and synthesis as a primary means of engaging with the work of others. Subsequent chapters extend these writerly skills by providing a focused view of how writers choose to shape and construct the arguments they set forth, and how those arguments hinge on the merits of the analysis they have conducted.

❧ ❧ ❧

Photojournalism: "Armenian Massacre, 1914" by Armin Wegner

Transfer Points: Visual Studies, History, Journalism, Holocaust and Genocide Studies, Criminal Justice, Human Rights

Armin Wegner braved great risk to take this photograph, keep it safe, and distribute it.

A volunteer nurse for Germany during World War I, Wegner had heard rumors about an Armenian massacre, so he took a two-month leave in 1915 to go and see for himself. At the time, the Young Turk government in the Ottoman Empire, a precursor to modern-day Turkey, at war with Russia, surmised that Armenians were sympathetic to the Russians. The Young Turk government thus ordered the Armenian people, a vast number of men, women, and children, to evacuate their historic homelands in Eastern Anatolia, and march to the Syrian desert.

As Wegner took photographs and otherwise archived these events, his superiors commanded him to stop. Wegner was eventually arrested and returned to Germany. But he hid the photograph negatives in his belt to prevent them from being confiscated. After Wegner's release, he went on to use his photographs and writing to advocate tirelessly for Armenian rights and, a few decades later, Jewish rights.

The Armenian forced relocation is estimated to have caused the deaths of 1.5 million people, or three-quarters of the Armenians living at the time in the Ottoman Empire (Javed). The title of Wegner's image, "Armenian Massacre," may seem self-evident, but it also gestures to great complexities regarding how language changes and how definitions matter, particularly with regard to human rights.

When the photograph was taken, the term *massacre* was the most extreme word available to describe the atrocities. The word *genocide* did not yet exist. A few decades later, though, emphasizing the inadequacy of the term *massacre* to describe such large-scale murder, Winston Churchill described the 1941 Nazi campaign in the Soviet Union as "a crime without a name":

> Whole districts are being exterminated. Scores of thousands—literally scores of thousands—of executions in cold blood are being perpetrated by the German Police-troops upon the Russian patriots who defend their native soil. Since the Mongol invasions of Europe in the Sixteenth-Century, there has never been methodical, merciless butchery on such a scale... We are in the presence of a crime without a name. (qtd. in Fussell)

Perhaps motivated by Churchill's "crime without a name" description, Raphael Lemkin, a professor, lawyer, and human rights advocate coined the term *genocide* in 1943. Lemkin then provided a more detailed definition in his 1944 book about Nazi atrocities, *Axis Rule in Occupied Europe*:

Armin Wegner (1886–1978) was a German intellectual, photographer, and writer. Born in Germany, he became a volunteer nurse during World War I and used a two-month leave in 1915 to investigate rumors he had heard about the Armenian massacre. He then became an eyewitness and captured the atrocities with his photographs. Through his writing, he was a champion of human rights, especially for Armenian and Jewish rights. In 2003, the Arpa Foundation for Film, Music, and Art in Hollywood founded the Armin T. Wegner award as a humanitarian honor to recognize a motion picture that fights for social conscience and human rights ("Biography").

By 'genocide' we mean the destruction of a nation or of an ethnic group. This new word...is made from the ancient Greek word *genos* (race, tribe) and the Latin *cide* (killing).... [G]enocide does not necessarily mean the immediate destruction of a nation, except when accomplished by mass killings of all members of a nation. It is intended rather to signify a coordinated plan of different actions aiming at the destruction of essential foundations of the life of national groups, with the aim of annihilating the groups themselves. (80)

Lemkin's writing and the term *genocide* have gone on to become cornerstones for the field of human rights. Lemkin's efforts, for example, helped initiate the 1948 United Nations Convention on the Prevention and Punishment of Genocide, an important milestone in the history of human rights.

Since Lemkin's development of the term *genocide* and its application to the Holocaust, scholars have reconsidered history. According to human rights scholar Ben Kiernan, genocide has existed since classical times, when Marcus Porcius Cato, the second-century Roman official, initiated the battle cry, "Carthage must be destroyed!" (49). Many have also deployed the term *genocide* to describe the plight of Native Americans (Fenelon and Trafzer). And the Armenian massacre has become more commonly referred to as the Armenian Genocide ("Armenian"). Subsequent twentieth-century genocides have also occurred, such as in Rwanda and Darfur.

The use of the term *genocide*, however, often breeds contention. In the case of the decimation of Native Americans, for instance, ongoing disagreement exists over the applicability of the term *genocide* (Fenelon and Trafzer). Similarly, arguments continue over whether genocide is or is not accurate in the context of the Armenian massacre ("Stanford").

Questions about what does or does not constitute genocide, research into the implications of and reparations for such atrocities, and efforts to prevent genocide, are all central to the field of human rights. Scholars in this field approach these sorts of questions from a wide range of disciplines, including cultural anthropology, sociology, history, documentary studies, journalism, public policy, and visual studies. Scholars of human rights also have training in law, as well as interdisciplinary fields such as African and African-American Studies, Jewish Studies, and Russian Studies.

The global and historical ubiquity of human rights abuses makes human rights not only a deeply interdisciplinary field, but one that relies on many modalities for writing and research. Human rights scholars publish peer-reviewed research in such journals as *Genocide Studies and Prevention*, *Genocide Studies International*, and *War Crimes, Genocide, & Crimes against Humanity*. This research includes diverse areas of focus, such as the impact of climate change on the genocidal impulse (Alvarez), the plunder of wealth in the Armenian Genocide (Kurt), historiography in the Indonesian Massacres (Henry), and economies of violence in Cambodia under the Khmer (Tyner and Rice).

Much of the writing in the field of human rights also involves more public forms of scholarship and public advocacy. Human rights scholars, policy makers, and activists create online networks such as *Prevent Genocide International*, and they write policy briefs for the United Nations and other government organizations. Scholars in this field also write op-eds and engage in public lectures and dialogues to raise awareness, educate people, and work to curtail and prevent ongoing genocides and human rights abuses.

These efforts demonstrate how those researching and writing about human rights must continually rely on their capacities for writing transfer. Across writing contexts, they must consider how to adapt, build, challenge, and extend knowledge and practices for different readers, from one occasion to subsequent occasions. They do so as part of a larger effort to advance knowledge that stands to better the human condition by exposing, exploring, understanding, and preventing the crimes without names.

Write Here

What is at stake in a term? What would be the implications of describing an image such as Wegner's with the caption "Armenian Massacre" or with the caption "Armenian Genocide"? In what ways do you see language intersecting with the field of human rights?

Armin Wegner
Armenian Massacre, 1914

Write Away

1. Using techniques of visual analysis (see Chapter 7), consider such questions as the following: What do you notice most about the image? What is in the background and foreground? What do you notice about the frame of the image? What is included? What do you think is excluded or exists right outside of the frame? What emotions does this image evoke for you? What argument might this image make about genocide? What might the photo suggest about the ethical complexities involved with documenting genocide?

2. Wegner's image serves as a primary historical artifact. Using a historical approach, locate other historical artifacts, evidence, and materials related to the Armenian genocide. These can be additional photographs, material artifacts, or documents, such as policies, newspaper articles, and letters. Compose a historical account of an aspect of the Armenian genocide, using as evidence the historical artifacts you have compiled.

3. What is the role of visual argument in the context of human rights? Using Wegner's image and/or other images related to human rights issues, historical or contemporary, write an argument that includes visual components about the role of visual argument in the context of human rights issues. Consider such questions as the following: What are the ethical complexities of visual documentation of human rights abuses or atrocities? What is the role of photojournalists in this context? What are the responsibilities of viewers of these images? What do these images accomplish? What are their limitations?

Business Marketing Report: "Myth, Adventure and Fantasy at the Frontier: Metaphors and Imagery behind an Extraordinary Travel Experience" by Jennifer H. Laing and Geoffrey I. Crouch

Transfer Points: Business, Management, Marketing

Restaurants, banks, shoes, computers, automobiles...when choosing among products or services, how do you decide which to purchase or use? What values and priorities motivate you in making consumer decisions? What factors contribute to your satisfaction with various products, goods, or services?

These are but a few of the questions that occupy scholars working in the discipline of marketing.

The American Marketing Association defines marketing as "the activity, set of institutions, and processes for creating, communicating, delivering, and exchanging offerings that have value for customers, clients, partners, and society at large" ("About AMA").

Nested most firmly within business, marketing also exists as a discipline in its own right. Sometimes it is termed *marketing management,* and it also intersects with fields such as hospitality management, or subfields such as event marketing or social media marketing. Jennifer Laing and Geoffrey Crouch are writing from within a subfield of marketing called *tourism marketing* or *tourism management,* a field that researches tourism practices and behaviors to better understand what motivates people to travel to particular destinations or seek various experiences.

As one of the most widely applicable disciplines, marketing draws knowledge from a variety of disciplines, including economics, business, psychology, art, literature, and rhetoric. Marketing research demonstrates the wide reach of this field. As an example, articles in the *Academy of Marketing Studies Journal,* a top journal in marketing, focus on such widely disparate issues as brand placement in novels (Brennan), a market analysis of doctoral programs for business degrees (Calegari, Sibley, and Turner), and online shopping motives (Kim and Song).

Marketing-related writing includes a wide range of genres and spans visual, written, and verbal texts, as well as professional, popular, and academic contexts. Specific examples include research articles and books, brochures, websites, and taglines. People in marketing also write market analyses for new or expanding ventures, proposals for marketing plans, brand/product reports, and marketing assessment reports. And, they make verbal pitches.

Throughout all of these writing and speaking occasions, form operates in a critical way within marketing. Choosing, for instance, whether to deliver a message orally or in writing, with or without visual components, bears an important impact on the message itself. Form is also vitally important in the context of market analysis and reports, where

Jennifer H. Laing is an Associate Professor of Management and Marketing in the La Trobe Business School in Melbourne, Australia. Her area of specialty is event management, and she has published widely across many areas of marketing, including research on travel narratives, heritage tourism, and gastronomic tourism. One of her articles addressed coffee culture and tourism in Melbourne. Her research interests also extend to film-induced tourism and royal events. **Geoffrey Crouch** is a professor of Tourism Policy & Marketing in the La Trobe Business School. He is the editor of the *Journal of Travel Research* and has served as Director of the MBA program at University of Calgary, Canada. His research interests include tourism marketing, tourism policy and planning, and tourism psychology. He has published on sustainable tourism, international tourism forecasting, and space tourism. As is often the case with research collaborators, Laing and Crouch have coauthored several research articles together. In addition to "Myth, Adventure and Fantasy," they have conducted research about the role of media in frontier travel experiences (Laing and Crouch, 2009, "Exploring") and about isolation and solitude in frontier travel (Laing and Crouch, 2009, "Lone Wolves").

readers tend to expect executive summaries, graphics, tables, and headings. At the sentence level, writing in marketing contexts is often deemed more effective when it demonstrates clarity and conciseness.

Writing in marketing also demands careful, deliberate thinking about readers. Writers in this field often work hard to understand readers' values, expectations, priorities, and goals—even in cases where these may be multivariable or even contradictory.

Composing practices in marketing require creativity and responsiveness, often in compressed time frames. A market analysis, for instance, may lose relevance if a writer extends the research, drafting, and revision process over too lengthy a time span. This does not mean that writers in marketing do not move through the stages of the writing process, but they may do so in a more compressed manner.

Across academic and professional contexts for marketing, ethics plays a central role. These ethical considerations involve the values and principals informing a product, brand, or service. Ethics also involves avoiding unethical marketing practices such as false advertising, the use of children in exploitative ways, spurious brand comparisons, or stereotyping people based on race, gender, class, or sexual orientation ("What is").

Writers in marketing, therefore, should take particular care to consider ethics in relation to how their words, images, and ideas might be interpreted by different individuals. They must think carefully about the values they are promoting and what the potential implications might be. And, they must also consider the risks involved with particular goods, products, and services. They must consider the degree to which they are or should be responsible for making those risks visible to potential customers.

Marketing, then, is grounded in *ethos*: When composing marketing-related materials, how can writers most responsibly convey expertise and confidence in the discipline, issues, or brands? Sometimes, this terrain can be especially difficult. Many industries, markets, or fields, for instance, have quite conflicted impacts, and writers in marketing must navigate these ambivalences deliberately and carefully.

All of this complexity makes writing in the field of marketing among the most varied, and interdisciplinary of fields in terms of form, methods, and inquiry. It is also among the most highly visible areas of writing, spanning scholarly, professional, and public contexts. And, the stakes involved with composing in marketing are especially high. Because of this breadth, writing in the field of marketing bears direct, significant impact on the choices, behaviors, and practices of people all around the world.

Write Here

What adventure would you embark on if you had no constraints? Why? Describe in as much detail as possible the adventure. Reflect on what would be appealing to you about it and what you would hope the experience might include or provide for you.

Jennifer H. Laing and Geoffrey I. Crouch
Myth, Adventure and Fantasy at the Frontier: Metaphors and Imagery behind an Extraordinary Travel Experience

INTRODUCTION

The role played by consumer fantasies and mental imagery in the consumption experience has been explored with respect to a number of extraordinary hedonic leisure or travel experiences to date, such as river rafting (Arnould and Price, 1993), skydiving (Celsi *et al.*, 1993) and ocean cruising (Macbeth, 2000). Recent research has focused on travel experiences in the most remote and unique locations on Earth, such as deserts, mountains, the poles or outer space, where individuals are challenged, both physically and psychologically, by 'life on the edge' (Cohen, 2004; Laing and Crouch, 2005). These frontier travellers journey largely without established tourist infrastructure in place, generally carry their own food, shelter and provisions, and must undergo extensive training beforehand to survive the rigours of the journey. These experiences are high cost and high risk and attract considerable public and consequently media interest because they are still relatively rare. Frontier journeys, with all their visceral delights as well as dangers, appear to be motivated or influenced by fantasies and myths, as well as long-held and deeply felt desires, as the traveller moves into unknown territories and situations. Adventure tourism experiences, even those at the very high or 'hard' end, are undertaken 'within a framework of myth and dramatic story line' (Trauer, 2006, p. 185). The myths and narratives associated with frontier travel may therefore help us to understand the 'mythology of adventure' (Cater, 2006, p. 322) more broadly, as well as current trends in tourism.

A qualitative study of frontier travellers, predominantly from Australia, the UK and the USA, has been conducted to explore their conceptualisation of their own travel experiences based on adventure mythology. This paper will consider some of the metaphors and imagery used by frontier travellers when describing their travel experiences and examines whether there are shared narratives or a common discourse expressed across the different journeys. This paper begins with a consideration of the literature on fantasy and mythical narratives behind travel, particularly focusing on the frontier or adventure experience.

LITERATURE REVIEW

It has been suggested that individuals organise and interpret their experiences, including tourism, through mythologies (Shields, 1991; Johns and Clarke, 2001; Shackley, 2001; Johns and Gyimóthy, 2002; Hennig, 2002), and myth may be an important part of the appeal of tourism destinations (Butler, 1990; Riley, 1994), as well as motivations to travel. Myth has been defined both in the sense of a narrative that is 'believed to be true by the people who tell it' (Hunter and Whitten, 1976, p. 279) and as a linguistic construct (Barthes, 1973; Johns and Clarke, 2001; Johns and Gyimóthy, 2002), where words can be associated with deeper and sometimes hidden meanings. Myths can also be viewed as collective expressions or representations of cultural beliefs and values, a form of 'cultural consensus' (Johns

and Clarke, 2001, p. 336) that can help to shape personal or national identity (Palmer, 1999). Hennig (2002) takes the view that tourism or travel straddles both the mythical and the physical world—tied to the former while taking place in the latter—and includes the frontier as a modern myth. This allows for the ritual re-enactment of these myths, often in the form of 'heroic journeys' or experiences. Hutt (1996, p. 49) also links myth to representations in the media and 'popular literature', particularly with reference to 'far-flung corners of the world'. Texts such as Henry Morton Stanley's *Through the Dark Continent* (1878) or Shackleton's *South* (1919) have 'set the imaginative pathways' (Zurick, 1995) for modern travellers. Bishop (1989, p. 3) observes that these travel narratives 'are an important aspect of a culture's myth-making'.

The frontier traveller is often recreating or retracing the expeditions of early explorers or travellers in remote and inaccessible places, and may be inspired by reading past accounts of exotic and dangerous landscapes, fueling childhood fantasies that persist in adulthood. Seaton (2002, p. 155) calls these texts, and the type of travel they are based on, 'metempsychotic', where 'the tourist takes on the persona of a significant other or group, as a role model for a particular repeated journey'. Many frontier travellers later write their own modern tales of adventure based on their journeys, which may serve as inspiration for a new generation of travellers. These past and present tales may also help to shape the personal narrative of the traveller, in the sense of 'sets of stories which unfold as life proceeds' (Voase, 2007, p. 49). The traveller makes reference to these narratives, consciously or subconsciously, in making sense of an experience or encounter (Voase, 2007).

Mythical narratives forming part of the frontier travel experience might therefore be based on links between these experiences and exploration or the heroic journey. The exploration myth is founded in what Goetzmann (1979) called the First Great Age of Discovery by Spain and Portugal in the 16th century, continuing in the second wave characterised by the great sea voyages of the 18th and 19th centuries—chiefly by the British and French—and on to the Third Age of exploration (Pyne, 1987, 2004; Sagan and Pyne, 1988; Pyne, 1993), covering the ocean depths, the icy landscapes of Antarctica and outer space. Many of the myths surrounding explorers have been perpetuated and embellished in literature (Haynes, 1998; Collis, 2000). The heroic journey, on the other hand, is associated with classical myths, such as Homer's *Odyssey* or Jason's search for the Golden Fleece, which involve the hero leaving their homeland for unknown hardships and trials and later returning, renewed and changed by the experience. 'To look death in the face and to return to the living is the ultimate proof of a hero's extraordinary stature' (Van Nortwick, 1992, p. 28). Both are part of the Western cultural legacy, although it might be argued that they are a more fundamental heritage of all human beings. As Allen (2002, p. xi) notes, 'We are all explorers. Our desire to discover, and then share that newfound knowledge, is part of what makes us human—indeed, has played an important part in our success as a species'.

This paper focuses on the use of mythic and fantastical metaphors and imagery associated with frontier journeys. The next section looks at the methods used in this study and provides definitions of some of the key concepts discussed in this paper.

METHODS

Transcripts of long interviews with 37 frontier travellers, together with 50 texts written by frontier travellers (mainly books and several Internet diaries) were analysed for their use of metaphors and imagery associated with fantasy, myth and dreams. Setting up interviews with these individuals mostly involved contact by email through their own websites, as many of these travellers attract media attention and are required to self-promote as a condition of sponsorship (Laing and Crouch, 2005). In a few instances in the latter part of the study, snowball sampling was used, where some individuals recommended approaching other frontier travellers for participation in an interview. Only limited use was made of this approach in the interest of accessing as diverse and representative a group as possible Taylor and Bogdan, 1998; Seale, 1999).

The choice of qualitative research and an interpretivist approach in this study was made in order to allow the participants' voices to be heard, to discover 'embedded meaning' and to explore reasons for behaviour (van Manen, 1977;

Crick, 1994; Miles and Huberman, 1994; Dann and Phillips, 2000). The interpretivist approach is often used in studies of lived experiences (Smith and Weed, 2007). Narrative analysis was used to investigate the 'stories' that were gathered in this study (both interviews and biographical texts). Morgan (2007, p. 367) observes that elements of an experience include the meanings created by an individual and derived from 'personal narratives and shared cultural values'. Other studies (e.g. Smith and Weed, 2007; Voase, 2007) also note the importance of narratives in understanding personal experiences. The interviewees were asked to tell the researcher how they came to undertake their first frontier travel experiences and were then asked about their reasons or motivations for doing so. They generally began to spontaneously tell the story of their frontier travel experiences, with the researcher taking the role of the listener and offering prompting questions where required. 'The listeners therefore immediately become active co-participants in the recounting of a narrative' (Elliott, 2005, p. 10). The interviewer tried to take a back seat as much as possible and let the stories flow without unnecessary interruption. Sometimes, these stories were lengthy, while others were more accurately characterised as vignettes or snippets, used by the interviewee to illustrate a particular motivation or key part of their travel experience. The plot might have been shaped by the occasional question asked by the interviewer, but largely this was left to the interviewee.

While the interviewer was the main intended audience for these stories, the fact that the interviews were taped suggests that the interviewees understood that there would be other potential audiences for their narrative (Bernstein, 1997; Elliott, 2005), i.e. through published academic works of the interviewer and any co-researcher(s), even though the interviewees' identity was concealed by a pseudonym. This fact might perhaps have influenced some of the stories being told, although the degree is hard to quantify. Some interviews were also conducted at public places such as local cafes, and interviewees might therefore have been influenced by the fact that other patrons could have overheard all or part of the interviews. It should also be borne in mind that many of these stories might have been 'well-rehearsed' as the interviewee had often presented accounts of their travels to the public through lectures or via media interviews, or the retelling may lead to changes in the original narrative (Gudmundsdottir, 2006, p. 225). This does not, however, make them any less meaningful as a way to understand the frontier traveller, given that adventure can be understood as a 'performed kinaesthetic experience' (Cater and Cloke, 2007, p. 14). These frontier experiences are arguably carried out in the knowledge that the general public will be interested in their exploits, with the latter acting as a form of audience, 'supporting and willing participants to successful completion of their adventure' (Cater and Cloke, 2007, p. 15). It is also the case that the retelling of stories may lead to exploration of the 'deeper meaning of events' (Gudmundsdottir, 2006, p. 225), created jointly through the voices of informant and researcher.

In the case of the books being analysed, the works were in the public domain and the stories were extracted from the literary texts by the researcher. The original audience was thus the readership of the book, which might perhaps have led to the stories being somewhat 'enhanced' to make them more interesting or readable. This, however, is consistent with the point made above; that these travel experiences are often undertaken with an eye to the interest of the general public, the media and their peers in these kinds of pursuits.

There is no single method of narrative analysis of qualitative material (Elliott, 2005) and a variety of approaches are potentially available to the researcher. The method selected for this study was a focus on *narrative content*, particularly the 'choice of metaphors and other images that are invoked' (Elliott, 2005, p. 38) when attempting to describe the frontier travel experience. This analysis therefore focuses on what the accounts of the participants tell us about these experiences, forming part of the social world (Smith, 2000; Elliott, 2005). The analysis can also be conceptualised as *paradigmatic* (Polkinghorne, 1995; Smith and Weed, 2007), in that the researcher conducts a type of content analysis to tease out themes from the narrative data, in order to produce overarching categories or typologies that unite these themes. 'The power of paradigmatic

thought is to bring order to experience by seeing individual things as belonging to a category' (Polkinghorne, 1995, p. 10).

The analysis of interview transcripts and texts used in this study revealed a number of references to metaphors or imagery. *Imagery*, according to Tannen (1989, p. 2), refers to visual images depicted within discourse or conversation, in the sense of 'previously experienced visual impressions, things and people seen rather than heard'. They can also be viewed more broadly as mental constructs or 'representations', which can derive from any of the sensory domains, not just the visual (Echtner and Ritchie, 2003; Featherstone and Hepworth, 2005). The latter definition has been used in the current study. The process and influences on image formation have been the subject of a number of tourism studies, primarily with respect to destination image, the role of image in the travel decision-making process and the factors influencing destination image formation (see for example Echtner and Ritchie, 2003; Beerli and Martin, 2004; O'Leary and Deegan, 2005). This paper, however, focuses on the way that imagery is conveyed by the frontier travellers taking part in the current study—in both oral and written discourse—particularly through the use of *metaphors*.

Metaphors can be understood as ways of comparing two 'different things on the basis of the characteristics they share' (Elgin, 1993, p. 146). Gibbs *et al.* (2004) note that the basis of metaphors is often *image schema*. The latter refers to 'dynamic spatial patterns' that are 'more abstract than ordinary visual mental images' and of an enduring nature, being 'permanent properties of embodied experience' (Gibbs *et al.*, 2004, pp. 1192–1193). Lakoff (1993, p. 202) observes that the term 'metaphor' should be reserved for the conceptualisation of 'one mental domain in terms of another', rather than mere linguistic expressions. This paper, however, will use the term 'metaphor' in its more colloquial sense to refer to the *metaphorical expressions* or language used by participants. It will be distinguished from 'imagery', which is used in this paper to denote the images or *imaginative comparisons* underpinning these metaphors.

Lengkeek (2000, p. 14) refers to the provision of 'new contexts and meaning' through metaphor, such that they can become 'everyday reality'. Metaphor can therefore be used to minimise unfamiliarity (Dann, 2002) by comparing one concept with something else better known or understood. This might explain their frequency of use in a frontier travel context, where the traveller is necessarily exploring or visiting places where few others have gone and may struggle to find words to make sense of what they have seen or experienced to others. Some metaphors are so ubiquitous and overused in everyday speech as to be almost cliché (Dann, 2002), but even the use of an overworked metaphor may suggest a particular way of viewing the world and be of interest in better understanding the way a particular individual draws meaning from an experience. The frontier traveller may be using well-worn metaphors such as the comparison of the frontier with a female, but their frequency of use and emphasis across the set of participants in this study suggests that they have a particular resonance for this type of traveller.

The next sections of this paper explore some of the imagery and metaphors used by frontier travellers in reference to their journeys. While these constructs have been dealt with separately, for ease of analysis, the final section of this paper will pull together the various strands and examine the relationship between myth, heroic journeys and fantasy for the frontier traveller in a holistic sense.

Quotes from interview participants will be attributed to pseudonyms in italics, to distinguish them from quotes made by authors of texts about frontier travel, another source of data used in this study. While data were collected with respect to a number of individuals, not all study participants are cited or referred to in this paper. Instead, the following analysis uses illustrative examples, based on data gathered, to explore the metaphors and imagery used by frontier travellers that were common across the data set in this study. The most commonly noted metaphors and imagery appeared to be those dealing with exploration/the explorer's journey and desire/passion within the frontier travel experience, which were often found in conjunction with each other. None of the metaphors and imagery discussed below were exclusive to a single frontier traveller.

DESIRE AND PASSION

Frontier travellers often paint the object of their travels in language reminiscent of a lover. The frontier is typically seen as a woman (Humberstone and Pedersen, 2001) either untouched or unspoilt like a 'virgin' or alluring and seductive, with the explorer Scott a case in point according to Sara Wheeler (1996, pp. 49–50). 'The Antarctic possessed a virginity, in his mind, that provided an alternative to the spoiled and messy world'. Wheeler (1996, p. 50) also notes of Scott, 'He wrote in his diary about, "the terrible vulgarising which Shackleton has introduced to the Southern field of enterprise, hitherto so clean and wholesome"'.

There are numerous examples of the 'virgin' metaphor used by frontier travellers when describing the landscape or the challenge of their endeavours. For example, Robert Anderson (1995, p. 187) describes the attraction of 'the unknown in making a first ascent' of a mountain in these terms: 'The feeling of treading virgin ground with surprises just around the corner, makes ascending unclimbed mountains like finding diamonds in the ice'. Sir Ranulph Fiennes similarly writes of the attraction posed by 'whole new ranges of virgin mountains' only recently 'made available to Western climbers' in China (Fiennes, 1993, pp. 11–12).

The use of metaphors like this is not just limited to mountaineers or trekkers. Sailor Jim Shekhdar 'wanted to do something nobody had done before, effectively to walk on virgin snow. That was my raison d'être and, after some debate, I settled upon the idea of rowing, unsupported and alone, across the Pacific Ocean' (Shekhdar with Griffiths, 2001, p. 3).

References to Antarctica are particularly rife with this metaphorical language, which may be in part a subconscious nod to its relatively peaceful history and avoidance of imperialistic conquest. *Karen* notes the attraction of Antarctica's 'purity' during a trek and *Rod* mentions the 'unblemished snowfield' of its coastline. David Lewis, discussing his solo sailing voyage to Antarctica, writes, 'The whole white continent lay virgin, entrenched behind pack and berg and the furious storms of the "screaming sixties"' (Lewis, 1975, p. 19).

The metaphor might be linked to a 'discourse of power' (Dann, 1996, p. 28), with the traveller wishing to subdue or dominate 'virgin territory'. The land could in fact be a metaphor for their own fears and subconscious desire to 'conquer' or master them through their travel experiences. Use of the virginity metaphor is, however, not confined to men. Bettina Selby (1988, p. 5–6), who journeyed to the source of the Nile in Africa, refers to uncharted regions she planned to visit in these terms:

> It didn't seem as if the available information about some parts of my route had increased all that much from the days when map-makers filled in the blank spaces with whatever came to mind; the thought that I might be pedaling through virgin territory gave me an anticipatory shiver of excitement.

Others use the metaphor of a 'siren' when describing the frontier, calling them to dangerous pursuits and not able to be easily resisted, again using feminine imagery. Humberstone and Pederson (2001, p. 24) note that 'wilderness places . . . may become symbols and markers for hegemonic masculinity', and this appears to be manifested in these examples of language of seduction, passion and desire. *Doug*, a mountain climber, uses language associated with love and sexual activity when describing his travel experiences ('totally swept away by it', 'romantically adventurous', 'gets my blood racing' and '(I) bask in the glow of another one over'). *Harry* likewise refers to his 'journeying through a place and trying to absorb it' as 'a difficult marriage' and *Rod* talks about the 'honeymoon period of being on a new (polar) expedition'. David Lewis observes that he 'had become embroiled in a love affair—with the sea. (Women and the sea have much in common, of course: both are subject to unpredictable change—and would be boring if they were not) . . . It was inevitable, I suppose, that the call of distant seas should become irresistible' (Lewis, 1975, pp. 14–15). The diver Pipín Ferreras compares the temptations of the sea to feminine charms (Ferreras, 2004, p. 139):

> Jacques Mayol used to say that entering the water for a free dive was like making love to the ocean. And, indeed,

the sea has often been described as a seductive siren, luring men into its often dangerous embrace. That was a lot to compete with . . .

These metaphors may be a way of explaining away or justifying the frontier travellers' fixation with or fascination for extreme travel experiences. The traveller, like an ardent lover, is swept away by their feelings and rendered powerless to resist the attraction of the frontier. Use of this metaphor appears to be more typically associated with male frontier travellers, with some females referring to their experiences in terms of a romance; potentially a less threatening and gentler experience. For example, Alexandra Tolstoy is 'greatly drawn by the romance of travelling' (Tolstoy, 2003, p. 4) along the Silk Road and explains some of the lure of her journey by the historical associations of some of the places she visits: 'To me Samarkand conjures up more romance than Paris or Rome ever could. Its very name suggests adventure, intrigue and the mystery of the Orient' (Tolstoy, 2003, p. 31). Sometimes the fantasy of romance disappoints and reality intrudes. Ben Kozel, for example, found that reaching the end of his river rafting journey was less charming or picturesque than he had originally dreamed of (Kozel, 2002, p. 313). 'There was none of the imagined romance in this moment. I was not standing on a golden beach, squinting into a rising sun. And no salty breeze ruffled the curls of my hair . . . I was cold. I was wet'.

These metaphors and imagery, conceptualising the frontier as a virgin, untouched and ready to be challenged or seduced or 'ripe' for romance, highlight an interesting mythical dimension to frontier travel. Ironically, this ideal of pure untouched wilderness is progressively being eroded in modern society, with Vince *et al.* (2005, p. 20) arguing that 'population numbers and affluence increasingly are making the old dichotomy between wilderness and development obsolete'.

FATE OR DESTINY

Frontier journeys may also be described as 'fateful' or the result of kismet or destiny, which adds to their numinous or magical quality in the minds of the traveller. *Harry*, an adventurer, describes how

'I had this great longing to fulfil what seemed like a destiny', while for Virginia Morell, a trip to find the source of the Blue Nile 'was, of course, my destiny' (Morell, 2001, p. 68)—something which was inevitable and thus could not be avoided. Morell recalls the Ethiopian word for destiny—*eddileh*—which she describes as 'a rainbow in one's life, where destiny has stepped in to hand you something rare and unexpected' (Morell, 2001, p. 68). She describes her destiny thus: 'as if something had to happen in a particular way; there was no other possibility' (Morell, 2001, p. 68). In a similar vein, *Aaron* related that 'I knew I'd go to the North Pole someday, even when I was a little six-year-old boy'.

This reference to destiny may be linked to dreams and fantasies of the frontier traveller, with the individual seeing himself or herself as a hero or heroine 'fated' or chosen to carry out a particular task or journey (Campbell, 1968, 1990). This makes the traveller feel unique or special, having been granted a responsibility or opportunity not open to or offered to others in the 'everyday' world, and might bestow upon the journey a mythic dimension.

MYTHS AND LEGENDS

The frontier journey, as well as the frontier itself, is often linked with mythical constructs. Butler (1996, p. 216), for example, notes that the 'myth of the frontier has been a powerful one', and argues that it may therefore 'be an important part of its appeal as a potential tourist destination'. Frontier travel experiences are described by exponents as 'quests' in almost Arthurian language, or as odysseys, evoking the heroic journey and a desire for transformation through trials, in places 'outside one's own common realm of experience' (Zurick, 1995, p. 137). *Doug* refers to having 'a great epic' when climbing mountains, while *Harry* conceptualises his frontier travel experiences as 'long quests':

> In a sense my journeys are the classic odyssey; Odysseus set out and came back, having had all these experiences, which tested him and so on. But I don't want to compare myself too much to a classical hero but there is that sort of element of setting out to learn and then coming back...

Myth and legend surrounding the deaths of climbers Mallory and Irvine on Mount Everest in the 1920s was a key motivation behind the more recent expedition undertaken by David Roberts and Conrad Anker to recover their bodies. Roberts labels this a 'quest' to 'rediscover Mallory himself, the visionary lost explorer whose body Conrad Anker found, and whose fate we may at last begin to divine' (Anker and Roberts, 1999, p. 16). Mallory's body takes on the guise of the Holy Grail, and even Roberts concedes that Mallory and Irvine's disappearance has been elevated, 'to the realm of the mythic' (Anker and Roberts, 1999, p. 139) due to historical conjecture as to whether they reached the summit before they died. Another climber, Thom Pollard, who discovered Mallory's body during that expedition, also expresses deep respect to a fallen 'hero' (Anker and Roberts, 1999, p. 139).

Tim Cope sought to ride a bike across Russia, Siberia, Mongolia and China, which he describes as 'a realm of mythical places, far off wonderlands...It was a prospect that tempted my imagination...' (Cope and Hatherly, 2003, pp. 1–2). David Breashears felt the same sense of the extraordinary as a child of ten living in Greece, confronted by Mount Olympus: 'I remember longing to climb it and search for traces of mythic gods and ancient warriors' (Breashears, 1999, p. 33). Bettina Selby refers to fabled tales of old when describing her journey to the source of the Nile (Selby, 1988, p. 8): 'I thought I would ride in a leisurely manner along the seaboard of the delta, from Alexandria to Port Said, seeing all the famous places that had been a legend to me for so long'. The legends, for Selby, give the destination a momentous, venerable quality, imparting a sense of significance and meaning beyond the place itself. This ties in with Rojek's (1997) view that myth is used by individuals to bring meaning to places visited.

THE EXPLORER'S JOURNEY

A subset of mythic journeys involves retracing historic expeditions or following in the footsteps of famous travellers or explorers. This desire of individuals to 'role play' and act out narratives has been identified in the travel context, and its importance in 'play' has been particularly noted by Gyimóthy and Mykletun (2004, p. 865), who describe how Arctic trekkers in their study used 'harsh environmental conditions and hard physical activities…to inscribe themselves into an idealized 'explorer' or 'pioneer' role'. Hall (2002, p. 295) cites ecologist Aldo Leopold as arguing that 'the opportunity to relive or imagine the experiences of pioneers or the "frontier" that formed national culture…was an essential component of the value of wilderness and wilderness recreation'. This is illustrated by the following comment of *Geoff*, a polar trekker and sailor: 'It actually motivates me in a way, to know that I'm not alone, in the fact that this is an old path that I take'. *Helen* refers to the 'first people' who attempted the ascent of Mount Everest and notes that she was climbing 'in their footsteps, hopefully with the same mindset'.

Some frontier travellers are careful to distinguish between their own exploits and those of famous explorers. As *Keith*, a pilot and balloonist, notes, 'I'm an adventurer…Mawson's an explorer. An explorer is a person who goes somewhere where no one has ever been and quite often is doing it for scientific reasons. And that's what Mawson was. I'm an adventurer…I do it for the spirit of adventure. And there's a big difference'. *Graham*, a desert trekker, observes that, 'I was born two hundred years too late…there's nothing left to explore…all I can do is go and retrace what someone's already done'.

Harry notes that there is 'an imperialistic thread running through Western tradition of exploration'. For Bettina Selby however, a fantasy of Empire and the 'golden age' of exploration are woven across part of her journey through Africa, which she describes as in the 'footsteps' of Victorian traveller and novelist Amelia B. Edwards. Prior to Selby's departure, she spent hours reading atlases and books of African exploration, leading to dreams that 'began to be peopled by long trains of porters bearing Fortnum and Mason hampers. Armies of fanatical "Fuzzy Wuzzies" boiled out of the desert behind their Mahdi, hurling themselves against "thin red lines" of pith-helmeted soldiers with Kitchener moustaches' (Selby, 1988, p. 7). This 'aura of empire' (Selby, 1988, p. 120) also encompasses following in the footsteps of the 'heroic' colonial explorers, whom she later refers to as 'my Victorian forerunners' (Selby, 1988, p. 228). Jamal

et al. (2003, p. 149), citing Gregory (2001), refer to the phenomenon of 'a nostalgia for colonialism itself, a desire to recreate and recover the world of late Victorian and Edwardian colonialism in all its majestic glory'. Selby's description of her travel experience evokes images of exploration and colonial splendour, a self-confessed 'dream state'.

DREAMS, MYSTERY AND ILLUSION

Many frontier travellers in this study referred to their travel experiences using the metaphor of a dream. For example, *Alex*, a round-the-world sailor, notes, 'Getting back, I say this fairly often, was just like waking up from a dream, as in the trip was a dream. So you wake up and you're in your normal world again…' Michael Asher also ascribes dreamlike qualities to the Sahara desert during his journey (Asher, 1988, p. 280–281): 'a place where conscious and unconscious, dream and reality, came together'.

Frontier travel experiences may also be described as magical or linked with mystery. This perhaps links to the propensity for frontier travellers to refer to their destinations as otherworldly or 'alien'—they are not quite 'of this world'. This is illustrated by Robyn Davidson, who describes her solo journey with camels across the Outback in illusory terms before she departs (Davidson, 1980, p. 95), and notes how its magic affected other people she knew or met:

> From the day the thought came into my head 'I am going to enter a desert with camels' to the day I felt the preparations to be completed, I had built something intangible but magical for myself which had rubbed off a little on to other people, and I would probably never have the opportunity to do anything quite so demanding or as fulfilling as that ever again.

The reality of what she sees and experiences in the Outback supersedes even her wildest imaginings. Davidson describes the enchantment of the desert as a magical realm from a fairytale (Davidson, 1980, p. 218): 'Nothing as wildly beautiful as that had I ever seen, even in my dream landscapes'. Bear Grylls uses similar language when discussing his emotions upon reaching the summit of Everest (Grylls, 2000, p. 254): 'The views I saw and the magic I felt during those precious few minutes will remain embedded in me for ever. They had surpassed my wildest imagination. I knew that I could never forget'. *Harry* sees his journeys as attempts 'to capture perhaps that magic that I'd sensed as a child'.

It is interesting that this element of illusion or a dream state exists alongside a strong desire for authenticity of experience for many frontier travellers (Hamilton, 2000; Hillary and Elder, 2003). This supports in part the contention of MacCannell (1976), that 'tourism is a metaphor for the general inauthenticity of modern life, where the tourist journeys away from modernity's artifices in search of authentic objects and experiences elsewhere', but also the view of Feifer (1985) that the post-tourist is seeking experiences that are unique, extraordinary and novel. The focus on the extraordinary as it relates to the imaginary world is also present in the metaphors and imagery linked to fantasies or fairytales.

FANTASIES AND FAIRY TALES

Zurick (1995, p. 61) notes that fantasy 'predates the journey and continually propels it along new courses', and the fairytale aspects of tourism have been considered by several academics, including Jafari and Gardner (1991) and Dann (1996). The latter observes that tourists 'are caught up in a fairy-tale world of childhood' (Dann, 1996, p. 123), and Gyimóthy and Mykletun (2004, p. 865–866) see this fantasy element manifested in travellers, such as Arctic trekkers, who 'invent substitute worlds, supplement versions of reality, or inscribe themselves into the new identities'; in their case, the 'explorer' or 'pioneer'. Dann (1996, p. 124) cites a number of accounts of exploration where individuals 'sometimes viewed the new territories they discovered in terms of fairyland' (see also Thomas, 1952; Cocker, 1992). This type of fantasy can form shared narratives within a community of travellers, as identified by Belk and Costa (1998, p. 220) with their focus on recreated mountain rendezvous: 'Certain fantasies have the benefits of scripts and motifs'.

Fairytales and fantasies were evoked by participants such as *Keith*, who says of ballooning, 'I'd visualised it being this wonderful magic carpet

ride', using language reminiscent of *The Arabian Nights*, and *Ross*, who refers to mountains looking 'like they were something out of a Tolkien novel…just like a fantasy'. *Evan* saw balloon flights as 'the stuff of fairytales', while Marinetta Asher (Asher, 1988, p. 265) describes the desert in terms of Perrault's *The Sleeping Beauty*. 'It's like an enchanted world—the colours, the rainbow, the stillness. It's like a place that is sleeping under a spell'.

For Bear Grylls, Mount Everest is a 'place of dreams' (Grylls, 2000, p. 41) and he describes his climb through the foothills in his diary using language straight from the Brothers Grimm (Grylls, 2000, p. 52): 'Vast mountains, the biggest in our world, rise straight up all around us, and when the wind blows through the valleys where we are, it feels as if the giants are stamping their heels'. *Alex* initially searched for 'a physical paradise' in the Edenic sense but found that ultimately it resided in companionship and 'the human interaction and the harmony and the working together' rather than a beautiful landscape: 'That is the closest you can get to paradise'.

Part of the fantasy connected to frontier travel experiences may be related to role play. Dann (1976, p. 22) notes that 'travel allows the individual the opportunity to build an environment for acting out psychic needs, and the playing of certain roles which cannot be fulfilled at home'. This is illustrated by round-the-world balloonist Brian Jones, who experiences a fantasy of being an astronaut as he prepares to board his balloon, and feels he is 're-enacting' heroic flights of the past (Piccard and Jones, 1999, p. 14):

> As we drive slowly towards it, with the balloon growing bigger and bigger in our eyes, my mind flew back thirty years to the launch of the Apollo 11 mission to the moon. In 1969 I had watched enthralled on television as the crew went aboard, and now I felt we were re-enacting the scene.

Using role play to re-enact fantasies is also echoed in the theatrical metaphors and imagery used by travellers when discussing their experiences and motivations behind frontier travel.

PERFORMANCE AND 'PLAY'

Frontier travel may involve an element of the theatrical, and the metaphors and imagery revealed in this current study support this. Celsi *et al.* (1993) refer to high-risk activities as being motivated, to a degree, by a 'dramatic world-view' in Western society, which has its roots in classical Greek theatre and involves conflict and tension-building finally released or solved through 'denouement', which leads to a purification or release known as 'catharsis'. Zurick (1995, p. 137) also uses performance imagery in his discussion of the 'back' of 'national frontiers', those remote peripheries that are contrasted with the 'front' or staged elements, such as enactments and ceremonies 'put on' for entertainment or 'amusement' of tourists. This imagery may not be unique to the frontier or independent traveller, according to the literature. Weaver (2005) uses performative metaphors in a study of the cruise industry, while Urbain (1993) considers the behaviour of some tourists returning home as akin to an actor, with 'roles' undertaken during travel 'carried over' and souvenirs likened to 'accompanying stage props' (Dann, 1996). Mordue (2005, p. 180) also refers to the recent focus of researchers on 'performance as a metaphor for tourist practice'.

Paradoxically, as discussed above, the frontier traveller appears keen to limit, if not eliminate, the 'front' stage, seeking a more authentic or 'real' experience, while still describing the experience using theatrical elements and imagery. For example, *Evan* expressly states that he enjoys the 'theatre' of frontier travel: 'The fact that it's perceived by the general public to be absolutely terrifying is fine, because that's all part of the theatre'. Creating theatre around frontier travel, for this individual, appears to involve playing up risks, highlighting the drama and involving the audience (the public) in an active way so that they take a personal interest in what is happening. They are not taken 'backstage' to discover the truth behind risks, that they are less dramatic than they appear to the 'audience'. Other potential audiences might be the media, sponsors or even peers. As round-the-world sailor Hugo Vihlen notes of his journey (Vihlen, 1971, p. 183): 'The trip has been a great experience and a test of myself in many ways, but it's not something that I would do if I thought no one else in the world

cared about it'. The ultimate audience of course for the frontier traveller is the self. Ian Brown saw walking to the South Pole as offering a chance for self-exploration: 'Our (polar) venture was a journey into ourselves as well as into a mysterious physical realm' (Brown, 1999, p. 14).

Mountaineers such as Robert Anderson often use theatrical language when describing their motivations, for example using imagery of being 'onstage' or in the 'spotlight' when climbing mountains. Anderson labels climbing Mount Everest 'the public finale' (1995, p. 201) to his attempt to climb the highest peak on each continent, while Andrew Lindblade (2001, p. 231) refers to 'the often serious scenarios played out when in the mountains'. For David Breashears, 'Bouldering was my rehearsal call; climbing was my performance' (Breashears, 1999, p. 53). He saw climbing 'not just as a sport, but as a form of expression…I wanted to make my climbing an expression of competence and grace' (Breashears, 1999, p. 46). The desert reminds adventurer Benedict Allen of a minimalist set (Allen, 1992, p. 282). 'Once, years ago at school, we had done a play, Beckett's *Waiting for Godot*. This camp had the same emptiness as the set, the inaction of the characters'.

Exploring the theatrical metaphors and imagery behind frontier travel might be a useful area for future research, as it appears to support the work of Gyimóthy and Mykletun (2004) on adventure as a form of 'deep play', following Ackerman (1999). It could also be linked to searching out new roles or identity within travel, providing the opportunity for a 'dislocation of self from the ordinary to the extraordinary…' (Beedie and Hudson, 2003, p. 625).

This paper will now consider the ways in which metaphors and imagery discussed in this section illuminate our understanding of the frontier travel experience, as well as the implications of these findings for the marketing of these experiences and tourism more generally.

DISCUSSION AND CONCLUSION

The analysis of the biographical texts and interview data used in this study reveals a common discourse or paradigm of the *performance of adventure*, where the traveller is following in the footsteps of explorers of old and performing a role based on heroic or mythic journeys of the past, as well as aspects of fairytale and fantasy. Within this metempsychotic approach to travel, the individual may be free to take on a new identity or enact a new role for himself or herself (Edensor, 2000). Each of the metaphors or imagery used helps to shape our understanding of the frontier travel experience, which appears to be based on the acting out or the re-enacting of stories or narratives from the past for a real or imagined audience that is eager to hear of their exploits. This adventurous role play is both a motivation and the frame for the travel experience. The traveller is the hero or heroine of his or her own mythological journey and must heed the 'call to adventure' (Campbell, 1968). This narrative or myth of adventure is then used by the traveller to enact and interpret their experiences at the frontier. Once home, the triumph of the returning hero is celebrated in print and in person, through public presentations and documentaries. The drama of the frontier travel experience is thus often re-enacted by the traveller when they return home and potentially inspires further mythic journeys, perpetuating the tradition of great explorers and the mythology of adventure.

This paper reveals the benefits of employing narrative analysis in research on tourist experiences. Polkinghorne (1995, p. 5) notes that the increasing interest in this research method is well deserved, as narrative is 'uniquely suited for displaying human existence as situated action', and thus exploring human behavior through the linguistic form. Analysis of the language used by travellers when describing travel experiences appears to be a useful way to develop a greater understanding of how and why people travel and the meanings that they bestow upon those experiences, given that travel often has a mythical dimension (Johns and Clarke, 2001; Johns and Gyimóthy, 2002) and myth is a 'type of speech' and form of expression (Barthes, 1973). The participants discussed in this paper used a common set of metaphors to describe their experiences. The use of metaphor is 'pervasive in everyday life [and] what we experience and what we do . . . is very much a matter of metaphor' (Lakoff and Johnson, 1980, 2003, p. 3). Metaphors can therefore help us to understand how people 'both think and act', even if they are largely unconscious

of these concepts, and how they govern our lives (Lakoff and Johnson, 1980). While this study focused on the frontier traveller, other forms of travel experiences might also be analysed using a similar technique to help illuminate our understanding of the tourist and their world.

Some of the metaphors and imagery uncovered during this study of frontier travel experiences might potentially be useful in future marketing of these experiences, as well as to adventure travel or tourism generally. For example, metaphors connected with theatre and performance might be able to be incorporated in marketing collateral, by the use of words such as 'arena' or 'stage' to describe the experience, given the fact that tourism is largely a performed experience (Cater and Cloke, 2007) and tourism marketers often sell 'stages and playgrounds' (Vester, 1987). Other metaphors such as sexual imagery revolving around feelings of desire and conquest or the fantasy of the frontier as pure and untouched could also be used to frame these intense experiences for its intended audience. These myths of adventure appear to be relevant for the frontier travellers participating in this study and potentially more widely held by other tourists, given the current fascination with risk and desire for novelty within popular culture and the growing demand for adventure tourism experiences (Puchan, 2004; Cater, 2006; Cater and Cloke, 2007; Schott, 2007). It could be argued that the mythology of adventure illustrates Barthes' (1973) contention that myths are essentially culturally constructed values or beliefs, invested in this case in the idea of the adventurer as the modern-day heir to the past luminaries of exploration.

While frontier travel is still largely available only to a small market niche, both because of the risky nature and high cost of these experiences and the fact that they take place in some of the most fragile environments on the planet (literally 'off the planet' in the case of space tourism experiences), they can also be seen as one end of a spectrum of activity or adventure tourism (Hill, 1995; Swarbrooke et al., 2003; Pomfret, 2006) or as a stage of adventure (Mortlock, 1984). This paper goes some way towards shedding some light on the extraordinary experiences of the frontier traveller and how the adventure myth that underpins them might be potentially linked to a broader travel context, based on a collective cultural narrative of heroism and exploration.

ACKNOWLEDGEMENTS

This research is the outcome of a project funded in part by the Sustainable Tourism Cooperative Research Centre, established by the Australian Commonwealth Government. The authors would also like to thank Fiona Wheeler and the anonymous reviewers for insightful feedback and comments on this paper.

REFERENCES

Ackerman D. 1999. *Deep Play*. Vintage Books: New York.

Allen B. 1992. *The Proving Grounds*. Flamingo: London.

Allen B. 2002. *The Faber Book of Exploration: An Anthology of Worlds Revealed by Explorers through the Ages*. Faber and Faber Limited: London.

Anderson R. 1995. *To Everest via Antarctica: Climbing Solo on the Highest Peak on each of the World's Seven Continents*. Penguin Books: Auckland, New Zealand.

Anker C, Roberts D. 1999. *The Lost Explorer: Finding Mallory on Mount Everest*. Touchstone: New York.

Arnould E, Price L. 1993. River magic: extraordinary experience and the extended service encounter. *Journal of Consumer Research* **20**(1): 24–45.

Asher M. 1988. *Two Against the Sahara: On Camelback from Nouakchott to the Nile*. William Morrow and Company Inc: New York.

Barthes R. 1973. *Mythologies*. Translated by Lavers A. Paladin: London (Original work published 1957).

Beedie P, Hudson S. 2003. Emergence of mountain-based adventure tourism. *Annals of Tourism Research* **30**(3): 625–643.

Beerli A, Martin, JD. 2004. Factors influencing destination image. *Annals of Tourism Research* **31**(3): 657–681.

Belk RW, Costa JA. 1998. The mountain man myth: a contemporary consuming fantasy. *Journal of Consumer Research* **25**(3): 218–240.

Bernstein C. 1997. Labov and Waletzky in context. *Journal of Narrative and Life History* **7**(1–4): 45–51.

Bishop P. 1989. *The Myth of Shangri-La: Tibet, Travel Writing and The Western Creation of a Sacred Landscape*. Athlone: London.

Breashears D. 1999. *High Exposure: An Enduring Passion for Everest and other Unforgiving Places*. Canongate Books: Edinburgh, UK.

Brown I. 1999. *Extreme South: Struggles and Triumph of the First Australian Team to the Pole*. Australian Geographic: Terrey Hills, New South Wales, Australia.

Butler RW. 1990. The role of the media in influencing the choice of vacation destinations. *Tourism Recreation Research* **15**, 45–53.

Butler RW. 1996. The development of tourism in frontier regions: issues and approaches. In *Frontiers in Regional Development*, Gradus Y, Lithwick H (eds). Rowman and Littlefield: Lanham, MA; 213–229.

Campbell J. 1968. *The Hero with a Thousand Faces*. Princeton University Press: Princeton, NJ

Campbell J. 1990. *The Hero's Journey. The World of Joseph Campbell II*. Harper and Row Publishers: San Francisco.

Cater CI. 2006. Playing with risk? Participant perceptions of risk and management implications in adventure tourism. *Tourism Management* **27**(2): 317–325.

Cater C, Cloke P. 2007. Bodies in action: the performativity of adventure tourism. *Anthropology Today* **23**(6): 13–16.

Celsi RL, Rose RL, Leigh TW. 1993. An exploration of high-risk leisure consumption through skydiving. *Journal of Consumer Research* **20**(1): 1–23.

Cocker M. 1992. *Loneliness and Time: British Travel Writing in the Twentieth Century*. Seeker and Warburg: London.

Cohen E. 2004. *Contemporary Tourism: Diversity and Change*. Elsevier: Kidlington, UK.

Collis C. 2000. *The edge men: narrating late twentieth century exploration on Australia's desert and Antarctic frontiers*. Unpublished PhD dissertation, La Trobe University: Melbourne, Australia.

Cope T, Hatherly C. 2003. *Off the Rails*. Viking, Penguin Books: Camberwell, Australia.

Crick M. 1994. *Resplendent Sites, Discordant Voices: Sri Lankans and International Tourism*. Harwood Academic Publishers: Chur, Switzerland.

Dann G. 1976. The holiday was simply fantastic. *Tourist Review* **31**(3): 19–23.

Dann G. 1996. *The Language of Tourism: A Sociolinguistic Perspective*. CAB International: Wallingford, UK.

Dann G. 2002. The tourist as a metaphor of the social world. In *The Tourist as a Metaphor of the Social World*, Dann G (ed). CABI Publishing: Wallingford, Oxon, UK; 1–17.

Dann G, Phillips J. 2000. Qualitative tourism research in the late twentieth century and beyond. In *Tourism in the 21st Century: Lessons from Experience*, Faulkner B, Moscardo G, Laws E (eds). Continuum: London and New York; 247–265.

Davidson R. 1980. *Tracks*. Picador, Pan Macmillan: London.

Echtner C, Ritchie J R B. 2003. The meaning and measurement of destination image. *The Journal of Tourism Studies* **14**(1): 37–48.

Edensor T. 2000. Staging tourism: tourists as performers. *Annals of Tourism Research* **27**(2): 322–344.

Elgin S. 1993. *Genderspeak: Men, Women and the Gentle Art of Verbal Self-defense*. John Wiley & Sons: New York.

Elliott J. 2005. *Using Narrative in Social Research: Qualitative and Quantitative Approaches*. Sage Publications: London.

Featherstone M, Hepworth M. 2005. Image of ageing: cultural representations of later life. In *The Cambridge Handbook of Age and Ageing*, Johnson ML, Bengtson VL, Coleman PG, Kirkwood TBL (eds). Cambridge University Press: Cambridge; 354–362.

Feifer M. 1985. *Going Places*. Macmillan: London.

Ferreras P. 2004. *The Dive: A Story of Love and Obsession*. Collins Willow: London.

Fiennes R. 1993. *Mind Over Matter: The Epic Crossing of the Antarctic Continent*. Sinclair-Stevenson: London.

Gibbs RW, Lenz Costa Lima P. Francozo E. 2004. Metaphor is grounded in embodied experience. *Journal of Pragmatics* **36**(7): 1189–1210.

Goetzmann W. 1979. Paradigm lost. In *The Sciences in the American Context: New Perspectives*, Reingold N (ed). Smithsonian Press: Washington, DC; 21–34.

Gregory D. 2001. 'Colonial nostalgia' and cultures of travel: spaces of constructed visibility in Egypt. In *Consuming Tradition, Manufacturing Heritage: Global Norms and Urban Forms in the Age of Tourism*, Sayyad N Al (ed). Routledge: London; 111–151.

Grylls B. 2000. *Facing Up: A Remarkable Journey to the Summit of Mount Everest*. Macmillan: London.

Gudmundsdottir S. 2006. The teller, the tale and the one being told: the narrative nature of the research interview. In *Narrative Methods, Volume II, Narrative Applications*, Atkinson P, Delamont, S (eds). Sage Publications: London; 220–234.

Gyimóthy S, Mykletun RJ. 2004. Play in adventure tourism: the case of Arctic trekking. *Annals of Tourism Research* **31**(4): 855–878.

Hall CM. 2002. The changing cultural geography of the frontier: national parks and wilderness as frontier remnant. In *Tourism in Frontier Areas*, Krakover S, Gradus Y (eds). Lexington Books: Lanham, MA; 283–298.

Hamilton C. 2000. *South Pole 2000: Five Women in Search of an Adventure*. HarperCollins Publishers: Sydney, Australia.

Haynes R D. 1998. *Seeking the Centre: The Australian Desert in Literature, Art and Film*. Cambridge University Press: Cambridge.

Hennig C. 2002. Tourism: enacting modern myths. In *The Tourist as a Metaphor of the Social World*, Dann G (ed). CABI Publishing: Wallingford, UK; 169–187.

Hill BJ. 1995. A guide to adventure travel. *Parks and Recreation* September: 56–65.

Hillary P, Elder JE. 2003. *In the Ghost Country: A Lifetime Spent on the Edge*. Random House Australia: Milsons Point, Australia.

Humberstone BJ, Pedersen K. 2001. Gender, class and outdoor traditions in UK and Norway. *Sport, Education & Society* **6**(1): 23–34.

Hunter DE, Whitten P. 1976. *Encyclopedia of Anthropology*. Harper and Row: New York.

Hutt M. 1996. Looking for Shangri-la: from Hilton to Lamichhane. In *The Tourist Image: Myths and Myth Making in Tourism*, Selwyn T (ed). John Wiley & Sons: Chichester, UK.; 49–60.

Jafari J, Gardner M. 1991. *Tourism and Fiction. Travel as a Fiction, Fiction as a Journey*. Cahiers du Tourisme, série C (119). Centre des Hautes Etudes Touristiques, Université d'Aix-Marseille III: Aix-en-Provence, France.

Jamal T, Everett J, Dann GMS. 2003. Ecological rationalization and performative resistance in natural area destinations. *Tourist Studies* **3**(2): 143–169.

Johns N, Clarke V. 2001. Mythological analysis of boating tourism. *Annals of Tourism Research* **28**(2): 334–359.

Johns N, Gyimóthy S. 2002. Mythologies of a theme park: an icon of modern family life. *Journal of Vacation Marketing* **8**(4): 320–331.

Kozel B. 2002. *Three Men in a Raft: An Improbable Journey Down the Amazon*. Pan Macmillan Australia: Sydney, Australia.

Laing JH, Crouch GI. 2005. Extraordinary journeys: an exploratory cross-cultural study of tourists on the frontier. *Journal of Vacation Marketing*, **11**(3), 209–223.

Lakoff G. 1993. The contemporary theory of metaphor. In *Metaphor and Thought*, 2nd edn, Ortony A (ed). Cambridge University Press: Cambridge; 202–251.

Lakoff G, Johnson M. 1980, 2003. *Metaphors We Live By*. The University of Chicago Press: Chicago and London.

Lakoff G, Johnson M. 1999. *Philosophy in the Flesh: The Embodied Mind and its Challenge to Western Thought*. Basic Books: New York.

Lengkeek J. 2000. Imagination and differences in tourist experience. *World Leisure* **3**: 11–17.

Lewis D. 1975. *Ice Bird: The First Single-handed Voyage to Antarctica*. William Collins Sons & Co/Fontana Books: Glasgow, UK.

Lindblade A. 2001. *Expeditions*. Hardie Grant Books: South Yarra, Australia.

Macbeth J. 2000. Utopian tourists—cruising is not just about sailing. *Current Issues in Tourism* **3**(1): 20–34.

MacCannell D. 1976. *The Tourist: A New Theory of the Leisure Class*. Schocken Books: New York.

Miles MB, Huberman AM. 1994. *Qualitative Data Analysis: An Expanded Sourcebook*, 2nd edn. Sage Publications: Thousand Oaks, CA.

Mordue T. 2005. Tourism, performance and social exclusion in 'Olde York'. *Annals of Tourism Research* **32**(1): 179–198.

Morell V. 2001. *Blue Nile: Ethiopia's River of Magic and Mystery*. National Geographic Society, Adventure Press: Washington, DC.

Morgan M. 2007. 'We're not the Barmy Army!': reflections on the sports tourist experience. *International Journal of Tourism Research* **9**: 361–372.

Mortlock C. 1984. *The Adventure Alternative*. Cicerone Press: Milnthorpe, Cumbria.

O'Leary S, Deegan J. 2005. Ireland's image as a tourism destination in France: attribute importance and performance. *Journal of Travel Research* **43**(3): 247–256.

Palmer C. 1999. Tourism and the symbols of identity. *Tourism Management* **20**: 313–321.

Piccard B, Jones B. 1999. *The Greatest Adventure*. Headline Book Publishing: London.

Polkinghorne DE. 1995. Narrative configuration in qualitative analysis. In *Life History and Narrative*, Hatch J, Wisniewski R (eds). Falmer Press: London; 5–23.

Pomfret G. 2006. Mountaineering adventure tourists: a conceptual framework for research. *Tourism Management* **27**(1): 113–123.

Puchan H. 2004. Living 'extreme': adventure sports, media and commercialisation. *Journal of Communication Management* **9**(2): 171–178.

Pyne SJ. 1987, 2004. *The Ice*. Orion Books: London.

Pyne S. 1993. Space: the third great age of discovery. In *Space: Discovery and Exploration*, Collins M J, Kraemer S K (eds). Smithsonian Institution, National Air and Space Museum and Hugh Lauter Levin Associates Inc: Washington, DC; 14–65.

Riley RW. 1994. Movie-induced tourism. In *Tourism: the State of the Art*, Seaton A V (ed). Wiley: Chichester; 453–458.

Rojek C. 1997. Indexing, dragging and the social construction of tourist sights. In *Touring Cultures*, Rojek C, Urry, J (eds). Routledge: London; 52–74.

Sagan C, Pyne SJ. 1988. *The Scientific and Historical Rationales for Solar System Exploration*. Space Policy Institute, The George Washington University: Washington DC.

Seale C. 1999. *The Quality of Qualitative Research*. Sage Publications: London.

Seaton AV. 2002. Tourism as metempsychosis and metensomatosis: the personae of eternal recurrence. In *The Tourist as a Metaphor of the Social World*, Dann G (ed). CABI Publishing: Wallingford, UK; 135–168.

Schott C. 2007. Selling adventure tourism: a distribution channels perspective. *International Journal of Tourism Research* 9(4): 257–274.

Selby B. 1988. *Riding the Desert Trail*. Sphere Books Ltd: London.

Shackley M. 2001. The legend of Robin Hood: myth, inauthenticity, and tourism development in Nottingham, England. In *Hosts and Guests Revisited: Tourism Issues of the 21st Century*. Smith VL, Brent M (eds). Cognizant Communication Corporation: New York; 315–322.

Shekhdar J with Griffiths E. 2001. *Bold Man of the Sea: My Epic Journey*. Hodder & Stoughton: London.

Shields R. 1991. *Places on the Margin: Alternative Geographies of Modernity*. Routledge: London and New York.

Smith B, Weed S. 2007. The potential of narrative research in sports tourism. *Journal of Sport & Tourism* 12(3/4): 249–269.

Smith CP. 2000. Content analysis and narrative analysis. In *Handbook of Research Methods in Social and Personality Psychology*, Reis HT and Judd CM (eds). Cambridge University Press: Cambridge; 313–335.

Swarbrooke, J, Beard, C, Leckie S, Pomfret G. 2003. *Adventure Tourism: The New Frontier*. Butterworth Heinemann: Oxford.

Tannen D. 1989. *Talking Voices: Repetition, Dialogue, and Imagery in Conversational Discourse*. Cambridge University Press: Cambridge.

Taylor SJ, Bogdan R. 1998. *Introduction to Qualitative Research Methods: A Guidebook and Resource* (3rd edition). John Wiley & Sons: USA.

Thomas L Jr. 1952. *Out of this World*. Travel Book Club: London.

Trauer B. 2006. Conceptualizing special interest tourism—frameworks for analysis. *Tourism Management* 27(2): 183–200.

Tolstoy A. 2003. *The Last Secrets of the Silk Road*. Profile Books Ltd: London.

Urbain J. 1993. *L'Idiot du Voyage. Histoires de Touristes*. Editions Payot et Rivages: Paris.

van Manen M. 1977. Linking ways of knowing with ways of being practical. *Curriculum Inquiry* 6(3): 205–228.

Van Nortwick T. 1992. *Somewhere I Have Never Travelled: The Second Self and the Hero's Journey in Ancient Epic*. Oxford University Press: New York.

Vester HG. 1987. Adventure as a form of leisure. *Leisure Studies* 6(3): 237–249.

Vihlen HS. 1971. *April Fool: Or, How I Sailed from Casablanca to Florida in a Six-foot Boat*. Follett Publishing Company: Chicago.

Vince SW, Duryea ML, Macie EA, Hermansen LA. 2005. *Forests at the Wildland-Urban Interface: Conservation and Management*. CRC Press: Boca Raton, FL.

Voase R. 2007. Visiting a cathedral: the consumer psychology of a 'rich' experience. *International Journal of Heritage Studies* 13(1): 41–55.

Weaver A. 2005. Interactive service work and performative metaphors: the case of the cruise industry. *Tourist Studies* 5(1): 5–27.

Wheeler S. 1996. *Terra Incognita: Travels in Antarctica*. Random House Inc: New York.

Zurick D. 1995. *Errant Journeys*. University of Texas Press: Austin, TX.

Write Away

1. Develop a marketing brochure (print or digital) for an adventure travel destination of your choosing. Decide which myths and fantasies, if any, you would like to incorporate and how you might do so. To prepare for this work, you might analyze marketing materials for other adventure travel destinations. Along with your brochure, include a reflection in which you discuss the choices you made, your target readers, and any ethical complexities you grappled with as you created the brochure.

2. Write a market analysis for a new travel adventure idea or for an expanded location of a current travel adventure opportunity. You can model your market analysis on the structure provided by the Small Business Administration: https://www.sba.gov/starting-business/write-your-business-plan/market-analysis. In consultation with your instructor, you can also integrate infographics into your market analysis and create a verbal presentation, or pitch, stemming from your analysis as well.

3. Using a search engine, locate a travelogue or travel narrative about a place, and write an essay in which you identify and analyze the use of myths and fantasies in that travelogue or narrative. How does the text deploy myths and fantasy? For what purposes? Can you identify any myths or fantasies in the text that are different, or which are used differently, from those discussed in the article?

Economic Analysis: "The Macroeconomic Aftermath of the Earthquake/Tsunami in Japan" by Ilan Noy

Transfer Points: Economics, Disaster Studies

"We are stuck in our offices because elevators are stopped. We are watching [on] TV the tsunami rushing landward … I am almost seasick from constant rolling of the building." –Jeffrey Balanag, Higashi-Shimbashi, Tokyo ("Japanese Earthquake")

"I have never felt such a strong quake in my life. My flat is on the fifth floor…and the building shook slowly at first, then more and more violently. It was really scary." –Yukiko, Tokyo ("Japanese Earthquake")

These are but two of the many eyewitness accounts from survivors of the March 11, 2011, Japanese earthquake. The earthquake, which began on a Friday at 2:46 p.m. local time, measured a magnitude of 9 and lasted nearly six minutes (Oskin). It then generated a widely destructive tsunami. The disaster also caused a "level 7 nuclear meltdown" (Oskin) at the Fukushima Daiichi Nuclear Power Plant, causing radioactive water to spread, with detection as far as North American coasts (Oskin). As of 2015, the number of confirmed deaths was 15,891, with more than 2,500 still reported missing (Oskin). As many as 500,000 people were displaced, 100,000 of them children (McCurry).

How do we measure the costs of such destruction? What are the different types of resources impacted by a disaster? How will such destruction impact the future? How can we transfer what we learn about the economics related to one disaster to others, so as to mitigate risk, minimize destruction, and strengthen recovery? What factors impact the types and degrees of economic devastation from disasters?

These are but a few of the important questions people research and write about in the field of disaster economics. Economist Ilan Noy, for instance, author of the article included here, explores the various economic impacts stemming from the 2011 Japanese earthquake and tsunami.

Research in disaster economics has had profound impacts on emergency preparedness and management. When considering different options for humanitarian aid or reconstruction, disaster economics can help policy makers and agencies identify what will be most cost-effective or efficient and what will have the most significant positive impact (Bull). Disaster analysis can also help us understand the cycles of risk and how to mitigate risk. For instance, some economists have found that insurance costs do not adequately cover disasters and that long-term policies would be in more alignment with the increasingly real threat of loss. Although such long-term policies would elevate costs to consumers, research indicates that cost would incentivize mitigation efforts and therefore mobilize people to do more with emergency preparedness and planning, thereby eventually driving down the threat of risk (Kunreuther and Michel-Kerjan).

Those in disaster economics have also brought research to bear on emergency-planning programs, enabling policy makers to distribute resources more effectively. For instance, in Oklahoma, the costliest aspect of tornadoes is not the tornadoes themselves, but the time spent doing nothing during warnings (Sutter and Simmons). And, researchers have also determined that tornado shelters cost $57 million per life saved, making them a relatively ineffective means of preparation (Sutter and Simmons).

Ilan Noy is the Chair in the Economics of Disasters and a Professor of Economics at Victoria University of Wellington, New Zealand. He has a B.A. from the Hebrew University in Jerusalem and a Ph.D. in International Economics from the University of California, Santa Cruz. Prior to joining Victoria University, Noy was an Assistant and Associate Professor of Economics at the University of Hawaii. Noy's research and writing focuses on the economics of disasters and financial crises. He has written about disasters and crises around the world, including the Christchurch earthquake, the Bangkok flood, the Fonterra food contamination, and the Kobe and Canterbury earthquakes. ("Ilan")

But disaster economics is only one specialty within the widely varied field of economics. The *Journal of Economic Literature* (*JEL*), in fact, has identified more than 30 subfields of economics, including transportation economics, game theory, bargaining theory, econometrics, macroeconomics, microeconomics, sports economics, cultural economics, and tourism economics.

Broadly construed, people researching, writing, and working in economics pursue questions about resources and the lack thereof. They ask the following sorts of questions: "Why are some countries rich and some countries poor?" "How will population aging affect life in the coming decades?" "What happened in 2008 to cause the worst recession since the 1930s?" ("What is").

The field of economics transgresses time, moving across past, present, and future.

Economists focusing on the past conduct research to better understand particular time periods, practices, or events. Such research might focus on the economics of banana production in Cameroon (Fonsah and Chidebelu), the economic history of child labor (Das), or the economics of the Great Depression (Parker). Economists also study the history of economic theory in particular regions and time periods, such as ancient Chinese economic thought (Lin, et al.) or the Whig party's approach to economics (Stasavage), or they infuse a historical study with an economic lens such as *An Economic History of Ireland Since Independence* (Bielenberg and Ryan).

Economists also explore contemporary events. The summer 2016 news section on the American Economic Association website, for instance, carried the following current items: "Are the Olympics ever worth it for the host city?," "The truth about the gender wage gap," and "Study: Legal Weed Could Raise $12 Billion a Year in Taxes" (AEA).

Economists also develop models to predict future events, scenarios, and practices. Such research might be focused around a particular field, such as future health care expenditures (Norton and Stearns), gas wells (Mohney and Mann), and passenger aircraft (Han and Choi). Or, such research might be about a particular region, such as the economic future of central Asia (Pomfret), Europe (de Lecea), or Romania (Stober).

Writing in the field of economics often integrates quantitative analysis, replete with frequent use of charts, graphs, and visuals. Economists write across many different genres and venues. They create peer-reviewed scholarship, but also regularly produce policy recommendations, op-eds, reports, and popular scholarship and literature about economic matters.

Increasingly, economists are forging interdisciplinary connections. Behavioral economics, for instance, fuses psychology and economics to explore what informs individual decision making and what shapes and limits economists' ability to accurately predict, measure, and explain economic cycles. Economic analysis also intersects with many other disciplines, including ethics, cultural anthropology, and literature.

This wide range of applicability across disciplines and contexts demonstrates the ways in which economics relies heavily on transfer. In the context of disaster economics, transfer-based thinking holds particular importance. Through transfer, economists can more effectively help policy makers and responders prepare for and respond to disasters and then build on that knowledge more effectively for future disasters.

Write Here

Think about a recent disaster and, with a small group of classmates, brainstorm all the possible economic impacts that this disaster might have had. What are the economic impacts from disasters? Which industries are impacted? What resources are impacted? What geographic region(s) experience those impacts?

Ilan Noy
The Macroeconomic Aftermath of the Earthquake/Tsunami in Japan

In the last 14 months, we have seen a spate of very large earthquakes which began with the unprecedented devastation caused by the earthquake in Haiti (1/10/10)—the most destructive natural disaster in modern history (relative to national population), continued with the unusually strong earthquake in Chile (2/27/10), to the most recent events generated by the earthquake in Sendai, Japan.

The horrific toll of this disaster is not yet clear (both in terms of fatalities and physical damage) and the nuclear crisis triggered by this event is still unfolding. Econbrowser readers, however, are probably already asking what will be the likely economic impact of this disaster. Remarkably, in spite of a spate of catastrophic disasters in the last decade (the East Asian tsunami of 2004, the Kashmir earthquake of 2005, and the Sichuan earthquake in 2008 to name a few), we have a fairly limited knowledge of the likely macroeconomic impacts of these events.

Before discussing these impacts, however, it is useful to note that while the most widely used dataset on disasters (EM-DAT) shows that their incidence has been growing over time, this increase is probably driven by improved reporting of milder events; truly large events do not show a similar trend.

Increasing Prevalence of Natural Disasters 1970–2007

—×— Total events   —○— Large events (right scale)

'Large events' refer to events the intensity of which is above the mean of the normalized killed distribution (source: authors' calculations from **EMDAT** data).

Figure 1 taken from Cavallo et al. (2010).

Direct Damage from Natural Disasters
Direct damages—i.e., the damage to fixed assets and capital, to raw materials and extractable natural resources, and most importantly mortality and morbidity—are typically much larger in less developed countries, and countries with a weakened institutional capacity. A comparison of the damages caused by the 2010 earthquakes in Haiti and Chile easily demonstrates this point. The dramatically different outcomes, 240,000 people dead as compared with around 500, originated at least partially from different policies, institutional arrangements, and economic conditions. This makes the Sendai earthquake unusual, since it caused very significant damage in a very prosperous country, and one that is typically considered very well prepared to mitigate these events. While the final death toll is still unclear, it appears it will be quite significantly larger than the Kobe earthquake of 1995, the most fatal natural disaster to hit a developed country in many years (when about 6400 people died).

Indirect Damages in the Short- and Long-Run
The indirect damages from a natural disaster refer to the impact on economic activity, in particular the production of goods and services, that will not take place following the disaster and because of it. These indirect damages may be caused by the direct damages to physical infrastructure (for example, the damage to the fishing fleet in the Sendai area), or because reconstruction pulls resources away from production (for example, the problems experienced by several industries as a result of rolling blackouts instituted to redirect electricity to the affected area). If significant enough, these costs can be accounted for in the aggregate by examining the overall performance of the economy, as measured through the most relevant macroeconomic variables, in particular GDP, the fiscal accounts, consumption, investment, the balance of trade and the balance of payments. Economists, remarkably, have only recently started attempting to quantify these costs and explain their magnitudes (recent surveys of this new literature are Cavallo and Noy, and Sharma).

As a result of several recent research projects (e.g., a World Bank project), the evidence on the short-run growth effects of disasters appears fairly clear by now. Findings in Noy (2009) are representative of this emerging consensus. Countries with higher per capita incomes, higher literacy rate, and better institutions are not only less vulnerable to the initial impact of the disaster, but their macro-economy is less affected as well (see table below). In particular, there is no evidence from recent data that even large natural disasters have any measurable adverse impact on the national economy of rich developed countries like Japan. In contrast, poorer less-developed countries do face significant short-run costs of disasters, and these can translate into significant income losses.

Disaster cost of estimated coefficients

Variable	(1)	(2)	(3)
	All	OECD	Developing
DDAMG-binary (big disasters)	-9.56	1.33	-9.72
DDAMG-binary (cumulative — big disasters)	-11.39	1.99	-11.68
DDAMGS	-0.96	1.58	-1.09
DDAMGS (cumulative)	-1.17	2.34	-1.33

Note: The table reports the change in GDP growth in percentage points that result from natural disasters in the short-run. Calculations are based on specifications presented in Table 4 columns 1–3. The first two rows measure the impact of an average large disaster (>mean direct damage) while the last two measure the impact of a disaster one standard deviation above the mean for direct damages. The cumulative effect is calculated based on the coefficient for the lag GDP growth as estimated in the dynamic panel.

Table taken from Noy (2009).

When compared to the research on short-run indirect impacts, the literature on the long-run effects of natural disasters is scant and its results inconclusive. The most recent attempts to evaluate the long-run impact of disasters on GDP suggest that there is no evidence of an adverse impact (if anything, a few papers argue that disasters provide an impetus for 'creative destruction' dynamics that lead to increased growth). For example, Cavallo et al (2010) construct counterfactual synthetic countries unaffected by disasters, and find no significant long-run effect of disasters on per capita GDP (even for very large disasters).

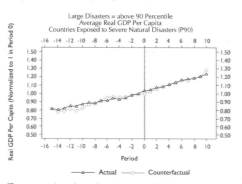

Figure 2 taken from Cavallo et al. (2010).

And What About Japan?

Given the findings described above, one can conclude that the likely indirect impacts of this horrific earthquake/tsunami event on growth in the Japanese economy will be quite minimal. The Japanese government and the Japanese people have access to large amounts of human and financial resources that can be directed toward a rapid and robust reconstruction and rebuilding of the affected region. Neither do we have any evidence to suggest that the earthquake is likely to have any enduring monetary effects. This observation, however, does not preclude enduring regional impacts. There is almost no research on this question, but some preliminary evidence suggests that similar large natural shocks can have important regional consequences. One widely mentioned prediction is that the population of New Orleans is unlikely to recover from the dramatic exodus of people from the region after Hurricane Katrina. Coffman and Noy argue that a similar and apparently semi-permanent decrease in population is observable for an Hawaiian island that was hit by a destructive hurricane in 1992.

In addition to these potentially permanent regional impacts, of course, this disaster may have impact on other macro-economic aggregates. The fiscal expansion that will follow this disaster will further increase the Japanese government's debt levels, but since this debt largely stays in Japan, and since households (especially credit-constrained households—see Sawada and Shimizutani) are likely to 'tighten their belts' and reduce consumption temporarily, these other affects are unlikely to be enduring as well.

One caveat is worth mentioning here: We still do not know what will be the impact of the enfolding crisis in the various nuclear reactors that have been affected. The analysis above ignored this danger, though the still present devastation in Chernobyl attests to its potentially destructive powers.

Write Away

1. How does analytic framework impact claims? Economists invoke many types of analysis in their research. Several of the most common include cost analysis, fiscal impact analysis, cost-effectiveness analysis, and cost-benefit analysis ("Types"). Define each of these different types of economic analysis, and, using evidence from Noy, identify which type of analysis Noy's work most closely resembles. Then, identify one or two other types of analysis and write a version of Noy's article that would be grounded on these other types of economic analysis.

2. Compose an annotated bibliography about research in one of the subfields of economics. You can choose, for example, macroeconomics, behavioral economics, sports economics, tourism economics, disaster economics, or any other subfield of economics as identified by the *Journal of Economic Literature*. For your subfield, identify trends, gaps in the literature, and areas for further research.

3. Noy argues that the economic status of a country has a significant bearing on the economic impact of a disaster. Using a database on economic loss, gather data about the economic impacts of disasters across several different countries. Position this data against other economic indicators of a country's status. What is the correlation between economic impact from disaster and economic status? Write a comparative analysis using economic data, integrating data visualization, and articulating a claim about economic status and disaster loss.

Chapter 7 Key Terms

analysis

analytic methods

rhetorical analysis

critical discourse analysis (CDA)

content analysis

visual analysis

scientific data analysis

statistical analysis

Big Data analysis

crosscultural analysis

Write Away

This activity asks that you engage in several different modes of analysis using the same object or text for analysis in order to gain insights into how different disciplinary contexts and different analytic modes yield different results from analysis.

Choose a somewhat brief or compact text that you can analyze in multiple ways. As in other instances throughout *Writing in Transit*, the concept of text should be as broadly construed as possible—an image, object, written text, etc.

Choose several analytic modes. From the different modes of analysis discussed in this chapter, select three or four to use. For example, you might analyze an advertisement that includes written and visual elements by conducting a rhetorical analysis, a visual analysis, and a content analysis. If you choose a mode of analysis that requires additional expertise, such as scientific data analysis, you can opt to instead identify the various elements of the text you would choose to analyze if you had more equipment and expertise, and ideas for how you might do so and what you would ostensibly learn.

Conduct and write the analyses. Conduct the different analytic approaches and write down what you discern—or think you would discern if you are analyzing in theory as opposed to reality—through each of these analyses.

Reflect on transfer and synthesis. After having had the opportunity to conduct multiple modes of analysis on the same text, reflect for ten minutes in writing on how you transferred analytic skills across the different analyses: What were the intersections and differences between your analytic processes? What divergent or similar kinds of conclusions did you reach as you conducted the various analyses?

Framing Arguments

Namoratunga, located in Kenya, dates from 300 BCE and is considered one of the oldest archaeoastronomical sites in sub-Saharan Africa. The location actually consists of two separate sites, both of which hold astronomical significance. Namoratunga pillars are aligned with astronomical precision, demonstrating that "an accurate and complex calendar system based on astronomical reckoning was developed by the first millennium BCE in eastern Africa." The stones of Namoratunga track "the movement of seven constellations in relation to the lunar cycle" (Chwanya; Lynch and Robbins; Martin).

Many different scholars have engaged in arguments surrounding Namoratunga. While some of them focus on the age of the stones or interpretation of their design, much like the arguments we encountered regarding petroglyphs in Chapter 7, the vast range of arguments about Namoratunga reflect what is an enormously wide array of possible disciplinary perspectives within and across which arguments emerge.

Timothy Clack and Marcus Brittain, for example, draw on Namoratunga as a site to argue for a more ethical approach to archaeology, a "participative archaeology research framework in which accountability is directed toward common ground between multiple 'stake-holders.'" Another team of researchers, led by astrophysicist Jarita Holbrook, includes Namoratunga as one of several sites around which they have developed a research conference and publication about African archaeoastronomy. One of their primary arguments is that, contrary to popular conception, tribal populations and ancient herdsmen in Africa had sophisticated calendar and astronomical knowledge.

Meanwhile, Barbara P. Nash, Harry V. Merrick, and Francis H. Brown, a team with geological and engineering expertise, examine black, glass-like volcanic rock called obsidian at localities in and around Namoratunga as a means of arguing about "patterns of source utilization within the region during the Later Stone Age and Pastoral Neolithic times."

The many questions surrounding Namoratunga—archaeology, ethics, power dynamics, cultural knowledge, history—illustrate the high stakes that can accompany arguments. Scholars develop and formulate arguments in order to advance knowledge, influence others, and draw attention to ideas that matter.

Although each argument about Namoratunga carries unique attributes, together they gesture toward two vital features of argument in academic writing worth emphasizing: significance and purpose.

These arguments show that even highly academic and somewhat nuanced topics, such as archaeological approaches or stone aging, have a larger significance and matter on a profound level. Similarly, while you might on occasion have the opportunity to argue in academic writing about a highly contentious issue, such as the death penalty or abortion, it is far more likely that across your academic career you will be asked to develop arguments about issues that might seem on the surface much less polarizing and perhaps initially somewhat less significant. Both occasions for argument have challenges: In the former, how do you convert opinion and emotion into a reasoned, effective, evidence-based argument? In the latter, how do you become intellectually and emotionally invested in less-contentious topics?

The Namoratunga arguments also convey a sense of what argumentative purpose may entail in the context of academic writing: namely that the purpose of arguments in academic writing is not usually to win so much as to advance knowledge. Joseph Joubert, an eighteenth-century French essayist, captures this version of argument quite well in a line from his famous text, *Pensées*: "The aim of argument...should not be victory, but progress."

As the Namoratunga arguments demonstrate, and as Joubert's quote advocates, argument in the context of academic writing is more often about progress than victory. Whereas the concept of victory seems harnessed to a desire to vanquish an opponent, arguments aimed at progress instead help us learn and grow; they enable us to move forward with our goals and dreams or reconsider our actions and change course when necessary.

Of course, progress itself is open to debate—progress according to one person might seem to be a lack of progress to another. Still, Joubert's larger point is that argument should move along our thinking. Argument should advance knowledge by examining questions, listening to others' ideas, and communicating what you have learned.

Write Here

Reflect on why each of the arguments about Namoratunga might be important. What is at stake in these arguments? Why might they be significant? A different, perhaps brasher, way to ask this question would be, "So what?" What difference might these arguments make? Who is, or should be, invested in these arguments? Can you think of any other kinds of scholarly arguments that might emerge around Namoratunga? What might their significance be?

---

೧ ೧ ೧

Correcting Common Myths about Arguments

Argument carries with it several pervasive misconceptions. In part, myths about argument emerge because argument itself is such a ubiquitous term used across so many diverging contexts, from personal to professional to academic. Conceiving of argument as a universal concept can negatively impact writers' transfer of argument across writing contexts by preventing them from examining how different contexts shape argument itself. So, as a point of departure for developing an in-depth, nuanced, and transfer-based approach to argument, let's begin by debunking some of these common myths about argument.

Myth #1: Arguments are about winning

Arguments in academic writing are not about winning, but rather about pursuing lines of inquiry, advancing knowledge, and making progress. Focusing too much on winning can divert attention away from other, more important considerations, such as what approach will best persuade others to enact change or think differently, or from examining carefully the evidence and research. Excessive attention to winning can also lead a scholar (accidentally or purposefully) to misinterpret or overlook evidence.

Just because arguments are not exclusively or primarily about winning, though, does not mean that academic writers do not care about influencing others to think differently or to take action (or to cease action). Academic writers across disciplines advocate for human rights and equality, and they construct arguments about important issues, from female genital mutilation to climate change. These arguments often focus less on "winning," so to speak, than on effectively addressing the causes and contexts for these systemic problems—as well as how people can be influenced to modify behaviors and enact policy changes.

Myth #2: Arguments involve only highly debated issues

Some issues are so contentious as to be considered hot buttons for arguments. For example, the top ten issues that lead to arguments between parents and children, according to Nolan Katkowski, include grades/school (#1), money and privilege (#5 and #6), and driving (#9). The "10 Topics Guaranteed to Start an Argument," according to Listverse, include the existence of God (#10), freedom of speech (#4), and abortion (#1). These issues register high value because there is much research readily available and they are issues about which people care deeply.

But the truth is people can argue about nearly anything. While academic writers do construct arguments about these kinds of hot-button issues, they also construct arguments about issues that may initially seem somewhat less divisive, such as how ancient art should be preserved or how the media discuss vaccines. The website Useful Science, which summarizes academic research across a range of fields, also illustrates the wide range of arguments academic writers construct:

> When people held hot beverages (hot coffee), they perceived strangers as friendlier and warmer than when they held cold beverages (iced coffee).

> Swearing increases pain tolerance: people were able to hold their hand in ice water longer if they swore (this effect was reduced for people who swore frequently).

> Red clothing may be a medium of sexual signaling: women expecting to meet an attractive man were more likely to select a red shirt than women expecting to meet an unattractive man.

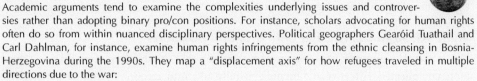

Transfer at Work

Academic arguments tend to examine the complexities underlying issues and controversies rather than adopting binary pro/con positions. For instance, scholars advocating for human rights often do so from within nuanced disciplinary perspectives. Political geographers Gearóid Tuathail and Carl Dahlman, for instance, examine human rights infringements from the ethnic cleansing in Bosnia-Herzegovina during the 1990s. They map a "displacement axis" for how refugees traveled in multiple directions due to the war:

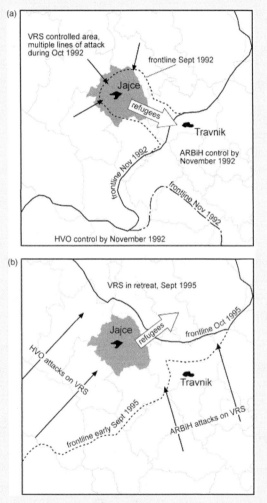

Taking a different disciplinary approach to human rights, philosopher Christopher Heath Wellman examines international ethics regarding how outsiders can respect a particular state's sovereignty, while still "intervening in its internal affairs if this interference will prevent just a single human rights violation" (119). And, offering an information-science-and-technology approach to human rights, Carleen F. Maitland, Trey Herschel, and Louis-Marie Ngamassi Tchouakeu explore why human rights organizations use censorship circumvention technologies as well as the implications and effects of doing so.

Although it is unlikely that any of these arguments will ever make it to a list of top ten issues likely to start a debate, they matter, nonetheless, and carry with them a measure of significance for a number of stakeholders.

Myth #3: Arguments have only pro/con positions

While certain arguments may seem pro or con, they are actually more often than not much more complicated. Effective arguments generally take into account alternative perspectives, make concessions, and qualify the circumstances under which a position is most applicable. As an example, let's look more closely at the issue of the Israel/Palestine question, which comes in, according to Listverse, as the ninth most likely topic to start an argument.

According to *procon.org,* the Israel/Palestine question is (somewhat ironically given the organization's name) not pro/con at all. The core question, according to *procon.org,* is, "What are the solutions to the Israeli-Palestinian conflict?" Within that question exists a number of other parameters to argue about: implications of one-state or two-state solutions, land disputes, refugees, international involvement, historical context. Each of these subcategories then have other elements, all of which can be and need to be argued about and all of which do not fit neatly into a pro/con format. Arguments that adopt a pro/con perspective tend to diminish the complexity of an issue and overlook many important aspects related to that issue.

Myth #4: Arguments are based on opinion

While academic writers certainly have opinions about the issues around which they construct arguments, they more often base their academic arguments on research and evidence than on opinion. Privileging opinion can have a counterproductive impact because opinion does not operate within the same framework as an effective argument. How can anyone really argue that you do or do not have a particular opinion? Why would people change their minds just because you have an opinion? Privileging opinion over argument can also have the negative consequence of limiting the capacity of academic writers to examine evidence and reconsider positions. Being overly invested in an opinion might prevent researchers from being open to changing their positions based on the evidence or on others' arguments they encounter.

Opinion does exist with academic argument, albeit in a limited and subsidiary manner. One example is the issue of the death penalty. Academic writers might have an opinion of whether the death penalty is warranted or not, or how it might be warranted to a greater or lesser degree in different cases. But the academic arguments they construct will instead be based on answers to research questions such as the following: What is the impact of the death penalty on deterring crime? What demographic data exist about death penalty decisions? How is the death penalty carried out? These would be the questions researchers would pursue rather than relying exclusively on their own opinions.

Myth #5: Arguments are about proving points

In the context of academic writing, an argument is not necessarily a final answer to a question. Instead, argument in academic writing might be conceived of as an occasion for a writer to communicate to others what he or she has learned by researching one or more questions.

Then, as others continue to learn more, subsequent questions and arguments can continue to emerge. Arguments are, at heart, about inquiry.

Thinking about argument as inquiry challenges commonly held assumptions that argument involves proving a point. Instead, asking what argument is in academic writing requires asking what the questions are that have given rise to a particular argument.

What is Argument?

Now that we have argued against several myths about what argument is not, let's turn to exploring what argument is.

At the most basic level, an **argument** in academic writing is the position a writer takes in a particular writing project, the evidence he or she includes for that argument, and the way he or she chooses to structure and format the argument. The term "argument" brushes against several other related terms, some of which you may have encountered before: **claim**, **thesis**, **proof**, and **position**. These terms help situate argument within the context of academic writing and begin to illustrate how the notion of argument shifts slightly depending on disciplinary context. Though discipline-specific definitions most certainly overlap and fluctuate, disciplinary perspectives provide particular inflections on how argument is defined.

Sociologist Greta Krippner, for example, defines argument based on her disciplinary perspective of sociology:

> Once you have developed a viable research question, your next task is to review the evidence in order to formulate an answer to your question. The answer to your question is your thesis, or your argument. Typically, researchers do original research at this point—they analyze statistical data, go to the field, administer surveys, conduct experiments, etc.

For Krippner, argument involves an answer to a research question based on original research. Arguments in the natural sciences, by contrast, might be defined more explicitly around evidence, accuracy, and logic:

> Taken together, the expectations generated by a scientific idea and the actual observations relevant to those expectations form what we'll call a scientific argument. This is a bit like an argument in a court case—a logical description of what we think and why we think it. A scientific argument uses evidence to make a case for whether a scientific idea is accurate or inaccurate.

Philosophy also has a discipline-specific definition of argument, perhaps one of the most extensive, since philosophy is in many ways grounded on logic, argument, and reasoning. Matthew McKeon, a philosopher from Michigan State University, defines argument:

> [A]rgument [is] a collection of truth-bearers (that is, the things that bear truth and falsity, or are true and false) some of which are offered as reasons for one of them, the conclusion. [P]ropositions [are] the primary truth bearers. The reasons

341

offered within the argument are called "premises," and the proposition that the premises are offered for is called the "conclusion."

Thus, in philosophy, according to McKeon, argument should be understood in relationship to truth-bearers, propositions, **premises**, and **conclusions**.

While you will not be expected to understand argument as it is defined in each discipline, you should be prepared to encounter varying approaches to argument across disciplines. Recognizing that argument can carry disciplinary conventions and expectations will equip you to learn more about argument within each new discipline and context you encounter.

Purposes of Argument

Academic writers construct arguments across disciplines for nearly as many purposes as there are arguments. The purpose of any given argument can be multiple and manifold, depending on the disciplinary context, the writer, and the writing occasion. As we will see later in this chapter, the structure of an argument also impacts purpose. For instance, Rogerian argument emphasizes common ground and compromise, which will be priorities of purpose for academic writers working with this mode of argumentation.

Disciplines also provide discipline-specific purposes for argument. Ian Johnston, of Malaspina University College in British Columbia, describes the purpose of argument in the context of liberal studies and English. Notice the emphasis on **persuasion**:

> Put most simply, an argument is an attempt to persuade someone of something. It is prompted usually by a disagreement, confusion, or ignorance about something which the arguers wish to resolve or illuminate in a convincing way.... The final goal of an argument is usually to reach a conclusion which is sufficiently persuasive to convince someone of something (a course of action, the reasons for an event, the responsibility for certain acts, the probable truth of an analysis, or the validity of an interpretation).

Arguments can also have an important negative purpose: to convince someone that something is not the case. Other disciplines refer to argument not so much as about convincing others but about justification. In a paper investigating students' use of argument in engineering courses, Sibel Erduran and Rosa Villamanan argue that "the nature of arguments in the applied field of Engineering [involves] appeals to scientific principles [in order] to justify the design of an industrial product."

Despite the many varying purposes for argument across disciplines, some purposes do seem to be more widely embraced by academic writers. Some of the more commonly deployed purposes for arguments are:

- to persuade others to think or act
- to communicate research and conclusions

- to share and interpret evidence and data
- to define one or more terms or ideas
- to push against, critique, or counter another idea
- to explain a relationship or cause
- to propose a solution to a problem
- to suggest a policy or proposal for future action
- to generate consensus or mediate conflict
- to raise questions

These, however, are only a few of the possible purposes for arguments, and they also often overlap. As you encounter other writers' projects, the best way to consider purpose is to ask the writer to describe his purpose (if possible), read his text to see whether the purpose is explicit, and/or discern on your own what you take to be the writer's aims and purpose based on his text (see also Chapter 4: Reading).

Featured Purposes of Argument

Some purposes for argument are widespread enough that they warrant a more extensive discussion. This chapter addresses and illustrates three common purposes of argument: causal argument, proposal argument, and definitional argument.

> ### Writer Insights
>
> **How do you argue in your field?**
>
> In advertising you write more than you would ever expect; from proposals, to follow up emails, to copy for clients, it is all very reliant on words... the right words. I never considered how much I wrote. It was just a way to communicate ideas and generate interest resulting in sales. I am more [conscious] of it now that I have realized I am a writer. Sales is a thinking sport; researching clients and their industry, planning out what would be best for the client and executing. It is all strategic. Away from work, I have started writing a blog following my passion, which is nutrition and the American food system.
>
> ~Cherie L. Dreves, Advertising Sales, Prescott Valley, Arizona, U.S.

> ### Writer Insights
>
> **What was the purpose of your most recent argument?**
>
> [W]riting…is a very important part of my daily job as a tax lawyer. I have to build up an essay whose goal is convincing the judge, so I have to write it in the most effective way. To reach the goal I have to divide the writing in three parts: introduce the matter, explain my arguments to support my final conclusions, and finally set my conclusions. Depending on your side (tax administration or taxpayer) the judge will probably know what the conclusion will be, so the important part of the essay is making up my arguments and quoting the part of court decisions that best support my position.
>
> ~Manuel Menchero, Tax Attorney, Madrid, Spain

Causal argument

A causal argument's purpose is to argue how something has become the way it is. Joseph Moxley at *Writing Commons* describes **causal arguments** as investigating the questions "Why are things like this?" "What is the effect, or result, of this?" and "What causes this?" Causal arguments appear in numerous ways across disciplines. These two examples can help illustrate causal arguments and their purpose.

Example 1: Causal Argument, Spanish Languages and Literature

This excerpt comes from a well-known book that critically examines the relationship between travel writing and colonialism, *Imperial Eyes: Travel Writing and Transculturation,* by professor of Spanish literature and culture Mary Louise Pratt. Pratt's line of inquiry asks, "what was the sociopolitical impact of travel writing in the twentieth century?" In the excerpt, Pratt presents a causal argument, in which she argues that European travel writing contributed to European colonization and expansionism.

Excerpt from *Imperial Eyes: Travel Writing and Transculturation* by M. L. Pratt

In the last decades of the twentieth century, processes of decolonization opened the meaning-making powers of empire to scrutiny, as part of a large-scale effort to decolonize knowledge, history, and human relations. This book is part of that effort. Its main, but not its only, subject is European travel and exploration writing, analyzed in connection with European economic and political expansion since around 1750. The book aims to be both a study in genre and a critique of ideology. Its predominant theme is how travel books written by Europeans about non-European parts of the world created the imperial order for Europeans "at home" and gave them their place in it. I ask how travel writing made imperial expansion meaningful and desirable to the citizenries of the imperial countries, even though the material benefits of empire accrued mainly to the few.

> Pratt locates her causal argument as significant in that it participates in a continuous effort to mitigate the long-term and ongoing impact of colonialism.

> Pratt notes here how her argument emerges from inquiry, having asked "how travel writing made imperial expansion meaningful and desirable."

> Here, Pratt specifies her causal argument. This strategy of naming her argument directly with the phrase "I argue" is frequently employed in disciplines dealing with languages and literature.

Travel books, I argue, gave European reading publics a sense of ownership, entitlement and familiarity with respect to the distant parts of the world that were being explored, invaded, invested in, and colonized. Travel books were very popular. They created a sense of curiosity, excitement, adventure, and even moral fervor about European expansionism. They were, I argue, one of the key instruments that made people "at home" in Europe feel part of the planetary project; a key instrument, in other words, in creating the "domestic subject" of empire.

From *Travel Writing and Transculturation*, 1992.

Write Now

In the previous selection, Pratt uses several related terms to describe her project: argument, effort, subject, inquiry, and theme. How does Pratt differentiate between each of these terms? Based on her text, how is she articulating the difference, for example, between an argument and a subject? Between a theme and an inquiry?

Example 2: Causal Argument, Marine Biology

Where Pratt relies on rhetorical analysis for her causal argument, this second example, from Hamish Campbell, et al., uses quantitative evidence. In this article, Campbell, et al. ask how crocodiles travel long distances. Their causal argument is that surface currents enable crocodiles to travel greater distances.

Excerpt from "Estuarine Crocodiles Ride Surface Currents to Facilitate Long-Distance Travel" by H. Campbell, et al.

Many anecdotal accounts exist of large crocodiles being sighted in open-ocean and on islands hundreds of kilometres from the nearest known population (Ditmars 1957; Allen 1974; Webb & Manolis 1989), yet their capacity for long distance ocean travel remains poorly understood and it is unknown if ocean voyages form part of their ecological repertoire or merely represent occasional mishaps of navigation....

> Here, the authors demonstrate that they are filling a gap in knowledge with their research because current research does not fully explain how crocodiles travel long distances.

The expansive geographical distribution of C. porosus suggests that long-distance ocean voyages are a regular occurrence between island populations. Certainly, large individuals have been sighted from vessels far out at sea (Ditmars 1957), but C. porosus cannot be considered a marine reptile, and primarily inhabits rivers and coastal systems. They live a low-cost energy lifestyle with limited capacity for sustained exercise (Pough 1980; Elsworth, Seebacher & Franklin 2003), and as such, their ability to purposefully traverse significant expanses of open-ocean seems extreme. This study provides an explanation as to how these remarkable feats of ocean travel may be achieved, by demonstrating that

> This segment occurs in the discussion section, after the authors have presented their results. Here, they articulate their causal argument.

From *Journal of Animal Ecology* (79.5), 2010.

C. porosus adopt behavioural strategies which utilise the momentum of surface currents to transport themselves long distances....

This study has shown that adult estuarine crocodiles dramatically increase their travel potential by riding surface currents. This observation has profound management applications because a problem crocodile translocated to an area where residual surface currents flow in the direction of the home-area will rapidly travel back home. Moreover, changes in coastal current systems, by either natural cycle or anthropogenically driven, may result in estuarine crocodiles travelling to locations without a recent history of their presence. Because adult estuarine crocodiles pose a significant risk to humans (Caldicott, et al. 2005), inshore current systems should be monitored in areas where humans and C. porosus may interact, and problem crocodiles should be translocated to areas where residual currents are not available for homeward travel.

> The authors emphasize again their argument in the first sentence of this paragraph and make its significance and applicability explicit, suggesting that demonstrating cause in this circumstance will help with crocodile management.

Proposal argument

Proposal arguments propose a solution for a problem or issue, often in such a way that has broader applicability. These arguments can include grant proposals, policy proposals, or development proposals, and because they might articulate the causes of a problem before proposing a solution, they can sometimes overlap with causal arguments. While fields such as business and public policy seem to lend themselves naturally to proposal arguments, many other disciplines also issue proposals. For instance, in English literature, an academic writer might propose that the field re-examine, or newly examine, an author, period, or genre of literature.

This example of a proposal argument comes from the field of management science. The authors propose a new method for determining time distribution models for emergency response vehicles. Their proposal will, they suggest, enable the creation of "probability-of-coverage maps for diagnosis and improvement of system performance."

Excerpt from "Empirical Analysis of Ambulance Travel Times: The Case of Calgary Emergency Medical Services" by S. Budge, A. Ingolfsson, and D. Zerom

The authors show how "past approaches" did not offer an adequate formula for predicting travel time. This background research establishes a need for a proposal.

Our paper provides the first thorough examination of the distribution of travel times in a way that can be easily incorporated into…models for EMS planning. Unlike the approach in this paper, past approaches often failed to account appropriately for the stochastic nature of travel time, which, even for a given origin and destination, will vary because of route choice, driver characteristics, traffic conditions, geographic aggregation of points into zones, and other known and unknown factors. This paper makes four main contributions. (1) We demonstrate that the KWH model for mean fire engine travel times is a valid and useful description of median ambulance travel times. We perform our validation by comparing the KWH function

The authors enumerate very clearly the "four main contributions" made by their proposal.

to the best-fitting nonparametric estimate of the median function; that is, we compare the KWH function to an infinite number of other possible functions, and find that it performs about as well as any of them. (2) We expand the KWH model to represent explicitly the full probability distribution of travel times conditional on travel distances. We propose a statistical model that allows the median travel time and its coefficient of variation (CV) to vary with distance, and we account for skewness and excess kurtosis (i.e., the distribution has a higher peak and fatter tails than a normal distribution). (3) We present and justify a parametric specification for how the CV varies with distance. (4) We show how our model of travel-time distributions can be used to create probability-of-coverage maps that facilitate decisions about where to locate stations and how to allocate ambulances to them.

The implications of this research extend beyond emergency services. Travel-time distributions are also critical in nonemergency applications, such as the routing of pickup and delivery vehicles…Delivery time is one of the operational dimensions on which private-sector firms

The authors here demonstrate the more extended significance and applicability of their proposal argument.

compete…A familiar example is the delivery-time guarantees offered by companies such as Domino's Pizza.

From *Management Science* (56.4), 2010.

Definitional argument

A third, especially frequent, purpose for arguments across disciplines involves definition. The primary purpose of **definitional arguments** is to define a new term or concept, expand the definition of an established term or concept, or challenge existing definitions.

One example of definitional arguments currently experiencing some measure of United States media coverage involves marriage, where many are arguing over the definition of what does or does not, or should or should not, constitute the definition of marriage. Some argue that marriage is defined as between one man and one woman; others argue that marriage is a civil union. Some argue as well over who holds the power to define: should the state hold the power to define what marriage is or isn't? Other arguments in this arena of definition might argue for how dictionaries are defining the very word "marriage." These examples of definitional arguments demonstrate that such arguments can hold significant impact.

The excerpted reading of a definitional argument comes from academic writer Yolanda Martínez-San Miguel, who argues for an expanded definition of the term "sexile."

Excerpt from "Female Sexiles? Toward an Archeology of Displacement of Sexual Minorities in the Caribbean" by Y. Martínez-San Miguel

> Martínez-San Miguel begins by offering what have been the more widely deployed definitions of the term "sexile." She therefore establishes that she will likely be challenging or expanding these definitions.

According to Manolo Guzmán, the term "sexile" refers to "the exile of those who have had to leave their nations of origin on account of their sexual orientation" (1997, 227). Yet sexile has a very different meaning for many contemporary university students in the United States. According to the Urban Dictionary, to sexile is "to banish a roommate from the room/dorm/apartment for the purpose of engaging in intimate relations with one's significant other/sex partner." It turns out that there is even an etiquette to sexiling, and some university newspapers have published articles educating students on the best way to sexile a roommate (Axelbank 2004). Proper warning, courtesy, timing, and consideration are among the most important elements in making sexile fall within the appropriate codes of conduct. In this sense, sexile is a paradoxical recognition of the ethical limits for negotiating a common domestic space. The other is excluded but only temporarily and as a result of an agreement, in order for sexual intimacy to take place. Thus, the other is complicit

---

From *Signs* (36.4), 2011.

with the self in the fulfillment of a desire that is not necessarily shared, and the other and the self negotiate the modes of appropriation and use of a common space.

Comparing some of the most common U.S. campus definitions of this notion, it became clear to me that "sexile," with its already double meaning, afforded an interesting point of departure in my study of the coloniality of diasporas in the Caribbean. In this essay I propose a working definition of sexile that refers to displacement in two simultaneous and complementary ways. The first is the displacement of subjects who are deemed misfits within the patriarchal, heteronormative discourses of collective identity formation in the Caribbean national states, neocolonial overseas territories, commonwealths, and departments that in many cases mimic the practices of exclusion found in the most traditional national discourses. The second form of displacement points to the negotiated and temporary exclusion of another from a shared communal space for the fulfillment of a diverging sexual desire. The aim of this essay is to extend the meaning of sexile as it has been used in Caribbean queer studies (Guzmán 1997; La Fountain-Stokes 2009): to propose it as a script to think about the configuration of alternative communal identities based on recent narratives that go beyond the heteronormative and homonormative matrixes (Martínez-San Miguel 2008).

> Martínez-San Miguel then offers her own working definition, which expands the term to include displacement and thereby applies the term to Caribbean sexual studies.

> At the end of this paragraph, Martínez-San Miguel explains the aim of her essay. Even though she frames it as a proposal, and it does have carryover with proposal arguments, her main purpose is to redefine a term. She also offers a sense of why this redefinition is important, and what the impact of it will be.

As evidenced by these examples, the purposes of argument have considerable overlap. This is in part because arguments are complex and often carry multiple implications. When constructing your own arguments, you can determine your own purpose(s) by considering what you hope to accomplish through the writing project. Understanding what makes for an effective argument will help you identify and shape your purposes.

Write Now

For each of the examples included in the featured purposes section, identify what the argument is, and evaluate it according to the criteria for effective arguments. Which criteria does it meet, and why? Are there any criteria it does not meet? If so, does this detract from the argument significantly? Based on each argument, can you identify any additional criteria you think should be added to the list?

Criteria for Effective Argument

Given the immense variety of argument, it is nearly impossible to develop an exhaustive list of criteria for what makes an argument more or less effective. Many disciplines have particular discipline-specific measures of effective argument. In some approaches to rhetoric, for instance, an argument might be evaluated on the basis of whether it achieves an equal balance of the three **argumentative appeals** (*ethos, pathos, logos*). In the sciences, an argument is often deemed effective if it is valid, reliable, and replicable.

Some disciplines even argue about what constitutes effective argumentation. For instance, in philosophy, scholars argue about whether the concept of "soundness" is a criterion (or not) for effective argument. Complicating matters further is the fact that the purpose of an argument impacts and shapes the criteria by which it can be determined to be effective; if you are writing a proposal argument, then the proposal should be explained thoroughly and should address the problem and offer a viable solution. If instead you are writing a definitional argument, then your approach to definition should be well researched and widely applicable.

As we shall see in Chapter 9, the structure of arguments also creates certain criteria for efficacy. If you are writing a Rogerian argument, identifying common ground is a key criterion. Finally, as Chapters 10 and 11 will demonstrate, format and evidence likewise generate additional criteria. If you are writing an op-ed, it is more effective not to include extensive citations and quoted evidence. If, on the other hand, you are writing a scholarly argument, then this kind of evidence is of vital importance.

Still, amid all the disciplinary and contextual variation, it is possible to identify several criteria for effective arguments that might be considered relatively applicable across contexts.

Complex

Most arguments in academic writing should be sufficiently complex that they are not entirely self-evident. If an argument is entirely obvious, or if it can be tidily wrapped up with one final answer, then it may lack sufficient complexity. For an argument to be worthy of your time as a researcher and others' time as readers, it should address meaningful questions and provide multiple avenues for exploration and research.

Fortunately, because all arguments have some inherent degree of complexity, your job is not to "make" arguments complex, but rather to uncover and articulate the complexity of the issues giving rise to these arguments. To do so, approach your argument from multiple perspectives, consider alternative conditions, or examine smaller

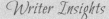
Writer Insights

How do you convince others through your arguments?

In Argentina we use the verb *chamuyar* and the noun *chamuyo* a lot. With its origin in local slang and a broad meaning, these terms can imply, for example, telling lies or improving a story you are telling, or even using pick-up lines with a girl. Of course you can do it when writing as well. Teachers here have to produce a lot of well-grounded planning that will be assessed by principals and inspectors. Peer assessment helps but *chamuyo* might save your day, not by lying but by putting some attitude and creativity into what you say. Dress up your words and bureaucracy will open its heavy gates for you.

~Fernando D. González Cordóba,
*ESL Primary and Secondary School Teacher–Translator,
La Plata, Buenos Aires Province, Argentina*

components of an issue. Other strategies involve thinking about the assumptions underlying a set of issues or ways in which terms are being defined. Most of the time, examining these sorts of matters will enable you to unpack the complexity of an argument in sufficient depth.

Contestable

You may be accustomed to thinking that the best argument is one that is so perfect nobody would be able to reasonably disagree, but in the context of academic writing, writers should actually welcome different or modified perspectives. This chapter has already emphasized that arguments are not about winning a debate. However, arguments do, and should, generate discussion and even disagreement. In this regard, contestability means the argument you are making is one with which reasonable people could disagree, but for which the position is not a simple pro or con.

An example of contestability might be found in the proposal argument previously excerpted with the time distribution model. Readers of that article could pick up on many potential threads for contestability. Perhaps they think a different model would work more efficiently. Or perhaps they would argue that the existing approach is already sufficient and instead more attention should be devoted to driver training or response team preparedness. Readers might also invoke contestability in terms of the ways in which the model was tested; perhaps the testing only involved one urban area that is not representative of others, or perhaps it involved only one type of response vehicle that may not be relevant to other response vehicles. All of these options for contestability demonstrate not so much that those researchers conducted flawed research or that their argument lacks value, but instead that their argument addresses an important issue and sparks productive, civic disagreement and debate about the matters under discussion.

Evidence-based

Your argument should be connected to and should emerge from the evidence. All claims that you make need to be grounded in evidence so readers do not have to take your word for granted, but can instead look at the evidence themselves. You might be interpreting the evidence in ways readers would disagree with, but you should nevertheless base your claims on evidence. If you do not have sufficient evidence to forward your argument or make a claim, then you should probably spend time identifying and collecting additional evidence. Additionally, you might consider changing your argument to one that can be grounded in available evidence.

Evidence can include any number of concepts, data, or texts. In literature, evidence often consists of passages from a text that demonstrate the points a writer is making in an argument. In history, evidence often consists of artifacts and materials that present a narrative account of a time period or event. In chemistry, evidence consists of lab results and outcomes. To properly ground your argument in evidence, be sure to include evidence for every claim you make, and be sure that the overarching argument you develop can be justified and explained based on the evidence you have at hand.

Rhetorically persuasive

Arguments should effectively persuade readers to appreciate your perspectives, take action, rethink ideas, or otherwise move forward productively based on your research and claims. The argumentative appeals discussed in detail in Chapter 4: Reading provide a variety of means for persuading your readers.

- **Ethos:** appeals made by establishing the character or image of the writer
- **Logos:** appeals based on evidence and reason
- **Pathos:** appeals to people's emotions and values

In some contexts, an argument might call for an equal balance across all three appeals. Other contexts might privilege one or two appeals. Regardless of which appeal or appeals gain prominence, however, arguments generally gesture in some meaningful way to each of the three appeals.

Using these forms of appeal can enable you to show you are an authority and have researched an issue thoroughly. You can demonstrate why people should care about an issue, and you can convince your readers by launching a reasonable, logical argument. Your argument should avoid lapses in logic or flaws in reasoning. Rhetoricians have developed the term "logical fallacies" to describe common flaws in reasoning. Effective arguments avoid logical fallacies and display reasonable logic and evidence so readers can be persuaded to agree with you or, at the very least, consider your perspective.

Timely

Timely arguments, in the dualistic sense of *kairos* as addressed in Chapter 4: Reading, are those that have contemporary currency and are appropriate in terms of the context. Effective arguments take into account both of these elements of timeliness. In terms of appropriateness, you will want to show that your argument fits within the disciplinary context and writing occasion. Deploying this tactic means you can demonstrate awareness of expectations and conventions in order to move your argument forward. It also means you are connecting your research to others' research in the same field.

Timeliness in the other sense of the term means you can demonstrate why your argument has particular value and significance at this specific juncture in time. Writers might emphasize why, more than ever before, particular questions or concerns must be addressed. Not all arguments are contemporary in nature, though, and these too can still be made to be timely. In these cases, writers might show how an issue has timeliness because a number of other scholars are also addressing it at this point in time. Attending to timeliness will motivate your readers with a sense of urgency to respond to your argument.

Qualified

Hardly any arguments in academic writing are applicable across all circumstances or universally true across all contexts. Holding arguments up to this expectation is unreasonable. Effective arguments generally include qualifications. Avoid making unnecessary generalizations or trying to develop arguments that fit all occasions. Instead, academic writers qualify their arguments or specify the circumstances under which their arguments best apply and the instances where those arguments make the most sense.

Sometimes qualifications entail defining terms carefully. Other times qualifying an argument means adding qualifying words such as *mostly, often,* or *usually.* Qualifications also involve raising questions about how an argument or claim might look under a different set of circumstances or with different assumptions. All these forms of qualification can help an argument be more reasonable and valid.

Linked to others' work

Arguments do not suddenly appear in a vacuum. Instead, they are situated within others' research and arguments and operate as parts of larger conversations. Arguments should be conceived of as contributing to an ongoing conversation that others have already been having and will continue to have after you contribute. Some writers feel disappointed if they discover that another writer has already written about a particular topic. While such feelings are understandable, it is actually a positive sign if you discover another writer has addressed your chosen topic. It actually means this topic is so worthy of conversation, debate, and attention that multiple people can address it. Even if it seems at first that this other writer has argued exactly what you were hoping to argue, it is likely that you have your own perspective and research to add and that your argument will be unique, even if it is related.

To link your argument to others' work, identify the scholars who have asked research questions related to your research questions. Discuss how their work emerged and how it has still left certain other questions unanswered. You can demonstrate how your argument moves in concert with or in contrast to others' ideas as well. Show how one or more scholars may have developed a shared approach or adopted a particular perspective that has influenced your own research. In these ways, you can demonstrate how your argument is linked to others' ideas.

Significant

While not everyone would agree about what constitutes significance, arguments should generally address ideas that matter to you and, preferably, to at least some number of other people. Connect your argument to a larger significance by articulating how an issue will impact people's lives. You might imagine a somewhat skeptical person responding to your argument by looking straight at you and asking, "So what?" What would you say in response to such a question? Why should people care about your argument?

Such questions invite you to identify why your argument matters. Your argument should address important issues that impact people's lives or the world around us. Not every argument is going to address world peace, poverty, health, and hunger, but every argument should have some larger significance attached to it. Articulate what this larger significance is for yourself and explicitly in your writing project as well.

Discipline- and context-specific

For every argument occasion, there are also likely discipline- and context-specific criteria for making an argument more effective. With philosophers, for instance, arguments should be valid and sound. Literary scholars deem arguments effective if they make original contributions to research. Scientists label arguments effective if they are replicable: "Scientists aim for their studies' findings to be replicable—so that, for example, an experiment testing ideas about the attraction between electrons and protons should yield the same results when repeated in different labs" ("Copycats"). Identify whether there are any discipline-specific criteria for arguments so you can work to meet them.

Keep in mind that readers also carry different expectations across disciplines for what an argument looks like and what makes it more or less effective. And, arguments look vastly different depending on whether they are published in contexts that are more academic, more public, or a combination of these. Of course, as you are learning in this text, writing contexts overlap, and we can transfer what we learn in one context to another. As you prepare to construct an argument, however, review examples of arguments in that writing context. You can choose to base your approach on these models or, if not, at least break with or modify their conventions in an informed and deliberate way.

Featured Criteria for Effective Argument: Avoiding Logical Fallacies

Logical fallacies denote common flaws in reasoning that can often (though not always) make arguments less effective, or sometimes ineffective. According to Charles Hamblin, "a fallacious argument…is one that *seems to be valid* but *is not* so." Fallacies might diminish an argument's efficacy by distracting readers from the main point or by inviting what is often unnecessary disagreement and resistance from readers.

Aristotle originally developed thirteen logical fallacies in his work *On Sophistical Refutations*. These, however, have since been expanded, with some sources naming as many as 150 unique logical fallacies. Because there are so many fallacies, they often overlap, have complex subcategories, or appear by varying names. For instance, the fallacies *post hoc* and slippery slope both address false conclusions: the *post hoc* fallacy yields a false conclusion based on a cause and effect, while the slippery slope fallacy has a false conclusion based on loosely connected or unconnected statements.

Fallacies can also be confusing in that sometimes they seem closely connected with aspects of argument that are actually effective. For instance, one logical fallacy is termed "appeal to emotion" (also sometimes subcategorized into "appeal to pity" or "appeal to sympathy"). This fallacy seems to be (and is) closely connected to the Aristotelian appeal to *pathos*. However, in the fallacious use of emotional appeal, a writer will be overly sentimental, use emotion in contexts that do not warrant emotion, or use emotion at the expense of *kairos, logos,* and *ethos*. Therefore, as you encounter what appear to be logical fallacies, be sure to evaluate the context in which they emerge to determine if they are indeed fallacious or, given the right context, they actually form an appropriate or strategic appeal.

Logical fallacies can occur across disciplines, but some disciplines might be more at risk for certain types of fallacies over others. For example, in disciplines such as development studies or human rights branches of public policy, academic writers might be particularly cognizant of how extensively they appeal to emotion. Because issues surrounding poverty, violence, and abuse are so inherently likely to evoke emotion in both readers and the researchers themselves, academic writers in these fields might need to work harder to remember to integrate appeals to *logos, ethos,* and *kairos* in order to make their arguments even more effective. This is not to say that these researchers should not also use *pathos,* but rather that they should devote extra attention or energy toward constructing arguments around *ethos, logos,* and *kairos,* in addition to the inherent *pathos* of their discipline.

Becoming familiar with logical fallacies and understanding more about how and when they emerge in arguments will help you avoid them in your own arguments as well as help you identify logical fallacies in others' arguments so you can contribute your own responses and ideas to ongoing debates in various fields. Take a look at several of the more common logical fallacies.

Hasty generalization

A **hasty generalization** fallacy is an overgeneralization based on incorrect, inadequate, or otherwise insufficient evidence. It may also describe an argument in which "exceptions are overlooked and not properly taken into account" (Walton). An example of a hasty generalization might look something like this:

> Susan is writing a public policy brief on public perceptions about the common core curriculum in K-12 education. For her research, Susan surveys her two closest friends, both of whom dislike the common core. She concludes that everyone in the United States dislikes the common core.

Susan has made a hasty generalization because she surveyed only two people, both of whom were friends (perhaps of similar ages), and she therefore does not have enough evidence to justify her conclusion. Moreover, her argument that everyone dislikes the common core has neglected to consider exceptions—it would take only one person to say he or she likes the common core, and Susan's argument would be discredited.

Ad hominem

Ad hominem arguments focus on a person's character. Sometimes arguments about character make sense, as when *ethos* matters: "Jones is not a fit candidate for public office, since he is a known embezzler" (Brinton). Other times, however, an *ad hominem* argument presents an irrelevant and/or overly venomous character attack, such as, "I refuse to listen to Senator Jones's proposals for amending the New Bank Bill; he cheats on his wife" (Hansen and Pinto). Note that some might still suggest that Senator Jones's marital fidelity is relevant, even for a bank bill. However, an *ad hominem* attack generally focuses on character at the expense of addressing other, more relevant aspects of the argument.

Straw Man

Straw man fallacies involve a writer misrepresenting an opposing position in order to refute that position more easily. This fallacy involves a dismissive attitude toward others' arguments, wherein a writer will minimize or mischaracterize another's ideas so they will seem ridiculous or illogical. Straw man fallacies can emerge deliberately, with someone deciding to discredit another's argument, or they can be unintentional in that perhaps someone actually misreads or misunderstands another's argument. Philosophers Robert Talisse and Scott F. Aikin argue that there are two forms of straw man fallacy: representation and selection. The first involves occasions when one misrepresents an argument in its entirety, and the latter involves mischaracterizing an argument by only selectively referring to certain components.

Representation Straw Man

Representation occurs "in an adversarial argumentative context between two speakers (A and B), where the proponent (A) represents her opponent's (B's) position in an inaccurate way which facilitates or strengthens A's case against B." (Talisse and Aikin). An example of this type of straw man argument might be:

> "Senator Jones says that we should not fund the attack submarine program. I disagree entirely. I can't understand why he wants to leave us defenseless like that."

Selection Straw Man

Selection forms of straw man involve researchers choosing too selectively what evidence they will include based on an assumption that readers will be unaware of other evidence that might possibly work against their argument. Talisse and Aikin argue that the selection form of straw man is even more vicious than representation straw man because it takes advantage of reader ignorance: "(A) correctly presents (B's) argument and legitimately refutes it, but she fails to countenance stronger objections from other sources.... Unless her audience is familiar with the better counter-arguments proposed by (A's) opposition, then (A) succeeds in winning their assent." An example of a selection form of a straw man argument appears in the excerpted article, in which the authors claim that the American Society of Reproductive Medicine Practice Committee is guilty of a straw man argument after basing their message on selective evidence and assuming general ignorance on the part of the public and funding organizations:

Transfer at Work

Fallacious arguments can (and do) emerge throughout all disciplines and can themselves become cause for disagreement among scholars. Alexandros Goudas and Hunter Boylan argue that a number of studies surrounding developmental education rely on fallacious reasoning. They suggest, for instance, that many researchers have misinterpreted data from a foundational paper in the field: "Disregarding all [the] caveats in Bailey, et al, later publications often seem to misinterpret the data. Scott-Clayton in her 2012 working paper on the placement tests cites Bailey et al. (2009) but disregards any of their positive statements" (6). Goudas and Boyland also claim that the influential 2012 publication by Complete College America (CCA) misinterprets and misapplies data and conclusions from recent research. Goudas and Boylan maintain that the CCA's fallacious arguments thus generate ill-advised and misguided policy recommendations for developmental education (8).

The American Society of Reproductive Medicine Practice Committee (ASRMPC) has suggested that DNA damage in spermatozoa should not be assessed because the correlation with pregnancy is inconsistent across independent studies. However this is a straw man argument. The reason why such assays should be undertaken is not just because they reflect the underlying quality of spermatogenesis but, more importantly, because the DNA damage they reveal may have detrimental effects on the developmental normality of the embryo and health of possible future children. (Aitken, et al.).

Some disciplines may lend themselves more readily to certain fallacies than others. In a field such as reproductive health, those making funding decisions (likely members of institutional or organizational administration or government) probably do not have the expertise that the members of the ASRMPC would have. Thus, these readers would be relying on the ASRMPC to provide a full consideration of the research, and a failure to include that evidence is considered a breach of trust. Aitken et al. claim that the ASRMPC is committing a straw man fallacy by refuting one justification for research when in fact another, better justification for research exists.

Other common logical fallacies

While the previous three are frequently occurring fallacies, there are a number of other logical fallacies, also worthy of your review and consideration.

Begging the Question: Using a conclusion that is already presumed to be true, or starting with an assumption that has not yet been proven

Many Questions: Posing numerous questions, some relevant, some irrelevant

False Dilemma: Suggesting there is no middle ground and one position automatically negates or directly opposes the other position

Equivocation: Using words that have multiple meanings as a way of confusing readers

No True Scotsman: Refuting counterevidence by discrediting it entirely and completely

Missing the Point: Arriving at a conclusion that is unconnected (or not closely linked) to the evidence provided

Post Hoc: Assuming that because one thing followed another, then the second thing was caused by the first. For instance, if you wear a blue shirt and get in a car accident, *post hoc* fallacy would say that the blue shirt caused the car accident.

Red Herring: Distracting readers by including an idea or concept that is irrelevant and therefore takes them away from the main issue

Slippery Slope: Stringing together a series of events and arriving at a conclusion that is extreme. For instance, a slippery slope argument would say that if you reduce fines for driving without a license, then more people will do so, and drunk driving will increase, and deaths from drunk driving will increase, until finally all civilian driving licenses will need to be revoked.

Again, this is but a partial, overlapping list, and as you explore these fallacies in more depth, you will likely encounter more complex variations of them. The main point is for you to think carefully about the conclusions you draw and the claims you make to ensure they are reasonable and relevant, and that they avoid these (or other) logical fallacies.

Write Now

Under most circumstances, academic writers try to avoid logical fallacies. But sometimes it's fun to purposefully create them if only as a way of better understanding how writers can accidentally fall into them. Review the logical fallacies discussed in this chapter, and do a quick Internet search to locate others. Then, practice purposefully, generating as many logical fallacies as you can for a general argument topic. For instance, with an argument about video games, a hasty generalization might be that all video games contain violence or no video games contain violence.

Transferring Argument Frames

While arguments across contexts are enormously varied, they nearly all should strive to have a defined purpose, demonstrate effective criteria, and avoid logical fallacies. These elements—purpose, efficacy, and logical soundness—provide a strong frame for arguments across context. The specifics of each of these elements might shift, however, according to context.

Across contexts, arguments integrate nearly all the aspects of the preceding chapters, from questions and reading to summary, synthesis, and analysis. This chapter is connected closely to the next two chapters, which will deepen your knowledge of argument by exploring, successively, particular argument structures (Chapter 9) and options for argument design (Chapter 10). By the end of Chapter 10, you will have a strong sense of argument in all its many complexities.

℀ ℀ ℀

Photographic Essay: "Syria's Victims Tell Their Stories" by Michael Friberg and Benjamin Rasmussen

> Transfer Points: Documentary Studies, Visual Studies, Journalism

In February 2011, five boys ages 13 to 15 spray painted anti-government slogans on a school wall in Daraa, a small Syrian town: "No teaching, No School, Till the End of Bashar's Rule"; "Leave, Bashar"; "The people want the fall of the regime"; "It's your turn, doctor" (Evans and Al-Khalidi). A security guard spotted them. Soon after, the boys were arrested, along with ten other school-age boys, and subsequently beaten and tortured. Outrage ensued. Anti-government protests in Daraa and across Syria began immediately, with increasingly violent responses on the part of the government.

The boys were released in late March 2011, but their experience, subsequently dubbed "the spark that started a revolution," soon escalated into a full-blown civil war, with horrific human consequences. Over the next five years, more than 250,000 Syrians died as a result of the conflict, and more than 11 million were forced from their homes to escape the violence, poverty, and devastation ("Syria"). The Syrian civil war has had widespread impacts across the world, perhaps most visibly in Europe, which faced political and humanitarian crises due to the migrant influx. Friberg and Rasmussen's photographic essay, from August 19, 2013, documents the lives of Syrians living in the Zaatari refugee camp in Jordan.

Documenting conflicts like the Syrian civil war enables people around the world to learn more about and respond to global events. Yet conflict journalism also carries particular challenges. The violence creates extreme risks for journalists, who must often work in life-threatening conditions. Journalists also face challenging decisions about what to include or not in the stories they tell. These decisions impact what the story conveys and shape people's perceptions about events, people, and places. The media journalists use to document conflict also impact what story emerges.

Friberg and Rasmussen's choice of media, a photographic essay, is part of a larger genre of visual documentary work known as photojournalism. Photographic essays are curated collections of photographs, usually by one photographer, that document an issue, event, person, or place.

While some photographic essays are entirely visual, many also include captions and narrative text. Photographic essays are often created by photographers and journalists, but sometimes they are generated by civilians and bystanders (Street), a practice termed citizen journalism.

The tradition of photojournalism extends far back in history: Ancient humans depicted events and ideas on cave walls. In the 1880s, a photographer in London took images of a fire, which were then used to report on the fire in the newspaper account (Kobre). Today, photographic essays, as well as multi-authored photo galleries, have become one of the most popular forms of journalistic media, especially with online news outlets (Caple and Knox). Photo essays have documented a wide variety of subjects, from North Carolina cotton production at the Matoaca Manufacturing company (English) and baseball (Walker), to tea processing in China circa 1885 (Gardella).

Michael Friberg is an editorial and documentary photographer based in Salt Lake City, Utah. His photographs have appeared in such media outlets as *Esquire*, *ESPN the Magazine*, *Rolling Stone*, and *TIME*. Friberg's projects have included Mormon culture in Utah, celebrity portraits, and the Acholi Tribe in Northern Uganda (Friberg). **Benjamin Rasmussen** is a freelance photographer based in Denver, Colorado. He grew up with an indigenous people group in Balabac, a small island in the Philippines (Flemming). Rasmussen's photographs, which often focus on social justice, human equality, and the human impacts of disaster and war, have appeared in such publications as *The New York Times*, *Wired*, *TIME*, and *Elle*. Rasmussen's projects have included Afghanistan's Wakhan Corridor, the Moro Islamic Liberation Front in the Philippines, and the Typhoon Haiyan disaster (Rasmussen). "Syria's Victims Tell Their Stories" appeared in *New Republic*, a monthly magazine publishing long-form investigative journalism about current issues. "Syria's Victims...," however, is part of a larger photographic essay, *By the Olive Trees*, which Friberg and Rasmussen developed in 2013 for a kickstarter campaign to raise money for those affected by the Syrian civil war.

The documentary and journalistic traditions from which photographic essays emerge foreground the unique ways in which images can tell stories and make arguments. Scholar Julianne Newton refers to this as "evidentiary power": the unique capability of images to serve as seemingly credible evidence, to influence public opinion, and to shape people's impressions. Photo galleries and photo essays can also offer a diverse account of an event or experience through the multiple images they feature (Caple and Knox). As with Friberg and Rasmussen's "Syria's Victims Tell Their Stories," photo essays often bring increased visibility to the experiences of those who are currently or historically oppressed, under-resourced, marginalized, or otherwise less visible.

Because many photojournalists work with marginalized groups, they bear a responsibility to consider carefully the ethics involved with how they represent others: When, if ever, might a photographer manipulate an image? What images should or should not be included in a photo essay? When suffering occurs, do photographers carry an obligation to help rather than to photograph? Will publishing images cause additional harm, shame, risk, or indignity to those being depicted?

As with those who create photo essays, those who use photo essays in their research must also take ethical considerations into account: Why are we looking at the photographs? How do we interrogate and honor the subject matter and the photographer? What do we do with the images we encounter? What, if any, obligations do we have to take action? What actions may be warranted?

Often with these very questions in mind, scholars from a number of fields research and write about photo essays. Photo essays play particularly important roles in the humanities and social sciences, in such disciplines as visual studies, journalism, documentary studies, art, English, history, and anthropology. When working with photo essays, scholars engage in deep visual analysis and explore the interplay between word and image. They also examine the complicated contexts surrounding photo essays, including the historical, socio-political, and personal contexts.

Such research illustrates the compelling stories photographic essays provide about the world around us. Bringing increased visibility to those who are often less visible and documenting in nuanced detail the lives and experiences of people all around the globe, photographic essays offer a unique, vitally important, and highly transferable mode of argument, research, visual communication, and writing.

Write Here

Locate and examine one or two photo essays or photo galleries documenting a place, group, or event of interest to you. What story emerges? What other versions of the story do you think might exist? What impressions do you have of the subject matter based on examining the photographs? What do you imagine might have been particularly challenging, if anything, for the photographer(s) in documenting and curating this material?

Michael Friberg and Benjamin Rasmussen
Syria's Victims Tell Their Stories

The Syrian civil war, now in its twenty-ninth month, has led nearly two million Syrians to flee their country. More than 500,000 of them have headed south to neighboring Jordan, a number that is expected to reach one million by year's end. Most Jordan-bound refugees pass through the Zaatari camp, whose current population of 130,000 makes it the second-largest refugee camp in the world. Considered as a city unto itself, it would rank as the nation's fourth largest, according to The Guardian.

The broader migratory pattern is being fed by the fraught calculus and often-harrowing journeys of individual exiles and displaced families. Here, 13 of those refugees talk about the places they abandoned, their new lives in limbo, and the homes they hope to find again.

Suleimah To'meh

Homs, 33 years old.

We left because of the problems that happened in our town. We talk, as they say, bluntly. The problems were that the people rose against the regime, and the regime started killing the people. We left from Homs, from the village we were in, and moved to another village, and from there we went with cars to the borders. From the border, we walked into Jordan, and from the border we went to the Jordanian police, and from there we came to the camp. We traveled early in the morning, when there would be no one around.

Mohammad Mounir Al-Zamel

Hirak, 23 years old.

I defected from the military and joined the FSA [Free Syrian Army] because of the killing and the criminality and destruction. A protest would start and the regime would start firing. I was serving in Aleppo, but when I went on leave I just stayed home. My friends in the military, they all defected as well.

There was a siege on my town that lasted five days. On the fifth day I was hit. I stayed there for two days after that without getting treatment. The bone was shattered. I had steadied my arm with a splint and I tried not to move it; when I moved it the bones would start rubbing each other and coming out from the flesh. They didn't know what to do with it. There was shrapnel in it but they couldn't get it out. They said it would be too dangerous to try to remove it.

I'll go back, no problem. My area is mostly liberated now. There are no more raids, just shelling and bombing from planes. I was there fighting for a year and a half. If I wasn't hit, I wouldn't have left.

Al-Zamel's nephews in the Zaatari camp.

Above: Eyad and Mo'ayad in the room they share with three other foreign laborers in an industrial area outside Amman, where the brothers have gone to find work.

Eyad Ghassan Al-Jughmani
Dara'a, 20 years old.

Mo'ayad Ghassan Al-Jughmani
Dara'a, 19 years old.

Eyad: My cousin was killed, he was 22 years old. A sniper with the regime security services killed him in the square. Another cousin was kidnapped at a security checkpoint and killed. A female cousin was also killed by a sniper. Another cousin from my father's family defected from the Syrian army and escaped to Dara'a. The govern-

ment grabbed him and killed him. My brother and I took only the clothes we were wearing and a change of clothes. That's it.

Mo'ayad: I came to Jordan about four months before my family. I stayed in the camp for one week and then left. I was in a really bad way, and then, thank Allah, I found work and fixed up my affairs. When my family came, we got them out of the camp as well, thanks be to Allah. It's not a good living in the camp. I'm a guy and I couldn't take it. How would it be for the families who live there?

Photos from an album kept by Eyad and Mo'ayad's sister, Safa'a. It was one of the few possessions the family brought with them to Jordan.

Intisaar Ghuzlaan
Dara'a, 37 years old.

Our neighborhood was in the center of town. It was full of people. During the first two years of the war, everything changed. It would be quiet, and we would go to get bread, and then there would be an air strike. The street would be full, then suddenly it would be empty. You would hide anywhere you could, in any house, until you could get home. We decided to leave when the regime decided to enter the houses and take the men for the army.

Our neighbors here are very good. It's as if you are still among your family and friends. But in your house, you feel like you're home. Here, this is not your home. This is not for you. The neighbors are good, but in one's country it is different.

Eyad and Mo'ayad visiting their mother and their four siblings in the home that a Jordanian family is letting Intisaar use.

Above: Wurood, photographed just days before her due date.

Wurood Al-Halabi
Hama, 23 years old.

My mother left before me, her and the girls, then my brother and I came. We had a lot of trouble on the Syrian border initially. It was raining and they wouldn't let us in. They wanted to send us back. They were asking "Where are you going, what are you doing, who do you know in Jordan?

"The camp was very strange to me. You are surrounded by people and you can't leave. It's like a prison. I think by the time my unborn son is able to return to Syria, he'll be aware of the world—he will be maybe four or five years old. I'll be naming him Mohamed, after my brother, the martyr with the FSA.

Raafy Al-Najaar
Dara'a, 36 years old.

I came into Jordan last December through the camps. I've been working for nearly five months as a volunteer with the UNHCR [the United Nations High Commissioner for Refugees], helping the Jordanian brothers in organizing the line and distributing numbers and helping them out. We help the Jordanians in helping the Syrians. It's difficult with the heat. We have humanitarian cases and we get them in quicker, but you see how it is here. People are coming to wait in line at 6 a.m.

Abdullah Ahmad Al-Heraaki
Dara'a, 30 years old.

The world outside the camp works and inside the camp we also work. My craft is to be a barber. I saw people putting up corrugated metal sheets, so I did the same and set up a place. I paid seventy-five dollars in the beginning for electricity and that was it. I did it with my hands, I did it all with my own two hands. Thanks be to Allah, we opened up a barbershop, and we're working. Since people here barely have any money, we only charge twenty-five cents for a haircut. We help each other out here.

A boy wheels an air-conditioner to the trailer where his family is staying.

One of the main roads cutting through the sprawling Zaatari camp. The gravel seen on the side of the road was trucked in and laid down to combat dust storms.

A fountain set up by a refugee family outside their trailer. In Syrian culture, fountains are symbols of stability.

A boy plays a video game in a cyber cafe started by one of the camp's residents.

One of the approximately 350 water trucks that makes deliveries to the camp each day.

Nasser Haamed Abdul Fattah
MZEREEB, 43 years old.

As a Palestinian in Syria, and a person from Gaza, you have no proof of identity. You can't go from one area to another. You want to go work, a checkpoint gets you, they arrest you, and you are put in the prison for a month, two, four, five, six, a year; no one knows.

We got out at night, at 7 p.m. approximately. We had nearly thirty children and five women with us. When we first crossed the Jordanian border we were received by the army—thank god for them—because we were fired upon by the security forces. For the first three months, we stayed in the Bashabsheh camp near the border. Then they opened up the Cyber City camp [a special camp for Palestinian Syrians].

Life here, compared to the other camps, is a thousand blessings. There is some restriction and noise, as you can see, but it's comfortable. Police from the Jordanian government, they've secured everything for the refugees. There is no harassment. We come in and out freely.

A pickup soccer game on the outskirts of Zaatari.

The entrance to Cyber City, an all-but-abandoned technology park that now houses Palestinian refugees from Syria.

Fattah with his family in their room in Cyber City.

Wajed Dhnie
Dara'a, 22 years old.

I was a student at Tishreen University in Latakia, a nice city near the sea where they have the most important port in Syria. I went home for Ramadan, and two days after I returned to the university, I had an exam. There was a message on the board: "Wajed has to go to the administration office as soon as possible."

I went to the office. The administrator told me, "Ah, don't be scared. It's a routine thing. It's normal." Then he asked me to go with him to a security station. I said, "I really can't. I have exams." So he said, "Can you come tomorrow morning at 11?" And he made me sign some sort of paper that I was informed I had to go and see the security detector or whatever. I didn't tell my parents because I knew they would freak out and tell me to come home. Since the administrator asked me so nicely, I thought they would ask me a couple of questions and then they would let me leave.

I arrived at the security station. They took my ID and asked me to turn off my mobile phone.

I thought that was normal because I was entering a governmental place. I was asked to have a seat. I waited for fifteen minutes, then a short guy came and asked me to follow him. Then he blindfolded me. I thought that was okay, because there are secrets inside the building they don't want me to see.

I followed him for, like, ten meters. I knew that we had entered someone's office. Then the short man asked me to kneel on the ground. The detective, or whoever was there, started to ask me questions: "Where do you live? What do you do? Do you write things on Facebook?" He started to read my posts. He said they were "against" Assad. They were not against Assad. I was just describing demonstrations that I saw and quoting from the songs they were singing there.

The detective ordered the short man to bring in a torturing machine called a flying carpet.

It's a wooden board with joints in the middle, and you get strapped from your hands to your chest to your legs, and then they bend it over. I don't know what they used to beat me with, but I guessed from the texture it was a metal rod.

Someone entered the room, a higher officer. Whoever the interrogator was, he asked me, "Have you ever participated in any of the demonstrations?" And I said no, because I really hadn't. They sent me down to the basement where they took off my blindfold. There were other teenagers sitting there, crying. I thought, My parents are now calling everyone they know. I will be out of here in two hours.

I spent eleven days in a cell. It was night when the prison keeper came. The next day they took us to the civilian court, where I had to be judged. The judge said, "I know that you wrote these things. I know that you're a student. I don't want to destroy your future. Because of the amnesty that Bashar Al Assad gave to all the prisoners, you'll be freed."

The next day, I took the first bus to Dara'a. It took me, like, twelve hours to get to there because of the checkpoints—normally it takes five. I had lost like ten or fifteen kilos.

I stayed with my family for two weeks before the security people called me again. They said, "Can you come in? We need to ask you a couple questions." I told the guy who was speaking on the phone, "It's an old trick, you should change it a bit," and I hung up the phone.

The next day I was in Jordan.

Muhmoud Ali Abo
Damascus, 70 years old.

When my land, Palestinian land, was occupied by Israel in 1948, we left our home and went to a village on the West Bank. We stayed in a big cave, my family and another family from my town. After three months, we left the caves and went to Jericho. We made camps from tents. We had schools in our tents. We stayed in this situation almost twenty years, until 1967. After that, we left for Jordan and then for Syria and then Libya.

In 1982, I lived in Beirut, where there was a war between the PLO and Israeli armies. We left for Tunis. Later we went to Yugoslavia where I studied a special course in flight engineering. We stayed in Yugoslavia for about six months and then came back to Beirut. I went to Libya and then to Syria in 1991.

I lived in Syria until 2012, in the Yarmouk camp in Damascus. But then there was a fight between the FSA and Syrian army in Yarmouk. So both armies were fighting over control over the camp. They were dividing the camp. Many people were killed in the attacks.

Since 1950, we Palestinians have had the nationality of Jordan. But the Jordanian government took my documents. They say to me: "You are not Jordanian. You have Palestinian roots." They took my documents, Jordanian documents, and kept them at the border when we came. I am without documents, and so is my son, and the son of my son. We are three generations without documents. This is the problem. I am very tired from constantly moving during my life. I am very tired, very, very tired.

Mohammad Al-Hariri
Dara'a, 45 years old.

I don't want to go back, but my aunt and her kids want to, so I'm waiting with them here until they get on the bus. The lift from here to the borders is free, but once you are inside Syria, it is out of your pocket. May Allah thank them, they have helped us, but there is no organization. No names, no receipts. Because there is no one to do those things, it has become an awful situation. The crowd attacks the bus. My aunt and her kids, they didn't want to push their way on, so they keep on standing.

Would-be passengers of one of the four buses, paid for by the Jordanian government, that ferry refugees back to the Syrian border.

Refugees carrying their belongings to the bus pickup area.

Abdul Rahman Mounir Al-Zalem
Dara'a, 22 years old.

In Syria we have a small orchard. Twenty four olive trees, five lemon trees, and three grape trees. We also have orange and mandarin trees. And mint and everything. It was a whole garden. I planted an olive tree here so we could feel like we were home.

Every week we say we will go back, and now it's been two years. Our house was shelled by the government airplanes—there is no trace, no trace. Maybe today we'll go back. Maybe tomorrow—if Bashar goes away, you know? We would go to Syria, to the Hirak, sit by the olive trees, and we would sleep and eat and drink there.

A TV in the apartment that Al-Zalem and his four sisters share. It is showing footage from a Free Syrian Army channel.

Al-Zalem's nieces and nephews. Their fathers remain in Syria, fighting with the FSA.

Write Away

1. What arguments does Friberg and Rasmussen's photo essay make? Use evidence from the photo essay, gathered through visual analysis, to write an essay in which you identify and respond to Friberg and Rasmussen's argument(s). Consider not only what is in the photos, but also what else might have been at the camp that Friberg and Rasmussen chose not to include or did not capture. Address as well how the text and images work together (or in opposition) to convey meaning and how the sequencing of the images also constructs meaning. To deepen the context for this essay, conduct research on what was happening in Syria during August 2013. How do these images extend, challenge, or otherwise modify our understanding about refugees and/or about the Syrian conflict?

2. Visual studies scholar John Berger describes photographs as follows: "A photograph is a meeting place where the interests of the photographer, the photographed, the viewer, and those who are using the photographs are often contradictory. These contradictions both hide and increase the natural ambiguity of the photographic image" (Berger and Mohr 7). Locate several photographic essays documenting refugee experiences (such as Friberg and Rasmussen's text) or another sociopolitical issue of your choosing. Then, write an essay in which you use the photo essays as evidence to discuss the "natural ambiguity" of photo essays in the particular context depicted. Are there contradictions among and between the various interests? If so, what are they? How might looking at these photo essays amplify, challenge, or otherwise extend Berger's ideas about "natural ambiguity"?

3. Create your own photo essay of a place, person, group, or event of interest to you. Take a variety of photographs and then curate them into a photo essay, making choices

about how many photos to include and which ones. What story do you want to tell? Make decisions about whether or not to include text in the photo essay, and, if so, what text. After you have created your photo essay, write a reflection in which you explain the choices you made, identify any challenges you encountered, and articulate your purposes and aims.

Technology Research Study: "What the Growth of a Space Tourism Industry Could Contribute to Employment, Economic Growth, Environmental Protection, Education, Culture and World Peace" by Patrick Collins and Adriano Autino

Transfer Points: Science and Technology Studies

"We will eventually build space science labs and hotels, prodding the capability for missions beyond the orbit of the Earth. Our space-hotel guests will be able to take breath-taking excursions, flying a couple of hundred feet above the Moon's surface in small two-man spaceships. In time, we will launch missions to Mars and beyond."

—Richard Branson, *The Economist Magazine*, December 2013

Patrick Q. Collins is a scholar of space economics, space tourism, reusable launch vehicles, and space solar power. He is a professor of economics at Azabu University in Japan, the Chairman of the Society for Space Tourism of Japan, and contributes research about space tourism in public and scholarly settings. His more publicly focused work includes, for example, guest appearances on *The Space Show* and a consulting firm titled Space Future Consulting, which also has a website titled Space Future. He has also published peer-reviewed scholarship on a variety of matters advocating for increased growth in space tourism, from space hotels ("Space") and artificial gravity swimming pools ("Artificial") to space stadiums ("Orbital") and gymnasiums ("Design"). His scholarship crosses disciplinary boundaries, but often transects civil engineering, aerospace engineering, and economics. **Adriano Autino** is president of Space Renaissance International and a Systems Engineering Consultant/Trainer at Andromeda Systems Engineering. His expertise is in systems engineering and project lifecycle management. In addition to coauthoring this article, Collins and Autino, with coauthor Alberto Cavallo, have also published the book *Three Theses for the Space Renaissance*.

With all the passion, innovation, and inspiration emanating from Branson's vision, it is easy to forget that space tourism involves discipline-based research across a wide range of fields, from economics, sociology, and business to aeronautics, physics, and civil engineering. More broadly, space tourism might be thought of as a component of a discipline known as science and technology studies.

Science and technology studies is a broad, multidisciplinary field with many subspecialties, such as environmental science and technology, agricultural science and technology, and engineering science and technology. People with expertise in engineering, sociology, economics, public policy, business, and physics conduct research at this interdisciplinary nexus.

Researchers in science and technology studies might, for instance, examine applications of robotics, public responses to Galileo or Darwin, or developments in water sanitation. Those with expertise in engineering, aeronautics, and astrophysics might pursue inquiries in the realm of space exploration and space tourism, as is the case of Collins and Autino.

As wide ranging as the potential applications are for space and technology studies, so too is writing in this field, which can vary immensely, from highly discipline-specific science and engineering papers, to public scholarship and popular discourse. Writing across these contexts, however, does have in common explicit attention to and knowledge about the social implications or dimensions of the science and/or technology being discussed. This might include attention to the political, social, ethical, cultural, environmental, and/or psychological factors that shape technological and scientific innovation, and which, by turn, are impacted by scientific and technological innovations.

The article by Collins and Autino addresses a number of positive social and political implications from the prospect of space tourism. Their article is published in the journal *Acta Astronautica*, which has a broader mission to publish research on "engineering, life and social space sciences, and space technology" (Acta). While a peer-reviewed scholarly journal, with particular ties to astronautics, an engineering-based field, *Acta Astronautica* is also open-access, suggesting that it aims to reach a wider range of potential readers across institutions, industries, and geographic locations.

The journal's stated aim has intentional ethical and social dimensions: "the peaceful scientific exploration of space, its exploitation for human welfare and progress, and the conception, design, development, and operation of space-borne and Earth-based systems" (Acta).

This explicit intentionality of promoting space exploration and looking for opportunities for progress raises important questions about the intersections between academic research and advocacy. Can people with an agenda for advocating toward a particular goal conduct research that is open-ended and earnest?

Such complexities operate in a number of fields, and challenge the idea that academic writing is purportedly objective and bias-free. In fact, those who write across academic contexts are often quite passionate about their research. Passion, subjectivity, and purpose, however, do not necessarily mean that these researchers are automatically writing with blind bias. Such passion, though, should encourage readers to consider how perspectives, passions, and ideologies might impact and shape the arguments scholars produce.

The degree to which authors Collins and Autino are invested in space tourism is evident in their conviction within this article, as well as in their other research and writing. This article is but one of many texts that the two authors, collaboratively or separately, have published that also advocate in different ways for the promises and potential of space tourism. Their professional lives, likewise, are highly invested in space tourism, with each serving as consultants for industry in space tourism. As discussed in the author footnote introduction, both have, in some ways, devoted almost all of their scholarly and professional efforts at promoting and researching space tourism. Collins, for instance, has been publishing articles about the possibilities and promise of space tourism since as early as 1988.

Again, such considerations highlight the importance of considering position and perspective alongside advocacy and argument.

Honoring their intentionality of purpose, and the broader aims of the journal in which they published, Collins and Autino do not focus in this piece so much on the scientific and technical aspects of space tourism, but instead advocate for a variety of positive advantages that might have been realized if space tourism had already been robust, and which might still be realized if space tourism grows.

Such an example is but one of many different kinds of texts that comprise writing in the field of science, technology, and society. This interdisciplinary field resists categorization even as it unites around common questions that, arguably, are among the most significant areas of inquiry past, present, and future: How do scientific advances impact human experiences? How and why do people use technology? With what industries or activities does technology intersect, and where else should it? What are the social processes that inform the development and growth of scientific advances? What are the political implications and dimensions of scientific developments? How does technology help, limit, and otherwise impact human experiences on the individual and collective dimensions?

Patrick Collins and Adriano Autino
What the Growth of a Space Tourism Industry Could Contribute to Employment, Economic Growth, Environmental Protection, Education, Culture and World Peace

1. Introduction: potential growth of space travel industry

Images of rockets launching satellites and crew into orbit, like the idea of space travel, are widely treated as "futuristic" in the media. However, it is noteworthy that such rockets are not only not futuristic, they are very old technology, developed in Germany during WW2. The first successful spaceflight was achieved on October 3, 1942, after which the project leader Walter Dornberger held a party for the team, who toasted the future of space flight with him:

> We have proved rocket propulsion practicable for space travel. This 3rd day of October, 1942, is the first of a new era in transportation, that of space travel.
> —Walter Dornberger, after the first successful space flight [1].

If German rocket development had continued as Dornberger envisaged, the V2 (of which a winged version reached Mach 4) and the Messerschmidt 163 piloted rocket-plane projects could well have led to the start of sub-orbital passenger space flights, using fully reusable, piloted spaceplanes, by 1950. In this case, passenger travel services to and from low Earth orbit (LEO) would presumably have started during the 1960s. Instead of this possible sce-nario, rocket development was dominated by the cold war competition between the USA and USSR, which led to the production of tens of thousands of long-range missiles. As a result, launch vehicles were derived from missiles, rather than being designed *ab initio* as passenger vehicles as aircraft had been, decades before. Government space agencies have continued to develop expendable rockets, of which the safety and cost/passenger are inevitably much closer to those of missiles than to passenger vehicles. (The space shuttle, as well as being partly expendable, was designed primarily to launch the "Big Bird" satellite and land within the continental USA after one orbit—not to achieve low-cost space travel.) As of mid-2009, sub-orbital passenger space flight services are expected to start in 2011: there has thus been more than a half-century delay in developing passenger space travel. In view of this history, the rockets used to launch satellites today, rather than being considered "futuristic" can reasonably be described as "obsolescent". That is, they could have been replaced by reusable launch vehicles several decades ago is policy-makers had so chosen, and they would have been if space technology investment was intended to earn commercial profits. This is because market research strongly suggests that there is much greater potential demand for reusable launch vehicles carrying fare-paying passengers than for expendable rockets. This is well exemplified by the study performed by Futron Inc. as part of NASA's "ASCENT" study (Analysis of Space Concepts Enabled by New Transportation) to identify and quantify possible uses of reusable launch vehicles [2]. Having considered numerous possibilities, it concluded that sub-orbital travel services in the USA alone might grow several times larger than world-wide commercial satellite launch services [3]. It is not possible to accurately predict future orbital travel growth rates even before sub-orbital passenger services begin, but the potential scale, to which orbital passenger space travel might grow, based on market research, is discussed in [4, 5]. For modeling sales of new services, the family of s-shaped "Gompertz curves" uses estimates of what percentage of households will eventually buy a new product or service, and how long it will take for a certain percentage of households to adopt it, in order to generate consistent scenarios of annual sales. An interesting precedent of rapid growth of a new services was the explosive growth of the mobile phone industry in Japan from 1994 through 1996. Starting from almost zero, new customers reached 40 million within 3 years, and the largest service supplier grew into a 50 billion dollar company. Some $30 billion were invested by the service providers during those 3 years, at a time during Japan's deepest post-war recession. All of the participating companies greatly underestimated how fast sales would grow. Another interesting precedent was the rapid growth of airline passenger traffic, sometimes called the "Lindberg Boom", which took place during the 1930s world depression. This was aided by a number of effective government policies designed to encourage passenger air travel. In 2008, the Tauri Group studied the personal spaceflight industry, and estimated total revenues of some $200 million in 2006 and $300 million in 2007 [6]. Although promising, this amount is barely 1% of what governments give to space agencies. Consequently additional investment of even several times this amount would be a trivial cost to governments—and utterly negligible compared to the trillions that they have given to banks during 2008-09. Consequently, if governments are sincere in their claims that they are trying to aid innovation and growth of new industries, then it is not only easy, but it would cost very little to accelerate the growth of passenger space travel services. Cost estimates by the Japanese Rocket Society [7], Bristol Spaceplaces [8], Bekey [9] and others, corroborated by the very low cost of "SpaceShipOne", indicate that once space travel grows to 1 million passengers/year, prices could fall to 5000 Euros for sub-orbital flights, and 20,000 Euros for orbital flights [7-9]. The latter is equivalent to some 200 Euros/kg or about 1% of launch costs today. We can estimate that if sub-orbital passenger travel had started in 1950, orbital travel could have grown to perhaps several million passengers/year by 2000.

Costs for the development of low-cost orbital passenger transportation systems are of the order of 10 billion Euros [7-9]. Even 10 times this amount would be less than 5 years of space agencies' current budgets. The economic benefits seem sure to greatly outweigh the cost, due to the much larger commercial markets that would be created as a result, in contrast to the very small markets created with 1 trillion Euro-equivalents invested in satellite and launch vehicle manufacturing to date. That is, there seem to be no technical reasons why rapid growth of space travel services could not be realised: the technology has existed for decades, and companies wishing to develop vehicles are hampered by only one obstacle, which is the easiest for governments to solve—lack of funds. Hence the rest of this paper assumes that over coming decades households will start to purchase space flight services, which will grow to reach 5 million passengers/year, out of worldwide middle-class population of more than 2 billion people, a few decades from now. Starting from today, in order to achieve the scale of activity shown in Fig. 1 over the next 30 years, government funding equivalent to about 10% of space agencies' budgets, or some 2 billion Euros/year would probably suffice to stimulate private investment in reusable orbital passenger vehicle manufacturing and operations. Thereafter most of the funding would come from private companies, just as airline and hotel companies finance their own growth today.

1.1 Implications of launch cost reduction
Reducing the cost of space travel to 1% of existing launch vehicles' costs, in combination with

the growth of a new consumer service market in space, would greatly aid the growth of many commercial space activities, thereby creating numerous new business opportunities both on Earth and in space. This process is already at work on a small scale in relation to sub-orbital flight services: in addition to a large number of travel companies acting as agents for sub-orbital flights (including JTB, the largest travel company in Japan), Zero-G Corporation supplies parabolic flight services, Bigelow Aerospace is developing the first space hotel, Spaceport Associates advises on spaceport design, Orbital Outfitters Inc. supplies customised flight suits, spaceports are being developed in several places, and several support organisations have been established. All of this activity is occurring some years before the first high-priced services even start, so a much wider range of different space travel-related businesses are sure to grow in future.

In the case of orbital services there will be an even wider range of companies with much larger revenues, including companies supplying various services to orbiting hotels. These will include services which terrestrial hotels typically purchase today, such as catering, cleaning, accounting, entertainment, plus such additional services as space-based window maintenance, air supply, solar-generated electricity, water supply, waste disposal services, and others.

As activities in orbit expand progressively, they could grow to include use of materials extracted from the Moon and near-Earth asteroids and cometoids, of which the potential has been researched for several decades [11]. Due to the much higher costs of activities in orbit than on the surface of the Earth, orbiting hotels seem likely to create the first market for non-terrestrial materials like ice, water, oxygen and hydrogen, as discussed in [12].

Another potentially major space-based industry, which has been held back for 40 years by high launch costs, is the supply of solar power from space to Earth. Although the potential of this system was recognised in studies by the US Department of Energy in the late 1970s, and confirmed in the 1990s [13], total funding has remained minimal. However, progress could be rapid once launch costs fall to a few percent of ELV costs [14]. Hence, as passenger space travel activities expand to large scale, a growing range of manufacturing activities in Earth orbit, on the lunar surface and elsewhere could develop spontaneously, driven by entrepreneurial effort to exploit new business opportunities opened up by the growth of new commercial markets in Earth orbit. These will in turn open the door to the large-scale space activities described in [11].

The growth of orbital passenger space travel to several million passengers/year over a few decades would represent a direct commercial turnover of some 100 billion Euros/year. In such a scenario of rapid growth, annual investment in new facilities, research and development might add the same amount again. Indeed, having reached such a scale, there would be no foreseeable limit to further growth—in particular it need not be limited, like terrestrial activities, by environmental or political constraints. Quite apart from the numerous opportunities which such a scenario offers for growth of the space industry, it also offers great potential benefits for humanity, in several different fields, as discussed in turn in the following.

2. Employment

In most countries, most of the population do not have economically significant land holdings, and so employment is the economic basis of social life, providing income and enabling people to have stable family lives. The high level of unemployment in most countries today is therefore not only wasteful, it also causes widespread poverty and unhappiness, and is socially damaging, creating further problems for the future. One reason for investing in the development of passenger space travel, therefore, is that it could create major new fields of employment, capable of growing as far into the future as we can see.

As of 2001, the hotel, catering and tourism sector was estimated to employ 60 million people world-wide, or 3% of the global workforce, and 6% of Europeans [15]. Hence we can estimate that the passenger air travel industry, including airlines, airports, hotels and other tourism-related work, indirectly employs 10-20 times the number of people employed in aircraft manufacturing alone. Likewise, passenger space travel services could presumably create employment many times that in launch vehicle manufacturing—in vehicle operations and maintenance, at spaceports, in orbiting hotels, in many companies supplying these, in services such as staff training, certification and insurance, and in a growing range of related businesses. This possibility is particularly valuable because high unemployment, both in richer and poorer countries, has been the major economic problem throughout the world for decades. Consequently the growth of such a major new market for advanced aerospace technology and services seems highly desirable, as discussed further in [16].

By contrast, in recent years employment in the traditional space industry in USA and Europe has been shrinking fast: a 2003 report by the US Federal Aviation Administration stated that employment in launch vehicle manufacturing and services fell from 28,617 in 1999 to 4828 in 2002, while employment in satellite manufacturing fell from 57,372 to 31,262 [17]. Likewise, European space industry employment fell by 20% from 1995 to 2005; the major space engineering company Astrium cut 3300 staff from 2003 through 2006; and in 2005 alone, European prime contractors cut 13.5% of their staff or some 2400 people [18]. Unfortunately, the probability of space industry employment recovering soon is low, because satellite manufacturing and launch services face both low demand and rapidly growing competition from India and China, where costs are significantly lower.

It is therefore positively bizarre that government policy-makers have declined to even discuss the subject of investing in the development of passenger space travel services, and have permitted no significant investment to date out of the nearly 20 billion Euro-equivalents which space agencies spend every year! This is despite the very positive 1998 NASA report "General Public Space Travel and Tourism" [19], and the NASA-funded 2002 "ASCENT" study referred to above [2, 3].

In the capitalist system, companies compete to reduce costs since this directly increases their profits. However, reducing the number of employees through improving productivity raises unemployment, except to the extent that new jobs are created in new and growing industries. In an economy with a lack of new industries, increasing so-called "economic efficiency" creates unemployment, which is a social cost. In this situation, governments concerned for public welfare should either increase the rate of creation of new industries, and/or slow the elimination of jobs, at least until the growth of new industries revives, or other desirable counter-measures, such as new social arrangements, are introduced. These may include more leisure time, job-sharing, and other policies designed to prevent the growth of a permanent "under-class" of unemployed and "working poor"—a development which would pose a major threat to western civilisation.

One of the many ill effects of high unemployment is that it weakens governments against pressure from corporate interests. For example, increased restrictions on such undesirable activities as arms exports, unfair trade, environmental damage, corporate tax evasion, business concentration, advertising targeted at children, and anti-social corporate-drafted legislation such as the "codex alimentarus", "tort reform" and compulsory arbitration are socially desirable. However, when unemployment is high, corporations' arguments that government intervention would "increase unemployment" have greater influence on governments.

As outlined above, the opening of near-Earth space to large-scale economic development, based initially on passenger space travel services, promises to create millions of jobs, with no obvious limits to future growth. At a time when high unemployment is the most serious economic problem throughout the world, developing this family of new industries as fast as possible should be a priority for employment policy. To continue economic "rationalisation" and "globalisation" while not developing space travel is self-contradictory, and would be both economically and socially very damaging.

3. Economic Growth

The continuation of human civilisation requires a growing world economy, with access to increasing resources. This is because competing groups in society can all improve their situation and reasonable fairness can be achieved, enabling social ethics to survive, only if the overall "economic pie" is growing. Unfortunately, societies are much less robust if the "pie" is shrinking, when ethical growth becomes nearly impossible, as competing groups try to improve their own situation at the expense of other groups. Continued growth of civilisation requires continual ethical evolution, but this will probably be possible only if resources are sufficient to assure health, comfort, education and fair employment for all members of society.

The world economy is under great stress recently for a number of reasons, a fundamental one being the lack of opportunities for profitable investment—as exemplified by Japan's unprecedented decade of zero interest-rates. This lack of productive investment opportunities has led a large amount of funds in the rich countries to "churn" around in the world economy in such forms as risky "hedge funds", causing ever greater financial instability, thereby further weakening economic growth, and widening the gap between rich and poor.

Increasing the opportunities for profitable, stable investment requires continual creation of *new industries* [16]. Governments today typically express expectations for employment growth in such fields as information technology, energy, robotics, medical services, tourism and leisure. However, there are also sceptical voices pointing out that many of these activities too are already being outsourced to low-cost countries which are catching up technologically in many fields [20]. Most of the new jobs created in the USA during the 21st century so far have been low-paid service work, while the number of US manufacturing jobs has shrunk rapidly [21]. It is thus highly relevant that aerospace engineering is a field in which the most technically advanced countries still have a substantial competitive advantage over later developing countries. Hence, if a commercial space travel industry had already been booming in the 1980s, the shrinkage in aerospace employment after the end of the "cold war" would have been far less. Consequently it seems fair to conclude that the decades-long delay in developing space travel has contributed to the lack of new industries in the richer countries, which is constraining economic growth and causing the highest levels of unemployment for decades.

The rapid economic development of China and India offers great promise but creates a serious challenge for the already rich countries, which need to accelerate the growth of new industries if they are to benefit from these countries' lower

costs without creating an impoverished underclass in their own societies. The long-term cost of such a socially divisive policy would greatly outweigh the short-term benefits of low-cost imports. The development of India and China also creates dangers because the demands of 6 billion people are now approaching the limits of the resources of planet Earth. As these limits are approached, governments become increasingly repressive, thereby adding major social costs to the direct costs of environmental damage [22]. Consequently, as discussed further below, it seems that the decades-long delay in starting to use the resources of the solar system has already caused heavy, self-inflicted damage to humans' economic development, and must be urgently overcome, for which a range of policies have been proposed in [23, 24].

3.1 Popular demand is the basis of economic growth
The continuing heavy dependence of the space industry on taxpayer funding, despite cumulative investment of some 1 trillion Euro-equivalents, is due to the simple fact that those directing the industry have chosen not to supply services which large numbers of the general public wish to buy. Yet it is elementary that only by doing this can the space industry grow into a normal commercial activity. Doing so will create an industry which raises private investment to develop new, better and larger facilities in order to sell better services to ever-more customers—in the familiar "virtuous circle" of business growth. Eventually this activity may even reach a scale sufficient for the tax revenues it generates to repay the public investment to date.

In successful companies, investment is skillfully judged so as to produce goods and services for which there will be large commercial (i.e. non-governmental) demand. If this earns sufficient profits, then the activity will continue to grow spontaneously for decades or more, like manufacturing of cars or airliners. If, instead, funds intended for investment are spent on developing non-commercial products, such as expensive surveillance satellites or a space station for which the only significant customer is government, then clearly the space industry is doomed to remain forever a small, taxpayer-funded activity—a hindrance rather than a help to economic growth.

Economic policy-makers responsible for deciding the public budget for space development must no longer rely exclusively on the advice of the space industry itself, which ever since its origin has had different objectives than the economic benefit of the general public. That is, economic policy-makers, who are responsible for tens of trillions of Euros of activity, must take the initiative to ensure that passenger space travel services are developed as soon as possible. There are many ways in which private investments in this field can be facilitated and supported, without governments themselves either planning or managing the projects.

Among other steps, this will require the important institutional innovation of collaboration between civil aviation and civil space activities. Since, even with today's knowledge, researchers foresee the possibility of economic development in space growing to a scale similar to terrestrial industry [11]. This field of industry must be considered as having the potential to become a major new axis for economic growth—equivalent in importance to the aviation industry, but with minimal environmental impact, as discussed below—and therefore deserving of the most serious and urgent attention by economic policy-makers.

4. Environmental protection

Economic development in space based on low launch costs could contribute greatly, even definitively, to solving world environmental problems. As a first step, substantially reducing the cost of space travel will reduce the cost of environment-monitoring satellites, thereby improving climate research and environmental policy-making.

4.1 Space-based solar power supply

A second possibility, which has been researched for several decades but has not yet received funding to enable testing in orbit, is the delivery of continuous solar-generated power from space to Earth. Researchers believe that such space-based solar power (SSP) could supply clean, low-cost energy on a large scale, which is a prerequisite for economic development of poorer countries, while avoiding damaging pollution. However, realisation of SSP requires much lower launch costs, which apparently only the development of a passenger space travel industry could achieve. Hence the development of orbital tourism could provide the key to realising SSP economically [14].

4.2 Carbon-neutral space travel

Clean energy produced by SSP could eliminate the environmental impact of space travel, and even make it "carbon neutral" if this is considered desirable [25]. Moreover, SSP has a much shorter energy pay-back time than terrestrial solar energy, due to the almost continuous supply of power which it can generate, rather than only in day-time during clear weather. Some critics claim that space travel will become a significant environmental burden [26]. However, while superficially correct in the short term, this is the opposite of the truth over the longer term. It would be a dangerous error to prevent the growth of space tourism in order to avoid its initial, minor environmental impact, since this would prevent a range of major benefits in the future, including the supply of low-cost, carbon-neutral SSP, and other space-based industry.

4.3 Space-based industry

If orbital travel grows to a scale of millions of passengers/year—as it could by the 2030s, with vigorous investment—it will stimulate the spontaneous growth of numerous businesses in space. These will grow progressively from simple activities such as maintenance of orbiting hotels, to in-space manufacturing using asteroidal minerals. For example, the development of SSP would enable a range of industrial processes using the advantages of space, including high vacuum, weightlessness, low-cost electricity and sources of both minerals and volatile chemicals in shallow gravitational wells.

If SSP grows to supply a significant share of the terrestrial energy market, more and more industry would operate outside the Earth's ecological system. While most industries cause growing damage to the Earth's environment as they grow in scale, industrial activities which are outside the Earth's ecosystem need not cause any such damage. Hence the growth of space-based industry to large scale offers the longer-term possibility of decoupling economic growth from the limits of the terrestrial environment. Indeed, it has been convincingly argued that only the use of space resources, including especially SSP, offers the possibility of protecting the Earth's environment while enabling sufficient economic growth to preserve civilised society [22, 27].

4.4 Severe weather amelioration and climate stabilisation

The use of solar power satellites for reducing the severity of hurricanes and typhoons, and/or ameliorating severe snow conditions has been discussed for some years. In the extreme case this application of SSP might even include a role in the stabilisation of climate. Earth's climate system is extremely complex, and is the subject of a great deal of ongoing scientific research, including collection of an ever-wider range of data, and ever-more detailed analysis of climate change in the past.

A positive-feedback cycle causing sudden onset of the cooling phase of the long-term cycle of "ice ages" has been hypothesized, whereby a winter with unusually low temperatures and/or unusually widespread and/or long-lasting snow cover would increase the probability of the following winter being even more severe [28, 29]. The beginning of such a trend would be similar to the sharply more severe winters seen over the two last years in North America (as well as the unusually cool 2009 summer).

Consequently, although such a possibility may seem remote, and although there are thorny legal problems concerning deliberate weather modification, it is nevertheless noteworthy that satellite power stations may be the only practical means of selectively melting snow over areas of thousands of square kilometres, possibly sufficient to prevent such a vicious circle, even in the event of terrestrial energy shortages.

4.5 Ethical consumption

Passenger space travel and its numerous spinoff activities have the important potential to escape the limitations of the "consumerism" which governments in the rich countries have encouraged in recent decades in order to stimulate economic growth, defined as GDP. Researchers now understand that this is resulting in "excess consumption" which causes unnecessary environmental damage [30], while reducing rather than increasing popular satisfaction [31]. That

is, "first world" citizens are increasingly trapped in a culturally impoverished "consumer" lifestyle which reduces social capital, social cohesion and happiness, while damaging the environment. By contrast, expenditure on the unique experience of space travel promises to play a more positive role in the economy and society, enriching customers culturally without requiring mass production of consumer goods and corresponding pollution. As such it could be a harbinger of a future "open world" economy [27].

5. Education

The educational value of space activities is well known: children and young people find the subject of space and space travel uniquely fascinating. A number of space-based, science-fiction films and television series have achieved extraordinary popularity, extending over decades. As a result, various organisations have created space-related educational programmes involving satellite design, small rockets and simulation of space flights. Unfortunately, while these activities are popular with the participants, it has to be recognised that they are not effective in increasing young people's scientific education overall, which continues to decline in most countries. That is, children who enjoy science classes find satellite projects inspiring, but these classes do not prevent the "flight from science" seen in rich countries, which is so dangerous for the successful continuation of civilisation. However, the possibility of being able to travel to space themselves at an affordable price is of much greater interest to young people than watching videos of other people traveling to space, or than simulating traveling to space. Hence the start of low-cost passenger space travel services holds unique promise for education in fields related to space travel. In particular, the expectation that the price of a sub-orbital flight could fall as low as just a few thousand Euros [8, 32] as the service grows to millions of passengers/year, offers the possibility of almost all children being able to take a flight sometime. This possibility can be used as a uniquely stimulating teaching tool. In addition, a scenario like that shown in Fig. 1 will employ tens of thousands of staff in orbit within a few decades—a uniquely exciting goal for young people to aim for.

6. Culture

The history and artefacts of the European Renaissance are still the subject of world-wide admiration today. One reason for this unique flowering—such as in 14th century to 16th century Firenze—was that there was a social ethic whereby the successful and wealthy had a sufficiently strong sense of civic duty that they used part of their wealth to enrich the community, particularly by building inspiring civic spaces— libraries, galleries, palazzi and other buildings— and by commissioning works of art and scholarship, with results which still inspire us 600 years later [33]. Such an ethic requires that those who are materially successful, however "self-made" and praiseworthy they may be, recognise that they are also all beneficiaries of good fortune—to have been born in a country, an era, a locale, and a family in which they have opportunities to learn language and manners, to accumulate formative experiences, to obtain useful knowledge, and then great opportunities to exercise their talents and grow into a great career. In a successful society, people who are blessed with such good fortune accept that they have a social duty to repay this— by creating a similarly nurturing environment for future generations. The enduring popularity of the achievements of the Renaissance surely illustrate the enormous value of such a deep ethical sense in society, and especially among its leaders.

61. The need for a new world-wide renaissance

By contrast, as societies became richer over the following centuries, they were increasingly disfigured by becoming more materialistic, a trend accompanied by more and more destructive and barbarous wars, including the horrific "world wars" and communist revolutions. This trend has continued with the recent shocking decline in ethics of the US and UK governments openly flouting national and international law—and even the Geneva Conventions, once seen as a bulwark of European civilisation by making war less inhumane through banning torture and the killing of civilians, *inter alia.*

The way of thinking of Renaissance leaders was strikingly different from today when the wealthy are encouraged to follow the rubric: "If you've got it, flaunt it", or appear to follow the frankly psychopathic: "Everything for us—and nothing for anyone else." In the USA since 2000, "…all of the real gains in national income, total net worth and overall growth in financial worth have gone to the top 1%"[34]. The result of this is that the gap between rich and poor has widened sharply so that the top 1% of the US population now holds more than twice as much wealth as the bottom 80% of the population [34].

The futility of such behaviour is well-known throughout the ages, as expressed in such sayings as: "You cannot take it with you when you die," or "There are no pockets in a shroud". The great universalist religions of Buddhism, Christianity and Islam are in agreement that material wealth is transient and acquisitiveness is not the path to happiness: to the contrary, having gratitude for good fortune, and making efforts to help others less fortunate than oneself are extolled. The reason why these teachings have lasted for millennia is because they help people to live satisfying lives, to raise healthy children, and to maintain stable, resilient societies. They are the basis of true civilisation.

Thus, while societies have grown far richer since the Renaissance, the way of thinking of the rich today seems far poorer. Despite almost unlimited opportunities for creativity and cultural contribution, most of the rich today leave behind little or nothing that will be remembered. They typically use their money to buy large numbers of possessions, which are redistributed on their death. Of course many people, including the wealthy, give generously to charitable organisations, many of which do very valuable work for numerous socially beneficial causes. However, much of this work does little more than offset some of the worst effects of the policies followed by the rich countries which are in fact rapidly widening the gap between rich and poor.

We can judge this behaviour. The great universalist religions as well as secular humanism would agree: the great benefactors of the Renaissance were more admirable human beings. Unless corrected soon, this futile materialism of "modern" societies seems likely to destroy civilisation. Yet under "neo-liberal" or "neo-con" dogma, instead of using the opportunity provided by wealth to contribute culturally to society, the already rich nowadays exert pressure on governments to reduce their taxes further, to remove remaining restraints on monopolies and illegal surveillance of the general public, while falsely blaming already deteriorating welfare systems for governments' fiscal crisis. The lack of new industries described above weakens governments against such pressures via the threat of increased unemployment, which is electorally unpopular. Such psychopathic greed and dishonesty among the upper levels of a society are surely the prelude to its destruction, and represent the most serious challenge to western civilisation. A new world-wide "Renaissance" is urgently needed, especially among the rich of the world.

6.2 "The Earth is not sick—she's pregnant"

Healthy societies can revitalise themselves. An interesting explanation of the potential of space travel and its offshoots to revitalise human civilisation is expressed in the idea that "The Earth is not sick: she's pregnant" [35]. Although this idea may seem strange at first sight, it is a surprisingly useful analogy for understanding humans' current predicament. According to the "Pregnant Earth" analogy, the darkening prospect before humanity is due to humans' terrestrial civilisation being "pregnant"—and indeed dangerously overdue—with an extra-terrestrial offspring. Once humans' space civilisation is safely born, the current stresses on the mother civilisation will be cured, and the new life may eventually even surpass its parent. This idea not only illuminates many aspects of humans' present problems described above, it also provides detailed directions for how to solve these problems, and explains convincingly how successfully aiding this birth will lead to a far better condition than before the pregnancy. A young couple may be happy in each other's company, but their joy is increased by the birth of children and life with them, from which many new possibilities arise.

Likewise, the birth of humans' coming extra-terrestrial civilisation will lead to a wide range of activities outside our planet's precious ecosystem. This evolution will solve not just our material problems, by making the vast resources of near-Earth space accessible, but it will also help to cure the emptiness of so-called "modern" commercial culture—including the "dumbing down" by monopolistic media, the falling educational standards, pacification by television,

obesity, ever-growing consumption of alcohol, decline in public morality, pornography, narcotics, falling social capital, rising divorce rates, and youths' lack of challenge and lack of "dreams". It will do this by raising humans' sights to the stars, and showing that the door to them is unlocked, and has been for decades—we have only to make a small effort to push it open forever.

In addition, re-opening a true geographical frontier, with all its challenges, will in itself be of inestimable value for the cultural growth of modern civilisation. The widespread sense that we live in a closed world which is getting more and more crowded will be replaced by an open-ended, optimistic vision of an unlimited future. Access to the cornucopia of space resources that await humans' exploitation can clearly make a unique contribution to this. To the extent that leaders of major industries are motivated by ambition in business competition, they will welcome this opportunity to extend their activities to new fields in the far wider arena of space. However, to the extent that they are motivated by the attempt to achieve monopolistic control and profits, they may try to hinder development in space, even at the cost of preventing its wide benefits, since this could be more profitable to them. Implementing the "Pregnant Earth" agenda can prevent this cultural regression and start a true world-wide Renaissance, an unprecedented flowering of civilisation of which human culture has been in need ever since the inspiration of the Italian Renaissance was followed by a decline into progressive materialism and war-mongering [35].

In pursuit of this goal, a growing number of space-related organisations are joining the "Space Renaissance Initiative" [36] started by the authors in June 2008. This has a programme to accelerate the expansion of human activities into space by advocating investment to specifically *reduce the cost of space travel*. That is, supporters recognise that space activities could contribute far more to economic growth than they have to date if even a small fraction of annual funding of space activities was targeted at making access to space much cheaper. At a time when the world economy is in the worst state it has been for more than half a century, the possibility of creating large numbers of jobs in commercially profitable, space-related work is very attractive, and should receive the attention of policy-makers world-wide.

7. World peace and preservation of human civilisation

The major source of social friction, including international friction, has surely always been unequal access to resources. People fight to control the valuable resources on and under the land, and in and under the sea. The natural resources of Earth are limited in quantity, and economically accessible resources even more so. As the population grows, and demand grows for a higher material standard of living, industrial activity grows exponentially. The threat of resources becoming scarce has led to the concept of "Resource Wars". Having begun long ago with wars to control the gold and diamonds of Africa and South America, and oil in the Middle East, the current phase is at centre stage of world events today [37]. A particular danger of "resource wars" is that, if the general public can be persuaded to support them, they may become impossible to stop as resources become increasingly scarce. Many commentators have noted the similarity of the language of US and UK government advocates of "war on terror" to the language of the novel "1984" which describes a dystopian future of endless, fraudulent war in which citizens are reduced to slaves.

7.1 Expansion into near-Earth space is the only alternative to endless "resource wars"

As an alternative to the "resource wars" already devastating many countries today, opening access to the unlimited resources of near-Earth space could clearly facilitate world peace and security. The US National Security Space Office, at the start of its report on the potential of space-based solar power (SSP) published in early 2007, stated: "Expanding human populations and declining natural resources are potential sources of local and strategic conflict in the 21st Century, and many see energy as the foremost threat to national security" [38]. The report ended by encouraging urgent research on the feasibility of SSP: "Considering the timescales that are involved, and the exponential growth of population and resource pressures within that same strategic period, it is imperative that this work for

"drilling up" vs. drilling down for energy security begins immediately" [38].

Although the use of extra-terrestrial resources on a substantial scale may still be some decades away, it is important to recognise that simply acknowledging its feasibility using known technology is the surest way of ending the threat of resource wars. That is, if it is assumed that the resources available for human use are limited to those on Earth, then it can be argued that resource wars are inescapable [22, 37]. If, by contrast, it is assumed that the resources of space are economically accessible, this not only eliminates the need for resource wars, it can also preserve the benefits of civilisation which are being eroded today by "resource war-mongers", most notably the governments of the "Anglo-Saxon" countries and their "neo-con" advisers. It is also worth noting that the $1 trillion that these have already committed to wars in the Middle-East in the 21st century is *orders of magnitude* more than the public investment needed to aid companies sufficiently to start the commercial use of space resources.

Industrial and financial groups which profit from monopolistic control of terrestrial supplies of various natural resources, like those which profit from wars, have an economic interest in protecting their profitable situation. However, these groups' continuing profits are justified neither by capitalism nor by democracy: they could be preserved only by maintaining the pretence that use of space resources is not feasible, and by preventing the development of low-cost space travel. Once the feasibility of low-cost space travel is understood, "resource wars" are clearly foolish as well as tragic. A visiting extra-terrestrial would be pityingly amused at the foolish antics of *homo sapiens* using long-range rockets to fight each other over dwindling terrestrial resources—rather than using *the same rockets* to travel in space and have the use of all the resources they need!

7.2 High return in safety from extra-terrestrial settlement

Investment in low-cost orbital access and other space infrastructure will facilitate the establishment of settlements on the Moon, Mars, asteroids and in man-made space structures. In the first phase, development of new regulatory infrastructure in various Earth orbits, including property/usufruct rights, real estate, mortgage financing and insurance, traffic management, pilotage, policing and other services will enable the population living in Earth orbits to grow very large. Such activities aimed at making near-Earth space habitable are the logical extension of humans' historical spread over the surface of the Earth. As trade spreads through near-Earth space, settlements are likely to follow, of which the inhabitants will add to the wealth of different cultures which humans have created in the many different environments in which they live.

Success of such extra-terrestrial settlements will have the additional benefit of reducing the danger of human extinction due to planet-wide or cosmic accidents [27]. These horrors include both man-made disasters such as nuclear war, plagues or growing pollution, and natural disasters such as super-volcanoes or asteroid impact. It is hard to think of any objective that is more important than preserving peace. Weapons developed in recent decades are so destructive, and have such horrific, long-term side-effects that their use should be discouraged as strongly as possible by the international community. Hence, reducing the incentive to use these weapons by rapidly developing the ability to use space-based resources on a large scale is surely equally important [11, 16]. The achievement of this depends on low space travel costs which, at the present time, appear to be achievable only through the development of a vigorous space tourism industry.

8. Summary

As discussed above, if space travel services had started during the 1950s, the space industry would be enormously more developed than it is today. Hence the failure to develop passenger space travel has seriously distorted the path taken by humans' technological and economic development since WW2, away from the path which would have been followed if capitalism and democracy operated as intended. Technological know-how which could have been used to supply services which are known to be very popular with a large proportion of the population has not been used for that purpose, while waste and suffering due to the unemployment and environmental damage caused by the

resulting lack of new industrial opportunities have increased.

In response, policies should be implemented urgently to correct this error, and to catch up with the possibilities for industrial and economic growth that have been ignored for so long. This policy renewal is urgent because of the growing dangers of unemployment, economic stagnation, environmental pollution, educational and cultural decline, resource wars and loss of civil liberties which face civilisation today. In order to achieve the necessary progress there is a particular need for collaboration between those working in the two fields of civil aviation and civil space. Although the word "aerospace" is widely used, it is largely a misnomer since these two fields are in practice quite separate. True "aerospace" collaboration to realise passenger space travel will develop the wonderful profusion of possibilities outlined above.

8.1 Heaven or hell on Earth?

As discussed above, the claim that the Earth's resources are running out is used to justify wars which may never end: present-day rhetoric about "the long war" or "100 years war" in Iraq and Afghanistan are current examples. If political leaders do not change their viewpoint, the recent aggression by the rich "Anglo-Saxon" countries, and their cutting back of traditional civil liberties, are ominous for the future. However, this "hellish" vision of endless war is based on an assumption about a single number—the future cost of travel to orbit—about which a different assumption leads to a "heavenly" vision of peace and ever-rising living standards for everyone. If this cost stays above 10,000 Euros/kg, where it has been unchanged for nearly 50 years, the prospects for humanity are bleak. But if humans make the necessary effort, and use the tiny amount of resources needed to develop vehicles for passenger space travel, then this cost will fall to 100 Euros/kg, the use of extra-terrestrial resources will become economic, and arguments for resource wars will evaporate entirely. The main reason why this has not yet happened seems to be lack of understanding of the myriad opportunities by investors and policymakers. Now that the potential to catch up half a century of delay in the growth of space travel is becoming understood, continuing to spend

20 billion Euro-equivalents/year on government space activities, while continuing to invest nothing in developing passenger space travel, would be a gross failure of economic policy, and strongly contrary to the economic and social interests of the public. Correcting this error, even after such a costly delay, will ameliorate many problems in the world today.

As this policy error is corrected, and investment in profitable space projects grows rapidly in coming years, we can look forward to a growing world-wide boom. Viewed as a whole, humans' industrial activities have been seriously underperforming for decades, due to the failure to exploit these immensely promising fields of activity. The tens of thousands of unemployed space engineers in Russia, America and Europe alone are a huge waste. The potential manpower in rapidly developing India and China is clearly vast. The hundreds of millions of disappointed young people who have been taught that they cannot travel in space are another enormous wasted resource.

We do not know for certain when the above scenario will be realised. However, it could have such enormous value that considerable expenditure is justified in order to study its feasibility in detail [5]. At the very least, vigorous investment by both private and public sectors in a range of different sub-orbital passenger vehicle projects and related businesses is highly desirable. Fortunately, the ambitious and rapid investment by the Indian and Chinese governments in growing space capabilities may finally jolt the space industries of Russia, America, Europe and Japan out of their long economic stagnation, and induce them to apply their accumulated know-how to economically valuable activities—notably supplying widely popular travel services to the general public.

Acknowledgements

The authors would like to thank the anonymous referees for their detailed comments which have considerably improved the paper.

References

1. T. Burnett, Who Really Won the Space Race?, Collins & Brown, 2005, p. 16

2. Futron Corporation, Analysis of space concepts enabled by new transportation, Analysis Study for NASA Marshall Space Flight Center, 2003.

3. D. Webber, Public space markets—what we know and what we don't know, STAIF 2003 Albuquerque; also at Hyperlink <www.spacefuture.com/archive/public_space_markets_what_we_know_and_what_we_dont_know.shtml>, 2003.

4. P. Collins, Economic benefits of space tourism to Europe, Journal of British Interplanetary Society 60 (11) (2007) 395-400 (also at www.spacefuture.com).

5. P. Collins, The economic benefits of space tourism, Journal of British Interplanetary Society 59 (11) (2006) 400-410 (also at www.spacefuture.com).

6. Tauri Group, Personal spaceflight industry summary, <www.commercialspaceflight.org/pressreleases/PSF%20Presentation%20Summary.pdf>, 2008.

7. K. Isozaki, et al., Status report on space tour vehicle Kankoh-Maru of Japanese Rocket Society, IAF paper no. IAA-98-IAA.1.5.06; also at <www.spacefuture.com/archive/status_report_on_space_tour_vehicle_kankoh_maru_of_japanese_rocket_society.shtml>, 1998.

8. D. Ashford, Spaceflight Revolution, Imperial College Press, 2003.

9. I. Bekey, Economically viable public space travel, in: Proceedings of the 49th IAF Congress, also at <www.spacefuture.com/archive/economically_viable_public_space_travel.shtml>, 1998.

10. P. Collins, Space activities, space tourism and economic growth, in: Proceedings of the Second ISST, also at <www.spacefuture.com/archive/space_activities_space_tourism_and_economic_growth.shtml>, 1999.

11. J. Lewis, Mining the Sky: Untold Riches from the Asteroids, Comets and Planets, Addison Wesley, 1996.

12. P. Collins, Tourism in low earth orbit: the trigger for commercial lunar development? in: Proceedings of the Space '98, ASCE, also at <www.spacefuture.com/archive/tourism_in_low_earth_orbit_the_trigger_for_commercial_development.shtml>, 1998, pp. 752-756.

13. J. Mankins, A fresh look at space solar power: new architectures, concepts and technologies, IAF paper no. IAF-97-R.2.03, in: 38th International Astronautical Congress, also at <www.spacefuture.com/archive/a_fresh_look_at_space_solar_power_new_architectures_concepts_and_technologies.shtml>, 1997.

14. M. Nagatomo, P. Collins, A common cost target of space transportation for space tourism and space energy development, AAS paper no. 97-460, AAS vol. 96, 1997, pp. 617-630; also at <www.spacefuture.com/archive/a_common_cost_target_of_space_transportation_for_space_tourism_and_space_energy_development.shtml>.

15. International Labour Organisation Human Resources Development, Employment and Globalization in the Hotel, Catering and Tourism Sector, ILO, Geneva, 2001.

16. P. Collins, Meeting the needs of the new millennium: passenger space travel and world economic growth, Space Policy 18 (3) (2002) 183-197 (also at www.spacefuture.com).

17. FAA, The economic impact of commercial space transportation on the US economy: 2002 results and outlook for 2010, FAA, Associate Administrator for Commercial Space Transportation, 2003.

18. P. deSelding, Industry, ESA air grievances during space days meeting, Space News 17 (23) (2006) 4.

19. D. O'Neil, et al., General public space travel and tourism volume 1—executive summary, NASA/STA, NP-1998-03-11-MSFC; also at <www.spacefuture.com/archive/general_public_space_travel_and_tourism.shtml>, 1998.

20. J. Rifkin, The End of Work, Putnam, 1996.

21. P. Roberts, The fading American economy: government is the largest employer, Hyperlink <www.counterpunch.org/roberts04092008.html>, 2008.

22. M. Bernasconi, C. Bernasconi, Why implementing the space option is necessary for society, Acta Astronautica 54 (2004) 371-384 (also at www.spacefuture.com/archive/why_implementing_the_space_option_is_necessary_for_society.shtml).

23. A. Autino, A plan for the mercantile astronautics, Paper presented to International Symposium on Space Travel, Bremen, 1999.

24. A. Autino, New credit tools and tax concepts for the opening of the space frontier, IAF paper no. IAA-2000-IAA.1.4.05, also at <www.spacefuture.com/archive/new_credit_tools_and_tax_concepts_for_the_opening_of_the_space_frontier.shtml>, 2000.

25. P. Collins, Synergies between solar power supply from space and passenger space travel, in: 4th International Conference on Solar Power from SPACE, SPS '04, Granada, also at <www.spacefuture.com/archive/synergies_between_solar_power_supply_from_space_and_passenger_space_travel.shtml>, 2004.

26. http://www.publications.parliament.uk/pa/cm200607/cmselect/cmsctech/66/7022101.htm.

27. A. Autino, The Copernican evidence—requirements for a space age philosophy, IAF paper no. IAC-02-P-P.23, also at <www.spacefuture.com/archive/the_copernican_evidence_requirements_for_a_space_age_philosophy.shtml>, 2002.

28. http://www.climatecooling.org.

29. J. Gribbin, M. Gribbin, Ice Age: How a Change of Climate Made us Human, Penguin Press Science, 2003.

30. J. Schor, Prices and quantities: unsustainable consumption and the global economy, Ecological Economics 55 (2005), 309-320.

31. R. Sato, The consumer paradox: scientists find that low self-esteem and materialism goes hand in hand, The Daily Galaxy, November 14, 2007.

32. D. Ashford, The aviation approach to space transportation, Aeronautical Journal of the Royal Aeronautical Society 113 (1146) (2009).

33. A. Sapori, Economic life, in: The World of Renaissance Florence, Giunti, 2007.

34. M. Whitney, Drifting downwards: the deflating economy, Counterpunch, <www.counterpunch.org/whitney07132009.html>, 2009.

35. A. Autino, La Terra non è malata: è incinta! ("Earth is Not Sick: She's Pregnant!"), Arduino Sacco Editore, Roma, 2008.

36. http://www.spacerenaissance.org.

37. M. Klare, Resource Wars: The New Landscape of Global Conflict, Owl Books, 2002.

38. www.acq.osd.mil/nsso/solar/SBSPInterimAssesment0.1.pdf.

Write Away

1. Using a library or popular search engine or database, search for books on science and technology studies. Write a book review for this book, in which you articulate its benefits and limits and position it within larger contexts of science and technology studies.

2. Identify an emerging area of science or technology or an imagined innovation in science and technology. Write an article modeled on Collins and Autino's that addresses the social, economic, political, and cultural implications of this innovation. Include relevant research in your argument.

3. Collins and Autino published this article in 2010. Much has happened in the space tourism industry since then. Write a market report in which you identify developments in

space tourism since 2010, and analyze their impacts on the social, cultural, economic, and political dimensions discussed by Collins and Autino. What have been developments in space tourism since 2010? Have any such developments created any new implications? In what ways have these developments impacted any of the political, social, or cultural dimensions discussed by Collins and Autino?

Literary Analysis of Collected Work: "(Author)ity Abroad: The Life Writing of Colonial Nurses" by Jessica Howell, Anne Marie Rafferty, and Anna Snaith

Transfer Points: Health Professions, Health Humanities, Literature

Medical students visiting art museums to analyze collections ... nursing students writing illness narratives ... care providers creating photographic essays ... health workers reading poetry about medicine. These are but a handful of the many intersections between health care and humanities, a nexus broadly referred to as health humanities. This area of research spans multiple disciplines, from literature, art, and creative writing to biology, chemistry, and neuroscience.

While those engaging in and conducting research about health humanities work across many contexts, the field can broadly be construed as the application of and intersection between humanities approaches to the understanding of health care alongside scientific knowledge. Examples might include research into the impact of music therapy for cancer treatment, narrative writing for healthcare providers, or examining race and class inequities or assumptions about aging.

"(Author)ity Abroad" involves a collaboration between scholars who have expertise, collectively, in public health, nursing, and literature. They have collaborated to apply literary analysis to the letters and other writings of colonial-era nurses who were working in such places as Africa and the Caribbean through an organization called the Colonial Nursing Association.

Colonialism in this case refers to the historical practice of colonization, as well as a conceptual framework regarding financial, cultural, and/or political control by one nation over another. As a conceptual framework, the concept of colonialism leads scholars across many disciplines to examine the implications, complexities, and consequences of colonialism. This might include narratives and acts of resistance, oppression, or violence. Or it might include psychological inquiries into the emotional impacts of subjugation or colonial aggression.

Jessica Howell Pratt is a faculty member in the Georgia State University School of Public Health. She also serves as the career coordinator by helping students with professional development through resumé development, practicum opportunities, and mock interviews. **Anne Marie Rafferty** is Dean of the Florence Nightingale School of Nursing and Midwifery at King's College London. Her research interests include nursing history and workforce research and policy. **Anna Snaith** is a Professor of Twentieth-Century Literature at King's College London in the Department of English. Her research interests include Virginia Woolf and Jean Rhys. She published a book about anticolonialism and feminism titled *Modernist Voyages: Colonial Women Writers in London*, 1890-1945. The *International Journal of Nursing Studies*, in which this article appeared, publishes peer-reviewed research about the education, training, and providing of health care in fields related to nursing and midwifery. Recent research in this journal included an article on compassion fatigue in oncology nurses (Hairong, Jiang, and Shen) and an article examining the efficacy of online learning for healthcare providers (Sinclair, Kable, Levett-Jones, and Booth).

Colonialism and its aftermath, often referred to as postcolonialism, also provide a theoretical framework for approaching power dynamics and hierarchies of privilege even outside of places or times when actual colonialism occurred. For instance, those conducting research into racial justice or class inequities might think about colonialism and postcolonialism as frameworks for understanding the mechanisms, structures, and implications of power hierarchies and networks of control.

The field of health care has complicated intersections with colonialism, and with power more broadly. During colonial encounters, the colonizing nation often provided health care to its own citizens in the colonized location. With great variation, these colonial powers may also have provided health care to the colonized people in those locations. Often this health care was either subpar, or even, in many cases, experimental and resulting in atrocities. Nearly always, this health care involved deliberate rejection of indigenous healthcare practices. Since health care is designed with and through cultural practices, colonialism, therefore, also impacted healthcare practices.

This cross-sectional framework of health care and culture, scientific and humanistic modes of knowing, forms the basis of health humanities. Scholars who conduct research and write in the field of health humanities may adopt interdisciplinary approaches, or may lean more heavily toward scientific approaches, or more heavily toward humanities approaches. As such, texts emerging from this field may be highly creative in nature, or may follow the traditional science format for peer-reviewed research.

This article was published in the *International Journal of Nursing Studies*, and so follows a more science-based form and structure, with detailed front matter (abstract, summary of the design, etc.), clear headings, discussion of methods, and an explicit call for further research at the end of the article.

Howell, Rafferty, and Snaith explore the writings of colonial-era nurses to help contribute to our understanding about what is involved in working in health care across cultural contexts. Such research also helps illustrate and remind us of the importance of working toward a model of justice and equity with health care, and the complications that too often impede such efforts. Such research also addresses the discipline itself, working to justify the field and emphasize the importance of expanding and continuing such forms of inquiry.

Such efforts are in fact vital. The questions scholars in health humanities examine help advance knowledge about healthcare practice and humanities: How do the arts intersect with health care? For what purposes can it be deployed, and in what ways? What role does social advocacy have in health care? How do power dynamics impact health care? How can we use perspective and creativity to reassess standards for what does or does not constitute healthiness and well-being?

Questions such as these, sparked by humanistic inquiry, enable patients, providers, policy makers, and family members to approach health care in more equitable, effective, careful, and compassionate ways.

Write Here

Imagine you are a healthcare provider and have the opportunity to travel abroad for an extended period of time in a working capacity. What factors would you consider as you made your decision about whether to go and/or where to go? What might be some of your concerns, if any? What, if anything, might be appealing to you about the prospect?

Jessica Howell, Anne Marie Rafferty, and Anna Snaith
(Author)ity Abroad: The Life Writing of Colonial Nurses

1. Introduction and background
In order to encourage empathy as well as a greater understanding of cultural difference, educators in healthcare and the humanities guide medical and nursing students through attentive encounters with art and literature (Shapiro et al., 2009). In

the past, however, more effort has been dedicated to discussing the experiences of doctors and, more recently, of patients, than the experiences of nurses and midwives. A growing body of scholarship in the history of nursing is correcting this imbalance. In order to contribute to such progress, this essay presents original research into nurses' life writing, outlining certain significant themes in their letters.

The words 'author' and 'authority' come from the same Latin root, auctor, meaning "creator" or "originator" (University of Notre Dame "Latin Dictionary," http://www.archives.nd.edu). Through writing letters, CNA nurses authored their own lives, claimed professional and personal authority, and helped authorize the imperial project. Though these women originally were sent in order to recreate a sense of home for British citizens stationed abroad—a seemingly traditionalist and delimited job—they also encountered new experiences and cultures and took on new professional responsibilities. In this sense, nurses not only travelled across national boundaries but also adapted and changed boundaries of propriety and gender expectations. By studying their correspondence, one may observe how these 'travelling' nurses reinvented themselves in the colonial setting.

2. Previous scholarship

Scholarship concerned with the figure of the nurse tends to fall into certain categories, which may sometimes overlap: research on wartime nursing, anthologies and literary analyses of contemporary nurses' poetry and prose, gender criticism, and Nightingale studies. Florence Nightingale had an intriguing and multifaceted personality; she also wrote a prodigious amount, including letters, books and tracts; further, her theories and plans strongly influenced modern nursing. It is no surprise that the work of such a key figure should be much studied. *The Collected Works of Florence Nightingale* edited by Lynn McDonald, as well as Mark Bostridge's biography *Florence Nightingale: The Woman and Her Legend* (2008), both attest to an ongoing interest in Florence Nightingale scholarship. Critical discourse has also acknowledged the importance of Nightingale in literature and culture, as shown in Mary Poovey's 1988 *Uneven Developments: the Ideological Work of Gender in Mid-Victorian England* and Catherine Judd's 1998 *Bedside Seductions: Nursing and the Victorian Imagination 1840–1880*, just to name two. By examining Nightingale scholarship from the perspective of life writing, however, we can begin to understand how biography and autobiography are both driven by the discursive imperatives of the day.

In order to better understand what life writing analysis has to offer in studying the figure of the nurse, let us briefly consider past biographies of Florence Nightingale, many of which over-simplified her personality. Even while she was still serving in the Crimean War, Florence Nightingale's reputation was growing to mythic proportions, bolstered by reports of her good deeds from family and friends, colleagues and patients. Deemed an angel, titled "The Lady with the Lamp," Nightingale became one of the Victorian era's biggest celebrities. She was memorialized even before her death (Poovey, 1988), and since her death has been the subject of a steady stream of biographies. Many of these have sought to reconcile or explain the contradictory impulses manifested in Nightingale's life and work. The majority of biographers or historians seem to have a certain unified theory about her identity. One may often guess by the title what each book's focus will be: *Florence Nightingale: Mystic, Visionary, Healer*; *Florence Nightingale: Avenging Angel*; *Florence Nightingale: Reputation and Power*; or *Creative Malady*.

As Ania Loomba explains, "historians and critics" are "part of a discursive order rather than outsiders—what they say, indeed what they can say, is also determined and shaped by their circumstances" (1998). Thus, each biography's own historical moment influences its tone. Early biographies such as Cook's *Life of Florence Nightingale* (1914) seem anxious to rescue Nightingale from any accusations of unfeminine character—[Along with] "The impelling power of a brain and a will" she "brought to her mission the tenderness of a woman's heart." However, mid-century biographies bring this 'flaw' to the fore: "There was something about Florence that chilled. . . She did not know what personal feelings were, in a private note she wrote that never in her life did she recollect being swayed by a personal consideration. She lived on a different plane, out of reach, frighteningly, but also infuriatingly, remote" (Woodham-Smith, 1955).

Though outside the scope of this essay, an important larger project will be to historicize the Nightingale historiography itself: for example, one could productively analyze the foregoing quotation in light of the 1950s cultural obsession with unreachable women. However, from a literary perspective, for the purposes of this paper it is most useful to notice Woodham-Smith's passing reference to "a private letter." Not only does he fail to quote the letter directly, he also neglects to tell us anything about its context. For example, imagine how differently we would perceive this letter and the author's resulting claims if we learned that it had been written to a colleague who accused Nightingale of favoritism, or as a reply to a family member who complained about her absence from a holiday function. By not letting Nightingale's words speak for themselves and by not acknowledging other relevant contextual factors, the biographer is able to portray Nightingale's identity in a one-sided manner that supports his theory of her personality. More recent biographers have acknowledged more shades of gray to Nightingale's identity. However, they often still use over-arching characterizations, calling her "stringent and complicated" or "a puzzle", contrasted with other figures who have "relatively unified" personalities, whose "actions, words and feelings tend in the same direction, complementing each other" (Boyd, 1982). Life writing critics would argue that there are often nuances to be found in the language of even the most straightforward authors.

The over-simplified treatment of Nightingale's life and personality may be following in the spirit of nineteenth-century essentialisms regarding nurses in general. The "character" of a good nurse—pious, sober, nurturing yet firm—was partly inculcated by Nightingale herself. Not only did she use pamphlets and tracts to set out the ideal behavior and characteristics of nurses, she also practiced quick judgment of other women, assessing their ability to succeed in the profession. As one may observe from her notes on probationers' reports, Nightingale terms the hapless Anne Cororan "Deficient in both management and steadiness, a coarse, low sort of woman." In contrast, Elizabeth Ford "under strict supervision may yet do well", in spite of "defects." Mary Yarnley is deemed "A clever woman but of a vulgar mind, somewhat inclined to hobnobbing where she likes and spitefulness where she does not. Too much on the level of the nurses she has to superintend". Nightingale asserts that Ellen Sparks is "Not to be trusted in a general hospital for her own sake; light in her conduct with men" (Baly, 1982). Nightingale evaluates nurses' characters in order to assess their professional promise. One notes certain social values encoded in these comments, which dictate that women, especially nurses, should be chaste and not encourage male attention; they should be refined and ladylike; and finally, they must differentiate themselves from their inferiors. These excerpts demonstrate how historical values and priorities affect written discourse, and that writers often reinforce one-sided perceptions of identity.

Our research attempts to counterbalance this trend in historical and literary nursing studies, whereby the ideal character of nurses is pinned down, and the identities of individual nurses are stabilized or summarized for the purpose of argument. Studying the representatives of the Colonial Nursing Association provides us the opportunity for this important corrective. CNA nurses travelled to far-flung colonies of their own accord, seeking novelty, adventure, professional opportunity, to give service, or all of these together, and their writing reflects these myriad motivations. Rather than defining them by one dominant, stable characteristic, we may consider these nurses as mobile or 'travelling' both physically and in their self-representation.

3. Methods of analysis for nurses' life writing

One takes into account several key considerations when studying life writing. First, one must reflect on the genre of the text, as each has different structures and conventions. Genres that fall under the label of "life writing" may include "autobiographies, biographies, case studies, diaries, memoirs, autobiographical novels, ethnography, blogs, profiles, and numerous other forms" (Lynch in Bradford, 2010). Next, one must be careful not to oversimplify the writer's identity and its influence on her writing. For example, a reader would be best served by taking into account the multiplicity of perspectives represented within women's writing, and nurses' writing in particular. As Linda Peterson explains in *Traditions of Victorian Women's Autobiography*, one should acknowledge "that gender may not be the crucial factor in some autobiography, that other allegiances (religious, regional, political or social) may be equally important, that some women may deliberately avoid a female literary tradition, or that some women's accounts may self-consciously invoke multiple traditions" (2001).

In order to remain alert for these subtleties, it may help to think of the context and situation in which the text was produced. To this end, Smith and Watson suggest one approach the writing as an autobiographical "act." Autobiographical "acts" are made up of the occasions (what caused the author to begin); sites (both historical and spatial); the "I", or speaker; the others of the "I" (may be other characters with whom the narrator relates, or the 'absent other', such as a beloved); patterns of emplotment (narrative strategies and storytelling); media; and consumers/audiences (2002). None of these elements are ideologically neutral. An author is both created by and participates in creating his or her culture. For example, "What is recollected and what is obscured" by the narrator creates our "knowledge about the past." In turn, a narrator is shaped by his or her own cultural background: "As we tell our stories discursive patterns guide, or compel, us to tell stories about ourselves in particular ways."

If "autobiographers incorporate and reproduce models of identity in their narratives as ways to represent themselves to the reader" (Smith and Watson, 2001), then to analyze nurses' writings one must identify the historical and political models of identity available to them. Nurses may draw upon and deploy any number of these models at a time—a reader should not necessarily look for one mould into which a nurse falls. In fact, nurses may have evolved to be particularly flexible in their self-representation. In "Reimagining Nursing's Place in the History of Clinical Practice," Fairman and D'Antonio argue that "Nurses'. . .class and gendered, structural place and authority has always made it necessary. . . to negotiate and form alliances to achieve ends, necessitating a positionality that is always shifting in response to the needs of patients and nurses themselves" (2008). This dynamic was no doubt heightened by the shifting political and economic power structures of the colonial setting. Also, CNA nurses necessarily improvised and adapted in response to the entirely new healthcare situations in which they founds themselves.

In the late nineteenth century, nurses could draw upon several models of identity when representing themselves to others. One was the "heroic nurse," made popular by Florence Nightingale and others who served in wartime. The heroic nurse was portrayed as bringing "morality and Purification" from the domestic realm to "the tainted public domain" (Judd, 1998). One may immediately observe how such a goal would be relevant in the colonial setting. Florence Nightingale herself linked hygiene and race when she said "On women we must depend, first and last, for personal and household hygiene—for preventing the race from degeneration" (quoted in Judd, 1998). In the colonial context, then, nurses might have perceived their role as two-fold—their mission was not simply to teach indigenous peoples 'good hygiene' but to prevent members of their own race from losing the civilised health practices of home and thus become like 'natives' themselves. Nightingale's model of wartime nursing service also blended the "Domestic narrative of maternal nurturing and self-sacrifice" with the "military narrative of individual assertion and will" (Poovey, 1988). This model seems especially relevant for nursing in the colonies, as imperialism uses the rhetoric of duty— the "white man's burden"—to mask underlying drives for profit and exploration.

At the same time, one would be well served to keep in mind both the "occasion" and "consumer" of the CAN nurses' letters home. Many of the letters to which we have access were written to the CNA secretary, an official representative of the nurses' employer. Only a very few of these letters were then chosen for publication in Nursing Notes (the magazine that ran 1888 through the 1940s and was comprised of letters, reports and advertisements of interest to fellow nurses). Therefore, it is perhaps not surprising when one comes across a letter espousing opinions exactly in line with both the CNA philosophy and the values of imperialism. In fact, though women's travel writing may seem "largely supportive of the imperial order, even though the voice and the tone may be more nuanced," censorship greatly "restricted what travel writing became available in print" (Travel Writing, Form and Empire Introduction, 2009).

CNA nurses recorded their impressions of the foreign lands and peoples they encountered; therefore, one may productively study their letters as a form of colonial travel writing. The over-arching purpose of 'colonial discourse studies' is to understand "how stereotypes, images and 'knowledge' of colonial subjects and cultures tie in with institutions of economic, administrative and biomedical contact" (Spurr, 1993). In other words, how does a colonist's perception of 'natives' reinforce colonial policy, and vice versa? As hospitals and clinics must surely be considered institutions of "biomedical contact," and as CNA nurses were sent to support the economic and administrative functioning of empire, their written impressions may be considered as valuable examples of colonial discourse.

When examining the letters from this perspective, one becomes especially attuned to representations of intercultural friction or misunderstanding. As Mary Louise Pratt argues in *Imperial Eyes*, much of colonial travel writing was written in the "contact zones" of empire—"social spaces where disparate cultures meet, clash and grapple with each other, often in highly asymmetrical relations of domination and subordination" (1992). Reading these texts, one must be alive to how "subjects are constituted in and by their relations to each other." When producing written texts, colonists commonly attempt to exert their superiority by expressing mastery over landscapes and bodies. For example, many explorers describe foreign landscape in three steps: first they estheticize it, painting a picture with their words and taking "esthetic pleasure" in the sights they encounter; then they imbue the landscape with "density of meaning", making it "rich in material and semantic substance". At the third stage, "mastery", the explorers "judge and appreciate" their environment and produce their "own vision of it for the readers (Pratt)".

In addition to the environment, it is common to find texts of exploration and travel that engage with the body as a "focal point of colonialist interest"—either its "material value as labor supply, esthetic value as object of artistic representation, ethical value as a mark of inno- cence or degradation, scientific value as evidence of racial difference or inferiority, humanitarian value of the sign of suffering," or "its erotic value as the object of desire" (Spurr, 1993). Instances appear where colonial nurses invoke bodies— their own, as well as both their white and native patients'—on all of these semantic levels except the erotic. For example, a nurse may mend a colonist's broken body so he can continue to labor in mines; she may judge a 'native's' level of civilisation and morality by his or her medical practices; but at the same time, she may feel it is her duty to relieve the suffering of members of both races. She may also depict the physical discomforts of life in the colonies, but downplay her own suffering out of a sense of duty. These are some of the key elements to which life writing and travel writing analysis draw our attention, to keep in mind when examining the letters themselves.

4. The Colonial Nursing Association

The Colonial Nursing Association began in 1896. It supplied over 8400 trained nurses to care for the sick and wounded abroad between 1896 and its termination in 1966. The Association was suggested by Mrs. Francis Piggott, who observed British subjects in need of adequate medical care in Mauritius, where her husband was posted. In her proposal letter to the Colonial Office in 1895, she wrote that "Recent experiences in this Colony and among the European Community in Japan, have brought home to me most forcibly and distressingly the utter impossibility which exists in these places of obtaining any skilled nursing in serious cases of illness." She continues by emphasizing the difficulties of life in the colonies, asserting that "men, delicate women and small children" must face "terrible risks and trials" because their "duties and avocations lead them year by year to these far-away tropical and often unhealthy climates." She creates a sense of urgency through dramatic diction—"forcibly, distressingly, utter impossibility, serious"—as well as by characterizing the colonial setting as threatening and foreign ("delicate," "small," "terrible risks," "far-away," "tropical," "unhealthy").

The letter portrays nurses as able to counteract negative attributes of the colonial environment by recreating the more civilised standards of medical care available at home, which will allow for the natural relationship between white men and women to be reestablished. Mrs. Piggot dwells most on examples of what she melodramatically terms "young married women to whom their hour of trial comes," or mothers in labor. She describes with distaste instances when it becomes necessary to engage a native nurse, such as "a helpless old China-woman", or for the husband to step in to assist with his wife's care. The nurse's presence can prevent these undesirable situations from occurring. Joseph Chamberlain, in his address at the 1899 annual CNA meeting, echoes these values: "hitherto our sick fellow countrymen have been left almost entirely to the tender mercies of the dirty, ignorant, and of course indifferent natives," he says, but now they can depend on wholesome, English women to care for them.

The Association's work was depicted as beneficial to both the project of empire and the professional development of nurses. Sir Alfred Jones, during the 1905 annual meeting, said, "Speaking from the point of view of a business man, he considered it wise economy to support the Association, as it was certainly diminishing the great waste of life in the tropical Colonies." In 1909, Mrs. Charles Robinson, a member of the CNA committee, wrote "The Story of the Colonial Nursing Association", in which she asserted that "Professionally, it is exceedingly rare for a nurse to fail, and certain of them develop qualities which not only double their value, but largely increase their personal happiness." Both of these excerpts are notable for their characterization of human life in terms of investment and "waste," reminding the reader that CNA nurses were hired to support colonialism, which was purportedly a moral but also fundamentally an economic venture. Similarly, nurses are encouraged to think of their own professional development as a commodity, which can be valuated, and which is enhanced by experience abroad.

Nurses were selected carefully for service in the CAN (later called the Overseas Nursing Association), as it was understood that their performance affected not only their personal reputations but also the reputation of the CNA and of British colonialism itself. Women who fell between the ages of twenty-five and forty were chosen. They were most often middle class or from "the new skilled working class." This selection process targeted spinsters and "ladies," who would "aim to replicate their sense of propriety abroad"; this demographic would perhaps benefit from opportunities beyond the domestic realm, and would (it was hoped) enhance the reputation of the CNA through good behavior (Rafferty, 2005).

Certain personality characteristics were also desired by the CNA: "The greatest qualifications for nursing abroad are cheerfulness and tact." Cheerfulness was considered necessary in the face of the challenges of climate, cultural difference and travel, and tact in the face of "awkward" or unexpected incidents. The same author appeals to nurses' sense of duty and heroism when he says, "The need is so great, the difference made by her service so incalculable in the lives of those whose lot is cast in a far country." A nurse who answers the call to serve in the colonies "can feel that she is not only fulfilling the highest aim of her career in helping the sick and suffering, but also doing her share as citizen of a great Empire in preserving the health of the pioneers and patient lonely workers."

The letters of those who served in the Colonial Nursing Association provide a rich resource for exploring nurses' life writing. In particular, one may analyze their self-representations in order to see to what extent they aligned with the expectations outlined by the CNA. Also, the colonial environment sometimes provided nurses with more opportunities for professional initiative and independence than they might have received at home, and it is useful to see what they did with their newfound freedoms. Of course, the letters provide a fascinating window into the day-to-day realities of colonial life. Perhaps most importantly, however, one may gain insight into these early nursing "pioneers'" values and emotions by examining what they chose to include in their letters home.

5. Letters by CNA nurses

Held by Rhodes House library at Oxford University is a substantial archive of documents related to the Colonial Nursing Association, including transcripts of annual meetings, official recruitment publications, and nurses' individual files, with their applications and letters to the CNA secretary (Colonial Nursing Association archives, Mss Brit Emp s400, hereafter CNAA,

Rhodes House, Oxford). This article will concentrate mainly on the models of identity created and adapted by nurses in their own writings. Excerpts from four letters are analyzed—one unpublished, three published—from Central Africa and the West Indies.

Though the entire history of the CNA is relevant to the fields of life writing studies, colonial and nursing history, this article considers letters written before World War I, because during wartime, well-rehearsed rhetoric of patriotism and service can dominate cultural discourse and block out other key considerations. This article focuses on Africa and the West Indies, colonial sites with complex legacies left over from slavery and the slave trade, in order to better understand CNA nurses' relationship to race and racial difference. Paul Gilroy suggests we consider the dynamics of cultural migration and contact between Africa, America and the Caribbean. He says that such study should not focus only on one strictly defined nation or ethnicity at a time, but instead on the whole region through which black bodies were transported for slave labor. He calls this region the "Black Atlantic" (1993). The CNA nurses could not help but participate in the legacy of the Black Atlantic, as they treated and trained the sons and daughters of former slaves. Though legally emancipated, these subjects were often still exploited—as Kevin Grant claims in *A Civilised Savagery*, "Slavery and freedom remained blurred even after emancipation, which commonly gave way to what abolitionists called 'slaveries in disguise'" such as indentured servitude, unfair wages and poor living conditions (3). The CNA nurses faced limitations posed by inadequate medical supplies and staff, as well as from poverty surrounding their stations. In Africa and the West Indies, they were often posted to struggling, former slave- and plantation-based colonies. Further, the nurses themselves were also transported back and forth across the Atlantic in the service of Empire; their travel was dictated by routes of colonial trade and economic demand.

Miss Alice E. Drewe is a useful subject of study because she served in the CNA for an extended period of time—from 1898 to 1923—and in many different locations, including Ceylon, Eastern Rhodesia, Sierra Leone, Southern Nigeria, the Gold Coast, British East Africa and Cyprus. She wrote the first letter under scrutiny here from North Eastern Rhodesia in 1906. Britain was interested in Rhodesia for its minerals and precious gems. From the late 1800s, British workers were sent to construct a railway system connecting South Africa with Rhodesia, in the interest of "colonial Capitalism" (Lunn, 1997). It was hoped that the railway system would eventually stretch "Cape to Cairo" in order to make exporting more efficient. White Britons who arrived to work on the railways or in the mines often had limited previous knowledge of or contact with other races. As historian John Lunn explains, unfortunately, "White railway workers were not slow to resort to ideas of 'native stupidity' and 'inferiority' to justify their relative privilege." In analyzing nurses' letters, then, let us remain attuned to the degree of influence such common colonial rhetoric may have had on their writing.

Miss Drewe begins by telling Secretary Miss Dalrymple Hay that she meant to write earlier, but has been too busy because there has been "no other nurse here besides myself" (CNAA). Her journey took three months. Nurses who served in Central Africa often had long treks before arriving at their final destination, as was Miss Drewe's experience: "On my arrival in Chinde I had to wait several days for the river steamer + the journey up the Zambesi took three weeks, twelve days of which were spent in a houseboat. The weather was hot + extremely dry + we were continuously landing on sandbanks which made our progress up the river very slow." She documents the practical difficulties of such a journey, as the party ran out of all provisions "except tinned salmon" several days before arriving on shore and then travelled over land for a further fourteen days while sleeping in tents. They lacked clean water: "The rivers + streams being very low there was scarcely any water to be had + it was usually thick + muddy + sometimes almost black." While these discomforts would be trying for any traveler, Miss Drewe states the problems matter-of-factly and does not dwell or express self-pity.

She explains further challenges of the job, including purchasing household supplies and paying for private servants out of her own wages, and often working double shifts: "There is only one nurse in the place + when I first came I did night + day work, but now in bad cases some of the officials relieve me in turn at night." While some of the patients she is called upon to treat are routine maternity cases, some are unique to the colonial environment: "There have been several patients in from the gold mines at Nussale (30 miles from here) one of them was a poor fellow who had been tossed by a buffalo. He had five ribs broken and four large wounds which were in a terrible state as he had travelled nearly 100 miles in a machilla. I am glad to say he is well again now and at work" (CNAA). While this narrative underscores the Miss Drewe's own professional competence and strong work ethic, it must also remind the reader of the over-arching purpose of her position, which is to maintain colonists' bodies, and their ability to work extruding natural resources for the profit of Empire.

In letters, nurses often describe their own homes, including details of the natural setting. While some, such as Miss Drewe, seem to take comfort in reproducing a botanical version of home—"I have made a garden since I came + have rose trees honeysuckle + other creepers round the verandah"—still others revel in the exotic quality of native plant life and the tropical environment, as demonstrated in the letter from Costa Rica. Miss Drewe emphasizes the elements of Fort Jameson that remind her of home, and judges it livable according to these standards: "There are generally about ten ladies in Fort Jameson + it is quite a sociable little place. There is a nice club + library also a sports and golf club + a Ladies tennis club." In her free time, she chooses to socialize in this insular simulated-Europe.

In contrast, in a letter published in February 1904s *Nursing Notes*, a nurse posted to Costa Rica emphasizes the delight she finds in her new circumstances. She travelled during a brief interim period of prosperity in the West Indies and adjoining countries, after the 1896 Royal Commission had investigated the status of these colonies and then pumped over three million pounds into the local economies and the trade infrastructure in order to make them profitable. Sugar cane and coffee exports were on the rise, supplemented by tropical fruits. However, uprisings over poor labor conditions in the 1920s and 1930s, and mid-century struggles for independence, had yet to

occur (Dookhan, 1988). One may observe in the following excerpts a sharp contrast in perspective regarding the West Indies between the pre-War years and mid-century. In the first excerpt, from *The British West Indies* (1912), author Algernon E. Aspinall enthuses, "By Englishmen all the world over the very name West Indies should be held dear, for it was in those colonies that the foundations of the British Empire were laid." He states "The scenery of the West Indies is exquisitely beautiful. That will be admitted by everyone who has been privileged to visit those colonies. . . [They are] Clothed with a wealth of tropical vegetation in which creepers and ferns of infinite variety predominate." By 1951, when W.L. Burn writes his *History of the West Indies*, cynicism and disgust have replaced the earlier enthusiasm and optimism: "An observer of the English mind on the eve of the last war must have found it hard to believe that the West Indies could ever have been objects of ambition and desire. . . Their wealth, once so splendidly tangible, which had built great families and altered the course of national politics, had been replaced by a dreary indigence."

However, in 1904, optimism still dominates. Our CNA nurse travelling to Costa Rica enjoys the Caribbean environment, noting, "We had a most pleasant voyage out, good weather all the time, and we touched in Barbados, Trinidad and Jamaica." She disliked the enclosed environment of the ship, so set out with a fellow traveler to "the Constant Spring Hotel", "nearly seven miles out of Kingston, near the Hills." She states, "We had a delightfully cool room and pineapples for breakfast, and we took back some lovely flowers to the boat. There were hummingbirds in the garden and clouds of butterflies." This tropical Eden continues "all the way up" to the post, as she passes "first bananas and then coffee plantations; rivers and waterfalls on either side and trees growing close to the line with all kinds of wonderful creepers hanging from them."

This nurse imbues her journey with a sense of adventure and happiness, related to the luxuriant, sensual beauty of the natural landscape. As previously mentioned, such themes are often found in colonial travel narratives wherein the writer "estheticizes" the tropical environments in order to make order and sense of it. In addition, one notes the mention of coffee and banana plantations, which indicates the colonial economy that the nurse's labor is intended to support.

Finally, whereas male explorers earlier in the nineteenth-century might have added to their descriptions of the landscape "density of meaning", namely references to the rich natural resources they hoped to mine, here the nurse invokes her professional role by listing her "cases". She leads with her professional accomplishments, speaking with a voice of authority and self-confidence: "I am at my second typhoid case already. The first was a little girl with typhoid, quite a mild case, but there is a great deal of typhoid about here, and always will be till they have a better water supply and drainage. I am now at a maternity case." Her tone is matter-of-fact and upbeat. She seems unfazed by the possibility that the winds of the dry season will be "rather trying"—she says that in her previous post "I had plenty of that before." This early published letter paints an appealing example indeed of life as a CNA nurse.

Some nurses go even further, to the extent that they profess a preference for the colonial to the domestic environment. In the next letter, from the May 1904 edition of *Nursing Notes*, a different nurse claims "One feels quite helpless in civilisation after living two years in the jungle. I love the jungle and am already longing to return and leave this terrible English cold. Life in Central Africa is just one long summer day, with a shower in the middle and a long cool evening after the rain." By saying she "feels quite helpless in civilisation" and longs to return to the jungle, the nurse allies herself with the colony, and, one could argue, depicts herself as an honorary native. She has completely acculturated to the new setting. This is an interesting rhetorical move practiced by many generations of colonial explorers whereby the colonist exerts superiority over her readers through having more intimate knowledge of an intimidating foreign locale than they do. However, her experience is dependent upon the speaker's position of privilege—she may revisit England whenever she wants, and she never encounters colonial life unfiltered or unprotected by her circumstance as a white woman.

This letter demonstrates the nurse's adventuresome and intrepid spirit. She enthuses, "We had a wonderfully entertaining journey coming out of the country":

> The river was too low for a boat to come up, and we had to travel overland nearly all the way to Chinde, almost a three weeks' journey through jungle where very few white women had ever been. The natives were most interested to see the 'Donas,' some of them never having seen white people before. We travelled the greater part of the way by night as it was too hot for the boys to carry us by day. We came through the big game country, and the natives told us they had been very frightened by hearing lions. We had not heard them I am glad to say, but the boys know the sound too well and are terribly afraid.

The nurse's experience takes on the romanticism and excitement of bushwhacking, even though she is in fact on an established trade route to a colonial outpost, being carried by native 'boys' so as not to overly exert herself. She even includes the scintillating detail of lions roaring in "big game country", hearkening back to Henry Morton Stanley and other hyper-masculinist discourses of African exploration.

Within the "contact zones" of the colonial environment, travelers often cement their superior status through their representation of natives. The CNA nurses express frustration with native 'superstitions' and traditions, as they feel such practices interfere with the work they are trying to accomplish. Ania Loomba, in her book *Colonialism/Postcolonialism*, explains that this is not an uncommon perspective: "Many nineteenth and twentieth century writers equated the advance of European colonization with the triumph of science and reason over the forces of superstition" (2005). Miss Drewe, the nurse posted to Central Africa, remarks "The natives here are extremely lazy + usually leave off work as soon as one's back is turned. I do a good deal of cooking myself as they are not to be trusted with invalid food neither are they to be trusted with patients who are very ill at night as they invariably go to sleep + it is sometimes difficult to wake them." This representation of locals as not trustworthy and lazy is common in colonial texts. Here, it emphasizes the divide between the nurse (competent) and the native (incompetent; in fact, a liability). It rests upon characterization of blacks, in this case, as immature or childish, inferior in sense as well as in training to their white counterparts. Such rhetoric also creates for the nurse a position of medical authority as distinguished from backward Others, who must be taught, punished or supervised.

As a further example, a nurse stationed in the West Indies wrote in June of 1904 "I have trained one woman, or perhaps 'trained' is too big a word for it. She is a middle-aged Carib woman and I have taught her that absolute cleanliness is necessary and that interference with any but normal cases is punishable" (*Nursing Notes*). Not only in Africa and the Caribbean but in other colonies as well, CNA nurses often recount forcefully displacing native nurses from caregiving situations in order to protect the health of the patient from their well-meaning but damaging ministrations. In this quotation, the native nurse is represented as incapable of true training; rather, she can only comprehend punishment and reward. It is not the purpose of this paper to question the merits of hygienic measures implemented by early twentieth-century British nurses in the colonial context, which doubtless saved lives, but rather to turn our attention to the identities these nurses forged, sometimes through contrast or opposition with other subjects.

6. Findings and future research

The colonial nurse, though ostensibly employed to create an ordered, hygienic and traditionally "British" treatment environment within the colony, was also a potentially transgressive figure—a single woman travelling to the outposts of empire and encountering unusual challenges and trials due to her situation. She blended characteristics of bravery and nurturing, kindness and ambition, service and self-interest, all of which can be best studied through careful consideration of her writings. Women who demonstrated such complex motivations and characteristics challenged the "angel in the house" stereotype. Coventry Patmore's 1854 narrative poem of the same name had introduced a popular ideal of femininity that was influential in the later Victorian period

and early twentieth-century, whereby a woman should be angelic, innocent and submissive to her husband ("Man must be pleased; but him to please/Is woman's pleasure"). For the CNA nurse to be accepted and celebrated for her strength and professional capability indicates that the frail and self-sacrificing 'angel in the house' was a model that could be broken or revised depending on context and the needs of the nation. In this sense, CNA nurses built upon the precedent set by Florence Nightingale and other wartime nurses, who breached the domestic setting thought to be most appropriate for women while still maintaining an air of propriety. Therefore, the CNA nurses' popularity should cause us to further reassess some of our current assumptions about the pervasiveness of historical gender limitations.

When studying nurses' writing, it is productive to employ methods of life writing analysis more generally, and specifically to consider their letters as colonial travel narratives. These approaches allow one to remain alive to the political as well as personal implications of autobiographical texts. The findings produced by such study enhance our understanding of nursing and colonial history. In addition, we gain insight into nurses' multivalent self-fashioning and identity formation. Namely, we observe that, in writing their own stories, nurses claim for themselves medical, cultural and narrative authority.

Our future research plans include seeking out unpublished and unofficial correspondence by CNA nurses posted to the West Indies and Africa. Fellow researchers at King's College are investigating CNA nurses' experience in Asia and during the World Wars. Collaboration with scholars who study the history of district nursing, or the writings of nurses travelling for work in a domestic context, would be valuable in determining the differences between the rhetorical methods nurses used at home and abroad. It also would be desirable to further investigate nurses' historical relationship to race and racial difference within healthcare environments, especially in traditionally segregated societies such as those found in colonial and slave-based economies. More fundamentally, however, this essay contributes to an ongoing and growing project of reclaiming and listening to nurses' voices, letting their own words speak for themselves.

References

Baly, M. (Ed.), 1982. As Miss Nightingale said: Florence Nightingale Through her Sayings: a Victorian Perspective. Baillière Tindall in Association with the RCN, Oxford.

Boyd, N., 1982. Three Victorian women who changed their world: Josephine Butler, Octavia Hill, Florence Nightingale. Oxford University Press, New York.

Aspinall, Sir A.E., 1912. The British West Indies: their History, Resources, and Progress. London

Burn, W.L., 1951. The British West Indies. Hutchinson House, London.

Colonial Nursing Association monthly letter, 1904. Nursing Notes: a Practical Journal for Nurses 17. Women's Printing Society, London. Held in closed stacks at Wellcome Library

Dookhan, I., 1988. A Post-Emancipation History of the West Indies. Longman, Harlow.

Fairman, J., D'Antonio, P., 2008. Reimagining nursing's place in the history of clinical practice. Journal of the History of Medicine and Allied Sciences 63 (4), 435–446.

Files of Individual Nurses, Colonial Nursing Association Archives, Mss Brit Emp s400 (CNAA), Boxes 128-30, Rhodes House, Oxford.

Gilroy, P., 1993. The Black Atlantic: Modernity and Double Consciousness. Verso, London.

Grant, K., 2005. A Civilised Savagery: Britain and the New Slaveries in Africa, 1884–1926. Routledge, New York.

Judd, C., 1998. Bedside Seductions: Nursing and the Victorian Imagination, 1830–1880. St. Martin's Press, New York.

Loomba, A., 2005. Colonialism/Postcolonialism. Routledge, London; New York.

Lunn, J., 1997. Capital and Labour on the Rhodesian Railway System, 1888–1947. Macmillan in Association with St. Antony's College, Basingstoke.

Lynch, C., 2010. The art of losing: the place of death in writer's memoirs. In: Bradford, R. (Ed.), Life Writing: Essays on Autobiography, Biography and Literature. Palgrave Macmillan, Basingstoke.

Patmore, Coventry (1854). The Angel in the House. Project Gutenberg, 2003. http://www.gutenberg.org/cache/epub/4099/pg4099.html.

Peterson, L., 2001. Traditions of Victorian Women's Autobiography: The Poetics and Politics of Life Writing. University Press of Virginia, Charlottesville.

Poovey, M., 1988. Uneven Developments: The Ideological Work of Gender in Mid-Victorian England. University of Chicago Press, Chicago.

Pratt, M.L., 1992. Imperial Eyes: Studies in Travel Writing and Transculturation. Routledge, New York.

Rafferty, A.M., 2005. The seductions of history and the nursing diaspora. Health and History 7 (2), 2–16.

Shapiro, J., Coulehan, J., Wear, D., Montello, M., 2009. Seeking common ground between medical humanities and basic sciences. Academic Medicine 84 (10), 1323–1324.

Smith, S., Watson, J., 2001. Reading Autobiography: A Guide for Interpreting Life Narratives. University of Minnesota Press, Minneapolis.

Spurr, D., 1993. The Rhetoric of Empire: Colonial Discourse in Journalism, Travel Writing, and Imperial Administration. Duke University Press, Durham.

Kuehn, J., Smethurst, P. (Eds.), 2009. Travel Writing, Form, and Empire: The Poetics and Politics of Mobility. Routledge, New York.

Woodham-Smith, C., 1955. Florence Nightngale. Penguin, Harmondsworth.

Write Away

1. This article situates nurses' letters within the colonial context. Using this article, write an extended summary about colonialism, both in terms of a historical practice as well as a conceptual framework: What is colonialism? Where and when does it or has it occurred? What are some of the conceptual implications of colonialism?

2. Choose a medical condition, patient experience, or health issue, and develop an artistic project about it. You can create a photographic essay, a fiction or nonfiction illness narrative, a scrapbook, a choreographed dance, a play, a dialogue, a spoken word performance, a musical composition, a structural design, etc. Write a reflection that discusses your choices in format, what you hope to have conveyed through the project, insights you garnered (about health, art, yourself, etc.) from the experience, and any limitations you encountered related to form and content.

3. Develop a literary analysis of the life writings of healthcare providers, modeling your work on Howell, Rafferty, and Snaith's article. First, locate and read personal accounts of people in health care in a particular area of the world and/or from a particular time period. Using the literary analysis techniques deployed by Howell, Rafferty, and Snaith, conduct your own exploration into the life writings of the healthcare providers you have selected. Address in your essay opportunities for future research, as well as a discussion about the advantages and/or limitations of examining this work from the perspective of humanities and health care.

Chapter 8 Key Terms

argument	conclusion	logical fallacy
claim	persuasion	hasty generalization fallacy
thesis	causal argument	*ad hominem* fallacy
proof	proposal argument	straw man fallacy
position	definitional argument	*post hoc* fallacy
premise	argumentative appeals	slippery slope fallacy

Write Away

Although you may feel relatively new to arguments, this activity asks you to take on an advanced role involved with publication: developmental editor. Developmental editors help authors (academic or not) prepare manuscripts for publication. These editors do not correct grammar but instead focus on ideas; they provide specific suggestions to authors for how to improve the content of their drafts-in-progress. You, as the developmental editor in this case, will work with an author to help make his or her somewhat-lacking argument into a highly effective one.

Find a partner in your class.

Each partner chooses a discipline and a topic. Each person should choose a particular disciplinary perspective and a topic to focus on for this Write Away. Pretend you are a biologist, for example, work-ing on plant photosynthesis. Or, pretend you are a cultural anthropologist studying agrarian societies.

Each partner writes a really "bad" argument. This is the fun part. Write the worst argument you can possibly imagine. Aim for an argument that is about as long as an abstract of 100-150 words. Try to include as many logical fallacies as possible, and stay as far away as possible from the criteria for effective arguments. Remember, though, developmental editors do not fix typos, so try to make your "bad" argument as grammatically accurate as possible.

Exchange "bad" arguments with your partner.

Developmental editors, get to work! Now it is time for you to assume your role as developmental edi-tor. You are tasked with getting your partner's bad argument into shape. Revise, rewrite, and improve the argument to make it as effective as possible. This may require at times taking a few liberties with the original argument, which is fine in this case. Your author can always decide to decline your suggestions. For now, do not be shy, and make any and all changes you think the argument needs to become as effective as possible.

Trade arguments back, and reflect. Return the now-much-improved argument to the original author, and then examine your returned argument. Reflect for ten minutes about what you learned about argu-ment from being a developmental editor and from seeing your "bad" argument become better. When providing and receiving developmental editing assistance, which changes made the biggest impact? What changes were deployed across both "bad" arguments?

Constructing Arguments

Pinpointing Chapter 9

This chapter extends the material about arguments introduced in Chapter 8 by examining how writers go about actually constructing arguments. Where Chapter 8 helped to frame what arguments accomplish and what makes them more or less effective, this chapter digs deeper to examine how writers structure their arguments. To provide you with strategies for *constructing arguments in transit*, this chapter addresses the following concepts:

- Questions that Shape Arguments
- Inductive and Deductive Reasoning
- Argument Structure
- Stasis Theory
- Classical Argument Structure
- Toulmin Argument Structure
- Rogerian Argument Structure

Chapter 10 builds on our exploration of argument by addressing the choices writers make regarding design and format, aspects that are, like structure, crucial to developing effective arguments.

In July 1911, explorer and Yale history professor Hiram Bingham (who has since become the prototype for Indiana Jones) suddenly came across the Peruvian site now known as Machu Picchu and declared it the "lost capital" of the Incas. Constructed in the fifteenth century, Machu Picchu sits at an elevated point between two mountains. From the sky the structural layout resembles a condor sitting in its lofty nest (Heaney; Magli).

Since Bingham's rediscovery of Machu Picchu, the site has sparked numerous debates across academic disciplines. Some even debate Bingham's role as rediscoverer, arguing that those accolades should instead go to a 1910 German exploration team or to Peruvians themselves long before (Eisner).

Research about the purpose of Machu Picchu occupies some of the most contentious scholarly terrain. Much about the site demonstrates that the Incas paid deliberate, sustained attention to the structure of Machu Picchu—be it for geometric, religious, astronomical, cosmological, or political purposes. Scholars, therefore, seek evidence for their arguments from Machu Picchu's structure itself.

Some scholars argue that it was primarily a royal retreat for a fifteenth-century Inca ruler. Recently, evolutionary anthropologists conducted mtDNA (mitochondrial DNA) analyses on skeletons Bingham had collected a century ago: "[Study] results support the hypothesis that the remains of residents of the Inca-period rural communities of Paucarcancha and Patallacta that were analyzed were native highlanders [and] we argue that they served roles of supporting the nearby Inca royal estate of Machu Picchu" (Verano).

Discrediting the notion of a royal retreat, other researchers argue that Machu Picchu served as an astronomical observatory. A team of Peruvian and Polish archaeologists used stone conservation and 3D documentation methods to argue that the building called El Mirador served as "a device used probably by a small group of Inca priest-astronomers for precise observations of the position of celestial bodies on the horizon, against the distinctive Yanantin mountain peaks." The Torreón structure, similarly, has been found to have a

window that opens in such a way as to track the solstices and equinoxes (Aveni; Dearborn and White; "New Archaeastronomical"; Reinhard).

Astrophysicist Guilio Magli argues that this astronomical function intersected with Machu Picchu's religious purposes: "[The geometry of the structural designs] lead[s] us to propose that Machu Picchu was intentionally planned and built as a pilgrimage center connected with the Inca "cosmovision." Travel blogger Julio Moreno explains how the archaeoastronomical planning might have impressed pilgrims as they arrived at Machu Picchu at particular points of the year: "[T]he sun rises exactly at a point between Machu Picchu Mountain, and the mountain next to it on June 21, the summer solstice. This is called the gateway of the sun, and the entrance to Machu Picchu as you come through the Inca Trail. During this day, some buildings are designed to cast shadows on altars or other religiously significant stones."

Constructing arguments across disciplines resonates with the mtDNA analyses conducted on the Machu Picchu skeletons. While the basic DNA building blocks of humans have universal, structural similarities, we all also have unique characteristics that make us more or less similar to one another and that ultimately make us each individual human beings. We can think of argument in the same vein; while there are nearly infinite opportunities for discipline-specificity, contextualization, and creativity for any given argument, there are also some structural similarities with argument construction that we can usefully identify across disciplines and contexts.

Drawing out the intersection between purpose and structure further, the scholars studying Machu Picchu create their very own arguments about the archaeological site with deliberate, sustained attention to structure. They choose how to construct arguments by considering disciplinary, historical, and individual context as well as purpose. Purpose deeply impacts choices made about construction, be it of an archaeological site or an archaeological argument.

Developing an awareness of the underlying structures for arguments as well as the ways in which they can be modified will help you recognize the choices academic writers make as they construct arguments and will help you make choices about constructing your own arguments.

Write Here

Identify an ongoing controversy surrounding Machu Picchu, and read an argument related to this controversy. Then, recreate that person's argument using objects (not words). To do so, find a variety of small objects you can use to represent the various components of that person's argument, and arrange them in such a way as to represent that argument. Explain the argument and your choices about constructional representation in writing. Share your construction and your written account of it with your classmates and instructor.

Questions that Shape Arguments

Chapter 3 emphasized that posing questions is a key feature of academic writing across disciplines and contexts. As writers construct arguments, they tend gradually to move toward posing a somewhat more focused range of questions. Developing refined and precise questions enables writers to craft more effective, targeted arguments. The questions that shape arguments include matters such as disciplinary perspective, publication context, and purpose. As you will see, many of the questions that help shape arguments are also those that readers themselves ask while engaging with others' arguments.

TABLE 9.1 Questions that shape arguments.

Research questions	What research questions are you asking? What do you need to learn in order to arrive at an argument? What issues or concepts have generated your research questions? What problems or concerns are you noticing, and what do you need to understand about them?
Disciplinary and publication contexts	What is the disciplinary context for your writing project? How do the conventions and expectations of that disciplinary context shape arguments? What is the publication context for your argument? How do the conventions and expectations of that publication context shape arguments?
Purpose	What do you hope to accomplish by writing this argument? What would you like readers to do or think after having read your argument? Why are you writing this argument?
Evidence	What evidence have you collected? What evidence do you hope to locate? What evidence do you have access to? How will you collect and analyze the evidence?
Assumptions	What assumptions may be impacting your argument? How might your political, social, cultural, or geographic values be impacting your argument? What assumptions might you have about the potential readers of your argument? How are you defining terms, and what assumptions might be shaping those definitions?
Audience	To whom are you directing your argument? What kinds of expertise do they have? Are they likely to agree with you already or disagree? What do you hope they do with or think about your argument? What perspectives might they have about your argument?
Qualifications	What qualifications exist for your argument? What are the specific circumstances in which your argument works? What other contexts or conditions might raise uncertainties with your argument? What are the limitations regarding your argument or the methods by which you conducted and analyzed research for your argument?
Alternative viewpoints	How might people disagree with your position? How might others offer alternative viewpoints? What points of contention might emerge from your argument?

Structure	What structure will best suit your argument? Should you focus exclusively on your own position or pay equal attention to conflicting viewpoints? What would be most effective for how you can organize your evidence, perspectives, and points?
Credibility	How will you establish your credibility? What steps will you need to take in order to acquire expertise about this area of inquiry? How will you convey to readers that you have authority and expertise? How will you establish a sense of trust and rapport with readers?
Format(s) or modalities	Should your argument appear in visual, verbal, multimodal, or written format? Is it a scholarly argument or a popular piece? Would it be better suited for multiple modalities? How might these varying forms impact your argument?
So what?	Why does your argument matter? Why should people care about this argument? What important issues does it address? How will it impact others' lives or the world around us?

Inductive and Deductive Reasoning

Arguments are developed through reasoning and proof. Chapter 8 already addressed reasoning in part through logical fallacies. But developing an effective argument entails deciding the way in which you will build your line of reasoning. Philosophers have created two general categories, or labels, for reasoning in arguments: inductive and deductive.

Inductive reasoning

Inductive reasoning involves moving from examples or observations (premises) to general assertions that are likely to be true (Figure 9.1). One can find inductive reasoning across disciplines. In the field of history, one might think about how the circumstances leading to one historical event might, if recreated, lead to another such event. Economists Mikko Ketokivi and Saku Mantere have studied inductive reasoning in the field of management and economics, where researchers collect data and then draw inferences and conclusions based on that data for future predictive models. Ketokivi and Mantere describe inductive reasoning, and its challenges, as follows:

> Inductive reasoning…runs…from particulars to generalizations. When one generalizes from data, one's inferences are always inductive…. [I]nduction is sometimes

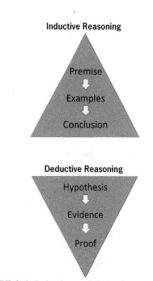

FIGURE 9.1 Inductive and deductive reasoning.

dubbed an ampliative form of reasoning (e.g., Salmon, 1966)—it "ampli-fies" our knowledge in that the conclusion is more than a restatement of the premises.

Ketokivi and Mantere make the point that in moving from particulars to generalizations, one risks applying ideas that might not necessarily be applicable or generalizable. Effective inductive reasoning, therefore, relies on a writer's capacity to recognize and address assumptions. As writers apply ideas from one setting to another, or move from particulars to generalizations, they must by necessity make certain assumptions about the circumstances or contexts that will enable the particulars to maintain applicability and continuity. Davis Oldham, a writing professor at Shoreline Community College, suggests that **assumptions** can involve facts, values, or analysis. Daniel Kies, a writing professor at DuPage University, argues that assumptions emerge from cultural, biological, intellectual, and idiosyncratic origins. With inductive reasoning, writers are extrapolating one premise to a more general context, and so must be sure that their assumptions about that general context are valid and explicit.

Deductive reasoning

In contrast to inductive reasoning, **deductive reasoning** moves from the general to the particular (Figure 9.1). Deductive reasoning has roots in the construction of hypotheses. For instance, if an academic writer develops a hypothesis to test, then she is approaching an argument through deductive reasoning. Deductive reasoning also presents challenges because ideas must be judged as being valid or invalid: if the premises (also termed evidence) hold truth, then the conclusion (also termed proof) will be true, and the argument can be understood as valid.

Like inductive reasoning, deductive reasoning is woven throughout disciplines. Because of its emphasis on validity, Michal Ayalon and Ruhama Even argue that "deductive reasoning is often used as a synonym for mathematical thinking." Mathematicians, that is, might start a proof with a premise or law and then apply it to a particular case in order to reach a conclusion. Offering another example of how deductive reasoning operates in a discipline, H. David Tuggle, Alex H. Townsend and Thomas J. Riley argue that the field of archaeology makes extensive use of deductive reasoning: "[the] identification of artifacts or features by archaeologists is accomplished by deductive reasoning."

Both forms of reasoning, therefore, have challenges and benefits, each affording academic writers with the opportunity to make claims based on premises and evidence and each having use across disciplines.

Writer Insights

What is the significance of your most recent writing project?

As a flute teacher, I create recital program notes to entertain, educate, and engage the audiences of my students. Listeners are more apt to connect with "Skip to My Lou" performed by a fledgling flutist if they know this popular American Frontier-era song encouraged the stealing of dance part-ners during its heyday. And what's the difference between a nocturne and a gavotte? The audience delights in such details. Writing is a valuable tool that I use to enhance the appreciation of music.

~June Newton, Flute Teacher and Freelance Musician, Augusta, Georgia, United States

Read an op-ed about an issue of interest to you. Write for ten minutes about why you think the argument relies on inductive reasoning, deductive reasoning, or a combination of both.

Argument Structure

Although academic writers situate arguments uniquely within particular writing occasions, they also draw from a shared array of structures as they construct arguments. Argument structure helps determine how academic writers organize and emphasize certain shared features of arguments, such as introductions, conclusions, opposing viewpoints, evidence, and articulations of the position. Developing awareness of these common argument structures, as well as the ways in which they can be modified, will help you recognize the choices academic writers make as you encounter and respond to others and as you generate your own arguments.

Four common approaches to argument structures that emerge across disciplines are stasis theory, classical argumentation, Toulmin argumentation, and Rogerian argumentation. Although each of these argument structures occurs across disciplines, certain structures might fit more readily in particular contexts. If you are working in a field such as ethics or development studies, for example, and your writing often tackles complex and ambiguous terrain, it might make sense to invoke Rogerian argument, which focuses on compromise. If you are writing in a field such as the health sciences and showing how a previous study reached a faulty conclusion, it might make sense to use the classical structure because this structure emphasizes refuting others' arguments. In disciplines such as English literature, history, or cultural anthropology, where writers often make use of in-depth analysis of texts to develop claims, the Toulmin argument structure might make sense given that it provides guidelines for carefully connecting evidence to a main argument. Of course, a writer in history might use classical argument structure to refute common perceptions about the narrative of a particular historical event. Still, it is important to consider how disciplinary context and writing occasion impact argument structure.

The upcoming sections introduce you to these four argumentation structures and provide examples of each. These examples demonstrate structure through written formats but can also be mapped onto and modified to other argument modalities, such as digital and in-person contexts, and for arguments that are visual or oral as well as written. Chapter 10: Designing Arguments will offer you the opportunity to think about how the platform and modality of an argument impacts the construction and design of an argument's structure. As you will also see, despite each of these structures having distinct features, they also have overlap, and academic writers often modify or blend these structures depending on the writing occasion. Thus, as you reflect on these structures, consider them not as strict templates, but as beginning points for constructing arguments.

Stasis Theory

Stasis theory provides a bridge between questions that shape an argument and argument structure. Where the questions in the prior section are more general in nature, stasis theory offers a structured set of questions—a heuristic—that can help you develop, refine, and shape your argument. It can be conceived of as a method of invention or discovery (or prewriting, as we discussed in Chapter 2: Research and Writing as a Process), specifically geared toward argument. Stasis theory can essentially help structure any argument by helping you determine what the main issues are, how significant they are, what the implications are, and what you think next steps should be related to the argument.

After using the stasis questions to generate a range of possible approaches to an argument, academic writers can then make choices about which aspects they think are most significant and/or which ones they may want to focus on for a particular argument.

Stasis theory, also known as issue theory, has its origins with "Hermagoras of Temnos, a rhetor of the second century BCE [and] Hermogenes of Tarsus" [a rhetor of the second century CE] (Fernández-Garrido). Stasis theory initially emerged in the context of judicial deliberations as a way for lawyers and judges to discover and determine what issues were at stake pertaining to a particular legal case. Those in judicial circles could, ostensibly, go through the questions to gain clarity on whether a crime had been committed, what that crime entailed, who was harmed, who was guilty, how significant the crime was, and what the punishment should be.

Now, stasis theory has found many realms of application beyond its legalistic, and arguably punitive, origins. For instance, Allen Brizee argues that stasis theory can help as a strategy for "workplace teaming and decision making." Kathryn Northcut has applied stasis theory to paleontology. And Charles Marsh has applied stasis theory to crisis communication.

In terms of its application to argument structure, stasis theory invites you to pursue four main areas of questioning, or issue seeking, as a way of discovering the potential contours of an argument. Arguing for the universal applicability of these questions or issues, Cicero maintained that "There will always be one of these issues applicable to every kind of case; for where none applies, there can be no controversy."

The four stases, or issues, and their questions, are as follows:

Facts (termed "conjectural"):
What has happened?
What has caused it?

Definition (termed "definitional"):
Has harm been done?
What type of harm is it?
To whom or what has this harm been done?
Who is responsible for this harm?

Quality (termed "qualitative"):
How severe is the harm or impact?
What is the degree of the harm or impact?

Policy (termed "procedural"):
Should something be done?
What should be done?

Considering each of these questions helps writers determine the parameters of their argument. Arguments can emerge through one or more stases, depending on not only the particular issue, but also the writer, the context for the argument, and the discipline.

As an example of how stasis theory can work to shape arguments across disciplines, let's consider an academic writer who is interested in questions about climate change. He might pursue any of the following stases related to climate change:

Facts/Conjecture: Academic writers might argue over whether the climate is or is not changing or about what is causing it. For instance, scholars David Stern and Robert Kaufman argue that "both natural and anthropogenic forcings cause temperature change."

Definition: Academic writers might also argue over what the impact of climate change is. For instance, Abigail Cahill and her coauthors argue in their article "How Does Climate Change Cause Extinction?" that "[a]nthropogenic climate change is predicted to be a major cause of species extinctions in the next 100 years."

Quality: Those interested in examining the degree of the impact of climate change would be making an argument about issues of quality. For instance, in their article "Climate Change Impacts on Marine Ecosystems," Doney, et al. argue about the severity of the impact of climate change, such as "shifts in the size, structure… and…abundance of populations [and] altered species interactions."

Procedure: The stasis of procedure asks what policies should be enacted, what solutions can be achieved, or what behaviors should be developed. Guy Dauncey, for instance, focuses the majority of his book, *Stormy Weather*, on practical solutions to climate change that utilize available technology.

Many arguments span multiple stases, even sometimes all four stases, and other times writers will instead demonstrate why they are focusing on one particular stasis over others, having perhaps shown that other stases are less relevant, less significant, or already resolved.

Transfer at Work

Academic writers use stasis theory in many disciplinary contexts, even outside of rhetoric. In "The Politics of Silence: Interpreting Stasis in Contemporary Eritrea," for instance, professor of history Richard Reid uses stasis theory to examine current conflicts between the Eritrean government and the broader population.

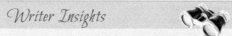

Writer Insights

What are the purposes of your arguments?

I am a nonprofit professional…. As someone with nine years of experience in campaigns, communications, policy and philanthropy, I have an eye for detail, a drive to impact the world, and a passion for leaving the earth, like a campground, better than I found it. I would like to think my writing is more than my work. The mission is always the same; I write to inspire, to teach, to share, to motivate, to communicate and to connect.

~Claire LaFrance, Nonprofit Professional, Washington, D.C., United States

In the excerpt from her book, *Kill the Messenger*, Maria Armoudian makes an argument about climate change and the media by systematically progressing through all four stases. In the text's annotations, I show how others could have argued alternative positions within each of the stases.

Excerpt from *Kill the Messenger: The Media's Role
in the Fate of the World* by M. Armoudian

In 2007, political changes fueled more robust media coverage. With the climate on their agenda, Democrats gained control of both houses of Congress; the U.S. Supreme Court decided the EPA's role in regulating greenhouse gases; and California passed groundbreaking climate legislation, signed into law by actor-turned-governor Arnold Schwarzenegger. To disambiguate the science, former vice president Al Gore dispelled the myth of a scientific debate in his film, *An Inconvenient Truth*. ...

> Armoudian is arguing about the facts (conjecture), building a case about what caused media to shift in 2007 to "more robust coverage" of climate change. Others might argue that different facts created this media shift, or that these facts tell only part of the story and that there are other facts leading to a conclusion that media coverage did not shift in 2007.

> Armoudian moves next to an argument of definition, arguing that the impact of this coverage generated a perception of "two sides to climate science." Others, presumably, could argue about a different impact.

Without checking the veracity of the naysayers' statements, many journalists gave equal footing to denialists and real climate scientists, ultimately framing an established climate science as "he-said-she-said" and creating an illusion that there were two sides to climate science....

Eager for controversy, some journalists seized upon a handful of words that turned errors in judgment into evidence of a conspiracy that unjustly tarnished climate scientists and misled the public on the seriousness of global warming. ...

> Armoudian now demonstrates the stasis of quality along with definition, arguing that this media coverage was severe in that it "unjustly tarnished climate scientists and misled the public." Those with different views could argue that this impact was not severe or problematic.

Media consolidation and concentration of ownership are the enemies of information diversity and pluralism, serving only media owners, not the public. To prevent narrow-minded discourse from dominating the public sphere, legal structures including antitrust laws, protections for net neutrality (unrestricted and unbiased Internet access and flow), treaties, and other thoughtful regulation are needed to help limit concentrated ownership and related forces that strangle the flow of independent information.

> Toward the end of her book, Armoudian moves to an argument of procedure. Here she argues for increased legislation to protect "information diversity and pluralism." Others might argue for different kinds of legislation.

From *Kill the Messenger: the Media's Role in the Fate of the World*, 2011.

Write Now

The preceding annotated example addresses climate, which seems to somewhat readily map onto the four stases because of its highly controversial and policy-driven nature. Choose another line of inquiry or discipline, perhaps one that seems less controversial, and develop questions and controversies for it based on the four stases. How would you develop stases, for instance, with arguments about sports psychology or the history of the plague?

Classical Argument Structure

Deployed since at least the fifth century BCE, the classical argument structure is most suitable when you are trying to make an argument convincing for readers who oppose your ideas, by addressing and refuting opposing viewpoints as a means of forwarding your own position. **Classical argument structure** may be familiar to you in the context of political debates, where candidates will argue for a particular agenda or approach—and in the process demonstrate why other candidates' approaches are less advantageous.

Classical argument has five primary components: introduction, narrative, confirmation, refutation and concession, and summary and conclusion.

Introduction

The introduction should accomplish several important objectives: secure the reader's interest, orient the reader to your argument, cultivate a positive relationship with the reader, and articulate your argument.

Securing readers' interest is one of the first aims for an introduction. Although your professors or teaching assistants are largely required to read your writing—it's part of their job—other readers have considerably more choice. Sometimes readers need encouragement to read, either because they may not know why an issue is important or interesting or because they may be choosing from among a number of different options for research on a particular topic. Given all the options and choices readers have, what will encourage them to read your writing project?

You might consider this a hook for your readers, where you put a line out and hope they take a bite. Perhaps you can begin with something surprising, or a narrative anecdote, or a relevant quote or concept. Whatever it is you choose, be sure your hook is relevant in content, purpose, and tone to your overall argument.

Write Now

With a current writing project of your own, try developing at least three different possible hooks for readers. You might try a compelling sentence, a narrative anecdote, a significant fact or observation, a relevant quote, or an unexpected fact. Developing several different hooks will enable you to see that there is great variety in options for how writers go about securing readers' interest.

Introductions should also orient readers to the overall argument. Help readers prepare for the argument by providing key terms, the main line of inquiry, your approach, and any other relevant information you think they will need to adequately consider your argument. You may decide to expand on these aspects later in the argument, but offer a glimpse now of the main concepts that will be under discussion.

Orienting readers to an argument serves as one way of cultivating a positive relationship with readers because it prepares them for what is forthcoming. Efforts to create a positive relationship between writer and readers also involve presenting yourself as ethical, trustworthy, knowledgeable, and courteous. You might think of this endeavor as a performance of sorts, even if it is an honest performance. Erving Goffman argues in his well-known book *The Presentation of Self in Everyday Life* that all presentations are a performance:

> When an individual plays a part he implicitly requests his observers to take seriously the impression that is fostered before them. They are asked to believe that the character they see actually possesses the attributes he appears to possess, that the task he performs will have the consequences that are implicitly claimed for it, and that, in general, matters are what they appear to be.

Goffman's notion of performance enables academic writers to think about their presentation of self and the various roles they play in relation to their readers.

Just as writers present themselves in an introduction, they must also present their arguments. Articulate for readers as clearly as possible what your argument, thesis, or position is. Your argument itself can consist of multiple sentences, one sentence, or even sometimes an entire paragraph; depending on the context, you might even say something like, "This article argues…" as a way of signaling to readers what the argument is.

Narrative

This second component of classical argument can be thought of as the story behind your argument. What other research has already been conducted about this issue? Why is your argument significant? Often this narrative section consists of the literature review (as discussed in Chapter 5: Summary, and Chapter 7: Analysis), where academic writers summarize and synthesize previous research. Include in this narrative section enough information for readers to feel fully apprised of the current state of research on a particular issue. One challenge of academic arguments is that readers often have varying levels of expertise. Writers must consider how they can bring those with less expertise up to speed without boring or talking down to those with more expertise.

Confirmation

This aspect of classical argument provides readers with the main reasons and evidence supporting your argument. This section confirms your thesis, position, or argument by showing readers how the evidence you have gathered makes your argument valid. The confirmation should be organized clearly and methodically so readers can understand the process by which you have arrived at your claim. This section might also include smaller arguments that are related to your overarching argument. If so, then you would also provide evidence and reasoning to support these smaller claims. The confirmation component is also the moment where you make sure to explicate all of your evidence fully so readers can see the connections between the evidence and the argument.

Refutation and concession

After offering evidence toward an argument, academic writers using classical arguments also address what are known as **counterarguments**. Academic writers anticipate what those with opposing views might argue, and they attempt to address and counter these views. Rather than dismissing them outright, though, academic writers often approach this through qualification or **concession**. A writer might acknowledge that an opposing view may have elements that are reasonable under certain circumstances. As we work to convince others to change their opinions, people rarely like to hear that they are completely wrong about something. More effective approaches will suggest that they are somewhat right or that they are right under certain contexts.

Summary and conclusion

The final section of classical argument summarizes your argument and the main points you hope to have made. Think of this as the final opportunity to provide readers with your takeaway points: What do you want your readers to be thinking about as they finish reading your argument?

Effective conclusions tend to include certain components: a recap of the main argument, hints at future research, and a call to action.

Conclusions, unfortunately, sometimes get short shrift. Writers can find themselves with insufficient time to focus on a conclusion. Instead, writers should devote significant energy to conclusions. They are critically important because they hold the final opportunity for you to address your readers in that particular writing occasion.

One of the central features of conclusions is a review or echo of the main argument. While it is important to summarize your main argument (some busy readers may read only your conclusion), you should never cut and paste text from earlier in the argument into the conclusion. Think about the conclusion as an echo of sorts, recasting the argument, but with just a slight variation in tone, content, or style.

Conclusions also should include ideas for future research and/or new questions. Since effective academic arguments contribute to ongoing conversations, furthering knowledge and making progress are often more appropriate than attempting to provide the final say-so. Effective conclusions should offer readers ideas for what remains to be considered or researched.

Finally, conclusions should make a call to action of some sort, even if that action involves thinking instead of doing. Now that readers have read your argument, what would you like them to do with what they have learned? Do you want them to think differently? Are you advocating for a policy or behavior of some kind? Provide readers with ideas for what they might do next.

In this example of a classical argument, David Corso, an undergraduate student majoring in biology and minoring in psychology at the University of South Carolina, Spartanburg, pursues the question, "What are the potential uses for video games in improving our lives?"

Corso perhaps adopts the classical style of argument because he anticipates that many readers will have opposing positions on video games, believing them instead to have deleterious effects on our lives. His strategy of refutation involves qualifying the context of others' research. This strategy of refuting others' claims based on methodology (what games they used in their experiments, for example) is a common strategy in the sciences and lends itself well to the classical argument structure because it offers the opportunity to develop both refutation and concession.

Excerpt from "The Psychological and Physical Effects
of Video Game Play" by D. Corso

From light and food to singing and dancing, our world is characterized by phenomena, events, and processes that have a physical and psychological effect on us. Our environment and our experience shape us—physically and mentally. Games work in a similar fashion. A game is any mental and/or physical activity that is defined by goals, rules, challenges, a feedback system, and voluntary participation (Game, n.d.; McGonigal, 2011; Prensky, 2001). A video game is a complex form of digital media that incorporates these gamic properties, and it requires the active interaction between a human and computer (Galloway, 2006; Wardrip-Fruin, 2009)....

> In the introduction, Corso provides a hook for readers, inviting us to think about light, food, singing, and dancing—universal human activities. The effect of this is also to link video games with other forms of enjoyment and leisure activities, thereby starting to link positivity with video games. Corso establishes goodwill and expertise by using a scholarly tone and invoking current scholarship.

Video games are the popularized, digital form of games, and through their inherent properties, video games are a perfect tool to quantifiably measure a number of physical and mental capacities, capabilities, and characteristics.... We have to understand the cognitive and physiological effects of video game play in order to understand how these processes can be utilized to help us interpret and navigate our world. By understanding these effects, we can begin to develop games that facilitate our lives, e.g. constructing beneficial stratagems for education and public health....

> Corso's thesis, his main argument, appears here, where he argues that video games can help us "interpret and navigate our world" and "facilitate our lives." Thinking in terms of stases, Corso's argument would fall under definition and quality.

From *Caravel, Undergraduate Research Journal*, 2014.

Cognitive Effects

Video games exercise and train cognitive skills. Cognition is defined as the mental processes associated with memory, language, perception, attention, problem solving, decision-making, and reasoning (Goldstein, 2011). Video games create engaging environments that allow for cognitive growth and development in mental rotational skills, object location ability, attention, visual attention, targeting, iconic and verbal representation of processes, verbal fluency, executive control, and both short and long-term memory skills (Boyan & Sherry, 2011).… Through their intrinsic qualities, video games promote cognitive growth and development.

A 2003 study by Green and Bavelier demonstrated cognitive growth through video game play.… They conducted five experiments…

> This section marks the beginning of Corso's narrative, where he offers a literature review of video game research. It is clear from the research he's citing that his disciplinary perspective is psychology and neuroscience. Corso uses summary and synthesis throughout this section.

> Corso blends narrative and confirmation, using Green and Bavelier as evidence for his own argument about the potential benefits of video games.

The State of Video Game Research: Problems and Solutions

Our lives and our world are characterized by complexity—the workings of a cell, law, quantum physics, etc.—and video games reflect these intricacies. … On the one hand, video games and video game play … have great utility in a number of areas, such as academia, research, and healthcare (Astle et al., 2011; Griffiths, 2002; Van Eck, 2006). On the other hand, video games and video game play create a number of problems that must be understood and resolved in order to utilize their full potential. … Through surveys, models, experimental tests, and correlational studies, video games have been shown to produce a number of negative effects (Carnagey et al., 2007; Gentile et al., 2012; Gentile et al., 2004; Wang et al., 2011). … Several studies have found correlation effects between aggressive behavior and video game habits (Gentile et al., 2004). …

The major factor in a number of these studies is the nature of video game play: the content of the game, i.e. fighting and death, the context in which people play, i.e. a lack of supervision, and the amount of time spent playing.… Since we know that video games will create this effect under specific environmental influences, i.e. violent video games produc-

> Corso now moves into refutation and concession, reviewing the literature that argues for the negative impact of video games. He summarizes and synthesizes fully, choosing not to refute it right away. This approach demonstrates judiciousness.

ing aggression and desensitization, then specific environmental influences on the other spectrum should be able to produce a different response, e.g. construction games producing cooperation and collaboration (Ito, 2009)....

Now Corso refutes the literature, conceding that these studies present solid evidence, but then stating that they address only certain types of video games. This approach qualifies the opposing point of view, showing that these arguments are valid, but only in certain circumstances.

The Potential Uses for Video Games

Corso now moves into a full section of confirmation, making specific points about how video games can facilitate "growth and success." He divides his confirmation into several categories (research, treatment/prevention, education), within which he argues that video games can have a strong impact.

Video games have enormous potential as tools to study human growth and development, as training simulators for various jobs and skills, for education at primary, secondary, and collegiate institutions, and so much more. ...

As Griffiths (2002) states, "Videogames can be used as research and/or measurement tools. Furthermore, as research tools, they have great diversity" (p. 47)....

Prevention and Treatment Strategies

Video games provide an effective prevention and treatment strategy for a variety of problems, such as with Alzheimer's and ADHD. ... Aart et al. (2007) report a number of problems that video game neurofeedback can be applied to as medication; these include alleviating attention and hyperactivity disorders, muscular tonicity recovery for cardiovascular patients, relaxation and meditation ...

Corso's confirmation continues, providing evidence for the positive impact and use of video games.

Educational Value

Video games are excellent pedagogical tools. As Gentile (2011) reports, video games can provide immediate feedback, motivate players, set specific goals, promote mastery, encourage distributed learning, teach for transfer, adapt themselves to the level of the learner, and provide various other teaching techniques. ...

Corso now moves into the conclusion, reminding readers of the contrasting positions as well, but encouraging a "holistic" approach and inspiring readers about the many possibilities video games can offer. This opens the door for readers to extend this research and explore these potential uses in more depth.

Conclusion

Video games have measurable effects—physically and cognitively. Video games produce cognitive improvements, e.g. visual attention processes, as well as physical changes, such as the brain areas responsible for processing and learning. However, video games also produce impairments that cause psychological deficits, e.g. inhibition and decision-making skills, from physical effects, i.e. prolonged stress mechanisms. As long as we approach video games in a holistic sense, we can design them to make us smarter and stronger while minimizing negative effects. There are no limits to the cognitive training and learning opportunities created by video games, and they can be developed to improve cognitive resources, such as memory, language, and problem-solving skills.

Toulmin Argument Structure

Toulmin argument structure emerged from a book by rhetorician and philosopher Stephen Toulmin (1922-2009) titled *The Uses of Argument* (1958). Toulmin arguments overlap with certain features of the classical argument structure, such as an introduction and conclusion, but Toulmin focuses primarily on how writers use evidence to move their argument forward. Where classical argument structures makes sense in contexts with oppositional readers, Toulmin argument structures might be applicable for more neutral contexts.

The Toulmin model involves six component parts: claim, evidence, warrant, backing, qualifier(s), and rebuttal.

Claim

The claim is the main argument or position of a writing project. Instead of labeling an argument a thesis, Toulmin refers to it as a claim. The word claim originates from the Latin root word of *clamare*, which can be translated as "to shout" or "to proclaim." Toulmin's terminology, then, illustrates that even in neutral contexts, writers should develop arguments that have significance, about which they feel compelled to "shout." The claim is the organizing principle around which the rest of the argument is structured. For claims to be effective, they should meet the criteria for effective arguments as articulated in Chapter 8, including such matters as complexity and contestability.

Evidence

Evidence works to move a claim forward or support a claim. Evidence, as we will see in Chapter 10, can include data, quotes, paraphrase, summary, and/or personal experience. Writers integrate evidence into their arguments so they can illustrate for readers how they arrived at their conclusions. If you make a claim about an issue, text, or concept, include evidence that attests to that claim. You might want to include an excerpt from a text, or results of a survey, or outcomes from an experiment. Evidence can also take the form of examples you provide that help illustrate a claim you are making. Academic arguments need to be evidence-based in order to reflect the careful research academic writers design and conduct.

Warrant

The warrant section is one of the most important components of Toulmin's argument structure. Without it, readers might not be able to understand why or how the evidence included works in support of a claim. The warrant can be considered the point of connection between the evidence and the claim. The warrant enables the writer to explain how the evidence is connected to the claim. Warranting includes explication, discussion, and reasoning. This section is also where a writer would address how he or she is interpreting the evidence so that it supports the claim.

Backing

Sometimes in the warrant section a writer will introduce ideas as part of his or her explanations that also need additional support or explication. These elements are referred to as backing because they are not directly connected to the evidence or claim, but they nonetheless play a crucial role in informing readers about important information related to the perspective or ideas. Backing might include background information or material that can help orient readers to various perspectives or frames of interpretation. Or, backing might include facts or historical narratives about certain issues pertinent to the evidence. Backing provides an additional layer of support for the warrant.

Qualifier

Qualifiers specify the circumstances under which an argument works, as well as those conditions under which an argument might not work. Qualifiers can include qualifying terms, such as mostly, often, or sometimes. But qualifications can also include entire concepts, such as naming the limitations of a research study or the parameters for selecting a study sample that might have impacted the results. Some arguments have entire sections labeled "Limitations" in order to explicitly address the qualifiers. Qualifiers might also include an occasion in which a writer addresses the assumptions undergirding an argument.

Rebuttal

The rebuttal is much like the refutation or concession of the classical argument structure. Rebuttals address counterarguments, potential disagreements, or alternative perspectives that might work against the claim. Rather than discounting alternative perspectives wholesale, writers often approach rebuttals by pointing out that certain portions of counterarguments are accurate or that under certain circumstances the counterarguments might be accurate. Rebuttals are an important opportunity in the argument to anticipate some of the disagreements and objections your readers might have. Sometimes a rebuttal section can also include a kind of reassurance to readers. For example, a writer can convey to readers that if they were to accept the claim of the argument, their concerns about the implications or challenges that lie ahead may be less critical than they perceive.

This example of a Toulmin-based argument is a literary analysis of George R.R. Martin's *A Game of Thrones*. Rebecca Jones, an undergraduate at the University of Wisconsin, River Falls, majoring in English, examines these questions: how are female characters depicted in Martin's novels? and how are female characters depicted in the television show?

Excerpt from "A Game of Genders: Comparing Depictions of Empowered Women between *A Game of Thrones* Novel and Television Series" by R. Jones

1. Introduction

The genre of fantasy has a long and sordid history in its depictions of women. Even today, female authors and positive female protagonists are still scarce. This is in part because the genre battles not only societal norms, but also the chivalric standards and gender roles of medieval times, which it often emulates. Knights and damsels-in-distress are often touchstones for male and female characters. Presently, "Feminist philosophy […] sees chivalry as oppressing women by formulating a specific role that not all women want for themselves, and, further, by devaluing the role that women are supposed to play." Recent fantasy novels have started to counteract this trend through the writings of female and male authors alike, refuting the former chivalric expectations for women within the genre by allowing women greater prominence within their novels. In the novel, *A Game of Thrones* by George R. R. Martin, the modern reader encounters Cersei Lannister, Catelyn Stark, Sansa Stark, Arya Stark, and Daenerys (Dany) Targaryen … Each of the aforementioned women is empowered through her political rank within the world Martin creates, while also possessing a strength of her own, which manifests through the various trials she faces…. While the series is a close adaptation of the novel, by noting the variations in depictions of … women, one sees the changing standards for women conveyed by the differences in portrayal between the two media, utilizing the lens of their respective archetypes. …

> Jones situates her claim within an ongoing conversation about the role of women in fantasy novels. In so doing, she broadens her potential range of readers to include those interested in feminist theory, women's studies, and fantasy fiction, as well as those interested in *A Game of Thrones* more specifically.

> Jones provides her claim at the end of this first paragraph in the final sentence. She argues that the archetypal portrayals in the novel and the show demonstrate an increase in power for female characters.

From *Journal of Student Research* (1.3), 2012.

2. The Women

2.1. Cersei Lannister: Shadow Queen and Mother

Cersei Lannister is the most powerful woman in both novel and show, and by far the most feared....

Four major scenes in the television show redefine Cersei's character and depict her as developed and complex, more so than Martin's presentation of her in the novel. The first of these scenes occurs in the episode "Kingsroad," when Cersei goes to the comatose Bran's room and consoles Catelyn telling of her own firstborn's death. The novel likewise mentions Cersei's first child, but much later and with a far different tone. When she tells Catelyn the story of her stillborn son in the show, it is with a quiet, somber voice. This change redefines her character and in the show's storyline gives her a different attitude and motivation than that of the poisonous, bitter Queen of the novel. This moment hints at the seeds of love she once had for Robert that have long since died: how there was a time when she bore his children, and rather than intentionally killing the child, as she does in the novel, he is already dead, and foreshadows the fate of her love for Robert. This moment gives the viewer some ground upon which to understand Cersei's later actions, as well as presenting her character as that of a Mother figure not just the Queen ...

> Jones includes evidence here for the show's depiction of a more complex character in the "Kingsroad" scene.

> Here, Jones provides the warrant for the evidence by demonstrating why this change is so significant in strengthening Cersei's character.

> Jones includes backing here as she provides information about Cersei's history with Robert that helps readers understand the warrant and evidence.

> Jones offers a qualification to her argument by admitting that Cersei also displays strength in the novel, just not as much as in the show.

In the show, [Cersei] is calm the entire time and in control. The novel, however, paints a different picture. She is still the strong woman but she shows her anger ...

While the show presents her as strong, unashamed, and unafraid..., Martin presents her as pathetic, disgusting, and [subordinate] in the novel. The differing lines in the novel and the actions presented in the show are what shape the difference between Cersei's two representations and allow her to be stronger in the show....

> Jones concludes this section by re-emphasizing her claim: that the show presents Cersei as a stronger, more complex female character than the novel does. In subsequent sections, Jones provides evidence, backing, and warrants about the other female characters in *A Game of Thrones*.

3. Conclusion

Fantasy has not always been kind in its depictions of women, such as its

Jones here offers a rebuttal to the counterargument that women are depicted in problematic ways in fantasy fiction shows and novels. Rather than suggesting this position is wrong, Jones instead reframes it by illustrating the opportunity for progress.

damsels-in-distress, passive ladies who do little but fill in the background space of the castle, or serving only as possessions who produce heirs for their lords. However, as society changes, so too must the literature it produces. Martin has already established strong and empowered women in his novel, yet in the show adaptation these women have often gained more strength, as fifteen years later he is now catering to a society whose standards for television have changed and is now able to have leading women who are strong, without objectifying them.… Allowing for [these changes], Martin reveals how society is more open to strong women, and looks for complex characters… In the end, [Martin] shows that while our culture has changed over the past fifteen years, there is still plenty of progress to be made …

Jones qualifies her argument by acknowledging that women are strong and empowered in the novel already, even though the show takes it to a greater degree. She further qualifies her argument by showing that more progress is yet to be made.

Rogerian Argument Structure

Rogerian argument, developed by psychologist Carl Rogers (1902-1947), is founded on compromise and understanding, resting on the premise that an argument should reach resolution. Rogerian argument focuses more explicitly on the refutation or rebuttal components of argument, and with more of a goal of compromise, than the classical or Toulmin argument structures. Approaching common ground and compromise may be more realistic or appropriate in some contexts. In the prior two examples, common ground might have been achieved if Corso had argued for increased regulation of violent video games even as he also argued for the positive impacts among other video games. For Jones, compromise might have emerged by exploring in more detail the lack of power among female characters in the show or the lack of power among female characters in another show.

Rogerian argument is composed of four components: catching the reader's interest, presenting the opposition's viewpoint, presenting the writer's viewpoint, and establishing common ground.

Catching readers' interest

As with other argument structures, Rogerian argument begins with an introduction that

Transfer at Work

Rogerian argument structures work in many disciplinary contexts, from political science and women's studies to computer engineering and biology. In "No Compromise: The Integration of Technology and Aesthetics," for instance, architects Robert Dunay, Joseph Wheeler, and Robert Schubert show how arguments against solar technology, which often center on their poor aesthetics, can actually be mediated by an approach to solar technology that accomplishes system integration and is therefore both sustainable and aesthetically pleasing.

captures reader interest. This introduction might point out the significance of an issue, raise important questions, or illustrate how an issue might concern the readers likely to be reading the argument. Rogerian argument emphasizes the importance of catching readers' interest and investment in an issue as a component of effective argument and deliberation. If readers do not perceive that anything is at stake in an issue, or if their attention is not fully present, then they may be less capable of listening to or reflecting on the ideas raised in the argument.

Presenting the opposing side's position

Because Rogerian argument is grounded on compromise, it positions, as an act of courtesy, the opposing side's position first. In presenting the opposing side's position, writers should spend considerable time discussing these opposing views and demonstrating an understanding of these positions. This section differs from a rebuttal in Toulmin's structure or a refutation in the classical structure because it values understanding and acknowledgement rather than criticism. Rogerian argument emphasizes the importance of listening carefully to others and then sharing with them what you heard them say. In so doing, this section of Rogerian argument is an opportunity for writers to indicate that they have listened to others and really can articulate those positions.

Present the writer's position

After extending the courtesy of addressing the opposing side's perspective first, a writer can then move to addressing his or her perspective, or any other perspectives that may contrast with the preceding one(s). In presenting the writer's position, or the second array of perspectives, the writer should rely on evidence-based reasoning. As with the other argument structures, Rogerian argument structure includes a full presentation of evidence and a full explication and discussion of the writer's point of view or position. In this section, writers can make appeals to *ethos, pathos, logos,* and also *kairos* as appropriate for the context.

Finding common ground

The culminating segments of Rogerian argument involve finding common ground between the perspectives or positions. Where other argument structures might lean more heavily toward concluding with the writer's position, Rogerian asks for an emphasis on compromise. Writers in this section will focus on shared values or goals or highlight a similar approach among the perspectives. The conclusion might also propose a solution that takes into account all the priorities and perspectives. Rogerian conclusions aim to resolve complicated issues by mediating between differences so that all parties can move forward productively rather than remain in a stalemate or perpetual disagreement.

The example of Rogerian argument comes from Eva Orbuch, who wrote this article while an undergraduate at Stanford University, where she majored in urban studies and minored in education. In the article on microfinance, published in the *Journal of Politics and Society,* Orbuch takes up the question, "[W]hat approach to service delivery is most effective in helping [microfinance institutions (MFIs)] achieve a balance between financial well-being and social impact?"

She explores the debate between two approaches to MFI service delivery: a financial approach or an integrated approach. While Orbuch ultimately advocates for an integrated approach, she forges a compromise with those who advocate for a financial approach.

Excerpt from "Toward an Integrated Approach to Microfinance: Sustainability in Bolivia and Peru" by E. Orbuch

Microfinance is a concept that has greatly expanded in meaning and practice since its inception.... One group of MFIs chooses to provide only financial products to their clients, primarily in the form of small loans, in order to maximize operational efficiency. This strategy contrasts with MFIs that choose to [use an "integrated approach"] and consider additional means of economic and social development...such as life insurance products, educational programs, and direct healthcare.

> Orbuch outlines the two positions here: one focused on "financial products" and the other, an "integrated approach." Orbuch does not malign or elevate either approach.

Current literature has called into question the previously touted effectiveness of microfinance and many in the microfinance community acknowledge the difficulty of fighting poverty through micro-loans alone.... Based on contemporaneous literature and on the perspectives of MFI leaders and employees, I conclude that the integrated service approach provides the best framework through which to balance the demands between financial sustainability and social impact.

> Orbuch captures reader interest by noting that the effectiveness of MFIs is being called into question.

> Orbuch here conveys her argument for the integrated approach, but, in Rogerian fashion, introduces the idea that this strategy offers a "balance" between financial and social interests.

Literature Review

...In 2005, the MIT Poverty Action Lab undertook a randomized evaluation of the impacts of introducing microcredit in a new market.... The results revealed that the introduction of microcredit has some varied and significant effects on business outcomes and the composition of household expenditure.... In a 2003 paper, researchers...gave the rationale that many other interventions such as employment, education, and healthcare depend on people's access to financial services, and that improvements in these other areas can only be maintained when households have increased control over financial resources.

> Orbuch offers a literature review of the financial approach. Notice there is no rebuttal or concession here, but, in a Rogerian manner, Orbuch is establishing common ground.

From *Journal of Politics & Society* (22), 2011.

While research focusing specifically on the effects of integrated microfinance is relatively rare, the work done has largely confirmed the positive nature of its impact. Institutions like Freedom from Hunger (FFH)…have performed several useful studies.… The results indicated that recipients of both credit and education services displayed greater business acumen and higher revenues than those who received only credit services.…

Next, Orbuch outlines the integrated approach, building on the common ground by showing that the integrated approach actually enhances the financial outcomes.

[S]ome organizations are being pressured into…leaving out non-credit products. There are also additional pressures for MFIs to "install complex accounting and managerial systems."… These pressures squeeze current practitioners of the integrated approach and discourage new MFIs from adopting service integration…Yet, as I will discuss later, my interviews also indicate that a strong social mandate and well-defined organizational policies could allow MFIs to continue to pursue their stated goals rather than face "mission drift," i.e., the gradual abandonment of the poverty-reduction aims of the microfinance sector.…I argue that this sought-after equilibrium between the banking and development aspects of MFIs can be translated into a more general balance between financial sustainability and social impact in the microfinance sector. While agreement among those interviewed was not unanimous, I believe that this balance is possible and the tradeoff is not inevitable.

Orbuch acknowledges the challenges involved with adopting the integrated approach, demonstrating a keen awareness of opposing viewpoints.

Orbuch establishes a "both/and" approach rather than an "either/or," suggesting that the integrated approach provides equilibrium and balance.

Project Methodology

To ensure a general amount of representation of the two sectors and a variety of service delivery approaches,…I visited thirteen MFIs and conducted interviews with thirty-one different MFI managers and employees.

Orbuch's methodology also achieves a Rogerian equanimity, as she specifically sought out MFIs that deliver both credit and educational services.

Organizational Benefits to Service Integration

1) Financial Sustainability and Cost-Effectiveness

Secondary data confirms the cost-effectiveness of the service integration approach.… Data from the Consortium of Private Organizations for the Promotion of Small and Micro-Enterprise (COPEME), a microfinance umbrella organization, shows that every Peruvian integrated organization studied had reached financial and operational sustainability.

Social Benefits of Service Integration

1) Client Health

...My interviews strongly suggest that health training and direct health interventions improve client health... [H]ealth education and direct delivery of health services are not only beneficial for clients, but also for the organization delivering them. According to Carmen Velasco,

"Even if you don't care about the social component of the program of what you do, if you're clever, you don't want to kill your clients..."

3) Economic Improvement

The final social benefit of integrated microfinance is the added economic progress for the clients.... [C]lients in solidarity loan groups are graduating out of their small group loan products, demonstrating that they are financially prepared to access a larger individual loan for their business....

Under What Circumstances Does Microfinance Integration Work?

Integrated microfinance will not work effectively in every context...Integrated microfinance can work well in countries that have consumer protections in the form of interest rate caps, but that have the flexibility to allow the rates required by integrated programs. Integration may not be possible in countries with rigid interest rate regulations, such as Venezuela....

As Orbuch moves to present her own position, she first discusses the financial sustainability of the integrated approach. This organization places emphasis on the financial aspects and forges a compromise with opposing perspectives. This section is then followed with more evidence about how the integrated approach increases organizational competitiveness and client loyalty.

Orbuch continues to offer evidence for her own position, but continues to speak in terms of financial benefit, showing how even health care offers financial reward.

Orbuch's final evidence returns to the common ground: financial improvement.

This section is key for Orbuch's Rogerian approach, as she suggests that the financial approach might in fact be more effective in some contexts.

Conclusion

…This paper argues that one of the most effective ways for MFIs to maintain [their] original social mission while also remaining financially sustainable is through a deliberate mix of financial and non-financial services.

> Even in her conclusion, Orbuch continues to establish common ground by showing that one can have an approach that is simultaneously social and financial.

Transferring Argument Construction

This chapter has built on the preceding chapter by deepening our consideration of argument, helping you discover how writers shape and construct arguments. Specifically, this chapter has provided guidance for how you might decide what to argue, what approach to reasoning you might use, and what structure will likely best suit your argument. These decisions will shift dramatically across writing occasions, with different situations inspiring you to tailor these choices in response to their circumstances.

Chapter 10 continues our exploration of argument by addressing the importance of format and design in shaping argument. As we will see, there are many modalities and formats—print, digital, and in-person, visual, written, or oral—within which arguments can emerge and which also shape writers' decisions about structure. Then, Chapter 11 continues to help you learn how to develop arguments by addressing how academic writers across disciplines integrate evidence. And, finally, Chapter 12 completes this foray into argument by providing guidelines on how to cite evidence effectively, again with an explicit focus on how writers actively engage in transferring their knowledge about citation across contexts.

℮ ℮ ℮

Sport Studies Commentary: "Race, Quarterbacks, and the Media: Testing the Rush Limbaugh Hypothesis" by David Niven

Transfer Points: Political Science, African and African-American Studies, Media Studies, Sports Studies

"Pants on Fire!" That's likely what Politifact's Truth-o-Meter would have registered over Rush Limbaugh's 2003 assertion that media coverage unfairly privileges African-American quarterbacks. Appearing on the September 28, 2003, ESPN *Sunday NFL Countdown* pregame show, Limbaugh made the following comments about media coverage of Donovan McNabb, an African-American quarterback for the Philadelphia Eagles:

> "Sorry to say this, I don't think he's been that good from the get-go ... I think what we've had here is a little social concern in the NFL. The media has been very desirous that a black quarterback do well. There is a little hope invested in McNabb, and he got a lot of credit for the performance of this team that he didn't deserve. The defense carried this team."

Limbaugh's comments set off a firestorm, resulting in charges that he was racist and culminating in his forced resignation from the ESPN show (Hiestand).

While much commentary throughout the controversy lauded the talents of African-American quarterbacks as a way of pushing back against Limbaugh, David Niven, then a political science professor at Florida Atlantic University, took a different approach. He wondered instead about Limbaugh's media assertion: Were media more inclined to favorably cover black quarterbacks?

The study Niven undertook to answer this question involved content analysis of more than 10,000 sports articles published during the 2002-03 NFL season. Niven's findings? Pants on Fire!: 2002-03 media did not cover black quarterbacks more favorably than white quarterbacks.

While it may seem curious for a political science professor to study media, race, and NFL quarterbacks, such research is in fact quite consonant with political science, which involves the study of power across many contexts. Political scientists often study media through the lens of race, ethnicity, class, religion, or gender to understand power hierarchies and institutional and structural power mechanisms. The mixed-research methods deployed by political scientists are also broadly applicable to many lines of inquiry.

Recent articles in the *Quarterly Journal of Political Science*, for example, address swing voters (Gelman, Goel, Rivers, and Rothschild) and partisan bias (Bullock, Gerber, Hill, and Huber), as well as issues of power and politics more broadly construed, such as ethnic favoritism in Kenya education (Kramon and Posner), aid policies in the Muslim world (Ahmed and Werker), and the origins of colonial institutions (Arias and Girod).

Niven's article appeared in the *Journal of Black Studies*, showing how political science often intersects with African and African-American Studies (AAAS). AAAS scholars study the history, culture, and experiences of black people in the United States as well as in other regions of the world. Also sometimes termed Black Studies, Africana Studies, and African Diaspora Studies, AAAS intersects with many disciplines, including literature, sociology, political science, history, art, and cultural anthropology, among others.

David Niven is an Assistant Professor of International Affairs at University of Cincinnati. He holds a Ph.D. in psychology from The Ohio State University and has also taught political science at Florida Atlantic University. Niven has published two scholarly books, *The Politics of Injustice: The Kennedys* and *The Freedom Rides and the Electoral Consequences of a Moral Compromise*. He is also the author of a popular book series that transfers scientific research into more accessible forms for a broader readership. The series includes such books as *The 100 Simple Secrets of Happy People* and *The 100 Simple Secrets of Great Relationships* (Niven).

Questions of vital importance to AAAS undergirded the complexities of media, race, and sports that Niven researched: How do media represent African-Americans? What is the role of media in shaping public perceptions about African-Americans? How might institutions such as the NFL or ESPN participate in, shape, and challenge structural inequities?

For Niven, these questions crystallized in the contentious persona of Rush Limbaugh. *The Rush Limbaugh Show*, started in 1988, is a nationally syndicated radio talk show in which Limbaugh discusses current events, daily news, and other observations. Limbaugh's show is framed around politics, with an explicit privileging of Republican, conservative perspectives. Estimates put *The Rush Limbaugh Show* as reaching anywhere from 1.4 to 20 million listeners each week (Edwards). In 1993, Limbaugh's success earned him induction into the Radio Hall of Fame ("Rush"), which may have been part of the reason ESPN hired him as a commentator.

Across the years, Limbaugh has often been affiliated with controversy, and frequently in matters involving gender and race. Limbaugh has asserted that Presidents Clinton and Carter had ugly daughters, he called a Georgetown law student a "slut" for taking birth control pills, and he purportedly once told a black caller to "take the bone out of your nose and call me back" (Jaffe).

Such matters are part of why social science research such as Niven's is so important. By examining the forms and consequences of social interactions and human behavior, social scientists like Niven can investigate a complex issue about NFL quarterbacks within a broader framework of power, race, politics, and media.

Write Here

Niven writes in his final paragraph that "the response to Limbaugh's comments makes it apparent that the media are not comfortable discussing race" (692). Why do you think the media may have been uncomfortable discussing race? What might be so challenging, dangerous, unpleasant, uncomfortable, or ill-advised about the media having race discussions? Do you think people more generally are uncomfortable discussing race, be it in the context of sports or in other domains? Why or why not?

David Niven
Race, Quarterbacks, and the Media: Testing the Rush Limbaugh Hypothesis

Conservative radio talk show host Rush Limbaugh was hired by the cable sports network ESPN to provide televised commentary on its National Football League pregame show. On September 28, 2003, just 3 weeks after he debuted on the air for ESPN, Limbaugh declared that the media are biased in favor of Philadelphia Eagles quarterback Donovan McNabb because he is African American.

Limbaugh said on ESPN's *NFL Countdown* that the media have "hope invested" in McNabb and gave him "credit for the performance of his team that he really didn't deserve" because "the media have been very desirous that a Black quarterback do well." When his remarks were later widely criticized in the media, Limbaugh did not retract his assertions. Instead, he said the controversy shows that "I must have been right about something."

Using content analysis data from newspaper coverage of the 2002 NFL season, this article compares coverage of seven African American quarterbacks with seven White quarterbacks. Collectively, the two groups of quarterbacks produced comparable results on the field. The results show, in stark contrast to Limbaugh's comments, that there was no tendency for African American quarterbacks in general, nor Donovan McNabb specifically, to receive partial treatment from the press.

RACE AND SPORTSWRITERS

The significance of media coverage of sports is twofold. First, various studies have found that the sports section is one of the few places where African Americans regularly receive coverage as newsmakers (DeLouth, Pirson, Hitchcock, & Rienzi, 1995; Lester, 1994; Martindale, 1990; Wenner, 1995). Indeed, given that one of the other contexts in which African Americans are prominently featured is in crime reports (DeLouth et al., 1995), sports coverage represents an especially important outlet for news that is not inherently negative.

This sports coverage then influences popular perceptions, especially of young people. Strudler (2000) links media coverage of sports stars to boys' notions of role models. Bierman (1990) and Sailes (1996-1997) have linked media coverage of athletics to the attitudes and career aspirations of young African Americans. Armstrong, Neuendorff, and Brentar (1992), meanwhile, have found that White college students' perceptions of African Americans in general are affected by their media consumption, with higher consumption of fictional television shows and sports producing a more robust estimate of typical African American prosperity. Thus, research suggests significant potential implications of sports coverage. Moreover, it is clear that Rush Limbaugh dramatically affected the topics being discussed in the sports media world with his comments. As Figure 1 illustrates, the number of articles in the nation's largest newspapers (major newspapers in the Nexis database) using the phrase "Black quarterback" or "African American quarterback" rose 4900% from September2 003 (the month before Limbaugh's comments) to October 2003.

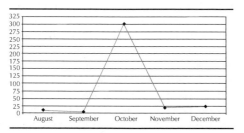

FIGURE 1 Newspaper References to African American/Black Quarterbacks, 2003 Season

Although the NFL (Schneider & Eitzen, 1986) and college football (Jones, Leonard, Schmitt, Smith, & Tolone, 1987) have long been found to dole out positions based on a nearly segregationist mentality reserving both marquee (quarterback) and some less notable positions (punter) for White players, that tendency is clearly waning.[1] There were many weeks during seasons in the early 1980s where not a single African American served as a starting quarterback for an NFL team, but in 2002, 7 teams (out of 32) had African American starting quarterbacks.

Would sports journalists be likely to be biased in favor of those African American quarterbacks as Limbaugh alleged? Research on sports journalism finds several forms of bias visible in their work.

Lau and Russell (1980), for example, find that football writers are prone to classic errors of attribution that psychologists have long documented in other contexts. For example, Lau and Russell find that positive outcomes for the local team are more likely to be credited to internal factors (such as ability and effort), whereas negative outcomes are more likely to be credited to external factors (such as luck, referees, or the weather).[2]

Imbalances in attribution have also been linked to race. Rainville and McCormick (1977) and Rada (1996) found that football announcers' attributions credit the innate physical ability of African American players, while crediting hard work and cognitive ability more often for White players. Murrell and Curtis (1994) limited their comparison to media coverage of quarterbacks—examining the attributions associated with three African American and three White quarterbacks in the NFL who had been matched based on comparable quarterback ratings. Murrell and Curtis also found attributions for African Americans consistent with the natural ability explanation, whereas Whites were more likely to be credited with hard work.

It is not surprising that evidence of this pattern is not limited to the sport of football or to the U.S. media (e.g., Wilson, 1997). McCarthy, Jones, and Potrac (2003) document the same racial attribution pattern in British television coverage of soccer.

Beyond the attribution process, other studies have found imbalances in sports coverage to the detriment of African Americans. Braddock (1978) found that White college football and basketball players received more coverage and more positive coverage than African American players in the sports pages of the *Washington Post*. Andrews (1996) and Simons (2003) both found disproportionate attention paid to unsportsmanlike behaviors of African American athletes.

Wonsek (1992) found that even the commercials shown during sports events feature an overwhelmingly White world where African Americans are seldom seen and even less frequently featured. With the exception of sports-related products such as sneakers, Wonsek found that African Americans were basically absent from the sales pitches for most major product categories.

Beyond race, studies of recent coverage of women athletes also find inequities. Women athletes receive less coverage than men, even when competing in comparable sports such as Olympic competition (Fink & Kensicki, 2002). Fink and Kensicki (2002) and Shugart (2003) also find a tendency to portray women in traditional sex roles and nonsports contexts emphasizing their appearance.

Just as there is no body of evidence showing media bias in favor of African American athletes, there is a similar dearth of evidence suggesting media bias in favor of African Americans in other contexts. For example, media coverage of African American political leaders has been found to be more narrow in scope than coverage of Whites and somewhat less positive (Zilber & Niven, 2000). Media coverage of African Americans in general has also been found to be more negative than for Whites (Byrd, 1997; Entman, 1994).

Nevertheless, there may be reason to suspect that there is an emerging equality in media coverage with regard to African American quarterbacks. First, research suggests that prominent African American athletes, most notably Michael Jordan, have achieved a position in the sports world and in our culture that transcends race (Kellner, 1996). Second, a line of psychological research called the distribution effect suggests that when a group is in a distinct minority in a profession, then it is likely to be treated quite distinctly, but as the group becomes less rare in the profession, perceptions become more equitable (e.g., Eagly, Makhijani, & Klonsky, 1992).

According to the theory, then, when African American quarterbacks such as Doug Williams were unique in the league, then reactions to an African American quarterback (from the media, fans, and other observers) would be highly attuned to race, to any differences perceived to exist between the lone African American quarterback and the many White quarterbacks, and to questions about the qualifications of the African American quarterback. Such a reaction would not necessarily indicate an overt bias but rather a subconscious process in which the attributes necessary for the job would be associated with the dominant demographic group.

As the minority demographic group becomes more prevalent in a profession, however, the assumptions of inferiority and difference and the attention to demographics in general weaken. According to the theory, as contemporary African American quarterbacks have become more common, they should be judged on similar terms as White quarterbacks by most observers.

METHOD

This study uses newspaper coverage of the 2002 NFL season to compare media treatment of African American and White quarterbacks.

Beginning with each African American starting quarterback in the league, an effort was made to create a matching sample of White quarterbacks for purposes of comparison. Using the NFL's official rating system of quarterbacks (in which every pass is factored into a formula assessing the positive or negative outcome), the seven African American quarterbacks who were rated by the NFL in 2002 (Donovan McNabb, Philadelphia Eagles; Aaron Brooks, New Orleans Saints; Rodney Peete, Carolina Panthers; Michael Vick, Atlanta Falcons; Jeff Blake, Baltimore Ravens; Daunte Culpepper, Minnesota Vikings; Steve McNair, Tennessee Titans) were collectively matched with seven White quarterbacks (Jeff Garcia, San Francisco 49ers; Jim Miller, Chicago Bears; Jon Kitna, Cincinnati Bengals; Tim Couch, Cleveland Browns; Kerry Collins, New York Giants; Trent Green, Kansas City Chiefs; Jake Plummer, Arizona Cardinals). As a group, the African American quarter-backs had a mean quarterback rating of 80.2, whereas the White quarterbacks had a mean rating of 80.3 (the quarterback rating scale ranges from 0 to 158.3).

The major U.S. newspapers index (in Nexis) was searched for every mention of each of the 14 quarterbacks during the 2002 regular season (from August 1, 2002, to December 31, 2002). This produced a sample of more than 10,000 newspaper articles. The number of articles mentioning each quarterback was noted, as was the number of headlines mentioning each quarterback.

Then, each of the articles was searched for key terms of praise or criticism in proximity (within three words) to the quarterback's name. For example, 25 phrases such as leader, success, strong, tough, and great were considered as praise. Phrases such as mistake, failure, struggle, poor, and erratic were considered as criticism.

TABLE 1

Newspaper Coverage of NFL Quarterbacks, 2002 Season

	Articles (Mean)	% Mentioned in Headline	% Criticized	% Praised
African American quarterbacks[a]	775	5.7	12.1	9.2
White quarterbacks[b]	765	5.4	11.7	9.1

NOTE: $N = 10,781$.

a. McNabb, Brooks, Peete, Vick, Blake, Culpepper, McNair.
b. Garcia, Miller, Kitna, Couch, Collins, Green, Plummer.

RESULTS

As Table 1 illustrates, the dominant thrust of the data suggests that African American and White quarterbacks were treated comparably.

For the mean number of articles published per quarterback, the African American group received 10 more mentions than the White quarterbacks over the course of the season, a difference of only 1.3%. That difference was almost entirely based on Donovan McNabb, who, as a three-time Pro-Bowl quarterback and member of one of the best teams in the game, drew the most attention of any of the quarterbacks in the sample.

Attention in the headlines was also close, with African Americans appearing fractionally more often than White quarterbacks. Despite the overall frequency of mentions, McNabb was not the most prominently featured in headlines among the quarterbacks sampled. Instead, Cleveland's Tim Couch, a former first overall pick in the NFL draft who was leading his team to its first playoff berth since the franchise had been awarded by the league, was most frequently in the headlines.

Critical comments about the quarterbacks again showed slightly higher results for African Americans, although in this case it is an "advantage" that would clearly not be desired. Reflecting, no doubt, the overall struggle of his team, which fell from a 13-3 play-off team in the previous season to a 4-12 campaign in 2002, Chicago's Jim Miller was the most frequently criticized quarterback in the sample.

Finally, positive comments were nearly identical in number for White and African American quarterbacks. The most highly praised member of the sample was San Francisco's Jeff Garcia.

Although there were slight differences in each of the four categories examined (three that essentially favored African American quarterbacks, and one that favored White quarterbacks), the data suggest that the coverage overall must be considered comparable. Indeed, each of the differences in the four categories fails to achieve statistical significance (using chi-square, $p > .05$ as a benchmark), which suggests that the modest differences visible in this data may be due to nothing more than chance.

DISCUSSION

The results make clear that there is no evidence to support Rush Limbaugh's assertion of a pro-African American conspiracy in newspaper coverage of quarterbacks. Nor is there evidence of a bias against African American quarterbacks. With a matched sample of White and African American quarterbacks who experienced comparable success on the field, and a national sample of newspaper coverage of those quarterbacks, the evidence shows that race is not driving coverage.

Surely, the media, when confronted with Rush Limbaugh's comments, offered a vigorous refutation. Indeed, they did. However, notable is how little attention was paid to the larger implications of Limbaugh's assertion.

Limbaugh said, in essence, that Donovan McNabb wasn't very good, and the media were lying about his talents because of their pro-African American bias. Of the two assertions—(a) McNabb's not very good, and (b) There's a racial conspiracy in the media—the first seems specious but of little true significance, whereas the second is specious but of great significance. That is, most experts likely consider Donovan McNabb to be among the best quarterbacks in football, but the implications of that assertion are trivial. At the same time, most experts likely consider the notion of a pro-African American media conspiracy as dubious, but the implications of that assertion are tremendous. Such a belief suggests a depth of effort to fictionalize the news that stretches, one would have to presume, from Donovan McNabb, to football in general, to sports in general, to all news.

Yet, from the outset of the controversy and continuing throughout the 2003 season, the media reacted primarily to the question of McNabb's talents. Typical was the presentation in the *Daily News* in New York. The paper headlined its story about the first Eagles game after Limbaugh's comments with, "Take That, Rush! McNabb Shows Heart as Eagles Hold On" (Gola, 2003).

Even after the Eagles defeated the Green Bay Packers in a play-off game more than 3 months later, the same mindset was still evident in the media. The *Star Tribune* in Minneapolis (Wicker, 2004) started their story on that game with, "Those who Rushed to judgment of Donovan McNabb were left chewing on their words after his fourth-quarter magic kept the Eagles' season alive." The article went on to note, "Don't look now, Rush Limbaugh, but Donovan McNabb is succeeding again."

Indeed, McNabb's success was often portrayed not only as a contradiction of Limbaugh's comments but as a direct answer to them. As a *Boston Herald* report on the same playoff game put it, "With his team down 14-7 . . . McNabb sent a telegram to a discredited Rush Limbaugh

with an eight-play, 89-yard drive in which he accounted for EVERY SINGLE YARD"(Bryant, 2004). *USA TODAY* added that McNabb's "play might've knocked Limbaugh out of his seat, if he didn't have much bigger problems" (O'Connor, 2004).

Ultimately, the response to Limbaugh's comments makes it apparent that the media are not comfortable discussing race. It was simply easier to highlight Donovan McNabb's statistics and belittle Limbaugh's position based on McNabb's success on the field than to honestly appraise the state of racial fairness in sports media coverage. Ironically, such an appraisal would seem to have produced a positive reflection on the media. Instead, any value of the dialogue that Limbaugh inadvertently started was muted because much of the reality of the situation went unexplored.

NOTES

1. Kooistra, Mahoney, and Bridges (1993) also find evidence that White players were disproportionately rewarded with regard to their contract status compared with African Americans in the NFL.

2. Roesch and Amirkhan (1997) note that athletes themselves often propagate these self-enhancing attributions.

REFERENCES

Armstrong, G., Neuendorff, K., & Brentar, J. (1992). Television entertainment, news, and racial perceptions of college students. *Journal of Communication, 42*(3), 134-152.

Andrews, V. (1996). Black bodies-White control: The contested terrain of sportsmanlike conduct. *Journal of African American Men, 2*(1), 33-59.

Bierman, J. (1990). The effect of television sports media on Black male youth. *Sociological Inquiry, 60*(4), 413-427.

Braddock, J. (1978). The sports page: In Black and White. *Arena Review, 2*(2), 17-25.

Bryant, H. (2004, January 12). Man on a mission: Quarterback carries Eagles toward shot at redemption. *Boston Herald*, p. 106.

Byrd, J. (1997). Blacks, Whites in news pictures. In S. Biagi & M. Kern-Foxworth (Eds.), *Facing difference: Race, gender, and mass media* (pp. 95-97). Thousand Oaks, CA: Pine Forge Press.

DeLouth, T-N., Pirson, B., Hitchcock, D., & Rienzi, B. (1995). Gender and ethnic role portrayals: Photographic images in three California newspapers. *Psychological Reports, 76*(2), 493-494.

Eagly, A., Makhijani, M., & Klonsky, B. (1992). Gender and the evaluation of leaders: A meta-analysis. *Psychological Bulletin, 111*, 3-32.

Entman, R. (1994). Representation and reality in the portrayal of Blacks on network television news. *Journalism Quarterly, 71*, 509-520.

Fink, J., & Kensicki, L. (2002). An imperceptible difference: Visual and textual constructions of femininity in *Sports Illustrated* and *Sports Illustrated for Women. Mass Communication & Society, 5*(3), 317-339.

Gola, H. (2003, October 6). Take that, Rush! McNabb shows heart as Eagles hold on. *Daily News*, p. 10. Jones, G., Leonard, W, Schmitt, R., Smith, D. R., & Tolone, W. (1987). Racial discrimination in college football. *Social Science Quarterly, 68*(1), 70-83.

Kellner, D. (1996). Sports, media culture, and race—Some reflections on Michael Jordan. *Sociology of Sport Journal, 13*(4), 458-467.

Kooistra, P., Mahoney, J., & Bridges, L. (1993). The unequal opportunity for equal ability hypothesis: Racism in the National Football League? *Sociology of Sport Journal, 10*(3), 241-255.

Lau, R., & Russell, D. (1980). Attributions in the sports pages. *Journal of Personality & Social Psychology, 39*(1), 29-38.

Lester, P. (1994). African-American photo coverage in four U.S. newspapers, 1937-1990. *Journalism Quarterly, 77*(2), 380-394.

Martindale, C. (1990). Changes in newspaper images of Black Americans. *Newspaper Research Journal, 77*(1), 40-50.

McCarthy, D., Jones, R., & Potrac, P. (2003). Constructing images and interpreting realities: The case of the Black soccer player on television. *International Review for the Sociology of Sport, 38*(2), 217-238. Murrell, A., & Curtis, E. (1994). Causal attributions of performance for Black and White quarterbacks in the NFL: A look at the sports pages. *Journal of Sport and Social Issues, 18*(3), 224-233.

O'Connor, I. (2004, January 14). McNabb's amazing career built on proving doubters wrong. *USA TODAY*, p. 2C.

Rada, J. (1996). Color blind-sided: Racial bias in network television's coverage of professional football games. *Howard Journal of Communications, 7*(3), 231-239.

Rainville, R., & McCormick, E. (1977). Extent of covert racial prejudice in pro football announcers' speech. *Journalism Quarterly, 54*, 20-26.

Roesch, S., & Amirkhan, J. (1997). Boundary conditions for self-serving attributions: Another look at the sports pages. *Journal of Applied Social Psychology, 27*(3), 245-261.

Sailes, G. (1996-1997). Betting against the odds: An overview of Black sports participation. *Journal of African American Men, 2*(2-3), 1 1-22.

Schneider, J., & Eitzen, D. S. (1986). Racial segregation by professional football positions, 1960-1985. *Sociology and Social Research, 70*(4), 259-262.

Shugart, H. (2003). She shoots, she scores: Mediated constructions of contemporary female athletes in coverage of the 1999 US women's soccer team. *Western Journal of Communication, 67*(1), 1-31.

Simons, H. (2003). Race and penalized sports behaviors. *International Review for the Sociology of Sport, 38*(1), 5-22.

Strudler, K. (2000). *The mass mediated sports hero as a role model for adolescent males.* Doctoral dissertation, University of Florida.

Wenner, L. (1995). The good, the bad, and the ugly: Race, sport, and the public eye. *Journal of Sport and Social Issues, 19*(3), 227-231.

Wicker, B. (2004, January 12). Monday morning quarterback. *Star Tribune*, p. 14C.

Wilson, B. (1997). "Good Blacks" and "bad Blacks": Media constructions of African-American athletes in Canadian basketball. *International Review for the Sociology of Sport, 32*(2), 177-189.

Wonsek, P. (1992). College basketball on television: A study of racism in the media. *Media, Culture & Society, 14*(3), 449-461.

Zilber, J., & Niven, D. (2000). *Racialized coverage of Congress: The news in Black and White.* Westport, CT: Praeger Publishers.

Write Away

1. Niven documents his research methods in the section labeled "Methods." Write a version of research methods modeled on Niven's for another study regarding race in a sport of your choosing. Be sure to include tables as well, modeled on Niven's.

2. Niven argues in his final paragraph that the media are not comfortable discussing race. This was in 2005. Are the media now more comfortable discussing race? If so, in which contexts? If not, in what ways, if at all, do they discuss race? And for what purposes? What can or do discussions of race accomplish? What might they not accomplish? Use Niven's article as a jumping-off point to write an essay in which you articulate an argument about contemporary media discussions regarding race. Use evidence from the media concerning race; you can do so in the topic of sports or in other areas. As you develop your essay, you might also consider the following questions: What would media discussions about race have looked like in the case of the Rush Limbaugh controversy? Why weren't conversations about McNabb's talents considered by Niven to be discussions of race?

3. Design and conduct a content analysis about media representations of a minority or underprivileged group of your choosing. Select a particular media source and a particular field on which to focus, such as sports, entertainment, business, crime, health, technology, etc. The media presentations you examine can be written or visual. Consider the following questions: In what ways do the media sources you have chosen to consider tend to represent this minority population? What is the impact of such representations? Use the IMRAD format for your article.

Satirical Journalism: *"Books Don't Take You Anywhere"* by The Onion

Transfer Points: Creative Writing, Journalism, Media Studies

Drugs Win Drug War … Study Reveals: Babies Are Stupid … Perky 'Canada' Has Own Government, Laws… Sony Releases New Stupid Piece of Shit That Doesn't Fucking Work.

These are but a few of the fake-news headlines created by *The Onion*, a satirical newspaper (Busis). Begun in 1988 by two college juniors in Madison, Wisconsin, *The Onion* started as a small print newspaper and is now one of the most widely read online satirical news platforms, offering fake news stories about daily observations and current events.

Relying on parody and satire, the fake news found in *The Onion* is but one example of a large range of fake news platforms and organizations across media sources. Verbal forms appear in podcasts such as *Welcome to Night Vale* and television shows such as *The Daily Show*, *Saturday Night Live*, and *The Colbert Report*. Print and online platforms for fake news include periodicals such as *The Onion*, as well as microblogs and online fake-news generators. Visual modes include internet memes and political cartoons.

While social media and cable news platforms have helped fake news proliferate over the past few decades, the genre itself has extensive historical roots. H. G. Wells's famous 1938 Halloween radio adaptation of *War of the Worlds*, for instance, induced mass panic through fake news bulletins about a purported Martian invasion. Benjamin Franklin wrote political satire (Poremba) and, in the eighth century, a bogus edict emerged purportedly by Roman emperor Constantine (Love).

Fake news also intersects with military propaganda, used to demoralize and confuse the enemy. World War II airplanes, for instance, dropped propaganda leaflets filled with fake news. And, during the Crusades, the Sultan Baibars concocted a fake-news letter indicating surrender that they could give to the enemy in order to gain access to a stronghold (Corbett).

The Onion is a news organization that produces satirical content about local, national, and international news, as well as everyday observations. It started in 1988 as a print publication, developed by two college juniors in Madison, Wisconsin (Busis). They sold it for $16,000 after about a year (Busis). It has since had headquarters in New York City and is currently located in Chicago. It moved to exclusively online content in December 2013 (Folkenflik). In 2016, *The Onion* was bought by Univision Communications, the company that owns America's leading Spanish-language broadcast station (Folkenflik).

As this range indicates, fake news not only entertains, but also serves important political and media functions. *The Onion* editors Joe Randazzo and Joe Garden stress that they aren't "just making jokes about horrible things with no context or no point or heart" (qtd. in Montagne). Fake news provides dissent against mainstream ideologies and mocks those in power (Jones; Reilly). It blurs boundaries between politics and entertainment, bringing more political knowledge to broader publics (Allan). Fake news also serves a watchdog function, holding journalism accountable for fairer, more robust coverage (Berkowitz and Schwartz). And, fake news influences contemporary media to integrate more humor and entertainment (Barnhurst).

Scholars across disciplines research fake news. Those in communication studies, journalism, and media studies explore the forms and impact of satirical news. For instance, communications scholar Regina Marchi interviewed 61 teenagers to learn how Facebook, blogs, and fake news impact teenagers' expectations about journalistic objectivity. Scholars in political science and public policy examine how satirical news impacts voter behavior and public opinion. An interdisciplinary team of professors from communications and political science, for example, asked 454 undergraduates to read news coverage of Stephen Colbert's Super PAC to see how fake news impacted the students' political trust, knowledge, and opinions about actual PACs (Brewer, Young, and Morreale).

Scholars in literature, American studies, and cultural studies also conduct research about fake news, exploring the role of fake news in cultural practices, values, and behaviors. American studies scholar Frank Russell, for instance, developed a typology of fake news sources, with such categories as "clones" and "citizen satirists."

Alongside these scholars, though, are those who actually write fake news. They too are trained across disciplines, with particular talents in creative writing, media studies, and journalism. Writing with humor is itself a discipline, formally established in 1973 with Ithaca College's groundbreaking course, Humorous Writing 336 (Rishel). While final versions of fake news may seem effortless, the creative process involves awareness of craft and painstaking patience, feedback, and revision.

Humor writers invoke established techniques such as over- and understatement, exaggeration, stark contrasts, and unique comparisons (Rishel). They also consider complex questions about humor: How do values and backgrounds impact what makes a text more, less, or not at all funny to different individuals? What is the role of humor in culture and society? What forms of humor work better or worse at different times? What even is a sense of humor, and how does it develop and change across time and context?

Such questions show how a humorous *Onion* headline like "Middle East Conflict Intensifies as Blah Blah Blah, Etc. Etc." is a deliberate critique of the political situation and mainstream media. Still, such a headline is, ultimately, also quite funny.

Write Here

Revise a set of current headlines from a news source of your choice to become fake news headlines. You can create fake news headlines about one issue or event or about several different events. Exchange your fake news headlines with one or more classmates, and write a reflection about the process of writing and reading fake news headlines: What issues seem especially ripe for fake news? Which ones are more challenging to transform into fake news headlines? Why? What are the fake news headlines critiquing, satirizing, or parodying?

The Onion
Books Don't Take You Anywhere

WASHINGTON, DC—A study released Monday by the U.S. Department of Education revealed that, contrary to the longtime claims of librarians and teachers, books do not take you anywhere.

"For years, countless educators have asserted that books give readers a chance to journey to exotic, far-off lands and meet strange, exciting new people," Education Secretary Richard Riley told reporters. "We have found this is simply not the case."

According to the study, those who read are not transported to any place beyond the area in which the reading occurs, and even these movements are always the result of voluntary decisions made by the reader and not in any way related to the actual reading process.

Phoenix-area 11-year-old Jennifer Gleason, who did not move in more than two hours of reading *The Wizard Of Oz.*

"People engaged in reading tend to be motionless," Riley said. "Not moving tends to make it easier to read."

In various field experiments, the study found that young readers are particularly susceptible to the reading-travel myth. One test subject, 11-year-old Justin Fisher of Ypsilanti, MI, began reading a fantasy novel by C.S. Lewis under close observation. After 40 minutes, the only trip Fisher took was to the bathroom, a journey he himself initiated because he "had to go." Further, at no point did Fisher's voyage to the bathroom involve evil witches, messianic lions or closet portals to other universes.

"I just stayed in my chair without moving that much," Fisher said. "I think I scratched my head a couple of times."

Another case documented in the study was that of San Diego 13-year-old Liz Kent, who read Robert Louis Stevenson's Treasure Island. Over the course of more than three hours reading the pirate-adventure tale, at no point did she make a new friend or travel to a distant land.

The study did note one exception to the findings, citing situations in which people read on buses, cars, trains or planes. Even in these cases, however, the reading-travel link is tenuous at best.

"Many people enjoy reading while traveling," Riley said. "But it is important to note that the traveling always results in the reading, and never the reverse."

As a result of the study, it is expected that many young people will call into question what Riley termed "the empty promises of library posters and other pieces of pro-reading propaganda."

"I hate it when you get excited about a place and then you don't go there," 10-year-old Ashley Brandes of Atlanta said. "Reading sucks."

Write Away

1. Using specific evidence from *The Onion* article, write an analysis that addresses the precise ways in which the author satirizes, parodies, ridicules, and/or dissents with mainstream and/or journalistic approaches to the topic. As you explicate specific evidence from the article, define any literary devices you discuss, such as satire, irony, and parody, and provide research about the circumstances related to education in 1997 as context for the article.

2. *The Onion* editors describe their ideation process as follows: "We see something … and say 'Well, that's kind of stupid. They're acting kind of stupidly here. We should make a joke about that'" (qtd. in Montagne). What do you see that seems "kind of stupid"? What would you like to make a joke about? Compose your own fake news article on a subject of your choosing for a publication such as *The Onion*. Select an issue, event, or observation that you think warrants fake news attention. As you develop your fake news article, explore and then deploy established techniques of humor writing, as well as your own strategies.

3. Media studies scholars have suggested that fake news impacts real news by exerting pressure to make real news more entertaining and humorous. Analyze articles in a news

source of your choosing—one that is not categorized as fake news—and respond to the following questions in a research-based argumentative essay: In what ways does the news source integrate entertainment and/or humor? For what purpose? What are the advantages and limitations of doing so? What differences might you note between entertainment in real news and in fake news? In what ways do these real news sources leave themselves vulnerable to the mockery that motivates fake news?

Chapter 9 Key Terms

inductive reasoning	classical argument	Rogerian argument
assumptions	counterargument	modalities
deductive reasoning	concession	
stasis theory	Toulmin argument	

Write Away

One of the best ways to improve your own ability to construct effective arguments is to unpack the structures of others' arguments. This activity asks you to do so with one area of argumentation across several different instances so you can begin to see the ways in which writers customize general structures for argument as demanded by particular writing occasions. This activity also enables you to gain an advance perspective on argument design and format, the next chapter's area of focus.

Decide on a general area of argumentation. Choose a general area of argumentation you would like to investigate. This can be any area in which you have an interest.

Select three to four different arguments in this area to examine. Locate three or four different examples of arguments in this area, being careful to choose different argument formats. For instance, if you are examining arguments about refugee issues, you might choose one peer-reviewed scholarly article, one YouTube video, and one op-ed. Or, you might choose a blog post, a homepage of a website, and a policy brief.

Identify the argument's structure. Carefully examine each of the arguments, and identify the structure. The concept of a reverse outline, the revision method introduced in Chapter 2, can also be applied to examining others' arguments: Identify what each paragraph is accomplishing with a key word or phrase. What does the writer do first, then, next? After developing the reverse outline for each argument, see if you can discern the argument structure. Does it seem to resemble classical, Toulmin, or Rogerian structure, or some combination of those, or a different structure altogether? What area of the stases do you see each argument operating within? What kinds of reasoning do you notice in the arguments?

Reflect on transfer and argument structure. Having seen several different arguments and their structures, reflect in writing for ten minutes about how writers tailor and customize argument structures for particular writing occasions. Did you notice that the writers employ, modify, or challenge one of the structures identified in this section? How and why do you think the writers chose their structures? In what ways do you think argument format and writing occasion might impact the choices writers make about argument structure?

Designing Arguments: Formats and Modalities

Several well-known Hollywood films, including *Raiders of the Lost Ark* and *Journey to the Center of the Earth*, have made use of archaeoastronomical features, elements, and designs. In one such film, *Cast Away*, the lead character, Chuck Noland (played by Tom Hanks), becomes stranded on a Pacific island for four years. He marks the passage of time by designing a measurement device called an analemma, carving it as an image onto a wall in the cave in which he sleeps. An analemma, a device emerging from ancient mathematics, tracks time by marking the sun's passage through the sky on a stationary object ("Archaeoastronomy").

Although Noland's analemma is fictional, moviegoers and film critics take matters of design seriously. Those with knowledge of analemmas have charged Noland's analemma with several design inaccuracies. Their commentary demonstrates that design is not merely a matter of surface-level aesthetic preference, but instead of choosing shapes that reflect meaning.

Posters to the website *science.blog*, for instance, have noted that the shape of Noland's analemma is inaccurate given his location in the Pacific: "Anyone who saw [*Cast Away*] with Tom Hanks would now recognize the error in the analemma drawn on the cave wall as being too vertical. Hanks's character was stranded on a tropic island, and the analemma should have been nearly horizontal."

Meanwhile, contributors to a discussion on *NavList*, an online community "devoted to the preservation and practice of celestial navigation and other methods of traditional position-finding," take issue with whether Noland would have even had the expertise to etch the analemma onto the cave wall in the first place. One *NavList* contributor argues that the analemma would have required Noland be able to differentiate between "Local Apparent Time" and "Mean Time," and then to have known how to read the analemma within the context of these varying notions of time. These online discussions about the intricacies of Noland's analemma may seem somewhat nitpicky, but they actually illustrate the importance of intentional design. Whether within the film, in which the character Noland hopes to rely on precise measurements to track time, or outside of the film, where accurate measurements really do take on even higher stakes, the analemma's design impacts perception and conveys meaning.

Analemmas thereby illustrate the ways in which design impacts the very nature of the argument itself. Change the analemma from horizontal to vertical, and the record of time shifts; design the analemma according to "Local Apparent Time" instead of "Mean Time," and, again, the way we understand the analemma, and its meaning, changes.

Just as Noland's analemma provides an illuminating perspective into argument by demonstrating that design shapes meaning, it also illustrates how design intersects with context to determine modality. Analemmas incorporate, simultaneously, several modes of communication—visual, written, mathematical, temporal, and even cultural and religious. Through this confluence of modalities, knowledge emerges.

So, too, with academic arguments. Academic writers can make use of multiple modalities for their arguments in order to convey them as robustly as possible, in addition to increasing the reach of those arguments to a wider range of people and learning styles.

Websites provide an apt example of the value of multiple modalities. The People for the Ethical Treatment of Animals website, peta.org, for instance, argues for animal rights through multiple modalities, from photographs and videos to written arguments. Similarly, photographic essays often argue by relying on the interplay between the written and visual. One of the most well-known examples of this form is James Agee and Walker Evans's photographic essay, *Let Us Now Praise Famous Men,* in which they argue through photographs and written text about the hardships endured by Depression-era tenant farmers in the southern United States.

Another more recent example of the value of overlapping modalities is a YouTube video that enjoyed some viral exposure in 2012, "The Ivy-League Hustle (I Went to Princeton, Bitch)." In this video, which combines written, visual, and verbal modalities, creator Nikki Muller makes the following arguments: "a college degree doesn't necessarily lead to a six-figure salary" ("Ivy League…Rap Pokes") and "[s]mart women are threatening to men and are expected to tone it down to be socially successful."

Like the case of the island location and the analemma in *Cast Away*, these examples of arguments using multiple modalities show that argument design intersects deeply with context. The choices that writers make are therefore dependent on a careful consideration and awareness of context. An argument advocating for HPV vaccines designed for a print journal, such as the *Journal of the American Medical Association*, for example, should include different components than if the same argument was designed as a photographic essay about people receiving, refusing, or delivering the vaccines. The very same argument would again incorporate different features if one redesigned it, by turns, as a TEDx Talk, a print ad, or a public service announcement.

As illustrated by analemmas, websites, viral YouTube videos, and print journal articles, the choices writers make about design shape the arguments themselves and are intertwined with the contexts in which the arguments will be developed and delivered. Far from being a small matter for afterthought, design should occupy a central, formative role for academic writers as they construct their arguments.

Write Here

Outline designs for two different versions of a research report on analemmas written for people unfamiliar with analemmas. Your options for design platforms include: verbal presentation, website, scholarly article, visual image, or moving image. Or you can design using a different or combined platform. What different design features would you include in each of the two platforms?

~ ~ ~

Written Modalities of Argument:
Scholarly, Public Scholarship, Popular Scholarship

Written arguments can range from popular to public scholarship to scholarly contexts and thereby emerge along every segment of the continuum of writing and reading contexts described in Chapter 4: Reading. Academic writers sometimes create written arguments for scholarly contexts, hoping to publish their arguments in specialized academic journals. They may then transfer those scholarly arguments to more public modes with a wider readership, such as a column for a popular magazine or online as a blog post. Each act of writing transfer involves reshaping the contours of an argument as well as the discourse conventions. Writing an argument in the form of an op-ed or letter to the editor, for instance, means that writers must distill their ideas into a relatively brief format, often without having the luxury of being able to rely on citations and full inclusion or explication of evidence.

Scholarly

Scholarly formats for written argument include peer-reviewed research, as in the examples in Chapter 9. Scholarly arguments of this sort use a full range of citation and research, as appropriate for the disciplinary context in which the text appears. Some written scholarly arguments are intended for particular readers, such as other experts in the field, while others are intended for a broader range of educated experts. Because they were published in multi-disciplinary undergraduate journals, the examples we read in Chapter 9 were likely directed toward a broader range of readers. By contrast, an article that appears in the *Quarterly Journal of Economics* is likely directed toward other economists.

Writer Insights

What formats or modalities do you use as a writer?

Letters, words, sentences, school essays, poems (deliberately stopped in early 20s: one must be a great poet—or silent), diary, letters, a short story (polished by editor, never published), exam papers, a play (read by a troupe, never performed), sketches performed for students by students, emails, Honours project, scientific articles, Ph.D. thesis, forum posts, personal blog (still going), Wikipedia articles and discussions, instant messages, conference theses, review, scientific articles again, paid professional blog contributions, media articles, molecular biology e-book (post-production stage), applied feminism book draft...some years later—epitaph.

~Victoria A. Doronina, Molecular Biologist, Manchester, Lancashire, United Kingdom

Public scholarship

Written arguments can also appear in the form of **public scholarship**, perhaps as an op-ed or blog. Op-eds (opinion pieces that appear in newspapers or news websites), for instance, rely on the expertise (*ethos*) of the writer but do not have the same rigor of citation or the expectation for quotes, data, and research. One example is Chelsea Carmona's July 6, 2012, op-ed that appeared in *The Washington Post*, "How AA Fails to Support Young Addicts." Carmona, who drafted the piece in conjunction with the "Op-Ed Project," begins with this captivating sentence: "I was 20 when I attended my first Alcoholics Anonymous meeting." She makes the argument that "some of the techniques that work for adults are much more challenging for the 46 percent of patients at substance abuse treatment centers who are age 18 to 24." Her evidence includes personal experience, which might also be included in a more scholarly version of her argument but would appear alongside scholarly published research as well.

Popular scholarship

Written arguments can also appear in more **popular** forums, often distinguished by a more narrative quality, though they often still include research and evidence. For instance, in "The Case Against Summer Vacation," published in *Time Magazine*, author David Von Drehle argues that summer vacation has a negative impact on economically disadvantaged children:

> Dull summers take a steep toll, as researchers have been documenting for more than a century. Deprived of healthy stimulation, millions of low-income kids lose a significant amount of what they learn during the school year. Call it "summer learning loss," as the academics do, or "the summer slide," but by any name summer vacation is among the most pernicious—if least acknowledged—causes of achievement gaps in America's schools.

Von Drehle's argument includes research (and he goes on to mention studies by researchers at Duke University and Johns Hopkins University), but the research is primarily presented as summary, without citations. Von Drehle also includes a number of photographs throughout the article, designed to maintain reader interest and enhance the reading experience of the argument.

Visual Arguments: Thinking Visually

Visual argument involves the use of visual components to make an argument. Sometimes visual arguments might include what Susan Hagan terms "visual/verbal collaboration," where images and text work together to "clarify, contradict, or challenge common understanding." But visual arguments can also be stand-alone arguments composed only of visual elements, such as photographs or animation. Visual arguments also include those texts that incorporate key visuals, tables, charts, graphics, and other infographics as a substantive part of the argument. While some disciplines, such as art, photography, or visual studies, seem to be particularly related to visual arguments, one nevertheless finds visual arguments applied across all disciplines.

Visual arguments should be approached with the same considerations as discussed in Chapter 7 regarding visual analysis. However, visual arguments also ask that academic writers engage in the art of **visual thinking**, which invites them to consider certain kinds of questions as they design visual arguments.

Visual options

Media options include animation, video, photography, and audio (although audio is not visual, it often accompanies a visual experience). Visual options also include charts, graphs, infographics, tables, and other visual elements. Those engaging in visual thinking will embed

Transfer at Work

Writers across disciplines develop visual arguments. In "New Colour Images from Old Planetary Photographs," for instance, astronomers Richard McKim and Johan Warell argue for a new method for digitizing and archiving older astronomical images. They include as evidence for their methodology the images they have digitized, which include a number of Mars photographs originally taken by E. C. Slipher at the Lowell Observatory from 1907 to 1963.

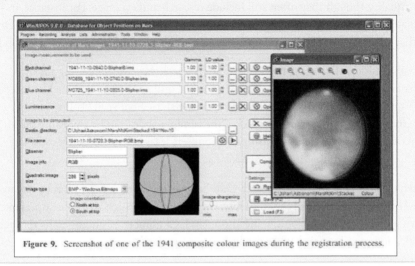

Figure 9. Screenshot of one of the 1941 composite colour images during the registration process.

in their creation process a phase devoted to brainstorming and experimenting with various forms of media so they can choose which medium is most advantageous for their purpose. Digital storytelling, for instance, often involves a storyboard element, in which the writer brainstorms script and media components in side-by-side columns.

Purpose of visual components

If you are designing a visual argument, the visual elements should serve a substantive function in advancing the argument itself. Visual components might include tables or charts that illustrate data in a vital manner, or they might consist of images depicting events or people of central importance to the text. In some writing contexts, visual components can be primarily supplemental and aesthetic, but in visual argument, the visual components should actually participate in efforts to inform or persuade readers. If the visual elements are solely a matter of enhancing reader engagement, then the argument would probably not be deemed a visual argument, but rather a written argument with visuals. To really constitute a visual argument, the visual components should feature strongly as an indispensible part of the argument itself.

Relationship between visual and written components

Do the visuals reinforce what the written text argues? Or, are the visuals such that they extend, challenge, or otherwise build on the written text? Another way of thinking about this would be to reverse the question and ask how the written text challenges, counters, or supplements the visual. A related aspect to consider is what the balance will be between the written and the visual. Will your text be mostly visual, mostly written, or balanced between the two? All of these involve choices that academic writers should consider as they embark on designing and constructing visual arguments.

Location of visual components

Choosing where to include visuals in your argument shapes and impacts the efficacy of your text. Location, in this capacity, can be regarded as both spatial and sequential. Spatially, writers must choose where on a page or document to include the visual components. Even visual components that do not appear with text must be placed deliberately within the spaces in which they appear. Sequentially, visual components can be integrated alongside ideas, or they can appear at the end or at the beginning of an argument. Deciding where to place images impacts the readers' experience with the visual components and their processing of your argument.

Common Forms of Visual Arguments across Disciplines

Because visual arguments come in so many different forms, from advertisements to public service announcements, photographic essays to tables, the sections below address only a few of the most common forms: photographic essays, graphics, academic posters, and presentation software. These forms of visual argument emerge across disciplines, as writers in many contexts integrate visual components into their writing or frame arguments exclusively through visual elements.

As visual arguments are both varied and complex, you should continue to explore and create other varieties of visual arguments as you move through your academic career. As you encounter these arguments throughout your undergraduate experience and beyond, stay attuned to recognizing and examining them. You might even keep a running list of the many sorts of visual arguments you encounter. Later, you can look here for inspiration when presented with future opportunities to work with visual argument.

Write Now

What forms of visual argument do you have experience creating or encountering? What forms of visual argument would you be interested in exploring further? If you have generated visual forms of argumentation, why did you do so? What kinds of argumentative occasions seem to warrant visual argument? Why do you think writers turn to visual argument in some instances and not in others?

Photographic essays

A **photographic essay** is an argument that emerges in the form of photographs. Often these photographs are documentary in nature. Photographic essays can stand alone as arguments, or they can be paired with written arguments. An example of a photographic essay is "Strong and Beautiful," by Brooke Kantor, Helen Clark, and Lydia Federico. They have constructed a written argument along with a photographic essay. The written component, titled "An Exercise in Body Image," makes the claim, "Our society lacks a significant space for body positivity. Fortunately, one area that has the potential to provide this space for young females is in women's athletics—in particular, the sport of rugby." The photographic essay that accompanies the argument includes a series of images, with brief captions, of members of the Harvard University women's rugby team (Figure 10.1).

HOT WON'T STOP BIG SQUAT MASTER
#feeling HUGE HEY QUADS Open Heart

BIG HUGE RIPPED

FIGURE 10.1 Images from "Strong and Beautiful," a photographic essay.

Being presented as a photographic essay separate from, though connected to, the written argument enables these photographs to make their own argument about athletics and female body positivity.

Graphics

The use of **graphics**, like the use of photographs in a photographic essay, can enable academic writers to construct an argument with particular efficacy. Graphics can be part of a written argument, such as the use of tables, charts, and other visuals, or they can stand alone. See these two brief examples of the use of graphics in visual arguments. In the first, Renée Farrar uses graphics as the arrangement for her poem, "Apple (a poem)," to make the argument that the icon for Apple participates in the disempowerment of the consumer (Figure 10.2).

Apple (a poem) | Renée Farrar

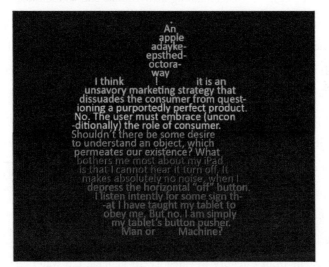

FIGURE 10.2 Graphic poem "Apple (a poem)."

Writer Insights

How do you use visual arguments in your discipline?

From the beginning of my academic career two years ago, I have coauthored four journal articles, two of which are review articles related to my field of life sciences.... One important feature common to most...articles [in my field] is the use of tables and charts in data presentation. Over time I realized that figures (and tables) do not only summarize and add to the beauty of one's writing but are necessary for the comprehensiveness of any text that involves much data and is actually preferred by peer reviewers.

~Murtala Isah Bindawa, Student, Biochemistry,
Bindawa, Katsina, Nigeria

The second example of graphics as visual argument demonstrates how graphics can participate as a critical aspect of a written argument. In the excerpt, undergraduate Benjamin Weia (Rice University) uses a chart as integral evidence in his argument that "bottled water is just as likely to have the same level of harmful chemicals as that of tap water, containing between 20,000 to 200,000 bacterial cells, and lack any beneficial minerals depending on water source."

Excerpt from "Do You Know Your Bottled Water?" by B. Weia

In terms of mineral composition, the amount of mineral content in bottled and tap water largely depends on source and treatment....

Three specific minerals important for a healthy body are calcium, magnesium, and sodium. Adequate calcium intake is important to maintain and restore bone strength for the young and to prevent osteoporosis in the old. Insufficient consumption of magnesium has been associated with heart disease including arrhythmias and sudden death. On the other hand, overly high sodium intake is well associated with high blood pressure and death from heart disease. The intake of all three of these minerals can be ensured by drinking water high in calcium, high in magnesium, and low in sodium. In fact, magnesium in water is absorbed approximately 30% faster than magnesium in food.

A comparative study in 2004 examined these three minerals in bottled and tap water across major U.S. regions. It concluded that drinking two liters per day of tap ground-water in certain regions or bottled mineral water of certain brands can significantly supplement a person's daily intake of calcium and magnesium (Figure 1).... While tap water sources showed wide variations in calcium, magnesium and sodium content, mineral levels of bottled water were more consistent from category to category. In general, tap water from groundwater sources had higher levels of calcium and magnesium than those from surface water sources....

> Weia includes the figure so that readers can begin to look at it, but notice that he does not actually refer to the figure until the next paragraph. This indicates how the graphic itself needs to offer a clear demonstration of the evidence or argument.

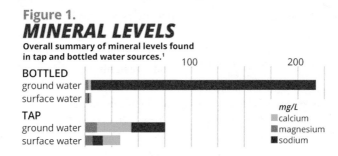

Figure 1.
MINERAL LEVELS
Overall summary of mineral levels found in tap and bottled water sources.[1]

From *Catalyst* (7), 2014.

Amongst the bottled waters, spring water consistently contained low levels of all three minerals, while mineral waters contained relatively high levels of all three minerals (Figure 1). Ozarka® spring water, produced in Texas, provides less than 2% of the three minerals' DRIs. In contrast, one liter of Mendocino® mineral water supplies 30% of the calcium and magnesium DRIs in women, and one liter of Vichy Springs® mineral water provides more than 33% of the recommended maximum sodium DRI. Based on these percentages, drinking bottled "mineral" as well as tap water from groundwater sources in certain cities can supplement food intake to fulfill calcium and magnesium DRIs.

> Weia spends considerable space explicating the graphic, necessitating that the reader examine it in some detail.

Academic posters

Academic posters are a visual representation of an academic argument. These can be created using a software program such as PowerPoint and then printed (a large-scale poster commonly runs 36" high and 48" wide), or they can appear as digital posters with interactive elements that users can control, such as the Prezi presentation interface. Academic posters are common in academic conferences, where researchers create a poster and display it at what is often termed a "poster session." Although conferences across disciplines include poster sessions, they are especially common in disciplines throughout STEM disciplines.

During a poster session, the writer stands by his or her poster, and other scholars review the poster and then can ask questions of the writer about his or her argument. Posters have the challenge of presenting complex amounts of information in readable, visually organized ways.

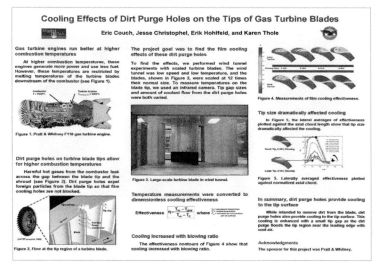

FIGURE 10.3 Academic poster design.

The academic poster in Figure 10.3 is successful in part because Couch, Christophel, Hohlfeld, and Thole have made careful use of white space and color. They included only the most essential elements on the poster, avoided crowding the information, and included graphics and images. For more information on designing academic posters, you can find a number of resources that provide templates for how to arrange the material and how to decide what sections to create for the poster.

Presentation software

Though **presentation software** might have been included in the section on verbal presentations, presentation software increasingly stands alone as an argumentative medium apart from the actual presentations that it might have originally accompanied. Designing the visual component of a presentation requires careful planning about how much to include on each slide or section, what order to arrange the material in, and how to integrate it with the presentation itself.

Several years ago, presentation software rarely appeared outside of the context of the presentation itself, which often included a written component or the physical presence of the writer. In that way, the presentation software was seen as a visual aid and did not have an expectation of presenting a full argument but operated as a supplement or visual enhancement to the main content of the presentation. Presentation software is now commonly posted online as an academic argument in and of itself. This creates an added challenge, because academic writers must now be careful editors of their visual content. To avoid an overcrowded or inscrutable presentation, they must strategically hold back some information while still including enough so that viewers can follow and appreciate the full complexity of the argument.

Figure 10.4 offers an example of such an argument. Prezi is a cloud-based online presentation tool that has rapidly gained popularity in the classroom and in business settings. Tanja de Bie argues in her Prezi that communities serve a vital role in the educational aspect of MOOCs (Massive Open Online Courses), while also presenting several key challenges. De Bie's Prezi, therefore, operates as an argument without the actual verbal presentation component, even if she had at some point made a presentation about this argument.

FIGURE 10.4 Prezi presentation software example.

Visual arguments, again, can emerge in many different modalities beyond photographic essays, graphics, academic posters, and presentation software, though these are likely among the formats you will encounter throughout your academic career. Explore visual arguments on your own to learn more about how to effectively design and construct them for your areas of interest and course assignments.

Write Now

What are your experiences using or viewing presentation software? What do you think accounts for their being more or less effective? If possible, try to recall an instance when you saw a presentation that used presentation software with particular efficacy. Describe what this person did to make it so effective.

Verbal Arguments

As prevalent as visual modalities are for argument across disciplines, so too are **verbal modalities**. By sharing arguments verbally through live, in-person encounters (including virtual meetings or calls), academic writers have the opportunity to exchange ideas with others. These interactions can not only advance others' thinking, but also influence that of the writer. While verbal arguments can sometimes emerge in a debate format, where a scholar is prepared to present and defend his or her argument at all costs, verbal arguments often have the characteristic of being exchanges, where scholars have an open mind to reconsider their own argument or take other viewpoints into consideration for future iterations of the argument.

Verbal arguments can occur at various stages of the writing and research process, from an interim stage, where scholars share works in progress, to a more polished stage, where the end result is a verbal argument. Nearly all disciplines hold academic conferences where scholars present their arguments orally.

Common Forms of Verbal Arguments across Disciplines

Learning how to present verbal arguments effectively requires attention to such components as body language, voice, and eye contact, as well as audio-visual handouts, slides, and materials. Many good resources are available for advice on how to deliver effective verbal presentations. These resources address choices you can make with how to prepare, how to dress, how to engage with your audience, and how to develop effective audio-visual components for the presentations. This section will provide an overview of several of the most common forms of verbal presentations you are likely to encounter during your academic career: academic presentations, elevator speeches or pitches, public service announcements, and films and videos.

Academic presentations

Academic presentations can be conceived of as a large umbrella concept for a wide variety of verbal presentations that occur across disciplines and contexts. An academic presentation can be as intimate as a seminar presentation to a small group of peers, or it can be more formal, consisting of a keynote lecture to hundreds of people or a panel presentation to twenty or thirty fellow scholars. Academic presentations are often between ten and twenty minutes, but can be even longer depending on content and context. They can also be briefer, such as in the context of lightning rounds or poster presentations, where people present their ideas to groups of viewers who typically travel around a room listening to a variety of presentations. These instances of academic presentations might consist of two- or three-minute time spans before people move on to the next presentation or poster. TEDx talks are yet another form of verbal academic presentations, a version that tends to combine scholarly and public scholarship contexts. In TEDx talks, speakers deliver a verbal argument about an issue and often call others to action.

Typically, academic presentations across all these occasions provide the opportunity for writers to interact with their audiences through conversation or questions and answers at the end of a talk. These interactions enable writers to get immediate feedback about their arguments and to respond immediately to audience contributions. While it is possible to engage with an audience through written contexts, such as the comments feature on a blog, these interchanges are often delayed and at a distance. Verbal academic presentations, on the other hand, tend to sponsor immediate exchanges.

Elevator speeches/pitches

People in some industries, such as those involved in startups, business, or nonprofit work, might do well to practice a form of verbal argument termed the **elevator speech** (also sometimes termed an elevator pitch). Many other academic contexts, however, also require facility with this form. The context for this format of verbal argument emerges from an imaginary scenario in which an individual who has the power to finance your project or influence others regarding your argument happens to be on an elevator with you. You have only the briefest amount of time to make your pitch to this influential individual. Perhaps your elevator ride will be ninety seconds, or it might, at the most, be three minutes. How will you convince this individual in such a brief amount of time?

The purpose of an elevator speech is not to convey the entire background and content of your verbal argument, but to convince the individual to be willing to learn more and continue the conversation. Such a scenario may seem unlikely and a bit farfetched. Indeed, you may not ever actually find yourself in such an elevator situation. However, you will likely find yourself in other contexts where you can draw upon these skills for great advantage. For instance, if you are interested in working with a particular faculty member or researcher, you can make your pitch to that individual in a brief hallway conversation. Or, you might have occasion at a social event or through a chance meeting in a professional context to convince someone about the merits of an innovative idea or the advantages of a potential collaboration. Many of these informal, happenstance interchanges can lead to robust collaborations and opportunities, if you can effectively deliver a brief but impactful elevator pitch.

Public service announcements

Public service announcements (PSAs) appear on television, radio, or online and offer an opportunity to convince and persuade people regarding your arguments. They tend to be quite brief in nature, somewhat similar to the length of a television advertisement. They generally range in length from ten seconds to one minute. Writers who create PSAs must whittle down arguments to the most essential elements. They also must distill the most broadly applicable and generalizable components of their argument because this form of verbal presentation assumes wide distribution through forms of mass media. PSAs often rely heavily on *pathos* and *ethos* for their arguments, since *logos* can be difficult to construct in such a short time span. PSAs often contain multimodal components, such as music, images, text, and voice, and writers must design these elements in such a way as to maximize the impact in a short time frame.

Those developing PSAs might construct *ethos* by illustrating the endorsement of influential people for a cause or by conveying expertise with shocking facts and figures that are largely unknown to members of the general public. Writers might appeal to *pathos* in PSAs by focusing on how the issue at hand harms or impacts humans in powerful, profound ways. In these approaches, the PSA can be a challenging form of verbal argument, but it is also one that can have broad impact by reaching a large range of viewers, who may then themselves go on to advocate for or influence others toward a cause or issue.

Films and videos

Although PSAs are technically verbal arguments that appear in video form, there are also a host of other occasions for shaping verbal arguments into the form of films and videos more broadly construed. These broader sorts of verbal arguments can include fictional films (both feature-length and short) that render an argument through video, animation, graphics, and sound. Verbal arguments can also appear in the form of documentary films, which are nonfiction films documenting an event, experience, or issue. Earlier in this chapter you had the opportunity to consider a YouTube video "The Ivy-League Hustle (I Went to Princeton, Bitch)," which makes an argument through video, lyrics, and music. Other films and videos have also been referenced throughout *Writing in Transit*. Morgan Spurlock's argumentative nutritional film, *Super Size Me*, is one such example. Spurlock uses his personal experience as evidence for a verbal argument in the form of a documentary film (Chapter 11, p. 469).

Where PSAs are inherently designed for mass distribution to reach a large public, films and videos can be constructed with similar distributive intent or they can be designed for release to a more specialized subset of people. Films and videos also provide a potentially expansive opportunity for writers to render their verbal arguments because they can take the time to persuade viewers through *ethos, pathos, logos,* and *kairos.* One challenge of films and videos parallels a challenge many writers encounter when developing written arguments: editing. Editing decisions include determining what to include or exclude, as well as the order and structure in which to arrange material. People engaging in video and film forms of verbal argument must also make complicated decisions about the intersections between sound, image, text, visual, and, sometimes, tactile components.

Depending on the context, films and videos can provide a powerful mechanism to construct and archive a verbal argument and then distribute it repeatedly and often for viewer consumption and consideration.

Write Now

Using a recent argument you have written, spend ten minutes reflecting in writing how you would transform it into a verbal argument in the form of a video or film. What might you include in your video or film? How would you construct your argument differently with this modality than you did for a written context?

Other Modalities for Argument

While the overlapping modalities, which primarily fuse written, visual, and verbal modes of communication, offer a large array of possible formats for argument, others also exist across disciplines and contexts. For instance, performance artists and choreographers construct arguments through dance and performance. Musicians construct arguments through sound, lyrics, and music, and architects make arguments through materials and structural design. Even silence or darkness can make an argument.

With so many design options available for arguments, you have the freedom to be highly creative in approaching their construction, even as you also stay attuned to their disciplinary conventions and expectations.

Transferring Argument Design

Chapter 10 builds on prior chapters by continuing our exploration into argument. While Chapter 8 introduced a framework for approaching argument and Chapter 9 addressed the construction of arguments, this chapter focused on how writers design arguments. As integral as concepts such as reasoning, significance, and structure are to argument, so too is design. The formats and modalities writers use to convey arguments have a deep impact on how their arguments are shaped. Writers must choose carefully how to design their arguments and what format to use by taking into consideration the writing occasion and the argument itself. And, while each design format carries particular considerations, writers also have the opportunity to transfer key skills and approaches to design across the many modalities and formats they may deploy.

Subsequent chapters extend our work with argumentation by focusing on, respectively, the integration of evidence and citation practices. These elements enable writers to fully develop their arguments and make them as effective as possible, whatever their particular purpose, structure, or designs are.

ཀྱི ཀྱི ཀྱི

Poem: "knee deep in N'awlins" by Rickie Elpusan

Transfer Points: Creative Writing, English Literature

As a result of Hurricane Katrina, 1,836 people lost their lives in 2005, most of them senior citizens. Seven hundred-five people are still considered missing. More than a million people were displaced from their homes. Katrina caused an estimated $150 billion of damage ("11 Facts").

This devastating Category 3 hurricane made landfall on the Gulf Coast of the United States during the morning of August 29, 2005. The levees in New Orleans soon failed, causing massive flooding. The hardest hit states were Louisiana and Mississippi.

The scale of Katrina's devastation and its wide-ranging impact have sponsored a vast array of scholarly research across disciplines. Engineers, for instance, have researched Katrina to understand the logistics of hurricane evacuation (Wu, et al.) and the impact of storm surges on bridges and buildings (Robertson, et al). Anthropologists and sociologists have written about the impacts of displacement from Katrina (Makiko, et al.) and such issues as post-traumatic stress among low-income Louisiana mothers (Paxson, et al). Chemists and ecologists have written about the concentration of metal in post-Katrina schoolyards (Presley, et al.) and about post-Katrina demolition and its effect on air quality (Ravikrishna, et al.). And, scholars in the arts have written about Katrina-related jazz funerals (Maxson) and about photographs and narratives emanating from Katrina (Neff).

Scholars have also written, and written about, poetry focused on Katrina. English literature scholar Robert Azzarello explores, for instance, "what is lost and what is gained" by the use of the poetic form regarding Katrina. He analyzes, among other texts, Martha Serpas's book of poetry about Katrina, *The Dirty Side of the Storm* (2007). Poet Brad Richard, similarly, offers close readings on a number of Katrina-related poems, examining such aspects as imagery, word choice, and the role of the reader. And, creative writing professor John Gery writes about the challenges facing poets who have composed poetry about Katrina.

These examples demonstrate some of the many intersections that occur more broadly between disaster and poetry. Across time and geographic region, people have composed and conducted research about such poetry. Known as disaster poetry, poetry of catastrophe, or poetry of witness, this subfield of poetry includes poems about political disasters, such as Walt Whitman's "When Lilacs Last in the Door-Yard Bloom'd," written as a response to President Abraham Lincoln's assassination (Tanenhaus), or about larger-scale disasters, such as Paula Bardell's poem about September 11, "Silence (over Manhattan)" (Weigle). This area of poetry also includes personal disasters and catastrophes, such as AIDS poetry written by Paul Monette, Thom Gunn, or Rafael Campo (Gorelik). Disaster poems may be focused explicitly on a particular disaster, or they might feature disaster as a lens to explore another event or concept. In Sandra Cisneros's "One Last Poem for Richard," for example, Cisneros invokes disaster to explore the demise of a personal relationship.

People who write or write about poetry focus on a range of aspects, including form, content, purpose, impact, structure, politics, and language. Those conducting research about poetry might also write about the history of a particular poetic form, such as the haiku form used by Elpusan. And, they might write biographical texts about particular poets, drawing on biographical and historical knowledge to deepen understanding about the poets, their historical context, and their texts.

Rickie Elpusan writes poetry that often appears on the website PoetrySoup. His poems emerge in many forms, from epigrams and free verse to senryu and haiku. He often writes about nature and the emotions. Some of his most frequently read poems, in addition to "knee deep in N'awlins," are "Liquid Little Stones," "Olive Trees," and "Carved on a Willow" ("Poems"). Elpusan is Lead Ophthalmic Technician at NVISION Eye Center in the greater Los Angeles area and also an artisan at The Olive Orchard, where he creates rosaries. He studied at Long Beach City College and volunteers for organizations and events related to disaster and humanitarian relief, children, and the alleviation of poverty ("Rickie").

Many people assume that poetry primarily fits within literature or creative writing contexts. However, because poetry addresses so many topics, it can be part of virtually any discipline. Poet Alice Major, for instance, writes about poetry and science, arguing that quantum uncertainty offers an apt metaphor for poetry (Chapman). Others have explored poetry's connection to business strategy (Healy), psychology (Mair), math (Bahls), and history (Ba 'albaki). People in medicine have researched the health benefits of writing poetry for people with serious illnesses (Rickett, et al.), and scholars have researched how poetry can promote social justice (Foster).

Poetry is not only transferable across and within disciplines, but it also transfers across scholarly, artsy, and public platforms. Through initiatives and websites such as PoetrySoup, where Elpusan publishes much of his poetry, virtually anyone can compose, publish, and access poetry. Those invested in poetry often recruit people in broader publics to experiment with poetry. Examples include the annual "Poem in a Pocket" day or the National Writers' Project focused on Hurricane Katrina.

One other transfer-based dimension of poetry is form. Elpusan writes in haiku, but poetry also appears in numerous other forms, from free verse and limerick to ode and rondeau.

Such examples illustrate the nearly limitless transfer associated with poetry, across time, region, language, context, genre, form, and discipline.

Write Here

Poetry such as haiku relies on skills of close observation and description. Engage with this dimension of poetic practice by finding an object and describing it in as much detail as possible. Consider all the senses in relation to the object, as well as the object's context and use. Then, transfer what you have described into a haiku about the object you have chosen.

Rickie Elpusan
knee deep in N'awlins

tempest stomps her feet
as she shakes her liquid skirt
knee deep in N'awlins

Write Away

1. Compose a synthesis essay about "knee deep in N'awlins" by applying concepts about disaster poetry to a reading of the poem. This synthesis essay requires that you first identify dimensions of disaster poetry or catastrophe poetry using an established resource about disaster poetry and/or other scholars' ideas about disaster poetry. Then, you'll also need to conduct a close reading of Elpusan's poem, including content and form. In your synthesis argument, use Elpusan's poem to address the following sorts of questions: What role does poetry play in our understanding about and processing of disaster? What are the limits of such expression? What are the possibilities? How does form intersect with disaster poetry?

2. Working individually or with a team, curate and introduce an anthology about the poetry of disaster. You might choose to focus on a particular disaster, or a particular type of poem, or you could fuse several such dimensions into one anthology. Compose an edi-

tor's introduction to the anthology in which you discuss your approach to selection and curation. You might even decide to create some of your own poems about disaster.

3. Compose a research-based argument about poetry that addresses a particular discipline, event, or concept. You can choose, for instance, to focus on poetry of engineering, poetry of business, or poetry of science. Or you can choose an event that is of interest to you, such as poetry about or from the Great Depression or poetry about or by refugees. Integrate relevant secondary literature into your argument. As you develop your essay, move through the entire research process, including a proposal, annotated bibliography of secondary literature, drafts, and revisions.

Public Policy Reporting: *"Is a Rural Area the Best Place for Surviving Disaster?"* by Don Staples and Fernando Aguirre

Transfer Points: Public Policy, Political Science, Journalism, Public Health

"[T]he world situation [is] highly threatening to humanity—so threatening that the hands of the Doomsday Clock must remain at three minutes to midnight, the closest they've been to catastrophe since the early days of above-ground hydrogen bomb testing" (Mecklin).

While this statement may seem like a quote from the latest science-fiction novel or post-apocalypse Hollywood film, it actually emerges from a group of informed science leaders and policy makers. Each year since 1947, these leaders evaluate world problems such as nuclear arsenals, climate change, international relations, terrorism, and emerging technologies. They then decide how dire these problems are, how close we are to near total destruction of humanity. They then represent the threat level by setting the hands on the Doomsday clock. Their assessment is grim.

The Doomsday clock is but one manifestation of ongoing fears and predictions about cataclysmic disasters that could befall humankind. An asteroid could hurtle into Earth. A pandemic such as SARS or H1N1 could decimate entire populations. Biological weapons could result in widespread illness and death. Artificial intelligence could spiral out of control, causing the launch of deadly weapons and the dismantling of infrastructure. Climate change could create ever more severe weather-related catastrophes, and overpopulation could put unsustainable pressures on natural resources. Nuclear Armageddon could instantaneously eliminate entire countries. Some maintain that a "snowball effect" is more likely, where multiple disasters would occur simultaneously (Ghose).

Any and all of these scenarios have prompted many people around the world to consider how to

Don Staples, when he wrote this text, was the manager of TruPrep retail outlets, located in Roswell and Marietta, Georgia. He also ran classes such as "Prepping 101" for local people on firearms and other doomsday prepping matters. Currently, he is content manager for a hotel restaurant supplier. He studied accounting at Lander University, in Greenville, South Carolina, and has a BSM in Management from Shorter University in Atlanta, Georgia. **Fernando "FerFAL" Aguirre** is an Ireland-based prepper author and blogger. He has written two books on survivalism: *The Modern Survival Manual: Surviving the Economic Collapse* and *Bugging Out and Relocating: When Staying is Not an Option*. He is also a regular blogger about prepping-related matters, such as firearms, politics, war, and first aid. His blogs include *Modern Survival Blog*, which boasts of having had more than 28 million visitors, and *Surviving in Argentina. Life In Argentina after the 2001 Crisis*. Aguirre is also involved with architecture and real estate, and has taught architecture courses at the University of Buenos Aires (Aguirre, "Modern").

prepare for possible disaster. Among those who take actual steps to prepare, there is a wide continuum. Toward the most active end of this spectrum are people known as "preppers," a group within which the two authors engaged in debate here about rural or urban settings identify.

Situated at the nexus of prepping and public policy, their pro/con discussion appears in a report titled "Preparing for Disaster" that was prepared for *Congressional Quarterly (CQ) Researcher*, a publication aimed at providing informed snapshots of contentious, significant matters of public policy. From fair housing and energy policy to death penalty and campaign finance, *CQ Researcher* provides 12,000-word reports on a wide range of contemporary and historic issues. Together, these reports comprise a widely used archive of public scholarship, helping those involved with government, education, politics, public health, and education understand the history and stakes involved with contentious, high-profile issues.

The writing that appears in *CQ Researcher* illustrates one of the more public forms of writing in the discipline of public policy. Such writing, often designed for both policy makers and broader publics, must capture complicated issues in a succinct manner and in such a way that showcases multiple perspectives. Those in public policy also frequently engage with other forms of writing, including policy memos, which outline and analyze a problem and provide recommendations, and reports, which provide assessments of initiatives and policies, as well as recommendations for the future.

Another common genre of writing in public policy is called a white paper, which consists of an authoritative and succinct approach advocating for a particular issue or approach to an issue. To develop these white papers, as well as other forms of writing in the discipline, writers will conduct policy analysis to understand the ramifications of various options or current policies. And, the article on preparedness in *CQ Researcher* resonates with a more public form of public policy writing known as a policy brief, which offers an overview of an issue for a decision maker. This latter genre is often also accompanied by a verbal briefing, demonstrating how, across these many genres, those in public policy also commonly engage in verbal modes of communication as well.

As these examples illustrate, writers working across these public policy genres must gather great amounts of information, and distill them in ways that honor complexity but are nonetheless accessible for busy people with diverging awareness, stakes, and perspectives. Writing in this context, therefore, tends to value concise, direct, and accessible language. Many texts integrate the use of document design as well, such as headings and text boxes, crafting texts in ways that invite readers to notice particular sections or jump around while reading.

Alongside these more public forms of writing, scholars in public policy also compose discipline-specific, peer-reviewed research. Examples from the *Journal of Public Policy*, for example, include "Offshore Financial Activity and Tax Policy: Evidence from A Leaked Data Set" (Caruana-Galizia and Caruana-Galizia) and "Low-Technology Industries and the Skill Composition of Immigration" (Rheault). Public policy scholars, as with those in other disciplines, also write book reviews, conference papers, literature reviews, and participate in scholarly lectures, debates, and dialogues.

Writing in public policy, be it public, scholarly, written, or part of a verbal presentation, involves key considerations that are salient to all writing occasions, but which take on particular complexity in the context of public policy. The rhetorical triangle, for instance, matters immensely to writers in public policy: Who will likely be reading the text, and why? What is a writer hoping to accomplish with a text? What is the writer's relationship with and attitude toward the issues under consideration, and how will these perspectives and roles impact the message being conveyed? How do writers establish credibility and expertise?

Write Here

If the world as you know it was suddenly facing inevitable, catastrophic decimation, what would you need to think about or prepare for to survive? Describe what your survival needs would be and what your plans would be for surviving.

Don Staples and Fernando Aguirre
Is a Rural Area the Best Place for Surviving Disaster?

Don Staples
Manager, TruPrep Retail Outlets, Roswell and Marietta, GA

Written for CQ Researcher, August 2013

The best location for surviving disaster depends on many variables. What type of disaster? Are you in the middle of a large city or in the suburbs? Is it a long-term situation like an economic collapse or short term like a tornado?

In the short term it makes sense to stay in your house, with all your possessions and comforts. No point in abandoning everything because a tornado knocked out power for a week. If nothing else, you need to be there to protect your investment.

If the disaster is going to last many months to a year or more, getting where you can subsist is essential. You need to be able to grow food, find clean drinking water and be safe from what may be happening in the city or spreading from the city to the suburbs. There will be many people totally unprepared, and most will become a problem for those who did prepare.

The first priority is water. If you are buying land in advance, do not buy anything without its own water. Space to grow food is the second priority. It is impractical for most people to store enough food to get through a long-term issue. You must also have seeds, hand tools, fertilizer, open space that gets plenty of sunlight and plenty of help from the family and/or friends you bring along. Shelter is hugely important as well. A tent will serve in the short term but building something more substantial will be important. You may also build a permanent shelter in advance or have a recreational vehicle onsite. The RV could also serve as transportation to the location. You will also need firearms and ammunition to deal with predators of the two- and four-legged variety. Getting out of densely populated areas will keep you and yours safe from most of the two-legged animals, and the four-legged ones will be food at some point.

I cannot over-emphasize the importance of groups for mutual support. The lone-wolf types will be the first to die, as no one can stay alert 24/7. The people in the group should have varying skills, including mechanical ability, hunting ability, medical training, etc. There should be people who know how to grow food as well, though everyone should pitch in to help with the farming labor.

Get these people together, preferably in advance, and the group should be able to survive any long-term disaster comfortably.

Fernando Aguirre
Ireland-based prepper author and blogger

Written for CQ Researcher, August 2013

The idea of a rural homestead being the best place to be during a disaster is usually fueled by Hollywood and fiction rather than history and logic.

A rural location has few advantages. In a pandemic, for example, being away from masses of people sounds like a good idea. But what about nonhuman vectors of disease? Some of the worst pandemics have been spread by rats and mosquitoes, and these are much easier controlled in urban areas.

What about an economic crisis or full economic collapse? Won't cities burn to the ground, with the brave survivors bugging out to the country? Again, history shows that people move to the cities when there's an economic crisis, not the other way around, and it's small towns that end up turning into ghost towns.

I've lived through an economic collapse while living in Argentina, and I can tell you from first-hand experience it's nothing like you see in movies.

What about social unrest and widespread rioting when police are helpless? In spite of the dramatic images of rioting, the truth is that other than full-blown war, violence from rioting and lawlessness is limited to a few days or weeks. In Argentina, following the financial meltdown of 2001-2001, widespread rioting lasted only a few days, with some additional incidents happening sporadically several weeks later. Riots in such places as London, Los Angeles and, recently, Brazil followed a similar pattern. Rioting looks eye-catching on TV, but it's not as impressive when you look at how long it lasts or the number of fatalities.

Being away from the city does reduce the chances of being victimized by vandalism, petty crime and occasional break-ins, but an isolated house is more often targeted than one where neighbors are closer by. In fact, in high-crime parts of the world like Latin America or Africa, isolated homesteads are impossible to defend from determined criminals. Instead, people choose to live in gated communities or apartment towers with good security.

In spite of all the doom and gloom, 90 percent of us will probably die from cancer or cardiovascular complications—common, ordinary illnesses that don't sound as cool as zombies or raiders. Being closer to quality medical care means that your chances of survival increase considerably, and so does your quality of life during treatment.

Write Away

1. Write a rhetorical analysis (see Chapter 7) of this pro/con debate. Consider the main components of rhetorical analysis, including author, audience, message, purpose, and appeals of *ethos, pathos, logos,* and *kairos.* Your rhetorical analysis can address all of these, or you can choose to focus in on one rhetorical component in particular that you find to be particularly pronounced or significant.

2. Write a policy brief about an issue of contemporary significance. To develop your brief, conduct research about the issue, drawing on reliable sources as well as varying sources. Aim to capture as many different perspectives as you can about that policy so that your brief will be as inclusive, reliable, informative, and expansive as possible. Design your brief by taking into consideration your potential readers as well as how to prioritize information and how to design information in such a way as to render your brief accessible and effective. Write a process reflection that addresses the readers you were targeting as well as aspects of the composition process that were challenging, surprising, and/or otherwise valuable for subsequent writing occasions you may encounter. In consultation with your instructor, you may also want to develop and deliver a verbal brief to accompany the written brief.

3. Compose a white paper about an issue of contemporary significance, designed for a particular reader or group of readers. Your white paper should provide a full description of the issues, the complexities and perspectives involved, and possible approaches. Your role in the white paper will also be to advocate for one of those possible approaches, demonstrating why it is advisable and what, if any, qualifications or limitations might still need to be taken into consideration. In the white paper, argue for a particular position.

Chapter 10 Key Terms

modalities	visual thinking	verbal modalities
scholarly	photographic essay	academic presentation
public scholarship	graphics	elevator speech
popular scholarship	academic poster	
visual argument	presentation software	

Write Away

This activity invites you to transfer an argument currently shaped for one modality into several other different formats. Doing so will help you experience how design choices impact argumentation and how you can work to transfer the art of designing arguments across different argument occasions.

Locate an argument. Locate an argument that is of interest to you. It can be in any format you choose: a written one in the form of a peer-reviewed scholarly essay, a print advertisement, a YouTube video, or any argument as long as the main claim of that argument is clear to you.

Choose two to three alternative design formats. Select two to three other formats or modalities, different from the one in which the argument currently appears, that you can use for this argument. For instance, you could decide to transfer a written scholarly argument into a song and a photographic essay. Or, you could transfer a YouTube video into an op-ed and a verbal presentation.

Whatever you choose, these should be design formats with which you would be interested in experimenting and that seem to lend themselves particularly well to the particular argument with which you are working.

Transfer the argument to each of those alternative design formats. Transfer the argument you have chosen to each of the other design formats. To transfer the argument, you will need to make decisions about which aspects of the argument should be transferred and how. You may also be called upon to introduce additional elements for the new formats. If so, do so to the best of your ability. Since you will be using the work of another, even as you transfer that argument to a different format, be sure to attribute those ideas properly to the original author at some point in the new format, indicating that you have adapted the original argument to the new format.

Reflect on your design process. Reflect in writing for ten minutes about this experience: Why did you choose the formats you chose for this argument transfer? Why did you think they might lend themselves especially well to the particular argument with which you were working? Which, if any, elements of the argument became reshaped as you moved from one format to others? What elements did you carry over or modify from one format to the others? What did you learn about designing arguments from this experience? What did you learn about transfer from this experience?

Share your argument formats and reflections with others. Share your arguments in their different formats, as well as aspects of your reflection (as relevant) with others.

Transfer Hub: Contribute your ideas and see what others have written at fountainheadpress.com/transferhub.

Choosing and Integrating Evidence:
Quotes, Paraphrases, Visual Materials, and Data

Pinpointing Chapter 11

Having explored in Chapters 8, 9, and 10 the various choices writers make in developing, structuring, and designing arguments, Chapter 11 focuses in depth on the hearty substance that drives argument: evidence. The evidence writers choose to advance their arguments, and the ways in which they integrate that evidence, enables them to accomplish the purposes they set out to achieve. To provide you with strategies for *choosing and integrating evidence in transit*, this chapter addresses the following concepts:

- What is Evidence?
- Purposes for Integrating Evidence
- Questions that Shape Integration of Evidence
- Criteria for Effectively Integrating Evidence
- Featured Strategy for Integrating Evidence: The MEAL Plan
- Examples of Integrating Evidence

Chapter 12 will then build on these aspects of evidence by addressing citation practices surrounding evidence. For writers, citation works in concert with the selection and integration of evidence as a way of conveying to readers as robustly as possible a full record of their research and the disciplinary perspective informing their approach.

I was there entirely alone. Not a soul stood even on the road below…. I was literally astounded. The light began as a thin pencil and widened to a band of about 6 in. There was so much light reflected from the floor that I could walk around inside without a lamp and avoid bumping [against]…the stones. It was so bright I could see the roof 20 ft above me…. I expected to hear a voice, or perhaps feel a cold hand resting on my shoulder, but there was silence. And then, after a few minutes, the shaft of light narrowed as the sun appeared to pass westward across the slit, and total darkness came once more. (Michael J. O'Kelly, 1967)

*S*o Michael J. O'Kelly, professor of archaeology, describes the moment he confirmed the local legends he had long been hearing about the mysterious illumination that purportedly transpired at Newgrange on each winter solstice. O'Kelly had witnessed a remarkable event at this Neolithic structure in Ireland where, at precisely, and only on, the winter solstice, for a period of approximately 17 minutes, a swath of direct sunlight enters through an opening in a small "roof-box" and "penetrate[s] down the passage to [fully] illuminate the central chamber." Tourists now flock to Newgrange each December to witness for themselves the annual winter solstice that so brilliantly marks the onset of winter (McKenna-Lawlor; Murphy).

The precise alignment visible each year at the winter solstice demonstrates keen Neolithic astronomical ability. Once thought to be exclusively a burial mound, Newgrange features a large, dome-shaped roof and a striking triple spiral design located at the entrance. Newgrange was constructed more than 5,000 years ago, in approximately 3200 BCE, by a "farming community that prospered on the rich lands of the Boyne Valley." Nearby, "wattled huts" remain, providing evidence for how these Neolithic settlers and their forebears also hunted salmon, eels, and waterfowl from nearby rivers (McKenna-Lawlor).

Farming and hunting, as it turns out, connect deeply to the winter solstice and help explain why those who built Newgrange did so with such archaeoastronomical precision. Some maintain that Neolithic farmers may have honored astronomical events, such as the winter solstice, and "worshipped...sky power" as a way to curry favor with the gods and therein "ensure better food supplies."

Other researchers have found evidence attesting to the hypothesis that food might have motivated ancient astronomical alignments (Munson). Archaeologist Maria Reiche, for instance, has found such evidence at the Nazca Lines in Southern Peru: "The geometric drawings [at Nazca] are directed toward horizon points marking the rising and setting of the heavenly bodies…[They] most likely served to mark the sowing and harvest time, and [guide the more conservative] distribution of food during the dry period of the year." Likewise, the winter solstice illumination at Newgrange may have served as a harbinger of winter for the hunters and farmers, signaling them to prepare for winter, store food, and adjust farming techniques to accommodate the change in season.

Each winter solstice, therefore, the ancient Neolithic people of Newgrange read evidence from the solstice alignment to conclude that the winter had begun. Today the archaeological evidence from Newgrange and the excavations of other such sites yield evidence suggesting that the archaeoastronomical alignments may have been part of ancient traditions affiliated with hunting, farming, and food storage and preparation.

Exploring the evidence surrounding food and the Newgrange winter solstice actually generates a productive lens through which to consider evidence more broadly, as in the context of academic writing. Evidence in this broader context retains a metaphoric affiliation with food: it fuels arguments, sustaining, nourishing, and generating them, thereby enabling scholars to continue learning and advancing knowledge. Evidence also resonates with Newgrange in another way. As with Newgrange's winter solstice alignment, evidence also sponsors alignments, forging connections between concepts so writers can construct their own insights, ideas, and arguments.

Considering evidence through the metaphor of food helps illuminate several additional and important features of evidence as well. One such feature pertains to the level of depth with which academic writers integrate evidence in their texts. Across and within different writing occasions, academic writers will sometimes examine evidence in an exceptionally in-depth manner: closely reading and analyzing evidence, and digesting evidence morsel by morsel, inside and through, as one might with an exquisitely crafted dessert. At other times, in a manner that seems to resemble a table of assorted cookies at a party, academic writers will **integrate** evidence in more sweeping ways, glossing quickly over a large quantity or range of research, or referencing another's work only briefly in the text.

Another way in which food serves as an apt metaphor in an examination of evidence is that evidence should be **sandwiched** effectively within the writer's ideas. That is, when academic writers integrate evidence, be it charts, images, tables, graphs, quotes, or **paraphrases**, they should position that evidence within their own argument, providing material before and after the evidence that helps readers understand the purpose of the evidence. Like the pieces of the bread that circumscribe the contents of a sandwich, the evidence one puts forth in an argument should be both framed and interpreted for readers. Think of the top piece of bread as introducing the evidence: helping readers understand why it is being included, what the evidence is, and how it relates to the point the writer is making. Following the evidence that makes up the "meat" of the writer's argument, so to speak, the bottom piece of bread is the further explication of that evidence, highlighting what the writer wants readers to notice. Without these metaphorical pieces of bread, evidence remains unframed (sometimes referred to as orphaned), and readers may not understand how that evidence is forwarding an argument or participating in the writer's larger aim.

Variety is a crucial aspect of integrating evidence. Without a variety of foods to choose from, eating would likely be somewhat boring; so too with evidence. Effective academic writing includes a variety of different voices and perspectives and offers readers a sense of the complexity and range of thinking for any particular line of inquiry. Academic writers integrate many different types of evidence, often from many different contexts. The best academic writers also deploy variety in the ways in which they integrate evidence into any given piece of writing, varying where they place evidence in the text and how they frame it.

Write Here

Although most contemporary people probably do not change their food gathering, distribution, or consumption practices across seasons as drastically as these Irish predecessors might have 5,000 years ago, it is likely that you do nonetheless make some adjustments to your diet. Reflect for ten minutes in writing on your own food practices as they are connected to the seasons. Do you eat more or less of certain kinds of food in particular seasons? Do you notice an abundance or scarcity of certain kinds of food across the seasons? Do you notice that you crave or desire different kinds of foods across seasons?

ల్ ల్ ల్

What is Evidence?

Evidence is the material academic writers draw from to advance their arguments. Evidence can take many forms, some quantitative (or numerical) and others text-based, field-based, or visual. Field notes, survey responses, interviews, experiment results, photographs, passages from texts, graphs, tables, charts, artifacts, objects, numbers—any of these (and more) might be considered evidence.

Evidence can serve many purposes in an argument, from being that which a writer analyzes to supporting an argument or by offering a counterpoint or contrasting view to an argument.

Evidence is situated deeply within disciplinary and publication contexts. Because readers approach writing through these frameworks, they carry both tacit and overt expectations about what kinds of evidence they will encounter and how that evidence will be integrated and presented. Do readers of a particular writing project expect peer-reviewed scholarship or more popular evidence? Does your intended audience prefer long quotes or paraphrase? Are tables and charts customary for a particular context? These are all discourse conventions that shape the ways in which academic writers integrate evidence into academic writing.

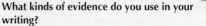

The range of evidence from which academic writers draw follows the kinds of research described in Chapter 2: Research and Writing as a Process. In that chapter, we discussed several different types of research: quantitative, qualitative, and mixed-methods, and we also discussed primary and secondary sources. Academic writers choose from among these options and generate evidence for their arguments.

Another area that shapes the evidence from which academic writers draw is the continuum of secondary materials discussed in Chapter 4: Reading. In that chapter, we discussed how academic writers choose what to read, which constitutes a choice of what evidence they will then collect and consider. Academic writers read primary and secondary materials; secondary materials exist along a continuum ranging from popular and public scholarship to scholarly secondary materials. All of this together serves as the range of evidence from which academic writers draw.

> **Writer Insights**
>
> **What kinds of evidence do you use in your writing?**
>
> As a historian, I like to employ two different types of "evidence" in my own writing. The first type of evidence I like to use is quotes. Quotes are easy to find and can help me "instantly" build theories in a reliable way. My second favorite type of evidence is anecdotes. When anecdotes are used carefully, they can help illustrate important points in a colorful way. Also, anecdotes help my readers connect emotionally to my scholarly thoughts about the people, places, and things of the past, which is pretty powerful.
>
> *~Derek L. Zboran, Writer,*
> *Rolla, Missouri, U.S.*

Chapters 6 and 7 also play key roles in establishing how academic writers work with evidence. Scholars conduct careful analysis and synthesis on data in order to make use of their evidence. Using these scholarly skills enables academic writers to transform data (text, images, artifacts, numbers) into evidence that forwards an argument or supports a position.

There are several ways in which evidence commonly appears in academic writing across disciplines: quotations, summary, paraphrase, visual evidence, data, and personal evidence.

Quotations

Quotations are portions of language from others' texts that writers replicate word for word in their own texts. Quotations are indicated with in-text citations, quotation marks, italics, and/or other accepted approaches to document design, as dictated by publication context, disciplinary context, and citation style. The use of quotations for evidence occurs most frequently in the humanities and the social sciences. In English, for instance, writers will include quotes from texts in order to provide evidence for their interpretation of those texts. In sociology, writers might include quotes from study participants to illustrate an important concept that their research has demonstrated. Although less common, writers in the natural sciences and engineering may also use quotes, particularly in the more popular versions of their arguments. Quotes serve many purposes as evidence, offering testimony for a claim, illustrating a point, capturing the unique stylistic elements of another's work, and adding variety to one's own text.

Quotes can appear in many different formats. They can consist of quoted key terms, partial phrases, full sentences, passages, or even entire paragraphs. Longer quotes are referred to as **block quotations**. Different citation styles each have different specifications for the

Transfer at Work

Evidence can look drastically different across disciplinary context and writing occasion. Researchers in Environmental Psychology and Social Psychology investigated how food reputation impacted consumer behavior. They collected their evidence from surveys asking how much particular factors of food reputation (product duration, territorial [a.k.a local] identity, product responsibility, and product claims for physical well-being) impacted consumers' choices. The researchers studied consumer likelihood to choose based on a first phase of consideration and a second phase of actual choice. They found that "territorial identity" impacted consumer choice about food and drink most significantly:

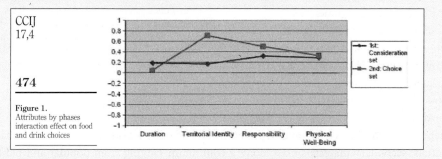

CCIJ
17,4

474

Figure 1.
Attributes by phases
interaction effect on food
and drink choices

Showing a contrasting approach to evidence, French professor Alison Murray Levine gathers her evidence from a close reading of a documentary and still shots for her article on French documentary films about food:

> The dialectical nature of the argument in this film—contrasting nature and industry, old and new— is also evident in its visual economy. The opening title appears over a close-up of a tuft of grass growing in a patch of asphalt (see Figure 3). Although isolated in a desert of asphalt, this grass does not appear to be suffering; it is vivid green, almost pulsing with life, even as a heavy truck rolls by in the background.... The people pursuing the 'old' methods—the grass farmers—are presented as more in touch with the future than those engaged in more 'modern' means of production ... Shots of the grass farm tend to be misty and quiet,... Shots of the modern farm focus more on the equipment and facilities and on interiors rather than landscapes. (187)

exact length a quote must be in order to be constructed as a block quotation. Writers should include block quotations only on occasions when many aspects of the quoted passage provide evidence for a claim and a shorter quote will not suffice. Whether quotes are block form or shorter, writers should integrate quotes as smoothly as possible within their texts. They do so by introducing the quote, presenting the quote, and then explicating the quote. Finally, they reference or cite the quote, using an accepted citation style for in-text citations (specifically discussed in Chapter 12).

Summary

Summary, as addressed in detail throughout Chapter 5, condenses larger amounts of material or ideas into smaller amounts of text. Summary appears as evidence perhaps most frequently when writers are developing literature reviews of prior scholarship about a concept or issue. In this capacity, writers might use summary as a way of providing evidence for a trend they have noticed in prior research or to identify a gap in knowledge they believe has been either overlooked or created by prior research. Summary can also serve as evidence when writers recount personal experiences, the plots of texts, historical events, or if they want to capture the tenor of a conversation or interview. Writers in many contexts also use summary as evidence when describing their research methods to support the claims they are making for the merits of how they collected data or analyzed materials.

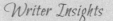

Writer Insights

When and why do you use personal forms of evidence in your writing?

My job is to inspire young adults who feel isolated and marginalized. I have found writing from my personal experience lifts the veil of fear and sometimes shocks them into telling their own truth. My life has been a perilous journey that has found merit in their eyes and hearts. Therefore, I use my stories often.

~Beverly Reed Scott, Original Voice® Storyteller,
Olympia Fields, Illinois, United States

When deployed as evidence, effective summary hinges on a writer's capacity to fully capture the main points of either events, other texts, or both, as well as any assumptions or contexts that shape those points. When writers integrate summary into their arguments in the form of evidence, they should clearly indicate that the reason is to exemplify their point or to illustrate a concept in more detail.

Paraphrase

Paraphrase involves borrowing the ideas of another and rephrasing them in your own words. It is related to summary but differentiated by the amount of text it captures. Summary captures a large amount of text and condenses it. Paraphrase, by contrast, rephrases a particular idea located at a particular moment in another text (rather than a snapshot of the entire text) and uses nearly the same amount of text for the paraphrase. So, if a writer paraphrases a particular sentence in a text, he or she will likely rephrase that idea in the form of another sentence. Paraphrase can be differentiated from quotations in that they are not exact replications of the original material. However, paraphrases, like citations, still require in-text citation.

There are many reasons why writers might choose to paraphrase others' material instead of quoting it directly. One such reason might be that the original text operates at a stylistic level that is out of alignment with a writer's current project. For instance, a writer might want to make an idea more accessible by paraphrasing it in his or her own language, or that writer might want to unpack the full complexity of a concept that may be originally phrased in a more general manner. Writers might also paraphrase in order to adhere more cohesively to disciplinary conventions. In this case, writers might choose to paraphrase others' ideas using terms and style choices that will resonate more effectively within the disciplinary or publication context in which they are writing. Or, writers might paraphrase because a particular disciplinary or publication context typically avoids the use of quotes.

Visual evidence

Visual evidence appears in many forms throughout academic arguments across disciplines. Writers might include art, images, screenshots, reproductions, photographs, sketches, illustrations, or drawings as evidence for their arguments. Sometimes writers will focus on one particular perspective or component of a larger visual text to isolate smaller segments of evidence. Visual

Writer Insights

Why does personal experience help you convince others?

Living in Malaysia, my students come from different backgrounds, and most of them learn English as a second language. It isn't easy for them to express their thoughts in English, so in class I would show them my blog posts or Facebook posts where I write about my experiences in life or at work. Through my writing, I'd like to inspire them to write, starting with themselves and gradually about the people and things around them. A love for writing can be nurtured. Like a gardener tending to his plants, I am committed to unearth the writer within my students with tender loving care.

~Chiew yen Dwee, English Language Teacher,
Batu Pahat, Johor, Malaysia

evidence also appears in the form of material artifacts of various kinds. Archaeologists, cultural anthropologists, ecologists, and physicists might research material artifacts and garner evidence from them for their claims, conclusions, or assertions. Writers might then include reproductions of these artifacts in their arguments as evidence or curate an exhibition of some kind to accompany their arguments. Other frequently used forms of visual evidence include charts, tables, and graphs, which are often referred to as forms of data visualization.

When working with visual evidence, writers face several key decisions. These include what format to use for the evidence, where to position it within the text, and how to integrate it with the other modes of communication, such as the written, auditory, and/or verbal components, depending on the context. When visual elements serve as evidence for an argument, they are best integrated in substantive ways throughout the argument. Visual evidence can be challenging because writers might assume that their readers will automatically see in the visual component what seems so evident to themselves. However, people can see drastically different elements in even the same visual image. This means that as you use visual evidence, be sure to fully explicate it and integrate it carefully and rigorously in your text.

Data

Data might be best considered an umbrella concept referring to many different pieces of information. Technically, one might even argue that quotes, summary, paraphrases, and visual components constitute data. Data as evidence also overlap with visual evidence because writers often visualize their data in the form of charts, graphs, and tables. But in this case, as a category for evidence, *data* refers to any set of information consisting of individual pieces that a researcher analyzes, synthesizes, and draws from in order to provide evidence for an argument.

Data can be qualitative or quantitative. For instance, qualitative data gathered from a survey or interview might include the quotes that participants provide in response to the survey or interview questions. Other examples of qualitative data might include an ethnographer's field notes or an evolutionary anthropologist's observations during a field study. Data also often consist of pieces of information that are quantitative in nature or that can be easily and beneficially quantified. Data might emerge from the results of a series of experiments, or data can be gathered from the measurements recorded during a study.

Some researchers refer to enormous quantities of data as **big data**. Big data typically require processing through technology and through intricate algorithms for selecting a subset of the data. Researchers also sometimes refer to data by the term raw data or unprocessed data: the bits of information collected through research that have not yet been arranged, analyzed, or interpreted. Once the data appears as evidence within an argument, it then might be termed processed data. Although data might be a term used more frequently in some disciplines, such as those affiliated with technology or natural science, it refers to any sort of information and materials collected, curated, analyzed, and synthesized throughout many fields in order to provide the evidence from which writers draw conclusions, articulate positions, and generate arguments.

Personal evidence

There is considerable disagreement about the use of personal opinion or experience as evidence. Some disciplines rely more extensively on the use of personal perspective, others not at all. Some writing occasions also make more extensive use of the personal, such as in blogs or op-eds, which are forms of public scholarship and academic writing. The personal is also becoming more apparent in scholarly writing as well. Composition professor Candace Spigelman argues about the use of the personal in academic writing:

> Personal writing can do serious academic work; it can make rational arguments; it can merge appropriately with academic discourse. Indeed, this "blended genre" is starting to appear in...professional literature...Nevertheless, the problem of the personal remains controversial.

Interviews are another moment when the personal is relevant, as in historical writing or some social science inquiries. In one well-known example of the use of the personal related to food, documentary filmmaker Morgan Spurlock ate only McDonald's food for 30 days as research for his documentary film *Super Size Me*. Here's a quote from Spurlock citing personal evidence:

> [I]n only thirty days of eating nothing but McDonald's I gained twenty-four and a half pounds, my liver turned to fat and my cholesterol shot up sixty-five points. My body fat percentage went from eleven to eighteen percent, still below the national average of twenty-two percent for men and thirty percent for women. I nearly doubled my risk of coronary heart disease, making myself twice as likely to have heart failure. I felt depressed and exhausted most of the time, my mood swung on a dime and my sex life was non-existent. I craved this food more and more when I ate it and got massive headaches when I didn't.

From an example like Spurlock's, we learn three important caveats about the use of personal evidence.

Academic writers generally combine personal evidence with other forms of evidence in scholarly work. Because readers vary in their receptivity to personal evidence, it is likely best in most writing occasions to use personal evidence in conjunction with other evidence rather than as stand-alone evidence.

Moreover, personal evidence should be differentiated from personal opinion. Instead, personal evidence is drawn from experiences and generally appears as narrative accounts of

Transfer at Work

Disciplinary context and writing occasion impact the efficacy of personal evidence. Sociologist Pamela Davies notes that personal evidence and personal experience rarely appear in her field: "With regard to the knowledge base informing child and family social work, with few exceptions, ... the personal has been abstracted. There is scant evidence of the personal or emotive, even within parental perception studies" (749). Hypothesizing that personal evidence can contribute importantly to her research, Davies experiments with using personal evidence and then describes the difficulties she encountered (by actually using personal evidence!):

> One of my difficulties ... arose from my being unpractised in writing in the first person—writing as 'I'. [A]another difficulty concerned my desire to offer authoritative criminological and victimological analysis on the experience.... A third difficulty arose in my attempt to overcome my inexperience in writing as 'I' whilst establishing an academic critique. How could I combine the intuitive and the intellectual in one account and where should I try to publish and disseminate? Where should I and could I publish? What journal might I choose? Who were my target audience?" (746)

Davies' efforts therefore simultaneously show the potential value of personal evidence and the challenges that can emerge from trying to use personal evidence effectively and in accordance with disciplinary conventions and expectations.

experience. As we discussed in Chapter 8: Framing Arguments, academic writers do have personal opinions, and it is important to reflect on and acknowledge opinions in order to understand potential biases or assumptions. However, academic writers must ground any opinions in evidence-based research in order to construct arguments effectively.

Finally, disciplinary context matters immensely when dealing with personal evidence. While disciplinary context impacts many dimensions of academic writing, it bears particular impact on the use of personal evidence. Some disciplines rely heavily on personal evidence (cultural anthropology, history) and others nearly always exclude personal evidence (engineering, chemistry). As with all such elements of academic writing, it is best to familiarize yourself with the discourse conventions present in each writing occasion so you can be sure you are adhering to them or, if you are challenging them, that you are doing so deliberately rather than accidentally.

Write Now

What kinds of evidence have you used in your academic writing (quantitative, qualitative, popular, scholarly)? How have you presented evidence in your academic writing (quotes, paraphrase, summary, visual, personal)? Are there any other kinds of evidence you have used? Which kinds do you find it easier to work with? Harder to work with? Why?

Purposes for Integrating Evidence

Academic writers use evidence for a variety of purposes and often do so with multiple purposes in mind simultaneously. One of the most foundational purposes for integrating evidence speaks to the very nature of academic writing itself. Academic research and writing rely on evidence-based claims whereby writers articulate arguments and draw conclusions based on evidence gathered through research. Without evidence, academic writers would lack the capacity to generate arguments, much less convince or persuade others regarding those arguments.

Writers choose what evidence to integrate, and how best to do so, based on their purposes and goals for the project, as well as the disciplinary and publication contexts surrounding the writing occasion. Despite the wide variety of purposes that inform these choices, a transfer-based framework enables one to identify certain strategies for integrating evidence across diverse contexts, even as those strategies are also influenced and reshaped by those contexts. Generally speaking, academic writers across disciplines integrate evidence in order to accomplish the following broad goals affiliated with academic writing and research.

Substantiate and advance arguments

As discussed in Chapters 8 and 9, academic arguments emerge from evidence. Evidence enables academic writers to draw conclusions, develop claims, and adopt positions. Integrating evidence enables scholars to communicate effectively the research they have conducted, showing readers the raw or unprocessed material they have interpreted in order to arrive at their conclusions. A writer's line of inquiry, purpose, and the disciplinary and writing context all help determine which kinds of evidence writers choose to include and how they might best integrate that evidence into their texts.

Most evidence requires an introduction before it and an explication after it. Some sorts of evidence or significant content in a writing project will require more extensive introductions and explications, while other projects might lend themselves to less lengthy approaches. For instance, when you include a block quotation, you should aim to spend a proportionate amount of time explicating that block quote.

Writers will generally integrate evidence throughout the entire writing project, and will identify the need for evidence whenever making a claim, assertion, or assumption. The claim, the length of the writing project, and the writer's purpose will also determine the amount and scope of evidence to include. These choices about integrating evidence will impact how successfully you persuade and inform the readers of your argument.

Build on, challenge, critique, or respond to others' evidence

Sometimes writers integrate (with proper attribution) evidence that other researchers have already collected, analyzed, or compiled. In these cases, writers will be doing so in order to make their own contributions based on that evidence. Writers might find they want to apply, extend, challenge, or otherwise respond to the evidence another writer has used. Sometimes a writer might show how that evidence can be interpreted differently, or the writer can demonstrate how that evidence leads to a different conclusion. Sometimes writers might include evidence from two or more different studies as a way of demonstrating unique connections among evidence across contexts. In these ways, a writer is essentially repurposing evidence from others.

Academic writers also use others' evidence to show that their own work exists within, alongside, and against prior scholarship about an issue or concept. By connecting their work to ongoing conversations and demonstrating those connections through evidence, writers can better advance knowledge. Situating one's own work within the work of others might also enable writers to demonstrate the significance of their research, showing that their research addresses important questions and concerns shared by others. Any instance of integrating evidence that others have used requires accurate citation and attribution in accordance with disciplinary and publication conventions.

Infuse credibility and authority

While personal opinion and personal experience can participate in academic writing in some disciplines, scholars more often use evidence from their research and that of others in order to infuse credibility and authority into their writing. Integrating evidence affords writers a way to show they have considered the work of established and respected scholars and thereby borrow this credibility as well.

The credibility of one's evidence is critical. Determining what makes evidence credible, though, hinges on writing context. If you are writing about the popular history and reception of a novel, for example, then posts to an online forum from the general public would constitute credible evidence. If, however, you are writing about hydroelectric development projects, then credible evidence will be found in government reports and scholarly, peer-reviewed research, though perhaps also alongside posts to an online forum. Credibility is also sometimes connected to how recently research has been published or presented. Some fields develop knowledge rapidly, and writers are expected to integrate evidence that is as current as possible—for many disciplines, this means published within the past one to three years. This notion of currency, though, changes with longer-term studies. Many disciplines also make use of historical evidence, and the evidence in this case becomes credible if it emerges from the appropriate historical context under consideration.

Add variety

Integrating evidence enables academic writers to add variety to their writing. If, for example, a text is primarily composed of prose, a writer can add variety by including evidence in the form of quantitative data. Depending on how this quantitative data appears, this evidence might also perhaps add visual components through data visualization. Similarly, a writer developing a text can infuse variety into that text by adding quotes, summaries, and paraphrases from the work of others. Any quotes that a writer includes, therefore, will not only serve as evidence for the argument, but will also add stylistic variety and diversity of ideas to a particular writing project. Evidence in the form of poetry or images can also add variety to one's writing, as appropriate for disciplinary and publication context.

Adding variety to one's writing enables a text to become more dynamic and engaging for readers. When texts are too static and monotonous, readers can get bored or lose interest. This may detract from their ability to focus on your arguments. Adding variety, though, also has the advantage of expanding perspective. Sometimes different forms of evidence can impact the perspectives through which we understand an idea, text, or issue.

Questions that Shape Integration of Evidence

Each writing occasion offers its own particular demands for integrating evidence. This discussion of questions builds on the questions provided in prior chapters, especially for how to critically read, how to analyze, how to synthesize, and how to summarize.

All of these strategies together enable academic writers to make sense of their data and research. Integrating it into a particular writing project requires another set of related strategies.

Elements of context that help determine the answers to effective integration of evidence include your primary questions, your arguments, disciplinary context, publication context, and other matters of the rhetorical triangle described in Chapter 4: Reading (purpose, audience, author). Integrating data effectively into your own work will involve your asking and considering certain questions for each particular writing project.

TABLE 11.1 Questions that shape integration of evidence.

Choose effective evidence	Does your research warrant qualitative evidence, quantitative evidence, or a mixture? Should you draw evidence from scholarly sources, popular sources, or public scholarship? Should your evidence include images, charts, tables, or graphics? When should you use block quotes, short quotes, paraphrase, or summary? What sorts of evidence do other writers in the field and/or publication context in which you are writing tend to use?
Explicate evidence sufficiently	How much explanation should you provide for your evidence? What do readers need to understand in order to fully appreciate how evidence is working to substantiate a claim? How might you most clearly explicate evidence so that readers will be unlikely to misinterpret or misunderstand it? What do you hope the evidence accomplishes, and how can you help readers see those aims?
Locate evidence appropriately	At which junctures in your argument will you need evidence? Where are you making claims or assertions? How do you differentiate between assertions considered to be common knowledge and claims that require evidence?
Determine appropriate amount of evidence	How much evidence do you need to include in the writing project? Is the writing occasion public, popular, or scholarly in nature? How many claims are you making? How much evidence do you need for each claim?

continued on next page

Choose credible evidence	How credible is your evidence? What do other writers and readers in this disciplinary context perceive as credible evidence? What evidence will readers be most likely to consider credible in this publication context?
Choose current and/ or time appropriate evidence	How recent should your evidence be? Should it all be from within the past five years? If you are using historical evidence, does that evidence emerge from the appropriate historical context?
Balance integration of evidence	Do you have an appropriate balance of evidence across your writing project? Is evidence clustered too extensively in one section of the writing project, or do you include evidence throughout the writing project? Have you created an effective ratio between evidence, explication, and your own arguments? Will readers be able to discern with relative ease which portions of your essay are evidence, which are explication, and which are your own contributions based on that evidence?

Criteria for Effectively Integrating Evidence

As with criteria in the other aspects of academic writing across disciplines, what makes effective integration of evidence in one writing context does not necessarily map onto all writing contexts. The National Council of Teachers of English describes the ways in which disciplines impact the efficacy of integrating evidence in a policy brief:

> [T]he assessment of whether evidence "counts" also depends upon how a writer uses evidence to support an argument. Writers carefully select evidence based on their chosen stance, purpose, and audience. Then writers use their chosen evidence to warrant, or justify, their stance. In literary analysis, for example, evidence from a literary text counts when citations include specific details that support a particular argument about the literature and when the writer sufficiently connects the textual evidence with his or her stance. In historical writing, too, determining the quality of evidence is equally about how well the writer analyzes and interprets its significance.

Thus, what counts or what is effective in one context does not necessarily apply to all contexts. Still, although disciplines and writing projects vary widely in the kinds of evidence used and the way that evidence should be integrated, it is possible to identify some important criteria for effectively integrating evidence.

Use evidence accurately

While it's perfectly fine to include only portions of evidence (and in fact we must always make these choices), the portions we include should not be taken out of context. As indicated

Transfer at Work

Methods for data collection and analysis also impact data accuracy. Danielle A. Becker and Lauren Yannotta conducted a usability study for an academic library website, learning that a newly designed website gave users more success performing a number of tasks:

Table 1. Percent of Tasks Answered Correctly

Task	Old Site	New Site
Find a book using online library catalog	80%	86%
Find library hours	100%	100%
Get help from a librarian using QuestionPoint	40%	93%
Find a journal article	20%	66%
Find reference materials	0%	7%
Find journals by title	40%	66%
Find circulation policies	60%	53%
Find books on reserve	80%	73%
Find magazines by title	0%	73%
Find the library staff contact information	60%	100%
Find contact information for the branch libraries	40%	100%

Studies such as this must follow rigorous methods in order to ensure accurate data. Jennifer Emanuel argues in "Usability Testing in Libraries," for instance, that those conducting usability studies must be aware of and address potential limitations. According to Emanuel, these limitations include a lack of resources, such as time, human capital, financial support and research skills to adequately analyze data or use multiple methods for triangulation. Emanuel also argues that usability studies can yield inaccurate data due to difficulties defining and obtaining a representative sample for one's study population. And, Emanuel argues that other potential limitations with usability studies involve different personalities of researchers that can include possible biases or assumptions that impact study design or analysis: "Researchers who are more attentive and reflective about the research process and data collection tend to be better usability testers than those who want immediate research results and want to be able to fix problems immediately" (210).

in Chapter 5: Summary, imagine that the author of the evidence is reading your work. Would he or she agree that you have accurately represented the evidence? If someone examined your entire data set, would that individual agree that you have, to the extent possible, accurately represented your evidence? Accuracy means you have attributed the evidence appropriately and cited it correctly. Accuracy also means you have not ignored counterevidence or other data that would work against conclusions.

Accuracy of evidence is particularly important because readers rely on your conclusions and arguments by assuming your evidence is correct. Some disciplines, such as science, emphasize the fundamental importance of accuracy in relation to evidence:

> Falsification in science is loosely defined as publishing or reporting misleading facts associated with a study, research or experimentation. Scientific falsification can be considered as: Falsifying data; Falsifying evidence; Fabricating data; Fabricating evidence; Plagiarism. ("Scientific Falsification")

After explaining more about each of these types of evidence falsification and citing some well-known cases of falsified evidence, the authors of this article offer an injunction against inaccuracy in scientific evidence: "Scientific falsification goes against everything that the scientific method stands for. It is unethical, immoral and dangerous. It is one of the worst acts that anyone in research can commit. It is severely punished."

Select evidence appropriately

Even as we accurately portray evidence, writers must also appropriately select it. We do this by selecting which evidence to include based explicitly on writing goals. A discussion about popular diet plans in the United States, for example, would benefit from including evidence in the form of both scholarly and popular sources to illustrate how much consumer research goes into the creation of diet fads. Such a study would have to especially consider which forms of visual evidence will be most impactful; the writer may have to choose between analysis of advertisements or nutritional science graphs, depending on the study's goal.

Analyze evidence sufficiently

Writers must analyze their evidence thoroughly and with methods that are appropriate to the disciplinary context and writing occasion. Valid arguments, claims, and positions rely on rigorous evidence of analysis through sound methods. Incomplete or inadequate analysis will lead researchers to jump to conclusions hastily and may contribute to logical fallacies and erroneous claims. Repeating and conducting analysis over time will further contribute to the thoroughness with which a writer's work is regarded. Researchers should choose a frame or method for analysis that others in the field accept as valid, and they should carry out that analysis with scrupulous attention to detail.

Much analysis relies on interpretation and inference, so thorough analysis does not necessarily mean that all researchers conducting the same analysis must draw the same conclusions. One portion of evidence can lead to disagreement and debate. But, thorough analysis means that you have, to the best of your ability, awarded full attention and care to the data and evidence before you. This can mean you have analyzed a subset of the evidence, rather than every single part of it. But you should select that subset in such a way that you can then justify how you made that selection.

Distinguish evidence from opinion

Academic writers certainly have opinions, but their arguments are generated with research-based evidence. Historian Elizabeth Shown Mills, for instance, describes the rigor that historians use as they work with evidence and why it matters:

> As history researchers, we do not speculate. We test. We critically observe and carefully record. Then we weigh the accumulated evidence, analyzing the individual parts as well as the whole, without favoring any theory. Bias, ego, ideology, patronage, prejudice, pride, or shame cannot shape our decisions as we appraise

our evidence. To do so is to warp reality and deny ourselves the understanding of the past that is, after all, the reason for our labor.

Mills's point is that historians, and researchers from other disciplines, must use critical observation, analysis, and synthesis as they consider evidence. Otherwise, they run the risk of treating evidence erroneously. While all humans have opinions, biases, and subjective perspectives, researchers must try as much as possible to differentiate these from the evidence they are using and be transparent about their own agendas, assumptions, and perspectives.

Contextualize evidence

As much as possible, sandwich your evidence in such a way that readers understand where your evidence is coming from and what the important elements of context are for that evidence. Introduce evidence clearly with what is called a "signal phrase." The Writing across the Curriculum program at Loyola University New Orleans describes signal phrases:

> Effective use of quotations requires that you include quotations in your paper in a way that allows the reader to understand the relevance of the quoted material to your own argument. You should never drop a quotation into your paper unannounced and apparently unrelated to the ideas around it. The quotation must always be embedded into one of your own sentences.

A common way to do this is to use a signal phrase that incorporates the quotation smoothly into your writing and, just as importantly, provides context for the material. Very often a signal phrase will also name the author of the quoted material, thus serving at once to include the quotation smoothly and to attribute the idea to its source ("Quotations").

Although the guidelines above connect signal phrases explicitly to quotations, embedding evidence in this way applies to academic writing more broadly. Paraphrase, summary, and visual evidence also benefit from an introduction and description of relevance when included in a writing project.

Relate evidence to writing purpose

Evidence must be related to the overall aims and purpose of your writing project. This connection is termed "warrant" under Toulmin's conceptualization of claims, as discussed in Chapter 9: Constructing Arguments. Different writing occasions demand varying approaches to evidence, but in general, academic writers must work to explicitly connect evidence through explication, analysis, synthesis, or other interpretation. While it might on occasion be reasonable to add an image or visual without explicitly referring to it, most other forms of evidence (quotes, paraphrase, summary, tables, charts, figures, etc.) must be discussed explicitly as they are integrated into a writing project. Sometimes this means that sources should be recent, sometimes historical.

Attend to discipline and context

Different writing occasions carry different discourse conventions. In scientific papers, for instance, readers are not accustomed to seeing large amounts of quoted text. Similarly, in the humanities, readers might be less familiar with tables and graphs. Neither occasion excludes the use of these, but writers should be aware of the discourse conventions that define the particular writing occasion.

Publication context also impacts the evidence writers use and the ways in which that evidence is integrated. If you are seeking publication in a scholarly journal, you should integrate scholarly evidence, even if you also use personal or popular evidence. By contrast, if you are instead writing a blog post, you might be more authorized to rely exclusively on personal experience. Being aware of discipline-specific and context-specific criteria, however, does not mean that one cannot sometimes challenge convention. Some of the most exciting scholarship is that which brings in new and different kinds of evidence to a question that has previously been primarily addressed through a different angle. Often, though, those who challenge conventions in these ways do so explicitly and by addressing why the other, more discipline-specific and context-specific kinds of evidence have limitations.

Vary evidence appropriately

Most writing projects benefit from a multipronged approach to evidence. Some writers find that their arguments naturally call for a variety of different sorts of evidence, including visual, written, and quantitative forms. In sociology, for instance, a writer might include summary and paraphrase while reviewing the literature, quotes for illustrating a few key concepts, and then charts and tables with quantitative evidence to depict aggregated data. Each different type of evidence will bring a new perspective to bear on the research questions. Even those working primarily with written evidence can still achieve variety by including written evidence in varied ways: some block quotes, some shorter quotes, some summaries, and some paraphrases. Varying evidence also refers to varying the ways in which writers integrate evidence. Writers can aim for introducing quotes, for example, with a colon, a comma, or by embedding quotes directly within sentences. Writers using visual evidence can choose to integrate charts in varying positions as well throughout a document.

Varying evidence in these ways, through form and integration, makes a reading experience more amenable to readers in terms of maintaining their engagement. Varying evidence also expands the likelihood that more of your readers, each of whom have varying strengths and preferences, will be able to grapple deeply with your evidence. Readers who are more visually oriented, for instance, can appreciate visual evidence and use that evidence to understand your argument. Readers who have more facility with quantitative evidence are better equipped to approach arguments through quantitative evidence. Varying evidence enables writers to accommodate a wider range of reader strengths and preferences and, therefore, to increase the potential reach of their arguments to a wider range of people.

Manage ratio between evidence, explication, and argument

Different writing occasions warrant different ratios between evidence, explication, and a writer's own contributions around that evidence in the form of an argument. Some popular contexts for writing require much greater inclusion of argument, very little evidence, and perhaps almost no explication of that evidence. More scholarly contexts might warrant an equal balance among the three. If you include too much evidence and explication at the expense of space for your own argument, then readers might not be able to fully appreciate your contributions. Alternatively, if you include only evidence and argument but do not effectively explicate that evidence, then readers might not see the connections between the evidence and the argument. A writing project that avoids inclusion of evidence but includes copious explication and argument prevents readers from having the opportunity to work with the evidence themselves.

As important as it is to manage an appropriate ratio between evidence, explication, and argument, it is also of critical importance to help readers differentiate among these as well. Will readers be able to discern with relative ease which portions of your essay are evidence, which constitute explication, and which comprise your own contributions based on that evidence? Blurring the distinctions between your evidence, explication, and argument may prevent readers from being able to recognize your contributions and process your ideas. To emphasize the elements that comprise your argument, writers can use signposts in their sentences, such as, "This evidence yields…" "The evidence suggests…" or "The evidence indicates…" These sorts of signposts will help readers navigate through your text and recognize the moments when your argument about the evidence is emerging.

Ensure credibility

Often, the writing context will dictate what is or is not credible evidence for a particular writing project. Sometimes personal anecdotes and opinions, on the part of the writer or from his or her research, are credible. Other times, writers need to rely on scholarly evidence that is deemed credible in that it has been published in a peer-reviewed journal or conducted with research methodologies that are valid. Much has been said about the credibility of online sources. Attempting to generate a global argument about whether online sources are credible is complicated by the question of what constitutes online sources: online research databases? blogs? online newspapers? Wikipedia? It might be more fitting, therefore, to suggest that writing occasion dictates credibility. Read the texts of others who have published in your field, and look to see what sources they have deemed credible for their research. It's fine to depart from convention, but always do so with full knowledge that you are making a departure, and explain why you are doing so.

Featured Strategy for Integrating Evidence: the MEAL Plan

Because integrating evidence can be so challenging, involving so may different choices and criteria, writers can benefit from considering structures that aid in these efforts. One such strategy for integrating evidence is a concept referred to by many writing centers with the acronym MEAL, or, more colloquially, as the **MEAL plan**. The MEAL plan provides a way of organizing paragraphs with evidence. While the MEAL plan works particularly well with text-based evidence, it can also be adapted to include visual and quantitative forms of evidence. It's especially well suited for scholarly contexts that carry the expectation of full integration of evidence, explication, and argument. This structure ensures that writers keep evidence focused, introduce evidence, explicate it, and then show how the evidence supports the main argument. The MEAL plan consists of a recommended order for writers to present the following four components of each paragraph: the Main Idea, Evidence, Analysis, and Link.

M: Main idea

The main idea is the focus of the paragraph. Paragraphs generally have one main idea in order to be considered unified. Paragraphs might be thought of as individual, perfectly proportioned bites of food—enough to chew on and enjoy, and not so much as to be overwhelming or so little as to be frustrating. If a writer puts too many ideas in a paragraph, then readers have a difficult time processing the information. If a writer has one main idea but hasn't explored that idea effectively, then a reader may be left feeling dissatisfied and the argument will not be sufficiently advanced.

E: Evidence

Evidence in the MEAL plan appears directly after the main idea. This would entail the moment that a writer would include a quote or a chart, or, if the evidence is located separately from the paragraph, the moment where a writer would refer to an image or table. Placing evidence at this juncture, as the second component of a paragraph, emphasizes that readers expect evidence directly after a main idea or claim. If the main idea offers the organizing focus for the paragraph, then readers right away will be interested in seeing evidence about that idea. The evidence section of the paragraph also includes the writer sufficiently introducing and framing the evidence so readers understand where the evidence comes from and what the evidence is.

A: Analysis

Because one cannot expect all readers to automatically notice what you want them to notice from evidence, the third section of the MEAL plan involves analysis. Analyzing the evidence, otherwise known as explicating it, enables writers to point out what is significant or compelling about the evidence. Writers can direct attention to certain facets or features of the evidence. Through analysis, writers offer their interpretation of the evidence. The strategies writers use for analyzing the evidence should be appropriate for the disciplinary context and the writing occasion in which they are writing. And, because this analysis occurs within the same paragraph, as has already been established, that analysis should be moving toward the same main idea that has opened the paragraph.

L: Link

As the fourth and final component of the MEAL plan, the link invites writers to connect the evidence and analysis to the main idea of the paragraph and, more broadly, to the main idea of the larger writing project. All evidence in a writing project should work in the service of the larger point, and so the link section offers writers an opportunity to explicitly demonstrate how their evidence advances their arguments. Its placement as the fourth element in the paragraph works well because it in some ways offers circularity, a return to the main idea. In linking the evidence and analysis to the main idea and main claim, writers will by necessity remind readers of the overarching purpose of the paragraph and how that paragraph connects to the larger argument. The link component also works well as the final element because it signals the completion of one stage of the argument, paving the way for a new paragraph to further develop or advance the argument.

As with many writing guidelines, strategies such as the MEAL plan are meant to be a beginning structure writers can further develop to fit their own purposes and writing projects. Sometimes, paragraphs have one primary piece of evidence, sometimes multiple; sometimes the analysis and the link are combined. And sometimes several paragraphs in a row will have the same main idea. Some writers will also opt to include in their writing on occasion a paragraph that consists entirely of only one main idea and nothing else. Doing so can, at times and when done so sparingly, be effective at drawing readers' attention to that idea.

One aspect that might usefully be added to MEAL is a transition at the beginning of a paragraph, rendering our acronym, more fittingly, T-MEAL. Transition sentences, the first sentence of a paragraph must accomplish several critical aims: to move the reader from what was discussed in the prior paragraph to what is coming in the new paragraph, to provide a topic sentence or overview of the new paragraph, and to connect the new paragraph to the larger claim of the writing project so readers can see how the paragraph is advancing the argument.

As an example of the T-MEAL plan, please see the third paragraph of Example 1, which includes annotations according to T-MEAL.

Examples of Integrating Evidence

This section provides examples of integrating evidence across disciplines. Since evidence is in so many ways like food, it seems apropos to use food as the multidisciplinary anchor to show how academic writers across disciplines select and integrate evidence for their arguments about food. This section contains examples from seven different disciplines.

Example 1: History

The excerpt comes from an article in a peer-reviewed scholarly journal about the use of taste in historical research. The authors, Gerald J. Fitzgerald and Gabriella M. Petrick, make the argument that taste helps historians understand culture. The paragraphs show Fitzgerald and Petrick integrating evidence from a variety of sources: primary historical sources and scholarly secondary sources. You will see them also using a variety of formats for their evidence, from block quotes to paraphrase and summary.

Excerpt from "In Good Taste: Rethinking American History with Our Palates"
by G. J. Fitzgerald and G. M. Petrick

Fitzgerald and Petrick here introduce a primary source: Fisher. They provide her full name and her book title as part of their signal phrase. They also show that they are integrating Fisher in order to illustrate their point about how food writing can "spark gustatory imaginations."

Good food writing can make the mouth water, the nose tingle, and the stomach growl. It invites readers to reconstruct a dish or a meal so that they may reflect on or imagine its taste, flavor, and texture. M. F. K. Fisher is probably the best known of the literary gourmands who helped spark gustatory imaginations and linked words to taste. In her book *An Alphabet for Gourmets*, she evokes the essence of a pea. "I watched the head-waiter, as skilled as a magician, dry peas over a flame in a generous pan, add what looked like an equal weight of butter, which almost visibly sent out a cloud of sweet-smelling hay and meadow air." In describing her own perfect garden peas she wrote,

Notice that the authors choose to include one quote that is shorter and a block quote as well. They have inserted ellipses in the text, which indicate that they are omitting certain words that are less relevant for their point. Even though they have omitted words, they have not taken the quote out of context or misrepresented the quote.

> Small brown roasted chickens, the best ones I have ever eaten, done for me that afternoon...and not chilled since but cooled in their own intangibly delicate juices. There was salad of mountain lettuces. There was honest bread.... But what really mattered, what piped the high unforgettable tune of perfection, were the peas, which came from their hot pot onto our thick china plates in a cloud, a kind of miasma, of everything anyone could ever want from them, even in a dream.[1]

After the quote, the authors explicate the words, highlighting for readers the exact parts of the quote that offer evidence for their claim. Notice that the quote itself is shorter than the explication of the quote.

What is striking about Fisher's work is that she not only places the reader at the table with her, but engages all the reader's senses to evoke taste. To convey the perfection of the peas, she relies on the readers' previous experiences with the foods (and their imagination of what they could be), conjuring the sensuality of peas freshly picked from the garden, cooked for only the briefest moment in boiling water, and brought steaming to the table with all their vegetal sweetness bursting in our mouths. Although only Fisher and her table mates actually tasted the peas and knew the delight they brought and

From *The Journal of American History* (95.2), 2008.

while her description assumes a universal experience with taste that is unlikely to exist, her vivid descriptions and attention to flavor can evoke a simulacra of the peas based on readers' previous experiences, especially if those readers share a common gustatory heritage. Rather than arguing for some universal or a historical sense of taste, we are suggesting that reading and writing with a sense of taste, one that is both sensitive to context and experience and also infused with historical imagination, can help historians think through the contingent nature of taste and its historical meanings.

Transition and Main Idea: The phrase "historians of food and taste" forges a transition from the prior paragraph; the phrase "previous gastronomic experiences" both provides a topic sentence for the paragraph and serves as the paragraph's main idea.

As historians of food and taste, we find that we depend on our previous gastronomic experiences to try to taste the past. Whether we are reading a grandmother's cryptic recipes, a technical paper, a cookbook, tasting panel notes, or a dietary survey, when it comes to food, we try to taste it in our minds if we can, and sometimes one of us, Gabriella M. Petrick, even prepares foods to give us a better understanding of the techniques used to produce them and of their flavor.... Tasting allows historians to place the sensory experience in historical context and to utilize an often-ignored analytical tool: the body's senses. Just as historians of art or music use their senses to analyze material, so too can historians of food and taste.

Evidence: This list of details serves as the evidence for the paragraph, along with the evidence of Petrick preparing food.

Analysis: The writers now analyze the evidence, discussing what the tasting affords them as scholars.

Link: Lastly, the writers provide the link here, linking the evidence to their overall claim and to the paragraphs' main idea.

However, using the sense of taste to investigate the past has its limits (we will never know what Fisher's peas really tasted like), but exercising historical imagination while attending to how people described past flavor experiences can help us approximate the nature of taste historically.[2]

In short, to understand a culture, past or present, we should endeavor to understand how a society feeds itself. It is the ubiquity and everydayness of eating that makes understanding it historically so important. The taste and flavor of food play an important part in social relationships, and a food's taste can embody meanings well beyond what is put into the mouth. It is only within the past ten years or so that food history—and the access it allows us to the history of taste—has become a field of inquiry. Many of the

Here the authors summarize the relevant literature that is mentioned again in a footnote at the end of the text. The sentence makes a claim about pre-1990s histories, and the footnote provides evidence for that claim.

Because the authors are building on Mintz's work more deliberately than on the work of the other scholars they mention, they take time to quote his argument.

books written before the 1990s were popular histories tracing the origins and dissemination of dining rituals, culinary traditions, and foodstuffs.[3] Historians who wrote academic texts about food in the 1980s, including Sidney W. Mintz, Harvey A. Levenstein, and Warren J. Belasco, asked complex questions about food's relationship to industrialization. In *Sweetness and Power*, Mintz explored the nexus between the metropolis and the colony through Britain's desire for sweetness. By focusing on sugar as an export commodity, Mintz examined how political and economic power was wielded in interactions between the colonial West Indies and Britain from the seventeenth to the nineteenth centuries. According to Mintz, the rise of the British factory system reinforced Caribbean sugar production. He explained that "cheaper sugar came at a time when its increased consumption was guaranteed not by the sugar habit itself, but by the factory world and machine rhythms which were the background of its use." Mintz concluded that readily accessible cheap calories (in the form of sugar) fueled industrial economies. Furthermore, this proliferation of sweetness ultimately transferred control over the foods workers ate to large corporations, thus transforming not only the British working-class diet but also the country's palate by separating the source of food production from the locus of its consumption.

[1] M. F. K. Fisher, *An Alphabet for Gourmets* (New York, 1949), 135, 138-39.
[2] For a critical examination of sensory history, see Mark M. Smith, "Producing Sense, Consuming Sense, Making Sense: Perils and Prospects for Sensory History," *Journal of Social History*, 40 (Summer 2007), 841-58.
[3] Good examples of the pre-1990 popular literature are Margaret Visser, *Much Depends on Dinner: The Extraordinary History and Mythology, Allure and Obsessions, Perils and Taboos of an Ordinary Meal* (Toronto, 1986); and Reay Tannahill, *Food in History* (New York, 1973). Notable popular food histories from the early 1990s include Raymond Sokolov, *Why We Eat What We Eat: How the Encounter between the New World and the Old Changed the Way Everyone on the Planet Eats* (New York, 1991); and Martin Elkort, *The Secret Life of Food: A Feast of Food and Drink in History, Folklore, and Fact* (Los Angeles, 1991).

Write Now

Fitzgerald and Petrick, like many academic writers, use footnotes in multiple ways. In the example, readers see them using footnotes as a form of citation (see Chapter 12) as well as a space to provide additional scholarship for readers to consider. Reflect on your experiences encountering footnotes. Do you often read them? Under what circumstances are you more or less inclined to read them? What kinds of readers do you think are interested in reading particular footnotes?

Example 2: Biology

The excerpt comes from an article in a peer-reviewed scholarly journal that is investigating the question, "What causes food hoarding in animals?" The authors have written a review of the literature, a synthesis of prior research, in order "to integrate what is known about the neuroendocrine mechanisms" related to food hoarding and food foraging. They make use of several published secondary scholarly sources and, in keeping with the purpose of a historical review of scholarly literature, they begin with sources that are from earlier in the twentieth century.

Excerpt from "Physiological Mechanisms for Food-Hoarding Motivation in Animals" by E. Keen Rhinehart, M. J. Dailey, and T. Bartness

> Since Wallace Craig is the person who has initiated the field of inquiry, the authors devote more space to his work, not only summarizing it, but also outlining several of his contributions.

Ingestive behaviour has a long history of study and currently has a place in the fields of animal behaviour, learning and memory, psychology, physiology and neuroscience. In 1918, Wallace Craig, an animal behaviourist, coined the terms 'appetitive' and 'consummatory' for the two-part sequence of behaviours required for eating, drinking and reproduction (Craig 1918). More specifically, he defined appetitive behaviours as motivated, species-specific behaviours involved in seeking a goal object (e.g., food, water, a mate), ultimately bringing the animal into physical contact with the goal object (Craig 1918). By contrast, the consummatory behaviours (from consummate not consume) are reflexive, stereotyped and are the final act once the goal object has been obtained (Craig 1918), in the case of ingestive consummatory behaviour—eating.

The primary purpose of this review is to focus on the appetitive ingestive behaviour of food hoarding, and to a lesser extent, food foraging, and attempt to integrate what is known about the neuroendocrine mechanisms controlling these behaviours.... More specifically, we will focus our review on the offspring of wild trapped animals that are considered 'natural food hoarders' because they are documented hoarders in nature, but

> In this series of sentences, the authors cite prior studies that have researched various kinds of animals, such as the five studies of laboratory rats cited here.

have been studied in the laboratory, such as Syrian hamsters (Mesocricetusauratus; Murphy 1985) and Siberian hamsters (Phodopus sungorus). Occasionally, we will supplement this information with studies of laboratory rats, which are not natural hoarders (Pisano &

From *Philosophical Transactions: Biological Sciences* (365), 2010.

Storer 1948; Calhoun 1962; Lore & Flannelly 1978; Takahashi & Lore 1980; Whishaw & Whishaw 1996), but instead carry food from the source to a safe place to eat. A paper by Wolfe in 1939 opened the door to the laboratory study of food hoarding by demonstrating that it was quantifiable. Several years later, Morgan et al. (1943) generated a 'deficit hypothesis' that continues to guide many hoarding studies today. The deficit hypothesis proposes that animals hoard owing to a growing energetic deficit that eventually reaches a threshold that triggers food hoarding (Morgan, Stellar & Johnson 1943).

> As earlier in the excerpt, when the authors refer to a groundbreaking study, they spend more space introducing the study directly in the text and summarizing in more detail the research.

Example 3: International Development

This excerpt comes from a scholarly book that is investigating the question, "How [will we] feed a growing global population in the face of a wide range of adverse factors, including climate change?" In the excerpted section, Gordon Conway, a Professor of International Development at Imperial College London, is examining what hunger is and how it is calculated. Specifically, he is discussing the spike in food costs from 2007-08. He cites the work of Anthony Young, who has critiqued data that suggests arable land is increasing. Notice also how Conway integrates visual evidence into his argument, positioning it alongside his own ideas and explicating it carefully for readers.

Excerpt from *One Billion Hungry: Can We Feed the World?* by G. Conway

> Conway is building on the work of Young, showing that, like Young, he believes the earlier estimates about the growth of cultivable land are in error.

Yet these [data about expansions in arable land and crops] seem to be overestimates. The results have been trenchantly criticized by Anthony Young, who has a long and extensive experience of soil and land surveys.[58] He believes the estimates suffer from the following flaws:

- Overestimation of cultivable land (not accounting for features such as hills and rock outcrops when the maps are reduced in scale)
- Underestimation of presently cultivated land (illegal land occupation; e.g., forest incursions, not recorded)
- Failure to take sufficient account of land required for purposes other than cultivation (underestimates of human settlements and industrial use)

From *One Billion Hungry: Can We Feed the World?*, 2012.

A more recent [Food and Agriculture Organization of the United Nations (FAO)] analysis in 2000 accepts these criticisms [about flawed estimates of cultivable land] as possibly valid and acknowledges that much of the cultivable but uncultivated land is under rainforest or needed for purposes such as grazing land and ecosystem services. [59]

> Here, Conway adds his own evidence to the evidence from Young, drawing on FAO reports.

Probably the most telling data is the area harvested over time. Total cropland has increased by only 10 percent over the past fifty years, while population has grown by 110 percent. [60] Given the pressures to increase food production, we would expect to see much greater land expansion if it were readily available. The only exceptions are for oil crops (Figure 1.7). Soybeans and oil palms have each increased by over 300 percent in area and by over 700 percent and over 1,400 percent, respectively, in production over the past fifty years. Presumably this is a result of clearing the Cerrado in Brazil and rainforests in the Amazon, Africa, and Southeast Asia. Permanent meadows and pastures (the land used to grow herbaceous forage crops) have increased somewhat, by nearly 9 percent in an area from 1961 to 2008. [61]

> In this paragraph, Conway continues to build the evidence he is using to show that cultivable land has not grown. He introduces the chart next.

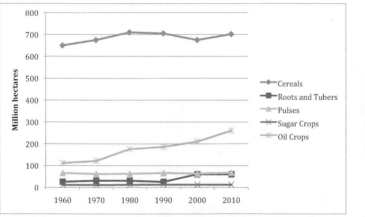

> Conway has preceded this chart with an explication of some of the figures, even explaining the one anomalous line.

Figure 1.7 Trends in harvested area for selected food crops, million hectares.[62]

> Following the chart, Conway continues to discuss the prospect of creating more cultivable land. What follows are the footnotes citing the sources Conway uses as evidence in this section.

More land could be brought into cultivation by clearing tropical rainforests, but this would be at the expense of biodiversity and would add considerably to greenhouse gas emissions.... A further factor in the equation is the large amount of land being degraded as a result of erosion, loss of fertility, and desertification.

[58] Young, A. 1994. *Land degradation in South Asia: Its severity, causes and effects upon people*. FAO World Soil Resources Report 78. Rome: FAO

Young, A. 1998. *Land resources: now and for the future*. Cambridge, UK: Cambridge University Press.

Young, A. 1999. "Is there really spare land? A critique of estimates of available cultivable land in developing countries." *Environment, Development and Sustainability* 1:3-18.

[59] FAO. 2000. World soil resources report 90. Land resource potential and constraints at regional and country levels. Based on the work of Bot, A., Nachtergaele, F., and Young, A. Rome: FAO

[60] Heldt, M. 2010. Science and innovation can help farmers meet global challenges. Presentation given at Investing in Science. London: Chatham House, 22 November

[61] FAO. 2009. Statistical yearbook, 2009. Rome: FAO

[62] FAO. 2010. FAOSTAT

Example 4: Engineering

The preceding example shows an author integrating a graphic and explicating it in detail. In Chapter 7: Analysis, we saw Anita Helle closely analyzing several photographs as evidence. Scholars also integrate evidence as a form of illustration, as in the example excerpted here, which is from an engineering article written by Parisa Pouladzadeh, Shervin Shirmohammadi, and Rana Al-Maghrabi. In this article, the authors are proposing a food imaging system that can use an image of food to identify how many calories and other nutritional elements are in the food. This is part of a larger inquiry into how technology and imaging can facilitate healthier living.

Excerpt from "Measuring Calorie and Nutrition From Food Image"
by P. Pouladzadeh, S. Shirmohammadi, and R. Al-Maghrabi

Fig. 6.   SVM module verifies with the user the type of foods it has determined [18].

In our proposed method,... the feature vectors of each food item, extracted during the segmentation phase, will be used as the training vectors of

The authors use the image as an example, or illustration, of how the interface will look to users. Demonstrating the interface as being user friendly and effective is key for the authors because this is a proposal argument. Notice that they refer to Fig. 6 in the text and describe it, so the image is a crucial component that works in concert with the text.

From *IEEE Transactions on Instrumentation and Measurement* (63.8), 2014.

SVM [Support Vector Machine]. For increasing the accuracy, after the SVM module has determined each food portion type, the system can optionally interact with the user to verify the kind of food portions.

For instance, it can show a picture of the food to the user, annotated with what it believes are the portion types, such as chicken, meat, vegetable, and so on, as…shown in Fig. 6. The user can then confirm or change the food type.…

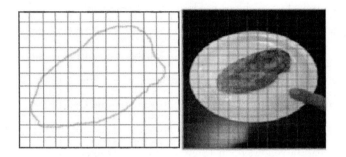

Fig. 7.   Methodology for food portion area measurement.

To calculate the surface area for a food portion, we propose to superimpose a grid of squares onto the image segment so that each square contains an equal number of pixels and, therefore, equal area. Fig. 7 shows an example with an actual food portion. The reason for using a grid is twofold. First, compared with other methods, the grid will more easily match with irregular shapes, which is important for food images because most of the food portions will be irregular.… Second, depending on the processing capabilities of the user's mobile device…, we can adjust the granularity of the grid…

Here too, the image plays a crucial role as a behind-the-scenes demonstration of the food-imaging system's grid methodology. Again, the authors refer directly to Fig. 7 in the text, so readers can toggle between reading the text and viewing the images. The images are also clearly labeled, though, so that readers can see which image is under discussion at a given moment in the text as well as to make it easier for readers who are interested only in the images to skim through the text.

Example 5: Literature/Women's Studies

The excerpt comes from a scholarly article that is investigating the question, "In what ways did community cookbooks shape and reflect cultural mores?" In the excerpt, Ferguson is conducting an analysis of a primary source, a community cookbook from 1878 in some depth, selecting particular portions of the text to provide evidence for her argument.

Excerpt from "Intensifying Taste, Intensifying Identity:
Collectivity Through Community Cookbooks" by K. Ferguson

Ferguson first outlines the claim that these community cookbooks "reinforce various class boundaries." Then Ferguson introduces in detail, with contextual information, the cookbook that will provide evidence for this claim.

One aspect of class difference is woven into the very egression and distribution of recipes. The sale of such cookbooks often served to raise funds for the impoverished and destitute, but the cookbooks themselves were aimed at those with the resources to make new, even unusual, foods (the main culinary attempts for which one needs direction). They thus create and reinforce various class boundaries, both in their purpose and in their instruction. One early community cookbook, written in 1878 not by a large community but by a committee of three women, epitomizes this ironic juxtaposition. Profits from *The Home Messenger Book of Tested Receipts,* the first page announces, benefited the Detroit Home of the Friendless. The authors warn, however, that in using the recipes, the lady of the house should "*stand by* her cook, to see that she follows them" (Steward, Sill, and Duffield 1878, ii, iv). [14]

The authors follow this with a notional dialogue:

Do you understand how to make muffins, Bridget?

I do that, mum. I makes illegant muffins; they're just as loight, as loight, etc. (iv)

This (conspicuously Irish) cook's muffins may be "loight," the authors warn, but this is likely because they are "poisoned with baking powder, and they taste like saw-dust and overeffervesced soda water" (iv). One must, they repeat, "stand by" one's cook to make sure she performs each step correctly; this, more than cooking itself, is the proper role of the lady of the house.

Ferguson explicates in the next two paragraphs the quoted material in depth to show readers how this evidence proves her claim.

What is being instructed, here? Not the cooking itself, although it is presumed that a supervisor should always be able to do the menial task being overseen. Instead, it is the proper way to engage and to assign one's servants—to keep them properly in line. Although this cookbook, like others of the time, is made up mostly of food recipes, these textual instructions are surrounded by a reticulation of authority and propriety; how to oversee and how to delegate are often presented as more important than how to cook.

[14] Italics in original. The title page also notes that the recipes therein apportion "TOTAL ABSTINENCE."
Stewart, Isabella G. D., Sally B. Sill, and Mary B. Duffield, comps. 1878. *The Home Messenger Book of Tested Receipts.* 2nd ed. Detroit: E. B. Smith.

From *Signs: Journal Of Women In Culture And Society* (37.3), 2012.

Example 6: Sustainability, Environmental Research Organization

The excerpt comes from a magazine article printed in a Worldwatch Institute publication and reposted on their website. Worldwatch Institute is an environmental research organization. Their mission statement as quoted on their website specifies their goals:

> Through research and outreach that inspire action, the Worldwatch Institute works to accelerate the transition to a sustainable world that meets human needs. The Institute's top mission objectives are universal access to renewable energy and nutritious food, expansion of environmentally sound jobs and development, transformation of cultures from consumerism to sustainability, and an early end to population growth through healthy and intentional childbearing.

This excerpted article investigates the question, "What is the Slow Food Movement and what is its impact?" Brian Halwell uses primarily personal evidence from his visit to a diner to help define Slow Food and why people adhere to it.

Excerpt from "The Argument for Local Food" by B. Halwell

Stop in at the Farmers Diner in Barre, Vermont, and you have landed in the middle of a revolution, although you might not see it at first glance.... Twelve green vinyl stools line the white linoleum countertop in this 60-seat eatery.... A pass-thru window to the kitchen frames the cooks as they flip omelettes and pancakes and push burnt bits of hash-browns and bacon towards the grill's gutter. Not too different from the original diner that opened in this long and narrow building 70 years ago.

The place has its early morning regulars—a retired farmer, a couple of state highway maintenance workers, electricians, plumbers, and other assorted craftsmen—who on this gray winter morning are already cradling their bulky white coffee mugs by 7 a.m. Booths are illuminated by 1930s style pendent lights....

Linger a bit longer, though, and you find that this isn't any ordinary diner. The milk in the blenders and dispenser is certified organic, which means the cows it came from weren't given shots of antibiotics, and weren't given feed grown with chemical fertilizers and pesticides. It's also from a local dairy, which means it didn't arrive in a tank truck from a place most of the folks in Barre have never seen.

From *World Watch Magazine* (16.3), 2003.

The eggs in the omelettes are local too. The berries and flour in the muffins and pies are from local berry patches and wheat fields. The diner cuts all its own French fries and grinds all its own hamburger meat—the beef too coming from local farms. In fact, while most of the food that Americans eat travels at least 1,500 miles from farm to plate, most of the food served in this place was grown within 50 miles, and Murphy's goal is 100 percent....

> Notice that because this is a popular publication, Halwell does not provide citations for his evidence about how far most of the "food that Americans eat travels."

I notice that the menu covers feature pictures of the farmers who supply the food. (Who would have thought that the food you eat in a restaurant could come from individual people?) The plastic place mat reads like a Who's Who of radical thought on the state of the modern food system, which is decidedly not about individually responsible people. I chuckle at the quote from Columbia University nutritionist and suburban homesteader Joan Gussow: "I prefer butter to margarine because I trust cows more than chemists." There is Wendell Berry's famous declaration that "eating is an agricultural act." And there's a quote from Murphy himself: "Think Locally, Act Neighborly." He tells me he won't hold it against anyone for acting or thinking globally, but it seems too complex to him. "Acting neighborly is something we know," he says.

> Halwell invokes the use of the personal voice here, using "I" and relaying his experience and conversations. Again, Halwell does not cite the quotes on the place mats because this is a popular publication format.

Write Now

Halwell's article makes use of personal evidence. What impact does the use of personal evidence have on you as a reader? What other kinds of evidence might Halwell need to include and integrate alongside (or instead of) the personal evidence in order to influence your perceptions about the Slow Food movement?

Example 7: Anthropology

Ethnography is a research methodology that is a subset of anthropology. As a discipline interested in individual cultures and their customs, personal evidence is often utilized as a component to ethnographers' research. Ethnographer Brian Hoey describes the ways in which ethnographers use personal evidence as follows:

> Ethnographers generate understandings of culture through representation of what we call an emic perspective, or what might be described as the "insider's point of view." The emphasis in this representation is thus on allowing critical

categories and meanings to emerge from the ethnographic encounter rather than imposing these from existing models.

The excerpt comes from an article, an ethnography of Alaska, specifically of the Arctic National Wildlife Refuge. Ganapathy pursues the questions, "What is the role of place in culture?" and "What role does the Arctic Refuge play in understanding the culture of the people who engage with it?" Ganapathy discusses food as a particular aspect of her ethnography. Notice how Ganapathy blends personal evidence with critical perspective and other forms of scholarly secondary evidence.

Excerpt from "Imagining Alaska: Local and Translocal Engagements with Place" by S. Ganapathy

In August of 2010, during the course of fieldwork in the village of Vashraii K'oo, Alaska, I was casually speaking to Jeanie—a Gwich'in Athabascan woman whose family I was staying

> Ganapathy provides personal evidence in the form of a narrative anecdote about berry picking. Where she could have instead offered a statistic about how many blueberries are picked by Gwich'in Athabascan women, Ganapathy instead depicts the scene more vividly.

with—about our recent berry-picking endeavors.[1] On the previous day, I had joined Jeanie and four other women to pick wild blueberries from the expanses of tundra surrounding the village. To access the most productive patches, we arranged for someone to ferry us across an adjacent river and then hiked for about a mile over rough terrain, picking plump berries along the way. Jeanie and I chatted about the previous day's outing, our bountiful harvests as well as the unfortunate berry-picking injuries I had sustained: sore knees, achy ankles, and an eye nearly swollen shut from a poorly placed mosquito bite. Jeanie also recounted stories from her youth of berry picking and being out on the land and mentioned that she now tries to encourage young people in the village to maintain these activities....

This brief anecdote serves as a starting point to further examine the concepts of "space" and "place" as well as processes of place-making from afar—and, more specifically, to consider how "local" populations engage with places that are, in large part, translocally constituted. Alaska is an ideal location for examining concepts of space and place across multiple scales. For Native communities in Alaska, surrounding landscapes have long been imbued with cultural, spiritual, and economic significance (Catton 1997; Nelson 1973;

> Ganapathy uses the personal evidence as a way into formulating her claim, and she also begins to insert relevant secondary materials as additional evidence for how landscapes in Alaska hold "cultural, spiritual, and economic significance."

From *American Anthropologist* (115.1), 2013.

Peter 1981; Thornton 2008).... The Arctic Refuge is one case in point. Adjacent Native groups, specifically Gwich'in Athabascan communities located to the south and west of the refuge and Inupiaq Eskimo settlements along the northern coasts, have engaged with surrounding landscapes for millennia in the pursuit of customary subsistence activities, seasonal migrations, trade, and sociability (Burch 1998; Chance 1990; McKennan 1965; Nelson 1972, 1973; Peter 1981)....

The Arctic Refuge exemplifies a place of translocal contestation.... The Arctic Refuge is sometimes portrayed as "America's Serengeti" (evoking colonial fantasies of distant exotic landscapes) or a place that is "too special to drill." The Gwich'in are presented through essentializing (albeit strategic) tropes as one of the last surviving subsistence cultures, whose members depend on the Arctic Refuge for food, clothing, and meaning in their lives. These narrative framings of the Arctic Refuge and the Gwich'in circulate widely. For instance, while at a muliticulturalism festival in Stevens Point, Wisconsin, in May of 2011, I attended a featured lecture and photo presentation about a local resident's recent travels through the Arctic Refuge and his Arctic Refuge environmental activism. The striking images, descriptions of rugged landscape and encounters with bears, and portrayals of the Gwich'in as authentically traditional Native Americans captivated the attendees and enabled them to connect to a

> Ganapathy again draws on personal evidence to show how the Arctic Refuge is often framed as a place that the Gwich'in people rely on for "food, clothing, and meaning."

place and cause that would otherwise be well outside their frames of reference. Such narrative framings, in conjunction with extensive lobbying, have been successful in forestalling development for over 20 years.

[1] The majority of my ethnographic vignettes derive from fieldwork conducted in Alaska between 2005 and 2010....

Transferring Evidence

As with many aspects of academic writing, integrating evidence affords academic writers across disciplines a wide variety of choices. Prior chapters examined these choices from the perspective of argument—why we argue, how we argue, how we construct arguments, and how we design arguments. But even the most effective and confident decisions in these domains would be hampered without also making keen decisions regarding evidence.

Evidence, as with other aspects of argumentation, is also one of the most varied. Writers can choose from numerous potential sources for evidence, from data and visual images to prior scholarship, primary evidence, and personal evidence. Amid this great variety of options for what evidence to choose and how to integrate it, one habit evidence writers can transfer across writing occasions is to always base those decisions on careful discernment of what you are claiming, how you are structuring that argument, and the format you are using to shape that argument. Doing so will help your evidence be as effective as possible for the particular context in which you are currently arguing.

This consideration of how to choose and integrate evidence, though, would be incomplete without also examining the practicalities of how writers cite evidence. Citation practices, then, will be the area of focus for Chapter 12.

❧ ❧ ❧

Environmental Impact Study: *"Homestays in Korzak: Supplementing Rural Livelihoods and Supporting Green Tourism in the Indian Himalayas"* by Anupam Anand, Pankaj Chandan, and Ram Babu Singh

Transfer Points: Human Geography, Environmental Studies

As navigation systems and digital maps become increasingly sophisticated, it is easy to relate mapping primarily to computer science and computer engineering. Mapping, however, also involves significant social and political considerations. Maps of the world, for instance, used to feature Europe in the center and now more often feature Africa in the center, part of a larger re-orientation to how Westerners conceive of themselves in relationship to the rest of the world. Mapping congressional districts impacts voter turnout and representation, often along class and race dimensions. Mapping drives migration and spawns conflict, as in the creation of East and West Germany, the partitioning of India, and the establishment of Israel. Mapping also intersects with the environment, creating ownership of, or barring access to, water and natural resources, which can prove critical for health and economic sustenance.

These important concepts, with significant human consequences, sponsor much of the work in geography. Broadly conceived, geography can be divided into two primary subdisciplines: physical geography and human geography. Physical geography is scientific in orientation. It involves scientific inquiry into historical and contemporary interactions between people and the environment and between different areas of the environment (geolounge). Scientists measuring polar ice caps or pollution levels in Paris, for instance, would be working within the discipline of physical geography.

Like physical geographers, human geographers also examine interactions between humans and the environment, but they do so with attention to the political, social, and cultural dimensions of these interactions. For instance, scholars in human geography might examine how ongoing drought impacts human migration, how viruses spread across urban spaces, and how oil drilling, coal mining, or tourism impact the environmental, economic, and cultural welfare of people living in nearby communities.

This latter line of inquiry—What is tourism's impact on communities and place?—is the central area of research in "Homestays in Korzak," in which the authors research how tourist homestays impact the people of Korzak and Korzak itself. This foundational inquiry relates to larger questions that human geographers often ask and that carry great significance: How do humans impact the environment? How does the environment impact humans?

As geographers pursue these questions, they write across many diverse forms, from policy reports

Anupam Anand is a graduate student at the University of Maryland in the Department of Geographical Sciences. He holds a M.Phil. degree in Geography from the University of Delhi and an M.S. in Ecology and Environment and Geography. His doctoral work examines human interactions with the environment, and he has a particular interest in methodologies within geography, such as GIS, remote sensing, and spatial analysis methods. Pankaj Chandan has a Ph.D. in Wildlife Sciences and works in the Species and Landscapes Programme for the World Wildlife Federation in New Delhi. His research has examined the impact of grazing practices in the Himalayas, tourism in Ladakh, and the status and distribution of the black-necked crane in India. Part of his work involves developing policies, such as a management plan for the wetlands in Ladakh. Ram Babu Singh is Vice President of the International Geographical Union and has served as the Head of the Department of Geography at the University of Delhi. He has conducted research all over the world and has published widely on such issues as disaster management, environmental studies, and climate change. Their article appeared in the journal *Mountain Research and Development*, which has been publishing peer-reviewed research "devoted to mountains and their surrounding lowlands—ecoregions of particular global importance, in which communities are often marginalized" (MRD).

to public scholarship. This article, published in a research-based journal focused on mountainous regions, includes several features that resonate with larger patterns of academic writing in human geography.

One such feature is the research methodology used by the authors: the qualitative case study. Human geographers use many research methods, from Google Earth to Remote Sensing, but they also use case studies. Dawson Hancock and Bob Algozzine define case studies as "intensive analyses and descriptions of a single unit or system bounded by space and time." Case studies involve collecting and analyzing qualitative data, such as observations, interviews, artifacts, and documents. Numerous fields use case studies as a research methodology. In criminal justice, a case study on police interrogation practices, for instance, included observations of 76 police interrogations over six months in the Brighton, England Police Department. In psychology, another case study, comprised of in-depth description and interviews with five people, yielded research about internet and computer addiction (Griffiths). In human geography, researchers have used case studies for many areas of research, including transportation in contemporary Beijing (Shen, Kwan, and Chai) and prehistoric human adaptation to and exploitation of the Ozarks (Wood and McMillan).

Another aspect of "Homestays in Korzak" indicative of writing in human geography involves the structure and organization of the text. The article includes an abstract, and is divided into several different sections, each labeled clearly with a subheading. The article also includes a variety of visual elements—photographs, graphics, and boxes—features common throughout human geography research as well as across many other disciplines.

Finally, the collaboration between the authors deserves mention since many scholars across the social and natural sciences publish co-authored research. These collaborations take numerous forms, and range in size from two people to seven or more. Each author's contributions vary across context, where some actually co-write while in other cases each person contributes in a different way, such as conducting qualitative analysis, designing the research methodology, or visualizing data. The order of author names can be alphabetical, or it can signal who is the "lead author" (or "first author") and who has seniority of rank (which often attends the last name or first name in the list of authors).

Authors in disciplines such as geography tend to collaborate because their research often requires multiple forms of expertise and involves large-scale projects. This sort of collaboration, while presenting its own unique challenges, also enables human geography to ask complex, varied questions about the many dynamic intersections between humans and place.

Write Here

In a tourism homestay, a tourist resides with a family instead of camping or staying at a hotel. In so doing, the tourist experiences, even if only for a few days, that family's lifestyle and cultural practices. Imagine a tourist from a vastly different culture and location were coming to your home for a week-long homestay. What would the experience be like for the tourist? What activities, in the home and out of the home, would the tourist likely participate in over the week? What sorts of meals would you provide? How would you orient that tourist to your culture and lifestyle?

Anupam Anand, Pankaj Chandan, and Ram Babu Singh
Homestays in Korzak: Supplementing Rural Livelihoods and Supporting Green Tourism in the Indian Himalayas

Introduction

Development of responsible tourism, especially in the fragile high-altitude Himalayan region, is fraught with significant challenges. These challenges include operational and infrastructural barriers as well as issues related to adverse impacts on the local environments. However, tourism is also one of the few available alternative pathways that can create new jobs and reduce poverty for the communities in the remote and resource-scarce region of Ladakh. By providing supplementary income to the rural communities, ecotourism can also prevent land abandonment and subsequent rural–urban migration.

People in the Ladakh Himalaya led a secluded and subsistence form of life until 1974. Outsiders were not allowed to enter the region before then. The Srinagar-Leh road came into existence in 1960s (Rizvi 1998). Although Ladakh opened to tourism only recently, the sector is rapidly advancing on an unsustainable course. Of the various conservation and development organizations that work in the area, the Snow Leopard Conservancy pioneered the homestay model in Ladakh and demonstrated a need to integrate development and conservation goals (Jackson and Wangchuk 2004). This homestay model is now being adopted by various agencies that are working in the region.

Box 1: Location and characteristics of Korzok

- Location: 32⁰58'N and 78⁰15'E u159E; altitude: 4595 masl.
- The temperature ranges from 30⁰C in summer to -40⁰C in winter. Absence of frost-free season results in formation of extensive permafrost.
- The nearest urban center is Leh, 215 km away.
- Connectivity by a single-track road, which has limited accessibility during winter.
- Population: 179 households; 22 households live in permanent structures, but they also migrate seasonally; the rest of the households live in tents called Rebos.
- One primary health center at the village.
- No school; there used to be one primary school, but now all students have been shifted to a centralized school in the Puga Valley.
- No electricity or running water; recently the village was provided with a diesel generator by the local hill council, which is used to provide electricity to the local villagers for 4 hours in the evening.

- Seventy percent practice subsistence agriculture during a short cultivation season and are nomadic pastoralists.
- Barley, wheat, and peas are grown mainly for fodder.
- This village is one of the very few highest permanent settlements and one of the very few such places in the world where agriculture is practiced.

With growing global awareness and initiatives to preserve the environment, in tourism, conservation, and rural development sectors, community-based ecotourism is being promoted as a low-impact, environmentally sensitive way to travel (Honey 1999; Kiss 2004; Jones 2005; Nelson 2007). In recognizing the threats posed by unplanned tourism, the World Wide Fund for Nature (WWF-India) felt the need to integrate a community-based ecotourism project in Korzok that would protect Lake Tsomoriri and offer supplementary income-generating opportunities to the Changpa population. Situated at about 4595 m, Korzok (Box 1) is a small picturesque village on the northwestern shores of Lake Tsomoriri, in the Rukchen Valley of Leh district in Ladakh, India. The lake, situated at 4586 m and 140 km² in area, is designated as a wetland of international importance or Ramsar site (Gujja et al 2003). Significant numbers of endemic and migratory species found in the area, including the vulnerable black-necked crane, *Grus nigricollis* (BirdLife International 2009), are protected by the Wildlife Protection Act of India (1972). Korzok's resources, like the rest of the Changthang plateau, are scarce, and the terrain is physically challenging, with a harsh and fragile environment, but it is endowed with unique and beautiful landscapes, unique biodiversity, trekking routes, and cultural assets, which are all major tourist attractions. It has been pointed out that locally based monitoring and enforcement of resources use generates strong ownership and positive conservation outcomes (Chhatre and Agrawal 2008). Given the long tradition of democratic decision-making and common resource use practices among the Changpas, the initiative had to be embedded in the local cultural context in order to generate benefits for the inhabitants and the surrounding environment at the same time.

The central development issue in Korzok was to create conditions for an enabling environment that would reconcile the needs of generating alternate livelihood opportunities and high-altitude wetland conservation to support the local economy and reduce poverty through a socially inclusive green tourism project. The main development issue, the evolution of the initiative, and some of the early impacts of the project constitute the focus of the present article. The case of Korzok is unique due to the site and situation, demography, and the history of the region. Hence, the early impacts of the project and the few general recommendations gleaned from it are not meant to be prescriptive in nature but could serve as an aggregated checklist for similar small-scale initiatives.

The Korzok homestay initiative

WWF-India launched a project in 1999 to "develop a strategy and plan for conservation" of high-altitude wetlands in the Indian Himalaya. Conservation of high-altitude wetlands is of prime importance in view of their role as water reservoirs, as a source of ecosystem goods and services, and in terms of adaptation to climate change (Chatterjee et al 2010). Tourism offered the potential for reducing poverty in Korzok, but it also was creating immense threats to the local environment and biodiversity in the absence of any regulatory framework. Apart from meager cash income from collecting camping fees from the tourists or hiring out animals for trekking purposes, tourism neither provided economic incentives to the Changpas nor any motivation for the Changpas to get involved in activities for conserving the wetlands. The villagers nonetheless felt the adverse impacts of unplanned and unregulated tourism activities beginning to put pressure on their pasturelands because of the presence of pack animals such as horses, donkeys, and mules. Tourist vehicles were causing noise and water pollution, and camping on surrounding grasslands was disturbing the pastures as well as the breeding sites of various birds. Campers were leaving behind nonbiodegradable wastes on the

virgin land. The absence of designated camping grounds and proper accommodations led tourists to camp irresponsibly

Economic incentives for conservation are particularly essential in isolated areas because inaccessibility and the lack of strong authority makes monitoring and regulation difficult (Wunder 2000). Tourism clearly provided additional income-generating opportunities, but the principal development challenge was reconciling the creation of alternate livelihood paths for the Changpas and conservation of Lake Tsomoriri. Responsible and sustainable tourism or ecotourism is widely viewed as an ecologically, economically, and culturally sustainable alternative to traditional tourism activities that were not sensitive to local culture and environment (Hvenegaard 1994). WWF-India with its long-standing experience in the region needed the support of the Changpas to conserve the high-altitude wetland, and the resident population needed the support of WWF-India to increase their stake in the tourism industry.

Initial consultations by the WWF-India staff with community leaders and surveys conducted in all 23 permanently settled households in July 2005 revealed the interest of the villagers in homestays. Changpa societies follow a complex system of customary tradition of reciprocities, rules, and regulations. Before independence, village headman or goba wielded considerable social and financial power, but, over the years, the institution of goba or headman has weakened. Instead of entrusting one person with the responsibilities of representing the village, the position is passed on at short intervals to the next family under a roster system. The absence of a distinctive class hierarchy among the Changpas in Korzok and a revolving locus of authority within the village helped avoid elite capture at the beginning of the project.

The cultural disposition of the Ladakhi people to host visitors and the convenience of running a homestay without major investments generated interest in the initiative. However, before instituting a full-fledged sustainable community-based tourism project, Participatory Rural Appraisal exercises and visitor surveys were conducted to explore the technical and economic dimensions of the planned activity. The tourism surveys, conducted from 2004 to 2006, during the peak tourist season of July–September, helped to clarify attitudes concerning the visitors' experience and to assess the homestay potential, accommodation preferences, and budget considerations. Both visitor surveys interviewed tourist groups: 450 in 2004 and approximately 300 in 2006, each group comprising 3 to 25 members. The survey data were analyzed, and the results were used internally by WWF-India to inform subsequent project design. The initial groundwork also helped clarify tourists' perception of the ecotourism potential at Korzok, the impact of tourism-related activities on the wetland ecosystem, and the threats to the ecosystem and possible conservation measures. The tourist surveys showed that more than 60% of the tourists expressed interest in the homestay initiative and believed that it would encourage responsible tourism in the area and minimize adverse impacts on the surrounding environment.

The indigenous Changpas who live in this challenging cold desert environment are pastoralists, with livelihoods deeply embedded in nature. They practice subsistence agriculture on marginal lands, and raising "pashmina goats" or Changra goats has been a mainstay for more than 4 centuries (Ahmed 2004). Yet, with the rapid pace of development and environmental changes, the traditionally nomadic Changpas are struggling for work and access to resources. A territorial dispute between India and Pakistan has resulted in a large and lasting military presence that has catalyzed change from the traditional subsistence economy and trade to dependence upon a market economy and subsidized goods imported by the central government (Goodall 2004). The Changpas, like other indigenous populations in the region, are compelled to choose a sedentary lifestyle (Chaudhuri 2000; Goodall 2004) and are seeking alternative forms of employment to supplement their incomes, although they do not necessarily possess the skills or required training to make these transitions. Understanding the gap in required skills, WWF-India facilitated a series of capacity-building exercises for the Changpa community with homestay facilities. The resource persons were fellow Ladakhis who had experience with running successful homestays near the Hemis National Park. The capacity-building exercise included hands-on experience with a wide range of subjects such as hygiene, waste segregation, developing marketing strategies, handling finance, and drawing up and finalizing guidelines for tourists. Selected youths from the village were trained as wildlife guides, and financial assistance was provided to the women's self-help group to start a parachute cafe´ in the village. The training programs stressed the close and clear link between ecological conservation of the area and the livelihood sustenance of the villagers.

Ten permanent dwellings were initially selected for homestays by the Tsomoriri Conservation Committee, based on the ability of households to assign at least one room for lodging throughout the year (Box 2). The Tsomoriri Conservation Committee was the initial management committee of a few villagers, monks from the monastery, and the WWF project officer. This committee later evolved to form the Tsomoriri Conservation Trust. Once a house is approved for homestay by the committee, the family is provided with furnishings and assistance in setting up the room for guests.

The unique concept of local conservation trusts gives regulatory and financial power to local actors for maintaining conservation measures (Gujja 2007). These representative decision-making bodies are also more accountable and responsive to local needs in terms of resource management and delivery of tourism-related services. The initial working committee of villagers was legally registered as the Tsomoriri Conservation Trust (TCT) in 2002.

The Tsomoriri Conservation Trust

The TCT's conversion to a trust in 2002 gave it more institutional power. Its members are the Changpas of the village and lamas of the 400-year-old Korzok monastery. As per the constitution of the Trust, any resident of Changthang can become a member of its General Body by paying a nominal admission and membership fee as long as the member adheres to the code of conduct of the TCT. The lamas or the Buddhist monks are much respected and have authority in Ladakhi society. The spiritual leader and head lama of the monastery is the chairman of the TCT. The general body members of the trust meet every month and the meetings are presided over by the chairman or deputy chairman of the TCT. The board of trustees meets every 6 months. WWF or any government officials are not present during the trust meetings. TCT instead has a provision for an advisory committee that consists of government officials, academicians, and elected officials whom the TCT may approach for consultation. The decisions are taken through consensus. Some of the aims and responsibilities of the TCT are the following:

Box 2: The homestays
Homestays in Korzok have been named after various faunal species found around the lake, such as golden eagle, shelduck, black-necked crane, redshank, etc. Starting with 10 in 2000, Korzok now has 15 homestays. Fees have been fixed by the TCT and are strictly adhered to by the owners; room charges are INR 800 (US$ 16.40) per person and INR 150 (US$ 3.10) for 3 meals a day, which consist of traditional Ladakhi food such as noodle soup thup-ka and roasted barley or yos and salty butter tea, rice with lentils, and vegetables. Boiled spring water is available for drinking. Posters are displayed in each homestay listing the key dos and don'ts for the tourists. One room with bedding and basic furnishings is provided.

1. A regulatory and supervisory body for the Ladakh homestay initiatives. It manages the flow of tourists to the area.
2. Conservation and monitoring of the high-altitude lake ecosystem. It regulates the camping and parking areas around the lake.
3. Providing support to the ecotourism initiatives by providing tourist information facilities.
4. Support to traditional industries, for example, shawl making.
5. The management of tourists in homestays is on a rotational basis and is regulated by the TCT. This ensures equal distribution of money to all the homestays. For this management the trust charges 10% of the income of each homestay, which becomes income of the TCT.
6. The income generated by the TCT is spent on the day-to-day activities of the TCT, for managing the camping sites and for garbage cleaning. Some income is spent on repair work in the village and also for restoration

and repair of cultural features, such as *stupas* and *manay* (prayer) walls, etc.

Any violation of the rules warrants a hearing by the TCT. The TCT decides on the penalty, which might be monetary or other disciplinary action. One particular homestay owner converted the traditional dry toilet system into a European style system and thereby violated the homestay guidelines of adhering to environmentally friendly practices. On this occasion, the TCT decided not to allow the homestay to operate any further.

Green tourism in practice: a path to sustainable development
The operating framework of the Korzok homestay project is a green initiative based on equity, accountability and cooperation, and participation, a few of the guiding principles for a Green Economy (Stoddart et al 2011). The Changpa community has ownership of its natural resources and runs various community-based tourism activities. The project demonstrates its sustainability and green approach through the following practices:

(1) Use of green, efficient, and renewable energy sources: Excluding the tourism-related transport to Korzok, the onsite energy usage is very low. The homestays are not luxuriously designed but provide the necessities required for a comfortable stay and hence do not consume huge amounts of energy as do hotels. The houses are based on traditional designs constructed from rammed earth, which keep the interiors warm without the need for additional heating by burning fossil fuels or wood. Solar panels provide electricity for heating and lighting.

(2) Efficient water consumption and usage: The homestays use a minimum of water because there is no need for landscape maintenance or wellness facilities. Water for drinking and washing is sourced from nearby springs and boiled by using solar energy, which lessens the pressure on fuelwood and also discourages the use of bottled water.

(3) Efficient waste management: The homestays have traditional toilet systems. The traditional dry closet toilet system has evolved as a means of adaptation to the harsh environment. It is a practical solution for scarce water and freezing temperatures. Cold dry air aids in rapid decomposition of waste matter, which is used as manure in the agricultural fields.

(4) Conservation of fragile ecosystem and biodiversity: No tourism activities such as camping or hiking are allowed in the key feeding and breeding areas of the black-necked crane and bar-headed goose. Restrictions that prohibit camping in the nearby grasslands (Figure 4) have provided benefits both to the nomadic community by preserving pasture grounds and by maintaining the health of critical wildlife habitats. Currently, the preventive measures of strictly enforcing zero tourism activities in the pasture and breeding grounds have restored the health of these pasture lands. Another long-term goal is to gradually reduce the dependency of Changpas on livestock, which is a major source of income, through the sale of *Pashmina* wool. With the adoption by the Changpas of a sedentary lifestyle in many parts of Changthang (Namgail et al 2007), which has led to population growth in the area, there is an urgent need to establish a sustainable alternate livelihood system so that the numbers of livestock upon which the population depend do not increase with the increase in population. To reduce the impact of pack animals on pasture lands, some areas have been designated for grazing.

(5) Effective management of cultural heritage, traditional values, and promotion of intercultural understanding: The homestays promote cultural sensitivity. Both the host and the visitors have to be aware of each other's cultural practices. Visitors can take part in various Ladakhi festivals, get first-hand experience of people's lifestyles, enjoy traditional cuisine, and gain knowledge of the material and spiritual culture of Ladakh.

(6) Improving livelihoods and poverty reduction: On average, during the tourist season (June to September), the occupancy rate for these homestays is 80%. Presently, each homestay charges INR 800 (US$ 16.40) per room, and the present camping fee is INR 50 (US$ 1) per tent. Many village youths have found jobs as porters, cooks, and guides for the tourists who trek in the area.

In Korzok, the main source of livelihood is livestock rearing and income from *pashmina*. It is difficult to calculate the exact income from selling wool, because the market demand fluctuates greatly (Ahmed 2004). The average yearly income from pashmina can range between INR 16,000 (US$ 320) and INR 24,000 (US$ 480), which is dependent on flock size, production, etc. A part of the income is lost to bribing government officials if they sell through the government-established system and to middlemen if they adopt the traditional system (Ahmed 2004). Through the homestays, each family earns between INR 35,000 ($700) and INR 60,000 ($1200) during the summer months, and the income stays within the household. The success of this integrated sustainable tourism and conservation enterprise in Korzok attracted major funding of INR 1.5 crores ($307,629) from the government of India in 2009 to develop infrastructure and make the village a model village in the Ladakh region. Although economic access to consumer goods is not an indicator of livelihood success, households that participate in the homestay initiative now have the capacity to buy material assets such as televisions, liquefied petroleum gas (LPG), and vehicles for transportation, things that were not common in 1999. These minor changes through the ecotourism initiative at least open up new spaces for people to explore alternatives when only a few are present, such as livestock rearing and pack animals for tour operators.

To quote Sonam Gyaltson, who has been running the black-necked crane homestay for the past 7 years and who supports a family of 8 persons, "After I started the business of running a homestay, the condition of my family has improved and now we are living a much better life."

(7) Supporting women's income: The homestays are mostly run by women. Operating the homestays causes no interference with other household chores, such as weaving, milking the goats and yaks, cooking, cleaning, or grinding barley. The tourists eat at fixed times, which are explained

to the tourists upon their arrival. Overall, all the activities are woven into their regular activities so they continue playing their traditional roles of taking care of children and managing the homefront. Mrs Tsering, who runs the Magpie Homestay, said "My husband died last year and now the income from the homestay is the only source of livelihood for me." Her husband died in 2010 and depended on pashmina trade for income. She now supports a family of four.

(8) Shared learning and diffusion of ideas: The Changpas share their knowledge about their culture and environment with the tourists and visitors. Many nongovernmental organizations and schools in Ladakh bring students and other community members to see the wildlife of the area and to stay in these homestays to experience the lifestyle lived by the Changpas. Research institutions in Jammu and Kashmir and other community-based organizations, such as farmers' cooperatives, also organize meetings at Korzok, which provides the homestay owners with an opportunity to share their experiences through the platforms provided by other organizations.

At present, apart from the 15 homestays in Korzok, there are 2 guesthouses, 21 tented accommodations, and 1 resort. These facilities, although not designed on sustainability principles, are required to adhere to camping and trekking regulations. They have accountability relationships with the TCT and cannot flaunt environmental regulations.

Box 3: The Changpas are already touching hearts...

"Thank you for hospitality and good caretaking. We hope very much that the excellent Korzok homestay system will help local people as well as conserve the wonderful flora and fauna of Tsomoriri. You live in a very special place."
Wendy and Davis Durlime, Switzerland

"To our dear host! Thank you so much for our wonderful stay. The room was nice and your hospitality exceptional. Thank you also for the fantastic food and for giving us the feeling of being welcome as part of the family. Exactly how one would expect homestay to be. One night was far too little. Best of luck for the future."

Frances Daniel
"Julley! Thank you for your kindness, wonderful food and constant attention. Good luck with homestay. I hope that earning more money will not create problems and tension for you. Your values are very precious. We in the West have so much to learn from you and your sense of hospitality. Namaste!"
Alescne, Switzerland

"To the greatest family possible. We cannot thank you enough for your generosity and warmth for the last two nights. You make the best curd in the world. We hope that you will continue to show visitors the traditional way of life, including the food. We wish you all the best for the future and hope that if we return to this beautiful lake one day we can repay your kindness. Never change, stay strong and good luck with all our love."
Laura Page and So Patterson, England

"It was lovely to stay at this beautiful place with a local family. We tasted some really good Ladakhi food."
Laura & Thomas, Czech Republic

Apart from regulatory measures enforced by the TCT, WWF-India systematically monitors the progress of the project through its field office situated at Korzok. The field staff interacts with the villagers on a daily basis and reports to the project leader about the on-ground activities. The field office mostly works in cooperation with the TCT to ensure that minor conflicts are amicably mediated by community leaders. The TCT as a representative body of the community also works in cooperation with the Jammu and Kashmir Wildlife Department. Although initial phases of the project required many external inputs from WWF-India, now that the various actors and institutions involved in the project are aware of their power and accountability relations with each other, the result has been an internal mechanism that helps to achieve the project outcomes.

Early impacts

Multiple stakeholder interests; issues of identity and representation; and the interrelationships between various actors, institutions, and policies influence the outcomes of community-based conservation (Belsky 1999). Community-based enterprise strategies do not necessarily lead to conservation and are contingent upon context (Goodwin 1996; Salafsky et al 2001). Although perfect examples of Integrated Conservation and Development Projects are difficult to find, the Korzok initiative offers a good case, because the Changpas have some measure of control over their natural and cultural resources, and they are on a path to share the benefits of tourism equitably. The Korzok homestay initiative has shown some initial success in addressing local livelihood needs through biodiversity conservation in the area by bringing environmental, economic, and livelihood benefits to the people. The homestays also have supplemented women's income in Korzok households. Women are mainly engaged in running these facilities because this allows them to play their traditional role as primary caregivers to children and the elderly (Belsky 1999). This case study presents a practical example that tourism, if integrated in the local context, can also help in the conservation of a particular ecosystem and can be used to raise the economic standard of poor and marginalized communities. The homestays have been a positive experience for many tourists (Box 3). Concrete examples in the forestry sector have shown that shifting control of forest resources to the community level reduces costs and enhances management effectiveness (Gibson 2001; Brown et al 2002). Ensuring participation and representation of the community in tourism has helped them secure rights, in this case, through the assistance of a nongovernmental organization and the state government; the benefits of tourism were not monopolized by affluent outside actors. Entrusting responsibilities to the villagers of Korzok for running the enterprise has allowed for a more equitable, steady, and sustainable flow of monetary benefits. Homogeneity in cultural background at Korzok has minimized conflicts and issues that could arise from identity politics and that could have hampered the progress of the homestay initiative. The institutional choice of WWF-India to work with traditional authorities has enhanced representation of local interests.

The adoption of homestays is limited to households that have extra space and a permanent dwelling in the village, so not everybody in the village benefits equally. The absence of any mechanism that regulates the investment of income from ecotourism activities in nongreen tourism activities may create problems in the future. Increased income has undoubtedly given the Changpas more choices about where to invest and what to spend on. Although some have invested in their children's education, others have purchased consumer goods. The Changpa households that live in tents in and around the Korzok settlement are also not benefitting economically from the homestay initiative, unlike their counterparts who live in permanent dwellings. Even if the seminomadic Changpas decide to join the homestay venture, it will invariably increase pressure on the ecosystem as well as competition. The TCT will need to evaluate and assess the optimal number of tourists the area can support in the future. Efforts such as banning trekking and camping in the grazing land in the surrounding areas have been undertaken to minimize impacts, but the rapidly growing tourism industry will continue to exert pressure on this fragile ecosystem. This calls for an evolving strategy for addressing future concerns. There also is a need to integrate traditional and spiritual belief systems with sustainable practices that have had documented impact on restoring habitats. For instance, Changpas depend on Tibetan astrological predictions recommended by monks for herd movements to different pastures (Namgail et al 2010), which can be attuned to the phenological cycle of fodder species, regeneration status, and grazing pressures.

Further reflection and conclusions

This project demonstrates the possibility of establishing pro-environment sustainable mountain tourism enterprises and equitable development in spite of inadequate infrastructure and skills, meager income-generating opportunities, and environmental challenges characteristic of many mountain regions of the world. As argued by Okazaki (2008), the success of a participatory project can be evaluated only after critical evaluation to identify the level of community participation. A good case of the perception and acceptance of this integrated conservation and ecotourism development model is how it has captured the interests and promoted entrepreneurship among other Changpas in the region. Inspired by the Korzok model, the Changpa inhabitants of Tso Kar, a high-altitude wetland in Changthang, have shown interest in developing a project along similar lines. The villagers established the Tso Kar Conservation Trust in 2007 and now regularly interact with their counterparts at Korzok to engage in, share, and learn from each other's experiences.

However, sites of conservation and development are dynamic, with various actors and agencies continually exerting influence and thereby influencing outcomes (Bebbington 2000; Perreault 2003). Therefore, this model, which demonstrates success in the particular Ladakhi context, may not be widely applicable across mountainous regions. The case of Korzok might be an ideal setting, where agencies such as WWF and the governments of Jammu and Kashmir are merely catalyzing and assisting in connecting the place-based practices to the larger ecotourism discourse. Some early impacts are already visible because local resource governance systems were in place before the beginning of the project; moreover, no significant social and economic differences can currently be seen among the Changpa households in Korzok. Also, due to the relative isolation of the location there is an absence of external actors with interests that might not align with the interests of the Changpas. Early impacts as seen in this case have been seen in similar ecotourism based projects elsewhere, but those impacts were not long-lasting (Belsky 1999) or found to have only marginal impact on household income (Bookbinder et al 1998) or inequitable distribution of benefits among different stakeholders (Walpole and Goodwin 2000; He et al 2008). Ecotourism is also found to be less sustainable in mountain habitats (Kruger 2005) and tends to open up areas most vulnerable to cultural disturbance and environmental degradation (Cater 1993). Other empirical studies on community- based conservation and development

projects have shown long-term institutional support and funding to be a requirement for ensuring success (Archabald and Naughton-Treves 2001). It would be interesting to see, a few years from now, whether the homestays create different economic classes or differences between homestay owners and seminomadic pastoralist Changpas and affect the seemingly stable current social setting among the residents of Korzok, and how this project fares in the absence of any institutional support from external agencies. There is also a likelihood of an increase in localism and local identity politics, given the assertions of Changpas that only the residents of the Korzok should be involved in the homestays or work as local guides. Although local stakeholder involvement is crucial for maintaining accountability in these initiatives, it might also lead to conflicts between various groups, local versus migrants, Changpas versus non-Changpas, etc.

The case offers some key insights gained through regular stakeholder consultation meetings with the Changpas and individual feedback given by the inhabitants to the on-site project officer and one of the authors. These also include feedback from tourists who visited the area and experienced homestays. However, the unique site and place-based context of this case study might limit its relevance elsewhere.

1. Members of the local population must have the awareness, information, and opportunities to participate and choose from in order to make decisions about their livelihoods. This initiative gave the Changpas this choice, and it remains to be seen where it will take them in the long run.

2. Equitable access to natural resource tenure, use, and management for various stakeholders involved at the project sites is essential for accountable outcomes with minimal conflict.

3. Social and economic incentives are a must for community involvement in the conservation process.

4. Communities should be empowered through financial and technical assistance, and skill-building exercises for a fair and smooth

transition to adopt alternative sources of income based on pro-environment policies.

5. Cultural competence and sensitivity is required for aligning local livelihoods with the broader goals of poverty reduction, development, and conservation.

6. Local cultural and spiritual value systems should be represented and integrated in the projects. Because the communities have been in these areas for centuries, they are appropriately positioned for nature conservation activities in the area.

7. As this green tourism initiative is adopted by a greater number of communities, a certification system will be required to institute compliance standards across the region and at various operational scales for green economy projects; currently, a system by WWF-India is underway, wherein initial stakeholder consultation was conducted for designing the certification system.

This project was conceived and initiated with the aim of promoting high-altitude wetland conservation along with supporting the local economy and reducing poverty. So far, it has managed to generate awareness among the sedentary Changpas of Korzok and piqued their interest in the potential of homestays as an alternative source to supplement their income. At this point, it is premature to state whether this green initiative will be a sustainable alternative to their traditional sources of income, which revolve around livestock. A way forward will be to conduct a comprehensive livelihood impact assessment through household surveys, along with carrying out in-depth analysis of how the local site conditions have changed over time in Korzok in terms of their social, economic, and the environmental aspects. Detailed data on household income, employment, resource use, traditional rights, and rules are not available, and, therefore, local-level household surveys would help clarify this initiative and to what extent it has impacted the people of Korzok, and whether it has changed the existing and historic dynamics in resource use, income generation, and distribution of benefits. Detailed interviews with the homestay owners and other residents of Korzok will be required to understand the underlying nuances of the project

and to understand the probable causes that could make them opt out of the project. Their narrative will be required to understand whether the process of creating a green tourism-based initiative has given power to some people at the expense of excluding others. An explicit understanding of these place-based processes will help generate a dynamic strategy for ensuring sustainable impacts in the future. Currently, consultations are underway among the various participating institutions and stakeholders in the Korzok initiative to conduct impact assessments of the project by an external agency every alternate year. A greater need in view of global climate change is also to understand the vulnerability and resilience of this fragile high-altitude ecosystem, because the co-benefits of conservation and development will only emerge if the local ecosystems are resilient.

REFERENCES

Ahmed M. 2004. The politics of pashmina: The Changpas of Eastern Ladakh. *Nomadic Peoples*, 8(2):89–106.

Archabald K, Naughton-Treves L. 2001. Tourism revenue-sharing around national parks in Western Uganda: Early efforts to identify and reward local communities. *Environmental Conservation* 28(2):135–149.

Bebbington A. 2000. Reencountering development: Livelihood transitions and place transformations in the Andes. *Annals of the Association of American Geographers* 90:495–520.

Belsky JM. 1999. Misrepresenting communities: The politics of community based rural ecotourism in Gales Point Manatee, Belize. *Rural Sociology* 64(4): 641–666.

BirdLife International. 2009. Grus nigricollis. In: IUCN [International Union for Conservation of Nature]. 2011. *IUCN Red List of Threatened Species*. Version 2011.2. http://www.iucnredlist.org; accessed on 15 December 2011.

Bookbinder MP, Dinerstein E, Rijal A, Cauley H, Rajouria A. 1998. Ecotourism's support of biodiversity conservation. *Conservation Biology* 12(6): 1399–1404.

Brown D, Malla Y, Schreckenberg K, Springate-Baginski O. 2002. From supervising subjects to supporting citizens: Recent developments in community forestry in Asia and Africa. *ODI Natural Resources Perspectives*. http://www.dfid.gov.uk/r4d/PDF/Outputs/NatResSys/R7889Pap.pdf; accessed on 25 October 2011.

Cater E. 1993. Ecotourism in the Third World: Problems for sustainable tourism development. *Tourism Management* 14(2): 85–90.

Chatterjee A, Blom E, Gujja B, Jacimovic R, Beevers L, O'Keeffe J, Beland M, Biggs T. 2010. WWF Initiatives to Study the Impact of Climate Change on Himalayan High-altitude Wetlands (HAWs). *Mountain Research and Development*, 30(1):42–52.

Chaudhuri A. 2000. Change in Changthang: To stay or to leave? *Economic and Political Weekly* 35(1/2):52–58.

Chhatre A, Agrawal A. 2008. Forest commons and local enforcement. Proceedings of the National Academy of Sciences 105(36):13286–13291.

Gibson C. 2001. Forest resources: Institutions for local governance in Guatemala. In: Burger J, Ostrom E, Norgaard RB, Policansky D, Goldstein BD, editors. *Protecting the Commons: A Framework for Resource Management in the Americas*. Washington, DC: Island Press, pp 71–89.

Goodall SK. 2004. Rural-to-urban migration and urbanization in Leh, Ladakh: A case study of three nomadic pastoral communities. *Mountain Research and Development* 24(3):218–225.

Goodwin H. 1996. In pursuit of ecotourism. *Biodiversity and Conservation* 5(3): 277–291.

Gujja B. 2007. Conservation of high-altitude wetlands: Experiences of the WWF Network. *Mountain Research and Development* 27(4):368–371.

Gujja B, Chatterjee A, Gautam P, Chandan P. 2003. Wetlands and lakes at the top of the world. *Mountain Research and Development* 23(3):219–221.

He G, Chen X, Liu W, Bearer S, Zhou S, Cheng LY, Zhang H, Ouyang Z, Liu J. 2008. Distribution of economic benefits from ecotourism: A case study of Wolong Nature Reserve for Giant Pandas in China. *Environmental Management* 42(6):1017–1025.

Honey M. 1999. *Ecotourism and Sustainable Development: Who Owns Paradise?* Washington, DC: Island Press.

Hvenegaard G. 1994. Ecotourism: A status report and conceptual framework. *Journal of Tourism Studies* 5(2):24–35.

Jackson R, Wangchuk R. 2004. A community-based approach to mitigating livestock depredation by snow leopards. *Human Dimensions of Wildlife* 9(4): 307–315.

Jones S. 2005. Community-based ecotourism: The significance of social capital. *Annals of Tourism Research* 23(2):303–325.

Kiss A. 2004. Is community-based ecotourism a good use of biodiversity conservation funds? *Trends in Ecology and Evolution* 19(5):232–237.

Kruger O. 2005. The role of ecotourism in conservation: Panacea or Pandora's box? *Biodiversity and Conservation* 14(3):579–600.

Namgail T, Bhatnagar YV, Mishra C, Bagchi S. 2007. Pastoral nomads of the Indian Changthang: Production system, land use and socioeconomic changes. *Human Ecology* 35:497–504.

Namgail T, van Wieren SE, Prins HHT. 2010. Pashmina production and socioeconomic changes in the Indian Changthang: Implications for natural resource management. *Natural Resources Forum* 34(3):222–230.

Nelson F. 2007. *Emergent or Illusionary? Community Wildlife Management in Tanzania*. Drylands Issue Paper No. 146. London, UK: International Institute for Environment and Development.

Okazaki E. 2008. A community-based tourism model: Its conception and use. *Journal of Sustainable Tourism* 16(5):511–529.

Perreault T. 2003. "A people with our own identity": Toward a cultural politics of development in Ecuadorian Amazonia. *Environment and Planning D: Society and Space* 21(5):583–606.

Rizvi J. 1998. *Ladakh, Crossroads of High Asia*. 2nd revised edition (1st edition 1983). New Delhi, India: Oxford University Press.

Salafsky N, Cauley H, Balachander G, Cordes B, Parks J, Margoluis C, Bhatt S, Encarnacion C, Russell D, Margoluis R. 2001. A systematic test of an enterprise strategy for community-based biodiversity conservation. *Conservation Biology* 15:1585–1595.

Stoddart H, Riddlestone S, Vilela M. 2011. *Principles for the green economy: A collection of principles for the green economy in the context of sustainable development and poverty eradication*. http://cmsdata.iucn.org/downloads/green_econ_principles.pdf; accessed on 20 October 2011.

Walpole MJ, Goodwin HJ. 2000. Local economic impacts of dragon tourism in Indonesia. *Annals of Tourism Research* 27(3):559–576.

Wunder S. 2000. Ecotourism and economic incentives: An empirical approach. *Ecological Economics* 32:465–479.

Write Away

1. "Homestays in Korzak" offers a case study that fits within a broader initiative that the authors refer to as "green tourism" (135). Write your own case study about a place related to, or facet of, green tourism. Address such questions as: What are the goals of green tourism? What has been working or not working with regard to your case study? What are the limitations or drawbacks of green tourism? Where and in what contexts are various green tourist practices applicable? What are future directions for green tourism? Where might green tourism expand?

2. Geographers use many tools in their work, from Geographic Information Systems (GIS) to Global Positioning Systems (GPS). Google Earth is another such tool, with wide applicability across disciplines. Using a disciplinary interest of your own (literature, language, geography, culture, health, business, etc.), write a blog post on how Google Earth can be used in connection to that discipline. Provide an example of the usage with Google Earth in your text. You can also consider compiling your blog post with classmates' posts as a way of creating a collaborative website of the multidisciplinary uses of Google Earth.

3. Compose a research proposal for a case study that would examine the impact of tourism on a particular place. Your research proposal should include the following components: a literature review of prior and relevant research related to tourism in that place, an indication of why additional research would be important or significant, a description of the kinds of data collection you would use during your case study research. You may also want to include a list of proposed collaborators, a proposed timetable, and a proposed budget.

Media Studies: "Articles" by News Bias Explored

> Transfer Points: Media Studies, Rhetoric, Journalism, Communications

How much do you trust the news? Do you have more or less confidence in particular news items, news sources, or news reporters? According to a September 2015 Gallup poll, Americans' confidence in the media has steadily declined over the past ten years, such that only four in ten adults now indicate trust in mainstream media (Riffkin). An even deeper challenge exists, though. Results reveal that Democrats tend to trust the media *more* than in the past while Republicans and Independents trust the media less than in the past ("Poll").

This mistrust emerges from an impression, perceived or factual, that media are biased.

News Bias Explored is a website developed by a team of students at the University of Michigan. The website functions as a form of public scholarship in media studies, outlining for a general readership various forms of media bias, with accompanying examples and analysis. The undergraduate and graduate students who developed the website include people in the discipline of English and those with computer science and engineering expertise, demonstrating the value of collaboration across disciplines to work toward a common goal.

It matters not only in terms of generating mistrust, but because media have incredible impact on public opinion and awareness. One of the founding scholars associated with media studies, Friedrich Kittler, emphasized the breadth of this impact by suggesting that media essentially shape our entire understanding of the world: "Media determine our situation" (qtd. in Mitchell and Hansen, vii).

Media bias can be deliberate or unintentional, subtle or overt, pervasive or isolated. Some of the more common forms of media bias include occasions where journalists omit facts, misrepresent source quotes, or rely on a limited range of sources to generate content. Media bias also seeps through with word choice in texts, captions, and headlines, as well as placement and visibility of news items (Parker Bass).

Many who study media bias work within the discipline of media studies, which, depending on the institution, can sometimes be termed journalism or communications. Media-studies scholars research and write about many different questions: What role do media play in shaping public opinion? What are the forms in which media bias emerges? How does media bias impact perceptions of events, places, or people? What news stories gain visibility and which ones remain invisible or less visible? Why? Which people tend to be more or less privileged across media coverage? How might word choice, in a headline or in the text itself, impact public perceptions?

Pursuing these questions across many different media sources—media are plural and diverse, not a single entity—scholars have researched media bias in print, and on television, radio, and the internet. Much of this research is highly interdisciplinary. Media studies scholars deploy quantitative methods, such as data mining, using digital software and statistical analysis, to gather and analyze big data; they also use qualitative methods, conducting in-depth content analysis, visual analysis, discourse analysis, interviews, and focus groups; media scholars also use mixed-methods strategies.

While media studies exists as a discipline, with its own body of knowledge, history, and research methods, scholars from many other disciplines also conduct research that can be situated at the nexus between media studies and their own disciplines. For instance, those in anthropology, public policy, or political science work with media studies quite prolifically. Many interdisciplinary fields that explore groups or regions, such as gender and sexuality studies, race studies, or cultural studies, also include research that intersects frequently with media studies. And, scholars in the sciences also conduct research pertaining to media bias, looking at how media bias, for example, functions in health-related news or environmental news.

The discipline of rhetoric overlaps extensively with media studies. Rhetoric examines arguments, structures, and symbols in written, visual, and auditory discourse. Because research in media bias so closely relies on in-depth analysis of discourse, rhetoricians often deploy their expertise in this area. Rhetorician Douglas Walton, for instance, has investigated a series of media case studies to explore rhetorical devices such as appeals to fear and pity, and fallacies, such as ad hominem arguments and arguments based solely on public opinion.

Those who conduct media-bias research, though, do more than merely point out the existence of media bias. They also ground their inquiries within complexities of communication writ large: Is it possible to communicate in a way that is not motivated by a particular perspective or agenda? Can anyone develop a narrative of events that is purely objective or exclusively informative? Are all instances of media bias equally insidious? Is the notion of "trust" an impossible ideal? What are the responsibilities of consumers of news with regard to media bias? Might the development of trust be in some ways just as dangerous as media bias itself? These are among the most compelling questions circulating at the center of research into media bias, and that drive the important work that scholars in this field pursue.

Write Here

Reflect in writing on your relationship with the news, your perceptions of media bias, and your degree of trust in the news. Consider the following sorts of questions: From what sources do you get news? Why have you chosen those sources? What media biases might impact the news you encounter? How much do you trust the news? Which types of news stories do you find to be more or less credible? Which news sources do you find to be more or less trustworthy? Why?

News Bias Explored
Articles

The purpose of this section is to pull together as many influences and manifestations of bias as possible, in a single example. As you read the following two articles, mark up sections which you think could have an effect on potential biases. Once you have done this, consider how the same analytical process can be applied to other news stories that you come across.

U.N. Withdraws U-2 Planes
By REUTERS

UNITED NATIONS (Reuters)—U.N. arms inspectors said Tuesday they had withdrawn two U-2 reconnaissance planes over Iraq for safety reasons after Baghdad complained both aircraft were in the air simultaneously.

Ewen Buchanan, spokesman for the U.N. Monitoring, Verification, and Inspection Commission, said he was unaware if the Iraqi air force had tried to intercept the planes.

But a U.S. official said Iraq "informed us when the planes were in the air that only one was acceptable and the second would be viewed as 'hostile.'"

He said the inspectors asked Washington to temporarily suspend the flights, flown on behalf of the United Nations, until U.S. and U.N. officials could meet on the incident in New York. Iraq, the U.S. official said, had been told about the two aircraft 48 hours in advance.

Should Iraq be found to have interfered with the flights, chief U.N. inspector Hans Blix, executive chairman of UNMOVIC, is obligated to report the incident to the U.N. Security Council immediately.

But Russia's U.N. ambassador, Sergei Lavrov, whose country opposes military action against Iraq, contended that "UNMOVIC is not considering it a provocation." He said the incident was a "misunderstanding" and "blown out of proportion."

Buchanan told reporters, "I can confirm that two U-2 reconnaissance aircraft operating on behalf of the UNMOVIC operated in Iraqi air space this morning."

"Although Iraq had been notified of a flight time window, they expressed surprise and concern that two flights were operating simultaneously. In the interests of safety, UNMOVIC requested the aircraft to withdraw," he said, adding that further U-2 and Mirage flights were still planned.

U.N. sources said there was no agreement that only one U-2 aircraft could fly at one time, although that had been past practice.

WASHINGTON (AP)-Iraqi fighter jets threatened two American U-2 surveillance planes, forcing them to return to abort their mission and return to base, senior U.S. officials said Tuesday.

A Pentagon official said the decision to end the mission "in the interest of safety."

The U-2 planes were flying missions at 2 a.m. Iraqi time for the U.N. weapons inspectors when Iraq launched fighter jets. According to two of the officials, the threat was directed against one of the two planes, said the officials, speaking on condition of anonymity.

Multiple flights are permitted under a U.N. Security Council resolution approved last November, and the Bush administration sought clarification from U.N. inspectors after the U-2 flights were suspended.

The U.N. inspection agency, known, as UNMOVIC, had given advance notice to Iraq of the flights, said the U.S. official.

The Iraqi threat is fresh evidence of Baghdad's unwillingness to cooperate with U.N. inspectors, another U.S. official said.

Two American U-2 planes were already in the air, the senior official said. He said they were the seventh and eighth sent on a surveillance assignment since the council approved the resolution unanimously, and that the flights had been coordinated with the U.N. inspection agency.

But Iraq "raised a fuss," this official said, and the two flights were recalled. American diplomats are checking with the U.N. agency before resuming U-2 flights, the official said.

The dispute punctuated a behind-the-scenes effort by the United States and Britain to win support for a new resolution designed to back the use of force as a last resort to disarm Iraq.

U-2 flights are conducted as part of an elaborate inspection arrangement designed to determine whether President Saddam Hussein has secretly stored chemical and biological weapons in defiance of U.N. resolutions.

Typically, Iraq is notified in advance of overflights of Iraqi territory.

Write Away

1. Develop a verbal presentation about a form of media bias. First, working individually or with a small group, develop a comprehensive list of different types of media biases, such as those related to fairness bias, visual bias, or narrative bias. Then, choose one of these types of media bias to explore in more depth by developing a presentation about this form of media bias. Your aim in the presentation is to educate others about this form of media bias and use examples from across current media sources to help illustrate the concept in detail.

2. The American Press Institute (API) discusses bias as an inherent component of media reportage. They say that bias might not always be bad; instead, it might "create narrative texture or make a story understandable" ("Understanding"). As such, API encourages journalists not to eradicate bias but instead to "manage" it. Working with others or individually, develop a list of strategies journalists might use in managing bias. Then, compose a piece of long-form journalism about an issue of your choosing. In your article, draw on the list of strategies to manage bias as effectively as you can. After you have completed your long-form journalism piece, write a reflection about how you managed bias, what was challenging about doing so, and how bias may have shaped your piece even though you worked to manage the bias.

3. Write a case study of media bias surrounding a particular issue, event, person, media source, or group. Include in your case study a variety of primary sources in the form of media coverage about the topic as well as relevant secondary sources to provide necessary context and to build on prior research about that topic. Work with your instructor and classmates to select and define a case study that is manageable in scope. Consider the following questions in your case study: What forms of media bias impact this case most prominently? Why? What are the stakes involved with this particular case, and how might these stakes influence media bias in this context? What recommendations, if any, do you have for moving forward with media coverage in this context?

Chapter 11 Key Terms

integrate	evidence	block quotations
sandwiched	quotations	MEAL plan
paraphrase		

Write Away

This activity asks you to work together in a small group with a "round-robin" of evidence integration—a method that allows all group members to write—so you can consider how you will transfer the art of choosing and integrating evidence across diverse writing occasions.

Form a small group, consisting of approximately four people.

Collaborate to create an argumentative claim. Together with your group members, collaborate on an argument you can set forth, perhaps even one about an aspect of food (sustainable food practices, hunger and food, dietary trends, health and food). It might be the case that not all members of the group fully agree with the argumentative stance, but that is fine. Your task is merely to develop a claim for the purposes of this Write Away.

Refine the argument according to disciplinary perspective and writing occasion. Together determine a disciplinary perspective for the argument, and decide details about the writing occasion. What is the publication context? What format are you using? What disciplinary perspective is informing the argument? These decisions are critical for the next step because they will impact the kinds of evidence you and your group members choose.

Assign each group member a different form of evidence to choose and integrate. Each group member should be responsible for choosing and integrating evidence toward that argument, but each group member should do so with one primary form of evidence. For example, one person could use personal evidence, another visual evidence, and another previous scholarship.

Using the MEAL plan as a format, each group member composes one evidence-based paragraph. Using the MEAL plan and the assigned form of evidence as determined by your group, each group member develops a paragraph of evidence. This will include choosing the evidence for that paragraph and integrating it as effectively as possible. For example, if one group member is responsible for including personal evidence, he or she will decide what kind of personal evidence to draw on (which experiences, how much, what sorts, etc.) and create a paragraph that advances the argument by integrating that personal evidence.

Repeat the entire cycle one or two more times. Using different arguments and rotating the forms of evidence each group member is responsible for, repeat the cycle one or two more times so that every group member gains experience with a few different kinds of evidence and a few different arguments.

Reflect on evidence and transfer. Reflect for ten minutes about the process of choosing and integrating evidence across contexts: What did you learn about choosing evidence and how it is nested within the disciplinary context and writing occasion? What forms of evidence seemed easier or harder to find and integrate? In what ways did the MEAL plan apply across writing occasions? Did you find it necessary to modify your approach in any ways? If so, describe these modifications.

12

Citing Resources

Beijing, China features two exceptional archaeoastronomical sites: the Ancient Beijing Observatory and the Forbidden City.

The Forbidden City, also known as the Imperial Palace or the Purple City, emerged during the Ming Dynasty in 1404 CE designed to signify an alignment between astronomical power and imperial power:

> the Forbidden City...was approached along the meridian, directly toward the north celestial pole, which was seen as the very heart of the heavens.... [S]ubjects permitted to visit the emperor...were required...to approach his throne—the center of the earthly realm—from due south.

Mirroring the Forbidden City's meticulous alignment, the Ancient Observatory, built during the fifteenth century, yielded such accuracy that lead astronomer Guo Shou Jing could "establish the length of the tropical (seasonal) year with an error of only twenty-six seconds" ("Chinese Astronomy").

Curiously, these Beijing sites stand apart in some ways from the dominant Western framework often invoked to categorize archaeoastronomical research: the "'green' v. 'brown' methodological debate," so named in reference to the different-colored covers binding two separate volumes of research papers delivered at the 1981 Oxford archaeoastronomical conference (Carlson, et al.; Ruggles).

According to the green/brown debate, green archaeoastronomers research European sites and, because these sites often lack robust historical and cultural records, tend to focus on statistics and mathematics. Brown archaeoastronomers, meanwhile, research sites in the Americas and, because these sites often have more extensive records, tend to rely on ethnography and historical evidence (Ruggles, "Lecture 7"; Dalgleish).

Because Beijing is neither located in Europe nor the Americas, sites such as the Forbidden City and the Ancient Observatory exemplify how alignments can be not only divisive or unifying, but also exclusionary. Where and with whom would those researching Beijing archaeoastronomy align their methodological approaches?

The answer, likely, is that archaeoastronomers probably move with more flexibility across methodological lines than the green/brown debate would suggest, and that categories are nearly always fluid. But, considered from this perspective, these Beijing sites are note-

worthy not only for their astronomical alignments, but also because they raise important questions about research and alignment: When scholars cite evidence, whom do they align themselves with—and why? How do they make those alignments visible? What are the implications? Who gets included? Who gets excluded?

These questions signal the underlying, complex power dynamics that often motivate academic writing citation practices. Too often, citation seems a matter of rules, indicating how writers should format a document or whether they should use endnotes or footnotes. Fortunately, though, learning citation is not so much about memorizing rules (many resources are available to help with the rules). Instead, learning about citation demands a conceptual understanding of why writers cite, why citation styles vary across disciplinary and publication context, and why decisions about citation can have high stakes.

Scholars decide with each writing occasion whom to cite and how to cite and, in so doing, align themselves with particular discourse communities (and differentiate themselves from others). Contrary to what the green/brown debate might suggest, scholars have many different discourse communities from which to choose and blend. As a result, scholars can also select from among many different citation styles. Each of the acronyms and names depicted here, in fact, represents a different citation style.

These citation styles, though, and the choices writers make about which citation style to use for any given writing occasion, are not arbitrary. Rather, the values and priorities within a discourse community shape citation styles. Writers deploy a particular citation style so their readers can clearly discern the key bibliographic information they will need in order to extend, challenge, or otherwise modify the arguments they encounter.

While some writers may often write within one particular discourse community or citation style, most writers move among discourse communities, and thereby also use different citation styles for different writing projects, depending on the disciplinary and publication context of any given writing occasion.

Although citation styles and discourse communities can at times create division, as suggested by the green/brown debate, they can also be much more useful. When deployed in effective ways, citation enables academic writers to reach out, connect with others' research and writing, and forge new intersections. Clear and accurate citation also allows scholars to disrupt unproductive alignments in favor of exploring those that might be more illuminating and enriching for their research and writing.

Write Here

Locate a peer-reviewed article on the Forbidden City or the Ancient Observatory. Looking only at the references, hypothesize whether the article would be categorized as "brown" or "green" archaeoastronomy, as a mixture of the two methodological approaches, or as something different altogether. What scholars and prior research are being cited? What disciplinary frames do you see motivating the author's approach in the article?

ᏽ ᏽ ᏽ

What is Citation?

Citation involves attributing the words of others in academic writing. Different disciplines typically use different strategies for citation; these strategies are referred to as **citation styles**, **citation guides**, or **schools of citation**. While there are many citation styles, and disciplines do not map rigidly into particular citation styles, you will find below some of the more often-used citation styles, along with the disciplines with which they are commonly affiliated.

Modern Language Association (MLA)
Often used in English, Literary Studies, Performance Studies, and Art

American Psychological Association (APA)
Often used with social sciences, such as Public Policy, Sociology, and Psychology

American Anthropological Association (AAA)
Often used with Cultural Anthropology

American Sociological Association (ASA)
Often used with Sociology

Council of Science Editors (CSE)
Often used in Health Professions

American Chemical Society (ACS)
Often used with Chemistry, Physics, and Biology

Institute of Electronics and Electrical Engineers (IEEE)
Often used with Engineering

Chicago Manual of Style (CMS)
Often used with Economics, History, and some social sciences

Although each citation style offers unique guidelines for how to cite, all generally provide guidelines for these three aspects of academic writing: document format, bibliographic citations, and in-text citations.

Citation styles are developed and maintained by members of varying governing organizations of disciplines. For instance, in the case of the MLA citation style, a committee of individuals involved with MLA, likely academics from a broad range of institutions, will periodically examine and, as needed, modify, the MLA citation style. They then publish these guidelines in a guide called the *MLA Handbook for Writers of Research Papers*. These citation styles are updated as research and writing practices change, and new, updated editions emerge periodically. For instance, older editions of the *MLA Handbook* had very little guidance on how to cite electronic references because, at the time, few academic writers used websites or electronic versions of articles. Now, of course, guides such as the *MLA Handbook* have large sections on how to cite electronic sources.

The rules, conventions, and guidelines for citation and formatting, however, are not arbitrary. Instead, they are deeply embedded in the knowledge-making practices that shape disciplinary inquiry. For example, scholars in biology may use the CSE citation style, which asks for author last name and year of publication to be included in the text whenever a source is referenced. In biology, it is of crucial importance to know what year a study was published so readers can discern how current the research is.

By contrast, scholars in English literature often use the MLA citation style, where references in the text usually include a quote, followed by the author last name and page number specified in the parenthetical citation. While the year of publication matters and is included in the works cited at the end of a paper, scholars affiliated with MLA are often interested in language and words and therefore emphasize quotation and page numbers. Moreover, scholars in biology do not normally include quotations in their academic writing; it is much more customary for them to summarize others' research findings and then include the author last name and year of publication.

To briefly illustrate in-text citation and how it shapes knowledgemaking, Table 12.1 offers the same two sentences as they might appear in several different citation systems.

Please note that Table 12.1 offers only a general sense of in-text citations. Citation styles shift across time, and particular contexts change the ways in-text citation look. Some publishing houses and journals also create "in-house" citation styles, unique to that organization or forum, intended to simplify or standardize citations across their offerings.

In-text citations vary not only according to the citation style, but also according to how much material a writer cites and how the writer integrates the evidence. For instance, in-text citation in MLA looks different when a writer includes a block quote as opposed to a shorter quote. Block quotes, defined differently according to citation style, generally refer to longer portions of excerpted text. According to MLA citation style guidelines, block quotes, unlike shorter quotes in MLA formats, are indicated not by quotation marks, but by additional indentation from the left margin. Other citation styles also specify the particular ways in which writers should cite block quotes. Additional aspects of in-text citations also shift depending on the ways in which writers integrate and frame the evidence they are including. One of the more common occasions in which writers must

Writer Insights

What is important about citation in your discipline?

Switching my career from finance to stress management, I felt something was missing. I didn't know what.... Instead of figures, I write words now, and I learned to write psychological and neuroendocrine research in a clear way. I became such a fan I plan to spend a lot more time on writing about stress management. Therefore, I gladly invested many hours on the APA school of citation.

~Karin de Wulf, Health Coach,
Fabas Ariège, France

TABLE 12.1 In-text citation comparison.

Modern Language Association (MLA)	David Bartholomae illustrates the challenges students face with writing in the disciplines: "Every time a student sits down to write for us, he has to invent the university for the occasion" (273).	Ken Hyland conducted research on citation practices across disciplines: "Writers in the humanities and social sciences employed substantially more citations than scientists and engineers, and were more likely to use integral structures, to employ discourse reporting verbs, and to represent cited authors as adopting a stance to their material" (1).
American Anthropological Association (AAA)	David Bartholomae argues, "Every time a student sits down to write for us, he has to invent the university for the occasion" (1986:273).	As Ken Hyland notes, "Writers in the humanities and social sciences employed substantially more citations than scientists and engineers, and were more likely to use integral structures, to employ discourse reporting verbs, and to represent cited authors as adopting a stance to their material" (1999:1).
American Sociological Association (ASA)	Students "invent the university" each time they write. (Bartholomae 1986:273).	"Writers in the humanities and social sciences employed substantially more citations than scientists and engineers, and were more likely to use integral structures, to employ discourse reporting verbs, and to represent cited authors as adopting a stance to their material" (Hyland 1999:1).
American Psychological Association (APA)	According to David Bartholomae (1986), "Every time a student sits down to write for us, he has to invent the university for the occasion" (p. 273).	According to Ken Hyland (1999), "Writers in the humanities and social sciences employed substantially more citations than scientists and engineers, and were more likely to use integral structures, to employ discourse reporting verbs, and to represent cited authors as adopting a stance to their material" (p. 1).
Council of Science Editors (CSE)	David Bartholomae (1986) outlines the challenges students face as they write in the disciplines.	Ken Hyland (1999) identifies different citation practices across the humanities, social sciences, sciences, and engineering.
American Chemical Society (ACS)	Students face many challenges trying to figure out how to write within disciplines (Bartholomae, 1986).	Scholars in different disciplines deploy different citation practices (Hyland, 1999).
Institute of Electronics and Electrical Engineers (IEEE)	Students face many challenges learning how to write within disciplines [1].	Disciplinary discourse conventions shape citation practices [1].
Chicago Manual of Style (CMS)	David Bartholomae illustrates the challenges students face writing in the disciplines.[1]	Ken Hyland's research demonstrates divergences in citation practices across disciplinary context.[1]

further tailor their in-text citations involves the use of signal phrases, which we'll look at in more detail later in this chapter.

Still, as these examples illustrate, citation styles are quite varied and emerge from a set of practices that reflect the way knowledge is created among various disciplines.

Purposes for Citation

Chapter 11 addressed why academic writers integrate evidence; this chapter extends those ideas by examining why academic writers cite that evidence. One commonly identified reason for citing evidence involves avoiding plagiarism. While matters of academic integrity are crucial, there are also a variety of other reasons writers cite the works of others. They do so as a means of giving credit to those who deserve that credit and also in order to provide the mechanism by which scholars can build on one another's work. This section describes the many different purposes writers have for citing the work of others.

Create a road map for other scholars

Academic writers read others' research so they can build, expand, adapt, modify, reconsider, or otherwise make use of it for their own research. As academic writers read others' research, they rely on those academic writers to provide bibliographic and citation information so that they

Transfer at Work

Although citation styles vary across disciplinary context and writing occasion, academic writers share similar purposes for citing. Xiao Tang, Lei Want, and Rajiv Kishore argue that "Citation behavior is a form of knowledge seeking ... Citing the work of experts in certain domains is necessary for strong theory building" (3). They researched 1,034 authors who published papers in ten top information systems (IS) journals. They found that the likelihood of an author citing another author is positively correlated to whether they have coauthored before and whether they have cited that author previously. However, they also found that, likely due to competition, these positive associations are weakened when the authors have the same institutional affiliation:

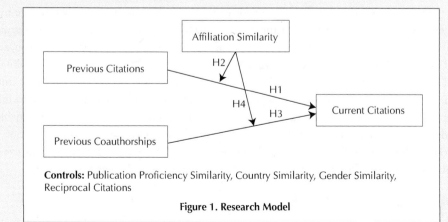

Controls: Publication Proficiency Similarity, Country Similarity, Gender Similarity, Reciprocal Citations

Figure 1. Research Model

Writer Insights

What is the importance of citation in your field?

[W]riting academic papers [are] essential in my career.... I [have recently] realized the importance of proper citation and different type[s] of citation format: MLA, CSE, and APA. I found that I have paid so little attention to bibliographies before, while I have a totally different attitude towards it now.

~Xinyan Xie, Student and Physician,
Tianjin, China

too can then build, respond, counter, or modify those ideas. Sometimes readers use your citations in order to get a fuller sense of the shape of research in a particular field.

Citations can reveal a considerable amount about your project; they can communicate to readers what disciplinary perspective you are using. They also, in a collective way, work to bring certain research into more prominence than other research. If enough scholars cite a particular person's research or a particular research paper, then that person and his or her work become more central to research in that field. Over time, one can observe that scholars are likely to cite a particularly prominent scholar or important study that has been cited by many others already writing on that subject. Some disciplines refer to this as impact, meaning how significant the impact of that particular research has been. Higher impact means that more people have cited that scholar's work. Some research databases even provide statistics on how many others have cited a particular text.

Provide consistency for readers

Adhering to a citation style specified by the publication context in which you are writing means your readers will likely be familiar with that citation style. Providing consistency in citation enables readers to process your research more readily. It would likely be distracting for readers if they had to learn a new style of citation when they encountered each new text. Busy researchers come to recognize what citations typically look like in their fields, and through citation they can quickly find what they are looking for in others' research. Since you are providing a road map for readers by networking your ideas with those of others, citation enables your road map to be as consistent and easily navigable as possible.

Of course, what may be consistent for your readers does not necessarily translate into consistency and ease of navigation for you as a writer. As you move through courses and writing projects, you will likely be asked to write with citation styles that are new to you, and you may, therefore, need to adjust your citation styles accordingly with different disciplinary and publication contexts. Although this process may take some effort on your part until you become more accustomed to a range of citation styles, the benefits make it worthwhile. Deploying a citation style that is appropriate to your discipline or publication context enables readers to approach your arguments with a greater focus on your ideas. When citation is inconsistent or unfamiliar, readers may become distracted by trying to figure out your use of footnotes, for example, or why there are (or are not) parenthetical in-text references.

Acknowledge others' work

When you cite properly, you are acknowledging the work of others. This means you are awarding credit to people who deserve that credit. In one sense, such acknowledgement is a matter of professional courtesy. Citation paves the way so you can then go on and extend, challenge, reconsider, or otherwise respond to their work. But acknowledgement has a more substantive impact as well. Most people want to be recognized for the work they have done, including those who conduct research, write, and publish. Imagine, for a moment, how you might feel if an idea from one of your written arguments was cited in another researcher's work. Receiving recognition enables people to see that their contributions matter, and this courtesy will likely inspire them to continue their efforts to contribute. In this way, your acknowledgment of their efforts may translate into support for them to continue conducting research and advancing knowledge.

Writer Insights

Why is citation important in your field?

As a technical writer, I rely heavily on style guides to ensure that my writing is interchangeable with the writing of others on my team. When our writings are merged together into one user manual, our styles, grammar, and voices need to appear as one. This may sound difficult to achieve, but its success lies in the preparation. The technical writing field frequently relies on the Chicago Manual of Style, and each project will then set additional style guidelines relevant to the company or industry we are working with (healthcare, manufacturing, etc.). These additional style guides may address acronyms and their use or colloquial terms.

~Stacey Wagner, Software Technical Writer,
Seattle, Washington, United States

Doing your part to cultivate a culture where people's contributions are acknowledged and valued means your work will likely be recognized and valued as well. Citing the work of others enables you to engage ethically, professionally, and courteously by awarding credit to those who deserve it and by recognizing their contributions. In so doing, you can also optimize the likelihood that you and your work will likewise receive such acknowledgment.

Avoid plagiarism

Plagiarism is using the work of others without attributing it. This includes words, ideas, images, visuals, audio recordings, music—anything that is the work of someone else. Academic writing is reliant on creating a community of high ethics so that researchers build on the work of others rather than steal from the work of others. Citing properly enables academic writers to attribute what is the work of others and to differentiate that from their own research contributions. Improper or absent citation is plagiarism—stealing. It carries with it severe consequences, including academic suspension or expulsion at many campuses. In academic communities, plagiarism also has severe consequences, including professional loss of career and public humiliation.

Write Now

Imagine a circumstance in which you learned that someone else had plagiarized your writing. How would you feel about someone using your work without attributing it to you? What impacts do you think plagiarism has on authors?

Differentiate others' ideas from your own

Citations within texts create visual markers of the extent of research in the text as well as the moments of transition between others' ideas and the writer's explications and arguments. When you include an in-text citation, whether it is marked with a footnote, an endnote, a parenthetical citation, or simply embedded within the text, that moment of citation shows readers you are using the work of others. By turn, the moments in a text that do not include those visual cues about citation convey to readers that these are the writer's contributions to the research. Academic writers should differentiate their ideas from others' ideas so readers can discern how the writing project is advancing knowledge.

Citations as visual cues of research can also help writers identify whether they have clustered citations too heavily in one area of the document, if they have included too many citations throughout, or if they have not included enough. Every disciplinary and publication context warrants a different approach to the number of citations and the distribution of citations. Scanning a text for the citations can help writers in their revision processes. For instance, if you look through a text or at the bibliographic references and see only a very few citations, then you might decide to include more research. Similarly, if you notice that your text's sentences are filled with citations, then that will likely be a signal that you will need to create more space to develop your own arguments in that text.

Document format

Document format addresses a host of different specifications regarding the layout and design elements of writing projects. These specifications include heading information, such as where on a document to place your name, the date, the class and professor name, and the title. Document format elements of citation styles even specify the format to use for the date, as well as how to format page numbers and whether pagination should appear on the upper right, upper left, or on the bottom center of a page. Document format also involves specifications about margin size and the sequence for appendices and acknowledgements. Citation styles also dictate through document format whether a writer should use footnotes, endnotes, or parenthetical in-text citations, and whether the list of bibliographic resources at the end of a document should be named References, Resources, Bibliography, or Works Cited.

Bibliographic citations

Bibliographic citations are the items used and cited within a document. Depending on the citation style, bibliographic citations can appear in footnotes or endnotes or in a separate bibliographic section at the end of a document. Bibliographic citations tend to include much of the same information for each item across citation styles, but citation styles dictate what order that information appears in and what format. For instance, all bibliographic citations include author name, but some citation styles ask for full first and last names, while others call for full last name with only the first name initial instead of the entire first name. Bibliographic citations also specify how to craft the publication information for many different types of texts. Each citation style provides unique templates, for example, specifying how to construct a bibliographic citation for a book, a book chapter, a journal article, a newspaper article, a movie, a website, an image, a legal document, and a variety of other types of resources ranging from performances to tweets.

In-text citations and signal phrases

In-text citations are the occasions within the actual text (as opposed to the references section) when academic writers integrate evidence, quoting or paraphrasing others, or summarizing relevant research. Whenever this occurs, academic writers cite where the information came from in order to make their research trail visible to readers. Some citation styles rely on author last name and page number (i.e., Comer 220); others require author last name and year of publication (i.e., Comer, 2014). In-text citations are connected to the bibliographic citations; readers use in-text citations to

Transfer at Work

Linguistics scholar Ken Hyland found considerable variation in the amount of in-text citations appearing in research across disciplines:

Table 1: Rank order of citations by discipline

Rank	Discipline	Av. per paper	Per 1000 words	Total citations
1	Sociology	104.0	12.5	1,040
2	Marketing	94.9	10.1	949
3	Philosophy	85.2	10.8	852
4	Biology	82.7	15.5	827
5	Applied Linguistics	75.3	10.8	753
6	Electronic Engineering	42.8	8.4	428
7	Mechanical Engineering	27.5	7.3	275
8	Physics	24.8	7.4	248
	Totals	67.1	10.7	5,372

Hyland also found variation in the form writers use across disciplines for their in-text citations:

Table 3: Presentation of cited work (%)

Discipline	Quote	Block Quote	Summary	Generalization
Biology	0	0	72	38
Electronic Engineering	0	0	66	34
Physics	0	0	68	32
Mechanical Engineering	0	0	67	33
Marketing	3	2	68	27
Applied Linguistics	8	2	67	23
Sociology	8	5	69	18
Philosophy	2	1	89	8

quickly recognize the attribution without getting distracted from what they are reading, and then they can go to the bibliographic section to learn the full bibliographic information should they need or want it.

Signal phrases, as discussed in Chapter 11: Choosing and Integrating Evidence, refer to a variety of strategies writers can use to introduce cited material and explicitly name the author and/or text. In some citation styles, such as MLA, the inclusion of a signal phrase impacts the way a writer cites the material. Since a signal phrase provides bibliographic information up front for readers, writers who use signal phrases do not then need to also reproduce that same bibliographic information in the parenthetical in-text citation. For instance, the Bartholomae example used to illustrate MLA in-text citation in Table 12.1 includes a signal phrase. Because the introductory material leading up to the quote signals to readers who the author is, the only item needed in the parenthetical citation is the page number:

MLA In-Text Citation, with Signal Phrase

David Bartholomae illustrates the challenges students face with writing in the disciplines: "Every time a student sits down to write for us, he has to invent the university for the occasion" (273).

One more detail to add regarding signal phrases involves whether a writer is including material from a source for the first time in a text or if the writer is referring to this source a second, third, or subsequent time. For instance, in MLA, the first time in a writing project when a writer refers to a resource, it is customary for the writer to use the resource's first and last name:

MLA In-Text Citation, First Reference to a Resource

David Bartholomae illustrates the challenges students face with writing in the disciplines, explaining, "Every time a student sits down to write for us, he has to invent the university for the occasion" (273).

However, according to MLA, the signal phrase should look different if a writer has already referred to the reference at a prior point in the text. In the case of subsequent references to cited material, the writer would refer to Bartholomae in the signal phrase only by last name (unless the writing project includes multiple resources by authors with the same last name, and the first initial is needed in order to avoid reader confusion):

MLA In-Text Citation, Second or Subsequent Reference to a Resource

Bartholomae illustrates the challenges students face with writing in the disciplines, explaining, "Every time a student sits down to write for us, he has to invent the university for the occasion" (273).

In some disciplinary and citation style contexts, it is exceedingly rare (or even perceived as unseemly) to use author first names in signal phrases, regardless of whether it is the first reference or a subsequent reference. Please review the discourse conventions for the context in which you are writing to get a sense of how writers approach signal phrases with multiple references to the same resource.

Many writing occasions do not lend themselves to writers using signal phrases every time they introduce and frame cited material, and some writing occasions invite the use of signal phrases only under the very rarest of conditions. Writers have many reasons for not choosing to use signal phrases every single time they cite in a text. Such reasons might include efforts to adhere to disciplinary conventions, writing occasion expectations, or stylistic preferences. Or, perhaps a writer aims to accomplish a particular purpose with the cited material that would be waylaid by a signal phrase.

Look at the following example of MLA citation without a signal phrase:

MLA In-Text Citation, without a Signal Phrase

Students face many challenges when writing. Among them is that they need to "invent the university for the occasion" (Bartholomae 273).

Since the source was not named in a signal phrase, the parenthetical citation in this case includes both author last name and page number. Signal phrases apply not only to quotations, but also to paraphrases and summaries.

To determine where and when to use a signal phrase, you might consider such matters as purpose, clarity for readers, and the types of sources and citations you will integrate into your writing project. You can also review the discourse conventions for the context in which you are writing to get a sense of whether writers tend to include signal phrases or not, as well as the circumstances in which signal phrases are likely to be used.

Write Now

Which citation styles have you used for your research and writing? What do you find challenging about citation? In what writing occasions have you found citation to be most valuable?

Citation Guides

Given the great complexities involved with citation, writers should be reassured that they do not need to learn every intricacy about every citation style. Fortunately, many resources exist for citation styles. Collectively, these are referred to as citation guides. They can be published from the organization that has developed the citation style, such as APA or MLA, or they can be published and maintained by third parties. Citation guides must be updated continually to reflect changes in the citation styles. These guides come in print forms and online versions. Some are more comprehensive than others. You should choose a citation guide that

Transfer at Work

All citation guides offer templates for how to cite, but they do so in different formats and with different arrangements, even those that provide guidance on the same citation style. Sarah Park, Lori A. Mardis, and Connie Jo Ury researched the citation guides provided on library websites. They note that librarians "often create their own extensions of [official] style manuals via their library web pages [in order to] provide ... tailored resources ... for specific courses and subject areas" (48). Their research with Google analytics suggests that these librarian-created citation guides are among the most popular pages on their library's website:

Ranking	Page title	Page views
1	B.D. Owens Library, Northwest Missouri State University	1,250,234
2	Owens Library Hot Paper Topics	246,094
3	Owens Library APA Citation Style Examples	214,915
4	Owens Library MLA Citation Style Examples	200,398
5	Owens Library Science Fair Projects	95,251
6	Owens Library Directions for Off-Campus Access	71,215
7	Owens Library Citing Sources	68,639
8	Owens Library Turabian & Chicago Citation Style Examples	51,701
9	Owens Library Scientific (CBE) Citation Style Examples	51,642
10	Owens Library Computers and Information Technology	25,775
11	Oral Communication Homepage	22,486
12	B.D. Owens Library Search Results	17,724
13	Owens Library Recommended Psychology, Sociology & Counseling Databases	17,209
14	Owens Library Help with Citing	16,270
15	Practice Academic Honesty	14,145

not only is readily accessible and that matches the writing or disciplinary context, but that is also reliable and up to date.

Citation style guides

Each citation style has an official style guide, often in print and online. MLA, for instance, publishes its guidelines in the *MLA Handbook for Writers of Research Papers*. The Chicago citation style publishes its guidelines in the *Chicago Manual of Style*. These style guides provide the most current and official guidelines. Be sure, though, to secure the most recent edition of the style guide since that will include the most up-to-date and accurate information.

Library and writing center websites

Most libraries and writing centers offer guidelines for citing the work of others; many of these are available publicly online. Be aware that not all websites are updated to reflect new editions of citation styles, however. As you use these resources, look to see when the site was updated, and try to discern the reliability and credibility of the site. For more on the reliability of sources, see Chapter 11: Choosing and Integrating Evidence.

Research and library databases

Many research databases (i.e., JSTOR, Google Scholar, ScienceDirect) will have an icon on the page near an article that enables a citation pop-up and provides options for various styles of citation, which you can then copy and paste into your document. Beware, however, that not all research databases provide accurate citations, so be sure to proofread them in consultation with a more official citation style guide.

Citation management software

These software programs enable you to enter bibliographic information into the program so that it stores your sources in an organized manner. Many of these programs, such as Endnote or Zotero, can also generate citations in the citation style you specify. As with research and library databases, these programs are not always accurate with the citations they generate; sometimes they do not include pertinent information, and other times, since they rely on user input, they include inaccurate information. Always proofread if you use a bibliographic citation manager.

One form of citation style guide conspicuously absent from the preceding list would be citation generator software available for free or for a fee online. These citation generators market their products by suggesting that citation will be simple because they will automatically provide the citations. Beware, however, that these citation generators produce uneven and unreliable citations, often mixing citation styles or providing inaccurate or incomplete information in the citations. The better options for citation style guides are likely to be from among the more reliable categories identified above.

Questions that Shape Citation

Writers shape their approaches to citation by considering a variety of matters, including disciplinary and publication context. Different disciplines use different citation styles, and citation conventions also change based on how popular or scholarly a text is. Even within these contexts, citation is not a simple matter. Writers within the same discipline may need to develop familiarity with multiple citation styles because different journals in which they publish may each request that authors adhere to different citation guidelines. Some journals even create their own citation styles that are unique to that journal and are not necessarily in accord with any of the formal, more universal citation styles.

Fortunately, becoming adept at citation does not involve copiously memorizing every specific rule across all the various styles of citation. Citation styles include entirely too many rules for anyone to memorize them all, and there are a vast number of different types of sources writers use in their writing, and each different type of source carries different specifications regarding citation. Even if one did memorize all of these specifications, the rules for citation change over time, adjusting as needed to developments in research, communication, and language. Strengthening your abilities with citation does not even necessarily involve memorizing any rules. Instead, the way you can get better with citation is by learning what questions to ask with each new writing occasion so you can tailor your approach to citation in the most effective way possible (Table 12.2).

TABLE 12.2 Questions that shape citation.

Acknowledge disciplinary context	What is the disciplinary context of your project? What citation styles are commonly deployed in that discipline? How might certain citation styles provide more relevant or effective information for that disciplinary context? In examining any prior research you have included in your project, what citation styles do those authors tend to use?
Address publication context	What is the publication context within which you are writing? Is it popular or more academic? What citation styles and practices do other writers in that publication context tend to use? What are readers in that publication context likely to expect regarding citation conventions and practice?
Choose a citation style	Has the professor, journal editor, or publisher indicated a citation style for your writing project? If not, can you inquire of someone what the citation style should be? If you have flexibility with your choice of citation style, even after taking into account disciplinary and publication contexts, what citation style are you most accustomed to using?
Adjust citations based on resource	What different types and forms of resources are you citing? Are your resources print or digital? Are they popular or scholarly? Have you accurately indicated the different forms of resources included in your writing project?
Find and use citation guides	What citation guide(s) will you use with this project? How will you access the citation guide? How reliable and up to date is your chosen citation guide? In using this citation guide as a resource, will you need to then proofread or verify the citations again to ensure accuracy?
Address amount of cited material	How much material from a particular reference are you citing? Do you need to cite multiple pages in an in-text citation? How do you differentiate between summary, which does not require a page number, and paraphrase, which does?
Decide when to use signal phrases	Have you included appropriate signal phrases before citations as needed? Does the citation need a signal phrase of some sort? Do the disciplinary and publication contexts call for extensive use of signal phrases?
Change citations based on reference frequency	With a particular citation, is it the first time you have cited this source, or is it a subsequent reference? Does the citation style you are using require adjustments in citation between the first mention and subsequent mentions?

Criteria for Effective Citation

Many aspects of writing include multiple criteria that writers aim for in order to create effective texts. As illustrated in prior chapters, for example, writers must consider multiple criteria as they craft effective summary, synthesis, analysis, argument, design, and integration of evidence. With citation, however, writers must really acknowledge only two principal criteria: appropriateness for the writing occasion and accuracy. Keeping these criteria in mind will help you cite effectively across the many varying writing occasions that rely on citation as a part of a larger scholarly conversation. Still, effective citation can be quite complicated, and even meeting these two key criteria requires considerable deliberation about citation practices and conventions, a nuanced awareness of writing transfer, and a careful attention to detail.

Accurate

Whichever style of citation you choose, be sure you are using it accurately. Check and double check, and allow time for it. Avoid waiting until the end of a writing project to cite things because you may forget where you located certain information.

Accurate citations should include the correct scholar, bibliographic information, and text. Find out for certain what the year of publication is, and make sure you are spelling the author's name correctly. Be sure to attribute ideas to the correct author.

The correct format according to the citation style, including location of the citation for in-text citations, must be utilized. While you may think it shouldn't matter whether a comma appears inside quotes or whether the year of publication appears after an author's name or at the end of a reference, these matters are important in helping provide consistency among a community of researchers so they can read one another's work without being distracted by how to find the information they need.

Appropriate for the writing occasion

When citing others' work, writers must choose a citation style that is appropriate for the writing occasion. Sometimes the citation style is dictated by a professor or, in the case of a writer aiming for publication, the journal or publisher to whom you are submitting your writing project. In these cases, though, it is important to recognize that the citation styles specified are not arbitrary but emerge out of disciplinary context and writing occasion. Citation styles impact the ways readers process information. When readers encounter in-text citations that show the year of publication, they may prioritize that as a component of their receptivity to the research. Disconnects between citation styles and writing occasion can leave readers distracted, unable to focus on your arguments and unable to trace how your research is participating in your argument.

Disciplinary context is not the only important context, however. Writing occasion dramatically impacts the citation style one will use as well as the conventions for that style. In more popular contexts, writers might use fewer citations, or include footnotes in formats that are more accessible to general readers. Popular writing that appears in online contexts might invoke a style of citation that involves links rather than publication information. In textbooks, as another example, you might see approaches to citation that look different than academic writing in other contexts, perhaps exhibiting fewer citations throughout and holding to "in-house" citation styles. In all of these cases, writers choose citation styles that fit appropriately within the disciplinary context and writing occasion in which they are writing. In so doing, their citation choices align with the ways in which knowledge is created within those contexts.

Examples of Citation across Disciplinary Perspectives

To illustrate how citation styles vary and the impact they have on academic writing, this section provides examples of citation styles, many of which cross disciplinary contexts:

- Institute of Electrical and Electronics Engineers (IEEE), Physics
- American Psychological Association (APA), Information Science
- Modern Language Association (MLA), English Literature
- Chicago Manual of Style (CMS), History of Science
- American Chemical Society (ACS), Chemistry
- American Anthropological Association (AAA), Archaeology
- American Sociological Association (ASA), Sociology
- Chicago Manual of Style (CMS), with Digital Resources Art
- Chicago Manual of Style (CMS), with Images, Art

As you explore these different examples, keep in mind that citation guidelines may have shifted since the time when a particular author was preparing his or her manuscript. Thus, these examples are not necessarily intended to show you how to cite so much as to help you learn why people cite, what citation entails, and how to locate the resources that will enable you to accurately and appropriately cite the work of others. Keep in mind as well that hardly any citation style is exclusively connected to one particular discipline. For example, chemists might often use ACS, but they are also likely to use other citation styles as well, such as APA or CSE. Consider these examples, then, as a beginning point for you to consider how academic writers approach citation and how citation looks across contexts and disciplines.

Example 1: Institute of Electrical and Electronics Engineers (IEEE), Physics

In this example, physicist Sidney Redner is pursuing the question, "how often is a paper cited?" He examines the impact factor of citation, and how that impact, or frequency of citation, is calculated. Faculty gain more prestige if they have an article that is distributed and cited more widely, so Redner is researching how papers get distributed and what the implications are of that popularity. He is using the IEEE citation style, primarily because he is publishing it in a journal that asks for that citation style, but also because he is a faculty member in physics, which makes use of IEEE at times.

Excerpt from "How Popular is Your Paper? An Empirical Study of the Citation Distribution" by S. Redner

Redner uses brackets with the numbers 1 and 2 to show that he is referring to research in references 1 and 2, as indicated in his references section. If readers want to read that research, they can then go to the references section and find items 1 and 2.

Redner names the study and the author in a signal phrase. Notice that Redner includes citations right after the author's name, a feature of IEEE.

Notice that the references from the end of Redner's paper include some discursive information as well as citations. Citations appear with the author's first initial and then the last name.

I consider a question which is of relevance to those for whom scientific publication is a primary means of scholarly communication. Namely, how often is a paper cited? While the average or total number of citations are often quoted anecdotally and tabulations of highly-cited papers exist [1, 2], the focus of this work is on the more fundamental distribution of citations, namely, the number of papers which have been cited a total of x times, N(x). In spite of the fact that many academics are obliged to document their citations for merit-based considerations, there have been only a few scientific investigations on quantifying citations or related measures of scientific productivity. In a 1957 study based on the publication record of the scientific research staff at Brookhaven National Laboratory, Shockley [3] claimed that the scientific publication rate is described by a log-normal distribution. Much more recently, Laherrere and Sornette [4] have presented numerical evidence, based on data of the 1120 most-cited physicists from 1981 through June 1997, that the citation distribution of individual authors has a stretched exponential form, $N(x) \propto \exp[-(x/x0) \beta]$ with $\beta \approx 0.3$. Both papers give qualitative justifications for their assertions which are based on plausible general principles; however, these arguments do not provide specific numerical predictions. Here, the citation distribution of scientific publications based on two relatively large data sets is investigated [5].

IEEE does not call for article titles, and it makes extensive use of abbreviations. For instance, item 3 is citing an article written by William Shockley titled "On the Statistics of Individual Variations of Productivity in Research Laboratories." It appeared in the proceedings of the IRE (Institute of Radio Engineers).

[1] See e.g., Science Citation Index Journal Citation Reports (Institute for Scientific Information, Philadelphia) for annual lists of top-cited journals and articles (web site: http://www.isinet.com/welcome.html).
[2] For example, current lists of top-cited articles in high-energy physics are maintained by the SPIRES High-Energy Physics Database at SLAC (web site http://www.slac.stanford.edu/find/top40.html).
[3] W. Shockley, Proc. IRE 45, 279 (1957).
[4] J. Laherrere and D. Sornette, cond-mat/9801293.
[5] The PRD data was provided by H. Galic from the SPIRES Database. The ISI data was provided by D. Pendlebury and H. Small of the Institute for Scientific Information. These two data sets and related citation data are available from my web site http://physics.bu.edu/~redner.

From *The European Physical Journal B-Condensed Matter and Complex Systems* (4.2), 1998.

Example 2: American Psychological Association (APA), Information Science

Michael Levin and his team examine here how large research databases learn to differentiate between authors of the same name, known by the phrase "author disambiguation." The authors use APA citation style.

Excerpt from "Citation-Based Bootstrapping for Large-Scale Author Disambiguation" by M. Levin, et al.

The authors include a footnote for the Web of Knowledge, a research database. They choose not to include it in the references section at the end because it is not a research study, but a database.

Large bibliographic databases often fail to distinguish authors with similar names. Consider "J. Lee," attributed with over 56,000 articles in Thomson Reuters' Web of Knowledge[1], or "Kim, J.H.," with over 11,000. Clearly there is not just a single J. Lee or J.H. Kim who published all of these articles. But although distinguishing the different authors with similar names is important for any research that makes use of networks of scientific publications, the task is quite difficult. Publication databases are huge, requiring methods that can scale up to millions of articles, and methods must be capable of handling partial and conflicting metadata. ...

The first line of the second paragraph has another footnote; although it is citing a study, it is also communicating additional information, so the authors chose to include it as a discursive footnote, and they also include the study in the references section.

The authors name several studies that refer to "supervised machine learning train classifiers" and their year of publication. Notice that APA calls for a list of multiple authors to include a comma and an ampersand before the final name in the list, followed by the year. According to current APA guidelines, if there are one to five authors, they are all named; if there are six or more, the citation includes just the first author's name plus the phrase et al. (and others).

There have been three classes of algorithms for author disambiguation.[2] Methods relying on supervised machine learning train classifiers (support vector machines, random forests, etc.) on a hand-labeled training set containing pairs of articles where similarly named authors are identified as being the same or different persons (Han, Giles, Zha, Li, & Tsioutsiouliklis, 2004; Huang, Ertekin, & Giles, 2006; Kanani, McCallum, & Pal, 2007; Chen, Kalashnikov, & Mehrotra, 2007; Culotta, Kanani, Hall, Wick, & McCallum, 2007; Yang, Peng, Jiang, Lee, & Ho, 2008; Treeratpituk & Giles,

On the bottom of the page in the publication appear what are known as discursive footnotes. As opposed to bibliographic footnotes, discursive footnotes add extra information to what appears in the text itself. They are almost like parenthetical asides that direct readers to additional literature or to further explain points. Writers generally decide what can or cannot go in a discursive footnote based on how central the information is to the actual argument. These can also sometimes be organized as endnotes, which appear at the end of a text, instead of footnotes at the bottom of pages.

[1] http://www.webofknowledge.com/
[2] See Smalheiser and Torvik (2009) for a comprehensive summary of this literature.

From *Journal of the American Society for Information Science and Technology* (63.5), 2012.

2009). Supervised algorithms require large handlabeled training sets, especially for huge databases like MEDLINE or Web of Knowledge that contain tens of millions of articles. Such large quantities of manually annotated training data are not easily available, would be hard to make representative, and would be expensive to collect. For this reason, supervised algorithms may not be the best solution for such databases....

Although these previous studies have shown that high precision features may be useful for bootstrapping, a number of open issues remain. It is not clear how effective feature-based bootstrapping is on large-scale collections—only Torvik and Smalheiser's (2009) study was large scale, and they combined feature-based bootstrapping with additional hand-labeled training data, so it is not possible to see the effect of feature-based bootstrapping alone. It is also unknown whether existing findings about feature-based bootstrapping will hold with very large datasets—for example, contrasting with the work of Bhattacharya and Getoor (2007) and Ferreira et al. (2010) on smaller datasets, our results will show that coauthorship is not effective for bootstrapping author disambiguation on Thomson Reuters' Web of Knowledge.

Here, the authors focus on specific studies, naming them within the body of the text as they hold more important findings relevant for their research. The Ferreira study entry, because it includes et al., indicates that study included six or more authors.

This is a partial listing of the references, which illustrate that APA asks for references to have the last name, followed by the first initial, then the year. Titles capitalize only the first letter, and this citation style includes more publication information than does the IEEE. Notice that references appear with a "hanging indent," whereby the second and subsequent lines of each entry are indented. This is so that busy readers can quickly scan through the names to find the reference they are looking for. Notice that references are alphabetized rather than appearing in chronological order of publication or of when they appeared in the text.

References

Andrew, G., & Gao, J. (2007). Scalable training of 11-regularized log-linear models. In *Proceedings of the 24th International Conference on Machine Learning (ICML '07)* (pp. 33–40). New York: ACM Press.

Bagga, A., & Baldwin, B. (1998). Algorithms for scoring coreference chains. *Recall*, 5(1), 2.

Banko, M., & Brill, E. (2001). Scaling to very large corpora for natural language disambiguation. In *Proceedings of the 39th Annual Meeting of the Association for Computational Linguistics* (pp. 26–33). Stroudsburg, PA: Association for Computational Linguistics.

Bhattacharya, I., & Getoor, L. (2006). A latent dirichlet model for unsupervised entity resolution. *In Proceedings of SIAM International Conference on Data Mining* (pp. 47–58). New York: ACM Press.

Bhattacharya, I., & Getoor, L. (2007). Collective entity resolution in relational data. *ACM Transactions on Knowledge Discovery from Data*, 1(1), 5.

Example 3: Modern Language Association (MLA), English Literature

In this example, Amy Robillard poses the inquiry, "How do scholars make use of student writing in scholarship about writing studies, and what are the implications?" Robillard uses the MLA citation style; she is publishing in a journal called *College English*.

Excerpt from "'Young Scholars' Affecting Composition: A Challenge to Disciplinary Citation Practices" by A. E. Robillard

In their article, "When Peer Tutors Write about Writing: Literacy Narratives and Self Reflection," Heather Bastian and Lindsey Harkness demonstrate that composition scholars have constructed "an image—a critical image—of students," and that such critical images of students are further supported by the type of student the discourse community of composition chooses to discuss in their essays. Struggling or poor writers remain the focus. The preoccupation with "poor" and "struggling" students establishes these writers as the norm and disregards other students, such as competent college writers (81).

> Robillard provides a signal phrase here by naming the full article title and the authors' first and last names. She includes a parenthetical citation at the end of this section, indicating to readers that all the sentences preceding the citation are from Bastian and Harkness's article. She combines paraphrase with quotation, all from page 81 of their article.

Bastian and Harkness suggest that students ought to be provided opportunities "to engage in the rhetoric of the composition field, so that they can create more accurate representations of themselves" (91), a suggestion that makes sense when one considers the extent to which composition studies—unlike, say, astronomy or biology or economics—has relied upon student writing as the subject of so much of its research…. In WPA-L listserv discussions, Doug Downs, Christina Fisanick, and Elizabeth Wardle advocate a focus in first-year composition courses on the very questions underpinning composition studies itself—especially student empowerment. This small trend represents a shift in the central question of composition studies, as John Trimbur notes in his article "Changing the Question: Should Writing Be Studied?" In the 1960s and 1970s, the central question of composition studies

> Here, Robillard continues to cite their article, this time with a longer quotation from page 91; notice that she includes the parenthetical citation directly after the quoted material, even though it is not the end of the sentence. This signals a shift from the ideas of Bastian and Harkness to her own ideas. The material after the parenthetical citation is Robillard's analysis. MLA does not call for year of publication in the in-text citation.

> Robillard now turns her attention to another scholar whose work applies to her research: John Trimbur. Again, Robillard names him and includes the full title of his article.

From *College English*, 2006.

Throughout this paragraph, as with the former one, Robillard includes page numbers after quotes and names authors and their works within her sentences. Notice how much more frequently Robillard addresses particular quotes and passages in the texts she's citing. This is characteristic of research in MLA citation style.

was "Can writing be taught?" (16). The process movement, in what Trimbur calls "a kind of trickster operation," revised the question to "How can writing be learned?" shifting the subject of the question from teacher to student and leading to "a proliferation of answers with no end in sight" (22). The question that seems now to be at the forefront of composition studies is "Should writing be studied?" and the answer that the process movement, with the writing workshop at the center of undergraduate writing instruction, seems to be providing is a resounding "no" (22). Trimbur cites the pedagogical imperative—on the part of not just teachers but also students who expect to become better writers through classroom practice—as the reason the question "Should writing be studied?" has met with such negative responses. The pedagogical imperative fixes writing as a verb, whereas Bastian and Harkness's work—and the publication of *Young Scholars in Writing* more generally—forces us to see writing as a noun, an object of study for students as well as for teachers. More recently, Nancy Dejoy argues in her book, *Process This: Undergraduate Writing in Composition Studies*, that engaging students in the questions of composition studies is essential to reconceiving students' current positions as consumers of composition's disciplinary knowledge and seeing them as participants in and contributors to such knowledge.

MLA asks for a Works Cited section instead of References or Bibliography. Each entry has a hanging indent, and the full name of each author (rather than an initial) is included. MLA Works Cited pages are double spaced.

Works Cited

Bardies, Roland. "The Death of the Author." *Image, Music, Text.* Trans. Stephen Heath. New York: Noonday, 1977. 142-48.

Bastian, Heather, and Lindsey Harkness. "When Peer Tutors Write about Writing: Literacy Narratives and Self Reflection." *Young Scholars in Writing* 1 (2003): 77-94....

Example 4: Chicago Manual of Style (CMS), History of Science

Yves Gingras explores in this article how scholars define "impact" regarding a scientific publication. Gingras writes in the CMS style.

Excerpt from "Revisiting the 'Quiet Debut' of the Double Helix:
A Bibliometric and Methodological note on the 'Impact' of Scientific Publications"
by Y. Gingras

In the field of the history of molecular biology we have observed, over the past ten years, a tendency to "revisit" the dominant narrative that made the double helix papers of 1953 by Watson and Crick a crucial event that transformed modern biology. Soraya de Chadarevian recently wrote: "it is now widely accepted that James Watson and Francis Crick's model of the structure of DNA did not make immediate impact."[1] Though the term "impact" is not defined, her statement is backed by a reference to a brief paper by Robert Olby published in *Nature* on the occasion of the 50th anniversary of the publication of the DNA structure and to the author's own previous work where she argued, on the basis of interviews, press coverage and archival documents that the discovery of the DNA structure was not considered important until the 1960s. She writes, for example, that "a letter addressed to the secretary of the MRC by Bragg at the end of the 1950s confirms the relative oblivion surrounding Watson and Crick's work on the double helix."[2]

Though it may be true that DNA was not a big thing in Bragg's laboratory, one can hardly generalize from such a local reaction to the whole community. In the same vein, Robert Olby titled his contribution "Quiet debut for the double helix." Its headline stated that "the historical record reveals a muted response by the scientific community to the proposal of [the DNA's] structure in 1953."[3] Three months later another historian, Bruno Strasser, repeated the same message that "we usually think that the double-helix model acquired immediate and enduring success" but that "on the contrary, it enjoyed only a 'quiet debut,'" the author then referring the reader

> Gingras includes quotes, but CMS has the citations as footnotes. These footnotes indicate the pages where the quote appears.

> In CMS, footnotes usually have the full bibliographic citation the first time a resource is cited. This journal has modified CMS slightly (which journals often do) and includes only an abbreviated reference here.

> Gingras makes use of signal phrases here but most often includes only the author's first and last name, omitting the titles of the works.

> Footnotes appear at the bottom of each page and are used with superscript numbers.

[1] de Chadarevian, 2006, p. 707.
[2] de Chadarevian, 2002, p. 243, our emphasis.
[3] Olby, 2003, p. 402.

From *Journal of the History of Biology* (43.1), 2010.

to Olby's piece.[4] Finally, a few years later, biologist Peter A. Lawrence, in an opinion piece criticizing "the mismeasurement of science" based on citation analysis, took that new wisdom as a fact and wrote that "the most important paper of the 20th century was cited rarely for the first ten years" again sending the reader to Olby's piece in Nature for the "proof of that assertion.[5]

> Whereas the footnotes contain the individual page citations, or in-text citations, the References section contains full bibliographic information. The year appears directly after the author's name. As with the other citation styles, books and journal titles appear in italics. In this citation style, articles appear in quotation marks.

References

de Chadarevian, S. 2002. *Designs for Life: Molecular Biology After World War II.* Cambridge: Cambridge University Press.

---- 2006. "Mice and the Reactor: The 'Genetics Experiments' in the 1950s Britain." *Journal of the History of Biology* 39: 707-735.

Olby, Robert. 2003. "Quiet Debut for the Double Helix." *Nature* 421: 402-405.

> When citing more than one work by the same author, CMS uses dashes rather than a repetition of the author's name.

[4] Strasser, 2003, pp. 803-804, our emphasis.
[5] Lawrence, 2007, pp. R584-R585, our emphasis.

Example 5: American Chemical Society (ACS), Chemistry

This fifth example comes from an editorial section of the *Journal of Medicinal Chemistry*. Editors Georg and Wang are discussing plagiarism as it relates to their journal. In the sciences, plagiarism can be complicated since many researchers publish multiple papers based on one large research project. These editors are clarifying the question "What is self-plagiarism?"

Excerpt from "Plagiarism" by G. I. Georg and S. Wang

At the *Journal of Medicinal Chemistry*, the annual number of suspected plagiarism cases is very low, which we credit in part to the thorough reviews of our Associate Editors and reviewers but most especially to the self-vigilance of our authors. We are pleased that our authors remain upstanding scientists and are being careful to avoid such egregious errors.

As Editors of the *Journal of Medicinal Chemistry*, we wish to provide our readers, authors, and reviewers with some guidance. Plagiarism is defined as the "wrongful

From *Journal of Medicinal Chemistry* (56.1), 2013.

appropriation or purloining and publication as one's own, of the ideas, or the expression of the ideas ... of another."[1] Many instances of plagiarism are committed because of authors' unfamiliarity regarding what constitutes plagiarism. It is on this topic we wish to provide additional information, specifically on self-plagiarism.

> Georg and Wang quote the Oxford English Dictionary definition of plagiarism and include a footnote for the reference.

The *Journal of Medicinal Chemistry* publishes original research; therefore, authors should not include lengthy discussions of their prior work. Authors should include only as much material as necessary to make the reported work clear and understandable.

(1) Wherever possible, new language should be used to present material rather than copying from previous publications.

(2) Partial or whole sentences taken from a prior publication should be placed in quotes and the reference given. This does not mean that large amounts of information should be repeated from other publications.

(3) It is acceptable to reuse figures as long as permission and acknowledgment has been received from the copyright owner. If the American Chemical Society is the sole owner, permission is not needed to publish in an ACS journal as long as credit is given to where the figure originally appeared in the ACS journal. If credit is given to another source in the figure caption, permission must be obtained from that source.

(4) As it is difficult to create unique ways to describe procedures and equipment, it is acceptable to reproduce language for these items in the experimental section.

(5) If you are in doubt as to whether or not material would be considered self-plagiarism, it is best to reword the text.

Because of the serious nature of the plagiarism, we continue to take all suspected cases very seriously. Allegations of plagiarism are thoroughly investigated according to established best practices (http://publicationethics.org/resources/guidelines). When we have reasonable concern, we ask authors to respond. If a satisfactory response is not forthcoming and there is adequate evidence to establish

> Here, the editors refer to another text and again include a footnote for the reference.

that self-plagiarism or plagiarism has occurred, we proceed per definitions and guidelines stated in the Ethical Guidelines to Publication of Chemical Research, American Chemical Society.[2]

References

(1) *Oxford English Dictionary*, 2nd ed.; Oxford University Press, Oxford, U.K., 1989.

(2) Ethical Guidelines to Publication of Chemical Research; American Chemical Society: Washington, DC, 2012; http://pubs.acs.org/userimages/ContentEditor/1218054468605/ethics.pdf.

> In these references, the page numbers are included for the entire article, not just the particular page from which the citation was pulled.

Example 6: American Anthropological Association (AAA), Archaeology

This example comes from Scott Hutson, an archaeologist, who is writing an inquiry into gendered citation practices in archaeological journals. Hutson makes the argument that "citations serve as a measure of structural inequalities, but may also act to reproduce or transform such structures." He examines citations spanning ten or more years in four academic journals in his field, finding that in several of the journals, women are cited less frequently than men, and that this "under-referencing of women might imply a devaluation of women's archaeological labor."

Hutson also makes the important point that some citation systems make gender inequities less visible than do others: "Because patterns in citations can be subtle, not easily detectable without tally sheets and statistics, they can operate below the level of awareness." For instance, in the AAA citation style in which Hutson is writing, first names are not included in the references, but only initials. While it is not possible to detect gender from first names all the time, sometimes one can, and omitting first names reduces the level of awareness of the gender of those who are cited.

> Excerpt from "Gendered Citation Practices in American Antiquity and Other Archaeology Journals" by S. R. Hutson

Personal networks might also be expected to affect the frequency at which women are cited. For example, Margaret Nelson (1994:201) reports that female archaeology graduate students "do not form peer groups that include women within their graduate departments"…and, therefore, "feel isolated and unable to gain answers to professional, non-academic questions." Roundtable discussions for women at the SAA annual meetings

> Hutson includes in the parentheses the year of Nelson's text, a colon, and the page number from which the ensuing quote comes. Notice that AAA calls for the page number prior to the quote rather than after.

From *American Antiquity* (167.2), 2002.

and at other conferences allow women to gain a network of female colleagues that might be reflected in their citations (e.g., also Ford 1994:72). Of course, other forms of networking, such as that which occurs between one's peers and professors at graduate school, have significant though not always gendered effects on citation (see Kehoe 1992 on citing circles). The existence of citing circles reminds us that citation is also a form of communication. By citing certain writers and not others, authors communicate, consciously or unconsciously, their alliances, alignments, and scholarly self-identities. Furthermore, citation may obliquely flatter...or affront.

> In the parenthetical citation of Ford, Hutson is paraphrasing something from page 72 of Ford's text. When Hutson refers to Kehoe, he uses only the year because he is summarizing the entire publication on citing circles rather than a specific idea on a specific page.

References Cited [abridged]

Ford, A.

1994 Women in Mesoamerican Archaeology: Why are the Best Men Winning? In *Women in Archaeology*, edited by C. Claassen, pp. 159-172. University of Pennsylvania Press, Philadelphia.

Kehoe, A.

1992 The Muted Class: Unshackling Tradition. In *Exploring Gender through Archaeology*, edited by C. Claassen, pp. 23-32. Prehistory Press, Madison, Wisconsin.

Nelson, M. C.

1994 Expanding Networks for Women in Archaeology. In *Equity Issues for Women in Archaeology*, edited by M. Nelson, S. Nelson, and A. Wylie, pp. 199-202. Archaeological Papers of the American Anthropological Association No. 5.

Example 7: American Sociological Association (ASA), Sociology

In the example, authors Nina C. Heckler, David R. Forde, and C. Hobson Bryan examine how assignment design potentially reduces the likelihood of plagiarism among students, specifically in digital environments. They use a combination of print and digital sources and are writing in the ASA citation style.

Excerpt from "Using Writing Assignment Designs to Mitigate Plagiarism"
by N. C. Heckler, D. R. Forde, and C. H. Bryan

In sum, faculty have the most important role in mitigating plagiarism in higher education (Van Gundy et al. 2006). To the topic of this research, the first line of defense for faculty is

From *Teaching Sociology* (41.1), 2013.

course design. In fact, some authorities maintain that faculty can and should be "designing out" plagiarism (Gannon-Leary, Trayhurn, and Home 2009:446).... Numerous research-ers point to course design as a potentially important factor in prevent-ing plagiarism (e.g., Compton and Pfau 2008; Gannon-Leary et al. 2009; Parameswaran and Devi 2006; Samuels and Bast 2006). Among the most integral elements of course design are assignment strategy and structure. Specific strategies include designing assignments for collaborative work (Hart and Friesner 2004; Kasprzak and Nixon 2004; McCord 2008; Ped-ersen 2010), having students turn in the actual sources used in research as-signments (McCord 2008; Samuels and Bast 2006; Sterngold 2004), col-lecting students' field notes (Pedersen 2010), having students submit work through plagiarism detection software (Batane 2010; Gannon-Leary et al. 2009; Walker 2010), having students turn in progressive work products for large projects (Gibson et al. 2006; McCord 2008; Samuels and Bast 2006), varying the nature and frequency of assign-ments (Batane 2010; Bernardi et al. 2008; McCord 2008; Sutherland-Smith 2008), and de-veloping assignments that require evaluation and reflection of material rather than collation of materials (Batane 2010; Howard and Davies 2009; Sutherland-Smith 2008).

> ASA calls for the author-date form of in-text citations; notice in the Gannon-Leary, Trayhurn, and Home citation that the authors have included a specific page number because they quoted a phrase directly from the text as opposed to just referring to it generally.

References [abridged]

Gannon-Leary, Pat, Deborah Trayhurn, and Margaret Home. 2009. "Good Images, Effective Messages? Working with Students and Educators on Academic Practice Understand-ing." *Journal of Further and Higher Education* 33(4):435-48.

Gibson, Jane Whitney, Charles W. Blackwell, Regina A. Greenwood, Ingrid Mobley, and Raquel Whitney Blackwell. 2006. "Preventing and Detecting Plagiarism in the Written Work of College Students." *Journal of Diversity Management* 1(2). Re-trieved March 20, 2011 (http://journals.cluteonline.com/index.php/JDM/article/view/5033).

McCord, Alan. 2008. *Improving Online Assignments to Deter Plagiarism*. Paper presented at the Proceedings of the 12th Annual Technology, Community & Colleges Worldwide Online Conference. Retrieved April 12, 2011 (http://etec.hawaii.edu/proceedings/2008/Mc-Cord2008.pdf).

Van Gundy, Karen, Beth A. Morton, Hope Q. Liu, and Jennifer Kline. 2006. "Effects of Web-Based Instruction on Math Anxiety, the Sense of Mastery, and Global Self-Esteem: A Quasi-Experimental Study of Undergraduate Statistics Students." *Teaching Sociology* 34(4):370-88.

> Several of the sources are from electronic versions, noted by the inclusion of websites in the references. In Gibson, the authors write "retrieved" and include the database from which they retrieved the article; in McCord, the website is the address where the papers are available.

Example 8: Chicago Manual of Style (CMS), with Digital Resources Art

The excerpt appears in an article documenting "how The Phillips Collection, a small museum of modern and contemporary art [in Washington, D.C.], desired to share its reputation as a welcoming and comfortable environment with remote audiences by launching a grassroots-style blog." The author, Sarah Bender, describes the deliberations involved in deciding about citation practices for the blog. She uses Chicago style of citation, but notice how many different kinds of resources she cites in this section, from conference papers and published papers to blogs, emails, and even a personal conversation.

Excerpt from "History, Identity, and Twenty-First Century Skills: Experiments in Institutional Blogging" by S. O. Bender

The blogs that served as a model for The Phillips Collection were the Los Angeles County Museum of Art's Unframed, the San Francisco Museum of Modern Art's Open Space,[9] the Brooklyn Museum's blog, and the Smithsonian American Art Museum's blog Eye Level.[10]

> Bender cites the blogs that informed her approach to blog development. CMS requires footnotes, so the actual blogs are cited in the footnotes according to the standards laid out in the *Chicago Manual of Style* for blogs.

Based on this research, contact was made with fellow museum professionals who oversaw some of the blogs on the spreadsheet. Amy Heibel, then director of Web and Media Strategy for LACMA, provided generous insight and support.[11] She emphasized the value of staying non-promotional in building an authentic relationship

> Bender cites a conversation she had with Heibel, again, using CMS guidelines.

---

9. See Rebecca Nath, "Social Media Tool Case Study: The San Francisco Museum of Modern Art's Blog, Open Space" (paper presented at the California Association of Museums Conference, San Jose, California, March 3–5, 2010), http://www.calmuseums.org/_data/n_0001/resources/live/FINAL_RNathSFMOMA.pdf.

10. See Jeff Gates, "Case Study: New World Blogging within a Traditional Museum Setting," in Museums and the Web 2007: Selected Papers from an International Conference, ed. Jennifer Trant and David Bearman (Toronto, Ontario: Archives & Museum Informatics, 2007), http://www.archimuse.com/mw2007/papers/gates/gates.html; Jeff Gates, "Clearing the Path for Sisyphus: How Social Media is Changing Our Jobs and Our Working Relationships," Museums and the Web 2010: Selected Papers from an International Conference, ed. Jennifer Trant and David Bearman (Toronto, Ontario: Archives & Museum Informatics, 2010), http://www.archimuse.com/mw2010/papers/gates/gates.html; Jeff Gates, "Confessions of a Long Tail Visionary," Life Outtacontext (blog), consulted August 14, 2013, http://outtacontext.com/articles/confessions/.

> The Gates article, though published in a collection of papers, was retrieved by Bender from archimuse.com, a website called *Archives and Museum Informatics,* which provides resources for members of those fields. CMS asks for the full website to be provided.

11. Amy Heibel (vice president, Technology, Web, and Digital Media at the Los Angeles County Museum of Art), in discussion with the author, October 15, 2010.

> CMS specifies that references appear as footnotes at the bottom of the page on which the citation appears. In this article, there is no separate references section at the end of the document.

From *Art Documentation: Journal of the Art Libraries Society of North America* (33.1), 2014.

Bender cites an email from Gates. Since Bender is not using quotation marks, this indicates she is paraphrasing his ideas rather than quoting.

with readers, especially art critics and bloggers who would be likely to promote blog content if it offered a fresh perspective, but not if it echoed marketing materials. ... Jeff Gates,[12] lead producer of New Media Initiatives at the Smithsonian American Art Museum and managing editor of its blog, was also a valuable resource, offering two gems of wisdom in particular. In response to concerns, chiefly from curatorial staff, regarding citations on the blog, Gates clearly distinguished the venue of the blog from that of a scholarly publication. On the blog, the content is more conversational, and simply noting a source's title is sufficient. If a point needs a more detailed citation, it is an indication that either the post's tone is inappropriate for the blog or the content is better suited to a more formal article or essay. Regarding the intention to make the Phillips Collection blog media-heavy and low on article-length posts, Gates alleviated concern over access to enough quality photography. He said that images on the blog didn't necessarily have to be "beautiful"; what was important was that they be "interesting."[13] This straightforward perspective was liberating and inspiring on many levels related to content creation (72).

Citing another conversation, Bender now uses quotation marks, indicating that these were Gates's words.

12. Jeff Gates (lead producer, New Media Initiatives at the Smithsonian American Art Museum, and managing editor, Eye Level), in e-mail message to the author, February 2, 2011.
13. Jeff Gates, in conversation with the author, October 21, 2010.

CMS specifies exactly how to cite a conversation and an email, as well as many other kinds of resources that academic writers might use in their scholarship.

Example 9: Chicago Manual of Style (CMS), With Images, Art

The final example of this segment will offer you a glimpse of citation with images. Citation with images depends on the context in which the image is included. Often, if the image is included as an illustrative figure, then authors will attribute the image source near the actual image but not necessarily include the image in the References section. The example demonstrates this mode of citation with images. Here, Alexander Watkins is arguing for the citation tool Zotero as a strong tool for image resource management, which can help users organize, manage, and cite their personal image collections.

Excerpt from "Zotero for Personal Image Management" by A. Watkins

Each different type of item in Zotero has its own metadata schema, though many fields are shared between item types. Zotero's artwork item type has fields for the most important image data (Figure 2). The ability to document images fully makes the program much more than a way to store and view images. It becomes a place to keep important information, generate citations, and make the data available for analysis. Zotero's metadata for images is strong compared to other image-management software programs, but it is less robust than full-featured digital asset management systems. It lacks the complexity of a schema like VRA Core or the ability to integrate vocabularies (305–6).

Watkins includes a screenshot of Zotero and labels it as a Figure. He does not include a bibliographic citation for the image, but earlier in the article he did have a footnote directing readers to the Zotero website: "1. Readers unfamiliar with using Zotero as a citation manager can get a quick introduction here: "Quick Start Guide [Zotero Documentation]," https://www.zotero.org/support/quick_start_guide."

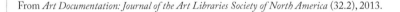

| Info | Notes | Tags | Related |

Item Type: Artwork
Title: Apollo and Daphne
Artist: Bernini, Gian Lorenzo
Abstract:
Medium: Marble
Artwork Size: 243 cm.
Date: 1622-1625
Language:
Short Title:
Archive: Borghese Gallery, Rome
Loc. in Archive: Room III
Library Catalog:
Call Number:
URL:
Accessed:
Rights:
Extra:
Date Added: Friday, March 08, 2013 4:38:22 PM
Modified: Sunday, March 10, 2013 2:56:43 PM

Figure 2. Artwork item type metadata in Zotero.

From *Art Documentation: Journal of the Art Libraries Society of North America* (32.2), 2013.

Citation Practices in the Twenty-First Century: Digital and Visual Formats and Materials

It is useful to keep in mind that citation practices have evolved considerably over the last twenty years to integrate the increasing prevalence of digital formats for academic writing and the increasing preponderance of digital and visual materials.

Most scholarship in the twentieth century emerged in either print or verbal formats, and relied on print resources. Since so much academic writing now appears in digital formats, from webpages and op-eds to online journals, academic writers need to be particularly attuned to citation practices related to these digital environments. Moreover, with increased access to digital materials of all sorts, writers must likewise be savvier at learning how to cite across many different kinds of materials.

Digital materials

All evidence and resources must be cited, including digital materials. Each citation style provides guidelines for how to cite a variety of kinds of materials, from an email or listserv posting to a photograph, whether it appears in an archive, a blog, or a website.

Still, because online contexts develop more quickly than the regular update cycles for citation styles, you should be prepared to encounter a resource at some point that a citation style does not address or does not fully address. In this case, you will need to adapt citation style guidelines to fit the resource. Do this in consultation with your professor and other writing-related resources, such as your institution's writing center, similar writing in that field, and/or reliable, official online writing guides.

Publishing online

Academic writers must use citation whether they are publishing in a peer-reviewed journal, a blog, or a website. Still, the specific strategies for citation can shift across these various platforms.

Some digital platforms, for example, cite by using weblinks instead of standard academic in-text citation formats. In the excerpt, from an article titled "The Play's The Thing," published in the online journal *Hybrid Pedagogy*, author Sarah Heidebrink-Bruno embeds several links, reprinted here in blue, in much the same way that they appear in the online article.

> When reading aloud in class, always do the voices. I know, you don't want to be "that teacher," but trust me, do the voices. Do you remember the first time someone read to you, or you listened to an audio book, and you heard <u>a voice so wonderful, so adaptable</u> that it made the storytelling come alive for you? Chances are, so do your students. If they haven't had that moment yet, create it for them. Be their <u>Alan Rickman</u>.

The first of the links brings readers to a YouTube video featuring an audio book: *The Hobbit*, read by Nicol Williamson (Haamurabi). The second link takes readers to a YouTube video featuring Alan Rickman reading Shakespeare's Sonnet 130 (Kedavra). Heidebrink-Bruno is providing examples of strong reading voices.

In a print journal, these citations may have instead appeared as discursive footnotes, where Heidebrink-Bruno might have offered readers examples of strong reading voices with something along the lines of:

> For examples of the power generated from strong reading voices, see Alan Rickman's reading of Shakespeare's Sonnet 130 and Nicol Williamson's reading of *The Hobbit*.

Then, in her works cited or references, Heidebrink-Bruno would have included full bibliographic citations for these two audio texts. However, because Heidebrink-Bruno is publishing in an entirely digital platform, she instead opts to link out directly to these sites.

Through its approach to citation more broadly, Heidebrink-Bruno's article also illustrates another feature of academic writing in digital platforms. While, as indicated earlier, many online peer-reviewed journals maintain the same discourse conventions for citation as in print publications, using one of the citation styles exemplified in the section toward the end of this chapter, some online publication formats require a modified approach to citation. *Hybrid Pedagogy*, in particular, adopts citation practices that might seem more characteristic of a blog, web-based article, or a more popular print article. That is, Heidebrink-Bruno does not include bibliographic citations at the end of her text. Instead, any resources she uses are attributed through embedded links in the text.

As an example of her modified approach to citation, Heidebrink-Bruno discusses at one point a photographic image as an instance of how students will enjoy examining and creating captions for visual images as a writing activity. Heidebrink-Bruno includes the image along with a caption (Figure 12.1).

**"In 1937, two women caused an accident
by wearing shorts in public for the first time."**

FIGURE 12.1 Example of an image and caption.

Importantly, Heidebrink-Bruno does not include a text-based citation for the photograph. She instead includes a live link embedded within the image, leading readers to the source where she found the image (a Tumblr blog titled stability.tumblr.com, run by blogger and photographer Nick Avallone).

In this case, the original photograph is an archival image located in the City of Toronto archives. The *Huffington Post* reported on the photograph, documenting that it went viral after a blogger posted it with the caption on Reddit because of the way the caption blames the women instead of the driver. Heidebrink-Bruno includes the photograph, but her embedded link does not take readers to the City of Toronto archives, nor to the initial Reddit posting, nor even to the *Huffington Post* article discussing the photograph. Instead, the link takes readers to another blogger on Tumblr who had reposted the photograph. This kind of networked approach to citation reflects the discourse conventions present in some (not all) digital environments and contrasts with citation practices in print-based scholarly contexts.

Photo credits in online platforms provide another distinctive feature of citation practices when publishing online. Heidebrink-Bruno includes another image in her article, with the following photo credit, again with embedded links (depicted in blue here): "[Photo, Minimalism outside by 55Laney69, licensed under CC BY 2.0.]" This approach enables Heidebrink-Bruno to attribute her resources, but not necessarily in accordance to any specific citation style as enumerated by, for instance, MLA, CMS, or APA.

By contrast, the bibliographic citations, excerpted from an article by Anita Helle (also excerpted in Chapter 7: Analysis), show how photographs are cited in a print-based scholarly format:

Lange, Dorothea. Doctor examining children in trailer clinic. FSA (Farm Security Administration) mobile camp, Klamath County, Oregon. Washington, DC: Library of Congress. http://www.loc.gov/pictures/item/fsa2000005393/PP/ (accessed September 9, 2011).

———. Fifty-seven-year-old sharecropper woman. Hinds County, Mississippi, 1937. Washington, DC: Library of Congress, Prints & Photographs Division, LCDIg-fsa-8b32018.

Despite the different citation approach illustrated in Heidebrink-Bruno's article, she is still attributing her resources; she is just doing so from within the established discourse conventions of the context and in accordance with the editorial guidelines of that journal.

Write Now

Find an online publication context, and examine the citation approach. How is the author attributing and referencing resources in this online format?

Transfer Hub: Share your ideas and see what others have written at fountainheadpress.com/transferhub.

Citing Your Own Work

Though it may seem surprising, if you borrow ideas from work you have previously produced, you need to cite yourself. This is alternately termed **self-citation** or self-reference. Citing yourself achieves the same purposes as citing others: it awards credit, offers a bibliographic trail for readers to follow, and enables academic writers to situate their current writing project within a larger, ongoing conversation. In educational settings, if students draw from prior writing projects they have produced, they must cite their prior writing projects (citation style guides even provide guidelines for citing unpublished writing).

An example of self-citation can be found within the article by David Corso on video games. Corso uses an idea from another of his writing projects and, therefore, cites it:

> If we maintain a holistic approach when dealing with video game play, we can investigate these effects and provide instruction on their implementation, i.e. incorporate less violence in video games while maintaining competition or making the player cognizant of these violent effects (Corso, 2013).

From the references section included with the article, readers learn that the work Corso cited was his honors college thesis:

> Corso, D. (2013). Holistic gaming: Using the physical and psychological effects of video games to better our lives. (Unpublished Honors College thesis). The University of South Carolina, Columbia.

Citing your own prior work is in many ways a positive strategy. Academic reputations with regard to publications can be in part determined by how many other articles have cited a particular publication. The more your text is cited, the more reputable it is (for more discussion about this phenomenon, known as impact factor, and the ensuing complexities, see Example 1). In scientific disciplines, where writers often publish multiple articles from one research project, the necessity for citing your own work becomes more complex. Citing their own work ensures that each publication has an original contribution rather than repeating the ideas of other prior publications.

Crafting Acknowledgments

Many academic texts include an Acknowledgments section as well as a References or Works Cited section. These sections enable academic writers to acknowledge the ways in which others around them have shaped the text, even if they might not have done so explicitly as in the case of evidence and actual works cited. Writers will often use this space to acknowledge feedback they have received from readers, editorial suggestions from editors, research assistance from librarians or archivists, and also funding support from grants or organizations.

Example 1: Acknowledgments

Excerpt from "'It's Medically Proven!': Assessing the Dissemination of Religion and Health Research" by S. M. Frenk, S. L. Foy, and K. G. Meador

Acknowledgments

The authors would like to thank Joe Mann, Director of the Rural Church Division at The Duke Endowment, Mary Piepenbringin, Director of the Health Care Division at The Duke Endowment, and Gene Cochrane, President of The Duke Endowment for financial support of the Caring Communities Health Ministries Assessment from which these data are drawn. The authors would like to thank Alexis T. Franzese and Whitney Arroyave for their assistance with the Caring Communities Health Ministries Assessment Project and Wendy Cadge, Linda K. George, and Harold Koenig for reviewing the manuscript. Finally, the authors thank the congregations that participated in the study. The content of this article is solely the responsibility of the authors and does not reflect the views or opinions of The Duke Endowment.

> The authors thank the people at the various sites they studied for their field research as well as the funder of their research. They also thank those who reviewed the manuscript.

From *Journal of Religion and Health* (50.4), 2011.

Example 2: Acknowledgments

Excerpt from "Responding to the Work of Others: There's a Better Way for Us to Live" by D. Wong

Acknowledgments

I'd like to thank Joav and Zach for their comments on my draft. Their input was very helpful in my revision. Their feedback on how I should add in a second rewrite at the end of the piece was insightful, and their encouraging comments gave me more confidence in writing my final draft. They did a

> Wong, an undergraduate when he published this article, expresses appreciation for his peers who read the draft, as well as a writing center tutor.

From *Deliberations* (9), 2008.

very thorough reading of my second draft, so I really appreciate their hard work. I'd also like to thank Timothy Wright from the Writing Studio, who gave me valuable feedback on ways I could improve my draft, especially with regard to my introduction.

Example 3: Acknowledgments

Excerpt from "History, Identity, and Twenty-First Century Skills: Experiments in Institutional Blogging" by S. O. Bender

Acknowledgments

I wish to express my gratitude to Amy Heibel and Jeff Gates who, as is evident in this article, provided early and essential guidance and support to this project. My unending thanks go to former public relations manager Cecilia Wichmann who, by bringing her blog idea to me, forever enhanced my relationship to my colleagues and my institution, and changed my belief in social media and its power to tell stories worth sharing.

> Bender thanks those who contributed intellectual inspiration and support to her project and those who influenced her thinking.

From *Art Documentation: Journal of the Art Libraries Society of North America* (33.1), 2014.

Transferring Citation

Citation practices build on the concepts covered in nearly all the preceding chapters. Citation makes it possible for writers to pursue questions, engage with the texts they read, develop arguments, and integrate evidence. While it may be true that accurate citation practices enable scholars to avoid plagiarism, a more productive approach to citation involves considering citation as a way of demonstrating your knowledge and of helping other researchers (your readers) build knowledge as well.

Transferring citation practices across writing occasions acknowledges that citation contributes to and reflects academic writing culture more broadly. Citation also has high political implications due to its power to establish, reinforce, or damage reputations across disciplines. Transfer is the essence of citation since citation practices exemplify the dynamic nature of academic writing.

❧ ❧ ❧

Exploratory Philosophy: *"On Habit"* by Alain de Botton

"Few things are as exciting as the idea of travelling somewhere else. But the reality of travel seldom matches our daydreams." De Botton thus begins "Art of Travel" with a premise: people hold great excitement at the prospect of traveling for pleasure, but they are often disappointed in the actuality of that travel.

From this premise, de Botton explores questions about why people have such enthusiasm for travel and why they tend to be disappointed. To conduct this exploration, de Botton relies on great thinkers of the past and personal experiences. He then arrives at various conclusions that help crystallize and clarify our thinking about the purpose of travel, our expectations of travel, and how we might avoid such disappointments in the future. De Botton thereby crafts an argument that can enable others, through these insights, to "be less silently and guiltily miserable on our journeys" ("Travel").

This approach to writing—using premises, considering others' and one's own experiences, clarifying and defining human behavior through deep, extended thought—emerges from and reflects, in many ways, de Botton's training as a philosopher. Those writing in the philosophical tradition take on big questions and address these questions by dissecting them with the aim of clarifying how we think about them. Philosophers' approach to writing often includes identifying the premises (the assumptions, attributes, or components) that inform and emerge from these questions and considering why and under what circumstances these premises might be applicable or not. Philosophers often aim to use these premises to develop conclusions about ideas that generate deeper understanding and that, ultimately, impact human experiences.

Writing in philosophy privileges reasoning and logic. Philosophical conclusions and arguments are often judged on their validity or soundness. De Botton, though, writes in a way that bridges writing in philosophy as described above with another, more exploratory reflective tradition in philosophy writing: the essay. While the essay as a genre extends across disciplines and has now come to designate many types of academic arguments, the essay originated as its own discrete genre of writing.

Most often, the origins of this essay genre of writing are attributed to Michel de Montaigne (1533-1592), a French philosopher and writer. He wrote a series of philosophical reflections—essays—on a variety of topics, including love, friendship, and religion. Montaigne's collections of essays were widely read during his life and have had enormous influence on many profound thinkers across the years, including philosophers and writers such as Jean Jacques Rousseau and Voltaire.

Carl H. Klaus and Ned Stuckey-French, scholars who have studied the art of the essay, note that people who have written within the essay tradition "typically conceive of the essay as a mode of trying out ideas, of exploration rather than persuasion, of reflection rather than conviction" (xvii-xvi). de Botton's text, then, reflects this long tradition of philosophical essayist writing. Predecessors include Montaigne but also such essayists as Samuel Johnson, Ralph Waldo Emerson, and Virginia Woolf.

Operating within the overlapping traditions of philosophical essayistic writing and academic argu-

Alain de Botton is a writer and philosopher. He has written numerous books examining a broad range of questions, from love and travel to religion and happiness. Among his most popular books are *How Proust Can Change Your Life* (1997), in which he argues that novels can be life-changing for readers, and *The Art of Travel* (2002), in which he examines how and why people travel. He once spent two years as a writer in residence at Heathrow airport, from which he wrote *A Week at the Airport* (2009). De Botton was born in Zurich, Switzerland, and moved to England at the age of 12. He lives in London and is integrally involved with the School of Life, which provides an innovative approach to education grounded on emotional and cultural intelligence. De Botton earned a B.A. in History from Cambridge University and an M.A. in Philosophy at Kings College. He regularly lectures on his books and owns a production company that generates material for YouTube.

ment in philosophy, de Botton's "On Habit" appears as the final chapter in "Art of Travel." Throughout the text, de Botton reflects upon many well-known travelers and travel experiences, as well has his own experiences, to explore the role of travel. For instance, he explores the disappointment of travel by relating a disappointing trip of his own to the Bahamas alongside an explication of disappointing trips in J.K. Huysman's novel *A Rebours*. He visits the Lake District to better understand William Wordsworth's assertions about the sublime, and he visits Provence and discusses Vincent Van Gogh's trip to Provence in order to examine what it means to use art as a way of understanding place (Yee).

Each chapter begins, as does "On Habit," with an indication of the place under consideration (i.e., Hammersmith, London), and the writer/traveler/philosopher whose ideas will be explored in that chapter (i.e., Xavier de Maistre). De Botton's own presence as a traveler wends its way throughout all chapters, and, as is customary in essayistic writing, he refers directly to himself and his experiences as he crafts his arguments.

The questions de Botton explores—What is the role of travel? What contributes to our happiness? What is the role of art in understanding place? How and why are people disappointed in expectations?—are examples of the broad, big questions that those writing and researching in the discipline of philosophy consider.

Write Here

Imagine you have unlimited time and an unlimited budget. Choose a place you would like to visit. This can be a place you have never been to or one that you have been to and would like to return. It can be a real place or an imaginary place. Describe in as much detail as possible the place and what you are hoping to experience in this location. Be as specific as possible, referring to all the sensory expectations you have (i.e., taste, sight, smell, touch, sound), as well as any more abstract ideas you are hoping to experience (i.e., happiness, love, adventure, etc.). What do you imagine going to that place will accomplish or provide for you? Why do you hold these expectations? Explore in writing why you are excited and enthusiastic about this place and why you value the expectations you hold about that place.

Alain de Botton
On Habit

1.

I returned to London from Barbados to find that the city had stubbornly refused to change. I had seen azure skies and giant sea anemones, I had slept in a raffia bungalow and eaten a kingfish, I had swum beside baby turtles and read in the shade of coconut trees. But my hometown was unimpressed. It was still raining. The park was still a pond; the skies were still funereal. When we are in a good mood and it is sunny, we may be tempted to impute a connection between what happens inside and outside of us, but the appearance of London on my return was a reminder of the indifference of the world to any of the events unfolding in the lives of its inhabitants. I felt despair at being home. I felt there could be few

worse places on Earth than the one I had been fated to spend my existence in.

2.

'The sole cause of man's unhappiness is that he does not know how to stay quietly in his room'—Pascal, *Pensées*, 136.

3.

From 1788 to 1804, Alexander von Humboldt undertook a journey around South America, later entitling the account of what he had seen *Journey to the Equinoctial Regions of the New Continent.*

Nine years before Humboldt set out, in the spring of 1790, a twenty-seven-year-old

Frenchman named Xavier de Maistre had undertaken a journey around his bedroom, an account of which he would later entitle *Journey around My Bedroom*. Gratified by his experiences, de Maistre in 1798 embarked upon a second journey. This time he travelled by night and ventured out as far as the window ledge; the literary result would be titled *Nocturnal Expedition around My Bedroom*.

Two approaches to travel: *Journey to the Equinoctial Regions of the New Continent*; *Journey around My Bedroom*. The first required ten mules, thirty pieces of luggage, four interpreters, a chronometer, a sextant, two telescopes, a Borda theodolite, a barometer, a compass, a hygrometer, letters of introduction from the king of Spain and a gun; the latter, a pair of pink-and-blue cotton pyjamas.

Xavier de Maistre was born in 1763, in the picturesque town of Chambéry, at the foot of the French Alps. He was of an intense, romantic nature and was fond of books, especially by Montaigne, Pascal and Rosseau, and of paintings, above all Dutch and French domestic scenes. At the age of twenty-three, de Maistre became fascinated by aeronautics. Etienne Montgolfier had, three years before, achieved international renown by constructing a balloon that flew for eight minutes above the royal palace at Versailles, bearing as passengers a sheep named Montauciel ('Climb-to-the-sky'), a duck and a rooster. De Maistre and a friend fashioned a pair of giant wings out of paper and wire and planned to fly to America. They did not succeed. Two years later de Maistre secured himself a place in a hot-air balloon and spent a few moments floating above Chambéry before the machine crashed into a pine forest.

Then, in 1790, while he was living in a modest room at the top of an apartment building in Turin, de Maistre pioneered a mode of travel that was to make his name: room travel.

Introducing *Journey around My Bedroom*, Xavier's brother, the political theorist Joseph de Maistre, emphasised that it was not Xavier's intention to cast aspersions on the heroic deeds of the great travellers of the past—namely, 'Magellan, Drake, Anson and Cook'. Magellan had discovered a western route to the Spice Islands around the southern tip of South America, Drake had circumnavigated the globe, Anson had produced accurate sea charts of the Philippines and Cook had confirmed the existence of a southern continent. 'They were no doubt remarkable men,' wrote Joseph. It was just that his brother had discovered a way of travelling that might be infinitely more practical for those neither as brave nor as wealthy as those explorers.

'Millions of people who, until now, have never dared to travel, others who have not been able to travel and still more who have not even thought of travelling will be able to follow my example,' explained Xavier as he prepared for his journey. 'The most indolent beings will no longer have any reason to hesitate before setting off to find pleasures that will cost them neither money nor effort.' He particularly recommended room travel to the poor and to those afraid of storms, robbers and high cliffs.

4.

Unfortunately, de Maistre's own pioneering journey, rather like his flying machine, did not get very far.

The story begins well: de Maistre locks his door and changes into his pink-and-blue pyjamas. With no need of luggage, he travels to the sofa, the largest piece of furniture in the room. His journey having shaken him from his usual lethargy, he looks at it through fresh eyes and rediscovers some of its qualities. He admires the elegance of its feet and remembers the pleasant hours he has spent cradled in its cushions, dreaming of love and advancement in his career. From his sofa, de Maistre spies his bed. Once again, from a traveller's vantage point, he learns to appreciate this complex piece of furniture. He feels grateful for the nights he has spent in it and takes pride in the fact that his sheets almost match his pyjamas. 'I advise any man who can do so to get himself pink and white bedlinen,' he writes, for these are colours to induce calm and pleasant reveries in the fragile sleeper.

But thereafter de Maistre may be accused of losing sight of the overall purpose of his endeavour. He becomes mired in long and wearing digressions about his dog, Rosinne, his sweetheart, Jenny, and his faithful servant, Joannetti. Prospective travellers in search of specific guidance on room travel risk coming away from reading *Journey around My Bedroom* feeling a little betrayed.

And yet de Maistre's work sprang from a profound and suggestive insight: the notion that the pleasure we derive from a journey may be dependent more on the mind-set we travel *with* than on the destination we travel *to*. If only we could apply a travelling mind-set to our own locales, we might find these places becoming no less interesting than, say, the high mountain passes and butterfly-filled jungles of Humboldt's South America.

What, then, is a travelling mind-set? Receptivity might be said to be its chief characteristic. Receptive, we approach new places with humility. We carry with us no rigid ideas about what is or is not interesting. We irritate locals because we stand in traffic islands and narrow streets and admire what they take to be unremarkable small details. We risk getting run over because we are intrigued by the roof of a government building or an inscription on a wall. We find a supermarket or a hairdresser's shop unusually fascinating. We dwell at length on the layout of a menu or the clothes of the presenters on the evening news. We are alive to the layers of history beneath the present and take notes and photographs.

Home, by contrast, finds us more settled in our expectations. We feel assured that we have discovered everything interesting about our neighbourhood, primarily by virtue of our having lived there a long time. It seems inconceivable that there could be anything new to find in a place where we have been living for a decade or more. We have become habituated and therefore blind to it.

De Maistre tried to shake us from our passivity. In his second volume of room travel, *Nocturnal Expedition around My Bedroom*, he went up to his window and looked up at the night sky. Its beauty made him feel frustrated that such ordinary scenes were not more generally appreciated: 'How few people are right now taking delight in this sublime spectacle that the sky lays on uselessly for dozing humanity! What would it cost those who are out for a walk or crowding out of the theatre to look up for a moment and admire the brilliant constellations that gleam above their heads?' The reason people were not

looking was that they had never done so before. They had fallen into the habit of considering their universe to be boring—and their universe had duly fallen into line with their expectations.

5.

I attempted to travel around my bedroom, but it was so small, with barely enough space for a bed, that I concluded that the de Maistrian message might prove more rewarding if it was applied to the neighbourhood as a whole.

So on a clear March day, at around three in the afternoon, several weeks after my return home from Barbados, I set out on a de Maistrian journey around Hammersmith. It felt peculiar to be outside in the middle of the day with no particular destination in mind. A woman and two small blond children were walking along the main road, which was lined with a variety of shops and restaurants. A double-decker bus had stopped to pick up passengers opposite a park. A giant billboard was advertising gravy. I walked along this road almost every day to reach my Underground station and was unused to regarding it as anything other than a means to my end. Information that assisted me in my goal attracted my attention; all else was judged irrelevant. Thus, while I was sensitive to the number of people on the pavement, as potential impediments to my path, their faces and expressions were invisible to me—as invisible as the shapes of the buildings or the activity in the shops.

It had not always been thus. When I first moved to the area, my attention was less jealously focused. I had at that time not yet settled so firmly on the goal of reaching the Underground quickly.

On entering a new space, our sensitivity is directed towards a number of elements, which we gradually reduce in line with the function we find for the space. Of the four thousand things there might be to see and reflect on in a street, we end up being actively aware of only a few: the number of humans in our path, perhaps, the amount of traffic and the likelihood of rain. A bus that we might at first have viewed aesthetically or mechanically—or even used as a springboard to thoughts about communities within cities—becomes simply a box to move us as rapidly as possible across an area that might as well not exist, so unconnected is it to our primary goal, outside of which all is darkness, all is invisible.

I had imposed a grid of interests on the street, one that left no space for blond children and gravy adverts and paving stones and the colours of shop fronts and the expressions of businesspeople and pensioners. The power of my primary goal had drained me of the will to reflect on the layout of the park or the unusual mixture of Georgian, Victorian and Edwardian architecture along a single block. My walks along the street had been excised of any attentiveness to beauty, any associative thoughts, any sense of wonder or gratitude, any philosophical digressions sparked by visual elements. In their place, there was simply an insistent call to reach the Underground posthaste.

Now, following de Maistre, I tried to reverse the process of habituation, to dissociate my surroundings from the uses I had previously found for them. I forced myself to obey a strange sort of mental command: I was to look around me as though I had never been in this place before. And slowly, my travels began to bear fruit.

Once I began to consider everything as being of potential interest, objects released latent layers of value. A row of shops that I had always known as one large, undifferentiated, reddish block acquired an architectural identity. There were Georgian pillars around one flower shop, and late-Victorian Gothic-style gargoyles on top of the butcher's. A restaurant became filled with diners rather than shapes. In a glass-fronted office block, people were gesticulating in a boardroom on the first floor as someone drew a pie chart on an overhead projector. Just across the road from the office, a man was pouring out new slabs of concrete for the pavement and carefully shaping their edges. I boarded a bus and, instead of slipping at once into private concerns, tried to connect imaginatively with other passengers. I could hear a conversation in the row ahead of me. Someone in an office somewhere—a person quite high up in the hierarchy, apparently—didn't understand: he complained about how inefficient others were but never reflected on what he himself might be doing to contribute to that inefficiency. I thought of the multiplicity of lives going on at the same time at different levels in a city. I thought of the

similarities of complaints—always selfishness, always blindness—and the old psychological truth that what we complain of in others, others will complain of in us.

The neighbourhood did not just acquire people and defined buildings through my reawakened attention; it also began to collect ideas. I reflected on the new wealth that was spreading into the area. I tried to think why I liked railway arches so much, and why the motorway that cut across the skyline.

It seemed an advantage to be travelling alone. Our responses to the world are crucially moulded by the company we keep, for we temper our curiosity to fit in with the expectations of others. They may have particular visions of who we are and hence may subtly prevent certain sides of us from emerging: 'I hadn't thought of you as someone who was interested in flyovers,' they may intimidatingly suggest. Being closely observed by a companion can also inhibit our observation of others; then, too, we may become caught up in adjusting ourselves to the companion's questions and remarks, or feel the need to make ourselves seem more normal than is good for our curiosity. But alone in Hammersmith in the middle of a March afternoon, I had no such concerns. I had the freedom to act a little weirdly. I sketched the window of a hardware shop and word-painted the flyover.

6.

De Maistre was not only a room traveller. He was also a great traveller in the classic sense. He journeyed to Italy and Russia, spent a winter with the royalist armies in the Alps and fought a Russian campaign in the Caucasus.

In an autobiographical note written in 1801 in South America, Alexander von Humboldt specified his motive for travelling: 'I was spurred on by an uncertain longing to be transported from a boring daily life to a marvellous world.' It was this very dichotomy, 'boring daily life' pitted against 'marvellous world', that de Maistre had tried to redraw with greater subtlety. He would not have suggested to Humboldt that South America was dull; he merely would have urged him to consider that his native Berlin might have something to offer, too.

Eight decades later, Nietzsche, who had read and admired de Maistre (and spent much time in his own room), picked up on the thought:

When we observe how some people know how to manage their experiences—their insignificant, everyday experiences—so that they become an arable soil that bears fruit three times a year, while others—and how many there are!—are driven through surging waves of destiny, the most multifarious currents of the times and the nations, and yet always remain on top, bobbing like a cork, then we are in the end tempted to divide mankind into a minority (a minimality) of those who know how to make much of little, and a majority of those who know how to make little of much.

There are some who have crossed deserts, floated on ice caps and cut their way through jungles but whose souls we would search in vain for evidence of what they have witnessed. Dressed in pink-and-blue pyjamas, satisfied within the confines of his own bedroom, Xavier de Maistre was gently nudging us to try, before taking off for distant hemispheres, to notice what we have already seen.

Write Away

1. De Botton wrestles with big questions in his writing: What is the role of great literature? How do people arrive at and maintain happiness? What causes disappointment? What is the nature of love? What is the purpose of travel? What is the role of art in understanding places? Choose a big question of importance to you, and write a philosophical essay about that question in the tradition of exploratory, reflective essayistic writing.

2. Writing in the discipline of philosophy requires an understanding of certain terms affiliated with philosophical argumentation. These concepts include premises, conclusions, reason, and logic. In addition, philosophers seek to render conclusions that are valid and/or sound. Write an academic essay in which you define these terms according to the way they are understood in philosophy and in which you map out de Botton's argument according to these terms. What are de Botton's premises? What are his conclusions? What forms of reasoning or logic does he rely on? Are his premises and conclusions valid and/or sound? If not, why?

3. One way that de Botton may have written chapters in "Art of Travel," is to have thought of a place and then identified writers who had traveled there or written about travel there; alternatively, he may have read of a place through a writer and then traveled there himself. Imagine you are conducting research for a similar endeavor. Create an annotated bibliography of literary or philosophical travel writing about a particular place. You can choose, in consultation with your instructor, whether and how you might limit the annotated bibliography to a particular period of time or type of travel writing. You can also decide how to organize your annotated bibliography. Imagine that your annotated bibliography might be helpful for others who would like to learn more about what travelers, thinkers, and writers have written about a particular place.

Oral History: "Train Travel through Young Eyes" by Kim Patterson

Transfer Points: History, Narrative

While it might seem that facts can provide sufficient knowledge about events such as the Vietnam War or September 11, a more in-depth understanding of the past hinges on personal accounts and stories. It is often these human experiences that add texture and nuance to the facts, enabling us to more effectively gain insights into history.

Oral history, such as that archived by Kim Patterson, is both a method of historical research and an archived product. It involves a well-prepared oral historian asking another person to verbally share recollections of her or his experiences. Oral history overlaps with journalism, in that journalism also involves personal interviews. But oral history puts particular emphasis on examining an historical period, event, or person through the lens of individual perspectives.

Oral histories have been conducted across many areas, from cloistered nuns (Reese) and Amish farms (James) to the disability rights movement (Pelka) and black Vietnam-era military officers (Hampton). As these examples suggest, oral history often involves archiving the voices of those who might otherwise go unnoticed or who tend to be less frequently heard. As such, oral histories often provide counternarratives to dominant conceptions of events and also generate more visibility for underrepresented people and issues.

Developing oral histories usually involves in-depth research about the time period or event in advance of the conversation. This research helps the historian design the interview questions and may help any framing material for the oral history. When developing interview questions, historians must think carefully about how to ask open-ended questions that facilitate the person's voice and own account rather than being overly prescriptive and shaping the narrative. And, while oral historians should be prepared with a list of questions, they must also be flexible enough to modify those questions if the story takes a new direction.

Oral historians also choose how to record the oral history. Using the best equipment possible will help preserve the oral history and will honor the person's time and story. Finally, when presenting, publishing, or archiving the oral history, researchers must determine whether or not to frame the material, and, if so, how to do so in a way that continues to privilege the person's story rather than the researcher's account of that story.

Those who write in the field of oral history do so in several different ways. They write the interview questions for the oral histories, they transcribe the oral histories, and they write analyses of the oral histories. Analyzing oral histories involves exploring in deliberate ways the features of oral histories. These include symbols, images, tone, silences, and nonverbal cues. All of these help contribute to our understanding of the past through the human experience.

Oral historians also conduct research into and write about the methods of oral history. They consider the ethics involved with how to most

Kim Patterson is the Associate Director at McLennan Community College University Center in Waco, Texas. She received her B.A. in Marketing and Journalism from Baylor University. Patterson has worked as an ongoing contributor to a series of radio segments called *Living Stories*, sponsored by the Institute for Oral History at Baylor University. In this capacity, she has conducted oral history radio segments across a wide range of subjects, most of which are connected to the region in which she lives and works, Texas. Her segments have included oral histories about the Ku Klux Klan, the 1900 Galveston Hurricane, and moonshine. She has also been on the board of contributors for the *Waco Tribune* and served as coordinator of communications and special events for the Montgomery County Community Foundation, which provides crisis assistance, scholarships, and assistance for families in Montgomery County, Texas.

responsibly conduct and preserve oral histories. And they explore how to train new oral historians to conduct oral histories responsibly and ethically.

While oral history does provide important insights and texture through the human experience, it is but one historical research method, and historians often use oral history in conjunction with other methods of the field. Scholars in history, for example, frequently conduct archival research, where they locate and analyze texts, artifacts, documents, or images from a particular time period or event.

Significantly, scholars in other disciplines also make use of oral history. For instance, researchers in African and African-American Studies, Jewish Studies, and Sexual and Gender Studies frequently use oral history, in part because the privileging of individual perspectives and human experiences is so central to research in these fields.

Across all these contexts, oral history is a vital research practice and archived product that helps us move closer to inhabiting the histories that have shaped our contemporary experiences of the world.

Write Here

If you could have a conversation with anyone, past or present, who would it be and why? What questions would you ask? What stories would you ask that person to share? What would you hope to learn from that individual?

Listen to the original broadcast here: http://edge.baylor.edu/media/163724/163724-audio.mp3.

Kim Patterson
Train Travel through Young Eyes

Passenger rail travel in America enjoyed its heyday in the early 1900s, carrying at its peak in 1920 an estimated 1.2 billion passengers that year. Trains made travel possible and relatively comfortable even in inclement weather, something no other method of transportation could offer at the time. In 1911, Texas became the state with the most railroad mileage, a position it has not relinquished.

Mary Sendón of Waco recalls a train ride she took around 1908:

"When I was about seven, my father and my Grandmother Kemendo took me with them to Houston on a train. And that, to me, was the most wonderful experience I ever had in my life. My grandmother had relatives there. And I had never been anywhere on a train. I didn't know what a train was like even. And I remember my grandmother got train-sick. She was riding backwards;

that's what did it. Well, there was a doctor on the train, and he said, 'Well, just let her lie down on this—' It wasn't a divided seat; it was kind of a bench. And they let her lie down to rest, you know. So there was a man and a woman sitting just close by. Turned out to be a Jewish couple, the Herzes, H-e-r-z. They had a cigar store in Waco. And they asked me to come and sit with them, so I went and sat with them. And I always remember the first time I ever had a Nabisco—you know, they used to sell little Nabisco wafers in little tin boxes? Just real thin wafers. I remember that the boy that came—they called the *butcher boy* that would come through selling things on the train. They bought me a box of those, and that was the first time I had ever tasted them. But they were friends of my dad's because they had business close to his shop."

East Texas native Avery Downing, former Waco ISD superintendent, recalls a train adventure from the 1920s:

"I remember going to the Dallas fair on a special assembled there in Marshall–Longview. I had a little experience there one time. I had spent all my money except a quarter. And I saw that I had a few minutes left before I got on the train to go back, so I decided I'd buy me a couple of pounds of grapes. I ran back down to this little old stand that had the grapes, bought them. When I got back, the train was moving out, and I had to catch that thing on the run.

I remember that. And I wonder till this good day—I considered myself a shy and timid fellow—I wonder what I would have done if I'd missed that train: no money and no acquaintances. I don't know." (interviewer laughs)

During its golden years, passenger trains seemed to be permanently ingrained in American culture, but they fell victim to the proliferation of cars, Interstate highways, and airlines as America prospered. By 1970 only the Santa Fe and Southern Pacific were still operating passenger rail service in Texas, and the following year remaining trains were turned over to Amtrak.

Write Away

1. Conduct an oral history. Steps entail choosing a subject, such as an issue, event, historical era, or person. Then, conduct research to understand the context. Design interview questions, stage a mock interview and incorporate feedback, choose a method of recording and archiving, and develop an informational sheet so that your interviewees understand the purpose of the oral history and where it will be archived. Conduct the oral history, transcribe as necessary, and include any framing material as you see fit. Curate the oral history so others can listen to it as well. Then, write a reflection about any insights you gleaned about oral history or about the subject matter. Note: if you are working with an issue or idea that is potentially sensitive, please consult with your instructor to understand the responsibilities and implications of oral history and sensitive subjects, both for you as researcher and for those you interview. http://www.oralhistory.org/about/principles-and-practices/

2. Oral history is one method of research that is key to historians. But those who are working in time periods older than the twentieth century might have limited capacity to use oral history. In these cases, they often conduct archival research. This involves looking at artifacts and items that have been collected and saved, usually by a university library, public library, museum, or private collector. Find an archive (either online or in person), and conduct archival research: Identify a few key archival pieces, observe and analyze them, and use them to develop a narrative about that time period or person or event.

3. Visit the Oral History Association's archive of various oral history collections, or an oral history collection at your institution or in your community, if available. Select a set of these oral histories and analyze them. For your analysis, use the following analytic questions, which have been developed from Luisa Passerini's *Fascism in Popular Memory* (1987): Do the speakers use metaphors, myths, or images? What might their significance or implications be? What is the function of humor, if any? Are there any moments of silence? What might be within those? Do any aspects strike you as possibly exaggerations or lies? If so, why might those be significant?

Critical Journalism: "Coverage of Cancer in Local Television News" by Walter Gantz and Zheng Wang

Transfer Points: Health Sciences, Public Health, Media Studies

When it comes to health information, it turns out most Americans are illiterate or barely literate. A 2003 survey by the U.S. Department of Health & Human Services found only 12 percent of Americans are proficient in health literacy. One might imagine that in the years since 2003, health literacy would have increased due to the abundance of health information available on the internet (72 percent of people who use the internet have used it for health-information purposes ("Health"). However, a 2015 survey found that, still, only 18 percent of Americans are proficient in health literacy (iTriage).

While health literacy rates are low for all Americans, the rates are even more concerning for people of color, minorities, and those in lower socioeconomic strata (HHS). This leads to ongoing, problematic inequities in access to health care in the United States with regard to race and class (Gee & Ford).

Low health literacy emerges from and highlights complex problems related to information access, clarity, bias, and visibility. How are health matters communicated to various publics? Who does and does not have access to such information? What is the role of ethics in health communication? How do people make health-related decisions based on the information they encounter? What biases shape health communication? What inequities impact health communication across various demographics?

These are the kinds of questions that occupy researchers in the field of health communication such as Gantz and Wang.

The Centers for Disease Control (CDC) define health literacy as "the degree to which an individual has the capacity to obtain, communicate, process, and understand basic health information and services to make appropriate health decisions" (CDC). Health literacy, therefore, requires the ability to access and process information, as well as evaluate the reliability and credibility of an information source. Health literacy also hinges on the ability to discern complicated, even ambivalent, implications and recommendations.

Responsibility for health literacy, though, is not exclusively located within the individual. It also hinges on the information itself. Health information can be confusing, incomplete, biased, inscrutable, outdated, and incorrect. Within and beyond these concerns, healthcare experts seeking to communicate grapple extensively with writing transfer: How can they effectively transfer health-related research and knowledge to broader publics in ways that will be accessible and understandable to an incredibly diverse range of people?

Walter Gantz is Chair and Professor of the Department of Telecommunications at Indiana University. He earned a B.A. from Brooklyn College and a M.A. and Ph.D. from University of Michigan (Eastman). His research interests include sports fanship, media dissemination, and advertising content (Lin and Atkin). He wrote a book called *Desert Storm and Mass Media* (1993). Zheng Joyce Wang is an Associate Professor of Communication at the Ohio State University and Director of the Communication and Psychophysiology Lab (CAP Lab). Her research interests include media behavior related to emotion and cognition processing and quantum probability models of cognition and decisionmaking (Wang).

As a field grounded in writing transfer, health communication is highly interdisciplinary. At the most foundational level, it relies on scientific knowledge and research about medicine. But, research in health communication is also informed by numerous disciplines, from sociology and ethics to literature, computer science, and engineering.

Since health information aims to "inform and influence individual decisions that enhance health" (CDC), health communications also intersects with marketing, a field that has deep expertise with influencing human behavior and decisions (CDC).

Gantz and Wang approach health communication from a social-science research perspective, conducting coding analysis of local television coverage of cancer. And, scholars in rhetoric have also conducted significant research about health communications. Increasingly, research in health communications relies on disciplines in the humanities. Medical schools, for instance, are incorporating programs focused around health humanities. These areas of inquiry, known as health humanities or medical humanities, examine health communication and medicine through the lens of art, narrative, and performance.

Demonstrating the impressive disciplinary range informing health communication research, one 2016 issue of the *Journal of Health Communication* includes articles about skin cancer coverage in magazines (McWhirter and Hoffman-Goetz), condom media campaigns in Pakistan (Beudoin, Chen and Agha), the impact of bullying blogs (Danielson and Emmers-Sommer), and eye tracking as an assessment measure for the effectiveness of online health messages (Bol, et al.).

Health information bears impressive power, influencing people about medical care and healthy living. Therefore, ethics plays an enormous role. Researchers in health communications examine aims and agendas, considering how any conflicts of interest might shape the ways in which information is communicated. Ethics also arises with matters of access and visibility: Which sorts of health issues gain more coverage? Which people tend to be more highly represented? Which demographics tend to have greater access and visibility to health communication?

Research in health communication emerges from and informs many entities, including the government, colleges and universities, media, and private organizations, such as insurance companies and medical providers. From personal blogs, government pamphlets, and public-service announcements to public lectures, marketing campaigns, and books and articles across popular and scholarly contexts, health communications stands as one of the most highly transfer-based fields. It also stands as one of the most wide-reaching and impactful because health communications has such a profound influence on nearly all the decisions we make about health.

Write Here

When you seek information about health issues, what sources do you turn to, and why? Think about all the different occasions when you have sought medical information, and identify the sources you turned to for each of these different contexts. Then, reflect on your impression of these sources: How reliable did you find the information? How did you evaluate reliability? What was the process of locating the information like? How did you decide what was or was not comprehensive or most relevant for you? How did the information influence your behavior or decisions? What else stands out for you about health information that you have sought?

Walter Gantz and Zheng Wang
Coverage of Cancer in Local Television News

The mass media play an important role in public health. This certainly is the case with cancer, as the media help increase awareness of cancer risks,[1-3] encourage people to undertake routine examinations and obtain medical advice,[1] and help people make better medical decisions.[4] Several studies[4,5] have suggested that adults tend to obtain most of their information about cancer from mass media channels. In this study, we examined the extent and nature of cancer information in American local television news from an information-seeking perspective, and we provide suggestions for more effective use of mass media in disseminating cancer information.

BACKGROUND
According to information-seeking theories,[6,7] cancer patients, their families, and close friends balance between information search and avoidance, whereas other members of the general public are

open to information about cancer even if they do not actively seek such information.

Cancer Information and Cancer Patients

Mills and Sullivan[8] identified 5 key information needs of cancer patients. However, cancer patients do not always seek information. Instead, under some conditions, some try to avoid cancer information, especially negative information that might remove hope.[9,10] Misinformation about cancer also has been cited as a factor that impedes active information seeking.[11] In addition, the mass media have been criticized for conveying negative and sensationalized cancer information, content that frightens, depresses, and discourages cancer patients from seeking information.[1]

The other side of the story is that research has suggested that media information may help cancer patients, even among those who try to avoid cancer information,[12] because "potentially consequential information may be [and is] acquired non-strategically" (p. 287).[12] Even when cancer patients try to avoid cancer related information, they are still likely to be exposed to, attend to, and process some of that information when they watch television for other purposes.

Cancer Information and the General Public

Compared to general news seeking, health information seeking is often triggered by significant, personally relevant discoveries.[13] Without feeling a significant cancer threat to themselves or to others they care about, people are unlikely to seek or avoid cancer information actively. Nonetheless, they are generally open to cancer information available on the media.

Information openness has received relatively little attention from health communication researchers, although several studies have focused on audience receptivity to pro-tobacco content.[14-16] An important byproduct of openness is incidental learning, the unintentional or unplanned learning that results from participation in other activities. Incidental learning can result in changed attitudes, self-confidence, and self-awareness.[17-19] Recent studies[20,21] have demonstrated that exposure to the media has the potential to induce incidental learning across an array of topic areas.

To maximize its value, cancer information on the media *should* do the following: cover a wide range of cancer sites and topics so that people with specific information needs can find what they need while the general public can incidentally learn about cancer and increase public awareness levels of cancer prevention and detection; not discourage information seeking by cancer patients and their families and friends; be easy for audiences to understand or follow during incidental learning; and provide follow-up options to encourage further information seeking. However, what cancer information actually *is* on mass media?

Cancer Information on Mass Media

Three decades ago, Greenberg et al[22] examined newspaper coverage of cancer using the 50 largest daily newspapers published during 6 composite weeks in 1977. Cancers with the highest incidence rates were not covered extensively. The authors also suggested that news stories might reinforce rather than change negative public attitudes about cancer (eg, emphasizing dying rather than coping).

Breast cancer has received considerable airplay. LM Schwartz and Woloshin[23] studied news media coverage of screening mammography for women and the use of tamoxifen as preventative strategies for breast cancer. Corbett and Mori[24,25] examined the role of celebrities in news coverage of breast cancer and the role of gender in gender-specific cancer reports. Andsager and Powers[26] shed insight on the ways in which breast cancer was framed in news and women's magazines.

Some researchers have examined mediated cancer information in a larger research context and have compared it with information about other diseases.[27,28] For example, Clark[27] compared the images of cancer, heart disease, and AIDS. Cancer and AIDS were described as evil predators, baffling enemies that brought hopelessness and despair. In comparison, heart attacks were viewed as mechanical rather than social failures that were very preventable.

Public service announcements (PSAs) about cancer have also been examined. Gantz and N Schwartz[29] analyzed 1640 hours of television content and found 32 PSAs related to cancer.

Most (63%) of the cancer PSAs actually were paid for by agencies seeking the coverage.

A small number of studies have examined cancer information in national news programs or news type programs on broadcast and cable television.[23-25,28,30] One limitation associated with many of the TV news analyses is their reliance on database summaries of the news. However valuable, these databases provide abstracts and limit inquiries to preestablished topic codes. Quantitative assessments[31] have documented the pitfalls associated with use of the Vanderbilt Television Archives.

Cancer Information in Local Television News

Local television news is an important and valued source of cancer information for the American public. People get most of their news from local television news.[32,33] The Health News Index Poll[34] showed that more than half (56%) thought they get "a lot" or "some" information about health issues from local television news.

Despite the public's attention to—and dependence on—local news, only 3 studies, to our knowledge, have included coverage of cancer on local newscasts. The Kaiser Family Foundation and the Center for Media and Public Affair[34] looked at 608 hours of local weekday evening news in 1996 to measure the amount and nature of coverage devoted to health. Among health issues, cancer attracted the second most coverage, drawing 12% of the coverage. Unfortunately, that study did not assess the nature of the coverage given to cancer. Pribble et al.[35] analyzed 1799 health news stories in 2795 local newscasts and found breast cancer was the most frequently reported topic. However, its sampling period included National Breast Cancer Awareness Month, making the popularity of a cancer topic no surprise. Pribble et al.'s[35] sample was limited in 2 other ways: It only included late evening news and stopped recording at 30 minutes even when those newscasts ran beyond 30 minutes. Wang and Gantz[36] examined 1863 news stories during a composite week in 2000 and found that illness and diseases received the heaviest coverage (39.5% of all news stories). Cancer was covered in more news stories (1.7% of all news stories) than any other single, specific topic. However, because that study was not specially designed to exam-ine cancer content, it did not offer information beyond that proportion.

We designed this study to provide the first systematic assessment of the extent and nature of cancer information in local television news in America. We examined the following research questions (RQs):

RQ1: How many stores and how much time is devoted to cancer news? How long generally does a cancer news story last?

RQ2: What time of the day do cancer stories appear most frequently in local newscasts—in the morning, at noon, in the early or late evening?

RQ3: Where are cancer stories located in television newscasts? For example, are they among the lead stories, or embedded in regularly scheduled health segments?

RQ4: What cancer sites and topics get coverage? To what extent do policy and law, application of policy and law (ie, specific cases related to law or policy), research advances, technology, and fundraising get covered?

RQ5: What are the demographics (ie, age, gender, and race) of the cancer patients featured? How often are these patients celebrities who happen to have cancer?

RQ6: What is the overall verbal and visual tone for these stories? Are health stories likely to worry the typical viewer who might be affected by the story?

RQ7: To what extent are varying viewpoints presented? (Do stories present contrasting prevention or treatment strategies?)

RQ8: How often do these news stories provide information that identifies where viewers can go for more information about cancer in general or about the specific cancer story covered?

RQ9: How accessible are cancer stories for the general viewing public?

RQ10: To what extent is market size related to the content associated with RQs 1 through 9?

METHODS

Each RQ was assessed using content analysis procedures.

Sample

Coders examined every news story on 1257 newscasts aired on 7 stations (the affiliates of ABC, CBS, Fox, NBC, UPN, WB, and Univision) in 4 Midwest US markets—Chicago, Illinois; Indianapolis, South Bend, and Terre Haute, Indiana—during 4 composite weeks from December 2004 to June 2005. We selected these markets to reflect a major-, large-, medium-, and small-size market in the United States. When we selected them, the 4 markets were the 3rd, 25th, 87th, and 150th sized markets in the United States.[37] We selected them from the same geographic area so as to control the influence of factors other than market size. We analyzed each channel's morning, noon, early evening, and late evening local newscasts.

Units of Analysis

The primary unit of analysis was the news story. We defined cancer stories as those that have at least some to half of the news content focusing on cancer (or oncology) in general or a specific cancer. Stories that only mentioned cancer (eg, 1 or 2 sentences in a lengthy news story) were not counted as cancer stories.

Measures

Each cancer story was coded in terms of duration (in seconds); location in the newscast; specific cancer sites, stages, and topics covered; overall visual and verbal tone; viewpoints presented; follow-up options provided; and language accessibility. SMOG was used to assess language accessibility.[36,38,39]

Intercoder Reliability

A total of 22 coders received approximately 40 hours of training over a 1-month period. Coders achieved satisfactory intercoder reliability at the end of training—modified Scott's pi[40] was greater than .90 on all coding items.

RESULTS

Distribution and Duration of Cancer Stories in Local News (RQ1)

The 1257 newscasts coded were 1382.5 hours long and included 40,112 news stories. A total of 347.2 minutes was devoted to cancer news—that is, 386 cancer stories. On average, there was less than 1 cancer story per 30 minutes (see Table 1). The average duration of a cancer story was 56.67 seconds (SE = 2.93). More than half (50.3%) of the stories were less than 30 seconds; 3 out of 4 (74.1%) lasted less than 1 minute. The shortest story was 7 seconds and the longest 7 minutes 3 seconds.

Air Time and Location of Cancer Stories (RQs 2 and 3)

As shown in Table 1, the largest proportion (40.9%) of the cancer stories was broadcast during morning newscasts and the least (15.0%) at noon. A different pattern emerged when newscast duration was considered. There was a significant difference in terms of the number of cancer stories per 30 minutes of news across the day ($F_{3,270} = 30.41, P < .001$). Bonferroni tests revealed that newscasts in the morning had significantly ($P < .05$) fewer cancer stories per 30 minutes than those at noon and in the early/late evening; newscasts at noon had significantly more compared to those in the morning and in the early/late evening; and there was no difference between those in the early versus late evening.

A total of 1 in 3 newscasts (34.9%) had a health segment in the program. The health segment contained more than half (57.0%) of the cancer stories coded. Of all the cancer stories coded, 7.0% appeared in the first 10 minutes of the newscasts.

Cancer Sites Covered in Local News (RQ4)

In terms of frequency of coverage, the top 5 cancer sites were breast cancer (25.1%), colon/rectum (12.7%), prostate (7.5%), brain (6.7%), and lung/bronchus (4.4%). This is somewhat at odds with the frequency that new cases of these cancers are reported in the population. According to the American Cancer Society,[41] the new case incidence rate was highest for prostate cancer, followed by breast, lung/bronchus, colon/rectum, and skin. Brain cancer received more coverage

TABLE 1. General Information on Newscasts and News Stories

	Chicago		Indianapolis		South Bend		Terre Haute		Total	
					Location					
General Information	N	%*	N	%	N	%	N	%	N	%
No. of newscasts and stories										
Newscasts	466	37.1	385	30.6	249	19.8	157	12.5	1,257	100.0
News stories	16,826	42.0	12,480	31.1	7357	18.3	3449	8.6	40,112	100.0
Health stories	1320	40.6	902	27.8	569	17.5	458	14.1	3,249	100.0
Cancer stories	159	41.2	101	26.2	75	19.4	51	13.2	386	100.0
News stories devoted to cancer		0.9		0.8		1.0		1.5		1.0
Health stories devoted to cancer		12.0		11.2		13.2		11.1		11.9
Time										
Newscasts (in hours)	536.4	38.8	440.4	31.9	268.9	19.5	136.8	9.9	1382.5	100.0
Health stories (in hours)	17.5	34.8	16.1	32.0	9.3	18.5	7.4	14.7	50.3	100.0
Cancer stories (in min)	118.9	34.2	101.2	29.2	73.9	21.3	53.2	15.3	347.2	100.0
News time devoted to cancer		0.4		0.4		0.5		0.7		0.4
Health time devoted to cancer		11.3		10.5		13.2		12.0		11.5
	Mean	SE	Mean	SE	Mean	SE	Mean	SE	Mean	SE
Average duration										
Health stories (in sec)	47.8	1.6	64.4	2.0	59.2	2.5	58.5	2.8	57.5	1.1
Cancer stories (in sec)	44.9	4.2	60.1	5.3	59.1	6.1	62.6	7.4	56.7	2.9
No. of cancer stories per 30 minutes										
In all the 1257 newscasts	0.28	0.02	0.15	0.02	0.21	0.03	0.27	0.03	0.22	0.01
In 274 newscasts with cancer stories	0.80	0.05	0.59	0.06	0.76	0.07	0.86	0.07	0.75	0.03
	N	%†	N	%	N	%	N	%	N	%
Location in a newscast										
Newscasts having a health segment	217	46.6	94	24.4	78	31.3	50	31.8	439	34.9
Cancer stories in a health segment	100	62.9	54	53.5	37	49.3	29	56.9	220	57.0
Cancer stories as a lead story‡	8	5.0	5	5.0	9	12.0	5	9.8	27	7.0
Air time of cancer stories										
Morning	57	35.8	50	49.5	35	46.7	16	31.4	158	40.9
Noon	30	18.9	10	9.9	8	10.7	10	19.6	58	15.0
Early evening	39	24.5	32	31.7	19	25.3	11	21.6	101	26.2
Late evening	33	20.8	9	8.9	13	17.3	14	27.5	69	17.9
	Mean	SE	Mean	SE	Mean	SE	Mean	SE	Mean	SE
Accessibility and follow-up options										
SMOG of cancer stories	10.7	1.7	10.5	1.6	10.5	1.4	11.2	1.5	10.7	1.6
	N	%	N	%	N	%	N	%	N	%
Lowest-highest SMOG	7-16		7-15		8-14		9-14		7-16	
Cancer stories with follow-ups	16	10.1	14	13.9	3	4.0	13	25.5	46	11.9

*Proportions across markets.
†Proportions within individual markets.
‡A lead story is defined as a story that appears in the first 10 minutes of a newscast.

in local news than a number of other cancers with higher incidence rates. On the other hand, skin cancer, which the American Cancer Society estimated to be No. 5, only received coverage in 2.6% of the cancer stories and ranked No. 7 in coverage frequency. Other undercovered cancer sites included urinary/bladder (No. 6 in new case estimation vs No. 15 in coverage), non-Hodgkin lymphoma (No. 7 vs 10), uterine (No. 8 vs 16), and kidney (No. 9 vs 18). When the time devoted to each cancer site was considered, the divergence between new case estimation and news coverage again also was quite clear (see Table 2).

Topics and Foci of Cancer Stories (RQ4)

Half of the cancer stories were about prevention (25.9%) or treatment (24.4%). A total of 1 of 4 cancer stories (25.6%) focused on advances made in research. Fundraising for cancer also was frequently covered (13.5%; see Table 3).

Cancer Patients in Cancer Stories (RQ5)

In total, 103 cancer patients were coded in 101 cancer stories that featured patients. (For each story, up to 2 cancer patients were coded.) The stories featured more male patients (63.1%) than female patients (36.9%). About 8 out of 10 were White (78.6%), and the remaining patients whose ethnicity could be identified were African American (17.5%) or Hispanic (1.9%). The most presented age groups were adults 44 to 65 years old (44.7%) and those older than 65 (30.1%). Of the cancer patients presented, about half (49.5%) were celebrities.

Tone and Viewpoints Presented by Cancer Stories (RQs 6 and 7)

More than half of the cancer stories (54.7%) were verbally neutral; and most cancer stories (93.0%) were visually neutral. Only a small proportion of stories (17.6%) were judged by coders as likely to worry those who might be affected by the disease. Almost all of the cancer stories (97.7%) offered a single viewpoint (see Table 3).

Follow-up Information Provided by Cancer Stories (RQ8)

A total of 1 out of 8 cancer stories (11.9%) offered follow-up information. The follow-up option most often provided was a Web site URL, featured in 5.7% of the cancer stories. Phone

numbers (toll free or non toll free) were the second most popular (2.3%), followed by mail address (1.0%), a corresponding television program (1.0%), and health professionals (.5%).

TABLE 2. News Stories Across Different Cancer Sites

Cancer Stories N (%)*	Estimated New Cancer Cases in 2006[†]	Story Duration (s) Mean (SE)[‡]	Total Time (in min)
Breast	97 (25.1)	214,640	48 (48)	77.6
Colon/Rectum	49 (12.7)	148,610	53 (59)	43.3
Prostate	29 (7.5)	234,460	38 (39)	18.4
Brain	26 (6.7)	18,820	65 (51)	28.2
Lung/Bronchus	17 (4.4)	174,470	86 (99)	24.4
Leukemia	14 (3.6)	35,070	38 (37)	8.9
Skin	10 (2.6)	68,780	61 (44)	10.2
Liver	9 (2.3)	18,510	20 (4)	3.0
Ovary	7 (1.8)	20,180	48 (43)	5.6
Non-Hodgkin Lymphoma	7 (1.8)	58,870	45 (26)	5.3
Oral Cavity	6 (1.6)	30,990	55 (46)	5.5
Pancreas	6 (1.6)	33,730	69 (69)	6.9
Esophagus	3 (0.8)	14,550	40 (19)	2.0
Thyroid	2 (0.5)	30,180	24 (7)	0.8
Urinary/ Bladder	2 (0.5)	61,420	27 (8)	0.9
Uterine	2 (0.5)	50,910	27 (9)	0.9
Bone	1 (0.3)	2,760	60 (--)	1.0
Kidney	1 (0.3)	38,890	201 (--)	3.4
Other specific cancer	17 (4.4)		64 (46)	18.1
Cancer in general	95 (24.6)		61 (54)	96.6
Total	400 (103.6)		57 (3)	347.2

*The proportion of cancer stories (n = 386) focusing on a particular cancer site. Note that because there were 14 stories focusing on 2 cancer sites, the total number of cases reported here (N = 400) is larger than the total number of cancer stories (N = 386).

†American Cancer Society (2006). Cancer Facts & Figures 2006. Available at: http://www.cancer.org/downloads/STT/CAFF2006PWSecured.pdf. Accessed August 12, 2006.

‡The mean and SE of story durations and the total time devoted to a certain cancer site are based on all the stories focusing on that cancer site. Up to 2 cancer sites could be coded for each story.

TABLE 3. Central Topics, Focuses, Tones, and Viewpoints of Cancer Stories

Central Topics*	Cancer Stories	
	N	%†
Prevention	100	25.9
Early detection	56	14.5
Diagnosis	14	3.6
Treatment	94	24.4
Life with cancer	28	7.3
End of life	26	6.7
Incidence statistics	23	6.0
Not Specific	76	19.7
Foci‡		
Policy/law	8	2.1
Application of policy/law	3	0.8
Fundraising	52	13.5
Technology	21	5.4
Advances	99	25.6
Verbal tone		
Positive	135	35.0
Negative	31	8.0
Mixed	9	2.3
Neutral	211	54.7
Visual tone		
Positive	22	5.7
Negative	2	0.5
Mixed	3	0.8
Neutral	359	93.0
The story is worrisome	68	17.6
Viewpoints presented		
No contrast	377	97.7
Contrast with conclusion	2	0.5
No conclusion	7	1.8

*Up to 2 central topics could be coded for each story. In total, 417 topics were identified for the 386 cancer stories.
†The percentage reported here is based on the total number of cancer stories (N = 386).
‡A story was judged "Yes" or "No" on each of the possible story foci.

Accessibility of Health News (RQ9)

SMOG scores for cancer news stories ranged from 7 to 16. (SMOG scores were not calculated for stories on Univision, all of which were presented in Spanish.) On average, cancer stories required at least a 10th-grade education (mean = 10.7, SD = 1.6) for the audience to understand the covered information. (See Table 4 for news story examples illustrating the minimum, mean, and maximum SMOG scores.)

Variation Across Markets (RQ10)

Significant differences across markets frequently emerged, but there was no clear pattern based on market size. Markets varied significantly ($P < .05$) in terms of (1) number of cancer stories per 30 minutes, (2) time of the day when cancer stories were aired, (3) average duration of cancer stories, (4) newscasts having a health segment (but not the number of cancer stories presented in a health segment), (5) cancer stories presented in the first 10 minutes of a newscast, (6) cancer sites covered, (7) story foci on fundraising and research advances, (8) verbal and visual tone, (9) number of authorities presented in each cancer story, (10) accessibility of stories indicated by SMOG scores, and (11) follow-up information offered.

DISCUSSION

This content analysis revealed that for the 7 channels in 4 markets coded, about 1% of all local news stories were about cancer. Cancer news stories were unevenly dispersed through the day's local newscasts. It is reasonable to speculate that those at home at midday were most likely to be exposed to cancer news.

Like other news stories, cancer news stories were short; 3 out of 4 cancer news stories in our sample lasted less than 1 minute. This is consistent with previous research on local news[42] and local health news.[36,43] At the same time, it suggests that local television news coverage of cancer will, by itself, not provide detailed coverage of the cancer issues it covers.

About 1 out of 7 cancer news stories focused on fundraising. Although fundraising is a critical function, stories about fundraising say little about cancer and may decrease air time for stories on available treatment regimes, the side-effects of existing and new therapies, as well as prognoses and the likelihood of cure, all of which have been identified as key information needs of cancer patients and those close to them.[8] The popularity of fundraising news is consistent with an earlier assessment that cancers news tended to focus on public awareness of cancer rather than on cancer itself.[44]

TABLE 4. Transcripts of News Story Examples to Illustrate Both Ends of the Range and the Mean of SMOG Scores

SMOG	News Title	Transcript
7	*Prostate Cancer*	Anchor: And doctors believe a drug normally used to fight breast cancer may actually help fight prostate cancer too. Doctors say men who took low doses of a hormonal drug for one year cut their chances of developing prostate cancer in half. But researchers say these findings need to be tested in longer studies.
10	*Colon Cancer*	Health Beat Reporter: People who take statin drugs to lower their cholesterol may be getting an extra benefit: protection from colon cancer. A new study found patients taking the drug dropped their risk of the disease by forty-seven percent. This latest finding updates a similar study last year that also found statins can protect from colon cancer.
16	*Teens, Sex, and Cancer*	Anchor: More sexually active teens might be at higher risk for cervical cancer than previously thought. An Indiana University study reveals that eighty-two percent of sexually active girls are infected with at least one type of HPV.* According to the research published in the *Journal of Infectious Disease*, thirty-nine percent tested positive for a particular string of the virus, which is associated with an increased cancer risk.

*HPV indicates human papillomavirus.

At least 3 media organizational factors were likely to play a role in the coverage of fundraising activities. First, compared with most other cancer topics, fundraising requires little investigative work since organizations readily provide information and personnel needed for news coverage of fundraising events so as to promote their events and strengthen their public images. Second, fundraising events tend to take place in a local community, an important news selection criterion for local news programs. Third, fundraising activities (eg, fun runs or walks) are very visual, providing newscasters with something to show their audiences.

Local television newscast coverage of cancer diverges somewhat from the real-life picture of cancer incidence rates and cancer patients. Such divergence is not new: Almost 3 decades ago, Greenberg et al[22] noted that cancers with the highest incidence rates were not covered extensively in newspaper. Local television news coverage of cancer patients also does not reflect the real-life demography of those with cancer. The divergence between the realities of cancer and TV coverage of it may affect public perceptions of cancer incidence rates and the viewer's own likelihood of developing cancer in their lifetime.

About half of the cancer patients in local news are celebrities. This is consistent with what has been found in earlier studies[22,24]—and understandable from a news organizational perspective: Celebrities attract viewers. On one hand, this suggests that the underlying purpose of covering cancer news is not to educate the audience but instead to attract and keep the viewing audience and increase program ratings (and thus to increase advertising revenue generated by the program). On the other hand, use of celebrities may be helpful in another way as well, much as coverage of Betty Ford's breast cancer when her husband was President of the United States reduced the stigma associated with breast cancer. When viewers see that celebrities are not immune to cancer, viewers may be more attentive to information related to cancer prevention and detection.[45]

A large majority of cancer news stories were verbally and visually neutral or positive in tone. This finding is consistent with recent studies on local health news in general[36] and refutes the concern that health news is depressing and as such, discourages viewers from information seeking.[1] This is important for cancer patients, as interest in seeking information beyond that offered by their physicians is affected by patient attitudes about avoiding negative information.[9,10]

Cancer stories on local television newscasts require at least a 10th-grade education to comprehend. Because news stories on television are short and fleeting, they often are more difficult for audiences to grasp than those in the print media and on Web sites. As a result, it is important that viewers be offered follow-up options that encourage information seeking. However, again, cancer news stories rarely provide follow-up information. As television stations increasingly encourage viewers to visit their Web sites, this situation may change.

Cancer research, care, and outreach professionals can take some comfort in knowing that cancer is a frequently reported topic in local television health news, and the presented information is likely to help viewers learn about—instead of inappropriately fearing—cancer. Yet, because cancer stories tend to be short, challenging for the average viewer to follow, and often focus on "soft" topics such as fundraising, cancer practitioners can not count on local television news as a primary vehicle for cancer information dissemination. In addition, the variability of cancer coverage across markets makes it unwise for practitioners to assume uniform coverage of any cancer topic across markets.

References

1. Rees CE, Bath PA. Mass media sources for breast cancer information: their advantages and disadvantages for women with the disease. J Documentation. 2000;56:235-249.
2. Schofield PE, Cockburn J, Hill DJ, Reading D. Encouraging attendance at a screening mammography program: determinants of response to different recruitment strategies. J Med Screening. 1994;1:144-149.
3. McCaul KD, Jacobson D, Martinson B. The effects of state-wide media campaign on mammography screening. J Appl Soc Psychol. 1998;28:504-515.
4. Johnson JD. Cancer-Related Information Seeking. Cresskill, NJ: Hampton Press; 1997.
5. Freimuth VS, Stein JA, Kean TJ. Searching for Health Information: The Cancer Information Service Model. Philadelphia: University of Pennsylvania Press; 1989.
6. Atkin C. Instrumental utilities and information seeking. In: Clarke P, ed. *New Models for Mass Communication Research.* Beverly Hills, CA: Sage; 1973:205-242.
7. Brashers DE, Goldsmith DJ, Hsieh E. Information seeking and avoiding in health contexts. Hum Commun Res. 2002;28:258-271.
8. Mills ME, Sullivan K. The importance of information giving for patients newly diagnosed with cancer: a review of the literature. J Clin Nurs. 1999;8:631-642.
9. Leydon GM, Boulton M, Moynihan C, et al. Faith, hope, and charity: an in-depth interview study of cancer patients' information needs and information-seeking behavior. West J Med. 2000;173:26-31.
10. Leydon GM, Boulton M, Moynihan C, et al. Cancer patients' information needs and information seeking behaviour: in depth interview study. BMJ. 2000;320:909-913.
11. Matthews AK, Sellergren SA, Manfredi CMW. Factors influencing medical information seeking among African American cancer patients. J Health Commun. 2002;7:205-219.
12. Berger CR. Strategic and nonstrategic information acquisition. Hum Commun Res. 2002;28:287-297.
13. Gantz W, Fitzmanrice M, Fink E. Assessing the active component of information seeking. Journalism Q. 1991;68:630-637.
14. Chen XG, Gruz TB, Schuster DV, Unger JB, Johnson CA. Receptivity to protobacco media and its impact on cigarette smoking among ethnic minority youth in California. J Health Commun. 2002;7:95-111.
15. Evans N, Farkas A. Influence of tobacco marketing and exposure to smokers on adolescent susceptibility to smoking. J Natl Cancer Inst. 1995;87:1538.
16. Gilpin EA, Pierce JP. Trends in adolescent smoking initiation in the United States: is tobacco marketing an influence? Tob Control. 1997;6:122-127.
17. McFerrin KM. Incidental learning in a higher education asynchronous online distance education course. Paper presented at Society for Information Technology and Teacher Education Conference in association with the Association for the Advancement of Computing in Education; March 1999; San Antonio, TX.
18. Mealman CA. Incidental learning by adults in nontraditional degree programs. Paper presented at The 12th Annual Midwest Research-to-Practice Conference; October 1993; Columbus, OH.
19. Ross-Gordon JM, Dowling WD. Adult learning in the context of African-American women's voluntary organizations. Int J Lifelong Education. 1995;14:306-319.
20. Paul B. Using multimedia: a descriptive investigation of incidental language learning. Comput Assist Lang Learn. 1998;11:179-201.
21. Tewksbury D, Weaver AJ, Maddex BD. Accidentally informed: incidental news expo-

sure on the World Wide Web. Journalism Mass Commun Q. 2001;78:533-555.

22. Greenberg RH, Freimuth VS, Bratic E. A content analytic study of daily newspaper coverage of cancer. In: Nimmo D, ed. *Communication Yearbook*. Vol 3. Somerset, NJ: Transaction Books; 1979:645-654.

23. Schwartz LM, Woloshin S. News media coverage of screening mammography of women in their 40s and tamoxifen for primary preventing of breast cancer. JAMA. 2002;287:3136-3142.

24. Corbett JB, Mori M. Medicine, media, and celebrities: News coverage of breast cancer, 1960-1995. Journalism Mass Commun Q. Summer 1999;76:229-249.

25. Corbett JB, Mori M. Gender-specific cancers, gender-specific reporters? Sci Commun. 1999;20:395.

26. Andsager JL, Powers A. Social or economic concerns: How news and women's magazines framed breast cancer in the 1990s. Journalism & Mass Commun Q. Autumn 1999;76:531-550.

27. Clarke JN. Cancer, heart disease, and AIDS: what do the media tell us about these diseases? Health Commun. 1992;4:105-120.

28. Hertog JK, Finnegan JR, Kahn E. Media coverage of AIDS, cancer, and sexually transmitted diseases: a test of the public arenas model. Journalism Q. 1994;71:291-304.

29. Gantz W, Schwartz N. Public Service Advertising in a New Media Age: A Report on Television Content. Menlo Park, CA: Henry J. Kaiser Family Foundation; 2002.

30. Keenan DP, AbuSabha R, Robinson NG. Content analysis of media coverage of the 1995 Dietary Guidelines for Americans. J Extension [serial online]. 2001;39(5).

31. Althaus SL, Edy JA, Phalen PF. Using the Vanderbilt Television Abstracts to track broadcast news content: possibilities and pitfalls. J Broadcasting Electronic Media. 2002;46:473.

32. Radio-Television News Directors Association. Americans rely on local television news, rate it highly, and consider it fair. Available at: https://www.rtndf.org/research/judg.html. Accessed December 15, 2006.

33. Radio-Television News Directors Association. The future of news. Available at: http://www.rtnda.org/resources/future/index.shtml. Accessed December 15, 2006.

34. Kaiser Family Foundation, The Center for Media and Public Affair. Health news index poll. Available at: http://www.kaisernetwork.org. Accessed December 15, 2006.

35. Pribble JM, Goldstein KM, Fowler EF, Greenberg MD, Neol SK, Howell JD. Medical news for the public to use? what's on local TV news. Am J Manag Care. 2006;12:170-176.

36. Wang Z, Gantz W. Health content in local television news. Health Commun. 2007; 21:213-221.

37. Nielsen Media Research. Nielsen Media Research Local Universe Estimates, Chicago, IL: Nielsen Media Research; 2006.

38. McLaughlin GH. SMOG grading: a new readability formula. J Reading. 1969;12:639-646.

39. National Cancer Institute. Readability Testing in Cancer Communications: Methods, Examples, and Resources for Improving the Readability of Cancer Message and Materials. Bethesda, MD: National Cancer Institute; 1979.

40. Potter W, Levine-Donnerstein D. Rethinking validity and reliability in content analysis. J Appl Commun Res. 1999;27:258-284.

41. American Cancer Association. Cancer Facts and Figures 2006. Available at: http://www.cancer.org/downloads/STT/CAFF2006PWSecured.pdf. Accessed March 17, 2007.

42. Project for Excellence in Journalism. The state of the news media 2004: An annual report on American journalism 2004. Available at: http://www.stateofthenewsmedia.com/2004/. Accessed May 19, 2005.

43. Schwitzer G. Ten troublesome trends in TV health news. BMJ. 2004;329:1352-1352.

44. Freimuth VS, Greenberg RH, DeWitt J, Romano RM. Covering cancer: newspapers and the pubic interest. J Commun. 1984; 34:62-73.

45. Chapman S, McLeod K, Wakefield M, Holding S. Impact of news of celebrity illness on breast cancer screening: Kylie Minogue's breast cancer diagnosis. Med J Aust. 2005;183:247-250.

Write Away

1. Compose a rhetorical analysis of this article. For details about how to conduct a rhetorical analysis, see Chapter 7. Address such questions as follows in your analysis: How do the authors incorporate appeals of *ethos, pathos, logos,* and *kairos*? What are the authors' aims and purposes? Who do you think are the intended and/or actual

readers? What are the main claims? You can focus on one of these rhetorical features or more, in consultation with your instructor.

2. Write a marketing proposal for a health-communications media campaign regarding a health issue of your choosing. Shape your marketing proposal with plans for how you intend to address each of the CDC guidelines for health-communications materials, which include the following: reviewing background information and current information already available, setting communication objectives, analyzing target audiences, developing and pretesting message concepts, selecting communication challenges, creating messages and products, developing a promotion plan, implementing the communication, and conducting outcome and impact evaluation ("What is"). For specifics from the CDC, see http://www.cdc.gov/healthcommunication/healthbasics/whatishc.html.

3. Develop a grant proposal to secure funding for a health-communications research project that will extend research such as Gantz and Wang's. Your project can be on a health issue of your choosing, but the research methods should include content analysis of a subset of media information related to that health issue. For your proposal, decide what health issue you would like to research and what media. Describe the intended significance of this research, your primary research questions, and your proposed research methods. Include a literature review to situate your proposed research within others' prior research. For certain segments of your grant, you can model your work on Gantz and Wang's, such as the research questions, the methods, and the literature review.

Chapter 12 Key Terms

citation styles	bibliographic citations	signal phrase
citation guides	in-text citations	self-citation
schools of citation	plagiarism	block quote
document format		

Write Away

Because you will be called upon throughout your undergraduate education and beyond to cite within different contexts, you should gain familiarity with how to transfer citation practices across writing occasions. This activity invites you to do so by transferring citation styles for the same text across disciplines and formats in order to reflect on citation and transfer.

Choose a two-page segment from a peer-reviewed text that includes citations. Choose a text you can use as an original citation starting point. The text you choose can be from any disciplinary perspective and in any citation style. Once you have selected the text, choose a two-page segment of it you can use to transfer citations.

Identify the text's current citation style. Using a library resource, citation guide, or authoritative online resource, identify which citation style the article is currently adopting. Be careful as some citation styles look similar to one another, and you might have chosen one that is a journal-specific citation style (which is fine). To discern citation style, look at both in-text citations and bibliographic information.

Choose two to three additional citation styles you can use for the transfer. Select two or three citation styles different from the one currently being used in the text you have chosen. If your text is using a journal-specific form of citation, just choose two or three other citation styles that look quite different from the current one. Aim to secure a mix of citation styles that ask you to examine citation from several different perspectives.

Transfer the citations across citation styles. Transfer the citation style from the original version to the other citation styles, one at a time. First, transfer all the citations in that two-page segment (in-text and any related bibliographic entries) into one of the other citation styles you have selected. Then, repeat that transfer for the second citation style, and the third if you chose three. You may find that in the process of transferring citation styles you will be called upon to reduce quoted material or change the style of signal phrases. Use a library resource, citation guide, or authoritative online resource to make sure you are citing as accurately as possible.

Transfer citations to a citation style for a weblinked blog. As a final transfer move, paraphrase the two-page segment of text as though you were posting the paraphrase to an online blog. As would be customary in that setting, opt as much as possible for weblinks instead of full in-text citations. Be sure to also cite that you are adapting/paraphrasing an article so your own citation attribution is accurate.

Reflect on citation and transfer. Reflect in writing for ten minutes on what you learned about citation and transfer from having completed this activity. Which citation styles seemed more difficult for you? Which ones fit better with the kind of disciplinary perspective you were using? What elements of citation carried over from one version to another? Which elements were drastically different?

Moving Forward with Writing Transfer

Writing in Transit has provided you with a transfer-based approach to writing, inviting you to approach each new writing occasion by considering the disciplinary and publication context, drawing on your prior experiences with writing, and cultivating and fortifying your writing-related strengths. To invoke Chapter 1's Chaco Canyon once again, your own Writing Great House has now become more expansive and nuanced as you have learned more about the key aspects of academic writing that transverse disciplinary contexts:

- Research and writing as a process
- Posing meaningful questions
- Reading
- Summary
- Synthesis
- Analysis
- Framing arguments
- Constructing arguments
- Designing arguments
- Choosing and integrating evidence
- Citing resources

Just as each of these aspects of academic writing move within and across disciplinary contexts, emerging as aligned, inflected, and distinctive, so too will you as a writer move throughout the varied terrain of academic writing, pursuing your curiosity and discovering new ideas.

The transfer-based approach featured in *Writing in Transit* empowers you to write with deep awareness and reflection, to survey and recognize that which you might apply, extend, reconsider, reject, or otherwise transfer from one writing and learning occasion to others. Challenging as this can be, you will likely have many opportunities to invoke and build on these transfer-based strategies throughout your undergraduate experience and beyond. In this way, *Writing in Transit* has prepared you to move forward with writing transfer, empowering you to make a difference and cultivate your aspirations as you encounter complexity, learn from and about yourself and others, advance knowledge, and otherwise contribute to the world around you.

References

"11 Facts about Hurricane Katrina." Do Something. www.dosomething.org/us/facts/11-facts-about-hurricane-katrina. Accessed 3 Sept. 2016.

"22 Chinese Inventions That Changed the World." *humansarefree.com*. Humans Are Free. Nov. 22 2014. Web. 22 May 2016.

"3 Ways Health Informatics is Cutting Patient Wait Times." *Health Informatics and Health Information Management.* University of Illinois at Chicago, n.d., healthinformatics.uic.edu/resources/articles/3-ways-health-informatics-is-cutting-patient-wait-times/. Accessed 2 Sept. 2016.

"A Chronology of the Elián González Saga." *pbs.org.* 2014. WGBH Educational Foundation. Web. 22 May 2016.

Aaij, Roel. "Roel Aaij." *linkedin.com*. LinkedIn. Web. 25 May 2016.

"About Alignments." *Exploratorium.* Exploratorium, n.d.

"About CERN." n.d. *home.cern*. Web. 20 May 2016.

"About Petroglyphs." *Zion Canyon Offerings.* Zion Canyon Offerings, n.d.

"About Sonoma County Law." *sonomacountylaw.com.* Web. 14 July 2016.

"About Stonehenge." *stonehenge.co.uk.* 3 Oct. 2014.

Abrams, Eleanor, Peter C. Taylor, and Chorng-Jee Guo. "Contextualizing Culturally Relevant Science and Mathematics Teaching for Indigenous Learning." *International Journal of Science and Mathematics Education*, vol. 11, no. 1, 2013, pp. 1-21. doi:10.1007/s10763-012-9388-2.

"Abstracts." The Writing Center at UNC Chapel Hill. *writingcenter.unc.edu.*

Acta Astronautica. International Academy of Astronautics. Web. 23 July 2016.

Adelson, Glenn, ed. *Environment: an Interdisciplinary Anthology.* New Haven: Yale UP, 2008.

Adriano V. Autino. *Lifeboat Foundation. lifeboat.com.* Lifeboat Foundation. Web. 23 July 2016.

Agee, Jane. "Developing Qualitative Research Questions: A Reflective Process." *International Journal of Qualitative Studies in Education* 22.4 (2009): 431-47.

Aguirre, Fernando. *Bugging Out and Relocating: When Staying is Not an Option.* Argentina: Fernando Aguirre, 2014.

Aguirre, Fernando. *Modern Survival Blog*

Aguirre, Fernando. *Surviving in Argentina. Life In Argentina after the 2001 Crisis.*

Aguirre, Fernando. *The Modern Survival Manual: Surviving the Economic Collapse* Based on a Personal FirstHand Experience of the 2001 Economic Collapse in Argentina. Argentina: Fernando Aguirre, 2009.

Ahmed, Hassaan, Omer Masood Qureshi, and Abid Ali Khan. "Reviving a Ghost in the History of Technology: The Social Construction of the Recumbent Bicycle." *Social Studies of Science* 45.1 (2015): 130-6. Web. 22 May 2016.

Aitken, R. John, et al. "The Source and Significance of DNA Damage in Human Spermatozoa; a Commentary on Diagnostic Strategies and Straw Man Fallacies. *Molecular Human Reproduction* 19.8 (2013): 475-85. *Oxford Journals.*

Akintola, Joe. "Major Sub-Disciplines of Geography." *geolounge.com*. Geolounge, 10 February 2015. Web. 22 July 2016.

"Alan Diaz Video/Interviews." www.ovguide.com. n.d. Web. 20 May 2016.

"Alan Diaz." *en.wikipedia.org.* 30 April 2016. Web. 20 May 2016.

Aleghfeli, Obaid Rashed. "Video Games." *Undergraduate Research Journal for the Human Sciences.* 11 (2012): n.p. *kon.org.*

Alexander, Jeffrey. *Classical Attempt at Theoretical Synthesis.* Berkeley: U of California P, 1983.

Alim, H. Samy. *Roc the Mic Right: The Language of Hip Hop Culture.* New York: Routledge, 2006.

"All Nobel Prizes in Physics." Nobel Prize. www.nobelprize.org/nobel_prizes/physics/laureates/. Accessed 18 November 2016.

Allan, Stuart. *The Routledge Companion to News and Journalism.* London and New York: Routledge, 2010. Print.

Alvarez, Alex. Borderlands, Climate Change, and the Genocidal Impulse." *Genocide Studies International* 10.1 (2016): 27-36.

Amarasingam, Amarnath, and Robert W. McChesney. *The Stewart/Colbert Effect: Essays on the Real Impacts of Fake News.* Jefferson, N.C.: McFarland, 2011. *amazon.com.* Web. 5 May 2016.

American Marketing Association. American Marketing Association. Web. 23 July 2016.

Anderson, Craig A., Douglas A. Gentile, and Katherine E. Buckley. *Violent Video Game Effects on Children and Adolescents: Theory, Research, and Public Policy.* Oxford: Oxford UP, 2007.

Anderson, Katharine. *Predicting the Weather: Victorians and the Science of Meteorology.* Chicago, U of Chicago P, 2005. *books.google.com.* Web. 22 May 2016.

Anderson, Robert S. *Nucleus and Nation. Scientists, International Networks, and Power in India.* Chicago: U of Chicago P, 2010. *books.google.com.* Web. 22 May 2016.

"Anupam Anand." *geog.umd.edu.* University of Maryland, n.d. Web. 22 July 2016.

Archaeoastronomy. Web.

"Archaeoastronomy." *scienceclarified.*

Aristotle. *On Sophistical Refutations.* 350 B.C.E. Trans. Arthur Wallace Pickard-Cambridge. Blacksburg, VA: Virginia Tech, 2001.

Ashton, Geoffrey. "Role Ethics or Ethics of Role-Play? A Comparative Critical Analysis of the Ethics of Confucianism and the Bhagavad Gita. Dao. A Journal of Comparative Philosophy. 13.1 (2014): 1-21. ProQuest. Web. 26 Aug. 2016.

"Assumptions about Learners and Teachers." *Position on the Teaching of English*. 1988-89. *ncte.org*.

Australia. Attorney General's Department. *Literature Review on the Impact of Playing Violent Video Games on Aggression*. Barton, Au.: September 2010. *classification.gov.au*.

Aveni, Anthony F. "Archaeoastronomy in the Ancient Americas." *Journal of Archaeological Research* 11.2 (2003): 149-91. *ProQuest*.

Aveni, Anthony F., and Robert M. Linsley. "Mound J, Monte Albán: Possible Astronomical Orientation." *American Antiquity* 37.4 (1972): 528-531. *JSTOR*.

Axis Rule in Occupied Europe: Laws of Occupation - Analysis of Government - Proposals for Redress, Washington, D.C.: Carnegie Endowment for International Peace, 1944, 670pp.

Ayalon, Michal, and Ruhama Even. "Deductive Reasoning: In the Eye of the Beholder." *Educational Studies in Mathematics* 69.3 (2008): 235-47. *edumatec.mat.ufrgs.br*.

Ayers, John W., et al. "Tracking the Rise in Popularity of Electronic Nicotine Delivery Systems (Electronic Cigarettes) Using Search Query Surveillance." *American Journal of Preventive Medicine*, vol. 40, no. 4, 2011., pp. 448-453. ScienceDirect, doi:10.1016/j.amepre.2010.12.007.

Babcock, Rebecca Day. *A Synthesis of Qualitative Studies of Writing Center Tutoring*, 1983-2006. New York: Peter Lang, 2012. *books. google.com*.

Bahls, Patrick. "The Mathematical Muse: Using Math to Construct Poetry." Math Horizons, vol. 17, no. 3, 2010., pp. 14-17. JSTOR, doi:10.4169/194762110X489251.

Barmé, Geremie. *The Forbidden City*. Harvard UP, 2008.

Barnett, Michael. *Eyewitness to a Genocide. The United Nations and Rwanda*. Ithaca: Cornell UP, 2003. *Ebrary Academic Complete*. Web. 25 May 2016.

Bartholomae, David. "Inventing the University." *Journal of Basic Writing* 5.1 (1986): 4-23. *wac.colostate.edu*.

Baudo, Renato, Gianni Tartari, and Mohiuddin Munawar, eds. *Top of the world environmental research: Mount Everest-Himalayan ecosystem*. Leiden: Backhuys, 1998. Print.

Bazerman, Charles. *Shaping Written Knowledge: The Genre and Activity of the Experimental Article in Science*. Madison, WI: U of Wisconsin P, 1988. Print.

Beach, King. "Consequential Transitions: A Developmental View of Knowledge Propagation Through Social Organizations." *Between School and Work: New Perspectives on Transfer and Boundary-Crossing*. Ed. Terttu Tuomi-Gröhn and Yrjö Engeström. Bingley, UK: Emerald Group, 2003. 39-61. Print.

Beaney, Michael. "Analysis." *The Stanford Encyclopedia of Philosophy* (Summer 2014). Ed. Edward N. Zalta. 25 March 2014. *plato. stanford.edu*.

Beaudoin, Christopher E., Hongliang Chen, and Sohail Agha. "Estimating Causal Effects with Propensity Score Models: An Evaluation of the Touch Condom Media Campaign in Pakistan." *Journal of Health Communication* 21.4 (2016): 415-423. *Taylor & Francis Online*. Web. 15 May 2016.

Becker, Ben. "PAX EAST 2012 Queue Room – Fisheye." Photograph. 7 Apr. 2012. *flickr.com*.

"Benefits of Electronic Health Records (EHRs)." 30 July 2015. healthit.gov. United States Government. Web. 2 Sept. 2016.

Benkler, Yochai, et al. "Social Mobilization and the Networked Public Sphere: Mapping the SOPA-PIPA Debate." *Political Communication* 32.4 (2015): 594-624. *tandfonline.com*. Web. 16 May 2016.

Berdahl, Loleen, et al. Exploring Perceptions of Credible Science Among Policy Stakeholder Groups: Results of Focus Group Discussions About Nuclear Energy." *Science Communication*. 38 (2016): 382-406. *scx.sagepub.com*. Web. 19 May 2016.

Berger, John, and Jean Mohr. *Another Way of Telling*. New York: Pantheon, 1982. Print.

Bielenberg, Andy, and Raymond Ryan. *An Economic History of Ireland Since Independence*. New York: Routledge, 2013. books. google.com.

"Biography." Armin T. Wegner Society of USA. armin-t-wegner.us. Web. 27 Aug. 2016.

Bitzer, Lloyd. "The Rhetorical Situation." *Philosophy and Rhetoric* 1.1 (1968): 1–14. *JSTOR*.

Blau, Soren. "One Chance Only: Advocating the use of Archaeology in Search, Location and Recovery at Disaster Scenes." *Australian Journal of Emergency Management, The* 20.1 (2005): 19-24. Web.

Bogich, Tiffany L., et al. "Preventing pandemics via international development: a systems approach." *PLoS medicine*, vol. 9, no. 12, 2012., pp. e1001354. General OneFile, doi:10.1371/journal.pmed.1001354.

Bol, Nadine, et al. "How are Online Health Messages Processed? Using Eye Tracking to Predict Recall of Information in Younger and Older Adults." *Journal of Health Communication* 21.4 (2016): 387-396. *Taylor & Francis Online*. Web. 15 May 2016.

Bolker, Joan. *Writing Your Dissertation in Fifteen Minutes a Day: A Guide to Starting, Revising, and Finishing your Doctoral Thesis*. New York: Macmillan, 1998. Print.

"Boudhanath Stupa, Kathmandu." *sacred-destinations.com*. n.d.

Bouvier, Paul. "Sexual Violence, Health and Humanitarian Ethics: Towards a Holistic, Person-Centered Approach. International Review of the Red Cross 96.894 (2014): 565-584. ProQuest. Web. 26 Aug. 2016.

Branson, Richard. Disruptors. *Virgin*, https://www.virgin.com/richard-branson/you-learn-by-doing-and-by-falling-over. Accessed 14 Dec. 2016.

Brennan, Ian. "Brand Placement in Novels and Competitor Recall: The Robustness of the Part-List Cueing Effect." *Academy of Marketing Studies Journal* 19.3 (2015): 63-72. *ProQuest*. Web. 24 July 2016.

Brewer, Paul R., Dannagal Goldthwaite Young, and Michelle Morreale. "The Impact of Real News about 'Fake News': Intertextual Processes and Political Satire." *International Journal of Public Opinion Research* 25.3 (2013): 323-43. Web. 21 May 2016.

Brinton, Alan. "The *Ad Hominem*." *Fallacies: Classical and Contemporary Readings*. Ed. Hans V. Hansen and Robert C. Pinto. University Park, PA: Penn State UP, 1995. 213-21. *books.google.com*.

Brizee, H. Allen. "Stasis Theory as a Strategy for Workplace Teaming and Decision Making." *Journal of Technical Writing and Communication* 38.4 (2008): 363-85. *Metapress*.

Brownstein, John S., et al. "Surveillance Sans Frontières: Internet-based emerging infectious disease intelligence and the HealthMap project." *PLoS medicine*, vol. 5, no. 7, 2008., pp. e151. ProQuest, doi: 10.1371/journal.pmed.0050151. *bubble.us.*

Bull, Ross. *Disaster Economics*. 2nd ed. Disaster Management Training Program. 1994. *pacificdisaster.net*. 20 Aug. 2016.

Bunn, Mike. "How to Read Like a Writer." *Writing Spaces: Readings on Writing*. Ed. Charles Lowe and Pavel Zemliansky. Vol. 2 Anderson, SC: Parlor P, 2011. 71-86. atleegoesto11.pbworks.com.

Burnette, Jeni L., Jeffrey M. Pollack, and Donelson R. Forsyth. "Leadership In Extreme Contexts: A Groupthink Analysis Of The May 1996 Mount Everest Disaster." *Journal Of Leadership Studies* 4.4 (2011): 29-40. *Business Source Complete*.

Bushman, Brad J., and L. Rowell Huesmann. "Twenty-Five Years of Research on Violence in Digital Games and Aggression Revisited: A Reply to Elson and Ferguson (2013)." *European Psychologist* 19.1 (2014): 47-55. *PsycINFO*.

Cahill, Abigail, et al. "How Does Climate Change Cause Extinction?" *Proceedings of the Royal Society of Biological Sciences* 280.1750 (2013): n.p. *RoyalSocietyPublishing.org.*

Calegari, Mary F., Robert E. Sibley, and Marlene E. Turner. "A Market Analysis Framework for Business Doctoral Education Opportunities." *Academy of Marketing Studies Journal* 19.3 (2015): 73-89. *ProQuest*. Web. 24 July 2016.

Calliope. "Alain de Botton. Biography." *imdb.com*. n.d. Web. 22 July 2016.

Campbell, Charlie. "Ten Years after a Historic Disaster Claimed the Lives of 230,000 People across Asia, Vibrations Can Still Be Felt." *Time*. 25 Dec. 2014. *time.com*. Web. 14 July 2016.

Canniford, Robin, and Avi Shankar. "Purifying Practices: How Consumers Assemble Romantic Experiences of Nature." *Journal of Consumer Research* 39.5 (2013): 1051-69. *JSTOR*.

Caple, Helen, and John S. Knox. "Online News Galleries, Photojournalism and the Photo Essay." *Visual Communication* 11.2 (2012): 207-36. Web. *Sage Journals*. 2 Apr. 2016.

Carlson, John B., David S. P. Dearborn, Stephen C. McCluskey, and Clive L. N. Ruggles. "Astronomy in Culture." *Archaeoastronomy* 14.1 (1999): 3-21. *honors.umd.edu.*

Carmona, Chelsea. "How AA Fails to Support Young Addicts." *The Washington Post*. 6 July 2012. *thewashingtonpost.com.*

Carr, Kurt, and Paul Nevin. "Petroglyphs of Pennsylvania." *Pennsylvania Historical & Museum Commission*. Pennsylvania, 2014.

Carr, Nicholas. "Is Google Making Us Stupid?" *The Atlantic Monthly* 107.2 (2008): 89-94. *Wiley Online Library*.

Carr, S. V. "ethics/psychology." *European Journal of Contraception & Reproductive Health Care* 9 (2004): 16. Web.

Carr, Stuart A., and Malcolm MacLachlan. "Interdisciplinary Research for Development: A Policy Paper." *global-health.tcd.ie.* Global Development Network. n.d.

Carroll, Laura Bolin. "Backpacks vs. Briefcases: Steps toward Rhetorical Analysis." *Writing Spaces: Readings on Writing*. Vol. 1. Ed. Charles Lowe and Pavel Zemliansky. Anderson, SC: Parlor P, 2010. 45-58. *1112dual.pbworks.com.*

Carter, Cassie. "Introduction to Syntheses." *msu.edu.*

Carter, David. "Computer & Video Game Archive." *lib.umich.edu*. University of Michigan.

Carter, Michael. "Ways of Knowing, Doing, and Writing in the Disciplines." *College Composition and Communication* 58.3 (2007): 385-418. *JSTOR.*

Cartwright, Guenther. "Photojournalism." In *The Focal Encyclopedia of Photography*. Digital Imaging, Theory and Applications, History, and Science. 4th ed. Ed. Michael R. Peres. Amsterdam, Focal Press, 2007. 339-341.

Caruana-Galizia, Paul, and Matthew Caruana-Galizia. "Offshore financial activity and tax policy: evidence from a leaked data set." *Journal of Public Policy* 36.3 (2016): 457-488. Cambridge Journals Online. Web. 1 Sept. 2016.

Cassa, Christopher A., et al. "No Place to Hide — Reverse Identification of Patients from Published Maps." *The New England Journal of Medicine*, vol. 355, no. 16, 2006., pp. 1741-1742. ProQuest, doi: 10.1056/NEJMc061891.

CDC. "Learn About Health Literacy." *cdc.gov*. CDC. 30 Sept. 2015. Web. 23 May 2016.

CDC. "What is Health Communications?" *cdc.gov*. CDC. n.d. Web. 15 May 2016.

Center for Material Culture Studies. materialculture.udel.edu. Web. 26 Aug. 2016.

Center for Reviews and Dissemination (CRD). *Systematic Reviews. CRD's Guidance for Undertaking Reviews in Health Care.* 2009. *york.ac.uk.*

"Chaco Culture." *World Heritage Center*. Unesco, n.d.

Chakrabarti, Amaresh, and Lucienne TM Blessing. *An Anthology of Theories and Models of Design*. London: Springer, 2014. *SpringerLink.*

Chapman, Robin. "Quantum Metaphors." N.d. American Scientist. Sigma Xi. http://www.americanscientist.org/bookshelf/pub/quantum-metaphors. Accessed 3 Sept. 2016.

Chen, Adrian. "We Need to Know Who Satoshi Nakamoto Is." 9 May 2016. *newyorker.com*. New Yorker. Web. 10 May 2016.

Chen, Jie-Qi, et al. "A Survey Study of Early Childhood Teachers' Beliefs and Confidence about Teaching Early Math." *Early Childhood Education Journal*, vol. 42, no. 6, 2014, pp. 367-377. *ProQuest*, doi:10.1007/s10643-013-0619-0.

Chiaet, Julianne. "Getting on the Ball: How the FIFA 14 Soccer Video Game Finally Got Its Physics Right." 27 Sept. 2013. Scientific American. www.scientificamerican.com/article/getting-on-the-ball-how-soccer-video-game-got-physics-right/ 13 Nov. 2016.

"Chinese Astronomy." n.d. *what-when-how.com.*

Ching, Frank, Mark Jarzombek, and Vikramaditya Prakash. *A Global History of Architecture*. Hoboken, N.J.: John Wiley, 2010. *books. google.com.*

Chomsky, Noam, and Edward S. Herman. *Manufacturing Consent. The Political Economy of the Mass Media*. 1988. New York, Pantheon, 2002. Print.

"Christopher Cassa, PhD." *Boston Children's Hospital.* Boston Children's Hospital, n.d., www.childrenshospital.org/researchers/christopher-cassa. Accessed 2 Sept. 2016.

Chunara Lab. New York University, 2016. wp.nyu.edu/chunaralab/. Accessed 2 Sept. 2016.

Chunara, et al. "Social and News Media Enable Estimation of Epidemiological Patterns Early in the 2010 Haitian Cholera Outbreak." *American Journal of Tropical Medicine and Hygiene,* vol. 86, no. 1, 2012., pp. 39-45. PubMed Central. doi:10.4269/ajtmh.2012.11-0597.

Chunara, Rumi, et al. "Why We Need Crowdsourced Data in Infectious Disease Surveillance." *Current Infectious Disease Reports,* vol. 15, no. 4, 2013., pp. 316-319.ProQuest, doi:10.1007/s11908-013-0341-5.

Chwanya, Matengo. "Namoratunga Like the Nabta Playa." *streamafrica.com.*

Ciottone, Gregory R. "Introduction to Disaster Medicine." 3-19. Web. books.google.com. 13 June 2016.

Cisneros, Sandra. "One Last Poem for Richard." Poetry Soup. Poetry Soup. http://www.poetrysoup.com/famous/poem/23148/one_last_poem_for_richard. Accessed 3 Sept. 2016.

Clack, Timothy, and Marcus Brittain. "Place-Making, Participative Archaeologies and Mursi Megaliths: Some Implications for Aspects of Pre- and Proto-History in the Horn Of Africa." *Journal Of East African Studies* 5.1 (2011): 85-107. *Political Science Complete.*

Clark, Catherine E. "Capturing the Moment, Picturing History: Photographs of the Liberation of Paris." *The American Historical Review.* 121.3 (2016): 824-860. doi:10.1093/ahr/121.3.824.

Clark, Liesl. "Who Built the Pyramids?" *NOVA,* 1997. pbs.org.

Coining a word and Championing a Cause: The Story of Raphael Lemkin. https://www.ushmm.org/wlc/en/article.php?ModuleId=10007050

Committee to Protect Journalists. cpj.org. Committee to Protect Journalists. Web. 16 May 2016.

"Computer Engineers. Who Are They and What Do They Do?" n.d. International Student Guide to the United States of America. Spindle Publishing Company. www.internationalstudentguidetotheusa.com/articles/computer_engineers.htm

"Condensed Matter Physics." University of Colorado. Regents of the University of Colorado. www.colorado.edu/physics/research/condensed-matter-physics

Conti, Ronald S., and Linda L. Chasko. "Technologies for today's mine emergency responders." *International Journal of Emergency Management,* vol. 1, no. 1, 2003., pp. 13-29. Inderscience.com. Web. 1 Sept. 2016.

Cooley, Nicole. "Poetry of Disaster." 20 Feb. 2014. Poets.org. Academy of American Poets. https://www.poets.org/poetsorg/text/poetry-disaster. Accessed 3 Sept. 2016.

Corbett, James. "Psyops 101: A Brief History of Fake News." *corbettreport.com.* 31 Oct. 2012. Web. 3 May 2016.

Corso, David. "The Psychological and Physical Effects of Video Game Play." *Caravel, Undergraduate Research Journal* (2014): n.p. *caravel.sc.edu.*

Courtney, Chris. Central China Flood, 1931. Disasterhistory.org.

Cox, Trevor. "Was Stonehenge Built for Rock Music?" *ShortCutsBlog. The Guardian.* 5 Mar. 2014.

Cuddy, Luke, and John Nordlinger, eds. *World of Warcraft and Philosophy. Wrath of the Philosopher King.* Chicago: Open Court, 2009. *books.google.com.* Web. 7 Nov. 2016.

Cultural Treasures of Nepal. Nepal Tourism Board, 2011. *Welcomenepal.com.*

D'Alessio, Dave. *Media Bias in Presidential Election Coverage, 1948-2008. Evaluation via Formal Measurement.* Lanham, MD: Lexington, 2012. Print.

Daily, Gordon. "Comment." 28 August 2009. "Starts with a Bang." Ethan Siegel. 26 Aug. 2009. *scienceblogs.com.*

Dalgleish, Hannah. "Delving into Archaeoastronomy." n.d. *thetribeonline.*

Dane, Hannah. "Who is Salam Pax and Why Was He Important?" *hannahdane.wordpress.com.* 27 Jan. 2015. Web. 23 May 2016.

Danielson, Carly M., and Tara M. Emmers-Sommer. "'It Was My Fault': Bullied Students' Causal and Controllable Attributions in Bullying Blogs." *Journal of Health Communication* 21.4 (2016): 408-414. *Taylor & Francis Online.* Web. 15 May 2016.

Darimont, Chris T., et al. "Faecal-Centric Approaches to Wildlife Ecology and Conservation; Methods, Data and Ethics." *Wildlife Biology in Practice,* vol. 4, no. 2, 2008., pp. 73-87.doi:10.2461/wbp.2008.4.7.

Das, Apama. Economics of Child Labour. A Case Study of Unorganized Sector in Raipur City of Chhattisgarh. New Delhi: Sunrise, 2010. Print.

Dauncey, Guy. *Stormy Weather: 101 Solutions to Global Climate Change.* Gabriola Island, BC: New Society P, 2001. *books.google.com.*

Dawson, Emily. "'Not Designed for Us': How Science Museums and Science Centers Socially Exclude Low-Income, Minority Ethnic Groups: Not Designed For Us." *Science Education,* vol. 98, 2014.

de Botton, Alain. *alaindebotton.com.* 2013. Web. 22 July 2016.

De Lecea, Antonio. "Europe's economic future: Europe can grow faster." *Global Economy Journal,* vol. 15, no. 2, 2015., pp. 187-197. De Gruyter. doi:10.1515/gej-2015-0026.

Dearborn, David S. P., and Raymond E. White. "The Torreón of Machu Picchu as an Observatory." *Archaeoastronomy.* 14.5 (1983): 37-49. *ProQuest.*

DeBose, Charles. "Codeswitching: Black English and Standard English in the African-American Linguistic Repertoire." *Codeswitching.* Ed. Carol Eastman. Clevedon: Multilingual Matters, 1992. 157–67. *books.google.com.*

DezhamKhooy, Maryam, and Leila Papoli Yazdi. "The Archaeology of Last Night .. what Happened in Bam (Iran) on 25-6 December 2003." *World Archaeology* 42.3 (2010): 341-54. Web.

"Digging Up the Present." Brown Alumni Magazine. July/August 2005. Brownalumnimagazine.com. Web. 27 Aug. 2016.

"Dimensional Analysis." *Department of Physics.* University of Guelph, n.d.

"Discourse Analysis." *Foundations of Qualitative Research in Education.* Harvard University, 2008.

Dodeman, Andre. "Crossing oceans and stories: Yann Martel's 'Life of Pi' and the survival narrative." *Commonwealth Essays and Studies,* 37.1 (2014): 35-44. *Vlex Global.* Web. 14 July 2016.

Doescher, Ian. *William Shakespeare's Star Wars: Verily, A New Hope*. Philadelphia, PA: Quirk, 2013. *amazon.com*.

"Don Staples." LinkedIn.

Doney, Scott C., et al. "Climate Change Impacts on Marine Ecosystems." *Annual Review of Marine Science* 4 (2012). 11-37. *annualreviews.org*.

"Dr. Jennifer Laing." *latrobe.edu.au*. La Trobe University. Web. 23 July 2016.

"Dr. Patrick Collins." *The Space Show. thespaceshow.com*. David M. Livingstone and One Giant Leap Foundation. Web. 23 July 2016.

Dreher, Axel, Jan-Egbert Sturm, and James Raymond Vreeland. "Development Aid and International Politics: Does Membership on the UN Security Council Influence World Bank Decisions?" *Journal of Development Economics* 88.1 (2009): 1-18. Web. *ScienceDirect*. Web. 25 May 2016.

Drehle, David Von. "The Case Against Summer Vacation." *Time Magazine*. 22 July 2010. *content.time.com*.

Dutton, William H. "The Fifth Estate Emerging through the Network of Networks." *Prometheus* 27.1 (2009): 1-15. *Academic Search Complete*. Web. 25 May 2016.

Eastman, Tyler, Ed. *Research in Media Promotion*. Mahwah, NJ: Lawrence Erlbaum, 2000. Print.

"Eckersley, Peter." *eff.org*. EFF. n. d. Web. 17 May 2016.

edge.org. John Brockman, 1996.

"Editorial Policy." *eurosurveillance.org*. Eurosurveillance. Web. 24 July 2016.

Edwards, Jim. "Rush Limbaugh's Audience May Be Much Smaller Than You Think." *businessinsider.com*. Business Insider. 13 Mar. 2012. Web. 5 May 2016.

Eisner, Peter. "Who Discovered Machu Picchu?" *Smithsonian Magazine*. March 2009. *smithsonianmag.com*.

Electronic Frontier Federation. *eff.org*. EFF. n. d. Web. 17 May 2016.

Elert, Glenn. *The Physics Hypertextbook*. 2016. physics.info/equations/. Accessed 17 November 2016.

Emdin, Christopher. *For White Folks Who Teach in the Hood ... and the Rest of Y'all Too: Reality Pedagogy and Urban Education*. Beacon Press, 2016.

English, Beth. "Matoaca Manufacturing Company: A Photographic Essay." *The Virginia Magazine of History and Biography* 114.3 (2006): 385. Web. *ProQuest*. 2 Apr. 2016.

Erduran, Sibel, and Rosa Villamanan. "Cool Argument: Engineering Students Written Arguments about Thermodynamics in the Context of the Peltier Effect in Refrigeration." *Educación química* (2009): 119-25.

Evans, Dominic, and Suleiman Al-Khalidi. "From Teenage Graffiti to a Country in Ruins: Syria's Two Years of Rebellion." *UK Reuters*. Reuters, 17 Mar. 2013. Web. 2 Apr. 2016.

Evans, Walker, and James Agee. *Let Us Now Praise Famous Men*. (1941) Boston: Houghton Mifflin, 2001. *books.google.com*.

"Executive Summary." University Writing Center. Texas A&M University. 2011. *writingcenter.tamu.edu*.

"Fajada Butte." *Evaluating Models of Chaco: A Virtual Conference. University of Colorado*. University of Colorado, 1997.

Fall, A., et al. "Sliding Friction on Wet and Dry Sand." *Physical Review Letters* 112 (175502): 2014. *journals.aps.org*.

"Fallacies: Alphabetic List (Full List)." *changeminds.org*.

Farrar, Renée. "Apple (a poem)." *Digital America*. 24 April 2014. *digitalamerica.org*.

Fazenda, Bruno. "Acoustics of Stonehenge." *University of Salford*. Acoustics Research Centre, University of Salford, 2012.

Fenelon, James V., and Clifford E. Trafzer. "From Colonialism to Denial of California Genocide to Misrepresentations: Special Issue on Indigenous Struggles in the Americas." *American Behavioral Scientist* 58.1 (2014): 3-29. *SAGE Journals*. Web. 28 Aug. 2016.

Fernández-Garrido, Regla. "Stasis-theory in Judicial Speeches of Greek Novels." *Greek, Roman, and Byzantine Studies* 49.3 (2009): 453–72. *Greek, Roman, and Byzantine Studies*.

Fichter, Darlene. "What is a Mashup?" *Library Mashups Exploring New Ways to Deliver Library Data*. Ed. Nicole Engard. Medford, NJ: Information Today, 2009. 3-17. *books.infotoday.com*.

Flipnomad. "Meet the Nomads: Cengiz Yar Jr." *Flipnomad*. Flipnomad. n.d. Web. 2 Apr. 2016.

Flottau, Jens. "Learning about Quicker Evacuation from Emirates Flight 521." 12 Aug. 2016. *aviationweek.com*. Web. 1 Sept. 2016.

Folkenflik, David. "Area Satirical Publication The Onion Sold To Univision (Seriously)" *npr.org*. npr. 19 January 2016. Web. 3 May 2016.

Fonsah, Esendugue Gregory, and Angus S.N.D. Chidebelu. Economics of Banana Production and Marketing in the Tropics. A Case Study of Cameroon. Bamenda: Langaa Research, 2011. books.google.com.

"For Teachers: 1001 Assignments." *Department of English*. Louisiana State University. 23 July 2013.

Foster, Aroutis, et al. "Mobile Learning: Technology as Mediator of Personal and School Experiences." *International Journal of Game-Based Learning (IJGBL)*, vol. 6, no. 1, 2016, pp. 30-42. *ProQuest*, doi:10.4018/IJGBL.2016010103.

Foster, Victoria. "What If? The Use of Poetry to Promote Social Justice." Social Work Education, vol. 31, no. 6, 2012., pp. 742-755. Academic Search Complete, doi:10.1080/02615479.2012.695936.

Frank, Russell. "Caveat Lector: Fake News as Folklore." *The Journal of American Folklore*128.509 (2015): 315-32. Web. 1 May 2016.

Freifeld, Clark C., et al. "Participatory epidemiology: use of mobile phones for community-based health reporting." *PLoS medicine*, vol. 7, no. 12, 2010., pp. e1000376. General OneFile, doi: 10.1371/journal.pmed.1000376.

Frost, Warwick, Jennifer Laing, Fiona Wheeler, and Keir Reeves. "Coffee Culture, Heritage and Destination Image: Melbourne and the Italian Model." In Coffee Culture, Destinations and Tourism. Ed. Lee Jolliffe. Bristol: Channel View Publications, 2010. 99-110. *books.google.com*. Web. 23 July 2016.

Fussell, Crime without a Name.

Game Over: Gender, Race & Violence in Video Games. dir. Nina Huntemann. Media Education Foundation, 2002. Film.

Garcia, Nelly Robles. "Land Use in the Environs of Monte Albán and Mitla." *The Management of Archaeological Resources in Mexico. Oaxaca as a Case Study. Society for American Archaeology.* Society for American Archaeology, 2000.

Gardella, Robert. "Tea Processing in China, Circa 1885—A Photographic Essay." *Business History Review* 75.4 (2001): 807-12. Web. *PubMed.* 2 Apr. 2016.

Gates, Henry Louis, Jr., and Abby Wolf. *The Henry Louis Gates, Jr. Reader.* New York: Basic Civitas, 2012. *amazon.com.*

Gee, Gilbert C., and Chandra L. Ford. "Structural Racism and Health Inequities." *Du Bois Review: Social Science Research on Race* 8.1 (2011): 115-32. Web. 24 May 2016.

Gee, James Paul. *James Paul Gee.* www.jamespaulgee.com/vita.html. Accessed 18 November 2016.

"General Information: Chichen Itza, The Great Ball Court." *American Egypt.* Mystery Lane Press, 2009.

Gentile, Douglas A., ed. *Media Violence and Children: A Complete Guide for Parents and Professionals.* Westport, CT: Praeger, 2003. *psychology.iastate.edu.*

"Geoffrey Crouch." *latrobe.edu.au.* La Trobe University. Web. 23 July 2016.

"George Washington Carver. National Historic Chemical Landmark." *acs.org.* American Chemical Society. 2016. Web. 22 May 2016.

Geraci, Robert. *Virtually Sacred. Myth and Meaning in World of Warcraft and Second Life.* New York: Oxford UP, 2014. *Oxford Scholarship Online.* Web. 7 Nov. 2016.

Gere, Anne Ruggles, et al. "Using Evidence in Writing. A Policy Brief Produced by the National Council of Teachers of English." Urbana, Ill: NCTE, 2012. *ncte.org.*

"Germans Told to Stockpile Food and Water for Civil Defense." 22 Aug. 2016. *bbc.com.* BBC. Web. 1 Sept. 2016.

Gery, John. "Katrina and Her Poets." Callaloo, vol. 29, no. 4, 2006;2007;., pp. 1541-1542. Black Studies Center, doi:10.1353/cal.2007.0022.

Ghose, Tia. "Doomsday: 9 Real Ways the Earth Could End." 30 May 2013. *livescience.com.* Purch. Web. 7 Aug. 2016.

Gibaldi, Joseph. *MLA Handbook of Research for Writers.* 7th ed. New York: MLA, 2009. Print.

Gibbs, Martin. "Cultural Site Formation Processes in Maritime Archaeology: Disaster Response, Salvage and Muckelroy 30 Years on." *International Journal of Nautical Archaeology* 35.1 (2006): 4-19. Web.

Gibson, Karen. "All Roads Lead to Chaco Canyon." *Cobblestone* 20.6 (1999): 26. *General OneFile.*

Gilbert, Sandra M., and Susan Gubar. *Norton Anthology of Literature by Women: The Tradition in English.* New York: Norton, 1985. Print.

Glascock, Jack, Curtis B. Livesay, and Thomas E. Ruggiero. "Religious Involvement, Audience Demographics, and Media Bias." *Journal of Media and Religion* 7.4 (2008): 256-70. Web. 20 May 2016.

Gleick, James. *James Gleick. around.com.* n. d. Web. 22 May 2016.

Goffman, Erving. *The Presentation of Self in Everyday Life.* Garden City, NY: Doubleday, 1959. Print.

Good, Byron J., et al., eds. *A Reader in Medical Anthropology: Theoretical Trajectories, Emergent Realities.* Chichester, West Sussex, UK: Wiley-Blackwell, 2010.

Goodin, Robert E. *The Oxford Handbook of Political Science.* Oxford: Oxford UP, 2009. Print.

"Google Transparency Report." *google.com.* Google. 16 May 2016. Web. 16 May 2016.

Gore, Albert. *An Inconvenient Truth.* Hollywood, Calif.: Paramount, 2006.

Gorelik, Aaron Bradly. *The AIDS Poets, 1985-1995: From Anti-Elegy to Lyric Queerness.* Dissertation. 2014. Scholarship. University of California. http://escholarship.org/uc/item/0vt3d1gr#page-2. Accessed 3 Sept. 2016.

Gould, Richard Allan. "Richard Allan Gould." vivo.brown.edu https://vivo.brown.edu/display/rgould

Gould, Richard Allan. *Disaster Archaeology.* Salt Lake City: U of Utah P, 2007. Print.

Graff, Nelson. "Teaching Rhetorical Analysis to Promote Transfer of Learning." *Journal of Adolescent & Adult Literacy* 53.5 (2010): 376-85. *ProQuest.*

Grahame-Smith, Seth. *Pride and Prejudice and Zombies: The Classic Regency Romance—Now with Ultraviolent Zombie Mayhem.* Philadelphia, PA: Quirk, 2009.

Grant, Ian. "Creative Approaches to New Media Research." *Young Consumers*, vol. 7, no. 3, 2006, pp. 51-56. *ProQuest*, doi:10.1108/17473610610705372.

Graphenea. Graphenea.com. www.graphenea.com/pages/graphene-uses-applications#.WC8QFzKZNao. Accessed 18 November 2016.

Graves, Roger, Theresa Hyland and Bob M. Samuels. "Undergraduate Writing Assignments: An Analysis of Syllabi at One Canadian College." *Written Communication.* 27.3 (2010): 293–317. *sagepub.*

"Great Ball Court." *Chichen Itza.* Chichen Itza, 2014.

Greitemeyer, Tobias. "Intense Acts Of Violence During Video Game Play Make Daily Life Aggression Appear Innocuous: A New Mechanism Why Violent Video Games Increase Aggression." *Journal of Experimental Social Psychology* 50.1 (2014): 52-56. *PsycINFO.*

Griffiths, Mark. "Does Internet and Computer Addiction Exist? Some Case Study Evidence." *CyberPsychology and Behavior* 3.2 (2000): 211-218. *Mary Ann Liebert, Inc. Publishers.* Web. 22 July 2016.

Griswold, Eliza. "How 'Silent Spring' Ignited the Environmental Movement." *The New York Times Magazine.* 23 Sept. 2012. *nytimes.com.* The New York Times Company. Web. 22 May 2016.

Groseclose, Timothy. *Left Turn: How Liberal Media Bias Distorts the American Mind.* New York: St. Martin's, 2011. Print.

Grossman, Dave, and Gloria DeGaetano. *Stop Teaching Our Kids to Kill: A Call to Action against TV, Movie & Video Game Violence.* New York: Crown, 1999. Print.

Gtaforums.com. GTANet.

Gubrium, Jaber F., and James A. Holstein, eds. *Handbook of Interview Research. Context & Method.* Thousand Oaks: Sage, 2002. *history.ucsb.edu.* Web. 23 July 2016.

"Guide to Boudhanath." *thelongestwayhome.com.* n.d.

Guinness World Records 2014: Gamer's Edition. London: Guinness World Records, 2013. Print.

Gunter, Heather. "Planning, training prepare hotels for disasters." *Hotel & Motel Management* 7 Feb. 2005: 3. *General OneFile*. Web. 2 Sept. 2016.

Guo, Yue, and Stuart J. Barnes. "Explaining Purchasing Behavior within World of Warcraft." *The Journal of Computer Information Systems*. 52.3 (2012): 18-30. *ProQuest*. Web. 7 Nov. 2016.

Haamurabi. " 'The Hobbit', Audio Book-Part I of III." Online video. *YouTube*. YouTube, 16 Feb. 2011.

Haas, Christina, and Linda Flower. "Rhetorical Reading Strategies and the Construction of Meaning." *College Composition and Communication* 39.2 (1988): 167-83. *JSTOR*.

Hafen, Ryan P., et al. "Syndromic surveillance: STL for modeling, visualizing, and monitoring disease counts." *BMC Medical Informatics and Decision Making*, vol. 9, no. 1, 2009., pp. 21-21. *BioMed Central*, doi: 10.1186/1472-6947-9-21.

Hagan, Susan M. "Visual/Verbal Collaboration in Print: Complementary Differences, Necessary Ties, and an Untapped Rhetorical Opportunity." *Written Communication* 24.1 (2007): 49-73. *SageJournals*.

Hamann, Cara J., et al. "Disaster Preparedness in Rural Families of Children With Special Health Care Needs." *Disaster Medicine and Public Health Preparedness* 10. 2 (2016): 225-8. *Cambridge Journals*. Web. 26 Aug. 2016.

Hamblin, Charles. *Fallacies*. London: Methuen, 1970. *scribd.com*.

Hampton, II, Isaac. The Black Officer Corps. *A History of Black Military Advancement from Integration through Vietnam*. New York: Routledge. 2013. *books.google.com*. Web. 23 July 2016.

Han, Jingyong, et al. "Modal density and mode counts of sandwich panels in thermal environments." *Composite Structures*, vol. 153, 2016., pp. 69-80. *ScienceDirect Freedom*

Han, Soonyoung, and Hae-Jin Choi. "Strategic conceptual design of mid-sized passenger aircraft based on future market performance prediction." *Concurrent Engineering*, vol. 22, no. 4, 2014., pp. 277-290. Sage Journals. doi:10.1177/1063293X14546671.

Hancock, Dawson R., and Bob Algozzine. *Doing Case Study Research. A Practical Guide for Beginning Researchers*. New York: Teachers College P, 2011. Print.

Hanganu-Bresch, C. & Berkenkotter, C. "Narrative Survival: Personal and Institutional Accounts of Asylum Confinement." *Literature and Medicine* 30.1 (2012): 12-41. *Project MUSE*. Web. 14 Jul. 2016.

Hanna Salman Sawalha, Ihab, Luai Eid Jraisat, and Kamal A. M. Al-Qudah. "Crisis and disaster management in Jordanian hotels: practices and cultural considerations." *Disaster Prevention and Management: An International Journal*, vol. 22, no. 3, 2013., pp. 210-228.

Hansen, Hans V., and Robert C. Pinto, eds. *Fallacies. Classical and Contemporary Readings*. University Park, PA: Penn State UP, 1995. 213-21.

Hanson, Stephen S. Ethics in the discipline(s) of bioethics. *HEC Forum, 23*.3 (2011): 171-92.

Harder, Jeff. "How Synthesizers Work." *howstuffworks.com*.

Harding, Sue-Ann. "Translating Eyewitness Accounts: Personal Narratives From Beslan, September 2004." *Journal of Language & Politics* 11.2 (2012): 229-249. *Political Science Complete*. Web. 14 July 2016.

Hawkins, Gerald S. "Stonehenge Decoded." *Nature* 200 (1963): 306-8. *nature.com*.

He, Jun, and Guijun Xian. "Debonding of CFRP-to-steel joints with CFRP delamination." *Composite Structures*, vol. 153, 2016., pp. 12-20.

"Health Fact Sheet." *pewinternet.org*. Pew Research Center. 2016. Web. 15 May 2016.

Healy, Nanci. "Poetry in the boardroom: thinking beyond the facts: a roundup discussion among Ted Buswick, Clare Morgan and Kristen Lange." Journal of Business Strategy, vol. 26, no. 1, 2005., pp. 34-40. Expanded Academic ASAP. Web. 3 Sept. 2016.

Heaney, Christopher. *Cradle of Gold: the Story of Hiram Bingham, a Real-Life Indiana Jones, and the Search for Machu Picchu*. New York: Palgrave Macmillan, 2010. Print.

Heidebrink-Bruno, Sarah. "The Play's the Thing: Lessons from Preschool Storytimes for College Classrooms." *Hybrid Pedagogy*. 29 May 2014. *hybridpedagogy.com*.

"Heliocentrism." *astro.unl.edu*. University of Nebraska-Lincoln. n. d. Web. 22 May 2016.

Hempstead, Colin A. and William E. Worthington, eds. *Encyclopedia of 20th-century Technology*. New York: Routledge, 2005. Print.

Henry, Adam Hughes. "Reflections on the Indonesian Massacres in Cold War Historiography and Political Economy. *Genocide Studies International* 10.1 (2016): 52-64.

Herman, Luciana. "Tips for Writing Policy Papers. A Policy Lab Communications Workshop." 2013. Law.stanford.edu. Stanford University. Web. Sept. 1 2016.

Herodotus. *"The Histories"—The Great Pyramid*. Transl. A.D. Godley. Cambridge: Harvard UP, 1920. *blog.world-mysteries.com*.

Hess, Gregory M. "Combating Online Software Piracy." *Journal of Internet Commerce* 2.3 (2003): 3-10. Web. 25 May 2016.

Hiestand, Michael. "Limbaugh Quits NFL Show Amid Race Flap." *USA Today*. 2 Oct. 2003. usatoday30.usatoday.com. usatoday. Web. 10 May 2016.

Higgins, Parker. "*parkerhiggins.net*. n. d. Web. 17 May 2016.

Historic Centre of Oaxaca and Archaeological Site of Monte Albán." *whc.unesco* UNESCO, n.d.

History & Culture." *Chaco Culture*. National Park Service, n.d.

History of Stupas." *Shambhala Mountain Center*. Shambhala Mountain Center, n.d.

Hoey, Brian A. *brianhoey.com*.

Holbrook, Jarita C., R. Thebe Medupe, Johnson O. Urama, eds. *African Cultural Astronomy: Current Archaeoastronomy and Ethnoastronomy Research in Africa*. Berlin: Springer, 2009.

Holmes, John. "LibGuide." University of Washington Libraries. *guides.lib.washington.edu*. University of Washington.

Hori, Makiko, et al. "Displacement Dynamics in Southern Louisiana after Hurricanes Katrina and Rita." Population Research and Policy Review, vol. 28, no. 1, 2009., pp. 45-65. ProQuest, doi:10.1007/s11113-008-9118-1.

Horning, Alice S. "Reading across the Curriculum as the Key to Student Success." Across the Disciplines 4. 14 May 2007. wac.colostate. edu.

Huckin, Thomas, Jennifer Andrus, and Jennifer Clary-Lemon. "Critical Discourse Analysis and Rhetoric and Composition." College Composition and Communication 64.1 (2012): 107-29. ProQuest.

Hyland, Ken. "Academic Attribution: Citation and the Construction of Disciplinary Knowledge." Applied Linguistics 20.3 (1999): 341-67. Oxford Journals.

IFJ. "IFJ Welcomes New Resolution of the United Nations Security Council on Protecting Journalists and Ending Impunity." 5 28 2015. ifj.org. Web. 15 May 2016.

"IGN Presents the History of Grand Theft Auto." ign.com. 6 May 2013. Web. 7 Nov. 2016. http://www.ign.com/articles/2013/05/06/ign-presents-the-history-of-grand-theft-auto-2

Ilan Noy. Ilan Noy. sites.google.com/site/noyeconomics/research/natural-disasters. Accessed 2 Sept. 2016

Imas, Olga, Viktoriya Kaminskaya, and Anna Sherstneva. Teaching Math through Blended Learning, IEEE, 2015. ProQuest, doi:10.1109/ICL.2015.7318081.

Ingram, Laura, James Hussey, Michelle Tigani, and Mary Hemmelgarn. "Writing a Literature Review and Using a Synthesis Matrix." writingcenter.fiu.edu.

Institute of Medicine. Committee on Building Bridges in the Brain, Behavioral, and Clinical Sciences. "The Potential of Interdisciplinary Research to Solve Problems in the Brain, Behavioral, and Clinical Sciences." Bridging Disciplines in the Brain, Behavioral, and Clinical Sciences. Ed. Terry C. Pellmar and Leon Eisenberg. Washington, D.C.: National Academies P, 2000. ncbi.nlm.nih.gov.

International Journal of Emergency Management

"Introduction and Overview of The Great Pyramid of Giza." gizapyramid.com. n.d.

"Ironyca Stood in the Fire." ironyca.wordpress.com.

Irving, Barrie, and Linden Hilgendorf. Police Interrogation: A Case Study of Current Practice. London: HM Stationery Office, 1980. Print.

"Israeli-Palestinian Conflict." 1 May 2014. procon.org.

Itriage. "Tracking American Health Literacy and Prescribing Improvement. Key Findings from an Independent Survey." about. itriagehealth.com. Aetna. 2015. Web. 15 May 2016.

Jaffe, Sarah. "Offensive is Nothing New: Rush Limbaugh's 5 Worst Remarks" alternet.org. Web. 5 May 2016.

James, Kyle. "Four Types of Web Analytic Data." doteduguru.com. 27 Oct. 2008.

James, Randy. Why Cows Learn Dutch. And Other Secrets of Amish Farms. Kent, OH: Kent State UP, 2005. books.google.com. Web. 23 July 2016.

Jamieson, Sandra. "Synthesis Writing." users.drew.edu.

Jamison, Brian. "Modeling Newtonian Physics in Space." Jumpdrive Studios. 10 April 2015. jmpdrv.com/2015/04/10/modeling-newtonian-physics-in-space/

Jamshidi, Ensiyeh, et al. "Effectiveness of Community Participation in Earthquake Preparedness: A Community-Based Participatory Intervention Study of Tehran." Disaster Medicine and Public Health Preparedness 10. 2 (2016): 211-18. Cambridge Journals. Web. 26 Aug. 2016.

"Japanese Earthquake: Eyewitness Accounts." BBCnews. BBC.com. 11 Mar. 2011. Web. 20 Aug. 2016.

Jarus, Owen. "Photos: Amazing Discoveries at Egypt's Giza Pyramids." 21 Jan. 2014. livescience.com.

Javed, Farhan. "Dodging history: Turkey One Century after the Armenian Genocide." Harvard International Review 37.1 (2015): 14+. Expanded Academic ASAP. Web. 12 July 2016.

Jaworski, Adam, and Nikolaus Copeland. The Discourse Reader. New York: Routledge, 1999. Print.

"Jessica Pratt." publichealth.gsu.edu. Georgia State University, 2016. Web. 23 July 2016.

"John S. Brownstein." Harvard University. Harvard University, n.d., http://scholar.harvard.edu/john/home. Accessed 2 Sept. 2016.

Johnson, Burke, and Larry Christenson. "Writing Quantitative Research Questions. Table 3.7." Educational Research. Qualitative, Quantitative, and Mixed Methods. 4th ed. Thousand Oaks, Calif.: Sage, 2010. 8 Feb. 2007.

Johnson, Ralph H. "ISSA Proceedings 1998—The Problem of Truth for Theories of Argument." Rozenberg Quarterly n.d. rozenbergquarterly.com.

Jolly, Roy, et al. "Cognitive Appraisals and Lived Experiences during Injury Rehabilitation: A Narrative Account within Personal and Situational Backdrop." Asian Journal of Sports Medicine 6.3 (2015): n.p. ProQuest. Web. 14 July 2016.

Jones, Jeffrey P. "'Fake' News versus 'Real' News as Sources of Political Information: The Daily Show and Postmodern Political Reality." In Politicotainment: Television's Take on the Real. Ed. Kristina Riegert. New York: Peter Lang, 2007. 129-50. googlebooks.com. Web. 21 May 2016.

Jordan, Nickolas. "World of Warcraft: A Family Therapist's Journey into Scapegoated Culture." The Qualitative Report. 19.31 (2014): 1-19. ProQuest. Web. 7 Nov. 2016.

Joubert, Joseph. Extracts from the Pensées of Joubert. 1925. Trans. Katharine Lyttelton. Pittsburgh, PA: Laboratory P, 1925. Print.

Journal of Business Ethics. link.springer.com. Springer. Web. 26 Aug. 2016.

Journal of Economic Literature

Journal of Ethics, Economics, Finance, and Society. Cambridgescholars.com. Cambridge Scholars Publishing. Web. 26 Aug. 2016.

Journal of Information, Communication and Ethics in Society. Emeraldinsight.com. Emerald Group Publishing. Web. 26 Aug. 2016.

Juul, Jesper. A Dictionary of Video Game Theory. half-real.net.

Kak, Subhash. "Visions of the Cosmos: Archaeoastronomy in Ancient India." Journal of Cosmology 9 (2010): 2063-77. journal of cosmology.com.

Kaktins, Uldis, et al. "Revisiting the Timing and Events Leading to and Causing the Johnstown Flood of 1889." *Pennsylvania History* 80.3 (2013): 335-63. Web.

Kantner, John. "Rethinking Chaco as a System." *Kiva* 69.2 (2003): 207-27. *JSTOR*.

Kantor, Brooke, Helen Clark, and Lydia Federico. "An Exercise in Body Image." *Harvard Political Review*. 28 June 2014. *harvardpolitics.com*.

Kastor, Peter. October 12 2016. *St. Louis on the Air*.

Katkowski, Nolan. "Top Arguments with Parents over School, Chores, and Curfew." 10 May 2005.

Katz, Sheila. ""Give Us A Chance To Get An Education": Single Mothers' Survival Narratives And Strategies For Pursuing Higher Education on Welfare." *Journal of Poverty* 17.3 (2013): 273-304. *Humanities International Complete*. Web. 14 July 2016.

Kay, Rob, and Andy Tudor. "An Artist's Eye." *Game Developer*. 1 June 2010. 13. *General OneFile* go.galegroup.com/ps/i. do?p=ITOF&sw=w&u=duke_perkins&v=2.1&id=GALE%7CA227785828&it=r&asid=e403c2bb039aa339a48115e2bbb 1b5da. Accessed 7 Nov. 2016.

Kedavra, Avada. "Alan Rickman Reads Shakespeare's Sonnet 130." Online video. *YouTube*. YouTube. 20 May 2013.

Kendall-Tackett, Kathleen. "Silence that Inner Critic and Start Writing!" *Meditations and More.* February 2009. *kathleenkendall-tackett.com*.

Kennedy, Carrie H., and Bret A. Moore. "Evolution of Clinical Military Psychology Ethics." *Military Psychology* 20.1 (2007; 2008;): 1-6. Web.

Kenneston, Aaron Robert. *Quantitative correlational study of Nevada resort hotel emergency plans, continuity plans, and security chief collaboration*. Diss. UNIVERSITY OF PHOENIX, 2012.

"Kenneth D. Mandl, MD, MPH, FACMI." American Medical Informatics Association. AMIA, 2016, www.amia.org/about-amia/leadership/acmi-fellow/kenneth-d-mandl-md-mph-facmi. Accessed 2 Sept. 2016.

Ketokivi, Mikko, and Saku Mantere. "Two Strategies For Inductive Reasoning In Organizational Research." *Academy Of Management Review* 35.2 (2010): 315-33. *Business Source Complete*.

Khan, Ali S. "Preparedness 101: Zombie Apocalypse." 16 May 2011. blogs.cdc.gov. cdc. Web. 1 Sept. 2016.

Kiernan, Ben. *Blood and Soil. A World History of Genocide and Extermination from Sparta to Darfur.* New Haven: Yale UP, 2007. *books.google.com*. Web. 27 Aug. 2016.

Kies, Daniel. "Underlying Assumptions." *The HyperText Books*. Department of English. College of DuPage. 10 Jan. 2012.

"Kim Patterson." *LinkedIn*. Web. 23 July 2016.

Kim, HyeKyoung, and Jihoon Song. "The Quality of Word-of-Mouth in the Online Shopping Mall." *Academy of Marketing Studies Journal* 19.3 (2015): 376-390. *ProQuest*. Web. 24 July 2016.

Kinzer, Heath, and Judith L. Gillies. "Cross-Cultural Analysis." *Department of Anthropology*. The University of Alabama, 2009.

Kirkland, Heidi. ""Maths Anxiety': Isn't it just a Dislike for Learning Mathematics?" *Mathematics Teaching*, no. 250, 2016, pp. 11-13. *ProQuest*, http://search.proquest.com.proxy.lib.duke.edu/docview/1807741656?pq-origsite=summon&http://www.nclive.org/cgi-bin/nclsm?rsrc=315. Accessed 14 Dec. 2016.

Klaus, Carl H., and Ned Stuckey-French, eds. *Essayists on the Essay. Montaigne in Our Time*. Iowa City: U of Iowa P, 2012. *books.google.com*. Web. 24 July 2016.

Klein, Kitty, and Adriel Boals. "Coherence and Narrative Structure in Personal Accounts of Stressful Experiences." *Journal of Social and Clinical Psychology* 29.3 (2010): 256-80. *ProQuest*. Web. 14 July 2016.

Kobre, Kenneth. *Photojournalism. The Professionals' Approach*. Boston: Focal, 2000. Print.

Kondrat, Xeniya. "Gender and Video Games: How is Female Gender Generally Represented in Various Genres of Video Games?" *Journal of Comparative Research in Anthropology and Sociology*. 6.1 (2015): 171-193. Retrieved from http://proxy.lib.duke.edu/login?url=http://search.proquest.com/docview/1712852612?accountid=10598

Kosenko, Kami, and Johanne Laboy. ""I Survived": The Content And Forms Of Survival Narratives." *Journal Of Loss & Trauma* 19.6 (2014): 497-513 17p. *CINAHL Complete*. Web. 14 July 2016.

Krakauer, Jon. *Into Thin Air: A Personal Account of the Mt. Everest Disaster*. New York: Villard, 1997. Print.

Krippner, Greta. "Making a Sociological Argument." 28 Sept. 2000. American Sociological Association. *asanet.org*.

Krupp, Edwin C. *Echoes of the Ancient Skies: The Astronomy of Lost Civilizations*. Mineola, NY: Dover, 2003. Print.

Kunreuther, Howard C. and Erwann O. Michel-Kerjan At war with the weather : managing large-scale risks in a new era of catastrophes. Cambridge, MA: MIT P, 2009. Print.

Kurt, Ümit. The Plunder of Wealth through Abandoned Properties Laws in the Armenian Genocide. *Genocide Studies International* 10.1 (2016): 37-51.

Laing, Jennifer H. and Geoffrey I. Crouch (2009). "Lone Wolves? Isolation and Solitude within the Frontier Travel Experience." *Geografiska Annaler* 91.4 (2009): 325-342. *JSTOR*. Web. 23 July 2016.

Lamott, Anne. *Bird by Bird: Some Instructions on Writing and Life*. New York: Random House, 2007. Print.

Lapidoth, Ruth. "The Misleading Interpretation of UN Security Council Resolution 242 (1967)." *Jewish Political Studies Review* 23.3/4 (2011): 7-17. *ProQuest Political Science*. Web. 25 May 2016.

Leach, Andrew. " 'One Day It'll All Make Sense': Hip-Hop and Rap Resources for Music Librarians." *Notes* 65.1 (2008): 9-37. *JSTOR*.

Lee, Carol D., and Anika Spratley. "Reading in the Disciplines. The Challenges of Adolescent Literacy." New York, NY: Carnegie, 2010. *carnegie.org*.

Lee, Seow Ting, and Iccha Basnyat. "From Press Release to News: Mapping the Framing of the 2009 H1N1 A Influenza Pandemic." *Health Communication* 28.2 (2013): 119-14. *Communication and Mass Media Complete*. Web. 19 May 2016.

Legal Ethics. www.tandfonline.com. Informa. Web. 26 Aug. 2016.

Leichman, Abigail Klein. "The Israeli Sharing His Mass Casualty Expertise in Boston." 24 April 2013. *Israel 21c. israel21c.org*. israel21c.org. Web. 11 June 2016http://www.israel21c.org/the-israeli-sharing-his-mass-casualty-expertise-in-boston/

Lekka, Vasia. "Normalizing Sexuality in Twentieth-Century Western Societies: A Critical Reading of the Diagnostic and Statistical Manual of Mental Disorders." *Journal of History of Science and Technology* 9 (2014): n. p. *johost.eu*. Web. 22 May 2016.

Leung, Rebecca. "Can a Video Game Lead to Murder? Did 'Grand Theft Auto' Cause One Teenager to Kill?" *60 Minutes*. 17 June 2005. *cbsnews.com*.

Levin, Henry, dir. *Journey to the Center of the Earth*. Twentieth Century Fox, 1959. Film.

Lieberman, Matthew D. "Education and the Social Brain." *Trends in Neuroscience and Education*, vol. 1, no. 1, 2012, pp. 3-9. *ProQuest*, doi:10.1016/j.tine.2012.07.003. Accessed 13 December 2016

Like, Christopher. "Harnessing Students' Interest in Physics with their Own Video Games." *The Physics Teacher*, vol. 49, no. 4, 2011., pp. 222-224, doi:10.1119/1.3566031.

Lin, Carolyn A., and David J. Atkin. *Communication Technology and Social Change. Theory and Implications.* Mahway, NJ: Lawrence Erlbaum, 2007. Print.

Lin, Cheng, et al. (eds) The History of Ancient Chinese Economic Thought London and New York: Routledge, 2014. Print.

Lindblom, Charles E. "Another State of Mind. The American Political Science Review." 76.1 (1982): 9-21. *JSTOR*. Web. 10 May 2016.

Liu, Ziming. "Reading Behavior in the Digital Environment: Changes in Reading Behavior over the Past Ten Years." *Journal of Documentation* 61.6 (2005): 700–12. *ProQuest*.

Livingstone, David. *A Practical Guide to Scientific Data Analysis*. Chichester, U.K.: Wiley, 2009. Print.

"Logical Fallacies." *logicalfallacies.info*.

lolmythesis. Angie. Dec. 2013.

Lopata, Peg. "Chichén Itzá." *Faces: People, Places, and Cultures*. July-Aug. 2008: 28+. *General OneFile*.

Lotan, Gilad. "Big Data for Breaking News: Lessons from #Aurora, Colorado." SocialFlow. 1 Aug. 2012. *blog.socialflow.com*.

Love, Robert. "Before Jon Stewart." *Columbia Journalism Review*. cjr.org. March/Apr. 2007. n. p. Web. 5 May 2016.

Lowe, George, and Huw Lewis-Jones. *The Conquest of Everest: Original Photographs from the Legendary First Ascent*. New York: Thames & Hudson, 2013. Print.

Luongo, Giuseppe, et al. "Impact of the AD 79 Explosive Eruption on Pompeii, II. Causes of Death of the Inhabitants Inferred by Stratigraphic Analysis and Areal Distribution of the Human Casualties." *Journal of Volcanology and Geothermal Research* 126 (2003): 169-200. *Science Direct*.

Lynch, B. Mark, and Lawrence H. Robbins. "Namoratunga: the First Archaeoastronomical Evidence in Sub-Saharan Africa." *Science* 200 (1978): 766-68. *JSTOR*.

Lynch, Ronan, Bride Mallon, and Cornelia Connolly. "The Pedagogical Application of Alternate Reality Games: Using Game-Based Learning to Revisit History." *International Journal of Game-Based Learning (IJGBL)*, vol. 5, no. 2, 2015, pp. 18-38. *ProQuest*, doi:10.4018/ijgbl.2015040102.

Macola, Giacomo. *The Gun in Central Africa. A History of Technology and Politics.* Athens, OH: Ohio UP, 2016. *books.google.com*. Web. 22 May 2016.

Madson, John. "The Deadliest Day on Everest: May 10, 1996." *Glide Magazine* 4 Mar. 2003.Web. *glidemagazine.com*.

Magid, Larry. "What Are SOPA and PIPA And Why All The Fuss?" 18 Jan. 2012. *forbes.com*. Web. 16 May 2016.

Magli, Giulio. "Akhet Khufu: Archaeo-Astronomical Hints at a Common Project of the Two Main Pyramids of Giza, Egypt." *Nexus Network Journal* 11.1 (2009): 35-50. *ProQuest*.

Mair, Miller. "Enchanting Psychology: The Poetry of Personal Inquiry." Journal of Constructivist Psychology, vol. 25, no. 3, 2012., pp. 184. Academic Search Complete, doi:10.1080/10720537.2012.679126.

Major, Alice. Intersecting Sets. A Poet Looks at Science. Edmonton: U of Alberta P, 2011. Books.google.com. Web. 3 Sept. 2016.

Major, Ted. "RhetoricalTriangle." Photograph. *flickr.com*.

Makuch, Eddie. "How Call of Duty: Infinite Warfare Handles the Lack of Sound in Space." 23 June 2016. Gamespot. www.gamespot.com/articles/how-call-of-duty-infinite-warfare-handles-the-lack/1100-6441178/

Malville, J. McKim. "Prehistoric Astronomy in the American Southwest." *The Astronomy Quarterly* 8 (1991): 1-36. *ScienceDirect*.

Mangen, Anne. "Hypertext Fiction Reading: Haptics and Immersion." *Journal of Research in Reading* 31.4 (2008): 404-19. *onlinelibrary.wiley.com*.

Mann, R., D. Ashton, and T. Mohney. "A Prediction on the Performance and Economic Viability of Future Gas Wells in the Western Canadian Sedimentary Basin." *Journal of Canadian Petroleum Technology*, vol. 44, no. 10, 2005., pp. 17-22. OnePetro, doi:10.2118/05-10-01.

Marchi, Regina. "With Facebook, Blogs, and Fake News, Teens Reject Journalistic 'Objectivity.'" *Journal of Communication Inquiry* 36.3 (2012): 246-62. Web. 21 May 2016.

Marcus, Joyce. "The Iconography of Militarism at Monte Albán and Neighboring Sites in the Valley of Oaxaca." In *The Origins of Religious Art and Iconography in Pre-Classic Mesoamerica*. Ed. Henry. B. Nicholson. Los Angeles: UCLA Latin American Center, 1976. 123-39. Print.

Marr, Andrew. "Ten Moments That Changed History—In Pictures." *The Guardian*. 15 Sept. 2012. *theguardian.com*. The Guardian. Web. 22 May 2016.

Marsh, Charles. "The Syllogism of Apologia: Rhetorical Stasis Theory and Crisis Communication." *Public Relations Review* 32.1 (2006): 41-6. *ScienceDirect*.

Martin, Denise. "Reflections on African Celestial Culture." *African American Consciousness: Past and Present.* Ed. James L. Conyers. New Brunswick, N.J.: Transaction, 2012. 109-26. *books.google.com*.

Martin, George R.R. *A Game of Thrones*. New York: Bantam, 1996. Print.

Martin, Nathalie, and Ozymandias Adams. "Grand Theft Auto Loans: Repossession and Demographic Realities in Title Lending." *Missouri Law Review*, vol. 77, no. 1, 2012., pp. 41-69.

Mastin, Luke. "The Basics of Philosophy." philosophybasics.com. philosophybasics.com. 2008. Web. 10 June 2016.

Matheson, Donald. "History of Citizen Journalism." *oxfordbibliographies.com*. Oxford UP. 25 February 2014. Web. 23 May 2016.

Mavridis, Apostolos, Thrasyvoulos Tsiatsos, and Theodouli Terzidou. "Designing and Deploying 3D Collaborative Games in Education." *International Journal of Game-Based Learning (IJGBL)*, vol. 6, no. 1, 2016, pp. 43-57. *ProQuest*, doi:10.4018/IJGBL.2016010104.

Maxson, J. David. "'Just a Closer Walk with Thee': Jazz Funerals, Second Lines, and Laying Hurricane Katrina to Rest." Southern Quarterly, vol. 53, no. 1, 2015., pp. 185-203. Project Muse. Web. 3 Sept. 2016.

"Mayan Ball Game." *ChichenItzaRuins*. chichenitzaruins.org, 2013.

McCauley, Marissa. "Probing Question: How Were the Egyptian Pyramids Built?" *Penn State*. Penn State, 15 April 2014.

McColm, Gregory. "Analysis, Synthesis, and Doing Homework."

McCullough, Jessica. "Identifying and Finding Scholarly Sources: A Web Tutorial." George Washington University. 7 Dec. 2009. *gwu.edu.*

McCurry, Justin. "Japan Earthquake: 100,000 Children Displaced, Says Charity." The Guardian. theguardian.com. 15 Mar. 2011. Web. 20 Aug. 2016.

McGrath, Kristine M. "Rush is Wrong. Study Finds Race Not a Factor in Media Treatment of Quarterbacks." fau.edu. Florida Atlantic University. Oct. 2003. Web. 22 May 2016.

McKee, Heidi A., and James E. Porter. "The Ethics of Archival Research." *College Composition and Communication*, 64.1 (2012): 59-81. JSTOR. Web. 26 Aug. 2016.

McKenna-Lawlor, Susan M. P. "Astronomy in Ireland from Earliest Times to the Eighteenth Century." *Vistas in Astronomy* 26.1 (1982): 1-13. *ScienceDirect.*

McKeon, Matthew. "Argument." *Internet Encyclopedia of Philosophy. iep.utm.edu.*

McLaren-Hankin, Yvonne. "'We Expect to Report on Significant Progress in our Product Pipeline in the Coming Year': Hedging Forward-Looking Statements in Corporate Press Releases." *Discourse Studies* 10.5 (2008): 635-54. *Sage Journals*. Web. 25 May 2016.

McLean, James G. Physics Writing Guide. How to Write a Physics Journal Article. December 2001. Department of Physics and Astronomy. Geneseo. State University of New York. www.geneseo.edu/~mclean/Dept/JournalArticle.pdf

McWhirter, Jennifer E., and Laurie Hoffman-Goetz. "Application of the Health Belief Model to U.S. Magazine Text and Image Coverage of Skin Cancer and Recreational Tanning (2000-2012)." *Journal of Health Communication* 21.4 (2016): 424-38. *Taylor & Francis Online*. Web. 15 May 2016.

Meadows, Dwayne. "Riding the World's Biggest Wave: 2004 Boxing Day Tsunami. A Personal Essay." nws.noaa.gov. noaa. Web. 29 Aug. 2016.

Mecklin, John, ed. 2016 Doomsday Clock Statement. Science and Security Board Bulletin of the Atomic Scientists. 2016. thebulletin.org. Bulletin of the Atomic Scientists. Web. 7 Aug. 2016.

MedicineNet.com. MedicineNet, 1996-2014.

Meltzer, Lynn, ed. *Executive Function in Education. From Theory to Practice.* Guilford, 2007. *Research Gate*, Accessed 13 Dec. 2016. Metaphor of the Living Dead

"MIA." *Wikipedia*. Wikipedia, 31 Mar. 2016. Web. 6 June 2013.

Michael. "Violent Video Games – What Does the Research Say?" Podcast. The Psych Files. *thepsychfiles.com.*

"Michel de Montaigne Biography." *biography.com.* A&E Television Networks, n.d. Web. 22 July 2016.

Mills, Elizabeth Shown. *Evidence Explained: Citing History Sources from Artifacts to Cyberspace*. Baltimore: Genealogical P, 2007. *amazon.com.*

Mishra, Rekha, and Kaushik, Neeraj. "Big Data: An Analysis." *International Journal of Science, Engineering and Computer Technology*3.1(2013): 29-31. *ProQuest.*

Mitchell, W. J. T., and Mark B. N. Hansen, eds. *Critical Terms for Media Studies*. Chicago: U of Chicago P, 2010.

Montagne, Renee. "'The Onion': Mocking All Who Deserve It Since 1988." *npr.org.* npr.org. 20 Nov. 2009. Web. 5 May 2016.

"Monte Albán." *ancient-wisdom.*

Montessori, Maria. *The Absorbent Mind.* Henry Holt, 1995.

Morales, Carlos E. "Central Texas Leadership Series: Kim Patterson." *kwbu.org.* Web. 23 July 2016.

Moreno, Julio. "10 Questions You Never Had about Machu Picchu." *travelworldheritage.com.* 26 Aug. 2013.

Morita, Tomohiro, et al. "Voluntary Medical Support Is Key After Nuclear Disasters." *Disaster Medicine and Public Health Preparedness* 10. 2 (2016): 186-7. *Cambridge Journals*. Web. 26 Aug. 2016.

Morrison, John, F. "Miracle Babes Survive Disaster. Among Them: An Infant Found Floating on a Mattress." 29 Dec. 2004. Philly.com. philly.com. Philadelphia Media Network. Web. 29 Aug. 2016.

Mountain Research and Development. Mountain Research and Development, February 2013. Web. 22 July 2016.

Muccio, Leah S., Rheta Kuwahara-Fujita, and Johanna J Y Otsuji. "Ohana Math: Family Engagement to Encourage Math Learning at Home." *Teaching Young Children*, vol. 9, no. 2, 2015, pp. 24-30. *ProQuest*, http://search.proquest.com.proxy.lib.duke.edu/docview/1621401678?pq-origsite=summon&http://www.nclive.org/cgi-bin/nclsm?rsrc=317. Accessed 14 Dec. 2016.

Muller, Nikki. "The Ivy-League Hustle (I Went to Princeton, Bitch)." *YouTube*. 20 May 2012. *youtube.com.*

Munson, Gregory E. "Mesa Verde Archaeoastronomy." *Handbook of Archaeoastronomy and Ethnoastronomy*. Ed. Clive N. Ruggles. New York: Springer, 2014. 565-75. *link.springer.com.*

Murphy, Anthony. "The Ancient Astronomers of Newgrange." mythicalireland.com. *mythicalireland.com*, 2002.

Murphy, Robin R. "A National Initiative in Emergency Informatics." 3 Nov. 2010. Computing Community Consortium. cra.org. Web. 2 Sept. 2016.

"Music Piracy Costs U.S. Economy $12.5 Billion, Report Reveals; the Study is One in a Series to Examine the Economic Impact of Copyright and Patent Infringement." Information Week. 22 Aug. 2007. *General OneFile*. Web. 25 May 2016.

Nadin, Peter. *UN Security Council Reform*. Abingdon, Oxon: Routledge, 2016. *books.google.com.* Web. 15 May 2016.

Nash, Barbara P., Harry V. Merrick, and Francis H. Brown. "Obsidian Types from Holocene Sites around Lake Turkana, and Other Localities in Northern Kenya." *Journal of Archaeological Science* 38.6 (2011): 1371-76. *ScienceDirect.*

National Press Photographers Association (NPPA). "NPPA Code of Ethics." *nppa.org.* 2016. Web. 20 May 2016. *NavList.*

Naydler, Jeremy. *Shamanic Wisdom in the Pyramid Texts: The Mystical Tradition of Ancient Egypt.* Rocherster, Vt.: Inner Traditions, 2005.

NCEI. National Centers for Environmental Information. *NGDC/WDS Global Historical Tsunami Database. www.ngdc.noaa.gov.* Web. 14 July 2016.

Neal, Mark Anthony. *NewBlackMan (In Exile).* n.d.

Neff, Thomas. "Holding out and Hanging on after Katrina: Photographs and Narratives." Callaloo, vol. 29, no. 4, 2006;2007;., pp. 1179-1184. Black Studies Center, doi:10.1353/cal.2007.0046.

"Nepal: Everest Base Camp Trek." *National Geographic Expeditions.* National Geographic, n.d.

"New Archaeoastronomical Alignments Found at Machu Picchu." *ancienthistoricalresearchfoundation.com.* 8 Oct. 2013.

Newell, William H. "The Role of Interdisciplinary Studies in the Liberal Arts." *LiberalArtsOnline* 7.1 (2007): n.p. *liberalarts.wabash. edu.*

"Newgrange." *newgrange.com.*

Newsad, Robert S. "An overview of developing tribal emergency management in the USA." *International Journal of Emergency Management,* vol. 7, no. 3-4, 2010., pp. 296-303

Newton, Julianne H. "Photojournalism." *Journalism Practice* 3.2 (2009): 233-243.

Newton, Julianne. *The Burden of Visual Truth. The Role of Photojournalism in Mediating Reality.* Routledge, 2013.

Nindang, Santi, and Teigan Allen. "Ahead of Flood Season, Thailand's Communities Demand Greater Preparedness. 8 Aug. 2012. The Asia Foundation. asiafoundation.org. Web. 27 Aug. 2016.

Niven, David. *davidniven.com.* davidniven.com. n.d. Web. 22 May 2016.

NOAA. "What is a Tsuami?" *oceanservice.noaa.gov.* Web. 14 July 2016.

Norris, Ray P., and Duane W. Hamacher. "Astronomical Symbolism in Australian Aboriginal Rock Art." *Rock Art Research* 28.1 (2011): 99-106. *Art & Architecture Complete.*

Northcut, Kathryn M. "Stasis Theory and Paleontology Discourse." Sept. 2007. *MoSpace.*

Nsoesie, Elaine O., David L. Buckeridge, and John S. Brownstein. "Guess who's not coming to dinner? Evaluating online restaurant reservations for disease surveillance." *Journal of medical Internet research,* vol. 16, no. 1, 2014., pp. e22.JMIR Publications. Accessed 2 Sept. 2016.

Nunberg, Geoffrey. "James Gleick's History of Information" *Sunday Book Review.* 18 Mar. 2011. *nytimes.com.* The New York Times Company. Web. 10 May 2016.

O'Dell, William. "Top 10 Arguments That Can't Be Won." *toptenz.net.* 13 Nov. 2008.

OAH (Organization of American Historians). "What Questions Do We Ask of the Past? Thinking Like a Historian." 2005. archive.oah.org. Web. 7 November 2016.

Ocampo, et al. "Using search queries for malaria surveillance, Thailand." *Malaria Journal,* vol. 12, no. 1, 2013., pp. 390-390. *Academic OneFile,* doi: 10.1186/1475-2875-12-390.

Okamura, Katsuyuki, et al. "The Great East Japan Earthquake and Cultural Heritage: Towards an Archaeology of Disaster." *Antiquity* 87.335 (2013): 258-69. Web.

Oldham, Davis. "Assumptions." *Shoreline Community College.* shoreline.edu.

Ollman, Bertell. "What is Political Science? What Should it Be?" *nyu.edu.* Web. 10 May 2016.

Olsen, Archaeology. Discipline of Things.

OMICS Publishing Group. "Peer Review Process." *omicsonline.org.*

"One Billion Hungry. Can We Feed the World?" *cornellpress.com.*

Oral History Association. Oral History Association, 2016. Web. 23 July 2016.

Oskin, Becky. "Japan Earthquake & Tsunami of 2011: Facts and Information." Live Science. livescience.com. 7 May 2015. Web. 20 Aug. 2016.

"Overanalyze." *Urban Dictionary.* 23 May 2008.

Ozanne, Henry. " 'Synthesis' in Social Science." *Sociometry* 8.2 (1945): 208-15. *JSTOR.*

Padgett, Tim. "How the Battle over Elian Gonzalez Helped Change U.S. Cuba Policy." *npr.org.* 28 June 2015. Web. 20 May 2016.

Pankaj Chandon. *Researchgate.net.* Research Gate, 2016. Web. 22 July 2016.

Panter, A. T., and Sonya K. Sterba. *Handbook of ethics in quantitative methodology,* Routledge, New York, 2011. doi:10.4324/9780203840023.

Panter, A.T. and Sonya K. Sterba. "Handbook of Ethics in Quantitative Methodology" . (Abingdon: Routledge, 20 Jan 2011), accessed 25 Aug 2016 , Routledge Handbooks Online.

"Paper Planes." *Wikipedia.* Wikipedia, 21 Mar. 2016. Web. 6 June 2013.

Parker Bass, Benjamin, et al. "What Forms Does News Bias Take?" *newsbias.* University of Michigan. n.d. Web. 2 May 2016.

Parker, Randal E. The Economics of the Great Depression: A Twenty-First Century Look Back at the Economics of the Interwar Years by. Cheltenham, UK and Northampton, MA: Edward Elgar, 2007. Print.

Parks, Perry, and Bruno Takahashi. From Apes to Whistleblowers: How Scientists Inform, Defend and Excite in Newspaper Op-Eds." *Science Communication.* 38 (2016): 275-302. *scx.sagepub.com.* Web. 19 May 2016.

Passerini, Luisa. *Fascism in Popular Memory. The Cultural Experience of the Turin Working Class.* Cambridge: Cambridge UP, 1987. Print.

Patton, Michael Quinn. *Qualitative Research and Evaluation Methods.* Thousand Oaks, Calif.: Sage, 2003. Print.

Pauwels, Luc. "Visual Sociology Reframed: An Analytical Synthesis and Discussion of Visual Methods in Social and Cultural Research." *Sociological Methods & Research* 38 (2010): 545-81.

Pax, Salam. "A Post from Baghdad Station." *Where is Raed?* 7 May 2003. *dear_raed.blogspot.com*. Web. 23 May 2016.

Paxson, Christina, et al. "Five years later: Recovery from post traumatic stress and psychological distress among low-income mothers affected by Hurricane Katrina." Social Science & Medicine, vol. 74, no. 2, 2012., pp. 150-157. ScienceDirect, doi:10.1016/j.socscimed.2011.10.004.

Pelka, Fred. *What We Have Done. An Oral History of the Disability Rights Movement*. Amherst: U of Amherst P, 2012. Print.

Pennebaker, James.

"Petroglyph National Monument New Mexico." *National Park Service*. National Park Service, n.d.

"Photography Alan Diaz Recalls Elian Gonzalez." www.steves-digicams.com. n.d. Web. 20 May 2016.

physics.org. Institute of Physics, n.d.

Pillans, Brad, and L. Keith Fifield. "Erosion Rates and Weathering History of Rock Surfaces Associated with Aboriginal Rock Art Engravings (Petroglyphs) on Burrup Peninsula, Western Australia, from Cosmogenic Nuclide Measurements." *Quaternary Science Review*s 69 (2013): 98-106. *ScienceDirect*.

Pillay, Anthony L. "Psychology, Ethics, Human Rights, and National Security : Editorial." *South African Journal of Psychology* 45.4 (2015): 424-9. Web.

"Piracy Cost Movie Industry $6.1 Billion; DVD and Internet Piracy Cost Movie Studios $6.1 Billion Last Year, the Motion Picture Association of America Inc. (MPAA) Says." *Internet Week* 3 May 2006. *General OneFile*. Web. 25 May 2016.

Plumer, Brad. "SOPA: How Much Does Online Piracy Really Cost the Economy?" 5 Jan. 2012. *washingtonpost.com*. Washington Post. Web. 16 May 2016.

"Poems by Rickie Elpusan." n.d. Poetrysoup. Poetry Soup. http://www.poetrysoup.com/poems_poets/poems_by_poet. aspx?ID=920, Accessed 3 Sept. 2016.

"Poll Shows Americans Don't Trust the Media." 7 October 2015. *studentnewsdaily.com*. StudentNewsDaily.com. n. d. Web. 1 May 2016.

Pomfret, Richard. "Modernizing Agriculture in Central Asia." *Global Journal of Emerging Market Economies*, vol. 8, no. 2, 2016., pp. 104-125. Sage Premier, doi:10.1177/0974910116634491.

Popovič, Anton, and Francis Macri. "Literary Synthesis." *Canadian Review of Comparative Literature*. 4.2 (1977): 117-32. *ejournals. library.ualberta.ca*.

Poremba, Sue Marquette. "Probing Question: How Old is Political Satire?" *news.psu.edu*. Penn State University. 20 June 2008. Web. 3 May 2016.

Porter, James E. *Audience and Rhetoric: An Archaeological Composition of the Discourse Community*. New York: Prentice Hall, 1992. Print.

Post, Robert M. "Biased Public Health Perspective on Depression Treatment: Media Bias on Publication Bias." *The American Journal of Psychiatry* 166.8 (2009): 934-5. Web. 20 May 2016.

Potts, Rolf. "Seth Stevenson." *Rolf Potts Vagabonding*. n.d. Web. 2 Apr. 2016.

Pratt, Mary Louise. "Arts of the Contact Zone." *Profession* (1991): 33-40. *JSTOR*.

Pratt, Mary Louise. *Imperial Eyes. Travel Writing and Transculturation*. London: Routledge, 2008. Print.

Pratt, Nicola. "Reconceptualizing Gender, Reinscribing Racial–Sexual Boundaries in International Security: The Case of UN Security Council Resolution 1325 on 'Women, Peace and Security'." *International Studies Quarterly* 57.4 (2013): 772-83. Web. *Wiley Online Library*. Web. 25 May 2016.

Prelli, Lawrence J. "Stasis and the Problem of Incommensurate Communication." *Rhetoric and Incommensurability*. Ed. Randy Allen Harris. West Lafayette, IN: Parlor P., 2005.

Preparedness 101: Zombie Apocolypse

Presley, Steven M., et al. "Metal concentrations in schoolyard soils from New Orleans, Louisiana before and after Hurricanes Katrina and Rita." Chemosphere, vol. 80, no. 1, 2010., pp. 67-73. ScienceDirect, doi:10.1016/j.chemosphere.2010.03.031.

Prevent Genocide International.

Previs, Kathy K. "Gender and Race Representations of Scientists in Highlights for Children: A Content Analysis." *Science Communication*. 38 (2016): 303-327. *scx.sagepub.com*. Web. 19 May 2016.

"Primary and Secondary Sources." Education Psychology Library. University of California, Berkeley. 2013. *lib.berkeley.edu*.

"Prof. Pinchas Halpern." http://www.tasmc.org.il/sites/en/Personnel/Pages/halpern-pinhas.aspx

"Prof. Ram Babu Singh." *interacademies.net*. iap, 2013. Web. 22 July 2016.

Professor Anna Snaith. *kclpure.kcl.ac.uk*. Kings College London, 2015. Web. 23 July 2016.

Professor Anne Marie Rafferty. *kclpure.kcl.ac.uk*. Kings College London, 2015. Web. 23 July 2016.

"Profile #11 Series #2: India: Pankaj Chandan." *aparchive.com*. The Associated Press, 2016. Web. 22 July 2016.

"Profiles." Forensic Archaeology Recovery (FAR). Forensicarchaeologyrecover.org. Web. 19 June 2016.

Psyonix_Dave. Reddit.com November 2015. www.reddit.com/r/RocketLeague/comments/3b00fn/rocket_league_physics_and_ field_size/

"Quotations: Using Signal Phrases to Integrate Quotations into Your Writing." *Writing Across the Curriculum*. Loyola University. *loyno.edu*.

Rampolla, Mary Lynn. *A Pocket Guide to Writing in History*. Boston: Bedford/St. Martin's, 2007. *books.google.com*.

Ramzi Ba 'albaki, et al., eds. "Poetry and History: The Value of Poetry in Reconstructing Arab History. Beirut: American University of Beirut Press, 2011.

Rao, N. Kameswara. "Astronomy with Buddhist Stupas of Sanchi." *Bulletin, Astronomical Society of India* 20 (1992): 87- 98. *adsabs. harvard.edu*.

Ravikrishna, Raghunathan, et al. "Air quality during demolition and recovery activities in post-Katrina New Orleans." Environmental Toxicology and Chemistry, vol. 29, no. 7, 2010., pp. 1438-1444. Wiley Online Library. doi:10.1002/ etc.210.

Reed, Frank. "The Analemma in Castaway." *NavList.* NavList. 10 Dec. 2006.

Reese, Abbie. *Dedicated to God. An Oral History of Cloistered Nuns.* New York: Oxford UP, 2014. Print.

Reilly, Ian. "From Critique to Mobilization: The Yes Men and the Utopian Politics of Satirical Fake News." *International Journal of Communication* 7 (2013): 1243-1264. Web. 1 May 2016.

Reinhard, Johan. *Machu Picchu: Exploring an Ancient Sacred Center.* Los Angeles: Cotsen Institute of Archaeology, U of California, 2007. Print.

"Religion of Nepal." *Royal Mt. Trekking.* royaltibet.com. n.d.

Reporters Without Borders. "United Nations—Further Steps to Enhance Resolution 1738 Needed More than Ever." 17 July 2013. *rsf.org.* Web. 16 May 2016.

Restall, M. "The Mysterious and The Invisible: Writing History in and of Colonial Yucatan." *Ancient Mesoamerica.* 21.2 (2010): 393-400. doi:http://dx.doi.org/10.1017/S0956536110000271

Rettberg, Jill Walker. *Blogging.* Cambridge: Polity, 2014. *books.google.com.* 23 May 2016.

Rettberg, Jill. *Blogging.* Cambridge, UK: Malden, 2008. Print.

Rheault, Ludovic. "Low-technology industries and the skill composition of immigration." *Journal of Public Policy* 35. 3 (2015): 387-420. Cambridge Journals Online. Web. 1 Sept. 2016.

Richard, Brad. "A Poetics of Disaster: Katrina in Poetry, Poetry after Katrina." New Orleans Review, vol. 36, no. 2, 2010., pp. 162-81. Academic OneFile.

Richardson, Robert, et al. "The 'Djedi' Robot Exploration of the Southern Shaft of the Queen's Chamber in the Great Pyramid of Giza, Egypt." *Journal of Field Robotics* 30.3 (2013): 323-48. *onlinelibrary.wiley.com.*

Rickett, Carolyn, et al. "Something to hang my life on: the health benefits of writing poetry for people with serious illnesses." Australasian Psychiatry, vol. 19, no. 3, 2011., pp. 265-268. SAGE Journals, doi:10.3109/10398562.2011.562298.

"Rickie Elpusan." n.d. LinkedIn. www.linkedin.com/in/rickie-elpusan-

Riffkin, Rebecca. "Americans' Trust in Media Remains at Historic Low." 28 Sept. 2015. *Gallup.com.* gallup.com. 1 May 2016.

Rishel, Mary Ann. *Writing Humor. Creativity and the Comic Mind.* Detroit: Wayne State University P, 2002. *books.google.com.* Web. 21 May 2016.

Robert G Azzarello Jr. "THE POETICS OF KATRINA." Race, Gender & Class, 2015., pp. 221-8. ProQuest.

Roberts, David. "Romancing the Stones." *Smithsonian* 33.4 (2002): 86-94, 96. *ProQuest.*

Robertson, IN, et al. "Lessons from Hurricane Katrina Storm Surge on Bridges and Buildings." Journal of Waterway, Port, Coastal, and Ocean Engineering, vol. 133, no. 6, 2007., pp. 463-483. ASCE Library, doi:10.1061/(ASCE)0733-950X(2007)133:6(463).

Robinson, Kerry H., and Cristyn Davies. "Doing Sexuality Research with Children: Ethics, Theory, Methods and Practice. Global Studies of Childhood 4.4 (2014): 250-263. Sage Journals. Web. 26 Aug. 2016.

Rodgers, Lucy, and Gerry Fletcher. *Indian Ocean Tsunami: Then and Now.* BBC News. 25 Dec. 2014. *bbc.com.* Web. 14 July 2016.

Rose, J. A., et al. "Gamification: Using Elements of Video Games to Improve Engagement in an Undergraduate Physics Class." *Physics Education*, vol. 51, no. 5, 2016.doi:10.1088/0031-9120/51/5/055007.

Rossiter, David. "An Introduction to Statistical Analysis." *itc.nl.* International Institute for Geo-information Science & Earth Observation (ITC). 9 Jan. 2006.

Rottenberg, Annette, and Donna Haisty Winchell. *The Structure of Argument.* New York: Macmillan, 2011. *books.google.com.*

Ruggles, Clive L.N. *Ancient Astronomy: An Encyclopedia of Cosmologies and Myth.* Santa Barbara, Calif.: ABC-CLIO, 2005. Print.

"Rumi Chunara." *NYU Tanden School of Engineering.* New York University, n.d., http://engineering.nyu.edu/people/rumi-chunara. Accessed 2 Sept. 2016.

"Rush Limbaugh." *biography.com.* Biography.com. n. d. Web. 5 May 2016.

Ryall, Jenni. *A Decade On, Thailand Remembers the Horrific Boxing Day Tsunami.* 26 Dec. 2014. *mashable.com.* Web. 14 July 2016.

Said, Edward. *Orientalism.* London: Penguin, 2003. Print.

Saint-Germain, Michelle A. "PPA 696 Research Methods Data Collection Strategies II: Qualitative Research." *csu.edu.*

"Salam Pax." *en.wikipedia.org.* n.d. Web. 14 May 2016

Salimian, Parissa K., et al. "Averting the Perfect Storm: Addressing Youth Substance Use Risk From Social Media Use." *Pediatric Annals*, vol. 43, no. 10, 2014., pp. e242. ProQuest, doi: 10.3928/00904481-20140924-08.

Salter, Irene Y., and Leslie J. Atkins. "What Students Say Versus What They Do Regarding Scientific Inquiry: What Students Say Versus What They Do." *Science Education*, vol. 98, 2014..

Salter, Mark B. "The Geographical Imaginations of Video Games: Diplomacy, Civilization, America's Army and Grand Theft Auto IV." *Geopolitics*, vol. 16, no. 2, 2011., pp. 359doi:10.1080/14650045.2010.538875.

Salter, Mark B. "The Geographical Imaginations of Video Games: Diplomacy, Civilization, America's Army and Grand Theft Auto IV." *Geopolitics*, vol. 16, no. 2, 2011., pp. 359doi:10.1080/14650045.2010.538875.

Samuels, Holly. "Brainstorming Research Questions. Tip Sheet 10." *CRLS Research Guide.* 2004. Web. *www.crlsresearchguide.org.* 21 Mar. 2014.

Sanchez, Haracio. *Education Revolution: How to Apply Brain Science to Improve Instruction and School Climate.* Corwin, 2017.

Sawyer, Miranda. "MIA: I'm Here for the People." *Guardian.* June 13 (2010) Web. 6 June 2013.

Schiffrin, Deborah, Deborah Tannen, and Heidi E. Hamilton, eds. *The Handbook of Discourse Analysis.* Malden, MA: Blackwell, 2001.

Schroer, Jeanine Weekes, and Robert Schroer. *Philosophical Studies* 171.3 (2014): 445-469. *SpringerLink.* Web. 14 July 2016.

Schwartz-DuPre, Rae Lynn. *Communicating Colonialism: Readings on Postcolonial Theory(s) and Communication.* New York: Peter Lang, 2014. *amazon.com.*

"Scientific Falsification." *explorable.com.* 5 Aug. 2010.

Seiler, Robert M. "Writing about Music." *University of Calgary.* University of Calgary, n.d. Web. 2 Apr. 2016.

Serpas, Martha. The Dirty Side of the Storm. New York: Norton, 2007.

"Seth Stevenson." *Amazon*. Amazon, n.d. Web. 2 Apr. 2016.

Shelby, Karen. "The Stupa." *Smart History*. Khan Academy, n.d.

Shen, Yue, Mei-Po Kwan, and Yanwei Chai. "Investigating Commuting Flexibility with GPS Data and 3D Geovisualization: A Case Study of Beijing, China." *Journal of Transport Geography* 32 (2013): 1-11. *ScienceDirect Freedom*. Web. 22 July 2016.

Shmueli, Efraim. "How is Objectivity in the Social Sciences Possible?: A Re-Evaluation of Karl Mannheim's Concept of 'Relationism.'" *Journal for General Philosophy of Science*. 10.1 (1979): 107-18. *JSTOR*.

Simic, Olivera. "Rethinking 'Sexual Exploitation' in UN Peacekeeping Operations." *Women's Studies International Forum* 32.4 (2009): 288-95. Web. *ScienceDirect*. Web. 25 May 2016.

Simic, Olivera. "Rethinking 'sexual Exploitation' in UN Peacekeeping Operations." *Women's Studies International Forum* 32.4 (2009): 288-95. *ScienceDirect*. Web. 15 May 2016.

Simmons, Kevin M., and Daniel Sutter. "False Alarms, Tornado Warnings, and Tornado Casualties." Weather, Climate, and Society, vol. 1, no. 1, 2009., pp. 38-53. Environment Complete, doi:10.1175/2009WCAS1005.1.

Sinclair, Peter M., et al. "The Effectiveness of Internet-Based e-Learning on Clinician Behaviour and Patient Outcomes: A Systematic Review." *International Journal of Nursing Studies* 57 (2016): 70-81. *ScienceDirect*. Web. 23 July 2016.

Singerman, David. "The Shady History of Big Sugar." 16 September 2016. *New York Times*. *nytimes.com*. Web. 7 November 2016.

Sipiora, Phillip, and James S. Baumlin, eds. *Rhetoric and Kairos: Essays in History, Theory, and Praxis*. Albany, NY: SUNY P, 2012. *books.google.com*.

Slattery, P. G., C. T. McCarthy, and R. M. O'Higgins. "Development of a novel cyanoacrylate injection repair procedure for composites." *Composite Structures*, vol. 153, 2016., pp. 1-11. *ScienceDirect Freedom*.

Slink, M. "United Nations Resolution 61/225 - What Does It Mean to the Diabetes World?: UN Resolution on Diabetes." *International Journal of Clinical Practice* 61 (2007): 5-8. Web. *Wiley Online Library*. Web. 25 May 2016.

Sollaci, Luciana B., and Mauricio G. Pereira. "The Introduction, Methods, Results, and Discussion (IMRAD) Structure: A Fifty-Year Survey." *Journal of the Medical Library Association* 92.3 (2004): 364-371. *ncbi.nlm.nih.gov*.

Space Future. Space Future Consulting, n.d. Web. 23 July 2016.

Sparavigna, Amelia Carolina. "Maria Reiche's Line to Archaeoastronomy." *Archaeoastronomy and Ancient Technologies* 1.2 (2013): 48-54. *arXiv.org*.

Spence, Kate. "Ancient Egyptian Chronology and the Astronomical Orientation of Pyramids." *Nature* 408.6810 (2000): 320-324. *ProQuest*. 9 Sept. 2014.

Spielberg, Steven, dir. *Raiders of the Lost Ark*. Paramount, 1981. Film.

Spigelman, Candace. *Personally Speaking: Experience as Evidence in Academic Discourse*. Carbondale, Ill.: Southern Illinois UP, 2004.

"Spinal Tap's Nigel Tufnel on Why Aliens Didn't Build Stonehenge." *Stonehenge Decoded*. National Geographic Channel. 2007. Television. *natgeotv.com*.

"Spotlight Interview with: Anne Marie Rafferty." *icn.ch*. International Council of Nurses, June 2010. Web. 23 July 2016.

Springen, Karen. "This is your Brain on Alien Killer Pimps of Nazi Doom." *Newsweek* 148.22 (December 11, 2006): 48. *ProQuest*.

Spurlock, Morgan, and Steve Horowitz, Dir. *SuperSize Me*. New York: Hart Sharp Video, 2004.

Stanley, Amy. "Maidservants' Tales: Narrating Domestic and Global History in Eurasia, 1600–1900." *The American Historical Review*. 121.2 (2016): 437-460. doi:10.1093/ahr/121.2.437.

Stasavage, David. "Partisan politics and public debt: The importance of the 'Whig Supremacy' for Britain's financial revolution." *European Review of Economic History*, vol. 11, no. 1, 2007. pp. 123-153. Cambridge Journals, doi:10.1017/S1361491606001900.

"Statistics on Literacy." *UNESCO*. United Nations. http://www.unesco.org/new/en/education/themes/education-building-blocks/literacy/resources/statistics. Accessed 14 Dec. 2016.

Stearns, Sally C., and Edward C. Norton. "Time to include time to death? The future of health care expenditure predictions." *Health Economics*, vol. 13, no. 4, 2004., pp. 315-327. Wiley Online Library, doi:10.1002/hec.831.

Sterling, Colin. "Photography, Preservation, and Ethics at Angkor." Future Anterior: Journal of Historic Preservation, History, Theory, and Criticism 11.1 (2014): 71-83. JSTOR. Web. 26 Aug. 2016.

Stern, David I., and Robert K. Kaufmann. "Anthropogenic and Natural Causes of Climate Change." *Climatic Change* 122.1-2 (2014): 257–69. *SpringerLink*.

Stevenson, Seth. "Trying Really Hard to Like India." *slate.com* 27 Sept. 2004. Web. 11 Nov. 2013.

Stober, Emmanuel O. "Aging Population-A Cloud On Romania's Economic Future." *Management Research and Practice*, vol. 7, no. 4, 2015., pp. 32-42. ProQuest.

Storm, Darlene. "Not Again: Stop Blaming Violent Video Games for Mass Shootings." 18 Sept. 2013. *blogs.computerworld.com*. Computer World.

Street, Richard Steven. "Everyone had Cameras: Photographers, Photography and the Farmworker Experience in California: A Photographic Essay." *California History* 83.2 (2005): 8-25. Web. *Academic OneFile*. 2 Apr. 2016.

"Student News Daily." *studentnewsdaily.com*. StudentNewsDaily.com. 2015. Web. 2 May 2016.

"Super Size Me Quotes." *imdb.com*.

Swarns, Rachel L. "272 Slaves Were Sold to Save Georgetown. What Does It Owe Their Descendants?" 16 April 2016. *New York Times*. *nytimes.com*. Web. 7 November 2016.

"Synthesis." *Biology Online*. 14 April 2011.

"Synthesis." *Oxford English Dictionary*.

"Syria: The Story of the Conflict." *BBC News*. BBC, 11 Mar. 2016. Web. 2 Apr. 2016.

Talisse, Robert, and Scott F. Aikin. "Two Forms of the Straw Man." *Argumentation* 20.3 (2006): 345-52. *ProQuest*.

Tanenhaus, Sam. "The Poetry of Catastrophe." 18 Mar. 2011. The New York Times. http://artsbeat.blogs.nytimes. com/2011/03/18/the-poetry-of-catastrophe/?_r=1. Accessed 3 Sept. 2016.

Tang, Haixu, and Sun Kim. "Bioinformatics: Mining the Massive Data from High Throughput Genomics Experiments." *Analysis of Biological Data: A Soft Computing Approach.* Ed. Sanghamitra Bandyopadhyay, Ujjwal Maulik, and Jason T L Wang. *Science, Engineering, and Biology Informatics.* Vol. 3. 3-24. *worldscientific.com.*

Teng, Scott K. Z., et al. "Grand Theft Auto IV Comes to Singapore: Effects of Repeated Exposure to Violent Video Games on Aggression." *Cyberpsychology, Behavior, and Social Networking*, vol. 14, no. 10, 2011., pp. 597-602doi:10.1089/ cyber.2010.0115.

Teng, Scott K. Z., et al. "Grand Theft Auto IV Comes to Singapore: Effects of Repeated Exposure to Violent Video Games on Aggression." *Cyberpsychology, Behavior, and Social Networking*, vol. 14, no. 10, 2011., pp. 597-602doi:10.1089/ cyber.2010.0115.

The Chicago Manual of Style. Chicago: U of Chicago P, 2010. Print.

"The Deadliest Tsunami in History?" 7 Jan. 2005. *National Geographic News. news.nationalgeographic.com.* National Geographic. Web. 14 July 2016.

"The Deadliest Tsunamis." SMS Tsunami Warning. Web. 14 July 2016.

"The Giza Plateau." *sca-egypt.org.* Supreme Council of Antiquities. n.d.

The Hastings Center.

The Journal of Religious Ethics. onlinelibrary.wiley.com. Wiley. Web. 26 Aug. 2016.

"The Logic of Scientific Arguments." *Understanding Science.* University of California Museum of Paleontology. Berkeley. *undsci. berkeley.edu.*

"The School of Life." *theschooloflife.com.* 2016. Web. 22 July 2016.

Thom, Alexander. "Stonehenge." *Journal for the History of Astronomy* 5.2 (1974): 71-90. *SAO/NASA Astrophysics Data System.*

Thu, Tran Nguyen Anh. Hanoi Flood (1971). Encyclopedia of Disaster Relief. Ed. K Bradley Penuel and Matt Statler. Sage Knowledge. Web. 27 Aug. 2016.

Timberg, Scott. *Culture Crash. The Killing of the Creative Class.* New Haven: Yale UP, 2015. *books.google.com.* Web. 25 May 2016.

"Title Summary." Sale, Richard, and George Rodway. *Everest and Conquest in the Himalaya: Science and Courage on the World's Highest Mountain.* Barnsley: Pen & Sword Discovery, 2011. *library.duke.edu.*

Tong, Mark Y., et al. "Automated validation of genetic variants from large databases: ensuring that variant references refer to the same genomic locations." *Bioinformatics*, vol. 27, no. 6, 2011., pp. 891-893. *Oxford Journals*, doi: 10.1093/bioinformatics/ btr029.

Torrence, Robin. "Social Resilience and Long-Term Adaptation to Volcanic Disasters: The Archaeology of Continuity and Innovation in the Willaumez Peninsula, Papua New Guinea." *Quaternary International* 394 (2016;2014;): 6-16. Web.

Toulmin, Stephen. *The Uses of Argument.* Cambridge: Cambridge UP, 2003. Print.

Trench, Brian, and Massimiano Bucchi. "Science Communication, An Emerging Discipline." *Journal of Science Communication* 9.3 (2010): 1-5. *jcom.sissa.it.* Web. 19 May 2016.

Tuggle, H. David, Alex H. Townsend, and Thomas J. Riley. "Laws, Systems, and Research Designs: A Discussion of Explanation in Archaeology." *American Antiquity* 37.1 (1972): 3-12. *JSTOR.*

Twenge, Jean M. "Yes, Violent Video Games Do Cause Aggression." *Psychology Today.* 21 Dec. 2012. *pscychologytoday.com.*

Tyner, James, and Stian Rice. "Cambodia's Political Economy of Violence: Space, Time, and Genocide Under the Khmer Rouge, 1975-79." *Genocide Studies International* 10.1 (2016): 84-94.

"Types of Economic Analysis." n.d. *chkb.org.* Vera Institute of Justice. Web. 20 Aug. 2016.

U.S. Wisconsin Department of Public Instructions. "Literacy in the Discipline and Disciplinary Literacy: A Place for Both." 2012. *standards.dpi.wi.gov.*

"UN Condemns Journalist Attacks." *news.bbc.co.uk.* 24 Dec. 2006. Web. 16 May 2016.

"Understanding Bias." *americanpressinstitute.org.* American Press Institute. 2016. Web. 21 May 2016.

United Nations Security Council. un.org. United Nations.Web. 16 May 2016.

United States. Department of State. Bureau of Democracy, Human Rights and Labor. *Nepal 2013 Human Rights Report.* 2014. *state. gov.*

Urban-Woldron, Hildegard. "Motion Sensors in Mathematics Teaching: Learning Tools for Understanding General Math Concepts?" *International Journal of Mathematical Education in Science and Technology*, vol. 46, no. 4, 2015, pp. 584-598. Proquest, doi:10.1080/0020739X.2014.985270.

Urcid, Javier, and Arthur Joyce. "Early Transformations of Monte Alban's Main Plaza and Their Political Implications, 500 BC-AD 200." *Mesoamerican Plazas: Arenas of Community and Power.* Ed. Kenichiro Tsukamoto and Takeshi Inomata. Tucson: U of Arizona P, 2014. 149-67.

Useful Science. usefulscience.

USGS. "Earthquakes with 1,000 or More Deaths 1900-2014." Earthquake.usgs.gov. USGS. Web. 26 Aug. 2016.

Vachette, Astrid. "The FRANZ agreement: France's complex involvement in South Pacific regional cooperation on emergency management." *International Journal of Emergency Management*, vol. 9, no. 3, 2014. pp. 229-247.

Van Buren, Mary. "The Archaeology of El NiñO Events and Other "Natural" Disasters." *Journal of Archaeological Method and Theory* 8.2 (2001): 129-49. Web.

Van Der Sluijs, Marinus Anthony, and Anthony L. Peratt. "Searching For Rock Art Evidence For An Ancient Super Aurora." *Expedition* 52.2 (2010): 33-42. *Academic Search Complete.*

Vassallo, Paul. "The Knowledge Continuum: Organizing for Research and Scholarly Communication." *Office of Information Services. United States Department of Commerce. National Institute of Standards and Technology.* Web. nist.gov.

Vayena, Effy, et al. "Ethical challenges of big data in public health." *PLoS computational biology*, vol. 11, no. 2, 2015. pp. e1003904. PLOS, doi: 10.1371/journal.pcbi.1003904.

Venner, Ed, Barny Revill, and Ed Wardle, dir. *Everest: Beyond the Limits*. Discovery Channel, 2006-2009. Film.

Verano, John W. "Human Skeletal Remains from Tomb 1, Sipan (Lambayeque River Valley, Peru); and their Social Implications." *Antiquity* 71.273 (1997): 670-82. *ProQuest*.

"Violence in the Media — Psychologists Study TV and Video Game Violence for Potential Harmful Effects." *apa.org*. Nov. 2013.

von Einsiedel, Sebastian, David M. Malone, and Bruno Stagno Ugarte. *The UN Security Council in the Twenty-First Century*. Boulder, CO: Lynne Rienner, 2016. *books.google.com*. Web. 15 May 2016.

Von Feldt, Rick. "About Rick Von Feldt." *hrfuturist.com*. n.d. Web. 14 July 2016.

Wagner, Alex. "Life in Exile: The Nomad Noise of MIA's Kala." *The Fader*. Aug. 7 (2008): Web. 6 June 2013.

Walker, James Robert. "Everything but the Game: A Photographic Essay." *NINE: A Journal of Baseball History and Culture* 14.2 (2006): 167-76. Web. *ProQuest*. 2 Apr. 2016.

Walker, Janice R. "Everything Changes, or Why MLA Isn't (Always) Right." *Writing Spaces. Readings on Writing*. Anderson, S.C.: Parlor P, 2011. 257-69. *wac.colostate.edu*.

Wall, Melissa. *Citizen Journalism, Digital Journalism*. 3.6 (2015): 797-813. *tandfonline*. Web. 14 May 2016.

Wallace, Carolyn S., And Lori Brooks. "Learning to Teach Elementary Science in an Experiential, Informal Context: Culture, Learning, and Identity: Learning To Teach Elementary Science." *Science Education*, vol. 99, 2015.

Walter, Bronwen. "Personal Lives: Narrative Accounts of Irish Women in the Diaspora." *Irish Studies Review* 21.1 (2013): 37-54. *Taylor & Francis Online*. Web. 14 July 2016.

Walton, Douglas. *Media Argumentation. Dialectic, Persuasion, and Rhetoric*. Cambridge: Cambridge UP, 2007. *library.duke.edu*. Web. 20 May 2016.

Walton, Douglas. *Fundamentals of Critical Argumentation*. New York: Cambridge UP, 2006.

Wang, Zheng Joyce. *The DOCC. Dynamics of Cognition and Communication. thedocc.com*. The Ohio State University. Web. 15 May 2016.

Ward, Christine. "The Bluff Great House. On the Periphery of the Chaco World." *Expedition* 45.3 (2003): 9-14. *penn.museum*.

Watchman, Alan, Paul Taçon, and Maxime Aubert. Correspondence on "Erosion Rates and Weathering History of Rock Surfaces Associated with Aboriginal Rock Art Engravings (Petroglyphs) on Burrup Peninsula, Western Australia, from Cosmogenic Nuclide Measurements" by Brad Pillans and Keith Fifield. *Quaternary Science Reviews* 69: 98–106. *Quaternary Science Reviews* 91 (2014): 70-73. *ScienceDirect*.

Weaver, Teresa K. "Maya Angelou's Final Chapter." *Palm Beach Post-Cox News Service*. 5 May 2002. *racematters.org*.

Weber, Cameron M. "The Economics of the Great Depression: A Twenty-First Century Look Back at the Economics of the Interwar Years by Randal E. Parker." *American Economist*, vol. 54, no. 1, 2010., pp. 135.

Weber, Florence F. "The Ethics of Ethnography Revisited: Learning from Documentaries." Revue de Synthèse 132.3 (2011): 325-349. SpringerLink. Web. 26 Aug. 2016.

Weber, Karin. "Outdoor Adventure Tourism: A Review of Research Approaches." *Sport & Tourism: A Reader*. Ed. Mike Weed. New York: Routledge, 2007. 57-71. Print.

WebMD. WebMD, 2005-14.

Weigle, Lauren. "Remembering 9/11: Top 10 Poems in Tribute to September 11th." 11 Sept. 2015. Heavy. Heavy. http://heavy.com/news/2015/09/9-11-poems-quotes september-11th-remembering-timeline-remembrance-2015-stories-2001-911/. Accessed 3 Sept. 2016.

"Welcome to the LHCb Experiment." n.d. *lhcb-public.web.cern.ch*. Web. 20 May 2016.

Welfare, Simon, John Fairley, and Arthur C. Clarke. *Arthur C. Clarke's Mysterious World*. London: Collins, 1980. *knowth.com*.

Wharton-Michael, Patty.

"What is Archaeology?" Society for American Archaeology. Society for American Archaeology. Web. 27 Aug. 2016.

"What is Biomedical Engineering." Department of Biomedical Engineering. Michigan Tech, n.d., www.mtu.edu/biomedical/department/what-is/. Accessed 2 Sept. 2016.

"What is Chemical Analysis." *Department of Chemistry*. University of Arizona. n.d.

"What is Civil Engineering?" *Civil Engineering and Engineering Mechanics. civil.columbia.edu*. Columbia University. 2012. Web. 24 June 2016.

"What is Economics? Understanding the Discipline." American Economic Association. American Economic Association, 2016. www.aeaweb.org/resources/students/what-is-economics. Accessed 2 Sept. 2016.

"What is English Studies?" *Department of English*. Illinois State U., 2009.

"What is Information Science?" *assist.org*. Association for Information Science and Technology. n. d. Web. 22 May 2016.

"What is Physics?" *physics.org*. Web. 19 May 2016.

What's in Blue. 26 May 2015. *whatsinblue.org*. What's in Blue. Web. 15 May 2016.

Wieland, Shannon C., et al. "Revealing the Spatial Distribution of a Disease while Preserving Privacy." *Proceedings of the National Academy of Sciences of the United States of America*, vol. 105, no. 46, 2008., pp. 17608-17613. PubMed Central. Web. 2 Sept. 2016.

Wikipedia: WikiProject Video Games. en.wikipedia.org.

Wilkinson, Joanne E. "Who is My Patient? Use of a Brief Writing Exercise to Enhance Residents' Understanding of Physician-Patient Issues." *Journal for Learning through the Arts* 2.1 (2006): n.p. *escholarship.org*. Web. 23 July 2016.

Wilson, Jason, and Jamaica Kincaid, eds. *The Best American Travel Writing*. Boston: Houghton Mifflin Harcourt, 2005. Print.

Wiwanitkit, Viroj. "Critical Guidelines for Health Care Workers Who Deploy to West Africa for the Ebola Response." *Disaster Medicine and Public Health Preparedness* 10. 2 (2016): 187. *Cambridge Journals*. Web. 26 Aug. 2016.

Woldu, Gail Hilson. "The Kaleidescope of Writing on Hip-Hop Culture." Notes. 67.1 (2010): 9-38. *Academic OneFile*.

Wolf, Mark J. P., ed. *Encyclopedia of Video Games: The Culture, Technology, and Art of Gaming*. Santa Barbara, Calif.: Greenwood, 2012. *ProQuest ebrary*.

"Women In Shorts (Maybe) Cause Car Crash In 1937 (PHOTO)." *Huffington Post*. 15 Mar. 2013. *huffingtonpost.com*.

Wood, W. Raymond, and R. Bruce McMillan, eds. *Prehistoric Man and His Environment. A Case Study in the Ozark Highland*. New York: Academic P, 1976. Print.

"Writing a Synthesis Essay." *Northern Virginia Community College*. n.d.

Wu, Hao-Che, et al. "Logistics of hurricane evacuation in Hurricanes Katrina and Rita." Transportation Research Part F: Traffic Psychology and Behaviour, vol. 15, no. 4, 2012., pp. 445. Science Direct, doi:10.1016/j.trf.2012.03.005.

Yar, Jr., Cengiz. "About Cengiz Yar, Jr." *Cengiz Yar, Jr*. Cengiz Yar, Jr. n.d. Web. 2 Apr. 2016.

Yar, Majid. *Cybercrime and Society. Crime and Punishment in the Information Age*. London: SAGE Publications, 2006. Web. *books. google.com*. 25 May 2016.

Yee, Danny. "The Art of Travel. Alain de Botton." Review. *dannyreviews.com*. 2006. Web. 22 July 2016.

Youngblood, Dawn. "Multidisciplinarity, Interdisciplinarity, and Bridging Disciplines: A Matter of Process." *Journal of Research Practice* 3.2 (2007): n.p. *jrp.icaap.org*.

Yu, Hairong, Anli Jiang, and Jie Shen. "Prevalence and Predictors of Compassion Fatigue, Burnout and Compassion Satisfaction among Oncology Nurses: A Cross-Sectional Survey." *International Journal of Nursing Studies* 57 (2016): 28-38. *ScienceDirect*. Web. 23 July 2016.

Zakaria, Fareed. *In Defense of a Liberal Education*. Norton, 2015. *Google Books*, https://books.google.com/books?id=_8YbBgAAQB AJ&printsec=frontcover&source=gbs_ViewAPI#v=onepage&q&f=false . Accessed 14 Dec. 2016.

Zebrowski, Ernest, and Judith A. Howard. Category 5: The Story of Camille. Lessons Unlearned from America's Most Violent Hurricane. Ann Arbor: U of Michigan P, 2005. *books.google.com*

Zebrowski, Ernest, and Mariah Zebrowski Leach. "Hydrocarbon Hucksters: Lessons from Louisiana on Oil, Politics, and Environmental Justice." Jackson, U P of Missiippi. 2014. EBL. Web. 27 Aug. 2016.

Zebrowski, Ernest. A History of the Circle. Mathematical Reasoning and the Physical Universe. New Brunswick, NJ: Rutgers UP, 1999. *books.google.com*

Zebrowski, Ernest. The Last Days of St. Pierre. The Volcanic Disaster That Claimed Thirty Thousand Lives. New Brunswick, NJ: Rutgers UP, 2002. *books.google.com*

Zemeckis, Robert, dir. *Castaway*. Twentieth Century Fox, 2000. Film.

Zheng, Yali, et al. "Unobtrusive and Multimodal Wearable Sensing to Quantify Anxiety." *IEEE Sensors Journal*, vol. 16, no. 10, 2016., pp. 3689-3696. *IEEE Xplore*, doi: 10.1109/JSEN.2016.2539383.

Zimmer, Michael, and Nicholas J. Proferes. "A Topology of Twitter Research: Disciplines, Methods, and Ethics." *Aslib Journal of Information Management* 66.3 (2014): 250-261. *ProQuest*. Web. 26 Aug. 2016.

Acknowledgments

Aaij, R. et al. Abstract from "Observation of J/ψp Resonances Consistent with Pentaquark States in Λob→J/ψK–p Decays," *Physical Review Letters*, 2015. All rights reserved.

Aleghfeli, Obaid Rashed. "Video Games" from *Undergraduate Research Journal for the Human Sciences,* 11 (2012). Reprinted with permission of Undergraduate Research Committee. All rights reserved.

Alim, Samy. Excerpt(s) from *Roc the Mic Right,* New York: Routledge, 2006.

Allin, Linda. Excerpt(s) from "Climbing Mount Everest: Women, Career and Family in Outdoor Education," *Australian Journal of Outdoor Education,* 8.2 (2004): 64-71.

Alridge, Derrick P. Excerpt(s) from "From Civil Rights to Hip Hop: Toward a Nexus of Ideas," *The Journal of African American History,* 90.3 (2005): 226+.

Anand, Anupam, Pankaj Chandan, and Ram Babu Singh. "Homestays in Korzak: Supplementing Rural Livelihoods and Supporting Green Tourism in the Indian Himalayas" from *Mountain Research and Development,* Vol. 32, No. 2 (2012). Published under Creative Commons licensing. All rights reserved.

Armoudian, Maria. Excerpt(s) from *Kill the Messenger: The Media's Role in the Fate of the World,* Amherst, NY: Prometheus Books, 2011.

Arthur, Damien. Excerpt(s) from "Authenticity and Consumption in the Australian Hip Hop Culture," *Qualitative Market Research,* 9.2 (2006): 140-156.

"Books Don't Take You Anywhere" from *The Onion,* Dec. 16, 1997. All rights reserved.

Bourg, David M. "How Physics is Used in Video Games" from *Physics Educations,* Vol. 39, Issue 5, 2004. Reprinted with permission of IOP Publishing. All rights reserved.

Budge, Susan, Armann Ingolofsson, and Dawit Zerom. Excerpt(s) from "Empirical Analysis of Ambulance Travel Times: The Case of Calgary Emergency Medical Services," *Management Science,* 56.4 (2010): 716-723.

Buxton, Bill. Excerpt(s) from "Books on History and Exploration, with a Focus on Central Asia…[and] The History of Climbing and Mountaineering," *billbuxton.com,* 2014.

Bynoe, Yvonne. Excerpt(s) from the Introduction to *Encyclopedia of Rap and Hip Hop Culture,* Westport, CT: Greenwood Press, 2006.

Campbell, Harnish. Excerpt(s) from "Estuarine Crocodiles Ride Surface Currents to Facilitate Long-Distance Travel," *Journal of Animal Ecology,* 79.5 (2010): 955-964.

Cassa, Christopher, Rumi Chunara, Kenneth Mandl, and John S. Brownstein. "Twitter as Sentinel. Lessons from the Boston Marathon Bombing" from *PLOS Currents Disasters,* July 2, 2013. Open access and all rights reserved.

Clarke, John R. Excerpt(s) from "Before Pornography: Sexual Representation in Ancient Roman Visual Culture," *Pornographic Art and the Aesthetics of Pornography,* Ed. Hans Maes. Reprinted with permission of Palgrave Macmillan. All rights reserved.

Collins, Patrick and Adriano Autino. "What the Growth of a Space Tourism Industry Could Contribute to Employment, Economic Growth, Environmental Protection, Education, Culture and World Peace" from *Acta Astronautica,* Vol. 66, Issue 11 (2010). Reprinted with permission. All rights reserved.

Condry, Ian. Excerpt(s) from "Cultures of Music Piracy: An Ethnographic Comparison of the U.S. and Japan," *International Journal of Cultural Studies,* 7.3 (2004): 343-363.

Conway, Gordon. Excerpt(s) from *One Billion Hungry. Can We Feed the World?* Ithaca: Cornell UP, 2012. Reprinted with permission.

Corso, David. Excerpt(s) from "The Psychological and Physical Effects of Video Game Play," *Caravel, Undergraduate Research Journal* (2014). Reprinted with permission.

Couch, Eric, Jesse Christophel, Erik Hohlfeld, and Karen Thole. "Cooling Effects of Dirt Purge Holes on the Tips of Gas Turbine Blades," from *The Craft of Scientific Presentations. Critical Steps to Succeed and Critical Errors to Avoid* 2nd ed., New York: Springer, 2013.

de Bie, Tanja. "MOOC Community. More than Weblectures," from *prezi.com,* Mar. 24, 2014.

De Botton, Alain. "On Habit" from *The Art of Travel.* Copyright © 2002 by Alain de Botton. Used by permission of Pantheon Books, an imprint of the Knopf Doubleday Publishing Group, a division of Random House LLC. All rights reserved.

de Wit, Emmie, et al. Excerpt(s) from "Middle East Respiratory Syndrome Coronavirus (MERS-CoV) Causes Transient Lower Respiratory Tract Infection in Rhesus Macaques," *Proceedings of the National Academy of Sciences,* 110.41 (2013).

Diaz, Alan. "Cuban Refugee Elián González" photographic image, Apr. 22, 2000. Copyright © 2000 by Alan Diaz. Reprinted with permission of the Associated Press. All rights reserved.

Dorothea Lange. "Doctor Examining Child. Kalmath County, Oregon, 1937" photographic image from the Library of Congress Prints and Photographs Division, LC-USF34-021833.

Dorothea Lange. "Fifty-Seven-Year-Old Sharecropper Woman. Hinds County, Mississippi, 1937. Thin Dimes around the Ankles to Prevent Headaches" photographic image from the Library of Congress, Prints and Photographs Division, LC-DIG-fsa-8b32018.

Elpusan, Rickie. "knee deep in N'awlins" from *poetrysoup.com*, Mar. 28, 2011. All rights reserved.

"Epidemiological Update: Middle East Respiratory Syndrome Coronavirus (MERS-CoV)." *European Centre for Disease Prevention and Control*, Nov. 23, 2013.

Faris, Suzanne B. "Roman Addiction: The Changing Perception of Problem Gaming in the Roman World." Microsoft PowerPoint Presentation from *digitalscholarship.unlv.edu*. All rights reserved.

Farrar, Renée. "Apple (a poem)," from *digitalamerica.org*. Reprinted with permission.

Ferguson, Kennan. Excerpt(s) from "Intensifying Taste, Intensifying Identity: Collectivity Through Community Cookbooks," *Signs: Journal of Women in Culture And Society*, 37.3 (2012) 695-717.

Fitzgerald, Gerald J. and Gabriella M. Petrick. Excerpt(s) from "In Good Taste: Rethinking American History with Our Palates," *The Journal of American History*, 95.2 (2008): 392-404. Reprinted with permission.

Frenk, Steven M., Steven L. Foy, and Keith G. Meador. Excerpt(s) from "It's Medically Proven!" Assessing the Dissemination of Religion and Health Research," *Journal of Religion and Health*, 50.4 (2011): 996-1006.

Friberg, Michael and Benjamin Rasmussen. "Syria's Victims Tell Their Stories" from *New Republic*, Aug. 19, 2013. Reprinted with permission. All rights reserved.

Ganapathy, Sandhya. Excerpt(s) from "Imagining Alaska: Local and Translocal Engagements with Place," *American Anthropologist*, 115.1 (2013): 96-111.

Gantz, Walter and Zheng Wang. "Coverage of Cancer in Local Television News" from *Journal of Cancer Education*, Vol. 24, No. 1 (2009). Reprinted with permission. All rights reserved.

Gee, James Paul. "Telling and Doing: Why Doesn't Lara Croft Obey Professor Von Croy?" from *What Video Games Have to Teach us about Learning and Literacy*. Copyright © 2003 by James Paul Gee. All rights reserved.

"The Geoff Ward Collection," hiphoparchive.org.

Georg, Gunda I. and Shaomeng Wang. Excerpt(s) from "Plagiarism," *Journal of Medicinal Chemistry*, 56.1 (2013).

Gingras, Yves. Excerpt(s) from "Revisiting the 'Quiet Debut' of the Double Helix: A Bibliometric and Methodological note on the 'Impact' of Scientific Publications," *Journal of the History of Biology*, 43.1 (2010): 159-181.

Ginsberg, Jeremy, Matthew H. Mohebbi, Rajan S. Patel, Lynnette Brammer, Mark S. Smolinski, and Larry Brilliant. Excerpt(s) from "Detecting Influenza Epidemics Using Search Engine Query Data," *Nature*, (2009): 1012-1014.

Gleick, James. Excerpt(s) from *The Information: A History, a Theory, a Flood*. Copyright © 2011 by James Gleick. Used by permission of Pantheon Books, an imprint of the Knopf Doubleday Publishing Group, a division of Random House LLC. All rights reserved.

Gould, Richard A. and Randi Scott. "Ethnoarchaeology and the Aftermath: The Process of Memorialization" from *Disaster Archaeology*. Reprinted with permission of the University of Utah Press. All rights reserved.

Halpern, Pinchas and Gregory L. Larkin. "Ethical Issues in the Provision of Emergency Medical Care in Multiple Casualty Incidents and Disasters" from *ResearchGate*, Jan. 2006. All rights reserved.

Halwell, Brian. Excerpt(s) from "The Argument for Local Food," *World Watch Magazine*, 16.3 (2003): 20-27.

Hansen, Peter H. Excerpt(s) from "Confetti of Empire: The Conquest of Everest in Nepal, India, Britain, and New Zealand," *Comparative Studies in Society and History*, 42.2 (2000): 307-332.

Heckler, Nina C. David R. Forde, and C. Hobson Bryan. Excerpt(s) from "Using Writing Assignment Designs to Mitigate Plagiarism," *Teaching Sociology*, 41.1 (2013): 94-105.

Heidebrink-Bruno, Sarah. "In 1937, two women caused an accident by wearing shorts in public for the first time" photographic image from *Hybrid Pedagogy*, May 29, 2014.

Heifferon, Barbara A. Excerpt(s) from "The New Smallpox: An Epidemic of Words?" *Rhetoric Review*, 25.1 (2006): 76-93.

Heilbrun, Margaret. Excerpt(s) from "*Review of The Conquest of Everest: Original Photographs from the Legendary First Ascent*," *Library Journal*, 138.7 (2013).

Helle, Anita. Excerpt(s) from "When the Photograph Speaks: Photo-Analysis in Narrative Medicine." *Literature and Medicine*, 29.2 (2011): 297-324.

Hesman, Tina. Excerpt(s) from "A Double Dose of Virus Scares," *Science News*, (2013): 18-35.

Howell, Jessica, Anne Marie Rafferty, and Anna Snaith. "(Author)ity Abroad: The Life Writing of Colonial Nurses" from *International Journal of Nursing Studies*, Vol. 48, Issue 9 (2011). All rights reserved.

Hutson, Scott R. Excerpt(s) from "Gendered Citation Practices in American Antiquity and Other Archaeology Journals," *American Antiquity*, 167.2 (2002): 331-342.

Interlandi, Sebastian. Excerpt(s) from "Review of *Top of the World Environmental Research*," *Quarterly Review of Biology*, 75.2 (2000): 209-10.

Jones, Rebecca. Excerpt(s) from "A Game of Genders: Comparing Depictions of Empowered Women between *A Game of Thrones* Novel and Television Series," *Journal of Student Research*, 1.3 (2012). Reprinted with permission.

Kantor, Brooke, Helen Clark, and Lydia Federico. "Strong and Beautiful," a photographic essay from *Harvard Political Review*, June 28, 2014. Reprinted with permission. All rights reserved.

Katel, Peter. Excerpt(s) from "Debating Hip-Hop: Does Gangsta Rap Harm Black Americans?" *Issues for Debate in Sociology: Selections from CQ Researcher*, Thousand Oaks, CA: Pine Forge Press, 2010.

Keen-Rhinehart, Erin, Megan J. Dailey, and Timothy Barness. Excerpt(s) from "Physiological Mechanisms for Food-Hoarding Motivation in Animals," *Philosophical Transactions: Biological Sciences*, 365 (2010): 961-975.

Krakauer, Jon. Excerpt(s) from "Death and Anger on Everest," *The New Yorker Online*, Apr. 21, 2014.

Krieger, Katharine. "Google Earth's Role in Marine Conservation through Biologging" from *Deliberations*, 2011, *twp.duke.edu/deliberations*. All rights reserved.

595

"United States Department of State, Bureau of Democracy, Human Rights and Labor." *Nepal 2013 Human Rights Report.*

Wald, Priscilla. Excerpt(s) from *Contagious: Cultures, Carriers, and the Outbreak Narrative*, Durham, NC: Duke UP, 2007.

Watkins, Alexander. Excerpt(s) from "Zotero for Personal Image Management," *Art Documentation: Journal of the Art Libraries Society of North America*, 32.2 (2013): 301-313.

Weed, Scott. Excerpt(s) from the Introduction to *Sport & Tourism: A Reader*, New York: Routledge, 2007.

Wegner, Armin. "Armenian Massacre, 1914" photographic image reprinted with permission of Getty Images. All rights reserved.

Weia, Benjamin. Excerpt(s) from "Do You Know Your Bottled Water?" *Catalyst*, 7 (2014): 7-8.

Wong, Daniel. Excerpt(s) from "Responding to the Work of Others: There's a Better Way for Us to Live," *Deliberations*, 9 (2008): 4-7.

Zebrowski, Ernest. "Johnstown, Pennsylvania, 1889" from *Perils of a Restless Planet*. Copyright © 1997 by Cambridge University Press. All rights reserved.

Index